The International Climate Change Regime

This book presents a comprehensive, authoritative and independent account of the rules, institutions and procedures governing the international climate change regime. Its detailed yet user-friendly description and analysis covers the UN Framework Convention on Climate Change, the Kyoto Protocol, and all decisions taken by the Conference of the Parties up to 2003, including the landmark Marrakesh Accords. Mitigation commitments, adaptation, the flexibility mechanisms, reporting and review, compliance, education and public awareness, technology transfer, financial assistance and climate research are just some of the areas that are reviewed. The book also explains how the regime works, including a discussion of its political coalitions, institutional structure, negotiation process, administrative base, and linkages with other international regimes. In short, this book is the only current work that covers all areas of the climate change regime in such depth, yet in such a uniquely accessible and objective way.

FARHANA YAMIN is a Fellow in Environment at the Institute of Development Studies (IDS), University of Sussex, England, specialising in global environmental issues with particular reference to climate change. Before joining IDS in 2002, she was Director of the Foundation for International Environmental Law and Development (FIELD) and led its Climate Change and Energy Programme from 1992 to 2001. She has coordinated several multi-partner research and policy collaborations for a number of governments and international organisations, including leading the team that advised the European Commission on the policy and legal framework for the European Emissions Trading Directive.

JOANNA DEPLEDGE is Sutasoma Research Fellow at Lucy Cavendish College, University of Cambridge, England. She has participated in the climate change regime process since 1996 and holds a PhD from the University of London on the organisation of the Kyoto Protocol negotiations. Dr Depledge is the author of several articles on climate change issues, and has taught both undergraduate and postgraduate courses on the climate change negotiations. She is a former staff member of the UN Climate Change Secretariat and, up to 2002, continued to work for the Secretariat as a consultant, providing support to the negotiations and preparing public information products. She has experience of other environmental regimes, and has worked as a writer for the Earth Negotiations Bulletin.

The International Climate Change Regime

A Guide to Rules, Institutions and Procedures

Farhana Yamin and
Joanna Depledge

PUBLISHED BY THE PRESS SYNDICATE OF THE UNIVERSITY OF CAMBRIDGE
The Pitt Building, Trumpington Street, Cambridge, United Kingdom

CAMBRIDGE UNIVERSITY PRESS
The Edinburgh Building, Cambridge, CB2 2RU, UK
40 West 20th Street, New York, NY 10011-4211, USA
477 Williamstown Road, Port Melbourne, VIC 3207, Australia
Ruiz de Alarcón 13, 28014 Madrid, Spain
Dock House, The Waterfront, Cape Town 8001, South Africa

http://www.cambridge.org

First published 2004

Printed in the United Kingdom at the University Press, Cambridge

Typeface Swift 9.5/14 pt   *System* LaTeX 2$_\varepsilon$ [TB]

A catalogue record for this book is available from the British Library

Library of Congress Cataloguing in Publication data

Yamin, Farhana.
The international climate change regime: a guide to rules, institutions and
procedures / Farhana Yamin and Joanna Depledge.
       p.   cm.
Includes bibliographical references.
ISBN 0 521 84089 9 – ISBN 0 521 60059 6 (pb.)
1. Climatic changes – Government policy.   2. Global warming – Government policy.
3. Environmental management – International cooperation.   4. United Nations
Framework Convention on Climate Change (1992). Protocols, etc., 1997 Dec. 11
I. Depledge, Joanna.   II. Title.

QC981.8.C5Y35   2004
363.738′74526 – dc22   2004049737

ISBN 0 521 84089 9 hardback
ISBN 0 521 60059 6 paperback

Contents

Figures

Tables

Boxes

Foreword

Addressing growing concerns about climate change requires a broad understanding of its social, economic, developmental, scientific, political and environmental aspects. Increases in temperature as a result of increasing emissions of greenhouse gases will have serious impacts on our economic well-being and on the ecosystems on which the health of our planet depends. With the expected increase in the intensity and frequency of extreme weather events such as floods and droughts, and their devastating effects, climate change needs continued urgent attention. Governments worldwide are engaged in constructive dialogue aimed at finding and implementing practical and efficient solutions to address the global problem of climate change. This includes mitigation measures for the reduction of GHGs, as well as identifying ways to reduce countries' vulnerabilities to the effects of climate change.

The United Nations Framework Convention on Climate Change was adopted in 1992 and entered into force two years later. Today, it enjoys almost universal membership, with 188 countries joining together in a unique example of multilateralism to confront the global challenge of climate change.

An intergovernmental process facilitates and supports the implementation of the Convention. In this process countries discuss and agree on action needed to stabilise our global climate. As part of this ongoing dialogue, in 1997 governments adopted the Kyoto Protocol to the Convention, which contains more specific, binding commitments and concrete reduction targets, with specific deadlines for industrialised countries.

Each year, countries meet to discuss and agree on further action. At the Conference of the Parties, nine sessions of which have been held so far, all countries that are Parties to the Convention are represented, as well as the private sector, civil societies, the scientific community, the media, international and national organisations. These annual meetings serve as a forum for participants to share ideas and experiences, and discuss strategies, policies and the rulebook for action. This has resulted, over the years, in a comprehensive framework of decisions containing rules, procedures and other guidelines designed to assist countries in their efforts to implement the Convention and its Protocol.

This Guide is therefore timely. It explains in clear, simple and succinct words the intergovernmental process – the institutions and procedures of the climate change negotiations, as well as the myriad rules, guidelines, actions plans and other decisions adopted by the Parties since the adoption of the Convention. It should serve as an objective and comprehensive reference guide to the 'rulebook' agreed by Parties, which I am confident will assist governments, researchers, policy-makers, civil societies and the public to learn more about and to implement activities designed to address climate change. Action against human-induced climate change must take place at every level of society.

I trust that this Guide will serve as a vital resource tool in the coming years and help to deepen the knowledge and understanding of all who are interested in and committed to global action against the destabilising effects of climate change.

JOKE WALLER HUNTER
Executive Secretary, FCCC

Preface and acknowledgements

The aim of this book is simple: to provide a comprehensive, authoritative, objective and accessible guide to the climate change regime. The book thus describes and analyses the rules set out in the Convention, Kyoto Protocol and COP Decisions, together with the institutions and procedures that govern the climate change negotiations.

This book responds to two trends in the climate change process: first, its growing complexity, which makes it difficult for newcomers, and even for negotiators familiar with the regime, to make sense of all the rules, institutions, procedures and practices that have developed over the past decade; secondly, the regime's increasing specialisation, which produces experts on individual topics (e.g. emissions trading, compliance), but few who have an overall picture of how the climate change process works. This guide is therefore targeted at newcomers to the negotiations, specialists wishing to broaden their understanding of the regime, and all those involved in the intergovernmental response to climate change, as negotiators, policy-makers, stakeholders, researchers or other interested professionals.

The book is based on an exhaustive review and analysis of primary materials, principally the Convention, Kyoto Protocol, COP Decisions and supporting documentation. We have also examined secondary materials to the extent these assist analysis and provide commentary on the rules, institutions and procedures of the climate change regime. Our work has benefited from discussions with experts in the climate change process, including FCCC Secretariat staff, negotiators, NGOs and IGOs, who have provided supplementary insights and information to help make this book comprehensive, authoritative and practically useful.

One result of these discussions is that producing this book has involved many partners. The authors wish to express their deep gratitude to the UK Department for International Development, the main financial sponsor of the book, along with the Governments of Australia and Switzerland. Without their financial support, this book could never have been written. The authors would also like to thank all the experts who have given of their valuable time to provide information and review chapters. These include: Roberto Acosta, Mozaharul Alam, Molly Anderson, John Ashe, Jon Barnett, Valentine Bartra, Kevin Baumert, Asfaha Beyene, Sue Biniaz, Barbara Black, Daniel Bodansky, Alan Boyle, Duncan Brack, Nick Campbell, Jan Corfee-Morlot, Paul Curnow, Suraje Dessai, John Eyles, Christiana Figueres, Don Goldberg, James Grabert, Stephen Gray, Kevin Grose, Erik Haites, Lars Haltbrekken, Bill Hare, Hanna Hoffmann, Christoph Holtwisch, Saleemul Huq, Lars Georg Jensen, Jackie Jones, Mark Kenber, Lee Kimball, Vitaly Matsarski, Meg McDonald, Damien Meadows, Malte Meinshausen, Axel Michaelowa, Zohra Moosa, Lwandle Mqadi, Erwin Mulders, Benito Müller, Youssef Nassef, Sebastian Oberthür, Janos Pasztor, Horacio Peluffo, Jim Penman, Martha Perdomo, Stelios Pesmajoglou, Olga Pilifosova, Espen Ronneberg, Chris Spence, Thomas Tanner, Greg Terrill, Dennis Tirpak, Jessica Troni, Karla Schoeters, Leonard Simanjuntak, Neroni Slade, Christopher Stone, Rob Swart, Dennis Tirpak, Avani Vaish, Everton Vargas, Yolando Velasco, Rachel Warren, David Warrilow, Philip Weech, Nattley Williams, Glen Wiser, Xuedu Lu and Michael Zammit Cutajar.

Many others have provided the authors with important insights and information. Special thanks are due to Richard Kinley for comments as well as for coordinating other members of staff of the FCCC Secretariat, who have been particularly helpful in going over the chapters with a fine toothcomb and responding to frequent requests for information. Former colleagues Philippe Sands, James Cameron, Jake Werksman, Ruth Mackenzie, Beatrice Chaytor, Carolina Lasén Diaz and Jürgen Lefevere at the Foundation for International Environmental Law and Development (FIELD) also deserve mention and thanks for their pioneering work on the climate change regime and other areas of international environmental law. In addition, the authors are very grateful to Cambridge University Press, in particular Finola O'Sullivan, for the strong support given to this project, and to staff at the Institute for Development Studies at Sussex University (UK), especially Oliver Burch, Alison Norwood and Julie McWilliam, for their indispensable help. Our deepest thanks go to Mike Yule and Michael Grubb for their limitless support and encouragement, and to four special little people, Aliya, Isaac, Safiya and Leonia, who have put up with quite a lot to help us complete this book. Needless to say, any remaining shortcomings, errors of fact or judgement rest with the authors.

Farhana Yamin and Joanna Depledge
1 March 2004

Abbreviations

4AR	Fourth Assessment Report
A6SC	Article 6 Supervisory Committee
AAU	Assigned amount unit
ADB	Asian Development Bank
AE	Applicant entity
AG13	Ad Hoc Group on Article 13
AGBM	Ad Hoc Group on the Berlin Mandate
AHTEG	Ad hoc technical expert group
AIJ	Activities implemented jointly
AIXG	Annex I Experts Group of the OECD/IEA
AOSIS	Alliance of Small Island States
ARD	Afforestation, reforestation and deforestation
ASEAN	Association of South East Asian Nations
BAPA	Buenos Aires Plan of Action (Decision 1/CP.4)
BCSE	Business Council for Sustainable Energy
BINGO	Business and industry non-governmental organisation
CACAM	Central Asia, Caucasus, Albania and Moldova
CAEP	Committee on Aviation Environmental Protection
CAN	Climate Action Network
CARICOM	Caribbean Community
CBD	Convention on Biological Diversity
CC	Compliance Committee
CDI	Capacity Development Initiative
CDIAC	Carbon Dioxide Information Analysis Centre
CDM	Clean Development Mechanism
CDR	Common but differentiated responsibilities
CEB	UN System Chief Executives Board for Coordination
CEE	Central and Eastern Europe

CEO	Chief Executive Officer
CER, lCER and tCER	Certified emission reduction, long-term CER and temporary CER
CERES	Coalition for environmentally responsible economies
CFC	Chlorofluorocarbon
CG	Central Group
CG-11	Central Group 11
CGE	Consultative Group of Experts on National Communications from Non-Annex I Parties
CH$_4$	Methane
CHF	Swiss francs
CITES	Convention on International Trade in Endangered Species
CO	Carbon monoxide
CO$_2$	Carbon dioxide
CO$_2$e	Carbon dioxide equivalent
COP	Conference of the Parties
COP/MOP	Conference of the Parties serving as the meeting of the Parties to the Kyoto Protocol
CPR	Commitment period reserve
CRF	Common reporting format
CSD	Commission on Sustainable Development
CST	Committee on Science and Technology
CTE	Committee on Trade and Environment
CTI	Climate Technology Initiative
DC	Developing Country
DNA	Designated national authority
DoD	Department of Defense
DSA	Daily subsistence allowance
e5	European Business Council for a Sustainable Energy Future
EAEO	Executing Agency with Expanded Opportunities
EB/CDM	Executive Board of the Clean Development Mechanism
EC	European Community
ECOSOC	Economic and Social Council of the United Nations
EDF	Environmental Defence
EGTT	Expert Group on Technology Transfer
EIA	Environmental Impact Assessment
EIG	Environmental Integrity Group
EIT	Economy in transition
EMA	Emissions Marketing Association
EMG	Environmental Management Group
ENB	Earth Negotiations Bulletin

ENGO	Environmental non-governmental organisation
ERT	Expert Review Team
ERU	Emission reduction unit
EST	Environmentally sound technology
ET	Emissions trading
EU	European Union
FAO	Food and Agriculture Organization of the United Nations
FAR	First Assessment Report
FB	Facilitative Branch
FCCC	Framework Convention on Climate Change
FIELD	Foundation for International Environmental Law and Development
FSP	Full-sized project
FSU	Former Soviet Union
G-77	Group of 77
GATT	General Agreement on Tariffs and Trade
GBF	Global Biodiversity Forum
GCC	Global Climate Coalition
GCOS	Global Climate Observing System
GDP	Gross domestic product
GEB	Global environmental benefit
GEF	Global Environment Facility
GHG	Greenhouse gas
GLOBE	Global Legislators for a Balanced Environment
GMEF	Global Ministerial Environment Forum
GRULAC	Group of Latin America and the Caribbean
GWP	Global warming potential
HCFC	Hydrochlorofluorocarbon
HFC	Hydrofluorocarbon
HWP	Harvested wood product
IA	Implementing agency
IBRD	International Bank for Reconstruction and Development
ICAO	International Civil Aviation Organization
ICC	International Chamber of Commerce
ICFTU	International Confederation of Free Trade Unions
ICLEI	International Council for Local Environmental Initiatives
ICSU	International Council for Science
IDA	International Development Association
IDR	In-depth review
IE	Independent entity; included elsewhere
IEA	International Energy Agency

IEG	International Environmental Governance
IETA	International Emissions Trading Association
IFC	International Finance Corporation
IGO	Intergovernmental organisation
IMO	International Maritime Organization
INC	Intergovernmental Negotiating Committee for the FCCC (1990–1995)
IOC	Intergovernmental Oceanographic Commission
IPCC	Intergovernmental Panel on Climate Change
IPE	Indicative Planning Figure
IPO	Indigenous peoples organisation
IPR	Intellectual property right
ITAP	Intergovernmental Technical Advisory Panel
IUCN	World Conservation Union
JI	Joint Implementation
JLG	Joint Liaison Group
JUSSCANNZ	Japan, US, Switzerland, Canada, Australia, Norway, New Zealand
JWG	Joint Working Group
KP	Kyoto Protocol
LCCP	Lifecycle climate performance
LDC	Least developed country
LEG	Least developed country expert group
LGMAs	Local government and municipal authorities
LNG	Liquefied natural gas
LUCF	Land-use change and forestry
LULUCF	Land use, land-use change and forestry
M & E	Monitoring and evaluation
M & P	Modalities and procedures
MCC	Multilateral Consultative Committee
MCP	Multilateral Consultative Process
MDG	Millennium Development Goal
MEA	Multilateral Environmental Agreement
MEPC	Marine Environment Protection Committee
MOP	Meeting of the Parties
MOU	Memorandum of Understanding
MSP	Medium-sized project
N_2O	Nitrous oxide
NAPA	National Adaptation Programme of Action
NC3	Third national communication
NCSA	National self-assessment of capacity-building needs
NCSP	National Communication Support Programme

NCSU	National Communication Support Unit
NGGIP	National Greenhouse Gas Inventories Programme
NGO	Non-governmental organisation
NIR	National inventory report
NMVOCs	Non-methane volatile organic compounds
NO	Not occurring
NOx	Nitrogen oxides
OBG	Open Balkan Group
ODA	Official Development Assistance
ODS	Ozone-depleting substance
OECD	Organization for Economic Cooperation and Development
OOPC	Ocean Observing Panel for Climate
OP	Operational Programme
OPEC	Organization of Petroleum Exporting Countries
OPS	Overall Performance Study
OS	Operational Strategy
PAMs	Policies and measures
PCF	Prototype Carbon Fund
PDF	Preparation and Development Facility
PFC	Perfluorocarbon
PIR	Project Implementation Review
POP	Persistent organic pollutant
ppp	Purchasing power parity
PPR	Project Performance Report
Preps	Poverty reduction strategy papers
PRINCE	Programme for Measuring Incremental Costs for the Environment
QELRC	Quantified emission limitation and reduction commitment
QELROs	Quantified emission limitation and reduction objectives
R & D	Research and development
REIO	Regional economic integration organisation
RINGO	Research and independent non-governmental organisation
RIVM	Dutch National Institute for Public Health and the Environment
RMU	Removal unit
SAR	Second Assessment Report
SB	Subsidiary body
SBI	Subsidiary Body for Implementation
SBSTA	Subsidiary Body for Scientific and Technological Advice
SBSTTA	Subsidiary Body for Scientific, Technical and Technological Advice
SCC	Small-scale CDM projects
SCCF	Special Climate Change Fund

SDR	Special Drawing Right
SF$_6$	Sulphur hexafluoride
SGP	Small Grants Programme
SIDS	Small Island Developing States
SME	Small and medium enterprise
SOx	Sulphur oxides
SPM	Summary for policy-makers of an IPCC Assessment Report
SPREP	South Pacific Regional Environment Programme
STAP	Scientific and Technical Advisory Panel
STO	Specific trade-related obligation
STRP	Scientific and Technical Review Panel
TAR	Third Assessment Report
TEAP	Technology and Economic Assessment Panel
TFI	Task Force on Inventories
TT: CLEAR	Technology information clearing house
UNCCD	UN Convention to Combat Desertification
UNCED	UN Conference on Environment and Development
UNCHE	UN Conference on the Human Environment
UNCLOS	UN Convention on the Law of the Sea
UNCTAD	UN Conference on Trade and Development
UNDP	UN Development Programme
UNEP	UN Environment Programme
UNGA	UN General Assembly
UNIDO	UN Industrial Development Organization
UNITAR	UN Institute for Training and Research
UNOG	UN Office at Geneva
UNOLA	UN Office of Legal Affairs
URF	Uniform reporting format
UV	Ultraviolet radiation
WBCSD	World Business Council for Sustainable Development
WEHAB	Water, energy, health, agriculture and biodiversity
WEOG	Western Europe and Others Group
WGGA	Working Group of the General Assembly
WHO	World Health Organization
WMO	World Meteorological Organization
WRI	World Resources Institute
WSSD	World Summit for Sustainable Development
WTO	World Trade Organization
WWF	Worldwide Fund for Nature

1

Introduction

This book is a guide to the rapid developments in international law in one of the most challenging and important areas of global concern: climate change. The climate system is the result of complex and dynamic interactions between the Earth's atmosphere, biosphere and oceans which human activities are beginning to throw out of balance. Atmospheric emissions of greenhouse gases (GHGs) have risen considerably due to fossil fuel burning, deforestation, livestock farming and other human activities. If current trends continue the concentration of greenhouse gases in the atmosphere will double by the end of the century. The scientific community has warned of the potentially serious effects of climate variability caused by increased concentrations. 'Business-as-usual' scenarios predict a rate of increase in global mean temperatures greater than that seen over the past 10,000 years.[1] Resultant climate impacts include sea level rise, changes in agricultural yields, forest cover and water resources and an increase in extreme events, such as storms, cyclones, landslides and floods.

These impacts will affect the environmental, social and vital economic interests of all states and have profound consequences for virtually every aspect of human society. The atmosphere knows no boundaries. Acting alone, no country can hope to arrest climate change, but collective action by sovereign states with disparate socio-economic and environmental circumstances is difficult. Yet environmental issues that require global cooperation challenge traditional paradigms of international law-making which are underpinned by concepts of state responsibility, sovereign equality and the paramountcy of state consent. A number of factors unique to climate change make such collective action more challenging still. These include potentially irreversible damages or costs, long planning

[1] IPCC, 2001a.

horizons, regional variations, time lags between cause and effect, scientific uncertainties and complexities inherent to climate change and geographical discrepancies between those who pollute and those subject to climate impacts.

Notwithstanding these difficulties, the international community has negotiated two major international treaties in less than a decade: the 1992 UN Framework Convention on Climate Change (FCCC) and the 1997 Kyoto Protocol (KP). Both treaties have been significantly elaborated through additional legal instruments and decisions adopted by the Climate Convention's governing body, the Conference of the Parties (COP), on the basis of developments in science and politics. The FCCC has been ratified by 189 Parties and thus enjoys near universal adherence. The Kyoto Protocol, widely regarded as one of the most innovative and ambitious international agreements ever agreed, has been ratified by over 120 parties, and is shortly expected to enter into force notwithstanding the decision by the United States of America not to proceed with ratification.

The international legal and institutional framework established by these legal instruments, and its relationship to other international issues, is as intricate and far-reaching as the climate problem itself. But it is also increasingly inaccessible to the wide range of affected interests. The underlying complexity of the climate problem and the sheer pace of scientific and legal developments are contributory factors. Newcomers to the climate issue, and even those familiar with the international climate regime, now find it difficult simply to follow the trail of documents and their significance for the interpretation and implementation of the two treaties negotiated to date. Rules governing aspects of the climate regime have become ever more technical and specialised, producing experts on individual topics but few who have an overall understanding of the complete picture. Additionally, documents alone give little insight into the functioning of the regime because it is difficult to glean the institutional practices, procedures and informal understandings that help define how the international climate process actually works. Transmission of such information from one generation of climate negotiators to the next is vital but time-consuming. Those with fewer financial and human resources suffer an additional disadvantage because they have limited access to documents and external expertise to draw upon in the first place.

Discussions with climate negotiators, and the broader constituency of climate policy-makers and stakeholders, including the professionals who advise them, convinced us that there was a need for an authoritative, balanced and readable guide to the rules, institutions and procedures of the international climate regime. The realisation that an ever greater share of our time was being taken up explaining the climate change regime to an increasingly diverse range of stakeholders and scholars, encouraged us to channel our expertise on climate issues in the form of a guide which we ourselves felt we needed. The imminent entry into force of the Kyoto Protocol, marking the conclusion of a ten-year cycle of regime development and heralding the beginning of another, provided the final impetus.

This introductory chapter sets out the scope, structure and analytical framework underpinning this guide to the climate regime. To assist readers to navigate their way around the guide, section 2 below explains how readers can find information of interest to them in the easiest and quickest manner.

1   Scope

Political and legal control over human activities contributing to climate change is fragmented between states, international organisations and an array of other actors. Climate change thus necessitates concurrent policy-making at multiple levels of governance. This book is concerned primarily with the body of international rules concerning climate change applicable to states and the institutions and procedures states have created to oversee their implementation, enforcement and further development. The Convention and the Kyoto Protocol constitute the core of the international climate regime and are therefore the central focus of this book. But states also have rights and obligations in respect of the environment which arise from legal sources other than the Convention and the Protocol. Additionally, institutions such as the Intergovernmental Panel on Climate Change (IPCC) and the Global Environment Facility (GEF), which have a remit that is broader than climate change, also play a role. Thus the climate regime encompasses these additional elements.

Climate change is a high profile political issue because GHG emissions currently arise from virtually all aspects of the global economy. International regulation of GHG emissions thus impinges on sovereignty which states are reluctant to concede, as evidenced by protracted debates on the need for legally binding reductions targets, the legal personality of the COP, majority-voting decision-making and procedures for determining non-compliance. Such debates also evidence a huge variation in the level of understanding among delegations about the consequences that flow from particular legal characterisations. Disparities in legal knowledge and lack of access to expertise characterise most areas of global concern and in this respect, climate change is no different. This book is intended to help level one small part of the knowledge playing field. This purpose has helped us frame its scope: to cover in a comprehensive manner all aspects of the climate regime which a country delegate unfamiliar with the climate issue and with limited resources and time might need to understand to function effectively in the international climate negotiations.

Our focus on the international climate regime means we do not cover national legislation relating to climate change. Because the majority of FCCC Parties have, or are in the process of developing, national programmes and legislation concerning climate change, with many incorporating elements of the FCCC and KP into their national frameworks, a compendium of national legislation would be a helpful tool for those concerned with implementation, but it is beyond the scope of this book. Nor do we examine matters covered by private international law, which concerns the rules developed by states as part of their domestic law to resolve disputes between private persons involving a foreign element, such as choice of applicable law and whether a national court has jurisdiction.

All rules, whether national or international, influence and are moulded by prevailing political, economic and geographical circumstances. Reference to these circumstances, and other 'real world' constraints, can advance understanding of the rules, and we have referred to such matters where appropriate. We have, however, limited inclusion of such material as other sources provide detailed negotiating histories. To help newcomers, a brief overview of the historical development of the regime and its key features is provided in chapter 2.

2   Structure and user's guide

This section explains the structure of this book and navigational tips to help users find information they need as efficiently as possible.

Chapters 1–3 serve as important orientation points for those not familiar with international negotiating processes generally and with the evolution of the climate regime. Chapter 1 explains the international legal foundations on which the climate regime is built, including how international rules come to be in existence generally and the implications of different kinds of binding, non-binding and soft law rules, all of which are used in the climate regime. Chapter 2 provides a historical overview of the climate change problem and the main features of the FCCC and KP. Chapter 3 explains the role of various participants in the climate change regime, including governments, inter-governmental and non-governmental organisations, research and academic organisations, business groups and negotiating blocs.

Chapters 4–12 cover the substantive rules of the climate regime. Chapter 4 examines the Convention's ultimate objective and principles. Mitigation commitments lie at the heart of the climate regime and are examined in chapter 5. The achievement of these commitments is linked to use of flexibility mechanisms such as emissions trading, joint implementation and the clean development mechanism which are described in chapter 6. Chapter 7 covers two issues which are vital to the effective development of the regime: research and systematic observation and cooperation on scientific information and education, training, public awareness and access to information. Chapter 8 explains commitments relating to adaptation to the adverse effects of climate change, and chapter 9 explains the issue of the impacts of response measures which concerns negative economic impacts one country might face when another takes mitigation action. Like other modern environmental treaties, the climate regime provides for capacity-building and the transfer of financial and technological resources to developing countries: these provisions are explained in chapter 10. The climate regime is at the forefront of developing non-confrontational mechanisms to monitor, verify and promote compliance with its rules. Chapter 11 explains the reporting and review provisions which underpin these processes, and chapter 12 describes the ground-breaking non-compliance mechanisms and procedures recently adopted by the regime.

Each of these substantive chapters is structured to cover all the rules relevant to a particular area, whether these are contained in the Convention or Protocol, because issue areas rather than article numbers correspond more closely to the underlying interests at stake. An article by article approach tends to fragment the substantive rules and processes that have emerged to track them. Because the Protocol is grafted onto the Convention but establishes a legally distinct regime, each chapter first explains the provisions of the Convention and then additional rules on that subject set out in the Protocol. Sections entitled 'rule development' describe the interpretation, guidance and further development of these rules agreed within the climate regime, usually in the form of COP decisions. This structure ensures legal clarity between the Convention and the Protocol, which is important because not all Convention Parties will become Parties to the Protocol, and also because there is a need to distinguish clearly between the legally binding rules set out in the texts of the Convention and the Protocol themselves and their subsequent iteration and elaboration as agreed by the COP through its decisions and practices. We have tried to keep the main discussion of the rules within the body of the text, with text boxes being largely devoted to providing historical and explanatory materials that might be of interest to some readers in need of additional background information.

Chapters 13–18 examine the institutions and procedures established by the regime to oversee implementation, enforcement and future development of its rules. Chapter 13 explains the mandate and working modalities of institutions directly established by the climate regime, including the role of the COP, the Kyoto Protocol's governing body, the Conference of the Parties serving as the meeting of the Parties (COP/MOP), and the various subsidiary bodies. Chapter 14 describes in detail the mechanics of climate negotiations, including the function and procedures of various kinds of negotiating groups, which many newcomers find daunting and complex. Chapter 15 looks at how the climate regime considers scientific and technical input, including from the IPCC. Chapter 16 explains the budgetary and administrative aspects of the regime, including the role of the Secretariat in the smooth functioning of the regime. Chapter 17 examines the increasing number of linkages between climate change and other policy areas, including links with regimes dealing with ozone, biodiversity and trade. Chapter 18 sets out provisions in the Convention and the Protocol, as well as more broadly, that are relevant for the evolution of the climate regime beyond the current commitments set out in these instruments. The final chapter, chapter 19, concludes by addressing the nature of future challenges facing the regime as it evolves beyond the current framework.

Appendix I provides an alphabetical table of Parties, listing their regional, political and Annex I/non-Annex I groupings together with key statistics (GDP per capita, total CO_2 emissions and CO_2 emissions per capita). These have been included in one table for ease of reference. The technical and graphical fact sheets in Appendix II set out detailed factual information for forty countries that have accepted quantified commitments under the climate regime, known as 'Annex I Parties', including each country's current and projected emissions, as these are critical for understanding the implications of each country's mitigation commitments. Appendix III provides a table organised according to articles and COP decisions to help readers quickly track down treaty provisions and related COP documents. Readers can also make use of the subject index at the back of the book to find key words and issues. Finally, the bibliography provides information on all official documents and all secondary literature to which we have referred in the book. To keep the referencing system as short as possible in the main text, the full titles of official documents and COP decisions, which are in all cases set out in the reports of the COP adopted by each session, are listed in the bibliography.

3   Analytical framework

This section explains what we mean by key terms such as regime, rules and principles and how we have identified the applicable rules. It also explains the role of soft law in environmental regimes such as climate change because this is important for understanding, inter alia, the way in which we used the term 'rule development'.

Political scientists and, in recent years, international lawyers have begun to use the term *regime* to refer to the rules, regulations and institutions relevant to a particular subject area. In international relations a regime has been defined as 'a set of implicit or explicit principles, norms, rules and decision-making procedures around which actors' expectations converge in a given area in international relations'.[2] A distinction is frequently made between principles and rules which prescribe norms relevant to the problem the regime addresses and those elements which deal with the more structural aspects such as institutions and decision-making processes. Of course, there is a close interplay between the substantive rules and the institutional and procedural 'tools' through which rules come to be implemented, enforced and further developed. We use the term *regime* here to refer to these normative rules together with the institutions and procedural tools established to oversee their implementation, development and enforcement.

There is general agreement that the term *norm* is a broad category covering any provision with prescriptive content and that the distinction between rules and principles relates to the specificity of the prescribed conduct.[3] *Rules* are more specific and seem to apply in an all-or-nothing fashion whilst *principles* denote more general standards of behaviour which might be consistent with a range of policy options.[4] In this book we have used the term *rule* as an umbrella term covering all types of legal norms. This is because labelling provisions as either rules or principles seems to prejudge, rather than explain, the crucial issues at stake: what is the scope and strength of the obligation under discussion and what legal consequences attach to particular provisions?

Binding legal rules entail international legal responsibility and a failure to comply can give rise to recourse to judicial proceedings. The sense of obligation, of being legally bound, distinguishes legal rules from other types of rules which states observe in their dealings with one another such as rules of politeness, convenience and goodwill.[5] Lawyers also tend to distinguish legal rules from rules of morality, which define how states or private persons ought to behave. Rules of morality appeal essentially to conscience rather than to enforcement by an external authority, as is the case with legal rules. The relationship between law and morality is complex. Although legal rules often reflect prevailing moral values and concepts, principles of morality must first have been derived from a valid legal source if they are to be recognisable as legally applicable to states. This is a particularly important point in the climate change context because developed and developing countries alike appeal to wider notions of social justice, equity and fairness in support of their positions, not all of which have a basis in existing law.[6]

Because the creation and enforcement of binding rules through treaties and customary international law, discussed below in the section on rule creation, is

---

[2] Krasner, 1982.   [3] Krasner, 1982: p. 2.   [4] Bodansky, 1993; and Sands, 1995b: p. 185.
[5] Oppenheim, 1996: p. 51.   [6] See e.g. Claussen and McNeilly, 1998; Yamin, 1999.

problematic for many reasons, in recent years lawyers have also paid considerable attention to the role of legally non-binding norms, sometimes referred to as 'soft law', in the international system.[7] Soft law instruments typically include ministerial declarations, memoranda of understanding, resolutions of international conferences, action plans and decisions by conferences of parties established by treaties, such as the COP of the FCCC. Soft law instruments contain a variety of legal norms: some are highly prescriptive whilst others are open-ended, indeterminate and incapable of creating precise standards of conduct. Soft law instruments can become binding if accepted as such by states.

Many multilateral environmental agreements (MEAs) now combine a framework convention with accompanying protocol(s) and/or 'secondary' or 'delegated' soft law resulting from the statements and practice that develop around a treaty to provide guidance to the interpretation, elaboration or application of hard law, typically in the form of further decisions adopted by Parties.[8] Climate change is typical of this approach.[9] Thus understanding when, why and in what circumstances Parties to the Convention use particular types of legal instruments is crucial to understanding both the implications of the outputs of the regime and sometimes the power asymmetries underlying it.

There are many good reasons for increased use of soft law in the field of environment. Typically global environmental issues involve large numbers of states as well as private actors, and are likely to give rise to differentiated standards that need continual adjustment to respond to changing scientific knowledge and political circumstances – matters which are typically more difficult to accommodate within traditional forms of law-making. Soft law instruments by contrast provide flexibility and their use avoids time-consuming ratification requirements, enabling decision-making that is responsive, or helps 'road test' complex policy solutions to provide experience for negotiating firmer commitments. The diverse nature of the interests involved means that global environmental issues often raise equity issues and demands for social justice. In these situations, soft law instruments can act as a 'half-way' stage in environmental law-making processes, bridging law with policy to which states wish to adhere but which they are reluctant to enshrine in binding, highly prescriptive forms.

Soft law also has some disadvantages because it is difficult to work out when soft law becomes 'hard', binding law.[10] The resulting fuzziness does not always sit well with the need for legal certainty. Thus whilst the flexibility and fluidity of

---

[7] For a more detailed discussion of the function, role and status of soft law see Shelton, 2000.

[8] Chinkin, 2000: p. 27

[9] Chapter 18 describes provisions relevant to the evolution of the regime.

[10] Chinkin, 2000: p. 37.

soft law in overall terms helps the progressive development of international law, in particular instances it can also generate uncertainty as well as simply providing states with an opportunity to be seen to be doing something whilst avoiding any obligation actually to comply.[11]

Because of the important role different kinds of legal norms occupy in the climate regime, in this book we have examined all types of rules, institutions and procedures agreed as applicable to states, whether or not states consider them to be legally binding or soft law. Thus, in sections on 'rule development' we have referred to COP decisions which are generally taken to be non-legally binding in form. We have also explained widely agreed practices and procedures. In our view, a book which focused only on the rules states currently considered to be legally binding would fail to convey the full measure of what states have agreed to adhere to in their dealings with each other in the climate context. Additionally, in a new area of international concern such as climate change, rules are at differing stages of legal maturity and state practice is highly dynamic with regard to expectations of standards of state behaviour. Thus limiting our subject matter to legally binding rules or 'hard law' would result in exclusion of legal norms which could, in due course, come to be regarded as binding.

We are conscious that in a highly politicised area such as climate change, presenting the current rules, institutions and procedures is not an easy undertaking. We have tried to be as objective as possible in our assessment of what has been agreed and acknowledge that our estimate of consensus may not always coincide with the view of any single state or group of states. Accordingly, in some areas that are particularly contentious, we have opted to report the divergent views that exist rather than to accord privilege to one viewpoint, as doing the former would, in our view, promote a better understanding of the existing framework, however inchoate this might be.

4   Legal foundations and structures

The world's 6 billion people and most of its geographical regions are divided into some 200 separate political units called states. These states are sovereign, in the sense that they control the individuals, natural resources and territory subject to their jurisdiction. Sovereignty implies equality and thus no state legally recognises another as a superior authority. Other actors (individuals, groups, transnational organisations, multinational corporations, financial structures and media networks) work across national borders. They drive political agendas, educate public opinion, provide sources of expertise for rule

[11] Chinkin, 2000: p. 26.

development and assist with implementation to an ever-greater extent but they cannot adopt binding rules for states.[12]

States have found it increasingly convenient to create international organisations and entrust them with a certain degree of legal autonomy necessary for carrying out specific tasks to achieve common goals. Some international organisations are empowered to take binding decisions for their members, but legally all international organisations are essentially creatures under the control of the group of states that created them and could cease to exist should they so decide. The international legal order is thus comprised principally of sovereign and independent states, international organisations endowed by states with international legal personality and bodies such as the FCCC COP whose legal character is discussed in chapter 13.

Historically, the freedom of states to decide upon their internal set-up, national legislation and foreign policy was virtually unrestricted, giving states maximum freedom to pursue their self-interest. Over time, legal constraints emerged as states began to accept, on a voluntary and reciprocal basis, a variety of restrictions. International law was seen as a series of rules restricting the freedom of action of states. Individuals and other kinds of entities were to be regulated through the quite distinct and formally separate system of municipal law. Today international rules are no longer regarded merely as limitations upon states and there is increasing, but not universal, recognition that rules of international law establish foundations upon which the very rights of states rest. International law is seen, in other words, as validating or invalidating all legal acts or any other legal system and in this sense is widely regarded as being at the top of the legal pyramid.[13] Although most national systems require international law to be transformed into national statutes before national courts apply it, the relationship between international law and municipal legal systems is now more 'porous' and integrated.[14]

Interdependency is a defining characteristic of the modern world and international rules shape a significant aspect of our daily lives. But the sovereign equality of states, and the voluntary acceptance of international obligations, still underpins the modern conception of international law.[15] States have established a number of international organisations and vested them with limited legal powers sufficient to achieve particular common goals. But there is no central legislative body at the international level. And there is no mechanism to determine at what level – bilateral, regional or multilateral – international rules should be created, nor what issues should be addressed by states, and with what level of priority. Disparities in wealth, power and influence between states, as well as the nature of the environmental problem, all help determine whether an issue will

---

[12] Yamin, 2001.   [13] Cassese, 2001.   [14] Cassese, 2001: p. 164.   [15] See Oppenheim, 1996.

give rise to an effective international regime or languish on the international agenda.

These structural features of the international system explain why existing environmental rules are a 'patchwork', reflecting a piecemeal, fragmented and ad hoc response to problems as they have emerged. The resulting rules and institutional arrangements maintain a narrow, largely sectoral focus and sometimes operate at cross-purposes. Elsewhere there are gaps in the international regulatory framework. This is particularly relevant for climate change because, although the majority of areas beyond the limits of national jurisdiction have specific regimes (such as Antarctica, outer space and the seas), there is no comparable 'law of the atmosphere'. There are instead more specific regimes that address, for example, the transboundary movement of acid-forming pollutants, depletion of the ozone layer, issues of nuclear testing, and now, finally, climate change.[16]

As discussed in chapter 17, it is arguable that the interconnected policy agenda demanded by sustainable development, and by climate change, could be served better with higher levels of institutional coordination and policy coherence than the current segmented rule-making structures allow.[17] The global priority accorded to climate change, compared to other problems, is also subject to stress. There is sometimes a perception, particularly among developing countries, that climate change gets too much international 'air time' compared to more immediate problems. UN summits mandated by the 1992 United Nations Conference on Environment and Development (UNCED) covering, inter alia, human rights, food security, women, social development, urban habitats and education, the adoption of the 2000 Millennium Development Goals and the Johannesburg Plan of Implementation adopted by the 2002 World Summit on Sustainable Development (WSSD) have introduced more balance to the international agenda.[18] But the multiple agendas and processes spawned by these conferences have only served to emphasise the need for greater institutional and policy coherence and additional finance, recognised at the 2002 Monterrey Conference on Finance for Development.

Integration of the environment, economic development and social justice components across the international system lies at the heart of sustainable development. The achievement of this goal, however, sits uneasily with an international legal order traditionally defined as a system of sovereign states cooperating to regulate their conduct so that each can pursue its self-interest more efficiently. The pursuit of sustainable development fits more naturally with modern paradigms of international law. These see the international legal

---

[16] Soroos, 1997.   [17] Hyvarinen and Brack, 2003.
[18] UN Millennium Declaration, A/RES/55/2, New York, UN.

order as one which 'is based on a universalist or cosmopolitan outlook which sees at work in international politics a potential community of mankind and lays stress on the element of trans-national solidarity'.[19] This more community-orientated approach has not 'uprooted or supplanted the old framework' but is superimposed on it and serves to mitigate some of the shortcomings of traditional structures.[20]

The climate regime is a global joint endeavour to protect a vital common interest. It is not difficult to see why the climate issue is seen as a test case for the ability of the current international order, comprising the traditional and modern strands, to meet the broader challenge of sustainable development.[21] This interest, the greater resources devoted to the climate change regime, the fact that the climate regime is grounded in two treaties and, of course, the vital economic interests bound up with climate change, will ensure that climate change remains a high profile affair within the international arena.

5   Rule creation

The climate change regime is comprised of rules generated from different kinds of sources which define how the institutions established under it function. Thus it is important to understand the nature and implications of the different legal sources and their 'hierarchy' or relationship to each other. The two main methods of rule creation are *treaties* and *custom*.[22] Other 'sources' cover general principles of law and judicial decisions and teachings of eminent jurists. Binding decisions of international organisations also generate rules governing states. Additionally, emerging legal concepts such as *jus cogens* and *erga omnes* obligations may come to impose additional constraints on state conduct.[23] These sources are discussed briefly below.

5.1   *Custom*

Although treaty law is far more prevalent than it was 100 years ago, a large part of the fabric of international law is made up of rules of customary status. Customary international law denotes state practice generally accepted as law by states. Such rules govern the way in which states make treaty law. They also provide substantive legal norms which are either of general application, such as rules of state responsibility, or else cover particular issue areas, such as the law of the sea.

---

[19] Cassese, 2001, citing M. Wight and H. Bull: p. 18.   [20] Cassese, 2001: p. 18.

[21] Gupta and Grubb, 2000.

[22] For a more detailed explanation of legal sources see Oppenheim, 1996; Sands, 1995b: p. 103; and Birnie and Boyle, 2002.

[23] Oppenheim, 1996: p. 7.

In order to establish the existence of a rule of customary international law two elements have to be proved: first, a *consistent practice or conduct* adopted by states, and second, a conviction on the part of states that such conduct is motivated by a sense of legal obligation (*opinio juris*). Practice must be extensive and virtually uniform, but individual instances of non-compliance do not negate the existence of a customary rule. Concurrence by a widespread and representative sample of states, particularly if they are the ones with specific interests affected by the rule, can suffice. It should be noted, however, that customary rules can also crystallise in a very short space of time. Provided state practice and *opinio juris* coincide, 'instant custom' can be created.[24]

Despite these shortcomings, customary rules provide an important reference point. Where there is no treaty law on a subject, customary rules, together with rules derived from other sources, prevail. Where a treaty has been concluded, and unless made clear otherwise, customary rules sit alongside treaty rules and thus are an independent, and ongoing, source of legal obligation that must be taken into account by parties to the treaties as well as non-parties.

The FCCC and KP do not contain an express provision explaining their relationship with customary international rules. The absence of such a provision has led several small island states to make declarations clarifying their understanding of the relationship between existing rules of international law, including customary law, and the regime established by the Convention.[25] Some have made identical declarations when ratifying the Kyoto Protocol, plus a statement that the Protocol's emission targets are inadequate to prevent dangerous anthropogenic interference with the climate system.[26]

5.2   *Treaties*

These are also known as conventions, accords, pacts, protocols, agreements or acts. The essence of such instruments is that they are written agreements among states creating rights and obligations for the parties concerned that are governed by international law.[27] There are no agreed rules prescribing their legal

---

[24] For examples, see Cheng, 1965: pp. 23–43.

[25] Declarations made by Fiji, Kiribati, Nauru, Papua New Guinea and Tuvalu, available from the FCCC website, are to the effect that signature/ratification of the Convention 'in no way constitutes a renunciation of any rights under international law concerning state responsibility for the adverse effects of climate change, and that no provisions in the Convention can be interpreted as derogating from the principles of general international law'.

[26] Cook Islands and Niue, as well as Kiribati, have also made declarations but these did not refer to the inadequacy of emission targets.

[27] Treaties can be agreed between states and international organisations. Although treaties are almost always written, it is possible to have an oral treaty. T. O. Elias, *The Modern Law of Treaties*, 1974.

form and no common nomenclature. Treaties derive their binding force from a fundamental principle underpinning the law of treaties, *pacta sunt servanda*, which requires states to perform obligations they have undertaken on the basis of good faith.

Treaties are the clearest form of consent by states to the creation of rules and for that reason are viewed as the most authoritative source on the subject matter covered by them. It is important to note that a legally binding treaty may contain a variety of legal norms, not all of which might be considered legally binding by its parties. Conversely, non-binding forms of agreement, such as oral agreements, unilateral acts, memoranda of understanding or statements or even minutes of a meeting or exchange of letters, may, in whole or in part, give rise to binding legal obligations.

Treaties create binding rules only for those states that become parties to them and then only where the treaty's entry into force requirements (usually a specific number of ratifications by states) have been met. Although usage of terms in not entirely consistent, in the climate policy literature, the rules contained in the Convention and the Protocol are called 'commitments' whereas the term 'obligations' tends to refer to legal norms that apply to states as a result of non-treaty-based rules.[28]

Because treaties developed as a means for states to give more specificity to customary rules, treaties have to be interpreted and applied against the background of customary rules.[29] The mechanics of treaty-making are covered by customary law as well as the 1969 Vienna Convention on the Law of Treaties, which largely codifies some of the customary international law in the area. This section provides instead a brief response to some of the frequently asked questions concerning the nature of treaties which are of particular interest to climate change.

5.2.1   Parties and non-parties

The FCCC and KP are *multilateral treaties* open to ratification by all states and regional economic integration organisations, such as the EU.[30] Recently, a number of climate observers have questioned whether all Parties to the Convention should be entitled to participate in all aspects of decision-making related to it.[31] So far as decision-making within the Convention is concerned, the

---

[28] See chapter 18.   [29] Oppenheim, 1996: p. 31.

[30] FCCC Article 22.1, KP Article 24.1. States become parties by depositing instruments of ratification, approval or acceptance with the Depository. See FCCC Article 19 and KP Article 23.

[31] See Bodansky, 2001, questioning whether developing countries should be able to participate in matters which essentially concern the commitments of developed countries. Oberthür and Ott, 1999, have argued that those willing to proceed with the KP, should go ahead with

expectation that all FCCC Parties will be able to participate in COP processes, individually or by representation through groups, is a strongly articulated norm in the climate regime – evidenced by, for example, the forceful objections raised on the few occasions when some delegations considered this had not been the case.[32] With respect to decisions outside the Convention, there would appear to be no legal reason why a group of states could not agree to take climate-related actions outside the Convention. It should be noted also that international law permits modification of a multilateral treaty between certain of the parties in certain circumstances.[33]

The relationship between parties to a treaty and *non-parties* has come to the fore since the announcement by the US and Australia that they will not proceed with ratification of the Kyoto Protocol. Parties to the FCCC who choose not to be parties to the KP will be non-parties to the Protocol. So far as substantive obligations are concerned, because treaties can only create obligations for those who choose to become parties, relations between parties to a treaty and non-parties continue to be determined largely by customary law.[34] Customary rules provide that rights and obligations for such states can be created if the parties to the treaty intend a provision to be the means of establishing an obligation for a third state and such a state 'expressly accept[s] that obligation in writing'.[35] They can also be created if matters covered by a treaty become accepted as rules of customary international law as described above.[36]

So far as procedural issues are concerned, the Kyoto Protocol makes clear that only Parties to the Protocol can take decisions relating to the Protocol.[37] Accordingly, elected posts for the various institutions serving the Protocol will be open only to such Parties.[38] So far as attendance at sessions is concerned, Parties to the FCCC that are not parties to the Protocol, such as the US, have a right to 'participate as observers' in sessions of the COP/MOP and the Subsidiary Bodies (SBs).[39] States that are not parties to the FCCC (and therefore not able to become parties to the Protocol either) may observe sessions of the COP/MOP and SBs if they give due notification to the Secretariat of this intention

---

a leadership initiative that does not involve those unwilling to proceed with the KP. Such an initiative is to be pursued 'within the framework of the climate regime but independent of the co-operation of those unwilling to proceed': p. 302. See also Flavin, 1998: 11–18, suggesting a leadership group outside of the climate regime.

[32] COP-4 report, Part I, containing concerns raised by Switzerland.

[33] Article 41, 1969 Vienna Convention.   [34] Article 34, 1969 Vienna Convention.

[35] Article 35, 1969 Vienna Convention.   [36] Article 38, 1969 Vienna Convention.

[37] KP Articles 13.2 and 15.2.

[38] KP Articles 13.3, 15.3 and 6 and Decision 16/CP.7, and Executive Board of the Clean Development Mechanism, Decision 17/CP.7.

[39] KP Article 13.2.

and no objections have been raised by more than one-third of the Parties present.[40]

Customary rules also cover the situation of a state that has *signed* a treaty but then chooses not to proceed with ratification, such as the US in relation to the Protocol.[41] Such a state must 'refrain from acts that would defeat the object and purpose of the agreement . . . until it shall have made its intentions clear not to become a party to the treaty'. Although the US has not taken a position on whether it continues to have any obligations under Article 18 of the Vienna Convention relative to Kyoto, it has in fact made clear its intention not to become a party within the meaning of Article 18. It has stated that it would refrain from participating in KP related negotiations unless these raised issues relating to international precedents or involved budgetary matters.[42]

5.2.2   Interpretation

The Vienna Convention provides that a treaty must be interpreted 'in good faith in accordance with the ordinary meanings to be given to the terms of the treaty in their context and in the light of its object and purpose'.[43] It also sets out what documents and factors should be considered in interpreting treaty rules which include the *travaux préparatoires*, prior drafts and any formal reports of negotiating sessions and any *interpretative declarations* made by Parties.[44]

---

[40] KP Article 13.8. Article 24.1 provides that only Parties to the Convention can become Parties to the Protocol.

[41] Article 18, 1969 Vienna Convention. Signature has two other legal consequences: (i) it signifies acceptance of the authenticity of the text, and (ii) it signals a political commitment to seek ratification of the texts unless and until a state makes clear its intention to do otherwise. See FCCC, Articles 20 and 26 on signature and authencity and Articles 24 and 28, KP. See also American Law Institute, 1987: section 312, Comment i at 174; Ackerman, 2001.

[42] See chapter 16.   [43] Article 31.

[44] See Articles 31–2, 1969 Vienna Convention. See also discussion of declarations made by island states to FCCC/KP at footnotes 25 and 26 above. Other declarations include: EU declaration on the division of competence and joint fulfilment; EU declaration in relation to the KP with additional declarations made by France and Ireland on Article 4 KP; by Cuba on settlement of disputes; by Solomon Islands on acceptance of compulsory arbitration; by Monaco, Czech Republic and Slovakia on acceptance of commitments under FCCC Article 4.2; by Hungary on its understanding of the term 'process of transition' and use of base years; by Bulgaria on use of base year; by Croatia on undergoing the process of transition to a market economy; the change of name of Serbia and Montenegro (formerly the Federal Republic of Yugoslavia); and by France, China and New Zealand on the territorial scope of application of the KP. For the text of all declarations made to date on ratification of the FCCC see http://UNFCCC.int/resource/conv/ratlist.pdf and for declarations relating to the KP see http://UNFCCC.int/resource/kpstats.pdf.

To date disputes over interpretation of key terms in the climate regime have been resolved at the political level of COP negotiations, rather than through recourse to impartial third-party proceedings.[45] Requests for legal advice, usually about particular legal issues rather than particular terms of the treaty, have been submitted by the FCCC Parties, or by the FCCC Secretariat, to the UN Office of Legal Affairs.[46] But the resulting advice has not always been followed, reflecting possible reluctance on the part of FCCC Parties to accept third-party oversight and a conscious preference to iron out legal differences through further political negotiation among themselves.

5.2.3   Relationship between treaties

The Convention and the Protocol are the core of the climate regime but regimes created by other treaties are important and are discussed in chapter 17. The relationship between the FCCC and the Protocol is discussed in chapter 13. There are complex rules governing the priority between treaties covering the same subject matter which are highlighted in relevant sections in the book.[47]

5.3   *General principles, judicial decisions and writings*

Treaties and custom constitute the bulk of international rules. Two other sources are also relevant: general principles of law and judicial decisions and writings. General principles of international law include, for example, the principle of good faith evidenced by *pacta sunt servanda*, the obligation to make reparations for breach of an international obligation; the principle that one may not be one's own judge, and elementary considerations of humanity and principles of humanitarian law.[48] Judicial decisions and writings of eminent jurists are considered to be a subsidiary means of determining the law rather than an actual source of new law. Although formal dispute settlement procedures have yet to be used in MEAs, it is not beyond the realms of possibility that, sooner rather than later, disagreements among Parties, or among Parties and non-Parties, will give rise to international litigation of some sort, including potentially through dispute settlement bodies such as the ICJ or bodies established under the WTO and UNCLOS.[49] There is already emerging interest in using both national and international climate litigation to press for greater climate mitigation.[50] Resulting cases will be influential in defining the rights and obligations of states to protect the climate system under international law.

---

[45] See, for example, chapter 10 on the request by countries from the CACAM about the meaning of 'developing country Party'.

[46] See chapter 13 p. 402.   [47] Article 30.2, 1969 Vienna Convention.

[48] Sands, 1995b: p. 123.   [49] See chapters 9, 12 and 17.

[50] Michael Christie, 'Lawsuits may be next weapon in climate change fight', 6 March 2002, Reuters report. For a discussion on the possibilities of climate litigation see Cameron and Zealke, 1990; Stone, 1990; Grossman, 2003.

5.4   *Other sources*

International organisations endowed with legal authority to enact delegated rules relevant to climate change will also be important sources of international rules for states that are members of such organisations, and are discussed in relevant chapters especially chapter 17. Rules deemed *jus cogens* and the related but legally distinct concept of obligations owed *erga omnes* are also relevant: although it should be said that both notions do not appear concrete enough presently to define the everyday rights and obligations of states in relation to climate change. They are explained here because of their potential future impact on constraining state conduct.

Jus cogens rules, also called peremptory norms of international law, are rules which are accepted and recognised by the international community of States as ones that are of such a fundamental normative character that states are not permitted to alter them through adoption of treaty law or customary practices.[51] There is currently no agreed definition of the category of rules agreed as having *jus cogens* status but candidates include, inter alia, rules relating to war crimes and crimes against humanity, prohibition of acts of slavery, piracy, apartheid and genocide.[52]

The concept of *erga omnes* refers to obligations owed to all states or to the international community 'as a whole'.[53] Massive pollution of the atmosphere or the sea has been put forward as an international crime and therefore potentially as an obligation owed *erga omnes* and one deserving further discussion, for example, by the International Law Commission.[54] The concept of *erga omnes* is closely linked to the issue of legal standing which bears upon how rules affecting the interests of the international community 'as a whole' come to be upheld, including whether a state is entitled to bring an action on behalf of the international community to enforce obligations owed to the whole community, without the need to show it is an 'injured state'. This issue is important in the climate change context because states may wish to protect the climate system which has been deemed to be 'a common concern of humankind' and they may wish to protect areas beyond national jurisdiction.[55] It should be acknowledged, however, that whilst the

---

[51] Article 53, 1969 Vienna Convention.

[52] Oppenheim 1996: p. 8; Cassese, 2001: p. 141; Ragazzi, 1997: p. 48.

[53] Ragazzi, 1997; Oppenheim 1996: p. 5; Cassese, 2001: p. 14; Birnie and Boyle, 2002: p. 196.

[54] See First ILC Draft Articles on State Responsibility which provide that 'prohibition of massive pollution of the atmosphere or the sea' is an obligation 'so essential for the protection of fundamental interests of the international community that [its] breach [was] recognized as a crime by that community as a whole'. See Article 19 (3) (d) of the Draft Articles on State Responsibility, Pt I, Yearbook of the International Law Commission (1980–II), Pt 2.

[55] Sands, 1995b: p. 153; Birnie and Boyle, 2002: p. 197; Cassese, 2001: p. 16.

recognition that massive pollution to the global commons is an international crime of fundamental interest to the whole international community and enjoys widespread legal support, there is currently no agreement on whether this should be accompanied by a procedural right of enforcement belonging to all members of the international community.[56]

---

[56] Cassese, 2001: pp. 141 and 200; Birnie and Boyle, 2002: p. 196, referring to the ILC Draft Articles on State Responsibility adopted in 2000.

2

Overview

This chapter consists of a brief overview of the climate change problem, the international response to it, and key elements of the climate change regime. The basic information provided aims to give readers the tools that are needed to understand and work with the more detailed chapters that follow.

1 The climate change problem

1.1 *Causes and projections*

Climate change is linked to the presence of greenhouse gases (GHGs) in the atmosphere. The natural greenhouse effect, however, which is essential to life on earth, is now being disrupted by human activity due to rising emissions of GHGs from the consumption of fossil fuels – coal, oil and gas – along with intensive agriculture. Forest clearance and other land-use changes are also releasing carbon stored in trees and other vegetation, while reducing the amount of CO_2 that is naturally absorbed by such carbon sinks. The man-made chemicals hydrofluorocarbons (HFCs), perfluorocarbons (PFCs), sulphur hexafluoride (SF_6) and other fluorocarbon gases are additional contributors to the growing cocktail of GHGs. The concentration of CO_2 in the atmosphere, for example, has risen by over a third since pre-industrial levels in 1750. All other things being equal, the greater concentration of GHGs in the atmosphere generates an enhanced greenhouse effect, trapping more heat and raising temperatures at the earth's surface.

The atmospheric concentration of GHGs, however, is only one factor among many that govern the climate system. The climate itself is subject to natural variability, and is also influenced by both natural and anthropogenic (human-induced) factors. Variations in the sun's output of energy, ocean currents and volcanic eruptions are all natural factors affecting the global climate. Additional human-induced factors include stratospheric ozone depletion, as well as emissions of sulphur dioxide and other very small airborne particles – known as aerosols – from fossil fuel and biomass burning. Aerosols, however, are short lived and do not mix so well in the atmosphere, so that their impact is largely regional and short term.

While awareness of the possible effects on the climate of fossil fuel consumption can be dated back to the late nineteenth and early twentieth centuries, it was only in the early 1980s that scientific concern was aroused by research results pointing to the potential severity of climate change. In 1988, the World Meteorological Organization (WMO) and the United Nations Environment Programme (UNEP) jointly established the Intergovernmental Panel on Climate Change (IPCC), with a mandate to assess the emerging science of climate change and subject it to intergovernmental scrutiny.[1] A central task for the IPCC was detection and attribution, that is, determining whether a warming trend could indeed be detected, and the extent to which this could be attributed to human interference. The consensus view of the IPCC, and therefore the vast majority of the world's scientists, is now that the climate is changing, and that human influence can indeed be detected against the background of natural variability.[2] Although there are still important uncertainties over the timing, rate and impacts of climate change, these do not challenge the fundamental conclusion that human-induced climate change is real.

The latest projection of the IPCC, set out in its 2001 Assessment Report,[3] is that global average temperatures will rise by 1.4–5.8°C by 2100. This implies a rate of change without precedent since the last ice age 10,000 years ago, when average temperatures were some 5–6°C lower than today. Temperatures, however, will continue to rise well beyond 2100, even if GHG emissions are drastically cut. One major consequence of global warming will be rising sea levels. These have already risen by 0.1–0.2 metres during the twentieth century, and the IPCC projects a further rise of 0.09–0.88 metres by 2100. The deep inertia of the oceans means that sea levels will continue to rise for centuries even after temperatures have stopped increasing.

1.2   *Impacts*[4]

The projected rise in global temperatures will translate into changes in day-to-day weather that will differ considerably across regions. A key concern for all regions, however, is that the weather is likely to become more variable and unstable. The impacts of climate change will also play out against the backdrop of

---

[1] On the IPCC, see chapter 15.   [2] See chapter 4.
[3] IPCC, 2001a.   [4] This section draws on IPCC, 2001b.

existing stresses and vulnerabilities, such as poverty, high population density and weak infrastructure. For this reason, adverse trends in the weather will disproportionately impact on poor countries and communities with limited resources to adapt. The same is true for natural ecosystems, where climate change will exacerbate existing pressures, such as habitat destruction and local pollution. Some particularly vulnerable systems (e.g. coral reefs) may be unable to adapt at all, and suffer irreversible damage.

The impacts of climate change will be far-reaching. While more intense droughts may exacerbate water shortages in arid and semi-arid regions, more frequent heavy rainfall events could threaten regions already prone to flooding. Many diseases – such as malaria and dengue – thrive in a warmer climate and could extend their geographical ranges. The agricultural sector is heavily dependent on climatic conditions, and is particularly important to many developing countries. Although some crops may benefit from the extra CO_2 in the atmosphere (the CO_2 fertilisation effect), research suggests this may be offset by damage from higher temperatures, water stress, more virulent diseases and pest attacks. Crops that are already growing close to their maximum temperature threshold (e.g. in tropical regions) would suffer from even a small degree of warming. Sea level rise, in turn, threatens low-lying islands and coastal areas, not just through submergence by the sea or ocean, but also through greater coastal erosion, periodic storm surges and the encroachment of salt water into irrigation systems and drinking water. The impacts of recent extreme weather events – cyclones, storms, drought-induced forest fires – demonstrate society's vulnerability to any increase in their intensity or frequency.

An underlying danger associated with climate change is that crossing certain (unknown) temperature thresholds might trigger abrupt, large-scale and catastrophic events. These could include the shut down of the Gulf Stream, which accounts for the present mild climate in North-western Europe, along with the disintegration of the massive West Antarctic and Greenland ice sheets. While the likelihood of these events occurring in the next hundred years or so is very low, warming this century could irreversibly set them in motion. Evidence from ice cores demonstrates that such abrupt events have occurred in the past within just a few decades or even years.

2   The international response to climate change

2.1   *The emergence of the climate change regime*

Climate change emerged onto the international political stage in 1988, when the UN General Assembly (acting on a proposal from Malta) took up the issue for the first time and adopted resolution 43/53, declaring climate change to be 'a common concern of mankind'. The debate in the UNGA came in the wake of the establishment of the IPCC, along with a confluence of other factors, including an unusually hot summer in the US, the discovery of the hole in the ozone layer in 1987 and the successful adoption of the Montreal Protocol on Substances That Deplete the Ozone Layer that same year.

By 1990, the IPCC had produced its First Assessment Report on the state of climate change science, warning that, although there were many uncertainties, human activity was leading to increased atmospheric concentrations of CO_2 and rising temperatures. This Report formed the background to the November 1990 Ministerial Declaration of the Second World Climate Conference, which recommended that negotiations on a framework climate convention begin without delay.[5] The UN General Assembly acted on this recommendation, formally launching negotiations on a framework convention on climate change. An Intergovernmental Negotiating Committee (INC) was convened under the UN General Assembly to conduct these negotiations.[6] The adoption of ambitious national GHG reduction targets by a number of OECD countries,[7] the publication of a supplementary report by the IPCC, and concurrent preparations for the forthcoming Earth Summit (UNCED) in Rio de Janeiro, provided political momentum to overcome the deadlock reached at the fifth INC session in February 1992.[8] The final text of the Convention was adopted at the close of the resumed fifth session of the INC held in May 1992 at a time when all OECD countries, with the exception of the US and Turkey, had set themselves stringent national GHG reduction targets.[9] The Convention was formally opened for signature at UNCED in June 1992. A summary of its key elements is provided in box 2.1.

This formative period coincided with a period of economic prosperity for most of the OECD countries resulting in widespread domestic support for increased environmental protection and development assistance. The adoption or opening for signature of five major international instruments at the Earth Summit attested to the global commitment to sustainable development at that time.[10] The break up of the former Soviet Union and entry of many developing countries into the global economy in the early 1990s appeared to herald greater levels of international cooperation, cutting across East–West and North–South political divisions. Regional economic integration, evidenced by the growth of the EU, and optimism

---

[5] See Ministerial Declaration contained in the report of the Conference in A/45/696/Add.1, Annex III (1990).

[6] UN resolution 45/221.   [7] See chapter 5.

[8] For a history of the INC negotiations, see Bodansky, 1993.   [9] See INC-5 part II report.

[10] The five instruments are: the Climate Change Convention, the Convention on Biological Diversity, Agenda 21, the Rio Declaration on Environment and Development, and the Non-Legally Binding Statement of Principles on Forests. Agenda 21 gave rise to further negotiating processes which concluded in the adoption in 1994 of the Convention to Combat Desertification and the 1995 Agreement on Straddling and Highly Migratory Fish Stocks.

over multilateral institutions in general triggered calls for numerous major UN summits and action plans. These trends counterbalanced apprehensions about the declining capacity of sovereign states to control economic forces unleashed by globalisation.

2.2   *Entry into force and the Berlin Mandate*

These factors contributed to the rapid entry into force of the Convention in March 1994. The first Conference of the Parties (COP-1) met a year later in Berlin where it adopted a number of decisions elaborating on the Convention, including, for example, guidance to the financial mechanism and guidelines for submitting national reports. The most important task facing COP-1, however, was to review the adequacy of the commitments of Annex I Parties, as required by the Convention.[11] After heated debate, COP-1 eventually adopted a decision known as the Berlin Mandate[12] (see box 2.2), finding the commitments to be 'not adequate', and launching a new round of negotiations on 'a protocol or another legal instrument'. The Berlin Mandate specified that the negotiations should revise the commitments of industrialised countries, but not introduce any new commitments for developing countries.

The negotiations were conducted within the Ad Hoc Group on the Berlin Mandate (AGBM), an open-ended group comprising all Convention Parties. The IPCC's Second Assessment Report, considered by COP-2 meeting in 1996 in Geneva, confirmed that human activities were indeed changing the world's climate. The Geneva Ministerial Declaration endorsing the IPCC's findings, although it was not formally adopted by COP-2, effectively silenced climate science sceptics, forcing the political pace of negotiations. The Kyoto Protocol was unanimously adopted by COP-3 meeting in December 1997 in Japan.[13] The key elements of the Kyoto Protocol are summarised in box 2.1 below.

Box 2.1   Key elements of the climate change regime

The Convention **(1992)**

- Defines an **ultimate objective** and **principles**, which also apply to the Protocol.
- Divides countries into:
    - **Annex I** (OECD countries and economies in transition – EITs)
    - **Annex II** (OECD countries only); and
    - **Non-Annex I** (mostly developing countries).

---

[11] See Article 4.2 (d) FCCC.   [12] Decision 1/CP.1.   [13] Decision 1/CP.3.

- All Parties: **general commitments**, including reporting obligations.
- Annex I Parties: **specific 'aim'** to return emissions to 1990 levels by 2000.
- Annex II Parties: must provide **financial assistance** to developing countries, and also promote **technology transfer**, including to EITs.

The Kyoto Protocol (1997)

- All Parties: **general commitments**.
- Annex I Parties: Individual **emission targets**, adding up to a total cut of 5%. Targets range from −8% (most countries) to +10%, and are listed in Annex B.
- Emission targets:
  - Cover CO_2, CH_4, N_2O, HFCs, PFCs, SF_6, counted together as a basket.
  - Also cover certain **carbon sequestration activities** in the land use, land-use change and forestry (LULUCF) sector, based on specific rules.
  - In most cases, use **1990** as a baseline.
  - Must be met by the 'commitment period' **2008–2012**.
- **Flexibility mechanisms** – joint implementation, clean development mechanism (CDM) and emissions trading – can be used to help meet targets. Groups of countries can also meet targets jointly (so far, only invoked by the EU).
- Stricter **reporting and review** procedures for Annex I Parties.
- **Compliance system** to address cases of non-compliance with the Protocol.
- **Regular reviews** of commitments.

Convention and Kyoto Protocol institutions

- **Conference of the Parties (COP)** serves as the 'supreme body' of the regime. COP will serve as the meeting of the Parties (**COP/MOP**) to the Kyoto Protocol.
- **Subsidiary Body for Scientific and Technological Advice** (SBSTA) and **Subsidiary Body for Implementation** (SBI) assist the COP and COP/MOP.
- The **Global Environment Facility** (GEF) serves as the financial mechanism for both the Convention and Kyoto Protocol.
- Permanent **Secretariat** serves both the Convention and Kyoto Protocol.
- **Rules of procedure** govern the negotiations. Due to disputes over the voting rule, these are not adopted, but applied at each session, except for the voting rule.

2.3   *The post-Kyoto era*

The period of rule development culminating in the adoption of the Kyoto Protocol was marked by economic recession in many OECD countries and financial crises across South Asia, which deepened significantly throughout 1998 and 1999. The crises experienced in the Asian Tigers and Argentina sent shock waves across the globe. Effects were felt by the fragile economies of Africa,[14] Latin American nations, and even the more resilient economic and political structures in the US, Japan and Europe.[15] The 'Rio partnership' between developed and developing countries soured in the face of aid fatigue at a time when the economies of the latter seemed especially vulnerable to the endemic instability of the world system driven by vast private financial flows. Impacts on former Soviet bloc countries were more modest, due only to the fact that many of these economies had already hit rock bottom as a result of their transition to a market economy. This economic turbulence, the skewed gains from globalisation, and disenchantment at the impact of international institutions on marginalised countries and vulnerable communities, gave rise to global civil protests, such as those at the Ministerial Conference of the World Trade Organization (WTO) in Seattle (US) in December 1999.

In the climate regime, too, divisions began to emerge in the post-Kyoto era between those (mostly developing countries) who wanted to focus on implementation of existing commitments under the Convention, and those interested in launching a post-Kyoto round covering developing countries. The stakes were raised by the fact that the US Senate had made the 'meaningful participation' of developing countries a condition for its ratification of the Kyoto Protocol.[16] Against this background, Parties meeting at COP-4 in Argentina adopted the so-called Buenos Aires Plan of Action (BAPA) (see box 2.2), which sought both to advance the implementation of the Convention (e.g. on issues such as technology transfer, adaptation and impacts of response measures), and to complete the unfinished business from Kyoto. Most Annex I Parties felt that this unfinished business – including rules for the three flexibility mechanisms, use of carbon sequestration to help meet emission targets and the design of the compliance system – was so important that it had to be resolved before they could ratify the Protocol. COP-6 was set as a deadline for reaching agreement on most issues under the BAPA. COP-4, however, mothballed the possibility of a post-Kyoto negotiating round covering developing countries. Nevertheless, by COP-5 in 1999, even the largest and best resourced delegations were starting to find the hugely ambitious BAPA taxing. COP-5, meeting in Bonn, conducted a stocktaking exercise that did little to adjust

---

[14] Harsch, 1998.   [15] Lannon, 1999; Kashyap, 2002; Chossudovsky, 1998.
[16] Senate resolution 98 (proposed by Byrd-Hagel) adopted July 1997.

the scope and timetable for completion of these increasingly complex negotiations. It also did little to address frustrations across the political spectrum caused by rising GHG emissions in most OECD countries on the one hand, and the refusal of developing countries to address the evolution of their commitments on the other.

In the face of such challenges, it is little wonder that COP-6, held at The Hague in November 2000, ended in spectacular failure.[17] The subsequent rejection of the Kyoto Protocol by US President George W. Bush in March 2001, which was no doubt intended to deal the Protocol a fatal blow, proved instead to be a form of shock therapy. The invisible glue of multilateralism, backed by sound science in the form of the IPCC's Third Assessment Report issued in early 2001, held the climate change regime together. The resumed sixth session of the COP (COP-6 part II), which met in Bonn in July 2001, broke the political deadlock. Against expectations, COP-6 part II struck a political deal known as the Bonn Agreements.[18] Building on the Bonn Agreements, COP-7, meeting in Marrakesh in November that same year, adopted the Marrakesh Accords,[19] a series of COP decisions that in effect brought the Buenos Aires Plan of Action to a close.

Box 2.2   Key decisions in the climate change process

Berlin Mandate: Decision 1/CP.1, adopted at COP-1 in 1995. The Berlin Mandate declared that the specific commitments for Annex I Parties under the Convention were 'not adequate', and launched negotiations on 'a protocol or another legal instrument', to be concluded by COP-3. These negotiations resulted in the adoption of the Kyoto Protocol.

Buenos Aires Plan of Action (BAPA): Decision 1/CP.4, adopted at COP-4 in 1998. The one-page BAPA served as an umbrella for decisions 2–8/CP.4. These seven decisions covered the financial mechanism (2 and 3/CP.4), technology transfer (4/CP.4), adverse effects of climate change/implementation of response measures (5/CP.4), activities implemented jointly (6/CP.4), the flexibility mechanisms (7/CP.4), and preparations for COP/MOP (including reporting and review, policies and measures, compliance and LULUCF) (8/CP.4). The BAPA umbrella decision helped to seal a political package, whereby all these issues – covering both the Convention and the Protocol – would be addressed in parallel. The deadline set by many of the BAPA decisions for action on their respective issues was COP-6.

---

[17] For analyses of COP-6, see papers in *International Affairs*, 2001.
[18] See report on COP-6 part II; also box 2.2 below.
[19] See report on COP-7; also box 2.2 below.

Bonn Agreements: Decision 5/CP.6, adopted at COP-6 part II in 2001, thereby restoring the momentum of the climate change process after the collapse of negotiations at COP-6 part I. The Bonn Agreements set out the political deal reached on the key points of contention (known as the 'crunch issues') in the BAPA negotiations. They established, for example, the penalties for non-compliance with emission targets, the individual limits for Parties' use of carbon sink credits, and the establishment of new funds to assist developing countries. Lack of time, however, meant that the Bonn Agreements could not elaborate further on more technical and less politically sensitive details, which were referred to COP-7 in Marrakesh.

Marrakesh Accords: Decisions 2–24/CP.7, adopted at COP-7 in 2001. This package of twenty-three decisions incorporates and builds on the Bonn Agreements, setting out very detailed rules, procedures, technical guidelines and work programmes. The issues covered by the Marrakesh Accords include those under the BAPA, along with related questions, such as capacity-building and the impact of single projects. The Marrakesh Accords thus brought to an end the post-Kyoto cycle of policy-making launched by the BAPA.

Some issues, however, were not fully cleared up by the Marrakesh Accords, notably certain technical questions relating to reporting and review (which were later resolved at COP-8 and COP-9), along with rules for sink projects under the CDM (eventually agreed at COP-9).

2.4   *The post-Marrakesh era*

The completion of Kyoto's unfinished business finally opened the way for ratification by almost all Annex I Parties. Several outstanding loose ends were then tied up at COP-8 (New Delhi, October 2002) and COP-9 (Milan, December 2003). These decisions, combined with the widespread ratification of the Kyoto Protocol, renewed optimism for the climate regime. Developments elsewhere in the international system contributed to this optimism. These included the Monterrey Conference on Financing for Development (Mexico, March 2002), which brought the trade, aid and financial institutions agendas together for the first time and resulted in the release of additional funds,[20] along with the World Summit on Sustainable Development (Johannesburg, September 2002) which generated a suite of development related targets, including for poverty eradication and energy, and

[20] See Monterrey Consensus of the International Conference on Financing for Development in A/CONF.198/11.

brought neglected issues, such as corporate responsibility and accountability, onto the international agenda.[21]

The delay in entry into force of the Kyoto Protocol, however, in the face of prevarication from the Russian Federation over whether or not to ratify, has left the climate change regime somewhat in limbo. Although the approval of the Kyoto Protocol by the Russian government in September 2004 sets the stage for the Protocol's entry into force, considerable unease over the very modest progress made by most Annex I Parties in cutting their emissions remains. In 2003, when full emissions data for 2000 first became available, the COP concluded that, although the emissions of Annex I Parties in 2000 were below their 1990 levels, this was largely due to cuts in the EITs and came despite considerable increases in several large emitters.[22] Unless much stronger action is taken, the emissions of Annex I Parties, including EITs, will rise over the period 2000–2010.

Notwithstanding these setbacks, the regime continues to evolve. Work has continued on the implementation of the Convention (e.g. on reporting and review, capacity-building and technology transfer), while the CDM Executive Board has become an established institution within the climate change regime, meeting regularly to develop and review the operation of the CDM. In addition to this more routine work, both the Convention and the Kyoto Protocol include provisions for the regular review of commitments and launch of new negotiating rounds. The first trigger under the Kyoto Protocol – assuming its entry into force – will come into effect in 2005, when negotiations must commence on the next set of emission targets for Annex I Parties. A further, more comprehensive review of the Kyoto Protocol's commitments is due for the second COP/MOP, probably soon after.[23] For now, however, the climate change regime is primarily in an implementation phase, with Parties focused on putting into practice the large body of rules that are now in place to guide their efforts to combat climate change. These include the rules of the Kyoto Protocol, which many Parties are putting into practice and writing into national legislation, pending entry into force. The remainder of this book provides an in-depth examination of these rules, along with the institutions and procedures that support them.

---

[21] See chapter 17.

[22] Decision 1/CP.9, National communications from Parties included in Annex I to the Convention.

[23] See chapter 18.

3

Regime participants

1   Introduction

The climate change regime enjoys one of the highest levels of participation in the international environmental arena among both states and stakeholder organisations, including non-governmental organisations (NGOs), intergovernmental organisations (IGOs), and UN bodies and specialised agencies. This chapter provides an overview of the climate change regime's diverse participants and how they organise themselves, focusing on those most directly active in the regime itself. Appendix I, which lists all the Parties to the Convention along with key statistics and their negotiating coalitions, complements this chapter.

2   Parties

The Convention[1] enjoys one of the highest rates of membership among MEAs, with its 189 Parties including 188 states plus the European Community, which participates as a regional economic integration organisation.[2] Only a handful of states have not yet ratified the Convention and remain non-Parties, including Andorra, Brunei Darussalam, the Holy See, Iraq and Somalia. At the time of writing, the Kyoto Protocol had been ratified by nearly two-thirds of Parties to the Convention, representing nearly three-quarters of the world's population.[3]

---

[1] Participation of countries that are not parties to the Kyoto Protocol in the climate regime is discussed in chapters 1, 13 and 14.

[2] See chapter 5.

[3] For up-to-date figures on Parties to the Convention and Kyoto Protocol, see www.unfccc.int.

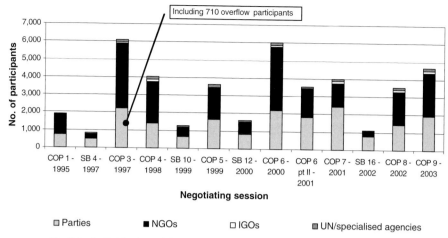

Fig. 3.1   Individual participants at selected negotiating sessions

The Secretariat asks each Party to the Convention to designate a 'national focal point', who then serves as the main point of contact for that Party concerning activities in the climate change regime on a day-to-day basis.[4] The great majority of Parties to the Convention regularly attend sessions of the regime bodies, with over 90 per cent typically represented at COP sessions and over 80 per cent at subsidiary body sessions. The size of delegations, however, varies significantly. While the average delegation at COP-6 part II in 2001 (a major, high-profile negotiating session) had ten members, this included twenty-two 'mega-delegations' of over twenty-five persons (some significantly more), along with sixty-six delegations of three members or less. Similarly, the average delegation at SB-16 in 2002 (a low-profile, technical session) consisted of five members, but included sixty-five delegations of just one person. Predictably, the smallest delegations are typically those from the poorer developing countries and EITs, and the larger ones from the wealthy, industrialised nations. Some developing countries with a considerable interest in the climate change issue, however, do also field large delegations. Brazil, China and Indonesia, for example, all sent delegations of over twenty persons to COP-9.[5] Figure 3.1 illustrates the number of *individual delegates* who have attended selected negotiating sessions. Predictably, the number of individual representatives is higher at COPs, especially high-profile COPs, than at subsidiary body sessions. Interestingly, there is no clear trend suggesting an increase in the number of participants over time.

---

[4] See document FCCC/CP/1996/6/Add.2, section B. The list of national focal points is available at http://unfccc.int/resource/nfp.html.
[5] See List of Participants at COP-9, FCCC/CP/2003/INF.1.

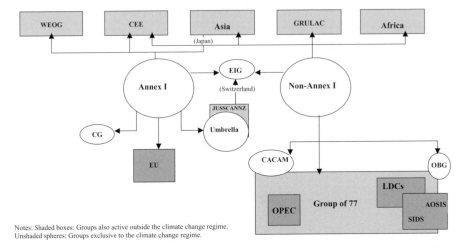

Notes: Shaded boxes: Groups also active outside the climate change regime.
Unshaded spheres: Groups exclusive to the climate change regime.

WEOG: Western European and Others group; CEE: Central and Eastern European group; GRULAC: Group of Latin America and the Caribbean; EIG: Environmental Integrity Group; JUSSCANNZ: Japan, US, Switzerland, Canada, Australia, Norway, New Zealand; CACAM: Central Asia, Caucasus, Albania and Moldova group; OBG: Open Balkan Group; CG: Central Group; LDCs: Least Developed Countries; SIDS: Small Island Developing States; OPEC: Organization of Petroleum Exporting Countries; AOSIS: Alliance of Small Island States. Parties that are members of AOSIS and SIDS correspond almost completely, although the two groups are not identical. Since this figure was drafted, two members of AOSIS – Cyprus and Malta – have joined the EU.

Fig. 3.2   Party groupings in the climate change regime

2.1   *Groupings*

The Parties to the climate change regime are organised into a number of different groups and coalitions, some of which stem from official UN listings, while others consist of more ad hoc political alliances. Figure 3.2 depicts the various groupings in place, with are then described in more detail below.[6] Appendix I summarises the groupings to which each Party belongs.

2.1.1   UN regional groups

Established practice in the UN system[7] divides UN members into five 'regional groups':

- Africa;
- Asia (which also covers the Pacific);
- Central and Eastern Europe;
- Latin America and the Caribbean (known as GRULAC); and
- Western Europe and Others (WEOG). This group includes Australia, Canada, New Zealand and the US, but not Japan, which is the only developed country member of the Asia group.

---

[6] This chapter does not directly discuss the lists of Parties in Annexes I and II of the Convention, and Annex B of the Kyoto Protocol. Given that such listings are directly related to the commitments of Parties, they are taken up in chapters 5 and 10.

[7] Some UN bodies use a different regional group system: WMO, for example, has six regional groups.

In practice, the exact composition of the regional groups varies between different parts of the UN system, due primarily to the differing membership of regimes. Non-UN members, for example, are nevertheless incorporated in the regional group system in the climate change context. Switzerland and Tuvalu, for instance, were considered part of the WEOG and Asia groups, respectively, before recently becoming UN members.

The regional group system is only of limited relevance to the substantive interests of Parties in climate change politics. The countries of Central and Eastern Europe, for example, include both Annex I Parties that are now members of the EU, and some of the non-Annex I Parties of the former Soviet Union. Asia is even more heterogeneous, encompassing Japan, Saudi Arabia and Samoa, all countries holding varying positions in the climate change negotiations, while the developed country group WEOG is split between the EU and non-EU countries, and excludes Japan.

The regional group system has, however, proved remarkably resilient in the regime, as indeed it has throughout the UN system. It is inscribed in the Rules of Procedure as the basis for electing Bureau members, and was also chosen as the main basis for electing members of most of the specialised bodies, including the CDM Executive Board and the Compliance Committee.[8]

With the exception of the African Group, which also serves as a negotiating coalition (see below), the regional groups are used almost exclusively to nominate candidates to the Bureaux and the specialised bodies, and not for the promotion of substantive interests. Regional ties, however, remain important and some of the regional groups occasionally make ceremonial statements at the opening or closure of a COP session. Meetings of the regional groups in the climate change regime are usually coordinated and chaired by whichever country holds the Chair of that regional group at the UN in New York.

2.1.2   Political negotiating coalitions

As well as UN regional groups, Parties also belong to political negotiating coalitions, some of which are supported by intergovernmental institutions. These coalitions are based on the common interests or cultural, economic or geographic affinities of their members, and vary considerably in their degree of cohesion, objectives and modes of operation. Some are active throughout the intergovernmental arena, while others are specific to the environmental or climate change context. Very few Parties do not belong to any coalition, but some belong to several, creating a multi-layered system of alliances that shapes the political dynamics of the climate change negotiations.

---

[8] See also chapter 13.

The existence of negotiating coalitions is pivotal to the functioning of the climate change regime, as well as the wider intergovernmental arena. By forming coalitions, Parties can pool their resources and negotiating clout, which is especially important for countries that do not hold much power and would otherwise find it difficult to get their views heard. The complexity of the climate change process also creates a major incentive for countries, particularly small ones, to join together to share information. Moreover, it would be logistically impossible to conduct negotiations among 150-plus individual delegations; the existence of coalitions, some of which speak with a common voice, thus helps to streamline the negotiation process and reduce its transaction costs. There are drawbacks, however. Large coalitions (such as the G-77), or those that face the political imperative of maintaining a unified position (such as the EU), can be ponderous in their internal proceedings and slow to respond to developments in the negotiations, thus hindering their ability to have an impact on the process. Likewise, coalitions themselves can become dominated by their more powerful members, drowning out the views of the weaker countries, or their positions can risk being dragged down to the level of the 'lowest common denominator'.

The post-Kyoto negotiations have seen a proliferation of new negotiating coalitions, with several groups having emerged over the past few years. This reflects the growing maturity of the regime, accompanied by an increasing awareness among countries of their specific and group interests relative to climate change, along with their desire to participate more actively in the regime. The demand by countries to form new coalitions also responds to the growing tendency of structuring negotiations based on coalitions. Invitations to 'Friends of the Chair' and other consultations, for example, are now typically issued via negotiating coalitions, rather than to individual countries.[9] There is no formal process for establishing a negotiating coalition; countries simply decide to do so, and then usually notify the COP Bureau, SBs or Secretariat of their actions. The various coalitions typically meet daily during sessions of the COP and SBs to share information, discuss strategies and, in many cases, elaborate common positions.

2.2   *Group of 77 and China*

The Group of 77 (G-77) is the largest negotiating coalition in the UN system.[10] The Group was formed in 1964, during negotiations on a 'new international economic order' held under the auspices of UNCTAD. These negotiations were aimed at redressing the unequal balance of global economic and political

---

[9] See chapter 14.
[10] For more information on the G-77, see www.g77.org; also Williams, 1997, and Mwandosya, 2000.

power in favour of the developing countries, many of which had recently become independent. The G-77, which now includes 132 members, remains active as the main advocate of developing country interests in the UN system, including in the climate change regime. China is an associate, rather than full, member of the G-77. It works very closely with the G-77 in the climate change regime, with statements from the Group invariably made 'on behalf of the G-77 and China'. Due to its associate membership, however, China itself does not speak on behalf of the Group. The G-77 has a permanent Secretariat and institutional structure in New York, along with regional chapters in the main UN centres, namely Geneva, Nairobi, Paris, Rome and Vienna.

Of the Parties to the Convention, all of them non-Annex I, 129 are members of the G-77 and China. These span a massive diversity of interests: the small island states that are most vulnerable to the impacts of climate change, the oil exporting countries who fear the impact of mitigation measures, least developed countries (LDCs), large industrialising nations and middle income nations (see range of statistics summarised in Appendix I). Despite their differences, however, G-77 members are united by the challenges they face in tackling poverty, achieving sustained economic development, and gaining power and influence in a world still dominated by the Western industrialised OECD members. This unity is strong, and is carried through to the climate change regime. The G-77 has only once publicly split, at COP-1 in 1995, where seventy-two developing countries joined what became known as the 'Green Group', advocating a draft text prepared by India (on a green piece of paper), which became the basis for the 'Berlin Mandate' that launched negotiations on the Kyoto Protocol.[11] The fact that most G-77 members also belong to other groups – such as the African Group, AOSIS and the least developed country coalition – has not seriously eroded this sense of unity, or at least its public face.

The G-77 in the climate change regime operates as a group in the context of the wider north/south divide in the UN system, including on environmental issues, where the industrialised countries are viewed as the main cause of environmental problems due to their consumption and lifestyle patterns. Slow progress by most OECD countries in cutting their GHG emissions, and the relatively small amount of financial assistance and technology transfer disbursed, has exacerbated this divide. Another feature of the G-77 is the lack of capacity of many of its smaller members to participate effectively in the negotiations, due to tiny delegations, lack of resources to conduct in-depth policy analysis and, in some cases, absence of a clear position or mandate from their governments.[12]

---

[11] See Mwandosya, 2000. On the Berlin Mandate, see chapter 2.

[12] For more on the problems faced by developing countries in the climate change negotiations, see Gupta, 1997.

Like any group, the G-77 and China has its more and less powerful members. Brazil, China, India and Saudi Arabia, for example, are among the most influential countries in the climate change context, and hold great sway over the decisions of the Group. This can lead to smaller countries feeling sidelined. Realisation that their specific concerns were not adequately reflected in the wider G-77, for example, prompted the LDCs to mobilise into a more organised political grouping in the climate change regime. Individual developing countries will, however, hesitate to go against a common G-77 position, or that of their powerful colleagues, for reasons of Group loyalty and awareness that they may require the support of the G-77 or its influential members on other issues, including in the wider intergovernmental arena.

The role of the G-77 Chair in the climate change context is performed by the country holding the Chair of the G-77 in New York, a position that rotates annually. Countries volunteer to hold the position, on the basis of rotation among the three developing country regional groups (Africa, Asia and GRULAC). Although it is a highly respected position, not all developing countries feel able or willing to take it on, due to the economic and institutional resources required, the difficulty of bringing members to a common position and the reality that the G-77 Chair may have to go against some powerful countries, which could trigger wider political repercussions. Five out of the seven most recent G-77 Chairs have been members of OPEC – Indonesia (1998), Nigeria (2000), Iran (2001), Venezuela (2002) and Qatar (2004) – countries that tend to have greater resources at their disposal and which recognise the significance of holding such a position in the climate change context.

The G-77 and China develop common positions on substantive issues wherever possible, and negotiate as a group on that basis. All decisions and common positions are agreed by consensus in plenary meetings of the G-77; if there is no consensus, there is no common G-77 position. Once agreed, the G-77 Chair will typically take the floor first in the negotiations to articulate the Group's position, and individual G-77 members then often intervene to support, and give their perspective on, that position. Given the diversity of views within the G-77, the common stance of the Group is often quite general, revolving around broad principles rather than specific points, thus allowing space for countries with strong or more detailed views to pursue their individual specific interests, providing these do not contradict the Group position.

Due to the logistical difficulties and expense of bringing all its members together, the G-77 does not meet inter-sessionally as a Group on climate change issues. However, the Secretariat does provide resources, including extra subsistence allowance for eligible delegates,[13] to enable the G-77 to meet for one or

---

[13] See chapter 16.

two days on the eve of negotiating sessions. The Secretariat also makes an office available to the G-77 Chair, along with a secretary and computing facilities. At particularly important negotiating sessions, the Secretariat has also sought to provide interpretation for Group meetings, at least into English and French.

Over recent years, the G-77 has developed a system of 'coordinators' who take the lead in negotiations on particular issues. Coordinators are chosen informally, based mostly on areas of expertise and expressions of interest from delegations, with the G-77 Chair seeking to balance the various factions within the Group. India, for example, coordinated the post-Kyoto negotiations on the flexibility mechanisms, while Brazil was coordinator for LULUCF. G-77 coordinators arrange meetings on their particular topics so that fellow Group members can express their views, and will often develop draft text for a common position. Common positions must be approved in the main Group, where the coordinators will receive a mandate to negotiate on behalf of the G-77 and defend the Group's position in negotiating forums. Coordinators will then report back on the negotiations to the main G-77, where they will seek a further mandate. Such specialisation has proved vitally important post-Kyoto, given the large number of issues on the table. It has also helped to improve transparency and accountability, as those G-77 members taking the lead on particular issues must report back on their actions as negotiators, and are then answerable to the main Group.

The work of the Group has been marked by the individual style of G-77 Chairs. The conciliatory style of the Tanzanian G-77 Chair for 1997, for example, is widely believed to have helped keep the G-77 united at a time of great latent divisions within the Group. Likewise, the outstanding diplomatic skills of the Iranian G-77 Chair for 2001, together with his country's strong commitment to multilateralism as a basis for international relations, contributed greatly to the constructive participation of the G-77 in the negotiations that led to the Marrakesh Accords. The effective managerial style of the Nigerian G-77 Chair for 2000, who drew on his private sector experience to lead the G-77, is credited by many as having consolidated the coordinator approach.

Most G-77 members also belong to other negotiating coalitions, reflecting the wide spectrum of views encompassed within the Group. These are discussed below.

2.3   *Alliance of Small Island States (AOSIS) and Small Island Developing States (SIDS)*

AOSIS, a coalition of small-island and low-lying coastal states that are highly vulnerable to climate change and associated sea level rise, was established in November 1990 during the Second World Climate Conference.[14] It now has a membership of forty-three states and four observers, most of which are also

---

[14] For more information on AOSIS, see www.sidsnet.org/aosis.

members of the G-77. The membership of AOSIS does not fully coincide with the forty-four countries officially classified by the UN as small island developing states (SIDS). AOSIS members also comprise low-lying states, such as Guinea-Bissau and Belize, as well as more developed nations, such as Cyprus and Malta, while the list of SIDS includes a number of countries that are not fully independent and do not generally participate in international treaties. With just one exception, however (the Dominican Republic), all SIDS that are Parties to the Convention are also AOSIS members.

AOSIS has been very active in the climate change regime from its inception, putting forward the first draft text in the Kyoto Protocol negotiations as early as 1994.[15] It is also active in other international environmental arenas, notably in the CBD and CSD/WSSD processes.[16] Although AOSIS has no formal constitution, its work is guided by clear principles, including the precautionary and polluter pays principles, equity, common but differentiated responsibilities, and a commitment to energy conservation and renewable energy.[17] To this end, AOSIS has striven to strengthen industrialised country emission targets, close loopholes, strengthen monitoring and compliance procedures, and establish channels for funding adaptation costs. The 'adaptation levy' in the CDM, for example, was mooted and supported by AOSIS members.

AOSIS operates mostly out of the diplomatic missions of its member countries to the UN in New York, with its work coordinated from the New York office of its Chair, a position now occupied by Jagdish Koonjul of Mauritius, and previously by ambassadors from Samoa, Trinidad and Tobago, and Vanuatu. An informal understanding exists that the position of Chair will rotate between the Pacific and Caribbean regions.

The UNSIDS unit provides some administrative support to AOSIS, including funding for workshops, while the South Pacific Regional Environment Programme (SPREP) and the Caribbean Community (CARICOM), two IGOs, also support the Alliance's work. In addition, AOSIS has drawn on legal advice and substantive input from the Foundation for International Environmental Law and Development (FIELD), a London-based NGO. FIELD lawyers have, on the Chair's request, prepared draft submissions or other inputs for the negotiations, which are then circulated to AOSIS members for comment. FIELD lawyers have also prepared briefings for AOSIS members prior to negotiating sessions, and even served on national delegations, again on request. AOSIS has therefore enjoyed relatively strong intellectual and institutional back up, which has helped to enhance its impact in the regime.

Positions are developed on the basis of consensus, and spokespersons are appointed to take the lead on particular issues, akin to the coordinator system

---

[15] See FCCC/AGBM/1996/MISC.2.   [16] See chapter 17.   [17] See chapter 4.

in the G-77. While the appointed spokespersons will articulate the AOSIS common position, other AOSIS members may also intervene to support it.

AOSIS countries are united by their shared development challenges and extreme vulnerability to the impacts of climate change. There are, however, inevitably differences of opinion among its members on certain issues, based on their varying national circumstances. States consisting of low-lying atolls (e.g. the Maldives), for example, are more immediately vulnerable to sea level rise than higher, volcanic islands (e.g. Papua New Guinea). Likewise, while some AOSIS members are least developed countries (e.g. Samoa, Vanuatu), others are comparatively wealthy (e.g. Singapore, Bahamas). Regional cultural and political differences are also part of the AOSIS dynamic, reflecting the wide geographical span of its members.

2.4   African Group

The African Group, the only UN regional group (see above) serving as an active negotiating coalition, provides an important forum for African countries to pursue their specific interests, especially on issues where their perspective may differ from that of the wider G-77. The African Group consists of fifty-three members who share common concerns, notably poverty, lack of resources, and vulnerability to extreme weather events. Indeed, Africa is the only region mentioned by name in the Convention, in the context of the impacts of drought, desertification and floods, and the need for adaptation.[18] The Group often makes common interventions in plenary on issues of particular concern to its members, such as capacity-building, finance and technology transfer. The African Group, however, is not entirely homogenous in its interests. Algeria and Nigeria, for example, are members of OPEC, while South Africa, with its relatively advanced industrialised economy, has much higher emissions per capita than other African nations. The Group must also contend with linguistic diversity, especially between anglophones and francophones, requiring most of its discussions and written papers to be translated informally by Group members.

The country holding the Chair of the African Group in New York does not necessarily assume the role of coordinator in the climate change regime, as some African countries are not active in the climate change regime or do not have the experience needed to take on that role. The Group has a system, however, to help build capacity among its members, whereby the Vice-Chair takes over from the Chair after one year, having gained experience of what the role entails.

2.5   Least developed countries (LDCs)

The UN maintains an official list of countries classified as LDCs, the first of which was agreed by the UN General Assembly in 1971. This list, which is

---

[18] FCCC Article 4.1 (e).

reviewed every three years, now defines LDCs according to three criteria, namely, low income, weak human resources and high economic vulnerability.[19] UNCTAD takes the lead in work relating to LDCs in the UN system. The LDCs, currently comprising forty-nine states, include most members of the African Group, along with some members of AOSIS and others.[20] Only one of the UN list of LDCs (Somalia) is not a Convention Party.

The LDCs first emerged as a formal group in the climate change context at SB-13 in September 2000. This was not without controversy. Some of the few African countries not classified as LDCs were worried that such a move would divide the African Group and argued that the poor in their countries were just as vulnerable as the poor in LDCs. Those AOSIS countries not classified as LDCs were similarly concerned that the formation of the LDC group would deflect attention – and potential funding – away from them, and limit the capacity of AOSIS to participate fully in the negotiations by diverting the energies of its members. Other developing countries were also nervous that the unity of the G-77 would be compromised. Formal statements of support for the new LDC group from the G-77 Chair and influential G-77 members at the final Plenary of SB-13 represented an important victory for the LDC delegations that had fought to gain acceptance for their new group.

Vanuatu (an AOSIS member) was appointed as the first coordinator of the LDC coalition. Coordinators are elected for a term of one year, with the possibility of re-election for a second year, with this annual rotation aiming to build up capacity for work on climate change among LDC members.

2.6   Organization of Petroleum Exporting Countries (OPEC)

Unlike the other coalitions discussed above, the ten Parties that are members of the Organization of Petroleum Exporting Countries (OPEC) do not negotiate as a group in the climate change regime, but they do coordinate their positions and strategies. All OPEC countries – Algeria, Indonesia, Iran, Kuwait, Libya, Nigeria, Qatar, Saudi Arabia, United Arab Emirates and Venezuela[21] – also belong to the G-77, with Saudi Arabia, in particular, holding considerable influence in that Group, helped by its economic ties to many developing countries, especially those of Islamic faith.

Many OPEC countries are highly dependent on income from the export of fossil fuels (mostly oil) (see chapter 9), and fear that this income may be at risk if serious policies are put in place to cut GHG emissions. OPEC countries have thus called on Annex I Parties to report on the adverse impacts of their climate policies on

---

[19] See www.unctad.org.   [20] See UNCTAD, 2002.
[21] Iraq, a non-Party, is the eleventh OPEC member.

developing countries and, more controversially, advocated financial compensation to offset these. They have also argued for the restructuring of energy markets
in OECD countries to reduce taxation on oil, while phasing out subsidies on coal
and nuclear power. The national circumstances of OPEC countries, however, are
not identical. OPEC members encompass differing regional, social, political and
cultural backgrounds, spanning Africa, Latin America, the Middle East and South
East Asia, as well as varying economic situations. Some members, for example,
such as Iran, possess important reserves of natural gas, a less carbon-intensive
fossil fuel than oil, while their per capita GDP also varies considerably.

Given their concerns over the economic impact of climate change policy, some
OPEC countries have questioned the need for strong action and highlighted scientific uncertainty. Some have also wielded procedural tools to delay negotiations,
including threats to veto advances in other areas if insufficient progress is made
on issues of concern to them. Just as their circumstances differ, however, the views
and strategies of OPEC countries are not uniform. Saudi Arabia, a formidable force
in the negotiations, is well known for adopting a particularly hard line.

OPEC members are among the better resourced of developing country delegations. They also receive administrative and analytical support from the OPEC
Secretariat, which is represented as an IGO at negotiating sessions.

2.7   *Central Asia, Caucasus, Albania and Moldova Group (CACAM)*

The CACAM group comprises several non-Annex I countries from
Central/Eastern Europe and Central Asia, including Albania, Armenia, Georgia,
Kazakhstan, Moldova and Uzbekistan, as well as Turkmenistan, which is also a
G-77 member. The raison d'être of the group is to clarify the status of its members in the climate change regime. The Convention, Kyoto Protocol and associated
decisions typically recognise Annex I Parties with economies in transition and
non-Annex I Parties that are developing countries, but not *non-Annex I Parties with
economies in transition*, which is what CACAM countries perceive themselves to be.
When the Convention was adopted in 1992, most CACAM countries either did not
exist or were reeling from the massive changes wrought by the demise of the Soviet
Union. The structure of commitments and classification of Parties into Annex I
and non-Annex I in the climate change regime thus fail to take account of these
countries' particular circumstances.

The idea of forming a group such as CACAM was first mooted at COP-3 in 1997,
and put into practice at COP-6 part I in 2000. CACAM's uniting force is its concern over the status of its members, and it seldom articulates common positions
on other issues. Indeed, its members are culturally and politically diverse, and
relations among many have historically not been friendly. Some lean more to the
EU, others to the Russian Federation, and still others to the Islamic world, while

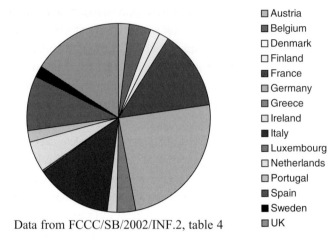

Data from FCCC/SB/2002/INF.2, table 4

Fig. 3.3   Share of aggregate GHG emissions in 2000 of the EU member states covered by the EU burden-sharing agreement (excl. LULUCF)

they also belong to different regional groups. The position of group coordinator rotates annually among the CACAM members, in English alphabetical order of their country names.

2.8   *European Union*

As the world's most ambitious experiment in regional integration, the EU is the most cohesive negotiating coalition in the climate change regime. Its twenty-five member states, plus the European Community (represented by the European Commission), articulate a common position on all issues, almost invariably speaking with a single voice. It is not always easy, however, for the EU to agree that single voice, as it spans countries with a range of political cultures, energy mixes and other individual circumstances, including its own divide between the generally more economically developed and energy efficient northern European states, the less developed south, and now the EITs of Central and Eastern Europe.[22] In terms of its GHG emissions, on adoption of the Kyoto Protocol in 1997, the EU was dominated by France, Germany, Italy and the UK (see figure 3.3), with these countries also playing leading roles in the EU's internal politics. This quartet of major emitters is now joined by Poland.

The ten Central and Eastern European states that joined the EU in May 2004 (see 'Central Group 11' below), have been involved in the Union's work in the climate change regime for some time. They have taken part in all EU climate change

---

[22] See Anderson et al., 1997; Gupta and Grubb, 2000; articles in *Climate Policy*, 2003; Househam et al., 1998.

meetings since April 2003, and have formally supported statements/written submissions made by the EU since this date. The expansion of the EU promises to create significant challenges for the Union in the climate change field, given the differing circumstances of the new entrants, including two non-Annex I parties.

The EU has sought to position itself as an 'environmental leader' in the climate change regime since the inception of the climate change process, proposing a 15 per cent cut in GHG emissions during the Kyoto Protocol negotiations and advocating limits on the use of the flexibility mechanisms and LULUCF in the post-Kyoto phase. EU countries tend to share a belief in the need for international cooperation to achieve collective goals, along with greater sympathy for the concerns of developing countries. Many also have active environmental NGOs and publics that are relatively supportive of environmental policies. EU countries are typically more willing to accept the need for government regulation to tackle climate change, with a tendency to view flexibility mechanisms, such as emissions trading, with greater caution than their 'Umbrella Group' colleagues (see below). As noted above, however, there are variations among the member states, with the UK, for example, closer to the more market-approach of the US than Germany or France.

The EU's six-month rotating Presidency takes the lead among EU member states in the climate change regime,[23] with its particular priorities and approach exerting influence over the Union's negotiating position and strategy. The Presidency usually speaks for the twenty-five member states and the Community. However, where a different state has expertise on a particular issue, it may be appointed as spokesperson on that issue, especially if the Presidency is a small country with limited capacity. Otherwise, and unlike the G-77 or other coalitions, it is extremely rare for EU countries other than the Presidency to speak in plenary sessions of the COP or subsidiary bodies, although in contact groups and other less formal settings a group of member states may speak in support of the Presidency. The Presidency receives support in its work from the European Commission (see box 3.1 below) and the forthcoming Presidency, together making up what is known as the 'Troika'.[24] The 'Troika' plays a key ambassadorial role, and typically represents the EU at high-level meetings both within the regime (e.g. on 'Friends of the Chair' groups) and outside (e.g. in bilaterals with other states and coalitions). In recent years, individual member states have also been appointed as spokespersons for

---

[23] This is not always the case in the intergovernmental arena. Where binding common legislation exists at the EU level, on ozone layer depletion or fisheries policy for example, the Commission will usually take the lead. See Oberthür, 2000.

[24] Prior to the 1997 Amsterdam Treaty, the Troika was formed by the current, past and future Presidencies.

bilaterals with other states and coalitions, with the aim of increasing efficiency and outreach.

The EU's work on climate change extends far beyond sessions of the regime bodies. Its *Working Party on International Environmental Issues* meets on a monthly basis to address climate change matters. It is composed of heads of delegation and relevant experts from each country, plus the Commission. *Expert groups* on specific issues (e.g. the flexibility mechanisms, sinks, policies and measures, scientific research) provide input to the Working Party, with the exact number and topics of these expert groups varying according to the issues on the table in the regime. These expert groups develop EU positions and statements, often based on drafts prepared by individual member states, which are then considered by the Working Party. In addition, EU Presidencies often organise workshops at the start of their Presidency, which may have participation from businesses and NGOs, to discuss the broad direction of EU climate change policy. Prior to important negotiating sessions in the climate change regime, the EU's member states will meet at ministerial level in the *Council of Environment Ministers* in order to agree the EU's overall negotiating position. This position is then set out in formal conclusions, which are decided by consensus, although statements by individual member states putting forward a particular perspective may also be noted.

During sessions of the regime bodies, the EU meets daily in coordination meetings to agree statements and proposals, and review the EU's position and strategies according to developments in the negotiations. The individual expert groups also continue to meet and deliver input to the coordination meetings as necessary. Again, decisions are always taken by consensus.

Box 3.1 below provides more information on the EU's institutions and policy-making process.

Box 3.1   EU institutions and policy-making[25]

The **Council of the European Union** is the EU's main decision-making body and meets at ministerial level. Environment ministers from the member states meet to decide EU climate policy and the EU's common negotiating stance. The Council shares legislative power to adopt European laws with the **EU Parliament**, which consists of directly elected members. The **European**

---

[25] Information from the third national communication from the European Community under the United Nations Framework Convention on Climate Change: European Commission, 2001; Dahl, 2000; and Wettestad, 2000. For more information on EU climate change policy, see articles in *Climate Policy*, 2003, and www.europa.eu.int.

Commission embodies and upholds the general interest of the Union, serving as its executive body. Unlike the civil service in most countries, the Commission is not required to stay neutral, having the right to initiate draft legislation and make legislative proposals to the Parliament and Council. The Commission represents the European Community, as a party to the Convention, in the climate change negotiations, and prepares the Community's national communication and other mandated reports.

EU laws vary in their force, from non-binding **recommendations** to binding **directives** and **regulations** that apply to all member states (directives must be incorporated into national legislation and allow some room for manoeuvre in their implementation).

Policy to implement the EU's commitments under the climate change regime is developed by both the EU and its individual member states. The extent of the EU's power – or **competence** – to act over and above member states is guided by the 1992 Maastricht Treaty and varies between policy areas. In commercial policy, for example, the EU has exclusive competence, while in most other areas, including the environment, competence is shared between the EU and member states. A key principle in determining and interpreting relative competence is that of **subsidiarity**, which requires that policies be developed and implemented at the most effective level. Because climate change policy encroaches on so many different areas, including energy and taxation, the relative competence of the EU and its member states to legislate and implement policy on the issue is not clear-cut, with countries differing in their enthusiasm for common EU measures.

2.9   *Umbrella Group and JUSSCANNZ*

The 'Umbrella Group' is a looser group of Annex I Parties, which operates exclusively in the climate change regime. It first emerged at COP-3 in 1997, initially to oppose the EU's attempt to restrict the use of the flexibility mechanisms, especially emissions trading. The 'Umbrella Group' – whose membership currently includes Australia, Canada, Iceland, Japan, New Zealand, Norway, the Russian Federation, Ukraine and the US – is brought together by a common motivation to ensure cost-effectiveness and flexibility in the Kyoto Protocol system. Displaying solidarity rather than unity, the Group operates to the mantra of 'working together but not tied together' and focuses on sharing information rather than developing detailed, common positions.

The Umbrella Group metamorphosed from the longer-standing JUSSCANNZ group. The key difference between JUSSCANNZ and the Umbrella Group is that the latter excludes Switzerland, whose position on the flexibility mechanisms is much closer to that of the EU. Additionally, the Umbrella Group includes the Russian Federation and Ukraine, which are supporters of unrestricted emissions trading. The acronym JUSSCANNZ thus stands for Japan, the US, Switzerland, Canada, Australia, Norway and New Zealand. Iceland is also a member, while Mexico and South Korea are observers. Other countries have participated as observers, notably Kazakhstan and Argentina. JUSSCANNZ's membership (and therefore the acronym used to denote it) has varied over time in the climate change regime, with Switzerland and Norway, for example, joining during the Kyoto Protocol negotiations. JUSSCANNZ is active throughout the UN, although with some differences in membership (and therefore in its acronym-based name), depending on the issue at stake. With the rise of the Umbrella Group, JUSSCANNZ is much less active than it once was in the climate change regime, although it still functions as an information-sharing coalition and usually meets once or twice during sessions.

Since its inception, the focus of the Umbrella Group has expanded to encompass issues other than the flexibility mechanisms, including reporting and review and also LULUCF, where, in line with its general support for flexibility and cost-effectiveness, the Umbrella Group has advocated the inclusion of a wide scope of carbon removal activities under the Protocol. The Umbrella Group has also pressed much harder than the EU to initiate a debate on developing country commitments.

Umbrella Group members are far from homogenous. In terms of their national circumstances, Iceland, Japan, New Zealand and Norway enjoy much lower emissions per capita and much higher levels of energy efficiency than do the remainder of the Group. Iceland and Norway, like other Scandinavian countries, tend to be more 'environmental' in their outlook, as well as more sympathetic to the concerns of developing countries, while Australia, Canada and Japan (and, before its repudiation, the US) tend to be more ardent in their quest for flexibility in the implementation of their Kyoto targets, including for individual concessions. For their part, the Russian Federation and Ukraine, as EITs, face a situation quite unlike those of their Umbrella Group partners. Since its repudiation of the Kyoto Protocol, the US, which previously played a very active role in the Umbrella Group, has become much quieter. Its negotiators have no mandate to speak on Kyoto Protocol issues, except if decisions have wider implications for US interests.

Such differences help explain why the Umbrella Group is only a loose coalition. The Group does put forward common submissions and statements, usually on the flexibility mechanisms, but individual group members are perfectly at liberty also to pursue their own specific interests. The position of spokesperson is allocated at random, depending on which country volunteers. Some countries with particular interests or expertise have also taken the lead on specific issues, such as Australia on sinks and Canada on developing country issues. In addition to its meetings during negotiating sessions, the Group also meets intersessionally, often on the margins of other meetings.

2.10   *Central Group and Central Group-11 (CG-11)*

The CG-11, which was active from 2000 to 2003, was composed of ten Annex I EITs in the process of joining the EU – Bulgaria, the Czech Republic, Estonia, Latvia, Lithuania, Hungary, Poland, Romania, Slovakia and Slovenia – plus Croatia. Cyprus and Malta (non-Annex I Parties also in the process of joining the EU, as well as AOSIS members) were observers to the group.

The Central and Eastern European EITs share many national circumstances and common interests, including sharp drops in their emissions in the late 1980s and early 1990s due to the economic downturn triggered by the dissolution of the Soviet bloc. Many are also still saddled with a carbon intensive and inefficient economic structure, and are thus keen to take advantage of investment opportunities presented by joint implementation under the Kyoto Protocol. Limited financial and institutional capacity means that several are also struggling to comply with their reporting obligations, and are likely to face difficulties in meeting the tighter rules under the Kyoto Protocol. The CG-11 was always closely allied to the EU, with the two groups holding regular meetings and consultations.

Following the successful conclusion of negotiations in December 2002 on the accession to the EU of most of its members and its observers, the CG-11 was dissolved. The remaining members of the former CG-11 – Bulgaria, Croatia and Romania[26] – stated that they would continue to cooperate as the 'Central Group'. On many issues, however, Bulgaria and Romania now ally themselves with EU positions. On certain matters of specific concern to the EITs as a whole, such as capacity-building where there is a separate decision for this group of countries (see chapter 10), the EITs negotiate as a group.

2.11   *Environmental Integrity Group (EIG)*

The origins of the Environmental Integrity Group (EIG) lie in the aftermath of the Kyoto Protocol negotiations where, with the formation of the Umbrella Group whose positions it did not share, Switzerland found itself outside of any group. Given the emerging tendency for closed negotiation meetings (e.g. 'Friends of the Chair') to be structured based on negotiating coalitions, Switzerland felt excluded from the final stages of negotiations, a situation which came to the fore at COP-4 in 1998. Switzerland thus joined up with two other 'outsiders', Mexico and South Korea, who are non-Annex I Parties but also OECD members, to form the

---

[26] See SBI-18 report, paragraphs 8 and 9. Negotiations between the EU and Bulgaria and Romania are still ongoing, with a view to these countries joining the EU in 2007.

Environmental Integrity Group, whose establishment was formally announced at SB-13 part I in 2000.[27] Switzerland usually coordinates for the group.

In many ways, the group's members, comprising both Annex I and non-Annex I Parties, are strange bedfellows, sharing little in terms of national circumstances except for the fact that they do not belong to any of the other main groups. As its name suggests, the avowed overall purpose of the EIG is to promote the environmental integrity of the climate change regime. Where the group does have a common position, the EIG will negotiate together, and where it does not, its members will negotiate individually.

2.12   *Open Balkan Group*

At COP-7 in 2001, Bosnia Herzegovina, the Former Yugoslav Republic of Macedonia and Yugoslavia (which has since become Serbia and Montenegro) expressed interest in forming their own negotiating coalition, the Open Balkan Group (OBG). The COP Bureau took note of this intention at SB-16 in 2002. Like CACAM, these countries are non-Annex I Parties, but consider themselves to be economies in transition, and not developing countries. Bosnia Herzegovina is also a member of the G-77.

2.13   *Other groups*

Other groups have a presence in the climate change regime, including the *League of Arab States*, which meets regularly during climate change negotiations, but very rarely speaks as a group. Delegations from *francophone countries* also meet once or twice during negotiating sessions, focusing mostly on procedural issues, such as availability of French language documentation, while also providing an arena for both industrialised and developing countries sharing a common language to exchange views.

3   Non-governmental organisations

The number of NGOs admitted as observers[28] to the climate change regime has more than trebled since COP-1, to 619 at COP-9 (see figure 3.4). The rise in admitted NGOs reflects a broader intensification in NGO activities in the multilateral arena, especially in the environmental field. The all-encompassing nature of

---

[27] Switzerland took a similar initiative in the negotiations on the Cartagena Biosafety Protocol, forming the so-called 'Compromise Group' bringing together countries outside the main groups, including Japan, Korea, Mexico, Norway and Switzerland, later joined by Singapore and New Zealand (see Nobs, 2002).

[28] In order to be represented at sessions of the regime bodies, NGOs must be formally admitted. This admission process is described in chapter 14.

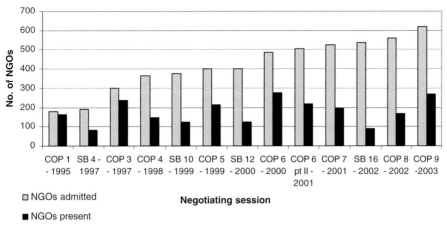

Fig. 3.4   NGOs admitted and present at selected negotiating sessions

climate change, in turn, means that almost any group within civil society could be considered a stakeholder, thereby generating great interest among NGOs, even by the high standards of global environmental issues.[29] Interestingly, however, the number of organisations actually *attending* negotiating sessions has remained relatively stable (see also figure 3.4) and there is similarly no clear trend towards any increase in the number of individual NGO delegates present at sessions (see figure 3.1 above), with individual participation fluctuating according to the political importance and profile of sessions.

NGOs participate in the regime in a number of ways, through both formal and informal channels. Rules for participation of NGOs in the formal proceedings of the regime bodies, along with the more established informal channels of holding side events and displaying exhibits on the margins of negotiating sessions, are discussed in chapter 14.

3.1   *Constituencies*

Although this is not inscribed in any official document, the climate change regime currently acknowledges five NGO constituencies:

- Environmental NGOs (ENGOs);
- Business and industry NGOs (BINGOs);
- Local government and municipal authorities (LGMAs);
- Indigenous peoples organisations (IPOs); and
- Research and independent NGOs (RINGOs).

[29] For analyses of the activities of NGOs in the climate change regime, see Newell, 2000; Carpenter, 2001; Yamin, 2001; Ecologic, 2002.

The constituency structure has evolved organically, as NGOs with specific interests or spheres of activity have organised themselves into groups and requested formal recognition from the climate change regime. The IPOs, for example, only emerged as a group in 2000, while the RINGOs were formally recognised as a constituency at COP-9 in 2003. NGOs, however, face no obligation to declare adherence to any constituency. Although the Secretariat does not maintain a comprehensive list of constituency members, it does require that each constituency choose a focal point who then acts as a point of contact. In parallel with the trend identified above for coalitions of Parties, recent moves to establish new NGO constituencies reflect the growing importance of the constituency structure as a means of involving NGOs in the climate change regime. Invitations for NGOs to attend workshops, for example, are managed principally through the focal points of the constituencies. Many NGOs, however, still do not belong to any constituency.

3.2   *Environmental non-governmental organisations (ENGOs)*

The environmental NGOs (ENGOs) active in the climate change regime are almost all members of the Climate Action Network (CAN), which was established in 1989 and is recognised by the Secretariat as the ENGO constituency coordinator. CAN's membership includes over 340 ENGOs from more than eighty countries, from the largest such as Friends of the Earth and Greenpeace, to tiny local groups. CAN international is organised into regional and some national offices, each with its own coordinator, and receives financial support from its members, governments and charitable foundations. Until recently, the coordinators of the EU and US regional offices played a dominant role in managing CAN's activities, reflecting the greater resources at their disposal. Since COP-8, however, CAN has started to develop a more global governance structure, electing its first board and adopting a charter. An international secretariat is now being established, while rules and procedures for CAN activities are also being developed.[30]

CAN's members are united by their aim 'to promote government and individual action to limit human-induced climate change to ecologically sustainable levels',[31] seeking strong commitments to reduce greenhouse gas emissions, the closure of loopholes, and effective implementation at the national level. Inevitably, however, there are differences among some ENGOs over specific issues in the negotiations, often reflecting regional perspectives. CAN members will try hard to agree a common position to advocate in the negotiations and, if this proves impossible, efforts will be made to develop regional positions. CAN is an organisation that places great value on unity, going to considerable lengths to present a common front to the outside world.

---

[30] See Schoeters, 2003.   [31] See www.climatenetwork.org.

Despite CAN's global coverage, ENGOs from OECD countries dominate its representation at sessions of the regime bodies. Although CAN tries to secure financial support to fund the participation of developing country ENGOs at climate change meetings, this is not always successful. Attendance levels by developing country ENGOs, as well as NGOs from EITs and the EU accession countries, have in fact risen gradually over the years, reflecting raised awareness of the importance of climate change, as well as CAN's efforts to forge links with, and support, these ENGOs. Where possible, CAN tries to ensure that formal Plenary statements on its behalf are made by both a northern and a southern representative. Increasing the involvement of ENGOs from a broad geographic span is critical to enhancing the legitimacy and influence of the ENGO constituency as a whole, especially in the eyes of non-Annex I Party delegates. CAN has long called for funding to be provided to NGO representatives, especially from developing countries, to facilitate their participation at negotiating sessions.[32]

The ENGOs that are members of CAN meet daily during sessions of the regime bodies, to exchange information on developments in the negotiations, and discuss positions and lobbying strategies. Smaller working groups coordinate CAN's work on particular issues, a practice that was formalised at COP-6 part I in 2000 in response to the increasing complexity of the negotiations. These working groups are headed by Annex I/non-Annex I Co-Chairs wherever possible, mimicking the practice in the formal negotiations.[33] Prior to major negotiating sessions, the ENGOs typically hold a strategy meeting over one or two days, including a briefing for developing country ENGO representatives and all ENGO delegates that are new to the process.

The work of ENGOs at sessions of the regime bodies covers a range of activities, including: lobbying government delegates; making interventions during debates; circulating information and position papers; monitoring developments in the negotiations; working with the media; holding side events; and organising eye-catching shows, such as 'fossil of the day',[34] where an award is given to the delegation considered by CAN to have taken the most environmentally regressive position that day. Some individual ENGOs will, of course, be more active than others in these pursuits. A highly visible element to CAN's work is the production of the tabloid-style newsletter *ECO*, which was first issued at the 1972 UN Conference on the Human Environment and continues today.[35] *ECO*, which typically includes serious analysis as well as satirical articles and humorous illustrations, is used as a lobbying tool, a source of information (including rumours on closed-door negotiations) and sheer entertainment.

---

[32] See, for example, FCCC/WEB/2002/14.   [33] See chapter 14.
[34] www.fossil-of-the-day.org.   [35] www.climatenetwork.org/eco/index.html.

CAN itself and individual ENGOs are also active in between sessions, running awareness campaigns, monitoring climate change policy and projects, lobbying governments and corporations at the national and regional levels, and preparing studies and position papers. CAN members are themselves in constant communication through electronic mailing lists. Ensuring effective information flow is an important part of the work of ENGOs.

3.3   *Business and industry non-governmental organisations (BINGOs)*

The business and industry NGOs (BINGOs) make up a much looser constituency and cover a far wider spectrum of views than the ENGOs. Given the non-profit requirements,[36] corporations wishing to be active in the climate change regime have organised themselves into a variety of groups, some of which were established specifically to campaign on climate change, and others of which are also active in other spheres. Informally, the constituency is characterised as divided between 'green' and 'grey' business. 'Green' business includes corporations that are concerned about the threat to business posed by climate change, such as insurance firms, or view climate change mitigation as a business opportunity, such as the 'sunrise' industries involved in renewable energy, energy efficiency and other environmental products. Green businesses are represented by such coalitions as the US-based Business Council for Sustainable Energy (BCSE), the European Business Council for a Sustainable Energy Future (e5) and the World Business Council for Sustainable Development (WBCSD).[37] 'Grey' business, on the other hand, comprises many fossil fuel, mostly US-based, industries, such as coal, oil, automobile and other energy intensive corporations, who fear that action to cut greenhouse gas emissions will negatively impact on their revenues. Until the US withdrawal from the Kyoto Protocol process, the main coalition among grey business was the US-based Global Climate Coalition (GCC), but it has now been 'deactivated'.[38] While green business urges clear and decisive action on the part of governments, grey business tends to support only the weakest measures, stressing economic costs and scientific uncertainty.

The boundaries between 'green' and 'grey' business, however, are fuzzy, with many groups and individual companies defying such broad categorisation. Many BINGOs have their own specific business interests to uphold, such as the nuclear and fluorocarbon industries.[39] Several coalitions have also sprung up recently to pursue business opportunities offered by the flexibility mechanisms, such as the Emissions Marketing Association (EMA) and the International Emissions

---

[36] See chapter 14.
[37] www.bscse.org, www.e5.org; www.wbcsd.org.   [38] www.globalclimate.org.
[39] See, for example, World Nuclear Association (www.world-nuclear.org) and Alliance for Responsible Atmospheric Policy (www.arap.org).

Trading Association (IETA).[40] In addition, there are differences within particular industries, with companies in the oil sector, such as BP and Shell, much more accepting of the need for action on climate change than, for example, Exxon Mobil.[41] In general terms, the BINGO constituency has become much more positive and engaged in the climate change regime since the adoption of the Kyoto Protocol.

Like the ENGOs, however, BINGOs do not like their (much greater) divisions to be highlighted, and are at pains to present themselves as a single constituency. Indeed, there are many issues that do unite all business groups, including the desire for policy certainty and clear legislation (whatever it may be), simple rules and minimum bureaucracy, as well as greater involvement in the negotiation process, the latter a concern shared by all NGOs.

BINGO groups and individual firms differ in their type and degree of activity. Some are highly active, lobbying governments in the corridors, holding hospitality events, proposing specific decision language to pass on to delegates, organising special events, and circulating information and position papers. Others, however, confine themselves to observing proceedings and reporting back to their head offices on developments that may affect their business. BINGOs generally do not intervene as much as ENGOs during formal debates, partly because of the greater differences between the various factions that make it difficult to agree a common statement. Much more so than ENGOs, BINGOs are dominated by representatives from the OECD, and US organisations in particular, and generally have far greater financial resources at their disposal.

The constituency is coordinated by the International Chamber of Commerce (ICC),[42] which works through a *climate change task force*, as part of its *energy and environment commission*. The task force is composed of forty to fifty members, plus observers, and is open to any ICC member wishing to attend. It meets twice a year, preparing draft 'business perspective' position papers on climate change issues, which are then sent to the broader ICC membership for comment, before being finalised and circulated, including at climate change negotiations.

During negotiating sessions, the ICC organises daily morning meetings, where members discuss developments in the negotiations and share information on their activities. Any delegation that considers itself to be a business organisation and does not attend the ENGO coordination may participate. There is rarely any attempt to develop common positions, except when the constituency has been invited to make a group statement, to the COP for example. While the work of BINGOs is facilitated by the ICC, individual coalitions and firms pursue their own interests and strategies in the climate change regime.

---

[40] www.emissions.org; www.ieta.org.
[41] See www.bp.com; www.shell.com; www.exxon.com.   [42] www.iccwbo.org.

3.4   *Local government and municipal authorities (LGMAs)*

Local government and municipal authorities first became active in the climate change regime at COP-1 in 1995, following a major meeting of municipal leaders that took place on the eve of the Conference. Strictly speaking, this group consists of *local*, rather than *non*, government organisations, and has sought a different status as such, both in the climate change regime and in the wider international arena.[43]

LGMAs in the climate change regime are coordinated by the International Council for Local Environmental Initiatives (ICLEI),[44] an organisation of almost 400 municipalities, counties and local government associations that functions as an international environmental agency for local governments worldwide. ICLEI's Climate Change Programme now engages over 350 municipalities, accounting for around 7 per cent of global greenhouse gas emissions, in concrete actions to tackle climate change. Many local governments, working through ICLEI or sometimes alone, have indeed been highly active 'on the ground', with some proving to be far more aggressive, and indeed successful, in addressing climate change than their national governments. Several Australian and US cities, for example, are highly active in ICLEI's Climate Change Programme. In October 2003, 155 mayors of US cities issued a joint declaration calling for stronger action on climate change by the federal government.[45]

Despite its considerable achievements at the local level, the LGMA constituency is only sparsely represented at sessions of the regime bodies, except at high-profile COP sessions, which attract attendance by municipal leaders as well as ICLEI staff. ICLEI usually delivers a statement during COP high-level segments and organises a side event at high-profile meetings, but is less active or visible than the other NGO constituencies in the climate change process.

3.5   *Indigenous peoples organisations (IPOs)*

Indigenous peoples emerged in the post-Kyoto phase as a small but vocal group in the climate change regime. This emergence was a response to the realisation that the climate change regime was addressing issues – in particular modalities for including LULUCF activities under the CDM – of great relevance to the lives of indigenous peoples, but without their input.

The indigenous peoples constituency is coordinated by the International Alliance of Indigenous-Tribal Peoples of the Tropical Forests. The various alliances that comprise the constituency cover indigenous peoples worldwide. This is the only NGO constituency where individuals from developing countries dominate.

---

[43] See FCCC/SBI/1997/MISC.6.   [44] www.iclei.org.
[45] See http://www.iclei.org/us/mayors_statement/.

Although the indigenous peoples are united in their efforts to increase their visibility and participation in the regime, there are some differences among the various alliances on substantive issues. Some indigenous peoples groups, for example, argue that the CDM should be used to gain income through forest activities, while others fear that it would threaten their way of life.

Since their first appearance in the climate change regime, at SB-12 in June 2000, the indigenous peoples groups have been active in organising side events, making interventions and holding meetings with the subsidiary body Chairs and COP Presidents, all with the aim of opening up more channels for their participation in the decision-making process. The indigenous peoples have received considerable support from the ENGOs, who perceive their interests to be similar. Like local governments, indigenous peoples consider themselves to be in a different category to other NGOs, on the grounds that they are territorially based, and in some cases exercise varying degrees of governmental control over those territories. Indigenous peoples are also active at the national and regional levels, again seeking to enhance the voice of this group in national decision-making on issues of importance to it.

3.6   *Research and independent non-governmental organisations (RINGOs)*

After the ENGOs and BINGOs, universities and research institutes make up the third major group of NGOs in the climate change regime, attracted by the complex and profound intellectual challenges posed by the issue. Researchers involved in the climate change regime cover a wide range of disciplines, from the natural sciences to law, economics and the humanities. They play a very dynamic role in the regime, injecting new ideas into debates through the distribution of research results and analytical papers, side events and direct discussions with delegates.

In the post-Marrakesh period, several research institutes organised themselves into a constituency of research and independent NGOs (RINGOs) and submitted a request to the Secretariat that they be considered as such. At COP-8, a spokesperson for thirty-five founding members of the RINGO group formally announced the launch of a new group seeking constituency status, which was later granted at COP-9. The RINGOs are coordinated by a steering committee, with focal point functions currently carried out at the Centre for European Policy Studies in Brussels.[46] The stated aim of the RINGOs is to 'engage in independent research and analysis aimed at developing sound strategies to address both the causes and consequences of global climate change' and, among the criteria for membership,

---

[46] See www.ringos.net.

is the requirement that members should be seeking 'constructive solutions' to the mitigation of climate change.

3.7   *Other non-governmental organisations*

A variety of other NGOs are represented at meetings of the climate change regime. Many take a largely environmentalist stance akin to those of the ENGOs, including *legislators and parliamentarians*, represented through the group Global Legislators for a Balanced Environment (GLOBE),[47] which, at COP-3, declared support for an equity-based regime and the concept of 'contraction and convergence',[48] along with *faith-based organisations*, in particular the World Council of Churches,[49] which has also emphasised the importance of equity issues. Both these groups have made formal statements to the COP high-level segment. *Youth groups* assumed a higher profile at COP-6 part I, where an International Youth Meeting was held on the eve of the conference, producing a declaration that was later presented to delegates.[50] Representatives of youth have since made powerful, environmentalist statements to COP high-level segments, including the presentation of a 'Children's Charter' at COP-8.[51] *Trade Unions* are also represented at negotiating sessions. The International Confederation of Free Trade Unions (ICFTU),[52] and other international trade union organisations (e.g. European Trade Union Confederation[53]) recognise the reality and importance of the climate change issue, focusing their efforts on ensuring that climate change policy takes account of employment and social issues. US-based trade unions, however, have traditionally taken a less positive stance, fearing job losses from climate mitigation action. *Lobby groups* are also active in the regime, notably the US-based Climate Council, which is widely thought to work closely with OPEC and other delegations.[54] A notable absence from the climate change regime is that of NGOs working on *development issues*. Very few are admitted, and those that are rarely attend meetings. Similarly, few *women's groups* are active in the climate change regime, although several are admitted.

4   **Intergovernmental organisations, UN bodies/specialised agencies**

4.1   *Intergovernmental organisations*

Over fifty IGOs are currently admitted to the regime, more than double the number at COP-1.[55] Many are also represented at negotiating sessions,

---

[47] www.globeinternational.org.   [48] See statement reproduced in Taalab, 1998: pp. 30–1.
[49] www.wcc-coe.org.   [50] COP-6 part I report, part I, paragraphs 102–4.
[51] COP-8 report part I, paragraph 139.   [52] www.icftu.org.   [53] www.etuc.org.
[54] See Oberthür and Ott, 1999; McCaughey, 1996; Brown, 1996; Gelbspan, 1997.
[55] On procedures for the admission of IGOs, see chapter 14.

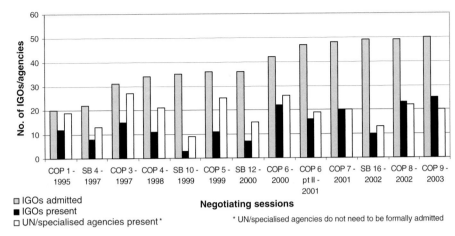

Fig. 3.5   IGOs admitted, and IGOs and UN/specialised agencies present at selected negotiating sessions

although there has been no obvious increase in this representation since COP-1 (see figure 3.5). Reflecting a similar trend among Parties and NGOs, the number of individual IGO delegates has also not risen noticeably over the lifetime of the regime (see figure 3.1 above).

IGOs typically do not engage in advocacy. Instead, they provide support to their member countries, undertake studies on climate change issues relevant to their members, and monitor developments in the negotiations. Studies by IGOs are often helpful to the wider climate change regime. The OECD and IEA,[56] whose members include the Annex II Parties plus several EITs and others,[57] have been particularly active in supplying analytical research to the climate change Parties. Much of their climate change work has been undertaken in support of the OECD/IEA 'Annex I Experts Group',[58] an ad hoc group of government officials from Annex I countries that meets regularly to discuss and analyse climate change policy issues of particular concern to industrialised countries.

A variety of other IGOs also regularly attend sessions of the regime bodies, supporting their member countries and monitoring developments of importance to them. These include the Secretariats of the South Pacific Regional Environment

---

[56] www.oecd.org and www.iea.org.

[57] At the time of writing, the OECD's thirty members include all the Annex II Parties, plus several EITs, namely the Czech Republic, Hungary, Poland and the Slovak Republic, as well as Mexico, South Korea and Turkey. The IEA, which shares twenty-six of the OECD's members (all except Iceland, Mexico, Poland and the Slovak Republic), is an autonomous agency linked to the OECD.

[58] www.oecd.org/env/cc.

Programme (SPREP), OPEC, the Asian Development Bank (ADB), the Association of South East Asian Nations (ASEAN), CARICOM and IUCN – the World Conservation Union.[59] Unlike the UN bodies and specialised agencies, most of which are global, or almost global, in nature, other IGOs are typically regionally based, with their members including only a limited cross-section of the Parties to the climate change regime.

4.2   *UN bodies, specialised agencies and related organisations*

A variety of UN bodies and specialised agencies also participate in the regime and are represented at negotiating sessions (see figure 3.5 and, for individual delegates, figure 3.1). Like most IGOs, these organisations do not play an advocacy role, but rather run programmes in support of the regime and its implementation by Parties, especially by developing countries. Some of these programmes are officially linked to, or mandated by, the regime, such as the activities of the World Bank, UNEP and UNDP as implementing agencies of the GEF.[60] Some UN bodies also undertake activities on behalf of the climate change Secretariat, such as UNEP on the implementation of education, training and public awareness activities under Article 6 of the Convention. Others provide input to the climate change regime in the field of research, analysis and technical work, some of which is officially requested or endorsed by the regime bodies. Chief among the providers of such input is the IPCC.[61]

In addition, several UN bodies have initiated climate-related activities outside of any official mandate by the climate change regime, but ostensibly in support of it. This has occurred as the wider UN system has recognised the significance of climate change, its potential implications for UN programmes and, no doubt, the funding opportunities that linking in with such a high-profile issue might open up, especially with the advent of the flexibility mechanisms. The climate change activities of UN bodies have certainly mushroomed since the adoption of the Kyoto Protocol, with many – including UNCTAD, UNDP, UNEP, UNIDO, UNITAR and the World Bank – having launched projects related to the flexibility mechanisms, often in partnership with other organisations.

Further discussion of the work of UN bodies linked to the regime is provided in the relevant chapters throughout this book, including discussion of the relationship to other MEAs (chapter 17) and the important link to the IPCC (chapter 15).

---

[59] www.sprep.org.ws/; www.opec.org; www.adb.org; www.aseansec.org; www.caricom.org; www.iucn.org.
[60] See chapter 10.   [61] See chapter 15.

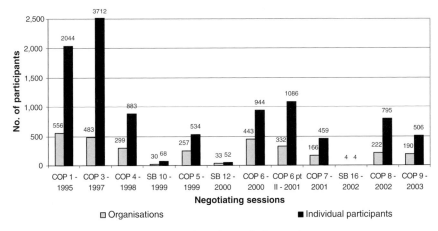

Fig. 3.6   Media presence at selected negotiating sessions

5   The media

The media play a critical role in the climate change regime.[62] Although their presence often goes unnoticed in the negotiating rooms themselves, journalists bring the climate change issue and developments in the regime to the attention of the public, and can place pressure on politicians to act. Intense media scrutiny undoubtedly played a vital role in pushing countries to reach agreement at both COP-3 on the Kyoto Protocol and at COP-6 part II on the Bonn Agreements.

To attend a session, a media organisation needs to receive accreditation from the Secretariat, for which it must provide proof of its bona fide media status in accordance with wider UN procedures.[63] Unsurprisingly, media presence varies greatly according to the profile of the negotiating session and expectations for its outcome, with peaks of media interest for the launch of the protocol negotiations at COP-1 and the adoption of the Kyoto Protocol at COP-3 (see figure 3.6). Lower media attendance at other critical negotiating sessions, notably COP-6 and COP-6 part II, can be partly attributed to the fact that the significance of their outcomes – rules for implementing the Kyoto Protocol and the Convention – were not as obvious as the adoption of a new protocol, and could not be so readily understood or explained by the media. Media representatives hail overwhelmingly from developed countries, with very low representation from EITs or developing countries. The Secretariat has, however, sought to encourage representation from the latter, in order to raise awareness of climate change in these countries.

[62] On the role of the media in the climate change arena, see Newell, 2000, and Carpenter, 2001.
[63] See http://www.un.org/geninfo/malu.htm.

4

Objective and principles

This chapter explains two foundational elements of the climate regime: its 'ultimate objective' as set out in Article 2 of the Convention and its principles, set out mainly in Article 3 of the Convention. Although Articles 2 and 3 intentionally do not establish concrete commitments for individual Parties, their constraining influence on the regime as a whole is palpable at many levels. In broad terms, Article 2 provides overall guidance for the basic values and scientific orientation for the climate regime whilst Article 3 provides guidance bearing more directly on implementation of the commitments Parties have accepted under the regime and their evolution. For these reasons, the implications of Article 2 are the focus of particular attention among scientists, policy-makers and stakeholders as climate policy-makers begin to grapple with the issue of defining what constitutes 'dangerous anthropogenic interference with the climate system'. The implications of the principles set out in Article 3 are also topical as policy-makers attempt to work out the potential implications of these principles for the design of the future climate regime, including who, when and in relation to what additional commitments should be formulated.[1] This section explains Articles 2 and 3, providing in each case an analysis of their implications, additional information about their historical development, current legal status and practical illustrations of their significance to the current policy context.

1 Ultimate objective

1.1 *Nature and scope*

The Convention establishes an objective for its Parties: the 'stabilization of greenhouse gas concentrations in the atmosphere at a level that would prevent

---

[1] See chapter 18 on procedural routes relevant to evolution of commitments.

dangerous anthropogenic interference with the climate system'. Like many other MEAs, this objective is framed in terms of an environmental quality standard, i.e., an environmental threshold, which Parties are obliged to ensure is not exceeded. Although many MEAs set thresholds that imply absolute bans on particular activities, such as banning dumping of radioactive waste at sea or the moratorium on killing or taking whales, others accept that human activities will create a certain level of environmental interference. In these cases they aim to establish a threshold beyond which the pollution or interference will not be permitted.[2] Climate change falls into this second category because the threshold that it establishes – dangerous anthropogenic interference with the climate system – allows activities causing such interference to continue up to this point. The stabilisation of concentrations to avoid this point being reached provides the common long-term objective of the climate regime.

The second sentence of Article 2, the significance of which is sometimes overlooked, provides additional guidance concerning the *timing* of actions to stay within this threshold. It states that 'such a level should be achieved within a time frame sufficient to allow ecosystems to adapt naturally to climate change, to ensure that food production is not threatened and to enable economic development to proceed in a sustainable manner'. The reference to allowing ecosystems to 'adapt naturally' means that the Convention provides that the Earth's ecological limits must be respected and that these set a constraint on both the timing and scale of changes human interference can unleash on the climate system. The Convention's objective thus has a preventative emphasis.[3] This is important because it means that mitigation scenarios that fail to provide for natural adaptation of ecosystems (generally those that defer mitigation into the future on cost-effectiveness grounds) must be evaluated in terms of the ultimate objective of the Convention. In other words, the objective implicates not only the ultimate GHG concentration level that can be reached but also the time path of achieving that concentration. This is also true of mitigation scenarios where resulting impacts mean food production is threatened and where economic development cannot proceed in a sustainable manner. Again this is important because many developing countries' economies are dependent on agriculture which means that this sector affects not only the food security of large parts of their populations but also their entire economic development.

The legal nature of the Convention's objective deserves clarification. First, Article 2 applies to the Kyoto Protocol. This is because the Convention itself states

---

[2] For example, the establishment of 'critical loads' in the acid-rain regime which allow a degree of pollution to occur. Sands, 1992.

[3] Sands, 1992: p. 272.

that 'any related instrument' shall share the ultimate objective set out in Article 2 and this is affirmed in paragraph 2 of the Preamble of the Protocol. Second, the ultimate objective is phased as a declarative goal rather than as a commitment or obligation for Parties.[4] Thus it is not clear if it creates substantive obligations for Parties. Additionally, as noted by Bodansky, the rationale for the use of the term 'ultimate' to qualify 'objective' is not entirely clear but perhaps stemmed from a desire to provide an overarching goal for the Convention, bearing in mind the provisions of Article 18 of the Vienna Convention.[5] The sections below discuss a number of important policy issues raised by Article 2 that have featured in climate negotiations in recent years.

1.2   *Detection and attribution*

The ultimate objective of the Convention is limited to 'anthropogenic' interference with the climate system, with Article 1.2 defining the term 'climate change' to mean a change in climate that is both:

- additional to natural climate variability observed over comparable time periods; and
- attributable, directly or indirectly, to human activity.

In the early years of the regime, uncertainties in climate science about these two issues provided many industry lobbies and laggard countries with opportunities to question whether the scientific basis for acting on the basis of the Convention's ultimate objective existed.[6] As a result these two issues, called 'detection and attribution', have been exhaustively researched in the last decade, with the IPCC then assessing whether a trend of increased temperatures against the background noise of natural variability can be detected and whether this can be attributed to human interference.[7] While the IPCC was hesitant to make a definite link between changes to the global climate and human activity in its First Assessment Report in 1990, in its 1995 Second Assessment Report (SAR), it was able to conclude that 'the balance of evidence suggests a discernible human influence on global climate'.[8] The IPCC confirmed this major scientific finding in the 2001 Third Assessment Report (TAR), stating that 'there is new and stronger evidence that most of the warming observed over the last 50 years is attributable to human activities'.[9] The

---

[4] Bodansky, 1993: p. 451.

[5] Bodansky, 1993: p. 451. Chapter 1 explains Article 18 of the Vienna Convention which is now of little consequence as almost 190 countries are now Parties to the Convention.

[6] Leggett, 1999: especially chapter 8.

[7] For a discussion of the 'detection and attribution' debate, see Brack, and Grubb, 1996.

[8] IPCC, 1995a: pp. 4 and 5. For a summary of the TAR, see Depledge, 2002.

[9] IPCC TAR, 2001a: p. 10.

IPCC further concluded that 'about three quarters of the anthropogenic emissions of CO_2 to the atmosphere during the past 20 years are due to fossil fuel burning', thus confirming the significance of fossil fuel emissions in the consideration of policy responses.[10] These findings represent the consensus views of scientists working within the IPCC and have been formally endorsed by the world's governments, even those initially sceptical of climate science.[11]

1.3   *Dangerous interference*

Increased scientific certainty that climate change is occurring has resulted in greater emphasis being given to issues concerning climate impacts. This shift is reflected both in the scientific literature assessed by the IPCC and in the greater attention given to adaptation issues by the COP since the adoption of the TAR in 2001. As a result there is emerging policy acceptance that information about climate impacts generated by the IPCC can play a vital role in helping policy-makers grapple with the value-laden questions that the COP, rather than the IPCC, must now focus on: what constitutes 'dangerous' anthropogenic interference with the climate system?[12]

The IPCC itself has signalled a greater willingness to engage with policy-makers on this issue in its Synthesis Report by stating that 'natural, technical, and social sciences can provide essential information and evidence needed for decisions on what constitutes 'dangerous anthropogenic interference', particularly by helping to reduce uncertainty and increase knowledge, thus serving as an input for considering precautionary measures'.[13] But it has also stressed that a decision on what constitutes dangerous interference must be determined through socio-political processes, such as the COP, taking into account considerations such as development, equity and sustainability, as well as uncertainties and risk.[14]

In practical terms, the IPCC TAR sought to advance understanding of what constitutes 'dangerous' climate change by devising a framework linking temperature rise with a qualitative assessment of risks in five areas:

- Risks to unique and threatened systems (e.g. coral reefs);
- Risks from extreme climate events;
- Distribution of impacts (across different countries and peoples);
- Aggregate impacts (on a worldwide basis); and
- Risks from future large-scale discontinuities (catastrophic events).

---

[10] IPCC TAR, 2001a: p. 10.

[11] The IPCC's Summaries for Policymakers are adopted line-by-line by governments: see chapter 15.

[12] Hare, 2001; Metz et al., 2002, *Climate Policy*, 2003; Berk et al., 2002; Arnell et al., 2002.

[13] IPCC, 2001d: Question 1.   [14] IPCC, 2001d: Question 1.

One of the most significant gaps in current impacts research, however, is that whilst the IPCC TAR projects temperature increases in the range of 1.4–5.8°C by 2100, scientific researchers have not yet examined what kinds of impacts might be expected at the top end of this range of temperatures (which in any case do not include feedbacks that might potentially increase the top end further).[15] Uncritical reliance on current impacts data therefore means implicitly taking a gamble that impacts associated with the top end of potential temperature increases can be discounted in COP policy-making. Extensions of impacts research to examine the full range of temperature-related impacts will help provide a sounder basis for policy-making on what constitutes dangerous interference. The issue of how the IPCC's work, in particular the TAR, could be used by policy-makers to address policy issues surrounding what constitutes 'dangerous' interference took place in the run up to and at COP-9. As a result COP-9 agreed that future SBSTA sessions should consider two new agenda items: the scientific, technical and socio-economic aspects of impacts of, and vulnerability and adaptation to, climate change and of mitigation.[16]

1.4   *Timing*

As stated above, the ultimate objective of the Convention provides guidance on timing by stating that safe levels must be achieved within a time-frame allowing ecosystems to adapt naturally, food production not to be threatened and economic development to proceed in a sustainable manner. Although the IPCC has not defined what a safe level of concentration would be, it has made clear that 'the projected rate and magnitude of warming and sea-level rise can be lessened by reducing greenhouse gas emissions. The greater the reductions in emissions and the earlier they are introduced, the smaller and slower the projected warming and rise in sea levels.'[17] It has also confirmed that for the most important anthropogenic greenhouse gas, CO_2, carbon cycle models indicate that stabilisation of atmospheric CO_2 concentrations at 450 and 650 ppm would require global anthropogenic CO_2 emissions to drop below year 1990 levels within a few decades or about a century respectively, and continue to decrease steadily thereafter. Eventually CO_2 emissions would need to decline to a very small fraction of current emissions.[18]

The IPCC has stated that 'stabilization of CO_2 emissions at near-current levels will not lead to stabilization of CO_2 atmospheric concentrations'.[19] Stabilisation of CO_2 concentrations at '*any* level requires eventual reduction of global CO_2 net

---

[15] Hare, 2001.   [16] Decision 10/CP.9.   [17] IPCC, 2001d: Question 5.
[18] IPCC, 2001d: Question 6.   [19] IPCC, 2001d: Question 5.

emissions to a small fraction of the current emission level.'[20] These conclusions are vital to understanding how and when actions to achieve the ultimate objection of the Convention might be structured and sequenced, including by whom, when and with respect to what mitigation actions should be undertaken, and suggest that there may be limited critical pathways or safe development corridors.[21] These policy issues could potentially be raised in discussions mandated by COP-9 at future SBSTA sessions on consideration of the TAR.[22]

1.5   *Developing long-term targets*

The desire to provide a long-term framework for negotiating future commitments, combined with political frustrations experienced to date in further defining the policy implications of Article 2, has led to calls that policy-makers discuss the merits and shortcomings of long-term quantified targets other than the one set out in Article 2 of the Convention.[23] A number of targets were indeed proposed during the negotiations of the Protocol, including further environmental quality standards that set quantified limits on the rate of warming and permissible levels of sea level rise (proposed by AOSIS) and proposals by the US, Japan and the EU to discuss the establishment of a long-term GHG atmospheric concentration target.[24] A number of Parties, notably France and Spain, advocated the gradual narrowing of the range of emissions per capita and per unit of GDP; these proposals resemble some of the concepts underlying the 'contraction and convergence' approach, which is premised on achievement of ecological limits.[25] None of these long-term targets was discussed in detail in the run up to Kyoto. This was due to three factors: Kyoto negotiations left little time for longer-term issues; the underlying scientific issues were poorly understood by the majority of COP delegates on the basis of information that had only recently become available from the IPCC in the SAR; and the institutional setting was not conducive to exploring some of these complex, value-laden issues given the frequency with which fossil fuel dependent Parties use climate negotiations to reopen scientific findings they have already agreed upon in the IPCC, in order to avoid discussion of their policy implications.[26]

---

[20] Stabilising emissions of shorter-lived greenhouse gases, however, such as methane, would lead to the stabilisation of their atmospheric concentrations within decades.

[21] See chapter 5.   [22] Decision 10/CP.9.

[23] Pershing and Tudela, 2003, examine a range of proposals, including previous approaches and some new ones.

[24] For details of proposals, see FCCC/TP/2000/2, paragraph 468.

[25] For details of proposals, see FCCC/TP/2000/2, paragraph 468.   [26] See chapter 9.

2   Principles

General principles are included in two different parts of the Convention: the Preamble and Article 3, with many shared conceptual connections.[27] Article 3 also allows principles not explicitly specified therein to guide Parties, thus recognising implicitly that other principles of international law (including those referenced in the Preamble) may be relevant.[28] This section explains the general nature and scope of the principles included in the Convention – whether in the Preamble or in Article 3. It then sets out an explanation of the main principles, such as common but differentiated responsibilities and the precautionary principle, with brief illustrations of their practical implications for climate policy.

2.1   *Nature and scope*

Proposals for including principles in the Convention resulted in many divergent views about the substantive meaning of the new principles upon which international actions should be based as well as the legal implications flowing from the inclusion of such principles.[29] Broadly speaking, the US along with other developed countries viewed the inclusion of an open-ended set of principles with caution, questioning their legal necessity and arguing instead for spelling out their practical implications, if any, in the form of commitments, or else relegating them to the Preamble where they would serve to indicate the policy rationale for collective action. Developing countries, on the other hand, led on this issue by China, pressed for inclusion of certain principles in the body of the text in the belief that these would provide useful guidance to Parties in implementing and developing the Convention in a manner that was more significant than reference in the Preamble allowed but which fell short of the specificity of commitments.[30] The final inclusion of Article 3 supports developing countries' view that in a complex new area of international cooperation like climate change, there may be need for a variety of legal norms: some detailed and capable of embodying precise standards, such as commitments, and others of a more general nature, which delineate shared understanding and expectations about the normative framework for subsequent action.

A number of general comments about the 'placement' of principles in the Convention and the nature of Article 3 are relevant. After realising that their initial

---

[27] Principles with specific application to particular issues have also been evolved by the regime. The annex to Decision 11/CP.7, for example, sets out a set of principles to govern the treatment of all LULUCF activities under the Kyoto Protocol which are discussed in chapter 5. Decision 15/CP.7 on the mechanisms contains a set of principles discussed in chapter 6.

[28] Chapter 1 explains what is meant by principles and their creation and role in international law.

[29] Bodansky, 1993: p. 501.   [30] Bodansky, 1993: p. 501.

response to delete principles or else move them to the Preamble was not going to be accepted, delegates that had had reservations about their inclusion decided to clarify Article 3 to limit its scope, legal implications and precedent-setting value. The reference to 'Parties' rather than 'states' is intended to limit the application of the principles to the Convention context, thus avoiding any implications that the principles are of broader relevance to the field of international environmental law generally.[31] The inclusion of 'inter alia' means that principles other than those set out in Article 3 may also be relevant. By saying that 'Parties' shall be 'guided by' the principles rather than observe them, the chapeau tries to ensure that the principles inform the implementation of commitments and other actions taken to achieve the objective of the Convention rather than give rise to additional commitments. The underlying intent of this provision is to limit the extent to which these principles can give rise to 'actionable' claims justifying recourse to dispute settlement proceedings.[32] It is not clear, however, whether the text actually achieves this, leaving such a possibility open to further consideration. Finally, the principles of the Convention also apply to Parties to the Kyoto Protocol in their actions under the Protocol because the Protocol provides that its Parties agree to 'being guided' by Article 3 of the Convention.[33]

It is important to bear in mind, however, that whilst understanding the general legal implications arising from the placement of principles in different parts of the Convention is important, state practice is also an important factor relevant to determining their nature, legal implications and status. The Convention Preamble, for example, contains some principles now regarded as binding, whilst some of the principles set out in Article 3 are considered to be emerging concepts whose legal status and implications remain to be developed. Additionally, the Preamble contains many principles 'jettisoned' from previous drafts because they were deemed too controversial but which remain linked to concepts now found in Article 3. And finally, in practice when they refer to principles, Parties do so without much regard to where the principles are found in the Convention. For these reasons, the following section discusses the substance of each of the main principles contained in the Convention, pointing out its legal implications and current legal status, rather than focusing on the 'placement issue'.

2.2   *Common concern of humankind*

Paragraph 1 of the Preamble recognises that 'change in the Earth's climate and its adverse effects are a common concern of humankind'. This implies that all states have a legal interest in the climate system, including legal responsibility to

---

[31] See chapter 1.   [32] See chapter 1.   [33] KP, Preamble, paragraph 4.

prevent damage to it.[34] In the climate regime, the extent of this 'common responsibility' is differentiated according to Parties' capacities and responsibilities and is fleshed out in more detail under the principle of common but differential responsibility discussed below. Whether the concept of 'common concern' provides a sufficient basis for a state, acting as a member of the international community, to enforce obligations to avoid damage to a global common, such as the climate system, remains open to discussion.[35] The concept of 'humankind' encompasses present and future generations and is thus linked to the concept of intergenerational equity set out in paragraph 23 of the Preamble which states that Parties are 'determined to protect the climate system for present and future generations' and which is referenced in Article 3.1 concerning common but differentiated responsibilities.

2.3   *Principle 21 Stockholm/Principle 2 Rio Declaration*

Principle 21 of the 1972 Stockholm Declaration/Principle 2 of the 1992 Rio Declaration is set out in full in paragraph 8 of the Preamble and provides that 'States have, in accordance with the Charter of the United Nations and the principles of international law, the sovereign right to exploit their own resources pursuant to their own environmental and developmental policies, and the responsibility to ensure that activities within their jurisdiction or control do not cause damage to the environment of other States or of areas beyond the limits of national jurisdiction.' This principle was confirmed as a binding principle of customary international law by the International Court of Justice in 1996.[36]

Principle 21 lies at the core of international environmental law and 'contains two fundamental objectives pulling in opposing directions: that states have sovereign rights over their natural resources and that states must not cause damage to the environment of other states or areas beyond national jurisdiction'.[37] Although paragraph 9 of the Convention's Preamble 'reaffirms the principle of sovereignty of states in international cooperation to address climate change', this affirmation does not override or undermine the obligation to avoid damage to the environment set out in Principle 21. This is because the principle of sovereignty affirmed in paragraph 9 allows states to conduct or authorise activities as they choose within their territories, including activities which may have an adverse

---

[34] Sands, 2003: p. 287. A similar formulation is found in the CBD which provides in its Preamble that 'biological diversity is a common concern of humankind'.

[35] See chapter 1.

[36] ICJ Advisory Opinion on the Legality of the Threat or Use of Nuclear Weapons, ICJ Reports 226 (1996).

[37] Sands, 2003: p. 236.

effect on their own environment, provided they observe limits established by international law.

Although Principle 21 is considered binding, this does not resolve more detailed issues that would arise in any practical dispute about its applications, including: What is environmental damage? What is the standard of care that must be observed by a state (absolute, strict or fault)? And what are the consequences of its breach and the extent of liability?[38] It is important to recall that the Convention was negotiated in part because the legal solutions Principle 21 could provide to such questions were deemed inadequate for protecting the climate system in the most effective manner possible, given that such protection requires a proactive, cooperative framework that provides legal clarity for a wide range of actors and seeks to avoid, rather than rectify, damage and ensures assistance for those adversely affected by climate change without recourse to costly litigation.

2.4   *Common but differentiated responsibilities*

The principle of common but differentiated responsibilities (CDR) is increasingly recognised in international law.[39] In essence it refers to the fact that certain problems affect and are affected by all nations in common, if not to the same degree, and that the resulting 'responsibilities' ought to be differentiated because not all nations should contribute equally to alleviate the problem.[40]

The concept of CDR is set out in Article 3.1 of the Convention, which states that Parties 'should protect the climate system for the benefit of present and future generations, on the basis of equity and in accordance with their common but differentiated responsibilities' and calls on developed country Parties to 'accordingly, take the lead in combating climate change and the adverse effects thereof'. CDR is thus a mixture of different concepts, including 'common concern' and acting for the benefit of present and future generations on the basis of equity.[41] The principle of equity requires taking into account all relevant considerations in the setting of responsibilities, in particular the needs and circumstances of developing countries. This aspect is brought out more fully in Article 3.2 of the Convention, which specifies that the special needs and circumstances of developing country Parties,

---

[38] Sands, 2003: p. 241.   [39] Stone, 2004; Rajamani, 2000.

[40] See also the formulation in Principle 7 of the Rio Declaration which provides that 'states shall cooperate in a spirit of global partnership to conserve, protect and restore the health and integrity of the Earth's ecosystem. In view of the different contributions to global environmental degradation, States have common but differentiated responsibilities. The developed countries acknowledge the responsibility that they bear in the international pursuit of sustainable development in view of the pressures their societies place on the global environment and of the technologies and financial resources they command.'

[41] Sands, 2003: p. 287.

especially those particularly vulnerable to adverse effects of climate change or those that would have to bear a disproportionate or abnormal burden, should be given full consideration. It is also stressed in Article 3.4 concerning the right to sustainable development discussed below.

The practical manifestation of the CDR principle is the structure of the Convention and the Protocol defining more detailed commitments for developed country Parties, with implementation of developing countries' less detailed commitments being related to the provision of financial and technical assistance as recognised in Article 3.7.[42] The reference to developed country Parties taking 'the lead' is frequently invoked by developing countries demanding that developed countries display effective leadership in combating climate change, such as bringing the Kyoto Protocol into force, before developing countries accept additional commitments.

It is important to clarify that Article 3.1 does not refer to historic contributions to climate change as originally proposed by some developing countries but presents a more balanced approach emphasising Parties' responsibilities as well as their present-day capabilities. The historically larger contribution of developed countries to climate change and their higher per capita emissions are, however, referenced as a factual statement in paragraph 3 of the Convention Preamble, which also recognises that the share of global emissions originating in developing countries will grow to meet their social and developmental needs. This is frequently invoked by developing countries in climate negotiations, particularly in discussions on evolution of mitigation commitments.[43] It has also informed thinking about the net effect of transfers and acquisitions under the Kyoto mechanisms, which led COP-7 to agree that Annex I Parties 'shall implement domestic action in accordance with national circumstances and with a view to reducing emissions in a manner conducive to narrowing per capita differences between developed and developing country Parties while working towards the implementation of the Convention'.[44]

2.5   Precautionary principle

The precautionary principle aims to provide guidance in cases where there is scientific uncertainty or where some risks are unknown, a condition known formally as ignorance, which even more than uncertainty underscores the need to plan for surprises. The precautionary principle is still an evolving principle of international environmental law and many formulations of the principle can

---

[42] See chapters 5, 8 and 9.   [43] See chapter 18.

[44] Decision 15/CP.7, Principles, nature and scope of the mechanisms pursuant to Articles 6, 12 and 17 of the Kyoto Protocol, Draft Decision/CMP.1 (mechanisms), Preamble, paragraph 6.

be found in a wide range of international instruments.[45] Its core requires that states not advance scientific uncertainty as a reason not to take action to prevent environmental damage or disasters, particularly if the harm may be serious and irreversible. Principle 15 of the Rio Declaration provides that 'where there are threats of serious or irreversible damage, lack of full scientific certainty shall not be used as a reason for postponing cost-effective measures to prevent environmental degradation'. The reference to 'cost-effectiveness' introduces an economic consideration limiting the extent of measures a state should consider undertaking.

Article 3.3 of the Convention provides that Parties

> should take precautionary measures to anticipate, prevent or minimize the causes of climate change and mitigate its adverse effects. Where there are threats of serious or irreversible damage, lack of scientific certainty should not be used as a reason for postponing such measures taking into account that policies and measures should be cost-effective so as to ensure global benefits at the lowest possible cost.

Thus, unlike the Rio Principle 15 formulation, the precautionary principle contained in Article 3.3 of the Convention does not introduce cost-effectiveness limitations into the environmental standard it sets out, although it requires such considerations to be taken 'into account'.[46] This slightly stronger version of the principle was no doubt influenced by AOSIS advocacy which then, and subsequently, emphasised its practical ramifications by pointing out that 'for us the precautionary principle is more than a semantic or theoretical exercise. It is an ecological and moral imperative. We trust the world understands our concerns by now. We do not have the luxury of waiting for conclusive proof, as some have suggested in the past. The proof, we fear, will kill us.'[47]

Whilst the core of the precautionary principle is well established, what this means in practical terms for implementation is still subject to disagreement, including on whether it is now a binding principle, whether it necessarily involves shifting the burden of proof to the person who wants to carry out an activity to show that it is safe (rather than opponents having to show it is unsafe) and what level of scientific certainty is needed to justify precautionary action.[48] Although opponents of the precautionary principle, usually industry groups, have decried the potential the precautionary principle has for over-regulation

---

[45] Sands, 2003: pp. 266–79. See also O'Riordan and Cameron, 1994; Freestone and Hey, 1995; Freestone, 1999; Harremoes et al., 2002; Stone, 2004.

[46] Bodansky, 1993: p. 503.

[47] Ambassador Robert van Lierop, Chairman of AOSIS, Permanent Representative of Vanuatu to the UN, Statement to Plenary Session of INC/FCCC, 5 February 1991.

[48] Sands, 1995b: pp. 272–3. See also Harremoes et al., 2002.

and limiting human activity, recent research appears to indicate that there is little empirical evidence documenting real life cases where regulatory action was taken on the basis of a precautionary approach that later turned out to be unnecessary.

The third sentence of Article 3.3 is not directly about the precautionary principle but provides that policies and measures should take into account different socio-economic contexts, be comprehensive, cover all relevant sources, sinks and reservoirs of greenhouse gases and adaptation, and comprise all economic sectors. These provisions are often cited by energy-exporting Parties as policy justifications for inclusion of sinks as a mitigation policy and against measures targeting fossil-fuel related emissions.[49] The final sentence of Article 3.3 endorses the cooperative flexibility mechanisms such as emissions trading, joint implementation and the clean development mechanism which have the potential to reduce global compliance costs and also can reduce economic impacts arising from response measures.

2.6   *Right to sustainable development*

Sustainable development is now a widely accepted international legal concept as evidenced by its widespread normative use in a wide range of international instruments and recent recognition by the ICJ.[50] Although it continues to be reaffirmed as an important, sometimes even the central, guiding principle of the UN, by states, IGOs, NGOs and even private institutions, progress to implement it has been modest because of the enormous substantive and governance challenges it poses.[51] There are four recurring elements of the concept:

- Preserving natural resources for present and future generations (intergenerational equity);
- Exploiting such resources in a sustainable manner (sustainable use);
- Balancing one state's use with needs of others in an equitable manner (intragenerational equity); and
- Integration of environmental considerations into economic, social and developmental issues and visa versa (integration).[52]

Article 3.4 of the Convention states that 'Parties have a right to, and should, promote sustainable development.' Traditionally the US has opposed the 'right to development' articulated by many developing countries since the mid-1970s as part of efforts to establish a New International Economic Order because this

---

[49] See chapter 9.

[50] Lang, 1995; Sands, 1995a; *Gabcikovo–Nagymaros Case*, ICJ Reports 78 (1997), paragraph 140.

[51] Pallemaerts, 2003.   [52] Sands, 1995b: p. 253.

implies entitlement to financial assistance from developed countries.[53] The wording in Article 3.4, which makes sustainable development a right to promote, was a compromise formulation to address these concerns.

Article 3.4 also provides that 'policies and measures to protect the climate system against human-induced change should be appropriate for the specific conditions of each Party and should be integrated with national development programmes, taking into account that economic development is essential for adopting measures to address climate change'. One practical manifestation of this is acceptance that states should enact effective environmental legislation, standards and management objectives 'that reflect the environmental and developmental context to which they apply and that standards applied by some countries may be inappropriate and of unwarranted economic and social cost to other countries, in particular developing countries'. This principle is set out in the Convention's Preamble in paragraph 10, which restates Principle 11 of the Rio Declaration. It is frequently invoked by both developed and developing countries, usually to argue against detailed international standards and in favour of approaches where Parties retain flexibility to determine how particular commitments will be implemented at the national level. More recently, fossil-fuel dependent countries have argued that 'minimizing the impact of the implementation of Article 3.1 of the Protocol is a development concern affecting both the industrialized and developing countries'.[54]

2.7   *Trade and environment*

Article 3.5 of the Convention promotes a supportive and open international economic system leading to sustainable economic growth and development in all Parties, particularly developing country Parties, and states that measures to combat climate change, including unilateral ones, should not constitute a means of arbitrary or unjustifiable discrimination or a disguised restriction on international trade. This provision, which reflects part of the wording of Principle 12 of the Rio Declaration, addresses the relationship between environmental measures and trade examined in more detail in chapters 9 and 17. The wording of Article 3.5 appears neutral since it neither endorses nor prohibits using trade measures of the sort contained in the Montreal Protocol as a means of increasing the effectiveness of the Convention in term of compliance and enforcement.[55]

---

[53] Bodansky, 1993: p. 504.   [54] See chapter 9.
[55] Bodansky, 1993: text and notes at footnotes 327–9.

5

Mitigation commitments

1 Introduction

The timing and stringency of mitigation commitments, and which Parties or groups of Parties should undertake them, lies at the heart of the climate regime. This chapter sets out the mitigation commitments agreed to date in relation to sources, sinks and reservoirs of GHGs. These, and other related mitigation terms, are explained in box 5.1 below. The provisions of the FCCC and the Kyoto Protocol are, of course, the most important source of rules in respect of GHG mitigation commitments. In each section the rules contained in the FCCC and KP are set out first, followed by a 'rule development' section which sets out how these rules have been further elaborated, defined or enhanced as a result of COP decisions. Customary international law and general principles of law help define the rights and responsibilities of states in respect of global environmental problems such as climate change and are discussed in chapter 1.

The mitigation commitments applicable to all Parties are found in Article 4.1 of the Convention. Informally, these are called 'general commitments' because Article 4.1 covers a broad range of issues relevant to addressing climate change, including planning, research and adaptation. The more stringent mitigation commitments of Annex I Parties are contained in Article 4.2 of the Convention and these are often termed 'specific commitments'. These are covered in detail in section 5. Articles 4.3 to 4.10 of the Convention contain commitments relating to the special situations of particular groups of countries, including EITs, developing countries and Parties dependent on the production/consumption of fossil fuels.

The Kyoto Protocol, which, unlike the Convention, does not formally have any titles for its articles, follows this pattern to a large extent. The mitigation commitments of all Parties are contained in Article 10, somewhat cumbersomely referred to as 'advancing the implementation of existing commitments'. The more stringent mitigation commitments of Annex I Parties are set out in Articles 2 and 3 of the Protocol and are referred to as 'quantified emission limitation and reduction commitments'. The special situations of particular groups of countries are incorporated in various provisions of the Protocol, and have subsequently been operationalised through more detailed provisions contained in the Marrakesh Accords adopted at COP-7. This is also true of the financial and technological assistance commitments.

For explanatory purposes, a useful distinction is whether mitigation commitments contained in the FCCC and the Kyoto Protocol can be seen as substantive or procedural in nature. Substantive commitments require action to control GHG emissions or enhance their removal by sinks. Substantive commitments can be qualitative in nature, such as a requirement to adopt particular policies and measures, or be framed in quantitative terms prescribing that a particular quantified result (a target) be achieved within a specified time-frame. Procedural commitments are, in essence, process focused and aim to advance preparatory efforts to address climate change, through requiring, for example, the preparation of inventories. Although such commitments do not mandate achievement of a particular GHG result, procedural commitments can exercise a strong catalysing effect capable of effecting policy change, and generate information necessary for taking more substantive actions. For this reason, the process of strengthening substantive commitments under the FCCC has evolved in tandem with the strengthening of procedural commitments.[1]

Mitigation commitments are linked to virtually every aspect of the regime. The FCCC and the Protocol allow groups of Parties, principally the EU, to fulfil their mitigation commitments jointly. For meeting their Article 3 commitments under the Protocol, Annex I Parties can also make use of the Kyoto flexible mechanisms: joint implementation, emissions trading and the Clean Development Mechanism.[2] All Parties must report on the implementation of their mitigation commitments in varying amounts of detail and frequency through submission of inventories and national communications. The preparation, reporting and review processes for national communications are described in chapter 11. Parties to the Protocol are also subject to the non-compliance procedure elaborated under the Marrakesh Accords which is described in detail in chapter 12.

---

[1] See chapter 18.   [2] See chapter 6.

Box 5.1   Mitigation: key concepts and definitions

Mitigation refers to human interventions to reduce emissions of greenhouse gases from sources or to enhance their removal by sinks. Under the Convention, *greenhouse gases* refers to gaseous constituents of the atmosphere, both natural and anthropogenic, that absorb and re-emit infrared radiation.[3] *Emissions* means the release of greenhouse gases and/or their precursors into the atmosphere over a specified area and period of time.[4] *GHG precursors* are emissions of nitrogen oxides, carbon monoxide and non-methane volatile organic compounds, also known as tropospheric ozone precursors. Although precursors are not strictly GHGs, they contribute indirectly to the greenhouse effect because they influence the rate at which ozone and other gases are created and destroyed in the atmosphere.[5] A *GHG source* is 'any process, activity or mechanism that releases a greenhouse gas, an aerosol, or a precursor of a greenhouse gas or aerosol into the atmosphere'.[6] *Aerosols* are airborne solid or liquid particles, of either natural or anthropogenic origin, residing in the atmosphere for at least several hours. Although not GHGs, aerosols influence climate through scattering and absorbing radiation and by affecting cloud formation. Man-made aerosols have had an overall cooling effect but cause acid rain and poor air quality problems. *Sinks* are defined as 'any process or activity or mechanism that removes a greenhouse gas, an aerosol, or a precursor of a greenhouse gas or aerosol from the atmosphere'.[7] Mitigation can also cover human actions to conserve or create *reservoirs*, sometimes also known as pools of carbon.[8] Reservoirs are defined as a component or components of the climate system, other than the atmosphere, where a greenhouse gas or a precursor of a greenhouse gas is stored.[9] Oceans and soils are reservoirs of carbon. Forests that absorb carbon from the atmosphere act as sinks whilst

---

[3] FCCC Article 1.5.   [4] FCCC Article 1.4.

[5] N_2O contributes to the formation of ozone in the lower atmosphere. CO elevates concentrations of CH_4 and atmospheric ozone through chemical reactions with atmospheric constituents which would otherwise destroy CH_4 and ozone. It eventually oxidizes to CO_2. NMVOCs participate along with nitrogen oxides in the formation of ground-level ozone and other photochemical oxidants.

[6] FCCC Article 1.9.   [7] FCCC Article 1.8.

[8] Because the atmosphere stores carbon, it is also a reservoir or pool of carbon. But the term 'reservoir' is used in the climate regime generally in a more restrictive sense to exclude the atmosphere.

[9] FCCC Article 1.7 refers to 'reservoirs' and does not make clear that this excludes the atmosphere, although in practice this is how the phrase is interpreted.

> forests whose carbon flows are in balance act as reservoirs. Forests can
> also become sources of GHGs, e.g. through deforestation. The absolute
> quantity of carbon held within a reservoir at a specified time is called the
> *carbon stock*.

This chapter is structured as follows. Section 2 sets out issues relating to coverage of the climate regime in terms of gases, sources and sinks. Coverage defines the scope of the subject matter to be regulated. Commitments refer to the range of actions states must undertake, or refrain from undertaking, in relation to the subject matter. Section 3 describes the rules relating to base years or base periods. The substantive and procedural mitigation commitments applicable to all Parties to the FCCC and to all Parties to the KP are set out in section 4. Section 5 provides an overview of the more stringent mitigation commitments of Parties included in Annex I of the FCCC and Annex B of the KP respectively. Reference should also be made to Appendix II which consists primarily of a series of graphical tables that set out in detail the country-specific commitments, and other particular considerations, applicable to individual countries listed in Annex I of the Convention or Annex B of the Protocol, including a brief overview of their current and projected emissions as these are critical for understanding the implications of each country's targets.

2   Coverage

2.1   *Sources of greenhouse gases*

Background: There was always broad agreement that the climate regime should cover all GHGs not otherwise regulated by other international treaties. The main policy issue was whether for the purposes of setting targets, gases should be considered individually or collectively. During the Protocol negotiations, AOSIS and Japan favoured regulating greenhouse gases individually on a gas-by-gas basis. The EU argued for a three-gas basket (CO_2, CH_4 and N_2O) and no sinks. The alternative, favoured by most JUSSCANNZ countries, would allow countries greater choice as they can select how to make reductions across a six-gas 'basket of gases' to suit their individual circumstances, utilising the concept of global warming potentials explained below, and use sinks.

FCCC: The broad definition of greenhouse gases set out in Articles 1.5. 1.7, 1.8 and 1.9 of the FCCC (see box 5.1) means that the Convention applies, in principle, to all sources and sinks of GHG emissions, including precursors. The exceptions or limitations in relation to specific gases/sources expressly agreed by Parties are greenhouse gases controlled by the Montreal Protocol.

Kyoto: The coverage of the Protocol is broadly similar to the Convention but more circumscribed and precise in relation to the sources covered under Annex I Parties' quantified commitments under Article 3 which explicitly endorses the 'basket of gases' approach in respect of the following six gases listed in Annex A of the Protocol:

- carbon dioxide;
- methane;
- nitrous oxide;
- hydrofluorocarbons;
- perfluorocarbons; and
- sulphur hexafluoride.

Strictly speaking, hydrofluorocarbons and perfluorocarbons are groups of gases, and along with sulphur hexafluoride are sometimes referred to as the 'industrial' or 'synthetic' gases. Emissions of all six types of gases from the following five sectors/source categories listed in Annex A can count towards Article 3.1 commitments:

- energy;
- industrial processes;
- solvents and other product use;
- agriculture; and
- waste.

Some greenhouse gases are more powerful per unit of emissions than others in terms of radiative forcing. The inclusion of six gases in a basket-of-gases approach has been made possible because of the concept of Global Warming Potentials (GWPs). GWP provides a common metric to compare and measure the relative radiative forcing of different GHGs without directly calculating the changes in atmospheric concentrations. GWPs are calculated as the ratio of the radiative forcing that would result from the emission of 1 kilogram of a greenhouse gas to that from the emission of 1 kilogram of carbon dioxide over a period of time (usually 100 years). The contribution of non-CO_2 greenhouse gases is then expressed in terms of Carbon Dioxide Equivalent (CO_2e). The basket-of-gases approach, combined with the use of GWPs, gives countries considerable flexibility to determine which gas from which sector to limit or reduce.

The IPCC can update GWPs on the basis of new scientific knowledge; however, Article 5.3 sets out a political decision to use the 1995 values for reporting purposes for the first commitment period. Table 5.1 below shows the original GWPs (assigned in 1990) and the most recent GWPs (assigned in 1995) for the most important greenhouse gases. To avoid inconsistencies in methodologies, Article 5.3 of the

Table 5.1   *Global warming potentials*

Gas	GWP 1990	GWP 1995
Carbon dioxide	1	1
Methane	22	21
Nitrous oxide	270	310
HFC-134a	1,200	1,300
HFC-23	10,000	11,700
HFC-152a	150	140
HCF-125	NA*	2,800
PFCs	5,400	7,850
SF$_6$	NA*	23,900

* Not Applicable. GWP was not yet estimated for this gas.

Protocol states that the GWPs 'used to calculate the carbon dioxide equivalence of anthropogenic emissions by sources and removals by sinks of the greenhouse gases listed in Annex A shall be those accepted by the [IPCC] and agreed upon by [COP-3]'. The COP/MOP is mandated to review and revise the GWPs but, to ensure legal certainty, any changes in the value of GWPs will only apply to commitments under Article 3 in respect of any commitment period adopted subsequent to that revision.

The adoption of multi-year targets in the Kyoto Protocol necessitated invention of a new term to refer to the maximum aggregate amount of carbon dioxide equivalent emissions to be emitted by a Party over a defined temporal period. Under the Protocol, this aggregate unit eventually came to be called the *assigned amount* and the temporal period as the *commitment period*, the first one covering the five years 2008–2012. The assigned amount for each Annex I Party is an absolute amount of emissions allowed for each Party over the five-year, first commitment period. This absolute amount is equal to the agreed base-year inventory amount (in CO_2e), multiplied by the share of allowable emissions outlined in Annex B, and multiplied by five years.[10]

Rule development: So far as estimation and reporting of sources and sinks is concerned, under the Convention and the Protocol, Parties should use the IPCC's Revised 1996 Guidelines for National Greenhouse Gas Inventories.[11] Paragraph 3 of Decision 2/CP.3, adopted alongside the Protocol, reaffirms that Parties to the Protocol should continue the Convention practice of using GWPs provided by the IPCC in its Second Assessment Report, known as the '1995 IPCC GWP values',

---

[10] Decision 19/CP.7, Annex, paragraph 5. There are special provisions relating to Parties that have reached an agreement in accordance with Article 4: see below.

[11] See chapter 11.

which are based on the effects of greenhouse gases over a 100 year time horizon. Taking into account the inherent and complicated uncertainties involved in GWP estimates, Parties to the Protocol may, in addition, use another time horizon for information purposes only. Table 5.1 above shows the GWP values accepted by the IPCC in 1990 and then in 1995 in its Second Assessment Report which must be used for the Protocol and current FCCC inventory reporting.

2.2   *Sinks*

In the global climate regime, policy choices about whether sinks should be included in the setting of commitments, particularly targets, have important consequences for flexibility to choose among various mitigation options and, ultimately, for compliance costs. The transparency and verifiability of different accounting approaches, such as the 'comprehensive approach' and 'gross' or 'net' accounting, is also important. These terms are not defined in the FCCC or Kyoto Protocol but are widely used in policy discussions and are explained in box 5.2.

Box 5.2   Sinks: comprehensive, gross and net accounting

Parties have debated the extent to which the carbon sequestered by sinks can be excluded from target setting or included through a number of accounting approaches. Canada, Australia, New Zealand, the US and OPEC have tended to support the *comprehensive approach* which refers to consideration of sinks as well as all sources of GHGs in the formulation of policy collectively. This approach has often gone hand-in-hand with advocacy of the concept of *net emissions* which is contrasted with the gross emissions approach. A *gross emissions* approach would define the target in relation to emissions from all GHG sources but excluding all removals (or emissions) from LULUCF. A *net emissions* approach would count all emissions and all sources, including from LULUCF, towards the setting of the target and its fulfilment. The *gross–net approach* refers to using the concept of gross emissions to define the base year from which the target is calculated but using the concept of net emissions at the end of the target period to assess compliance. Under the gross–net approach, targets are set on the basis of gross emissions in, say, 1990, but countries can get credit for removals of GHGs by sinks in meeting their targets because emissions would be measured on a net basis in the commitment period. A *net–net approach* uses the concept of net emissions both to define the base year and at the end of the target period.

FCCC: The FCCC does not explicitly endorse the comprehensive approach but some FCCC provisions refer to it favourably.[12] Parties to the FCCC are required to *report* annual emissions from sources and removals from sinks on a disaggregated basis using the IPCC 1996 Revised Guidelines.

So far as the quantified aim for Annex I Parties under Article 4.2 (a) and (b) is concerned, the FCCC refers to sources only as it states that Parties shall aim at returning 'to their 1990 levels these anthropogenic emissions of CO_2 and other greenhouse gases'.[13] It does not refer to inclusion of LULUCF.[14] To assess progress made by Annex I Parties in respect of the quantified aim, emissions in 1990 are compared with emissions in 2000 without inclusion of the contribution from the LULUCF sector which is shown separately from Parties' emission totals.[15] Although carbon dioxide is highlighted, the quantified aim covers all GHGs not controlled by the Montreal Protocol. Parties continue to debate whether the quantified aim requires gases to be controlled on a gas-by-gas basis or whether the basket-of-gases approach is permissible: a basket approach would tend to weaken the quantified aim because non-CO_2 gases are easier to control and would therefore take some of the pressure off CO_2 reductions. The interpretation that each Annex I Party is to return each gas to its 1990 level individually is favoured by some Parties, such as the UK and the EU.[16] Others, such as the US, have argued that this language in the context of the whole paragraph allows these gases to be considered collectively as a basket.[17] In practice, the IPCC 1996 Revised Guidelines require reporting on a gas-by-gas basis but also allow Parties to report aggregate emissions expressed in carbon dioxide equivalent terms, using GWP values provided by the IPCC.[18] This enables a clear assessment of the trends in emissions of individual gases. The FCCC Secretariat prepares reports examining the aggregate trends for each country and

[12] See e.g. Article 3.3. Bodansky, 1993: p. 518 at footnote 411; and chapter 4.

[13] See section 4 below on Article 4.2 (a) and (b) for an explanation of the quantified aim.

[14] Some Parties, such as the US, view the commitment to report on progress towards the quantified aim in terms of their 'net emissions', which would allow inclusion of the contribution of sinks. US Transmittal Document from the President to the Senate, Article-by-Article Analysis, p. 3. Bodansky, 1993: p. 520 and footnote 420.

[15] See e.g. FCCC/SBI/2003/7, Compilation and synthesis of third national communications from Annex I Parties. For example, the EU declaration on Article 4.2 (a) and (b) in its instrument of ratification of the Convention states that 'the Community and its Member States reaffirm the objective set out in the Council conclusions of 29 October 1990, and in particular the objective of stabilization of CO_2 emissions by 2000 at 1990 levels in the Community as a whole. The European Community and its Member States are elaborating a coherent strategy in order to attain this objective.'

[16] UK Department of Environment Note on FCCC, on file with the author, makes a similar point. See also text and footnote at 415, Bodansky, 1993.

[17] Bodansky, 1993: p. 519, text and footnote at 415.

[18] Decision 4/CP.1, paragraph (c). See also COP-3 report, part 1, FCCC/CP/1997/7, paragraphs 14 and 15.

across all Annex I countries both without and with sinks included, but for the purpose of monitoring progress with the quantified aim in Article 4.2 (a) and (b), they exclude sinks from the aggregate totals. This is because Article 4.2 (a) and (b) reflects the gross approach as it only relates to emissions and does not refer to inclusion of LULUCF.

Kyoto: The Protocol covers emissions/removals from sinks which are to be reported in accordance with the IPCC 1996 Revised Guidelines for National Greenhouse Gas Inventories.[19] However, the provisions relating to how emissions and removals from sinks should count towards Annex I Parties' Article 3 commitments are precise, complicated and the subject of extensive rule development as a result of the compromises that were agreed in Articles 3.3 and 3.4 of the Protocol, including through the Marrakesh Accords.

LULUCF is not included as a sector/source category in Annex A of the Protocol. At Kyoto, pressure to allow countries to take credit for particular categories of sinks led to inclusion of a limited number of sinks activities that could count towards Article 3 commitments. The inclusion of emissions/removals from particular LULUCF activities is covered by specific provisions of the Protocol, namely Articles 3.3, 3.4 and 3.7, and by decisions adopted pursuant to those Articles. These provisions, in effect, mandate a *gross–net approach* to accounting for Article 3.3 sinks for purposes of meeting Annex I Parties' Article 3.1 commitments. The gross–net approach under Article 3.3 means that emissions from LULUCF emissions/removals are not taken into account in defining Annex I Parties' quantified commitments or assigned amount. But they are taken into account when assessing compliance at the end of the commitment period. Under the Protocol, the gross–net approach applies to all Parties in Annex I except for countries whose LULUCF emissions constituted a net source in 1990. The Marrakesh Accords agreed a capped net–net approach for sinks under Article 3.4.

Article 3.7 states that Parties must include emissions from deforestation-related activities in the calculation of their base-year emissions. On the basis of current reported 1990 emissions, Article 3.7 can only apply to Australia, Greece and the UK. However, it is only of policy significance to Australia because emissions from the LULUCF sectors were of negligible significance to the other two countries when compared with their emissions from sources. Because Article 3.7 could potentially make achievement of Australia's Kyoto target less difficult, it is sometimes informally known as the 'Australian Clause'.

Rule development: The approach used in the Protocol relating to the use and accounting of sinks by Annex I Parties is discussed in section 5.3, with the inclusion of LULUCF activities under the CDM being discussed in chapter 6.

---

[19] Decision 2/CP.3, paragraph 1.

2.3   *Gases controlled by the Montreal Protocol*

FCCC and Kyoto: The FCCC explicitly states, at various points, that it does not cover greenhouse gases controlled by the 1987 Montreal Protocol on Substances That Deplete the Ozone Layer.[20] Without an explicit exclusion, Parties might count reductions of ozone-depleting substances mandated by the Montreal Protocol towards achievement of their FCCC and Kyoto commitments. The Kyoto Protocol follows the FCCC by explicitly excluding gases controlled by the Montreal Protocol from provisions relating to mitigation commitments.[21]

Rule development: Inclusion of HFCs and PFCs in Annex A of the Kyoto Protocol has necessitated greater cooperation between the climate and ozone regimes regarding policy coherence – an issue which is discussed in detail in chapter 17.[22]

2.4   *Fuels used for international aviation and maritime transportation*

Background: International aviation and shipping account for about 4 per cent of global CO_2 emissions, with the overall radiative forcing being higher due to other factors (build up of ozone and contrails) so that projections suggest a doubling of the share of global emissions (to 8 per cent) by 2020.[23] Fuels used for international aviation and marine transportation are often referred to as 'bunker fuels' even though this is a generic term referring to fuel carried by ships and aircrafts for their own use whether they are engaged in international or domestic transportation. The term 'bunker fuels' is not defined in the Convention or the Protocol but is defined in the IPCC GHG inventory guidelines which have been adopted by the COP to guide preparation of inventory reports under the Convention and the Protocol.[24] Fuels used for international aviation and marine transportation raise three separate issues: (1) adequate and consistent inventories, (2) allocation of emissions, and (3) policy options to control their emissions. The issue of allocation is difficult to agree upon because international transportation by definition raises international competitiveness issues and some countries are reluctant to count emissions from fuels sold for international aviation or maritime transportation towards their national total, particularly given the dramatic increase in these emissions since 1990. International cooperation in the field of aviation and shipping has a long history and many aspects of these industries are regulated at the international level through the International Civil Aviation organisation (ICAO) and the International Maritime organisation (IMO). In recent

---

[20] The exclusion is mentioned in Articles 4.1 (a)–(d), 4.2 (a), (b) and (e) (ii), 4.6 and 12.1 (a). The pre-existence and legal competence of the ozone regime is acknowledged in the Convention Preamble, paragraph 13.

[21] The exclusion is mentioned in Articles 2.1 (a) (ii), 2.2, 3.1, 3.2, 7.1 and 10 (a). See also Annex A.

[22] Decisions 13/CP.4, 17/CP.5 and 12/CP.8.   [23] Oberthür, 2003: pp. 191–205.

[24] See chapter 11.

years, these two organisations have begun to work in much closer cooperation with the climate regime to give assistance on the first two issues outlined above and, in principle, to advance solutions to the third policy issue.

FCCC: Although the term 'bunker fuels' does not appear in the Convention, the FCCC does address fuel sales by Parties, while specific rules relating to bunker fuels are embedded in decisions under the Convention relating to inventories on the basis of work undertaken by SBSTA, much of it done in recent years with the cooperation of ICAO and IMO.

Reporting of emissions from aviation and marine bunker fuels in the Convention is mandatory in the annual national inventories of Annex I Parties due under the Convention.[25] So far as reporting is concerned, a distinction is made between *domestic* and *international bunker fuels*. Emissions from domestic aviation and shipping are covered by transport emissions and included in a Party's national total whilst emissions from international aviation and marine bunkers are reported separately and not counted towards Parties' national GHG totals under the FCCC.[26] The distinction between domestic and international bunker fuels is also made by Non-Annex I Parties, who 'should' report on international bunker fuels 'to the extent possible, and if disaggregated data are available'.[27]

The Revised 1996 IPCC Reporting Guidelines for National Greenhouse Inventories and the 2000 IPCC Good Practice Guidance give practical guidance on what must be reported, how and by whom. Emissions from fuel sold to ships or aircraft engaged in international transport are reported by the country where the fuel is loaded but are excluded from that country's national totals. All civil domestic and freight flights inside a country (commercial, private, agricultural, etc.), including take offs and landings, are considered domestic and therefore are added to national totals. For shipping, emissions from fuel used in navigation by all vessels not engaged in international transport, including fishing, must be included in national totals. As pointed out in the IPCC Guidelines, this can include some lengthy journeys between two ports in a country (e.g. San Francisco and Honolulu). Despite this guidance, there are a number of definitional and methodological problems arising from the requirement to report bunker fuels emissions on the basis of the domestic/international split.

Kyoto: At Kyoto, Parties made three important decisions relating to international bunker fuels. First, they agreed that the FCCC practice of reporting domestic and international bunker fuels in national inventories but of excluding the latter from the national totals should also apply to the Protocol, pending decisions

---

[25] FCCC/CP/1997/7, Paragraph 18. FCCC Guidelines for National Inventories.

[26] Paragraph 18. FCCC Guidelines. And see Revised IPCC Guidelines, Common Reporting Format Guideline at sections 1 (A) (3) (a) (i) (aviation) and 1 (A) (3) (d) (i) (marine).

[27] Decision17/CP.8, Paragraph 19, Annex.

relating to the allocation of the latter.[28] Emissions from international bunkers are currently not included in national totals and thus are excluded from Annex I Parties' quantified commitments under Article 3.

Second, emissions from international bunker fuels shall be regulated through the ICAO and IMO respectively, rather than directly under the Protocol. Accordingly, Article 2.2 states that Annex I Parties to the Kyoto Protocol shall 'pursue limitation or reduction of emissions . . . from aviation and marine bunker fuels, working though the International Civil Aviation organisation and the International Maritime organisation, respectively'. This provision clarifies the international division of labour between the climate regime and the ICAO and IMO. It should be noted that Annex I Parties will be obliged to report in their national communications on their efforts to work through IMO and ICAO to fulfil this commitment.[29] Along with other provisions in Article 2, this commitment is subject to reporting and reviews by expert review teams and is subject to oversight by the facilitative branch of the Compliance Committee.

The third decision agreed at Kyoto is Parties' acceptance of the need for further work on the inclusion of bunker emissions in the national GHG inventories of Parties.[30] Negotiations within SBSTA in the run up to the adoption of the Protocol revealed that data relating to international bunker emissions was incomplete and hampered consideration of the politically thorny issue of emissions allocation. SBSTA-4 in December 1996, which commenced examination of this issue, concluded that four basic allocation options could be explored further. These were: no allocation to national inventories; allocation according to the country where the fuel is sold; allocation according to the nationality of the airline/vessel operator or aircraft/ship registration; and allocation according to the country of departure or destination of the aircraft/vessel.[31]

Rule development: Currently, three strands of work are discernible under the COP agenda item dealing with bunker fuels which supports both the Convention and the Protocol: work by the ICAO relating to aviation bunkers, work by the IMO relating to marine bunker fuel and work to improve reporting under the Convention and the Protocol. The adoption of Article 2.2 stating that the ICAO and IMO will take the lead in formulating policy options to control bunker emissions was intended to lessen the need for the climate regime to be proactive in the controversial policy issues surrounding allocation and control options. Advances on the allocation options discussed by SBSTA-4 in 1996 have been difficult because of a lack of consensus among Parties. Following the adoption of the Protocol, SBSTA's efforts have focused on work to improve the methodological

---

[28] Decision 2/CP.3, Paragraph 4. [29] FCCC/CP/1999/7, Paragraph 15.
[30] Decision 2/CP.3, Paragraph 4. [31] SBSTA-4 report, FCCC/SBSTA/1996/20, paragraph 55.

and reporting aspects of bunker fuel in order to improve transparency, accuracy and comparability of bunker emissions in accordance with the thrust of Decision 2/CP.3. At SBSTA-18, Parties will consider further the work on this issue.[32]

Since 1997, the ICAO and IMO have become more active in the climate regime, both in terms of assisting FCCC bodies in their efforts to improve the quality and comparability of data and in terms of studying policy options to control GHG emissions from international bunker fuels. The prospect of ICAO or IMO reaching agreement on mandatory controls limiting or reducing emissions from international bunker fuels remains, however, distant, as the work of both the ICAO and IMO, described in box 5.3 below, is currently focused on further analytical work and/or voluntary approaches. To date no concrete proposals for mandatory control of emissions from these sources have emerged from either organisation, nor is specific work underway to develop such proposals.

Box 5.3   ICAO and IMO work on bunker fuels

The International Civil Aviation Organization (ICAO) was established in 1947 to promote safe and efficient air transport on the basis of the 1944 Chicago Convention on International Civil Aviation. The ICAO Assembly meets once every three years in Montreal. The ICAO Council, composed of 33 of the 188 contracting states, is a permanent body endowed with legal authority to create binding international standards in respect of some of the areas covered by its mandate (e.g. air traffic) upon a two-thirds majority vote. Standards are adopted by the ICAO Council as 'international standards and recommended practices' in the form of annexes to the Chicago Convention. Climate issues are discussed within the Committee on Aviation Environmental Protection (CAEP) which comprises nineteen contracting states, including observers from business and environmental groups, and which reports to the Council.[33] Council representatives tend to be from states with significant aviation interests.

In 1999, the IPCC presented a Special Report on Aviation and the Global Atmosphere prepared by the IPCC and the Scientific Assessment Panel of the Montreal Protocol in response to a request from ICAO.[34] ICAO's current work on aviation emissions is governed by Resolution A33-7, particularly Appendices H and I, in force as of 3 October 2001. Resolution A33-7 mandates

---

[32] FCCC/SBSTA/2003/INF.3, Emissions resulting from fuel used in international aviation and maritime bunkers. ICAO 34th Extraordinary Meeting of Assembly in Montreal, April 2003.
[33] FCCC/SBSTA/2001/INF.1.   [34] IPCC, 1999.

the ICAO Council to continue to study policy options to reduce or limit the environmental impact of aircraft emissions, placing special emphasis on technical solutions and consideration of market-based measures, taking into account potential implications for developed and developing countries.[35] This work is being undertaken by CAEP. In January 2001, CAEP decided not to pursue an ICAO standard limiting carbon dioxide, citing diversity of operations and the fact that market pressures already ensure aircraft are fuel efficient.[36] The ICAO Council has encouraged contracting states to use voluntary measures and will facilitate this by developing guidelines.[37]

So far as shipping is concerned, the principal international body is the International Maritime Organization (IMO) which came into existence in 1958. The IMO is a UN specialised agency responsible for improving maritime safety and for preventing pollution from ships. The IMO Assembly meets every two years, with the IMO Council acting as the executive organ. IMO's climate work is undertaken by the open-ended Marine Environment Protection Committee (MEPC) which reports to the IMO Council. A Study on Greenhouse Gas Emissions from Ships, prepared for the IMO in 2000, concluded that shipping is a small contributor to the world total CO_2 emissions (1.8 per cent of world total CO_2 emissions in 1996).[38] The Study noted that efforts to improve reporting of emissions were needed to estimate the contribution of shipping to climate change more accurately and that policy options to reduce emissions from international shipping were available. At its forty-eighth session in October 2002, the MEPC developed a draft Assembly resolution on greenhouse gas emissions from ships and invited Members to submit comments to the next meeting of the MEPC. The draft resolution urges the MEPC to identify and develop the mechanism or mechanisms needed to achieve the limitation or reduction of GHG emissions from international shipping, and in doing so give priority to the establishment of a GHG emission baseline, the development of a methodology to describe the GHG-efficiency of a ship expressed as a GHG-index for that ship, recognising that CO_2 is the main greenhouse gas emitted by ships. The draft resolution also calls for Governments, in cooperation with the shipping industry, to promote and implement voluntary measures to limit or reduce GHG emissions from international shipping, when the GHG emission indexing scheme is developed by the MEPC.

---

[35] Paragraph 3, Appendix H, A33-7.   [36] FCCC/SBSTA/2001/INF.1, paragraph 17 (a).
[37] Paragraph 2, Appendix I, A33-7.   [38] IMO 2000.

2.5   *Military emissions*

Background: Military emissions for some countries are a significant GHG source. For the US, for example, the Department of Defense (DoD) used 1.4 per cent of the energy within the United States, of which about 58 per cent was used for operations and training in military tactical and strategic systems (i.e. equipment, vehicles, aircraft and vessels designed or procured for use in military operations) and the remaining 42 per cent was used at DoD installations by facilities and non-tactical vehicles.[39] Thus understandably the issue of whether military related emissions should be given special treatment or excluded from the Protocol's quantified commitments was discussed during the Protocol's negotiations.

FCCC: The FCCC does not mention GHG emissions from military use. But the wide scope of the definitions of GHG emissions under Article 1.5 means such emissions are, in principle, covered by the FCCC. Thus, as with other emissions, military emissions have been reported in national inventories. Article 12.10 of the Convention creates a presumption under the Convention that information contained in inventories is to be made 'publicly available' by the Secretariat. Article 12.9 states that 'information received by the secretariat that is designated by a Party as confidential . . . shall be aggregated by the secretariat to protect its confidentiality'. The designation of information as confidential is to be done by a Party 'in accordance with criteria to be established by the Conference of the Parties' and is discussed in chapter 11.[40] Practical guidance as to what is to be included in reporting on military emissions, including the level of aggregation permissible to maintain confidentiality, is given under the 1996 IPCC Reporting Guidelines on National Inventories and the 2000 IPCC Good Practice Guidance.[41]

Kyoto: Like the FCCC, the Protocol does not explicitly mention military emissions. But, for additional clarity, Parties at Kyoto agreed that emissions 'resulting from multilateral operations pursuant to the United Nations Charter shall not be included in national totals, but reported separately; other emissions related to operations shall be included in the national emission totals of one or more Parties involved'.[42] This COP decision clarifies that GHG emissions associated with military training and strategic planning exercises that are not multilateral operations are included in the KP and must be reported in national totals in inventories. Emissions from these types of activities thus count towards Article 3 commitments.

---

[39] Testimony by Frank J. Gaffney Jr, Director of the Center for Security Policy, the William J. Casey Institute of the Center for Security Policy, before the International Relations Committee, House of Representatives, 13 May 1998.

[40] FCCC Article 12.9.   [41] Paragraph 1 (A) (5).   [42] Decision 2/CP.3, Paragraph 5.

Decision 2/CP.3 also clarifies that *multilateral operations* expressly authorised by the UN Security Council (such as Desert Storm and Bosnia) are excluded from Article 3 commitments, although the associated emissions must still be reported. The normal accounting inventory practice is for each Party to report emissions occurring within its national jurisdiction. Parties involved in multilateral operations may decide among themselves how to account for emissions relating to multilateral operations (e.g. US manoeuvres in another NATO country). Thus this provision appears to sanction countries allocating military emissions between themselves (e.g. accounting for them through inventories) rather than relying on emissions trading and joint implementation. The implications of this provision have yet to be practically determined but may need to be addressed when Parties compile inventories for 2003 which will cover emissions resulting from the war against Iraq. One point to note is that the term 'multilateral operations pursuant to the UN Charter' is somewhat ambiguous as to whether multilateral operations not expressly authorised by the UN, but that are nonetheless pursuant to the UN Charter, are to be excluded from national totals.[43]

3   Base year

Background: In climate policy literature, there are two, logically distinct functions of the concept of a 'base year' or 'base period'. The first refers to the historic reference level to be used by Parties to report their GHG emissions and removals. The second, more politically controversial, function refers to use of a historic level to define mitigation commitments, particularly in terms of allocating emissions caps. Thus, issues concerning base years may be of fundamental importance in determining the long-term contribution each country might make towards mitigation.

FCCC: Since the earliest days of the climate negotiations, for Annex I Parties there has been widespread agreement that, in the absence of very special circumstances, 1990 ought to serve as the base year for reporting under the Convention. The FCCC does not explicitly state this but the implication that 1990 is the base year arises from the provisions of Article 4.2 (a) and (b) requiring Annex I Parties to aim at returning their GHG emissions to their 1990 levels. This provision, in combination with the subsequent adoption by the COP of guidelines on preparation

---

[43] In his testimony of 11 February 1998 before the Senate Foreign Relations Committee, the Under Secretary of State Stuart Eizenstat stated that this provision 'exempts from our national targets not only multilateral operations expressly authorized by the UN Security Council (such as Desert Storm or Bosnia), but also multilateral operations that the United States initiates pursuant to the UN Charter without express authorization (such as Grenada)'.

of national communications, confirms that 1990 is the base year for all Annex I Parties other than those with economies in transition.[44]

Article 4.6 of the Convention provides that in the implementation of their commitments under Article 4.2, the COP can allow Annex I Parties undergoing the process of transition to a market economy a certain degree of flexibility, 'including with regard to the historical level of anthropogenic emissions . . . chosen as a reference'. This provision was included because many countries with economies in transition experienced economic decline in the late 1980s, which meant that their 1990 GHG emissions were unusually depressed in relation to previous years. Basing their commitments on 1990 levels would have committed them to maintaining such lower levels of emissions into the future, despite expectations for economic and emission growth in coming decades. Accordingly some degree of flexibility to such Parties was considered appropriate. Parties with economies in transition who wish to invoke the provisions of Article 4.6 of the FCCC were requested to propose to the COP the kind of flexibility they seek in respect of Article 4.6, stating clearly the special consideration they are seeking and providing an adequate explanation of their circumstances.[45]

Rule development: On the basis of Article 4.6, the COP has allowed the following countries to use alternatives to 1990 as the base year:

- Bulgaria: 1988
- Hungary: average of years 1985–1987
- Poland: 1988
- Romania: 1989
- Slovenia: 1986

All other Annex I Parties, including those with economies in transition not listed above, use 1990 as the base year.

Kyoto: Under the Kyoto Protocol, base years (or base period in the case of Hungary) for Annex I Parties are the same as those agreed under the Convention, including those agreed pursuant to Article 4.6.[46] Any Party which wants flexibility to use a base year other than 1990 but has not yet invoked Article 4.6 must notify the COP/MOP and request acceptance by the COP/MOP of their intention to use a different base year.[47] This procedure also applies to any Party whose base year was agreed subsequent to adoption of the Protocol, such as Slovenia whose base

---

[44] Decision 9/CP.2, Annex, paragraph 6.

[45] Decision 9/CP.2, paragraphs 5–7. Apart from proposing a base year other than 1990, Parties with economies in transition can request flexibility in relation to, for example, use of the revised guidelines for the preparation of national communications and schedule of submission of national inventory data.

[46] FCCC Articles 3.1, 3.3, 3.5 and 3.7.   [47] KP Article 3.5.

year was agreed by the COP in 1998, and which must therefore request COP/MOP approval for its choice of base year.

Using the concept of the base year to define the mitigation commitments of Annex I Parties (and to determine their assigned amount) proved problematic during the Kyoto Protocol negotiations on a technical and political level. At the technical level, the Protocol's quantified commitments do not cover all of the sources and sinks reported in the inventories for the base year but are based on the gross–net approach to Article 3.3 and provisions relating to Articles 3.4 and 3.7 described above.[48] The level to be used for calculating a Party's assigned amount is actually specified in Article 3.7 of the Protocol which more accurately specifies that only the aggregate anthropogenic carbon dioxide equivalent emission of the GHGs from sources listed in Annex A of the Protocol in 1990, or the base year or period determined in accordance with Article 3.5, shall be used to calculate a Party's assigned amount.

Articles 3.7 and 3.8 add additional refinements to this formulation. Article 3.8 states that in calculating the assigned amount under Article 3.7, each Annex I Party may choose whether to use 1995 or 1990 as its base year in relation to the long-lived gases (HFCs, PFCs and SF_6).[49] Each Party is likely to choose the year in which its emissions of such gases, weighted by GWPs, were the greatest to maximise its assigned amount because this relaxes the stringency of their Kyoto target. It is not clear whether the same base year has to be chosen for all three gases or for each gas individually. Finally, for a limited number of Parties, the second sentence of Article 3.7 allows inclusion of deforestation-related emissions in the calculation of their base-year emissions.

Using historic levels of emissions to define emissions caps proved controversial in the negotiation of the Kyoto Protocol so far as developing countries were concerned, because basing future emissions limits on past levels rewards historically high emitters and penalises low emitters. This approach, known as grandfathering, is generally favoured by developed countries. Grandfathering is typically contrasted with a per capita emissions approach, favoured by a number of developing countries with large populations. The choice of approach to be adopted was a moot point under the Convention because it did not contain binding targets. By using historic levels to define the commitments of Annex I Parties, the Kyoto Protocol has resolved this issue for Annex I Parties, at least in relation to the first commitment period – although the fact that this favours some countries, such as EITs and to a certain extent the EU, remains a touchy issue with some US critics

---

[48] Depledge, Technical Paper, FCCC/TP/2000/2, Tracing the Origins of the Kyoto Protocol, An Article by Article Textual History, paragraph 454.

[49] Article 3.8.

of the Protocol because the US has experienced rapid economic and population growth since 1990.[50]

Non-Annex I Parties' base years: What then are the rules concerning base year(s) for non-Annex I Parties under the Convention and the Protocol? Since these Parties do not have quantitative commitments the issue of a base year is a non-issue for commitments in their current form, which are substantive but qualitative, and require the Parties to implement programmes and measures to limit emissions, protect and enhance sinks. Because monitoring increases knowledge about source/sink activities and provides insights as to how to limit (future) emissions, many such Parties are sensitive about setting base years, believing this will result in increased pressure for them to negotiate quantified commitments.

FCCC: There is no mention in the Convention of any particular historic reference level that might be used by non-Annex I Parties for reporting or for defining their mitigation commitments. The Preamble to the Convention does state, however, that 'per capita emissions in developing countries are still relatively low and that the share of global emissions originating in developing countries will grow to meet their social and development needs'.[51]

Article 4.1 (a) of the Convention requires all Parties to develop, and periodically update, national inventories of their GHG emissions and removals by sinks. Guidelines for the preparation of the initial communications adopted at COP-2, stated that inventory data should be provided for 1994 but that non-Annex I Parties can choose to provide data for 1990.[52] The guidelines adopted by COP-8 for preparation of second national communications state that such Parties 'shall estimate national GHG inventories for the year 1994 for initial national communications or alternatively may provide data for the year 1990'. For second national communications, non-Annex I Parties shall estimate national GHG inventories for the year 2000. The least developed countries could estimate their national GHG inventories for years at their discretion.[53]

Kyoto: As with the Convention, there is no mention in the Protocol of any historic reference level that might be used by non-Annex I Parties either to report emissions or to define mitigation commitments. The Protocol specifically provides that inventories should be prepared using comparable methodologies to be agreed upon by the COP and consistent with the guidelines for the preparation of national communications adopted by the COP.

---

[50] See Grubb and Yamin, 2001.

[51] Preambular paragraph 4.

[52] Decision 10/CP.2, Annex, paragraph 14.

[53] Decision 17/CP.8, Annex, Section I, paragraph 7.

4   Mitigation commitments: all Parties

4.1   *Differentiation*

Background: The commitments of all Parties, including their mitigation commitments, are contained in Article 4.1 of the Convention and in Article 10 of the Kyoto Protocol. These commitments are qualified in a number of ways.

FCCC: The chapeau of Article 4.1 states that Parties may take 'into account their common but differentiated responsibilities and their specific national and regional development priorities, objectives and circumstances'. This chapeau creates a highly differentiated regime as it means there is no common standard that is being laid down, leaving each Party, in effect, to determine its own level of implementation, taking into account its own specific goals and circumstances.

For developing countries, an additional qualification is that the FCCC recognises that implementation by developing countries of Article 4.1 will have to take into account the provision of financial and technological assistance by Annex II Parties under Articles 4.3 and 4.5 and that economic and social development and poverty eradication are the first and overriding priorities of the developing country Parties as stated in Article 4.7 of the Convention. The exact legal implication of this qualification is subject to interpretation. Some argue it means developing countries will retain their legal responsibility for such commitments but not be expected to fulfil effectively their Article 4.1 commitments if developed countries have not effectively fulfilled their financial and technology transfer commitments.[54] Others regard Article 4.7 as a factual statement only with, presumably, no implications for legal responsibility of developing countries.[55] The exact implications of Article 4.7 on the implementation of general commitments set out in Article 4.1 will, in all likelihood, be determined essentially at a political level.

Kyoto: Article 10 of the Kyoto Protocol aims 'to continue to advance the implementation' of the commitments set out in Article 4.1 of the Convention, stating explicitly that it does not create any new commitment for Parties not included in Annex I. The chapeau of Article 10 is virtually identical to that in Article 4.1 and states that Parties may take 'into account their common but differentiated responsibilities and their specific national and regional development priorities, objectives and circumstances'. The chapeau also makes reference to Articles 4.3, 4.5 and 4.7 of the Convention which means that, so far as developing countries are concerned, the implementation of Article 10 is also subject to the effective fulfilment by developed countries of provisions covering financial and technological

---

[54] Sands, 1995a: p. 376.   [55] US Transmittal Document, p. 6.

assistance.[56] Thus the Kyoto Protocol reinforces the differentiated structure, and conditionalities, of the FCCC.

4.2   Inventories

Background: The requirement to develop and update national inventories is a critical first step for national planning because the inventory process generates information policy-makers need to devise effective mitigation policies and to monitor their progress. Requiring inventories to be prepared periodically using comparable methodologies is critical to assessing patterns of emissions and removals over time as well as for assessing the overall effect of measures taken pursuant to the Convention.

FCCC: Article 4.1 (a) of the Convention requires all Parties to develop, periodically update and publish national inventories of anthropogenic emissions and removals by sinks using comparable methodologies to be agreed by the COP.[57] These inventories must be made available to the COP in accordance with Article 12.

Kyoto: There is no requirement for non-Annex I Parties to prepare national inventories under the Protocol as this is already required by the Convention. Article 10 (a) of the Kyoto Protocol does, however, require all Parties, to the extent possible, to formulate 'cost-effective national, and if appropriate, regional, programmes to improve the quality of local emission factors, activity data and/or models which reflect the socio-economic conditions of each Party for the preparation and periodic updating of national inventories'.

Article 10 (a) also requires all Parties to formulate and update national programmes to improve quality of local emissions factors, activity date and/or models, 'using comparable methodologies to be agreed upon by the Conference of the Parties and consistent with the guidelines for the preparation of national communications adopted by the Conference of the Parties'. By stating that methodologies for inventories must be those agreed by the COP, not the COP/MOP, this provision ensures that the preparation of non-Annex I Parties' national inventories remains under the FCCC.

Rule development: Rules determining the preparation, format, frequency and review of national inventories under the Convention differ according to whether Parties are listed in Annex I or not. These rules are explained in chapter 11.

4.3   National programmes

Background: Establishing national programmes addressing climate change is central to the implementation of the climate change regime. Under both the Convention and the Protocol, such programmes must include measures

---

[56] See chapter 11.   [57] Article 7.2 (d): see chapter 12.

to mitigate climate change as well as measures to facilitate adaptation. The section below focuses on the mitigation aspects.[58]

FCCC: Article 4.1 (b) is the pivotal commitment in the Convention because it requires all Parties to formulate national programmes containing measures to mitigate climate change by addressing all GHG emissions and removals by sinks and also to facilitate adequate adaptation to climate change. Parties are required to publish these programmes, implement them and also update them regularly. Parties may, where appropriate, undertake this commitment on a regional level, although none appears to have done so.[59]

It is important to recognise that due, in part, to the varied circumstances of Parties, the commitment in Article 4.1 (b) concerning national programmes does not say where the balance of effort between mitigation and adaptation should lie or whether adaptation and mitigation should be looked at in an 'integrated' manner. Article 4.1 (b) does not require that national programmes achieve specific levels of emissions reductions/limitations nor does it mandate the pursuit of particular mitigation (or adaptation) policies by a country. Article 4.1 (b) can thus be seen as essentially a qualitative commitment, albeit one that is highly significant because it leads to establishment of institutional processes charged with the important function of identifying, implementing and assessing measures to mitigate and adapt to climate change.

Kyoto: Advancing the mitigation commitments of all Parties under Article 4.1 was a politically divisive issue during the Protocol negotiations. Proposals which would have required all Parties to, for example, prepare annual inventories, consider 'no-regret' measures in the formulation of national programmes and consider adoption of particular mitigation policies and measures were not agreed as developing countries argued that these would have resulted in new commitments which, as was clearly agreed in the Berlin Mandate, were outside the terms of reference of the Kyoto negotiations.[60]

In the end, the chapeau of Article 10 (b) reproduces almost verbatim the text of Article 4.1 (b). The intent of subparagraph (i) of Article 10 (b) is to give greater guidance in terms of specificity of national programmes that are to be formulated by Parties by listing the various kinds of sectors such programmes could address. Article 10 (b) sets out these sectors to include, inter alia, 'the energy, transport and industry sectors as well as agriculture, forestry and waste management'. Subparagraph (i) also specifies that adaptation technologies and methods for improving spatial planning would improve adaptation to climate change. The wording of

---

[58] For adaptation aspects see chapter 8.

[59] The EU is a regional economic integration organisation (REIO) and a Party in its own right.

[60] Decision 1/CP.1, paragraph 2 (b).

Article 10 (b) (i), that national programmes 'would' concern the sectors listed above or 'would' involve use of adaptation technologies (rather than 'shall' or 'should') ensures that Article 10 (b) (i) does not create a new commitment additional to the Convention whilst giving Parties to the Protocol more specific guidance as to how they may implement the existing commitment contained in Article 4.1 (b) regarding national programmes addressing mitigation and adaptation.

Article 10 (b) (ii) requires Parties to report on the implementation of the Protocol, including on their national programmes, through their national communications and stipulates that non-Annex I Parties 'shall seek to include in their national communications, as appropriate, information on programmes which contain measures that the Party believes contribute to addressing climate change and its adverse impacts, including the abatement of increases in greenhouse gas emissions, and enhancement of and removals by sinks, capacity building and adaptation measures'.

Non-Annex I Parties had already agreed to inclusion of similar wording in the guidelines for the preparation of their national communications adopted at COP-2.[61] Because COP decisions are generally considered to be non-legally binding, the incorporation of this provision in the Protocol signals its acceptance as a mandatory commitment. Additionally, it also signals the formulation and implementation of climate policies as well as greater strategic assessment of the combined effect of their mitigation-related policies and measures and of capacity-building and adaptation measures in a manner not so explicitly emphasised in Article 4.1 (b) of the Convention. Thus, again, whilst the wording of Article 10 (b) (ii) does not appear to create significant mandatory obligations over and above those contained in the Convention, the central thrust is to refine the formulation, implementation and subsequent assessment by non-Annex I Parties of their national programmes, albeit on a more incremental and modest scale than some Annex I Parties which argued for quantified commitments for developing countries would have liked.

Rule development: Implementing Article 4.1 (b) requires each Party to utilise or establish domestic policy processes with sufficient institutional, administrative and legal capacity to formulate and implement their national programmes, to have ongoing oversight of such programmes, and to ensure their integration with a broader range of economic, social and development planning. Thus the commitment in Article 4.1 (b) for all Parties to formulate national programmes has had an important galvanising effect so far as advancing work on national planning for climate change is concerned. As reported in national communications, in the vast majority of cases, Parties to the FCCC have established new national

---

[61] Decision 10/CP.2, paragraph 15 (e).

bodies, comprising representatives of a range of ministries, with many reporting directly to the president or prime minister, to undertake the process of preparing a national programme addressing mitigation and adaptation.[62]

Actual formulation of national programmes requires each Party to undertake a strategic assessment of available mitigation options, including the benefits and costs of taking mitigation action, how to weigh these against the potential damages that may occur as a result of climate change, all within the context of sustainable development.[63] Although simple in concept, undertaking such a strategic assessment at a country (or global or regional) level requires human and institutional capacity as well as raising an array of complicated issues for policy-makers which the various academic and policy disciplines are only beginning to grapple with. Thus determining which policy instruments should be pursued to maximise mitigation opportunities within a particular country or region, and the timing of these policy interventions, is equally complex, in part, because the impact of implementing particular policies and measures is difficult to gauge and highly dependent on national circumstances. Balancing these against the expected costs and benefits of adaptation (in terms of damages avoided) makes it more complicated.

The guidelines on initial national communications from non-Annex I Parties requested such Parties to include a general description of steps taken or envisaged to implement their Article 4.1 commitments, including steps concerning 'programmes containing measures the Party believes contribute to addressing climate change and its adverse impacts, including the abatement of increase in greenhouse gas emissions and removals by sinks'.[64] Parties could, if they so wanted, draw upon the guidelines for Annex I Parties which contain more detail on information about mitigation programmes.

The guidelines for second national communications from non-Annex I Parties adopted by COP-8 require much more detailed information on the implementation of Article 4.1 (b). For example, Parties are encouraged 'to provide, to the extent their capacities allow, information on programmes and measures implemented or planned, which contribute to mitigating climate change . . . including, as appropriate, relevant information by key sectors on methodologies, scenarios, results, measures and institutional arrangements'.[65] Although this reporting requirement is not phrased in mandatory terms, it entails a significantly higher level of detail in reporting than previous guidelines for non-Annex I Parties' first (or 'initial')

---

[62] FCCC/SBI/2003/13.

[63] During the INC negotiations, the concept of national strategies being reported to the COP raised sovereignty concerns for some developing countries, so the term 'strategies' was dropped in favour of the term 'programmes'. Bodansky, 1993: p. 509, footnote 349.

[64] Decision 10/CP.2, paragraph 15 (e).   [65] Decision 17/CP.8, paragraph 40.

communications. This demonstrates that, like the commitments of Annex I Parties, the commitments of non-Annex I Parties are evolving, albeit in a slower, more discrete fashion.

To provide some degree of coherence and comparability, a number of intergovernmental agencies and UN bodies have devised methodologies, guidelines and technical resources to assist Parties to implement their commitments relating to national programmes. These methodologies, guidelines and technical resources were not referred to in the guidelines for national communications adopted by COP-2 but are referred in the most recent guidelines adopted by the COP-8 for the preparation of second national communications from non-Annex I Parties.[66] Currently, the most well-known and utilised mitigation-related guidelines and methodologies are:

- Technologies, Policies and Measures for Mitigating Climate (IPCC Technical Paper I)
- Greenhouse Gas Mitigation Assessment: A Guidebook by the US Country Studies Program
- Climate Change 2001: Mitigation (Contribution of Working Group III to the Third Assessment Report of the IPCC)

Use of the technical resources listed above to formulate and assess mitigation programmes is at the discretion of each non-Annex I Party.[67] To date, by using such tools, such Parties have identified numerous mitigation options across a range of sectors, as reported in their initial national communications.[68] As with Annex I Parties, it has been difficult to compare and gauge the impact of non-Annex I Parties' mitigation programmes.[69]

The expectation that Article 10 (b) of the Protocol would encourage actions over and above those undertaken by non-Annex I Parties to implement the Convention

---

[66] Decision 17/CP.8.

[67] Decision 17/CP.8, Annex, paragraph 30. Note that in the case of adaptation assessment, although use of methodologies and tools listed above is not mandatory, the guidelines for preparation of national communications allow use of any 'appropriate methodologies and guidelines' provided they are 'consistent, transparent and well documented'.

[68] See chapter 11 on how many non-Annex I Parties have submitted national inventories. See also FCCC/SBI/2003/INF.14, Fifth Compilation and Synthesis of Initial National Communications from non-Annex I Parties.

[69] One recent independent study has found that the combined impact of climate and non-climate related policies in six non-Annex I Parties over the past decade has reduced the growth of the emissions by nearly 300 millions tons a year, i.e., only 92 millions tons less than the 392 million tons of reductions mandated by Kyoto for all Annex I Parties based on Annex I Parties' emissions projection for 2010. 'Climate Change Mitigation in Developing Countries, Brazil, China, India, Mexico, South Africa and Turkey', Pew Center on Global Climate Change, October 2002, p. iii.

to date was an important element of the political deal struck at Kyoto about how existing commitments would be advanced, and thus pivotal to the inclusion of an article on the financial mechanism in the Kyoto Protocol (Article 11).[70] The second round of national communications, which will be prepared using the more detailed guidance agreed at COP-8, will provide some indication of the extent to which the implementation of commitments under Article 4.1 (b) of the FCCC and Article 10 (b) of the Protocol is being advanced.

4.4   Integration

Background: Integration of environment, development and social concerns lies at the heart of the concept of sustainable development.[71] Integration is thus central to efforts to incorporate climate consideration into other sectors, in particular the 'core areas' relating to economic development and social policy. The concept of integration requires assessment of the implications of climate change in any planned action, including legislation, policies and programmes. It would also cover assessing the climate friendliness of particular projects and, where appropriate, altering or even abandoning projects on the basis of their contribution to addressing climate change. Integration is thus closely related to the more recent concept of 'mainstreaming'. Although there is no uniformity in usage, the term 'mainstreaming' describes the consideration of climate issues in decision-making processes such as planning and budgeting. The term 'integration' is used where specific actions concerning climate change are added to the design and implementation of particular policies, programmes, projects or actions.[72]

FCCC: Article 4.1 (e) of the Convention concerns integration and planning specifically in relation to adaptation to the impacts of climate change. This provision is discussed in chapter 8 in more detail. Article 4.1 (f) requires all Parties to 'take climate change considerations into account, to the extent feasible, in their relevant social, economic and environmental policies and actions, and employ appropriate methods, for example impact assessments, formulated and determined nationally, with a view to minimizing adverse effects on the economy, on public health and on the quality of the environment, of projects or measures undertaken by them to mitigate or adapt to climate change'. This procedural commitment is designed to ensure the integration of climate change in all relevant fields of policy-making and of actions undertaken by Parties. Article 4.1 (f) is not limited to policy-making related to domestic issues but includes all policies and actions. The qualification of the term 'to the extent feasible' means it is up to each Party to determine the process of integration.

---

[70] FCCC/TP/2000/2, Paragraph 341.   [71] See chapter 4.
[72] See, for example, Sperling, 2003.

Article 4.1 (f) draws attention to the fact that unless they are designed carefully, policies and actions undertaken by Parties to mitigate or adapt to climate change could generate adverse effects on the economy, on public health and on the quality of the environment. Some technologies which address climate change may not necessarily always be environmentally sound, for instance, nuclear power or technologies for large hydroelectric plants, because they may have significant environmental impacts where they are deployed. Accordingly, one aspect of integrating climate change into planning is to ensure that particular projects and measures to mitigate or adapt to climate change minimise adverse effects.

Article 4.1 (f) requires Parties to employ 'appropriate methods' with a view to minimising such adverse effects. In this regard, environmental impact assessments (EIAs) are mentioned favourably in Article 4.1 (f), but their use is not mandatory under this Article. The scope of projects and measures referred to in Article 4.1 (f) would appear to include projects and measures undertaken by a Party within and outside its jurisdiction. It is important to remember, however, that the extent of Parties' commitment is limited to what they consider to be 'feasible' and by the general qualifications set out in the chapeau of Article 4.1. In addition, the use of appropriate methods to assess adverse impacts, including through EIAs, is subject to the phrase 'as formulated and determined nationally', making clear that it is up to Parties to determine the scope and application of this commitment at the national level.[73]

Kyoto: There is no direct equivalent to Article 4.1 (e) and (f) in the Kyoto Protocol. Article 10 (g) requires, however, that all Parties 'give full consideration, in implementing the commitments under this Article, to Article 4, paragraph 8, of the Convention'. Article 4.8, which is procedural in nature, requires all Parties to give full consideration to the specific needs and concerns of developing countries arising from the adverse effects of climate change and/or the impact of the implementation of response measures, especially on the countries listed in paragraphs (a)–(i) of Article 4.8.

One implication of Article 10 (g) of the Protocol is that it appears to prompt all Parties to consider the impact of response measures in their implementation of Article 10 in a way which was excluded, or left ambiguous, from the scope of operation of Article 4.1 (f).

Articles 2.3 and 3.14 of the Protocol require Annex I Parties to strive to implement mitigation-related policies and measures so as to minimise adverse effects, including the adverse effects of climate change, effects on international trade and social, environmental and economic impacts on other Parties, especially

---

[73] Decision 5/CP.7 *re* implementation of 4.6/4.9, paragraph 7 (iii) states that GEF is to fund training in, inter alia, EIAs.

developing country Parties, in particular those mentioned in Articles 4.8 and 4.9 of the Convention. These provisions are examined in more detail in chapter 9.

Rule development: Despite the importance of 'mainstreaming' climate change, the COP has not taken any decisions to provide further guidance on how this might be undertaken by Parties nor how international and multilateral organisations might be engaged in the process of mainstreaming climate change in their activities. Thus the task of how countries might begin the process of integration at a practical level, and what kinds of methodologies and tools might be deployed, has been left to individual Parties at the national level. Many have tried to do so by establishing institutional frameworks with interconnections between all relevant national institutions.

So far as impact assessment and other tools are concerned, the COP has not taken any specific decisions to facilitate Parties' implementation of this commitment, due, in part, to sovereignty concerns that inappropriate standards may be set.[74] Although the use of impact assessment and other tools is left largely to national discretion, developments under the Convention and the Protocol foresee their increased use. Paragraph 7 (iii) of Decision 5/CP.7, for example, concerning implementation of Articles 4.8 and 4.9 and Articles 2.3 and 3.14 of the Protocol, instructs the Global Environment Facility to provide funding for training in specialised fields, including environmental impact assessment, as part of the measures to address the adverse effects of climate change. Implementation of the project-based Kyoto mechanisms will also involve increased use of environmental impact assessments because, as part of the project approval process, project proponents of JI and CDM projects are required to submit analyses of environmental impacts, including transboundary impacts, of proposed projects.

4.5   *Sinks and reservoirs*

Background: The build up of greenhouse gases in the atmosphere can be lowered either by reducing the rate at which GHGs are added to the atmosphere (e.g. from burning fossil fuels and clearing forests) or increasing the rate at which carbon dioxide is removed from the atmosphere (e.g. through absorption in the terrestrial biosphere comprising forests, crops, agricultural lands and in wetlands). Forests are, for example, a major reservoir, containing some 80 per cent of all the carbon stored in land vegetation and approximately 20 per cent of the carbon stored in different types of soils.[75] Deforestation releases large amounts of carbon into the atmosphere, between 800 million and 2.4 billion tonnes of carbon

---

[74] This concern is reflected in the Convention Preamble at paragraph 10 (which reflects Principle 11 of the Rio Declaration), discussed in chapter 4.

[75] IPCC, 2000a: table 1-1.

annually, making it the second largest source of carbon dioxide emissions after fossil fuel combustion.[76] Carbon is also naturally stored in oceans. Carbon can, in theory, also be captured and stored in geologic formations including oil and gas reservoirs, unmineable coal seams and deep ocean (saline) reservoirs, but this kind of carbon sequestration has not been researched on a significant scale and climate policy has therefore focused on sequestration by natural terrestrial systems, such as forests and soils.

The role of terrestrial sinks in mitigation is complicated by scientific uncertainties about how much carbon can be stored in land (the 'saturation' issue), the risk that stored carbon will be re-emitted in the future (the 'permanence' issue) and methodological complexities surrounding monitoring and accounting. Additionally, as pointed out by the IPCC, use of sinks to offset emissions in the context of sustainable development raises broader questions of policy coherence in terms of synergies and trade-offs across a broad range of environmental, social and economic impacts, such as biodiversity, food security, employment, health, poverty and equity issues, necessitating institutional coordination between different international regimes.[77] All of these issues have come to the fore of climate policy because Kyoto sanctions the use of specific categories of domestic sinks towards achievement of Annex I Parties' commitments under Article 3, as well as allowing such Parties to invest in sinks projects overseas using the Clean Development Mechanism and joint implementation.[78]

FCCC: The Convention recognises that sinks and reservoirs can make a contribution to mitigating climate change.[79] The terms 'sinks' and 'reservoirs' are defined in the Convention and explained in box 5.1 above. Article 4.1 (d) requires all Parties to 'promote sustainable management, and promote and cooperate in the conservation and enhancement, as appropriate, of sinks and reservoirs of all greenhouse gases not controlled by the Montreal Protocol, including biomass, forests and oceans as well as other terrestrial, coastal and marine ecosystems'.

This commitment relates to promotion and cooperation and does not create a binding obligation to conserve or manage carbon sinks sustainably. Article 4.1 (d) does not single out forests for special consideration but places all types of sinks and reservoirs on an equal footing.[80] The FCCC, like other recent international environmental instruments, thus does not create obligations that would require Parties to arrest deforestation activities.[81] This reflects the resistance of countries

---

[76] Climate Change Information Kit, 'How Human Activities Produce Greenhouse Gases', Sheet 22.

[77] IPCC, 2000a: paragraph 84.   [78] Section 4 and chapter 6.

[79] FCCC, Preamble, paragraph 4. Articles 1.8, 3.3, 4.1 (a), and (b), 4.2 (b), 4.1 (d).

[80] Bodansky, 1993: p. 509, text at footnote 352.

[81] Other instruments which have sought to check deforestation include the Convention on Biological Diversity and the Rio Forests Principles.

with large forests, particularly developing countries, to perceived interference in the use of their natural resources. It mirrors the successful insistence of major oil producers that fossil fuels, the largest source of carbon emissions, also not be singled out in the Convention for special consideration.

Kyoto: The Protocol does not contain a commitment that directly advances the obligation contained in Article 4.1 (d) in respect of all Parties. Article 10 (a) includes references to improving inventory emissions factors, activity data and models, including for removals by sinks processes which may be particularly significant for developing countries. Article 10 (b) (i), concerning national programmes, mentions agriculture and forestry along with other sectors that should be covered by national programmes, but as with the FCCC, LULUCF activities are not singled out for special treatment. It should be noted that the term 'land use, land use change and forestry' is much broader than the term 'forests' because it encompasses a range of human activities that have impacts on forests and other types of terrestrial carbon sinks. The general extent to which these provisions advance commitments under the FCCC in respect of sources and sinks is discussed above.

Article 2.1 (ii) strengthens the obligations of Annex I Parties to protect and enhance sinks and reservoirs.[82] Additionally, Article 3.3 requires and Article 3.4 permits certain LULUCF activities to count towards the mitigation commitments of Annex I Parties under Article 3 of the Protocol. This flexibility has necessitated strengthened sinks-related inventory and reporting requirements spelt out in Articles 5, 7 and 8 of the Protocol. Sinks projects are explicitly contemplated under Article 6, joint implementation, and although not mentioned in Article 12, CDM have been included as a result of the Marrakesh Accords.[83]

Rule development: To date the emphasis in climate policy has been on reducing emissions at source because combustion of fossil fuels is the biggest source of atmospheric build up of carbon and can be reliably monitored and verified.[84] With the adoption of the Kyoto Protocol, use of terrestrial sinks to absorb emissions has come to be seen as a low-cost policy which 'buys time' whilst reducing the need to implement more expensive, and politically contentious, emissions reductions at source, and potentially providing conservation and biodiversity benefits.

Inclusion of LULUCF activities to meet Article 3 commitments of Annex I Parties, including through joint implementation and CDM sinks projects, has required an expansion of principles, rules and modalities governing the use and accounting of terrestrial carbon sinks beyond the rules contained in the text of the Protocol, and

---

[82] See section 5 below.   [83] See chapter 6.
[84] See chapter 4. Schlamadinger and Marland, 2000: p. 3.

this expansion is reflected in the Marrakesh Accords.[85] These principles, rules and modalities, some of which are still being elaborated, will affect the implementation of Annex I Parties' commitments in relation to their domestic sinks and those located in host Parties.[86] To the extent that non-Annex I Parties participate in CDM sinks projects, some of these principles and rules will also have an impact on non-Annex I Parties' commitments to conserve, enhance and sustainably manage their sinks.

Unlike LULUCF, the role of other non-terrestrial reservoirs, such as oceans, in climate mitigation has been fairly low on the COP agenda, and to date no decisions have been adopted by the COP giving further guidance on the duty to cooperate to conserve and enhance such reservoirs. In the case of ocean sinks, linkages between the climate regime and other legal instruments which could potentially cover disposal of carbon dioxide at sea (through injection or solid disposal of carbon dioxide in deep oceans) may need to be further examined as such activities may count as pollution under other legal instruments such as the 1982 Law of the Sea Convention and the 1972 London Convention.[87] For similar reasons, engineered geological disposal whereby carbon dioxide is injected or piped into large physical structures such as depleted oil and gas reservoirs, landfills, coal seams, mines and saline aquifers under the seabed, have also to be examined in detail.[88] Two developments that may affect future rule development in this area are worthy of note. First, Decision 5/CP.7, discussed in chapter 9, encourages Annex II Parties to 'cooperate in the development, diffusion and transfer of less greenhouse gas emitting advanced fossil fuel technologies, and/or technologies relating to fossil fuels, that capture and store greenhouse gases'.[89] The same Decision mandates the IPCC to prepare a technical report on the subject of geological sequestration prior to COP/MOP 2.[90] Second, although initiated outside the context of the FCCC, the announcement in 2003 of an international framework for cooperation for research and development of carbon capture and storage technologies, initiated by the United States with partners from Australia, Brazil, Canada, China, Colombia, India, Italy, Japan, Mexico, Norway, the Russian Federation, the United Kingdom, and the European Commission, may signal greater attention to this issue.[91]

---

[85] Decisions 11/CP.7 and 12/CP.7. See also Decisions 15/CP.7 (mechanism principles) 16/CP.7 (JI), 17/CP.7 (CDM) and 19.CP.4 (modalities for accounting of assigned amounts).

[86] See section 4 below

[87] The 1972 Convention on the Prevention of Marine Pollution by Dumping of Wastes and Other Matter the 1972 London Convention). See UK Royal Commission on Environmental Pollution (2000) and Purdy and MacRory, 2004, for a more detailed discussion of applicable legal instruments.

[88] Purdy and MacRory, 2004.   [89] Purdy and MacRory, 2004: Paragraph 26.

[90] Paragraph 27.

[91] Press release, 'US hosts inaugural forum for carbon sequestration research and development', July 2003 at http://energy.gov/HQPress/releases03/junpr/pr03135_v.htm.

5   Mitigation commitments: Annex I Parties

5.1   *Overview*

One practical manifestation of the principle of common but differentiated responsibility in the climate change regime is that Annex I Parties have assumed more stringent mitigation commitments than the commitments applicable generally to all Parties described in the previous section. The classification of countries as Annex I Parties under the Convention and the Protocol is explained in boxes 5.4 and 5.5 respectively. A full list of Parties included in Annex I/Annex B, including details of their mitigation commitments, is set out in Appendix II.[92] Annex I Parties' more stringent commitments can be clustered as follows:

- Enactment and coordination of policies and measures (PAMs) to mitigate climate change;
- Achievement of quantified targets within a specific time-frame;
- Joint achievement of mitigation commitments through domestic and overseas actions;
- Consideration of specific needs/circumstances of developing countries vulnerable to climate impacts and/or impacts of response measures in devising and implementing mitigation policies; and
- Reporting on all of the above in a comparable, transparent and verifiable manner.

Consideration of special needs/circumstances is explained in depth in chapters 8 and 9 on adaptation and impacts of response measures and the issue of reporting is taken up in chapter 11.

Box 5.4 Annex I Parties under the Convention and notifications

Parties with more stringent mitigation commitments are listed in Annex I of the Convention. The list of the thirty-five countries plus the European Union included in Annex I of the Convention has only been formally amended once since 1992. These amendments deleted Czechoslovakia from the list and added six countries: Croatia, Czech Republic, Liechtenstein, Monaco, Slovakia and Slovenia.[93] In accordance with Article 16.3 of the Convention, this amendment entered into force for all Parties on 13 August 1998, which now means that there are forty-one entries listed in Annex I. Apart from the agreed amendments to the list in Annex I, proposals to delete the name of

---

[92] See chapter 3.   [93] Decision 4/CP.3.

Turkey from the list in Annex I were not agreed but COP-7 invited Parties 'to recognize the special circumstances of Turkey, which place Turkey, after becoming a Party, in a situation different from that of other Parties included in Annex I of the Convention'.[94] It is not clear what practical ramifications will flow from this recognition now that Turkey has become a Party to the Convention. In practice this is likely to revolve around issues concerning the frequency, format and timing of national communications to be submitted by Turkey and perhaps its choice of base year.

Article 4.2 (g) permits any Party that is not listed in Annex I to assume the more stringent mitigation commitments of Annex I Parties specified in Article 4.2 (a) and (b) of the Convention by notifying the Depository of this intent, thus avoiding the need to amend the Convention formally.[95] The following countries have made such notifications: Monaco, Czech Republic, Slovakia, Croatia, Liechtenstein and Kazakhstan.[96] Apart from Kazakhstan, the notifications of the other countries are of historic interest because the COP-3 amendments formalised their inclusion in Annex I. So far as Kazakhstan is concerned, in recent negotiations Kazakhstan has stressed that, notwithstanding its notification under Article 4.2 (g), it will still be classified as a *non-Annex I Party* under the Convention because it will not be formally listed in Annex I of the Convention. Kazakhstan's notification is intended to ensure that it can benefit from the more favourable financial and assistance possibilities available to non-Annex I Parties under the Convention. Although considerable political pressure from other OECD members has been applied to them to accept more stringent mitigation commitments, Mexico and the Republic of Korea have not made declarations under Article 4.2 (g).

Article 4.2 (f) of the Convention mandated a review of the list of countries included in Annex I and Annex II not later than 31 December 1998. Proposals to add the name of Kazakhstan and to delete the name of Turkey from Annex I were not agreed because the addition and deletion of names of countries from Annex I is closely related to the broader issues raised by the evolution of mitigation commitments of non-Annex I Parties.[97] Kazakhstan stated at COP-7, however, that it was interested in negotiating quantified commitments under Article 3.1 and Annex B of the Protocol but it has yet to submit a second national communication to make its choice of target more readily understood or appreciated by the COP.[98]

---

[94] See chapter 10.   [95] See discussion on evolution in chapter 18.

[96] See Letter to Depository, 23 March 2000, FCCC website.

[97] Turkey was removed from Annex II: see chapters 3 and 18.   [98] COP-7 report.

Box 5.5   Annex I/Annex B Parties under the Protocol

Article 1.7 of the Kyoto Protocol defines the term 'Annex I Party' to mean 'a Party included in Annex I of the Convention, as may be amended, or a Party which has made a notification under Article 4, paragraph 2(g) of the Convention'. This definition was intended to ensure a high degree of coherence between the Convention and the Protocol in terms of which countries are classified as 'Annex I Parties'. A number of legal and practical anomalies, nevertheless, have arisen. Legally, Kazakhstan is in a unique position in being considered a non-Annex I Party under the Convention but an Annex I Party under the Protocol once it ratifies the Protocol (because it has made a declaration under Article 4.2 (g)). On a practical level, failure to ratify either the Convention or the Protocol has also given rise to discrepancies as to who is considered an Annex I Party under the Convention and the Protocol. Of the forty-one Annex I Parties under the Convention, thirty-nine have quantified commitments set out in Annex B of the Kyoto Protocol. Turkey and Belarus do not appear in Annex B as neither had ratified the Convention in 1997. If these countries, and Kazakhstan, ratify the Kyoto Protocol, and the latter enters into force, they will have the status of being Annex I Parties under the Protocol. They would thus appear to be bound by the mitigation and reporting-related commitments applicable to Annex I Parties under the Protocol even though they do not currently have quantified commitments pursuant to Article 3.1 and Annex B.

5.2   *Policies and measures*

Background: Article 4.2 of the Convention and Article 2 of the Kyoto Protocol contain commitments related to PAMs. The term 'policies and measures' is not defined in the Convention, the Protocol or any subsequent COP decision. The term 'policy' is widely understood to mean a prescriptive course of action, whilst the term 'measures' refers to corresponding legislative, administrative or other means through which policies are implemented. A fundamental rule of international law is that a Party to a treaty must enact appropriate domestic policies, legislation and administrative measures to ensure that activities under its jurisdiction and control conform to its international obligations.[99] In environmental treaties, the choice of policies, and institutional arrangements to oversee the implementation and enforcement of such policies, is generally left for each

---

[99] Article 26, Vienna Convention on the Law of Treaties.

Party to determine. In climate policy, three interlinked issues lie at the heart of negotiations about Annex I Parties' PAMs:

- Whether implementing particular PAMs should be obligatory rather than left to choice;
- Whether international cooperation on PAMs should focus on information exchange or on coordination; and
- How Parties should report upon, and the COP assess, the effectiveness of PAMs.

The view that implementation of certain PAMs should be mandatory for all Annex I Parties with quantified targets, championed in the early years of the regime by the EU, has not prevailed in the Convention and the Protocol. Diversity of mitigation options and national circumstances, stressed by JUSSCANZ countries, and sovereignty concerns, stressed by developing country Parties, militate against international prescriptiveness, however environmentally and economically justified more harmonised approaches might be in economic theory. The approach to PAMs taken under the FCCC and the Protocol shares many common elements. Additionally, as acknowledged by COP-7, 'implementation of policies and measures contributes to achieving the objectives of the Convention and the Protocol'.[100] Further work on PAMs is intended to support implementation of the Convention and the Protocol simultaneously.

5.3   *Scope and purpose of PAMs*

FCCC: Article 4.2 (a) and (b) of the Convention sets out more stringent mitigation commitments for Annex I Parties. These two subparagraphs combine mandatory, factual and permissive elements relating to PAMs which gloss over ambiguities and disagreements that could not be resolved when the Convention was adopted. Different interpretations of the commitments contained in Article 4.2 (a) and (b) are possible and, in view of the centrality of Article 4.2 (a) and (b) to the climate regime, these provisions are explained more fully in box 5.6.

Article 4.2 (a) of the Convention obliges each Annex I Party to 'adopt national policies and take corresponding measures on the mitigation of climate change by limiting its anthropogenic emissions of greenhouse gases and protecting and enhancing its greenhouse gas sinks and reservoirs'.[101] This first sentence contains an unambiguous, legally binding obligation for each Party to adopt PAMs to limit

---

[100] Decision 13/CP.7, Preamble, paragraphs 6 and 7.

[101] The footnote to Article 4.2 (a) clarified that the term 'national' includes 'policies and measures adopted by regional economic integration organisations' and thus covers policies and measures enacted by the EU.

that Party's anthropogenic GHG emissions and enhance its sinks and reservoirs. In terms of scope, the reference to 'its' emissions and 'its' sinks and reservoirs means that the basic focus of PAMs is to be on each Annex I Party's domestic sources and sinks.[102] The commitment to adopt PAMs has an ongoing temporal dimension and does not expire at a particular point in time but mandates continued policy efforts to mitigate climate change.

The purpose of such PAMs is to limit a Party's emissions or enhance removals by sinks. The word 'limiting' requires a Party through its PAMs to exercise some degree of constraint over its emissions. The appropriate degree of constraint is not clear. The word 'limiting' was used in preference to 'reducing' or 'stabilisation' because 'limiting' did not imply an obligation to reduce emissions below current levels or to maintain a downward trend into the future.[103] Actions to limit would thus appear to be consistent with some growth in emissions but not with business-as-usual emissions which would not be consistent with the objective of the Convention which is explicitly mentioned in this sentence. Article 4.2 (a) states that these PAMs 'will demonstrate that developed countries are taking the lead in modifying longer-term trends in anthropogenic emissions consistent with the objective of the Convention, recognizing that the return by the end of the present decade to earlier levels of anthropogenic emissions of carbon dioxide and other greenhouse gases not controlled by the Montreal Protocol would contribute to such modification'. The quantified aim to return to earlier levels of emissions, the earlier level being specified in Article 4.2 (b) as 1990, is qualified by the requirement to take 'into account the differences in these Parties' starting points and approaches, economic structures and resource bases, the need to maintain strong and sustainable economic growth, available technologies and other individual circumstances, as well as the need for equitable and appropriate contributions by each of these Parties to the global effort regarding that objective'.

The third sentence of Article 4.2 (a) is permissive: it provides that Annex I Parties may choose to 'implement such policies and measures jointly with other Parties and may assist other Parties in contributing to the achievement of the objection of the Convention, in particular, that of this subparagraph'. The COP's consideration of Article 4.2 (d) of the Convention which required the COP to adopt 'criteria for joint implementation' to enable Annex I Parties to meet their commitments under Article 4.2 (a) is discussed below.

---

[102] This links with reporting requirements as each Party is only expected to calculate emissions/projections in relation to its own sources. Reporting on actions to limit GHGs or enhance sinks implemented jointly with others is subject to 'activities implemented jointly' reporting guidelines, Decision 5/CP.1 discussed in chapter 6.

[103] Reinstein, 1994 and Sands, 1992.

Box 5.6   Commitments under Article 4.2 (a) and (b)

Article 4.2 (a) and (b) of the Convention contains commitments relating to PAMs, a quantified 'aim' and reporting. These subparagraphs also refer to joint implementation. The text and structure of Article 4.2 (a) and (b), in particular its deliberate separation into two subparagraphs, was intended to gloss over fundamental policy disagreements about (1) whether the Convention should contain legally binding targets for Annex I Parties, (2) whether these should be achieved domestically or overseas through joint actions, and (3) whether efforts should focus on controlling emissions of individual gases from sources rather than sinks. Since 1994, various textual commentaries,[104] COP decisions, Parties' statements and actual practices, and policy discussions about the Kyoto Protocol have clarified areas of agreement and resulted in working solutions. The passage of the year 2000, and preparations for the entry into force of the Kyoto Protocol, have also lessened the controversy surrounding Article 4.2 (a) and (b). There is broad acceptance that Article 4.2 (a) and (b):

- Requires each Annex I Party to adopt national policies and measures limiting its emissions and enhancing its sinks/reservoirs on an ongoing basis, with a view to demonstrating a modification of long-term emissions trends;[105]
- Does not establish a legally binding target for each Annex I Party to return its GHG emissions to 1990 levels by 2000 but establishes this as a quantified 'aim' which such Parties should strive to achieve;[106]
- In the achievement of the 'aim', steers each Annex I Party to focus on abatement efforts limiting CO_2 emissions but with flexibility to determine abatement efforts in terms of other gases, provided

---

[104] Bodansky, 1993; Reinstein, 1994; Sands, 1992; Asian–African Legal Consultative Committee, 1992; United States, Department of State, 1994; UK Department of the Environment, 1992.

[105] This is reaffirmed in the Delhi Declaration, Decision 1/CP.8, paragraph (m), which states that 'Annex I Parties should further implement their commitments under the Convention . . . and demonstrate that they are taking the lead in modifying longer term trends in anthropogenic greenhouse gas emission, consistent with the ultimate objective of the Convention.'

[106] Most legal writers are of this opinion, whether or not the two subparagraphs are read separately or combined: see e.g. Bodansky, 1993; Reinstein, 1994; and Sands, 1992. Additionally, the national communications of all Annex I Parties make reference to the 'aim' and confirm that they are striving to achieve this without referring to it as a legally binding target.

emissions from individual gases (and the contributions from sinks/reservoirs) are reported separately;[107]

- Permits Annex I Parties to fulfil their commitments jointly or through activities implemented jointly with non-Annex I Parties but without modifying their respective commitments and on the basis that no credits can accrue to any Party;[108]
- Requires each Annex I Party to report to the COP on its PAMs to implement Article 4.2 (a) and (b) commitments, including their projected effect for the period 1990–2000, and on future emission trends.[109]

Kyoto: Unlike the Convention, the Protocol separates PAMs and quantified targets into two articles. The chapeau of Article 2 makes clear that the purpose of PAMs is for each Annex I Party to achieve its quantified commitments, prescribed in Article 3, and 'in order to promote sustainable development'. Article 2.1 (a) of the Protocol requires each Annex I Party 'to implement and/or further elaborate policies and measures in accordance with its national circumstances' in areas such as those listed in subparagraphs (i)–(viii). Although inclusion of the words 'in accordance with national circumstances' and 'such as' ensures this list of PAMs remains indicative, not mandatory, in character, explicit referencing in the Protocol to particular policies and sectors generates strong expectations that consideration will be given by each Annex I Party to the listed PAMs in their implementation of the Protocol. The list of PAMs mentioned in Article 2.1 (a) covers certain gases, sectors and some cross-cutting policies which were rather jumbled up during the course of negotiations. In terms of gases and sectors, and bearing in mind the chapeau, Annex I Parties should implement/elaborate PAMs that:

- Protect/enhance sinks and reservoirs of greenhouse gases (taking into account any commitments under relevant international environmental agreements) and promote sustainable forest management practices, afforestation and reforestation (subparagraph (ii));
- Promote sustainable forms of agriculture (subparagraph (iii));
- Limit and/or reduce GHG emissions in the transport sector (subparagraph (vii));

---

[107] See e.g. paragraphs 14–15 FCCC/CP/1997/7. On whether removals of sinks/reservoirs count towards the 'aim' of returning to 1990 levels by 2000, see sections 2.2 and 4.5.

[108] Decision 5/CP.1, Preamble, paragraphs (a)–(d) and paragraph 1 (f).

[109] Articles 4.2 (b) and 12.2.

- Limit and/or reduce methane emissions through recovery and use in waste management, as well as in the production, transport and distribution of energy (subparagraph (viii)).

In terms of cross-cutting policies, Annex I Parties should implement PAMs that:

- Enhance energy efficiency in relevant sectors of the national economy (subparagraph (i));
- research, promote, develop and increase use of new and renewable forms of energy, of carbon dioxide sequestration technologies and of advanced and innovative environmentally sound technologies (subparagraph (iv));
- Progressively reduce or phase out market imperfections, fiscal incentives, tax and duty exemptions and subsidies in all greenhouse gas emitting sectors that run counter to the objective of the Convention and application of market instruments (subparagraph (v));
- Encourage reforms in relevant sectors aimed at promoting policies and measures which limit or reduce emissions of greenhouse gases (subparagraph (vi)).

Due largely to the sensitivities of some OPEC countries, the list in Article 2.1 (a) does not explicitly mention PAMs to reduce/limit carbon dioxide emissions from the energy sector despite the fact that such emissions are the largest and most readily verifiable source of global GHG emissions. Some of these emissions are covered elliptically, however, through the focus on transport emissions, enhanced energy efficiency, increased renewable energy, sequestration and phase out of market imperfections.

PAMs can be enacted nationally, locally and regionally and can concern domestic emissions or actions that lead to reductions outside a Party's jurisdiction. The principal focus of Article 2.1 (a) appears, however, to be on Annex I Parties' *domestic* GHG sources and sinks. It should be noted, however, that the Protocol leaves each Annex I Party free to determine the balance of efforts it will make to reduce/limit emissions domestically or overseas. Accordingly PAMs can (and do) include instruments making use of the Kyoto mechanisms, such as national or regional emission trading regimes, and other activities that have as their objective the reduction of emissions outside of that Party's jurisdiction.[110] Article 2.2 of the Protocol mandates Annex I Parties to pursue reduction of GHG emissions from aviation and bunker fuel, working through the ICAO and the IMO (discussed in section 3).

---

[110] See chapter 6.

5.4   *Coordination and review of PAMs*

FCCC: Article 4.2 (e) (i) of the Convention states that each Party included in Annex I shall 'coordinate as appropriate with other such Parties, relevant economic and administrative instruments developed to achieve the objective of the Convention'. At the time the Convention was negotiated, a number of countries, mostly European, were considering novel policy instruments such as environmental taxes and tradable permits which would have been environmentally and economically more efficient, and politically more feasible, if simultaneously implemented by, or coordinated with, other industrialised countries.[111] The text of Article 4.2 (e) (i) requires Annex I Parties to coordinate such instruments but only to the extent each considers it 'appropriate'. It should be noted that Article 4.2 (e) (i) does not use the term 'harmonisation', which implies a common policy or measure, but uses the weaker term 'coordination' instead, which can simply refer to countries pursuing different PAMs in a concerted and harmonious manner.

As a corollary, Article 7.2 (c) of the Convention defines one of the functions of the COP as facilitation of PAMs coordination but only when requested by two or more Parties (whether Annex I or not) and then only in relation to the PAMs adopted by the requesting Parties, taking into account their differing circumstances, responsibilities and capabilities and their respective commitments under the Convention. Article 7.2 (b) mandates the COP to promote and facilitate the exchange of information on measures adopted by Parties (whether Annex I or not) to address climate change and its effects, subject again to taking into account their differing circumstances, responsibilities, capabilities and commitments.

Article 4.2 (e) (ii) requires each Annex I Party 'to identify and periodically review its own policies and practices which encourage activities that lead to greater levels of anthropogenic emissions of greenhouse gases not controlled by the Montreal Protocol than would otherwise occur'. This provision requires examination of existing policies and practices, such as subsidies and export guarantees, which tend to distort markets by promoting GHG emitting activities that might otherwise become uncompetitive. The words 'subsidies' and 'export guarantees' do not appear explicitly in the Convention because many OECD governments were rather sensitive about their domestic track record on subsidies, particularly to the coal sector.[112]

Kyoto: By 1997 Parties were willing to include an explicit commitment in the Protocol for Annex I Parties progressively to reduce or phase out market imperfections, fiscal incentives, tax and duty exemptions and subsidies in all greenhouse gas emitting sectors that run counter to the objective of the Convention and application of market instruments.[113] Additional reporting on phasing out

---

[111] See e.g. EU proposed CO_2 tax (Com(92)226).   [112] See chapter 9.   [113] Article 2.1 (a) (v).

of market imperfections, fiscal incentives, tax and duty exemptions and subsidies is now mandatory under Article 3.14 of the Protocol.[114] The concept of coordination remained more sensitive. Proposals to elaborate COP/MOP's role by defining a time-bound process to facilitate PAMs coordination were not agreed at Kyoto but essentially deferred.[115] The remnants of this proposal are included in Article 2.4 which states that the COP/MOP, 'if it decides that it would be beneficial to coordinate any of the policies and measures in [Article 2.1 (a)] above, taking into account different national circumstances and potential effects, shall consider ways and means to elaborate the coordination of such policies and measures'.

At Kyoto, and subsequently, greater emphasis has been placed, instead, on information exchange. Accordingly, Article 2.1 (b) of the Protocol requires AIPs to

> cooperate with other such Parties to enhance the individual and combined effectiveness of their policies and measures adopted under this Article, pursuant to Article 4, paragraph 2(e)(i), of the Convention. To this end, these Parties shall take steps to share their experience and exchange information on such policies and measures, including developing ways of improving their comparability, transparency and effectiveness. The [COP/MOP] shall, at its first session or as soon as practicable thereafter, consider ways to facilitate such cooperation, taking into account all relevant information.

The reference to developing 'ways of improving their [PAMs'] comparability, transparency and effectiveness' is an oblique reference to the concept of 'policy performance indicators' which was introduced to the Kyoto negotiators at a late stage but not discussed in detail due to time-constraints.[116]

Rule development: Coordination of some PAMs among Annex I Parties could enhance efficiency gains of certain PAMs, and for Parties with significant trade in GHG intensive products, also minimise distortions of competition. For example, coordination of national emissions trading systems enabling coverage of more emissions sources would generate greater environmental and efficiency gains than uncoordinated national schemes alone. Coordination of national schemes could cover countries that had ratified the Kyoto Protocol as well as those that have not ratified.[117] Similarly, pooling of R & D in promising new technologies could enable pursuit of entrepreneurial risks beyond those acceptable to an individual Party,

---

[114] Decision 22/CP.7; see chapter 9.

[115] Yamin, 1998a. Proposals for a coordination mechanism were put forward by AOSIS and supported by the EU.

[116] Yamin, 1998a; Depledge, FCCC/TP/2000/2. Policy performance indicators were derived from proposals from Australia and Japan.

[117] See Haites and Aslam, 2000.

whilst avoiding duplication of efforts. Diversity of national circumstances and sovereignty concerns, however, continue to make international coordination of PAMs extremely contentious, as each Party wants to minimise external constraints on policy choices, particularly in sensitive policy areas, such as energy, transport, industry, agriculture and forestry. To date, therefore, no Party has sought to coordinate PAMs under the auspices of the COP and therefore no formal agreement has been reached as to how such a request could be facilitated by the COP or the COP/MOP.

More recently, Parties have come to appreciate that the COP and the Subsidiary Bodies can play an important role in facilitating 'learning by doing' by providing a useful forum to help Parties keep track of new climate policies in other countries and gain a better understanding of each other's circumstances, PAMs and experiences. Thus Article 2.1 (b) of the Protocol has received more attention in recent COPs even though the Protocol does not require the COP/MOP to take a decision on this issue at its first session. This interest has led to a body of work on 'good practices' in PAMs among Annex I Parties designed to support both the Convention and the Protocol. Additionally, growing pressure to show others that Annex I Parties are making 'demonstrable progress' to implement their quantified commitments under Article 3.1 of the Protocol, as called for in Article 3.2, has led to greater emphasis on improving the reporting of domestic PAMs and their likely impact on emission trends.[118] This has supported moves for greater analysis of how Parties design, evaluate and monitor individual PAMs and overall mitigation portfolios. Reporting and review of PAMs through national communications is examined in detail in chapter 11.

Consideration of how the COP/MOP could facilitate cooperation to enhance the individual and combined effectiveness of PAMs, as referred to in Article 2.1 (b) of the Protocol, commenced at COP-4 with the COP mandating SBSTA to prepare a report on 'best practices' in PAMs based on their national communications and other information.[119] Two workshops were held in Copenhagen, the first in April 2000, pursuant to Decision 8/CP.4,[120] and the second in October 2001,[121] pursuant to the request from COP-6 Part I.[122] The first focused on 'best and good practices'. The second workshop concluded that, the concept of 'best practices' appeared a useful and workable concept in the *domestic* context because it was possible to judge what might be best in a particular context. It also concluded that, given the differences in the national circumstances, the concept of 'good practices' rather than 'best practices' may prove to be more useful internationally in advancing implementation of the Convention and the Protocol.[123]

---

[118] See chapter 9.   [119] Decision 8/CP.4.   [120] FCCC/SBSTA/2000/2.
[121] FCCC/SBSTA/2001/INF.5.   [122] FCCC/CP/2000/5/Add.2, section III.F.
[123] FCCC/SBSTA/2001/INF.5, paragraph 2.

COP-7 adopted the 'good practices' approach, deciding that implementation of PAMs and information exchange furthers the Convention and the Protocol and that, in the run-up to the first session of the COP/MOP, Article 2.1 (b) of the Protocol could be furthered by Parties 'sharing experiences and exchanging information at the technical level'.[124] This work, to be undertaken by SBSTA, is to involve all Parties, cover all sectors, methodological and cross-cutting issues. Transparency, effectiveness and comparability are to be improved through work on 'criteria and quantitative parameters' – an oblique reference to policy performance indicators – as well as consideration of methodology, attribution and national circumstances issues which could help Parties design, monitor and evaluate PAMs more effectively. This work should also assist Parties and the COP in identifying further options for cooperation among interested Parties to enhance the individual and combined effectiveness of their PAMs an issue which has recently caused problems as a number non-Annex I Parties have argued that the work on PAMs should remain focused on Annex I Parties.[125] Finally, Decision 13/CP.7 stated that the work on 'good practices' should 'contribute to the elaboration of elements for reporting information on demonstrable progress pursuant to decision 22/CP.7'. This Decision has been further elaborated by Decision 25/CP.8 and will result in the submission of a report by 1 January 2006 by each Annex I Party that has ratified the Protocol describing, inter alia, its domestic PAMs and their expected impacts on emissions trends.[126] This is discussed in detail in chapter 11 on reporting and review. How the work on 'good practices' will result in sharing of information on how Annex I Parties are striving to minimise adverse impacts is discussed in chapter 9.

In the near term, the practical outcome of Decision 13/CP.7 is to mandate the Secretariat to produce a set of printed and web-based products designed to facilitate Annex I and non-Annex I Parties sharing information.[127] Analytical work to develop methodological tools to design, monitor and better evaluate the environmental, economic and social impacts of particular PAMs and portfolios has also been enhanced as a result of Decision 13/CP.7.[128] Additional workshops at future SB and COP sessions, and greater collaboration with international organisations with extensive experience in assessing the effectiveness of policies and developing databases of PAMs, such as the OECD and IEA, are among possibilities

---

[124] Decision 13/CP.7.   [125] ENB summary of SB 18, 16 June 2003.

[126] See the section below and chapter 10.

[127] Current outputs include (i) a web-based database on key PAMs reported in Annex I Parties' third national communications (NC3), FCCC/WEB/2002/7; (ii) a report from the Secretariat on 'good practices', FCCC/SBSTA/2002/INF.13; (iii) a submission from the OECD/IEA reporting their work and information databases on PAMs, FCCC/WEB/2002/11; and (iv) the Secretariat's compilation and synthesis NC3: addendum on PAMs, FCCC/SBI/2003/7/Add.2.

[128] FCCC/SBSTA/2002/INF.13.

being discussed.[129] The likely direction of rule development of these activities is an eventual tightening of reporting guidelines on PAMs to improve their transparency, effectiveness and comparability, including better methodologies to assess the underlying costs and impacts of PAMs to mitigate climate change as well as non-climate related PAMs contributing to increased emissions (for example, such as energy market liberalisation or energy subsidies). Decision 1/CP.9, for example, mandates SBSTA to consider ways of improving the transparency of GHG projections in time to contribute to the preparation of fourth national communications. Additionally, discussion of the scientific, technical and socio-economic aspects of mitigation which Parties at COP-9 agreed would be advanced by future SBSTA sessions is also likely to prompt greater information sharing and PAMs learning by doing and, given that this decision will be reviewed by COP-11, will feed into 2005 policy discussions.[130]

5.5   *PAMs and adverse impacts/response measures*

Articles 4.8 and 4.10 of the Convention require all Parties to take into consideration in their implementation of commitments the situation of particular groups of Parties. Articles 2.3 and 3.14 of the Protocol require Annex I Parties to consider adverse impacts of climate change and response measures on developing country Parties listed in Articles 4.8 and 4.9 of the Convention. These provisions are explained in more detail in chapters 8 and 9.

5.6   *Reporting of PAMs*

Reporting and review of the Convention and Protocol commitments, including how PAMs are to be reported, is covered in chapter 11.

5.7   *Quantified commitments*

Background: A number of policy choices have framed the elaboration of quantified mitigation commitments of Annex I Parties under the Convention and the Protocol. The first has been whether quantified targets, as opposed to PAMs, should be negotiated at all. This issue divided Annex I Parties in the early years of the regime and was resolved only with the adoption of the Kyoto Protocol. Other policy choices included whether quantified commitments should be:

- Defined in terms of coverage on a gas-by-gas or 'basket-of-gas' basis;
- Define to include sinks as well as sources;[131]
- Achieved over a single year or over a multi-year period;

---

[129] SBSTA-18 in June 2003 did not reach any conclusions on how to take forward the work on PAMs under Decision 13/CP.7.

[130] Decision 10/CP.9.   [131] For an explanation of the comprehensive approach, see box 5.2.

- Uniformly applicable to all Parties or differentiated;
- Achieved domestically or overseas; and, finally,
- Subject to compliance procedures and mechanisms with binding conse-
  quences or not.

Provisions in the Convention were silent, inconclusive or inadequate on a number of these issues. The Kyoto Protocol, supplemented by the Marrakesh Accords,
reached agreement on these fundamental issues, giving Annex I Parties considerable flexibility in meeting their quantitative commitments and resulting in
perhaps the most innovative and technically complex package of rules adopted to
date in international environmental law.

5.8   *The Convention's quantified aim*

Article 4.2 (a) and (b) contains three related commitments: those relating
to PAMs, to reporting and a 'quantified aim' requiring Annex I Parties to aim
at returning their emissions of carbon dioxide and other greenhouse gases (not
controlled by the Montreal Protocol) to their 1990 levels by the year 2000. As
explained in box 5.6, the commitments relating to the adoption and reporting of
PAMs are not time-bound but of an *ongoing nature* with a view to demonstrating
that Annex I Parties are taking the lead in the modification of longer-term emission
trends. Thus this element of the commitments in Article 4.2 (a) and (b) will remain
significant for Annex I Parties that do not ratify the Protocol who will continue to
be obliged to adopt and implement PAMs to limit their GHG emissions and enhance
removals to demonstrate modification of longer-term emission trends. For Annex I
Parties that ratify the Protocol, the 'quantified aim' is of less practical relevance
post-2000 because, for the majority of Annex I Parties, it has been overshadowed
by quantified commitments under the Protocol.

Rule development: Apart from the adoption of the Protocol, rule development
in relation to the commitments in Article 4.2 (a) and (b) has come mainly in the
form of amendments to the list in Annex I, discussed in boxes 5.4 and 5.5.[132]
No substantive conclusions have been reached by the COP as regards the second
review of the adequacy of these commitments, mandated by Article 4.2 (d), because
of disagreements about whether this review should examine the commitments of
developing countries or be limited to the commitments of Annex I Parties.[133]

Appendix II of this book sets out the progress made by each Annex I Party
towards the Convention's quantified aim as well as by groups of Annex I Parties
such as the EU, EITs and JUSSCANNZ. As a matter of record, inventory data submitted by Annex I Parties for the year 2000 confirmed that their total aggregated

---

[132] See chapter 18.   [133] See chapter 19.

GHG emissions (excluding land-use change and forestry, LUCF) decreased by 3 per cent from 1990 to 2000.[134] As noted in the Secretariat's compilation and synthesis report of the third national communications, 'Annex I Parties have jointly attained the aim of Article 4.2 of the Convention – to return their 2000 emissions to 1990 levels – although the extent to which Annex II Parties succeeded in reversing an increasing trend in GHG emissions varied widely.' After consideration of GHG inventories from Annex I Parties for the period 1990–2001, COP-9 noted that aggregate GHG emissions from Annex I Parties were below 1990 levels despite considerable increases by several Parties, largely because of the decrease in emissions from EITs.[135] COP-9 also noted that projections provided by Parties indicate that, in the absence of additional measures, aggregate emissions of Annex I Parties, including emissions of EITs, are expected to increase in the period 2000–2010.[136] Decision 1/CP.9 concludes with the COP stating that 'further action is needed by Annex I Parties to implement policies and measures that will contribute to modifying longer-term trends in anthropogenic emissions, consistent with the objective of the Convention and the commitments of these Parties, and strongly urges these Parties to intensify efforts to that end'.[137]

5.9   *Kyoto quantified emission limitation or reduction commitments*

The great achievement of Kyoto is the legally binding targets for the thirty-nine countries listed in Annex B of the Protocol. Article 3(1) states that these Parties

> shall, individually or jointly, ensure that their aggregate anthropogenic carbon dioxide equivalent emissions of the greenhouse gases listed in Annex A do not exceed their assigned amounts calculated pursuant to their quantified emission limitation and reduction commitment inscribed in Annex B with a view to reducing their overall emissions of such gases by at least 5 per cent below 1990 levels in the commitment period 2008–2012.

Article 3 introduces several new concepts not found in the Convention that are explained in box 5.7 below.

Article 3.1 establishes two different kinds of targets: differentiated targets for each Annex I Party and an overall Annex B cap, or collective target, for Annex I Parties.[138] Each Annex I Party's individual quantified emission limitation and

---

[134] FCCC/SBI/2003/7/Add.1.

[135] Decision 1/CP.9, National communications from Parties included in Annex I of the Convention.

[136] Decision 1/CP.9, paragraph 2.   [137] Decision 1/CP.9, paragraph 3.

[138] FCCC/TP/2000/2, paragraphs 131–3 and 216–21.

reduction commitments (QELRC) are to be worked out according to the percentage inscribed for it in Annex B of the Protocol. These individual targets distribute the effort needed to achieve the collective target of 5 per cent among the Annex B countries in a clear, legally binding manner. Responsibility for achievement of the collective target is expressed in softer terms, 'with a view to reducing the overall levels', leaving open various questions about the legal nature of the collective target and the distribution of responsibilities for achieving it.[139]

Under Article 3.1, the total amount of GHG emissions that each Annex I Party can emit over 2008–2012 must not exceed its assigned amount. The actual assigned amount each Party is entitled to emit is calculated in accordance with Articles 3.7, 3.8 and 7.4, as elaborated by Decision 19/CP.7. This Decision states that the assigned amount for each Annex I Party will be equal to the percentage inscribed for it in Annex B of its aggregate anthropogenic carbon dioxide equivalent emissions of the greenhouse gases, and the sources, listed in Annex A of the Protocol, in 1990 (or other applicable base year) multiplied by five, taking into account the following:[140]

- Base-year provisions explained in section 2;
- Assigned amounts of the EU and its member states are to be worked out using the respective emission level allocated to each of these Parties in the agreement reached pursuant to Article 4, rather than the percentages inscribed in Annex B;[141]
- Assigned amounts of Parties for whom LULUCF constituted a net source of GHGs in 1990 is to be calculated by including the net emissions from LULUCF in their base year, pursuant to Article 3.7.[142]

Box 5.7   Kyoto Protocol Article 3: concepts and terminology

The word 'target' is not used in the Protocol because of US sensitivities in the Protocol negotiations about binding commitments.[143] Instead, the Protocol uses the term 'quantified emission limitation and reduction commitments'

---

[139] For example, it may be possible for a country that had status as an 'Annex I Party' under the Protocol but was not listed in Annex B (currently Turkey, Belarus and Kazakhstan) to contribute to the achievement of the collective target without having an individual target legally in place. It is not clear, however, what incentives would exist for a Party to take such a course nor what consequences, if any, would result if inclusion of the emissions of such a Party resulted in a breach of the collective target of 5 per cent below 1990 levels in 2008–2012.

[140] Decision 19/CP.7, Annex, paragraph 5, chapeau.

[141] Decision 19/CP.7, Annex, paragraph 5 (c), and see below on joint fulfilment.

[142] Decision 19/CP.7, Annex, paragraph 5 (b), and see section 2 above on coverage.

[143] Chapter 18 explains what is entailed by binding commitments.

(QELRC). 'Commitment period' refers to the time-frame in which QELRCs must be achieved. Unlike the Convention's single-year target, Kyoto's first commitment period runs for five years, 2008–2012, giving Parties a sufficiently long lead time to plan sensible emission pathways as well as short-term flexibility within the five years to smooth out seasonal and economic fluctuations. The Protocol is silent on the commencement and duration of subsequent commitment periods. The adoption of multi-year targets and the basket-of-gases approach in the Kyoto Protocol necessitated invention of a new term to refer to aggregate amount of carbon dioxide equivalent emissions that the Protocol allowed each Party to emit over the entire commitment period. This aggregate unit eventually came to be called the *assigned amount* as this term did not have the property rights connotations associated with the term 'budget' and related US proposals for an international 'cap and trade' emissions trading scheme, both of which raise equity issues about historic (grandfathered) emission levels.[144] The Marrakesh Accords attempted to address some of these concerns by stating that 'the Kyoto Protocol has not created or bestowed any right, title or entitlement to emissions of any kind on Parties included in Annex 1'.[145] The actual assigned amount for each Annex I Party is to be calculated according to Articles 3.7 and 3.8 and Decision 19/CP.7.[146] Once calculated, the assigned amount for each Party shall remain fixed for the commitment period. Parties may, if they so choose, add and subtract from their assigned amount, four kinds of units: an emission reduction unit (ERU), a certified emission reduction (CER), an assigned amount unit (AAU) and a removal unit (RMU). The first three units are created pursuant to the Kyoto mechanisms under Articles 6, 12 and 17 respectively. The RMU is a unit created by the Marrakesh Accords to represent removal of emissions by LULUCF activities when undertaken in accordance with the provisions of the Protocol. Finally, the term 'individually or jointly' is important because, subject to the Article 4 provisions, it allows groups of Annex I Parties, such as the EU, to fulfil their QERLCs jointly.

5.10   *Gases/Sectors: Annex A*

The QERLCs set out in Article 3.1 cover emissions of the six greenhouse gases in a 'basket' approach, using GWPs, described in section 2 above.

---

[144] See section 2 above on base years and grandfathering. See also chapter 6; and Yamin, 1999.

[145] Decision 15/CP.7, Annex, draft COP/MOP decision on the principles, nature and scope of the mechanisms.

[146] Decision 19/CP.7, Annex, paragraph 5. There are special provisions relating to Parties that have reached an agreement in accordance with Article 4: see below.

5.11   *LULUCF activities*

Articles 3.3 and 3.4 set out the compromise reached at Kyoto after intense negotiations.[147] The provisions of Article 3.3 include *gross–net* accounting for forest areas established since 1990 and deforestation since 1990, except for Parties required by the second sentence of Article 3.7 to account for deforestation on a net–net basis. The approach agreed, at the resumed session of COP-6 and at Marrakesh, for Article 3.4 during the first commitment period includes *gross–net* accounting for forest management, but subject to a cap, and *net–net* accounting for agricultural activities (cropland management, grazing land management and revegetation). Forest management can also be used, up to an agreed limit, to compensate penalties arising from deforestation accounted under Article 3.3.

Article 3.3 defines a limited range of sinks activities that can count towards QERLCs in the first commitment period. It provides that only net changes over the commitment period in emissions and removals resulting from direct human-induced land-use change and forestry activities, limited to afforestation, reforestation and deforestation (ARD), count towards Article 3.1 commitments. Such activities will only count towards targets if they commenced after 1990, the net changes in carbon stock can be measured for each commitment period and can be reported in a transparent and verifiable manner and reviewed in accordance with Articles 7 and 8 of the Protocol. To facilitate estimation of carbon stocks, the first sentence of Article 3.4 mandates Annex I Parties to provide SBSTA with data to establish its levels of carbon stocks in 1990 prior to the first session of the COP/MOP, work on which commenced in August 2000.

The second sentence of Article 3.4 mandates the COP/MOP at its first session, or as soon as practicable thereafter, to decide how, and which, 'additional categories of human-induced activities in agricultural soils and the land-use change and forestry sector can be added to, or subtracted from, Parties' assigned amounts'. This decision must take into account uncertainties, transparency in reporting and verifiability, aspects stressed by those opposing the inclusion of sinks. It should also be based on the IPCC's methodological work on sinks, SBSTA advice on Article 5 (concerning methodologies for inventories and reporting) and decisions by the FCCC COP (not the COP/MOP). The third and final sentence provides that the COP/MOP's decision shall apply in the 'second and subsequent commitment period' and, if a Party so chooses, also in the first commitment period provided these activities have taken place since 1990.

Rule development: Articles 3.3 and 3.4 were unsatisfactory in that they do not define key terms, such as 'forests', and the meaning of other terms, such as

---

[147] See chapter 5, section 2.2.

'direct human induced', was left unclear.[148] Harvesting is not mentioned at all. It was also unclear how carbon stocks would be identified to allow calculation of the 1990 baseline on a consistent basis and what consideration should be given to the conservation and sustainable use of biodiversity and forest resources.[149] Supporters of the comprehensive approach (box 5.2), dissatisfied with the limited categories of sinks under Article 3.3, insisted on early consideration of additional sinks categories under Article 3.4 to provide greater flexibility and legal certainty for Annex I Parties through the inclusion of additional sinks that could be applied to the first commitment period. As a result of these considerations, Decision 1/CP.3 mandated preparatory work on these issues immediately after Kyoto. The technical complexity, and high political stakes, of sinks issues contributed significantly to the breakdown of negotiations at The Hague at COP-6 part I.[150] Decisions 11/CP.7 and 12/CP.7 of the Marrakesh Accords have clarified and significantly elaborated Articles 3.3 and 3.4 by promulgating principles, definitions, agreed activities, quantitative caps and additional methodological and reporting requirements aimed at ensuring that inclusion of LULUCF activities does not undermine the environmental integrity of the Protocol.

5.11.1   LULUCF Principles

The annex to Decision 11/CP.7 sets out a set of principles to govern the treatment of all LULUCF activities under the Protocol irrespective of who undertakes such activities or where these occur. Thus these principles apply to LULUCF activities undertaken by non-Annex I Parties in the context of the CDM. The overall intent of the principles is to ensure that credits cannot be earned for natural removals as very large amounts of carbon exchanges take place between the terrestrial and atmospheric carbon pools without any human intervention (box 5.1). A more specific aim is to ensure that the commitments of Annex I Parties under Article 3.1 are not weakened in any form or create perverse incentives for deforestation or other environmentally unsound practices (such as replacement of old biodiversity-rich forests with more-carbon-absorbing monoculture plantations). The principles thus:

- Support the use of 'sound science' in the treatment of LULUCF activities (paragraph 1 (a));
- Support the use of consistent estimation and reporting methodologies over time (paragraph 1 (b)); and
- Implement LULUCF activities which contribute to the conservation of biodiversity and sustainable use of natural resources (paragraph 1 (e)).

---

[148] Fry, 2002.   [149] See chapter 17.   [150] Grubb and Yamin, 2001.

To avoid credits for activities happening anyway (including increased natural sequestration levels resulting from higher atmospheric CO_2 concentrations), and with the aim of ensuring that the commitments of Annex I Parties are not weakened, the principles state that:

- The aim of Article 3.1 defining quantitative commitments not be changed by inclusion of LULUCF activities (paragraph 1 (c));
- The mere presence of carbon stocks be excluded from accounting (paragraph 1 (d));
- No transfer of Article 3.1 commitments to a future commitment period be implied (paragraph 1 (f));
- Reversals of removals from LULUCF be accounted for at the appropriate time (paragraph 1 (g)); and
- Accounting should exclude removals resulting from elevated carbon dioxide concentrations above their pre-industrial level, indirect nitrogen deposition and the dynamic effects of age structure resulting from activities and practices before 1990 (paragraph 1 (h)).

Proposed largely by developing countries, and initially resisted by many Annex I Parties, these principles provide broad policy guidance in this otherwise highly complex area where scientific and technical issues can all too easily obscure the fundamental policy concerns at stake. The Marrakesh principles are of relevance in the implementation of LULUCF rules, including methodological and reporting elements related to Articles 3.3 and 3.4 that remain to be elaborated. Unresolved policy issues include non-permanence, leakage, additionality, uncertainties and social–economic and environmental impacts, including impacts on biodiversity and natural ecosystems, of LULUCF projects under the Clean Development Mechanism.[151] The COP-7 agreement that the IPCC should develop methodologies to factor out direct/indirect and natural/anthropogenic changes in carbon stock levels, for possible adoption by COP-10, may represent a concrete way in which the principles will inform the next stage of rule development, including accounting procedures for the first commitment period.[152]

5.11.2   LULUCF definitions

Diversity of forest ecosystems and shifting geographical boundaries created definitional problems about what should count as 'Kyoto lands' under Articles 3.3 and 3.4. The Marrakesh definition of forests is set out in Decision 11/CP.7 and follows the FAO approach to defining forests because it allows each Party to select the lands that will count as forests, provided these fall within

---

[151] See chapter 6.   [152] Decision 11/CP.7, paragraph 3 (d).

the fairly broad limits specified in the decision. The alternative biome-specific approach would have classified forests in a more ecologically sound, and ultimately more verifiable, manner by setting out the tree height and crown cover for particular forest types, and then requiring Parties to identify lands that fit such categories.[153] This approach was not considered practically feasible for the first commitment period. Accordingly, Decision 11/CP.7 requests SBSTA to explore use of the biome approach for the second and subsequent period.[154] Concerns that Parties might try to define lands as forests to earn more credits than warranted have been partly addressed by requiring Parties to identify geographically land considered to be forests and to select a single minimum tree height, crown and land area value for the duration of the first commitment period prior to its commencement and report on how such values are consistent with information historically reported by them to the FAO, explaining the rationale behind any differences.[155]

The other definitions set out in Decision 11/CP.7, such as afforestation, reforestation, deforestation and revegetation, provide much needed clarification of the terms used in the Protocol. The term 'direct human induced' is not defined, but Parties are required to demonstrate through reporting that activities under Articles 3.3 and 3.4 'have occurred since 1990 and are human-induced'. Thus the degree of human intervention necessary to take credit for naturally occurring processes, such as regeneration, remains to be established through actual practices. Decision 11/CP.7 confirms the earlier clarification agreed by COP-4 in Decision 9/CP.4 that, so far as Article 3.3 is concerned, 'the adjustment to a Party's assigned amount shall be equal to verifiable changes in carbon stocks during the period 2008 to 2012 resulting from direct human-induced activities of afforestation, reforestation, and deforestation since 1 January 1990'.

The Kyoto Protocol does not mention reporting and taking credit for the carbon content of harvested wood products (HWPs) and emissions associated with the harvest cycle. Although HWPs constitute a significant carbon reservoir, HWP issues have not been fully resolved by the Marrakesh Accords. Current rules, derived from the IPCC Reporting Guidelines and Decision 11/CP.7, thus do not include HWPs either as a pool under Article 3.3 or as an activity under Article 3.4.[156] So far as reporting is concerned, the default approach in the IPCC methodologies, followed in Decision 11.CP.7, states that 'debits resulting from harvesting during

---

[153] Fry, 2002.   [154] Decision 11/CP.7, paragraph 2 (b).

[155] Decision 11/CP.7, paragraphs 16–20. This information is to be submitted in the report to establish a Party's assigned amount which is subject to review under Articles 7 and 8. See chapter 11.

[156] IPCC 1996b, *Reference Manual*, p. 5.17.

the first commitment period following afforestation and reforestation since 1990 shall not be greater than credits for that unit of land'.[157] This simplifies calculation of emissions and is necessary to correct certain anomalies that arise from the application of the gross–net approach under Article 3.3. Discussions at SBSTA-15 (meeting with COP-7) essentially concluded that HWP is a second commitment period issue. Parties have agreed to discuss the treatment of HWP after making submissions on this issue in 2003. On the basis of these submissions and other work, the Secretariat has been requested to prepare a technical paper to be considered at SBSTA-20 and 21 with a view to recommending a decision for COP/MOP.

5.11.3   LULUCF caps

In addition to ARD activities under Article 3.3, the Marrakesh Accords sanctioned four additional LULUCF activities under Article 3.4 that can be undertaken domestically within Annex I Parties to count towards emission targets.[158] These activities are:

- Forest management;
- Cropland management;
- Grazing land management; and
- Revegetation.

Degradation and devegetation are not currently included under Article 3.4 but their inclusion was examined by SBSTA-18 on the basis of the IPCC's work. Further discussions at SBSTA-19 and at COP-9 mean that a recommendation for inclusion in the first commitment period for consideration will be discussed in the future SBSTA-20.[159]

Article 3.4 allows Parties to choose which of the four activities they will count towards their QERLCs. Decision 11/CP.7 states that each Party must make this choice through its report to establish its assigned amount at the outset of the commitment period.[160] Once the selection is made, the decision by the Party will remain fixed for the first commitment period. Additionally, once land is accounted for under Articles 3.3 and 3.4, all emissions and removals on this land 'must be accounted for throughout the subsequent and contiguous commitment periods'. These provisions were designed to ensure that Parties did not pick and choose sink activities that had done well during the commitment period, and that it would be possible to track emissions and removals from the same piece of land across

---

[157] Decision 11/CP.7, Annex, Section B, paragraph 4.

[158] Chapter 6, section 6.4 describes the rules relating to inclusion of LULUCF activities under the CDM.

[159] Decision 11/CP.7, paragraphs 2 (a) and 3 (c).   [160] See chapter 10.

commitment periods even if a Party changed its decision about which activities it wanted to have included in subsequent commitment periods.

Inclusion of additional activities under Article 3.4 activities was heavily resisted by the EU and most developing countries at Marrakesh because it weakens the environmental stringency of the QERLCs agreed at Kyoto.[161] Unless restricted, use of such activities could actually have led to overall increases in emissions from many Annex I Parties (e.g. in the energy and industry sectors). The compromise that was reached at the resumed session of COP-6 and at Marrakesh restricts certain LULUCF activities that can be elected for counting towards the first commitment period to the following:

1   If a Party's ARD activities under Article 3.3 result in more emissions than removals, then the Party may offset these emissions through forest management activities under Article 3.4, up to a total level of 9 megatons of carbon per year for the five-year commitment period.
2   The extent to which forest management activities can be accounted for to help meet emission targets beyond tier 1 is subject to an individual cap for each Party, listed in the Marrakesh Accords set out and explained in Appendix II to this book. This cap includes joint implementation projects under Article 6 involving forest management.
3   Emissions and removals from cropland management, grazing land management and revegetation can be counted to help meet emission targets on a net–net basis (e.g. changes in carbon stocks during 1990, times five, will be subtracted from the changes in carbon stocks during the first commitment period, in the lands where these activities will take place).
4   This concerns LULUCF activities under the CDM.[162] Only afforestation and reforestation projects are eligible under the CDM. Greenhouse gas removals from such projects may only be used to help meet emission targets up to 1 per cent of a Party's base-year emissions for each year of the commitment period.

This system of limits does not apply to Article 3.3. Thus there are no quantitative limits on ARD activities undertaken in Annex I Parties that can count towards their Article 3.1 commitments.

Appendix II to this book provides information about the size of the various caps and their significance for achieving the Kyoto targets.

5.11.4   LULUCF methodologies, reporting and accounting

The extent to which Parties will actually be able to count both Article 3.3 and Article 3.4 activities towards their targets will depend on each fulfilling

---

[161] Meinshausen and Hare, 2003. See also Vrolijk, 2002.   [162] See chapter 6, section 6.4.

inventory methodological and reporting guidelines which will be subject to reporting and review procedures under Articles 5, 7 and 8 of the Protocol.[163] These requirements underpin the creation of RMUs – a new type of unit created by the Marrakesh Accords to represent removal of emissions by LULUCF activities – that can count towards Annex I Parties' targets and generate financial benefits if traded through the Kyoto mechanisms.

Inclusion of Article 3.3 and 3.4 activities, and their conversion into a valuable commodity, has necessitated elaboration of additional methodologies to estimate, monitor and report changes in the carbon stock levels of various activities as well as better guidance on what constitutes good practice, particularly in relation to management and reporting of uncertainties. Because accurate reporting and better handling of uncertainties are critical to the integrity of RMU issuance and use, Decision 11/CP.7 invited the IPCC to prepare two documents, one on estimation/reporting and one on uncertainty management, for possible adoption by COP-9.[164] Once adopted, it will be mandatory for Annex I Parties to follow the standards set in these documents.[165] At COP-9, Parties agreed to adopt the IPCC Report on Good Practice Guidance for LULUCF (as approved by the IPCC Plenary in November 2003), as well as the draft common reporting format tables for reporting emissions and removals of sinks for inventories due under the Convention.[166] The use of the IPCC Guidance for the Protocol will be discussed at COP-10 alongside other issues that COP-9 could not agree upon in the time available at Milan: namely the IPCC report on degradation of forests and devegetation of other vegetation types and the IPCC report on factoring out direct human-induced changes in carbon stocks which will consequently be examined at future SBSTA sessions.[167]

Rules governing the issuance (creation) and validity (use) of RMUs are set out in Decision 19/CP.7 concerning modalities for accounting of assigned amounts.[168] These accounting provisions make it impossible for a Party to issue RMUs unless inventory data and other required information to support the issuance has first been checked and verified by expert review teams and any outstanding 'questions of implementation' have been resolved.[169] To make the RMU accounting process transparent, prior to 2008 each Party has to select for each activity under Articles 3.3 and 3.4 whether it will issue RMUs annually or for the entire commitment period. A Party's selection will be fixed for the first commitment period.

---

[163] See chapter 11.   [164] Decision 11/CP.7, paragraph 3 (a) and (b).
[165] Decision 11/CP.7, Annex, paragraphs 2 and 3.   [166] Decision 13/CP.9. See chapter 11.
[167] See COP-9 Report and SBSTA-18 Report.   [168] Decision 19/CP.7, Annex, paragraphs 25–6.
[169] See chapters 11 and 12 for questions of implementation.

Where RMUs have been issued in accordance with Decision 19/CP.7, they may be added to and subtracted from a Party's assigned amount and traded under the Kyoto mechanisms. The Marrakesh Accords explicitly prohibit the carry-over (banking) of RMUs for future commitment periods, discussed below.[170]

5.12   Early action

The Protocol does not contain a legally binding target for 2005, as proposed by the EU and developing countries. As a compromise, Article 3.2 of the Protocol mandates Parties 'by 2005 to have made demonstrable progress in achieving [their] commitments under this Protocol'. The Protocol does not specify how this 'demonstration' is to be assessed, by whom or what kind of consequences might flow from such an assessment. The assessment process and consequences of fulfilling Article 3.2 were therefore negotiated as part of the Marrakesh Accords and at COP-8.

Although not a legally binding target, one of the potential functions of Article 3.2 was to serve as an 'early-warning system' for countries not taking sufficient action to meet their targets.[171] A second function was to provide a mechanism for Annex I Parties to share experiences and information on PAMs relating to implementation of the Protocol, as discussed above. During the Marrakesh Accords negotiations the early-warning function came to be overshadowed by the information-sharing function, largely as a result of pressure from JUSCANZ countries to de-link the 'demonstrable progress' commitment from any form of compliance assessment.[172] Accordingly, the reporting and review of Annex I Parties' commitments under Article 3.2 will now be handled by the Facilitative Branch of the Compliance Committee.[173]

Decision 22/CP.7 on guidelines for the preparation of national communications, and Decision 25/CP.8 which is directly on Article 3.2, elaborate how the assessment of demonstrable progress will take place. These decisions request each Annex I Party to submit a 'one-off' report on their progress in implementing the Protocol, discussed in chapter 11.

5.13   Calculating assigned amount

As explained in box 5.7, each Party's QELRCs are converted into a notional quantity called 'assigned amount' which can be divided up into units allowing Parties to participate in the Kyoto mechanisms explained in chapter 6. Articles 3.5, 3.7 and 3.8 provide instructions on how the assigned amount of particular Parties

---

[170] Decision 19/CP.7, paragraph 16.   [171] Anderson, 2002a: p. 156.

[172] Anderson, 2002a: p. 156.

[173] See chapter 12. Decision 24/CP.7, Annex, Section IV Facilitative Branch, paragraph 5 (b).

can be worked out and how particular gases or sinks are to be treated in the assigned amount calculation. All these provisions are discussed in more detail in section 2.

5.14   *Use of Kyoto mechanisms*

Chapter 6 discusses how Annex I Parties may use the mechanisms referenced in Articles 3.10, 3.11 and 3.12 of the Protocol.

5.15   *Carry-over*

Article 3.13 provides that 'if the emissions of a Party included in Annex I in a commitment period are less than its assigned amount under this Article, this difference shall, on request of that Party, be added to the assigned amount for that Party for subsequent commitment periods'. The rationale for carry-over (or 'banking') is environmentally sound because it encourages, rather than penalises, over-achievement of targets. Relatively uncontroversial at Kyoto, at Marrakesh carry-over was seen by developing countries as undermining the environmental integrity of the Protocol because banking on an excessive scale could detract Annex I Parties from reducing emissions at source and give such Parties large carbon budgets in future commitment periods.

The Marrakesh Accords impose two kinds of restrictions on carry-over. First, the carry-over of RMUs for future commitment periods is expressly prohibited.[174] Because RMUs are fully exchangeable (fungible) on a one-to-one basis with CERs, ERUs and AAUs that are bankable, it may be possible for an Annex I Party to circumvent the intent of the no 'carry-over of RMUs' rule by giving priority to using RMUs to meet their commitments. Whether this happens in practice, and leads to any subsequent 'anti-laundering' response from the COP/MOP, along the lines proposed by developing countries at Marrakesh, remains to be seen. A second restriction on carry-over relates to CERs and ERUs. Decision 19/CP.4 limits banking of CERs and ERUs to 2.5 per cent of a Party's assigned amount.[175] Again, given the fully exchangeable nature of the Kyoto units, under current rules an Annex I Party could circumvent these restrictions by, for example, retiring or cancelling all its CERs and ERUs for compliance purposes in order to bank AAUs for future use as the latter are not subject to carry-over restrictions.

5.16   *EITs and small economies*

FCCC: Articles 4.8, 4.9 and 4.10 of the Convention include provisions dealing with the special circumstances and needs of particular groups of Parties and are addressed in chapters 8 and 9. Article 3 of the Protocol provides the basis for

---

[174] Decision 19/CP.7, paragraph 16, and see below.   [175] Decision 19/CP.7, Annex, Section F.

special consideration for three other kinds of Parties: EITs, small countries that might be affected by the implementation of a single, large project and developing countries that might be affected by the adverse environmental and economic impacts.

So far as Parties that are EITs are concerned, the Protocol sets targets for many of them that are likely to result in surplus emissions which can be traded. In addition to this, Article 3.5 allows Parties that are EITs to choose a base year different to 1990, described in section 3. This provision mirrors Article 4.6 of the Convention. Article 3.6 of the Protocol provides that 'a certain degree of flexibility' shall be allowed by the COP/MOP to Parties with economies in transition 'in the implementation of their commitments under the Protocol, other than those under this Article'. The practical operation of Article 3.6 remains unclear but it was intended to provide some flexibility in, for example, the submission of national communications.[176]

When the Kyoto Protocol was adopted, Iceland raised a problem concerning its plans to construct an aluminium smelting plant that would have a significant impact on its ability to attain its QELRC. Decision 1/CP.3 requested the SBs to give 'consideration of, and as appropriate, action on suitable methodologies to address the situation of Parties listed in Annex B to the Protocol for which single projects would have a significant proportional impact on emissions in the commitment period'.

At COP-4, Iceland proposed that single projects that have a significant proportional impact on emissions during the commitment period should be reported separately, and not included in national totals, to the extent that they would cause a Party to exceed its assigned amount. Although Iceland's GHG emissions are extremely small in global terms, its proposal raised broader policy issues about global benefits produced by displacement of fossil fuels by renewables and competitiveness issues. It also raised concerns as it would weaken the QERLCs and collective target set out in Article 3. Finally, other Parties feared the legal precedent of allowing a Party to, in effect, renegotiate its target so soon after the Protocol's adoption, not least because in Iceland's case its target already allowed an increase in Iceland's emissions by 10 per cent over the commitment period, and it was not immediately clear why Iceland could not use the Kyoto mechanisms to offset the increase in its domestic emissions.

Iceland refined its proposals to address some of these concerns and pursued its proposal until agreement was reached at COP-7. Decision 14/CP.7 sets out strict conditions that must be met if a Party wants to exclude the impact of a single large project from its national emissions. These conditions were drafted to ensure that

[176] FCCC/TP/2000/2, paragraphs 235–40.

only a very limited number of countries could make use of them. Decision 14/CP.7 provides that only Parties that account for less than 0.05 per cent of total Annex I emissions in 1990 with single projects involving industrial processes that account for more than 5 per cent of the total greenhouse gas emissions of a Party in 1990, utilising renewable energy which leads to a reduction in greenhouse gas emissions per unit of production and where best environmental practice is used to minimise process emissions, can qualify for treating such projects separately from national totals. Qualifying Parties can exclude emissions from such single projects from their national totals, but the total amount of emissions that can be reported separately is capped at 1.6 million tons of carbon dioxide annually. To avoid abuse of this provision, this amount cannot be transferred by the qualifying Party (or acquired by another Annex I Party) using the Kyoto mechanisms. Finally, reliance on Decision 14/CP.7 is valid only if qualifying Parties give notice to the COP by its eighth session. Only Iceland and Monaco have given such a notification, thus they are the only Parties able to avail themselves of the special provisions of Decision 14/CP.7.

Article 3.14 of the Protocol, like Article 2.3 on PAMs, stipulates that Annex I Parties should strive to implement their QELRCs to minimise adverse impacts on developing countries listed in Articles 4.8 and 4.9 of the Convention. This is discussed in chapters 8 and 9.

5.17   *Joint fulfilment*

Background: The Convention and the Protocol use the term 'individually or jointly' to allow groups of Parties to fulfil their commitments jointly as well as Parties acting as members of a REIO of which the EU is the only example which is actually a Party (see box 5.8). As with many other concepts, the Convention's provisions as regard the rights and responsibilities of REIOs lacked clarity and have had to be dealt with in the Protocol.

Box 5.8   Regional economic integration organisations

Any REIO wishing to become a Party to the Convention or the Kyoto Protocol must declare, at the point of ratification, the extent of its competence on matters covered by the treaties, and must inform the Depositary of any substantial modification.[177] The requirement to make such declarations of competence applies to all REIOs but the only REIO that is a Party to the Convention is the EU. The rationale for such declarations is to ensure legal

---

[177] FCCC Article 22 and KP Article 24.

clarity with regard to the extent of competence of the REIO and its member states. Knowing who to hold legally responsible for compliance is particularly important when legally binding commitments are at stake. Accordingly, in its declarations made on ratifying both the Convention and the Kyoto Protocol, the EU has confirmed that it will fulfil its commitments jointly, together with its member states, 'within the respective competence of each'. On ratification of the Kyoto Protocol, the EU also submitted a copy of the agreement reached among the Community and its member states regarding the joint fulfilment of emission targets under Article 4,[178] as required by that Article.

FCCC: Article 4.2 (a) of the Convention is expressed in terms of national policies and measures. The footnote to Article 4.2 (a) confirms that the term 'national' includes 'policies and measures adopted by regional economic integration organizations'. Article 4.2 (a) also provides that Annex I Parties can 'implement such policies and measures jointly with other Parties and may assist other Parties in contributing to the achievement of the objection of the Convention, in particular, that of this sub-paragraph', Article 12.8 of the Convention allows a group of Parties to make a joint communication of their fulfilment of the Convention provided they have given prior notice to the COP, followed any guidelines adopted by the COP concerning such joint communications and ensured that such joint communications include information on the fulfilment by each of the Parties in the group of its individual obligations under the Convention. No separate guidelines for reporting have been elaborated under the FCCC regarding joint fulfilment of commitments by groups of Parties. To date, only the EU has submitted a joint report as part of its collective implementation of Article 4.2 (a) and (b).[179]

Kyoto: Article 3.1 uses the term 'individually or jointly' to allow groups of Annex I Parties to fulfil their QELRCs jointly. In the Protocol this term is clearly distinguished from the project-based mechanisms under Articles 6 and 12 and from emissions trading pursuant to Article 17.[180] Article 4 of the Protocol allows a group of Parties that want to fulfil their QERLCs jointly to do so by forming a 'bubble' equal to their collective QERLCs and then re-allocating their commitments

---

[178] See FCCC/CP/2002/2, Agreement between the European Community and its member states under Article 4 of the Kyoto Protocol.

[179] See section 3 on the EU declaration on Article 4.2 (a) and (b) in its instrument of ratification of the Convention, stating its commitments will be fulfilled in the Community as a whole through action by the Community and its member states, within the competence of each.

[180] See chapter 6, section 2.

among themselves.[181] Inclusion of this provision was necessary to accommodate the EU's adoption of its collective target at Kyoto based on its internal 'burden-sharing' arrangements which allow some of its member states to increase their emissions by up to 27 per cent whilst others assume more stringent reductions.[182] Pressure from JUSSCANNZ led to Article 4 being open, however, to any group of Parties, not just to regional economic integration organisations like the EU. An important additional reason for the inclusion of Article 4 was the need to allocate responsibility for achievement of binding targets in a legally clear manner, particularly where changes in REIO membership were anticipated, such as those resulting from EU enlargement.

Article 4 requires any group of Parties that want to achieve QELRCs jointly to conclude a written agreement setting out the respective emission level allocated to each Party by the agreement. The terms of the agreement must be notified to the Secretariat upon ratification, acceptance or approval, or accession by the Parties to the agreement. The Secretariat shall inform other Parties of the terms of any agreement which must remain in operation for the duration of the commitment period. To deal with the EU enlargement point, Article 4.2 provides that any alteration in the composition of a REIO, after the adoption of the Protocol, 'shall not affect existing commitments under this Protocol'.

On responsibility for failure to achieve the total emissions levels specified by the agreement, Article 4 distinguishes between two situations. If the Parties to the agreement are not operating under a REIO which is itself a Party to the Protocol, Articles 4.4 and 4.5 specify that each Party to the agreement is responsible for 'its own level of emissions as set out in the agreement' and that, in the event of joint responsibility declared under Article 4 and a subsequent failure to achieve their total combined level of emission reductions, each Party to the agreement shall be responsible for its own level of emissions as set out in the agreement.

Article 4.6 specifies that where a REIO is itself a Party (and so far only the EU falls into this category), the REIO shall be responsible together with each of its member states, as well as each individual member state also being responsible for the failure to achieve its level of emissions as notified in an agreement. This provision recognises the mixed competence of the EU in relation to climate change.

The EU's agreement pursuant to Article 4 was submitted to the Secretariat and notified to Parties in June 2003.[183] The agreement reallocates the QELRCs listed in Annex B as agreed by the EU Council in June 1998 and spells out who will bear

---

[181] Haites, 2000.

[182] 1990th Council Meeting, Environment, Brussels, 3 March 1997, 6309/97 (Press 60). On the history of EU burden-sharing, see Ringius, 1999.

[183] FCCC/CP/2002/2.

responsibility for their achievement in accordance with Article 4.6. This agreement is legally binding on member states under EU law, whether or not the Kyoto Protocol enters into force.[184] The agreement also contains the declaration of competence required pursuant to Article 24.3 of the Protocol. Finally, the agreement gives information about how the Community will calculate its base-year emissions to establish its members' assigned amount.

[184] FCCC/CP/2002/2.

6

Flexibility mechanisms

1   Introduction

The costs of climate change and adaptation to its impacts are unknown.
After sinks, the biggest factor influencing Annex I Parties' compliance cost is the
geographic availability of mitigation measures. As location of abatement measures
is climatically irrelevant, global cost-effectiveness prescribes that the cheapest
mitigation options should be undertaken wherever they are located. The principle
that groups of Parties with differential compliance costs could cooperate in jointly
implementing mitigation measures beyond their territories was accepted in the
Convention.[1] But widely divergent interpretations of what this principle should
mean in practice led Parties to launch the pilot phase of activities implemented
jointly.

The Protocol provided clarity by including three innovative mechanisms allowing Annex I Parties to achieve their Article 3.1 mitigation commitments by undertaking, financing or purchasing emissions reductions generated overseas. These
mechanisms are joint implementation (JI), the Clean Development Mechanism
(CDM) and emissions trading (ET) pursuant to Articles 6, 12 and 17 of the Protocol
respectively.[2] For those unfamiliar with the Kyoto mechanisms, table 6.1 provides
an overview of their key features.

Although inclusion of flexibility mechanisms enabled countries to commit
to more environmentally stringent targets at Kyoto than might otherwise have
been the case, their application to the international context on so large a scale was

---

[1] FCCC Article 3.3, chapter 1, and FCCC Article 4.2 (a) and (d), chapter 5.
[2] Burden-sharing of Article 3 commitments among REIOs pursuant to Article 4 of the Protocol
is discussed in chapter 5, section 5.17.

Table 6.1   *Kyoto flexibility mechanisms overview*[3]

| Name | Project-related mechanisms | | Non-project mechanism |
	Article 6/Joint Implementation	Clean Development Mechanism	Emissions trading
Parties (subject to participation/ eligibility criteria)	Annex I–Annex I	Non-Annex I–Annex I	Annex I–Annex I
Authorised Legal Entities (dependent on Party eligibility criteria	Yes	Yes	Yes
Kyoto unit	ERUs	CER, tCER and lCER	AAUs
Unit fungibility	Yes	Yes	Yes
Unit use restrictions	Refrain from using ERUs from nuclear facilities	CERs from afforestation and deforestation not to exceed 1% of Party's assigned amount. Annex I are to refrain from using CERs from nuclear facilities	No restrictions
Unit carry-over	Yes – 2.5% of a Party's assigned amount	Yes – 2.5% of a Party's assigned amount	Yes – without restriction
Unit availability	2008 to 2012	From 2000	2008 to 2012
Coverage of activities	All Kyoto eligible sources and LULUCF activities	All Kyoto eligible sources with priority to small-scale; sinks limited to afforestation/ reforestation	Not applicable
Responsible institutions	Accredited Independent Entities, Article 6 Supervisory Committee, COP/MOP	Designated Operational Entities, Executive Board, COP and COP/MOP	National Registries, Transaction Log, COP/MOP

[3] Adapted from Wollansky and Freidrich, 2003.

Table 6.1   (*cont.*)

| Name | Project-related mechanisms | | Non-project mechanism |
	Article 6/Joint Implementation	Clean Development Mechanism	Emissions trading
Adminstratrative support	Secretariat	Secretariat	Secretariat
Administrative costs	To be borne by Participants	To be borne by Project Participant and DEOs	No specific provisions

without precedent and raised novel moral, equity and environmental considerations explained in box 6.1.[4] Most of these could not be resolved at Kyoto. Fleshing out the details of the Kyoto mechanisms formed a central part of the negotiations leading to the Bonn Agreement and the Marrakesh Accords.

There are five main COP-7 decisions which define the principles, nature, scope and operational modalities for the three mechanisms.[5] Since Marrakesh, additional rules have been adopted by COP-8 and detailed technical guidance subsequently agreed by the Executive Board of the CDM (EB) on its own operational procedures as well as substantive matters needed to facilitate the prompt start of the CDM. Modalities and procedures regarding inclusion of LULUCF activities in the CDM were adopted at COP-9.[6] Even without including the mechanism-related rules covered in COP decisions dealing with reporting, review and compliance, mechanism rules agreed to date alone run to nearly 150 pages.

This chapter explains the most salient aspects of the COP decisions on the mechanisms and the adopted modalities set out in their annexes, including

---

[4] Yamin, 2000.

[5] Decision 15/CP.7 covers matters relevant to all three mechanisms, Decision 16/CP.7 covers JI, Decision 17/CP.7 covers the CDM and Decision 18/CP.7 deals with ET. Decision 19/CP.7 defines accounting modalities, including how transactions under the mechanisms may proceed and ultimately count towards compliance. For legal reasons explained below, all five decisions are set out in the form of COP decisions containing annexes that set out recommended draft decisions for the first COP/MOP to adopt. The terms 'mechanism modalities' or JI, CDM or ET modalities will be used in this chapter to refer to the annexes attached to the COP decisions which set out the recommended modalities for the COP/MOP.

[6] Decision 19/CP.9, Modalities and Procedures for afforestation and reforestation project activities under the CDM in the first commitment period of the Kyoto Protocol.

agreements reached on mechanisms issues at COP-8 and COP-9. Because eligibility to use the mechanisms entails significant linkages with the reporting and review requirements of the regime, as well as the procedures and mechanisms for compliance under the Protocol, readers unfamiliar with these aspects of the climate change regimes should read chapters 11 and 12.

Box 6.1   Flexibility mechanisms: origins, evolution and concerns

In the late 1980s a number of OECD countries began using market-based instruments such as trading, taxes and charges in environmental policy, in place of, or as a supplement to, traditional command and control techniques to reduce reliance on highly prescriptive technology-based regulations that had tended to stifle innovation. Two kinds of trading concepts are of significance to climate change: 'cap-and-trade' schemes which involve setting a limit on total emissions, distributing permits equal to allowable emissions and requiring entities to hold sufficient permits to cover their emissions during a given compliance period; and 'baseline-and-credit' schemes whereby participants receive 'credits' for emissions reductions achieved against a hypothetical baseline. A common feature of both schemes is that a financial asset, called a permit or an allowance, is created by governments, which is usually given (rather than auctioned) to polluters in a cap-and-trade scheme or issued in the case of baseline-and-credit schemes upon demonstration that emissions have been reduced. Because it is financially valuable, the allocation of the permit generates political 'buy in' and lessens the 'pain' of pollution control. The sulphur trading programme under the 1990 US Clean Air Act Amendments typifies 'cap-and-trade' trading and was held up as an innovative precedent for climate negotiators.

The Convention's use of the term 'joint implementation' referred to both kinds of trading scheme as well as a multitude of other forms of international cooperation, making it difficult to operationalise any one of them. Additionally, the creation of permits and credits at the international level, in particular distributional issues concerning their allocation among Parties with highly differentiated legal commitments, raised a number of fundamental moral, equity and environmental considerations. Many European and developing countries were, and remain, morally troubled by the notion that richer countries should be allowed to buy their way out of taking domestic action. Others emphasised that trading might entrench existing inequalities by endorsing the 'right to emit' of those historically responsible for the greatest share of greenhouse gas emissions whilst shifting the actual burden of pollution control to those who have contributed little, the South.

Environmental effectiveness concerns were also raised because, unlike domestic trading schemes which rely on high penalties and strict enforcement to deter non-compliance, monitoring, tracking and verifying GHG emissions in an international context is far more complex. Accurate and timely self-reporting by governments in the absence of an international authority enforcing compliance does not have a good track record. Because under the Convention many Annex I Parties had failed to keep pace with their reporting commitments, these considerations fuelled concerns that trading mechanisms that required governments to keep tabs on thousands of emission sources would prove too taxing for many governments and might give rise to fraudulent transactions. Additionally, the lack of stringent Kyoto targets for a number of EITs, such as the Russian Federation and Ukraine, gave rise to concerns that such countries might sell their surplus allowances. Such surplus allowances, which bore no relation to climate mitigation policies, were known as 'hot air' or 'paper tonnes', and could be used by richer, buyer countries to avoid making politically unpopular domestic reductions.

2   Activities implemented jointly

Article 4.2 (a) and (b) of the Convention mandates Annex I Parties to adopt policies and measures to limit their GHG emissions to achieve the 'quantified aim'. Article 4.2 (a) states that such Parties 'may implement such policies and measures jointly with other Parties', but this is subject to criteria the COP might adopt under Article 4.2 (d) regarding joint implementation. Cooperative measures to reduce or sequester GHGs can be undertaken between different governments, businesses and NGOs without sanction from the COP, so the intent of Article 4.2 (d) was to provide an internationally accepted way for Parties to earn credits for undertaking or financing joint measures. Because the Convention obliges Annex II Parties to provide funding and technological assistance to developing country Parties to help the latter meet their obligations, identifying which activities should be considered by Annex II Parties as fulfilling their mandatory Convention commitments and which should earn credits is problematic and continues to prove challenging in the context of consideration of how the issues of 'additionality' of AIJ or CDM projects should be assessed.

2.1   *Pilot phase*

COP-1 could not reach agreement on the fundamental issue of in what circumstances Annex I Parties should claim, and whether developing countries without emissions targets could grant, such credits. Accordingly, COP-1 agreed that 'no credits shall accrue to any Party' as a result of AIJ activities during the pilot phase. This phase was to be comprehensively reviewed and was originally scheduled to end not later than the end of 1999. The time-frame was chosen to allow the pilot phase to support sufficient 'learning by doing' as well as to enable completion of Protocol negotiations addressing thorny political issues about the overall size and burden-sharing agreements relating to Annex I Parties' emissions targets which many developing countries and the EU regarded as relevant to determining the overall balance of domestic and overseas mitigation abatement efforts by Annex I Parties.

COP-5 reviewed the pilot phase and decided to continue it beyond 1999, encouraging Parties that had not yet had experience with projects to take up such opportunities. Decisions to continue the pilot phase have also been adopted by COP-7 and COP-8. Until COP-8 Parties participating in AIJ projects were requested to provide AIJ information to the Secretariat to enable it to prepare an annual synthesis document considered by each COP. To simplify and reduce such reporting, COP-8 decided that in future the synthesis document should be prepared on a biennial basis, rather than on an annual basis as originally provided in Decision 5/CP.1.

2.2   *Uniform reporting format*

Decision 5/CP.1 called on the SBs to develop a framework for Parties to report in a transparent and credible manner on 'the possible global benefits and the national economic, social and environmental impacts as well as any practical experience gained or technical difficulties encountered'. Such reporting was critical for determining how baselines that met the financial and environmental 'additionality' criteria set by COP-1 (discussed below) were to be assessed. Because participation in AIJ is voluntary, such reporting was, and remains, distinct from information provided in Parties' national communications. COP-3 adopted the first 'uniform reporting format' (URF) which Parties could use to report, on a voluntary basis, on their AIJ projects.[7] A revised URF was adopted by COP-8 which incorporates experience with the first URF and takes into account the kind of information

---

[7] Decision 10/CP.3.

that would in future be needed to assess whether AIJ projects can meet eligibility criteria for CDM and JI.[8]

2.3   *Substantive AIJ criteria*

Although COP-1 could not reach agreement on credits, Decision 5/CP.1 was groundbreaking in setting out criteria for AIJ, many of which fed into, or were directly incorporated into, CDM and JI modalities. Experience of developing a URF for reporting of AIJ projects assisted negotiations on reporting and methodological issues related to the CDM and JI projects. The substantive criteria for undertaking AIJ projects remain as set out in Decision 5/CP.1 and provide as follows:

- AIJ in no way modifies the commitments of each Party under the Convention and AIJ projects are supplemental to, and only one subsidiary means of achieving, the Convention's objective;
- AIJ can proceed among Annex I Parties and with non-Annex I Parties that so request;
- Participation in AIJ for all Parties is voluntary and requires prior acceptance, approval or endorsement by the Governments of Parties concerned;
- AIJ projects should meet the 'environmental additionality' criterion which is policy shorthand for saying they 'should bring about real, measurable and long-term environmental benefits related to the mitigation of climate change that would not have occurred in the absence of such activities'; and
- AIJ projects should meet a 'financial additionality' criterion which states that 'financing of AIJ shall be additional to the financial obligations of [Annex II Parties] within the framework of the financial mechanism as well as to current ODA flows'.

The environmental and financial additionality criteria are incorporated in JI and the CDM modalities and explained in greater detail below. Decision 5/CP.1 does not limit the scope of AIJ. Thus, all types of projects that reduce or sequester emissions can, in principle, be AIJ projects. There are currently over 150 AIJ projects formally communicated to the Secretariat, with a large share being in EITs.[9]

2.4   *Relationship to Kyoto mechanisms*

Although the modalities and procedures for the CDM and JI do not mention AIJ explicitly, COP-7 agreed the following. For the CDM, 'a project activity starting as of the year 2000, and prior to the adoption of this decision, shall be eligible for validation and registration as a Clean Development Mechanism project

---

[8] Decision 20/CP.8.   [9] FCCC website. See also *JI Quarterly*.

if submitted for registration before 31 December 2005. If registered, the crediting period for such project activities may start prior to the date of registration but no earlier than 1st January 2000.'[10] COP-9 clarified that this wording inadvertently excluded the possibility for projects starting between the date of adoption of Decision 17/CP.7 and the date of the first registration of CDM project activities to be able to earn CERs and accordingly decided that such CDM project activities may use a crediting period starting before the date of its registration if the project activity is submitted for registration before 31 December 2005.[11]

JI projects starting as of the year 2000 may be eligible as Article 6 projects if they meet the requirements of the guidelines for the implementation of Article 6 of the Kyoto Protocol as agreed at COP-7. ERUs shall only be issued for a crediting period starting after the beginning of the year 2008 (as before then there is no assigned amount from which they can be issued).[12]

These provisions mean that there is no automatic conversion of AIJ projects to CDM or JI projects as some Parties had wished but that each project must fulfil the criteria set out for CDM and JI projects agreed at COP-7. The crediting start date of 2000 for CDM activities operationalises the provisions of Article 12.10 of the Protocol, which states that CERs obtained during the period 2000 to 2008 can be used by Annex I Parties for compliance with Article 3 commitments. There is no such equivalent start date for JI activities under Article 6. Thus AIJ projects carried out among Annex I Parties that qualify as JI projects will only generate ERUs from 2008 onwards because assigned amount does not exist before 2008.

3   Cross-cutting mechanisms issues

The Kyoto mechanisms share a number of cross-cutting features. Many of these are set out in Decision 15/CP.7, which deals with the principles, scope and nature of all three mechanisms. Others with a larger technical component are also included in rules relating to the accounting of assigned amount set out in Decision 19/CP.7, registry-related rules adopted by COP-8 and information-related reporting and review requirements pursuant to Articles 7 and 8 of the Protocol.

3.1   *Adoption and review of mechanism modalities*

Given that the COP and the COP/MOP have their own distinctive legal authority, there was a shared desire to provide a smooth legal pathway from the adoption of mechanism modalities by the COP to their eventual endorsement by

---

[10] Decision 17/CP.7, paragraph 13.   [11] Decision 18/CP.9, paragraph 1.
[12] Decision 16/CP.7, JI Modalities, paragraph 5.

the COP/MOP.[13] The transition is achieved by embedding the modalities for the mechanisms in the form of annexes that are attached to draft decisions that the COP recommends the COP/MOP to adopt. In the case of the CDM, the COP will assume the responsibilities of COP/MOP until the entry into force of the Protocol.

The review of mechanism modalities had to balance the need to provide legal and regulatory certainty to Parties and legal entities that wanted to use the mechanisms with the desire to make improvements based on the inevitable 'learning by doing' that will take place as Parties gain practical experience of these innovative mechanisms. Additionally, because all three mechanisms are related to the achievement of binding Article 3 Kyoto commitments, the timing and legal nature of revisions to mechanism modalities was also an issue. The modalities for all three mechanisms contain virtually identical review provisions which provide that:

- any future revisions of the modalities, rules and procedures for each mechanism shall be decided in accordance with the rules of procedure of the COP/MOP as applied;
- the first such review will be carried out no later than one year after the end of the first commitment period, based on recommendations by the SBI, drawing on technical advice from SBSTA, as needed; and
- further reviews shall be carried out periodically thereafter.[14]

The JI and CDM modalities make clear that any changes resulting from overall reviews shall not have retrospective effect for projects that have already commenced.

3.2   *Equity issues*

In response to moral and equity concerns (box 6.1), the Marrakesh Accords state that the 'Kyoto Protocol has not created or bestowed any right, title or entitlement to emissions of any kind on Parties included in Annex I'.[15] The US Clean Air Act contains a similar provision which was intended to ensure that the federal government could still take decisions about permits where this was deemed necessary to protect the public interest without having to worry about paying off polluters for possible infringement of their legal rights.[16] Although the reference in Decision 15/CP.7 is to 'emissions' rather than to the actual units created by the

---

[13] See chapter 13, section 3.1.

[14] Decision 16/CP.7, JI Modalities, paragraph 8. Decision 17/CP.7, CDM Modalities, paragraph 4 and Decision 18/CP.7, ET Modalities paragraph 2.

[15] Decision 15/CP.7, Preamble, paragraph 5 and Draft Decision – /CMP.1 (Mechanisms), Principles, nature and scope of the mechanisms pursuant to Articles 6, 12 and 17 of the Kyoto Protocol, Preamble, paragraph 5.

[16] Yamin, 1999.

Protocol, inclusion of this provision signals that Parties do not regard holdings of Kyoto units as property rights. Rather they see them simply as unitised and divisible embodiments of promises accepted by sovereign states in the context of a multilateral agreement which for that reason can be revoked, revised and altered through further negotiation.[17]

Concerns that use of the Kyoto mechanisms might entrench as well as exacerbate existing emissions inequalities by encouraging Annex I Parties to seek cheap reductions abroad led COP-7 to agree that such Parties 'shall implement domestic action in accordance with national circumstances and with a view to reducing emissions in a manner conducive to narrowing per capita differences between developed and developing country Parties while working towards achievement of the ultimate objective of the Convention'.[18] This provision will be taken into account in the review of demonstrable progress under Article 3.2 of the Protocol.[19] The Secretariat has been mandated to prepare a report on the implications of the per capita paragraph every time the review process under Article 8 of the Kyoto Protocol relating to national communications and supplementary information from Annex I Parties is completed.[20]

3.3   *Supplementarity*

Prioritising domestic action has moral as well as environmental effectiveness dimensions. The extent to which either trumped cost-effectiveness considerations and justified quantitative constraints on use of the mechanisms was one of the most divisive elements of post-Kyoto negotiations. The Marrakesh Accords provide that 'use of the mechanisms shall be supplemental to domestic actions and domestic action shall thus constitute a significant element of the effort made' by each Annex I Party in meeting its Article 3.1 commitments. The word 'significant' carries no quantitative connotations and was chosen in preference to words such as 'principal' and 'primary' which did. A qualitative assessment of whether Annex I Parties will meet the supplementarity condition was agreed and this requires Annex I Parties to submit information about their use of the mechanisms and domestic action as part of the information that must be submitted in accordance with Article 7 which will be reviewed under Article 8.[21] An additional report on how each Annex I Party is making 'demonstrable progress' under Article 3.2 of

---

[17] Werksman, 1999b.

[18] Decision 15/CP.7, Preamble, paragraph 6 and Draft Decision – /CMP.1 (Mechanisms), Preamble, paragraph 6. See also Decision 5/CP.6, Section VI.I, paragraph 4.

[19] See chapter 5, section 5.12.

[20] Decision 22/CP.7, Draft Decision – /CMP.1, Guidelines for the preparation of information under Article 7 of the Protocol, paragraph 4. See chapter 11.

[21] See chapter 11.

the Protocol will also form part of the information relevant to considering supplementarity.[22] For the first commitment period, the total additions to a Party's assigned amount resulting from eligible LULUCF projects under the CDM shall not exceed 1 per cent of base-year emissions of that Party, times five.[23] To the extent the rules limiting banking of CERs and ERUs, described below, constrain use of the Kyoto mechanisms, they could create more incentives for domestic action. Finally, questions of implementation raised by the qualitative assessment of supplementarity are to be addressed by the Facilitative Branch and cannot be addressed by the Enforcement Branch of the Compliance Committee.[24]

3.4   *Fungibility*

The term 'fungibility' embraces a range of issues relating to the nature of the initial 'assigned amount' allocated to each Annex I Party pursuant to the Protocol and the interchangeability of Kyoto units with each other and their relationship with the initial assigned amount.[25]

Articles 3.10 and 3.11 allow Parties to add to and subtract from their assigned amount ERUs generated through JI under Article 6 and AAUs under ET under Article 17. Article 3.12 on the other hand allows CERs to be acquired and added to a Party's assigned amount but does not state that Annex I Parties can transfer CERs to other Annex I Parties. The omission of the word 'transfer' from Article 3.12 was used by some developing countries to oppose CERs being traded among Annex I Parties after their initial acquisition. This also led to some of them opposing fungibility.

The Marrakesh Accords provide for full fungibility of ERUs, CERs, AAUs and RMUs.[26] Irrespective of how they are created, Kyoto units can be exchanged on a one-to-one basis with each other as Decision 19/CP.7 defines each of these units to equal one metric tonne of carbon dioxide, calculated using agreed GWPs.[27] Thus, for the purposes of compliance, these Kyoto units are equal. Units generated by CDM LULUCF activities, known as tCERs and lCERs, are equal to other Kyoto units in terms of compliance but, to address issues of permanence, are subject to a range of additional rules discussed in section 6.4.3.

Another aspect of fungibility is the differential ability to bank Kyoto units for the next commitment period. Decision 19/CP.4 limits banking of CERs and ERUs to 2.5 per cent of a Party's assigned amount and states that RMUs cannot be banked at all.[28] Thus there are restrictions on banking of all Kyoto units except AAUs. Because

---

[22] See chapter 11, section 3.8.5.   [23] Decision 11/CP.7, Annex, paragraph 14.

[24] Decision 15/CP.7, paragraph 4 and Decision 24/CP.7, Annex, paragraph 5 (b).

[25] Chapter 5, section 5.9 explains assigned amount.   [26] Decision 15/CP.7, paragraph 6.

[27] Chapter 5, section 2.1 explains GWPs.

[28] Decision 19/CP.7, Annex, Section F. See chapter 5.

there are no rules agreed otherwise, Annex I Parties will in practice be able to use enough other units for compliance purposes to meet the respective restrictions and then use AAUs for the balance.[29] Thus, the restrictions on banking have no practical impact on the fungibility of the Kyoto units.

So far as the legal nature of assigned amount and additions to it is concerned, a number of developing countries wanted to clarify the legal nature of Annex I Parties' 'assigned amount' and had thus pressed for inclusion of language stating that the Protocol does not create any rights, title or entitlement as explained above. Additionally, Parties agreed that, once recorded in the compilation and database established by the Secretariat as part of the accounting modalities under Article 7.4, the assigned amount of 'each Party shall remain fixed for the commitment period'.[30] The fixed nature of the assigned amount was also intended to address developing country concerns that the additions and subtractions of Kyoto units to the assigned amount would somehow weaken or alter the nature of Annex I Parties' legal commitments. Decision 15/CP.7, paragraph 6, provides that such additions and subtractions will take place 'without altering the quantified emission limitation and reduction commitments inscribed in Annex B to the Kyoto Protocol'.

Decision 19/CP.7 on accounting modalities provides the answer because it states that Kyoto units are not 'added to' a Party's assigned amount until it designates those units to be used for purposes of meeting its commitment – which will be done at the end of the commitment period (which for compliance purposes includes an additional period for fulfilling commitments). Prior to this point in time all Kyoto units are simply held in a national registry. Thus CERs can be freely transferred like the other Kyoto units and are as liquid as the other Kyoto units prior to being designated for compliance use. After that CERs can no longer be subtracted but other units could be in case the Party specified more units than necessary to achieve compliance with its commitment. By defining the point of 'addition' in this way, Decision 19/CP.7 aims to meet the concerns of developing countries but without practical impact on the transferability or liquidity of CERs.

3.5   *Stakeholder involvement*

Modalities for JI and the CDM contain a common definition of 'stakeholder' which means 'the public, including individuals, groups or communities affected, or likely to be affected' by the JI or CDM project.[31] To support the

---

[29] See chapter 5, section 5.11.

[30] Decision 19/CP.7, Draft Decision – /CMP.1 (modalities for accounting of assigned amounts), paragraph 2 and Annex, paragraph 9.

[31] Decision 16/CP.7, Annex, paragraph 1 (e) and Decision 17/CP.7, Annex, paragraph 1 (e).

participation of stakeholders in JI and CDM projects, the modalities for JI and CDM provide that certain types of information must be made publicly accessible. Additionally, such information is necessary because there are various points in the JI and CDM project cycle where stakeholders may intervene to ensure that decisions – whether by national authorities or international bodies – are in conformity with the modalities set out in the various COP decisions. These points of intervention, the types of information that must be available and the timing of their availability are vital for ensuring that stakeholders and others perform 'watchdog' functions for the two project-based mechanisms which, if successful, could result in thousands of projects worldwide.

Although the rules for emissions trading do not refer to stakeholders as such, rules on the establishment of national registries which will record Kyoto unit transactions provide that non-confidential information in national registries must be publicly accessible through a user interface available via the Internet that allows 'interested persons to query and view' information held in national registries.[32] NGOs and stakeholders, particularly businesses engaged in the mechanisms, will therefore play a vital function in spotting the frequency, types and implications of discrepancies that might arise, including whether the transaction log established by the Secretariat is itself functioning correctly. Modalities for constructing national registries to enhance their public accessibility have been further elaborated since Marrakesh and are to be considered further, including how issues relating to confidential data should be handled.[33]

4   Participation/eligibility requirements

Another common feature of the mechanisms is that Articles 6, 12 and 17 emphasise that Annex I Parties 'may' use the mechanisms to fulfil their Article 3.1 commitments. Although the decision to participate is entirely voluntary, once made each Party has to fulfil certain participation requirements. All the mechanisms set out certain legal and administrative provisions to ensure that Parties retain sovereign responsibility over mechanism-related transactions taking place under their jurisdiction.

All three mechanisms allow Parties to authorise private actors to participate in the mechanisms.[34] In each case the mechanism modalities specify that the Party

---

[32] Decision 19/CP.7, Annex, paragraph 44 and Decision 24/CP.8.

[33] Decision 24/CP.8. See also FCCC/TP/2002/3, Registries under the Kyoto Protocol and FCCC/TP/2002/2, Treatment of confidential information by international treaty bodies and organisations, and Decision 21/CP.9 concerning issues relating to the implementation of Article 8 of the Kyoto Protocol.

[34] Decision 16/CP.7, Annex, paragraph 29; Decision 17/CP.7, Annex, paragraph 33; and Decision 18/CP.7, Annex, paragraph 5.

that authorises legal entities shall remain responsible for the fulfilment of its obligations under the Protocol and shall ensure that such participation is consistent with the mechanism's modalities.[35] Legal entities may only transfer and acquire Kyoto units, however, where a Party itself meets the participation requirements set out in the mechanisms. From an economic perspective, the participation of entities in the mechanisms, under the responsibilities of Parties, was considered important because, whilst mechanisms open only to governments are more efficient than no mechanisms at all, mechanisms limited to governments are not as efficient as mechanisms open to a wider range of actors. This is because governmental trading equates national marginal costs but does not equalise marginal abatement costs across sources within each country and it is the latter that leads to more significant reductions in compliance costs.

All the mechanisms define minimum environmental integrity related standards that must be met by Parties that wish to participate in the mechanisms. The requirements are referred to here as 'eligibility conditions' to distinguish them from the broader legal and administrative participation requirements set out above. For Annex I Parties, these requirements will be assessed by the Enforcement Branch of the Compliance Committee.[36]

4.1   *Protocol ratification*

Whether participating as host or investor, an Annex I Party can only transfer and acquire ERUs under JI, and all kinds of Kyoto units under Article 17 emissions trading, if it is a Party to the Kyoto Protocol. This is simply because only Parties to the Protocol that have Article 3 commitments will have an 'assigned amount'. If countries that are not Parties to the Protocol, such as the US and Australia, establish national emissions trading schemes, the permits or allowances created by such national schemes will not form part of the Kyoto system.[37] Such non-Parties to the Protocol can unilaterally decide to allow the use of Kyoto units with their domestic obligations.

The CDM modalities specify that until the Protocol enters into force, all Parties to the Convention can participate in CDM projects.[38] After the entry into force of the Protocol, non-Annex I Parties may participate in the CDM only if they are Parties to the Protocol.[39] The CDM eligibility requirements for Annex I Parties are not as clear and refer to eligibility at the time when such Parties will *use* CERs for

---

[35] For emissions trading, a Party must maintain an up-to-date list of such entities and make it available to the Secretariat.

[36] See chapter 12, section 5.5.

[37] Mutual recognition arrangements between Kyoto units with non-Kyoto permits may, however, be possible. See Haites and Mullins, 2002.

[38] Decision 17/CP.7, paragraph 3.   [39] Decision 17/CP.7, Annex, paragraph 30.

compliance. Thus, whilst the CDM modalities are really focused on how Parties to the Protocol can engage in CDM activities, they neither excluded the possibility that non-Parties to the Protocol could participate in CDM project activities nor spelt out how they may do so.[40] To provide greater clarity, the CDM Executive Board at its eighth meeting clarified that, with regard to validation requirements to be checked by a designated operational entity, before entry into force of the Kyoto Protocol, all Parties to the Convention may participate in CDM project activities. Subsequently, in accordance with provisions of paragraphs 37 (a) and 40 (a) of the CDM modalities and procedures, the registration of a proposed CDM project activity can, however, only take place once approval letters are obtained from Parties to the Convention that have ratified the Kyoto Protocol.

4.2   *Designating national authorities*

Both project-based mechanisms require Parties to designate national authorities to provide oversight of JI and CDM projects. Any Party involved in an Article 6 project shall inform the Secretariat of its designated 'focal point' whilst the CDM modalities require all Parties to designate a 'national authority for the CDM'.[41] The functions of these bodies are explained below.

4.3   *Establishing assigned amount*

No Annex I Party can undertake JI and ET transactions, or use CERs towards compliance, unless its assigned amount pursuant to Articles 3.7 and 3.8 has been calculated and recorded in accordance with the annex on modalities for the accounting of assigned amount to Decision 19/CP.7.[42] To meet this condition, each Annex I Party has to submit a *pre-commitment period report* which contains all the information needed to calculate its assigned amount as well as other kinds of information necessary to demonstrate that the Party is able to monitor, track and record mechanism-related transactions. This report, to be submitted prior to the commencement of the commitment period, is subject to a thorough review by the expert review teams (ERTs) as described in chapter 11.

4.4   *National system*

No Annex I Party can undertake JI and ET transactions, or use CERs, unless it has in place by no later than 1 January 2007 a national system for the estima- tion of GHG emissions and removals pursuant to Article 5.1. Guidelines for the

---

[40] Wilkins, 2002.

[41] Decision 16/CP.7, Annex, paragraph 20; Decision 17/CP.7, Annex, paragraph 29.

[42] See chapter 5, section 5.11.

establishment of national systems and review processes which aim to ensure these are robust enough to meet mechanism requirements are explained in chapter 11.

4.5   *National registry*

Whether or not they choose to participate in the mechanisms, all Annex I Parties must designate an organisation that will serve as the 'administrator' of the national registry that must be established and maintained by all Annex I Parties as part of the accounting modalities necessary for tracking their assigned amounts.[43] These registries are a vital part of the administrative infrastructure for tracking transactions under the mechanisms and their effective functioning will thus be thoroughly reviewed and tested by ERTs as part of the pre-commitment period report review procedures.[44] Confirmation that they are working effectively will be part of the review of the pre-commitment period report, explained in chapter 11.

4.6   *Annual inventories*

Submission of accurate annual inventories, prepared in accordance with guidance adopted pursuant to Articles 5.2 and 7.1, and submitted and reviewed annually and according to schedule, together with the supplementary information described below, is the backbone of the mechanisms eligibility requirements for Annex I Parties. The threshold conditions of failing to meet Article 5.2 and 7.1 eligibility conditions are set out in Decision 22/CP.7 which provides that any Annex I Party shall fail the mechanisms' methodological and reporting eligibility requirements for JI, the CDM and ET as follows:[45]

- If it has failed to submit an annual inventory of anthropogenic emissions by sources and removals by sinks, including the national inventory report and the common reporting format, within six weeks of the submission date established by the COP;
- If it has failed to include an estimate for an Annex A source category (as defined in the IPCC Good Practice Guidance and Uncertainty Management in National GHG Inventories) that individually accounted for 7 per cent or more of the Party's aggregate emissions, defined as aggregate submitted emissions of the gases and sources listed in Annex A to the Protocol, in the most recent of the Party's reviewed inventories in which the source was estimated;
- If, for any single year during the commitment period, the aggregate adjusted GHG emissions of the Party concerned exceed the aggregate

---

[43] See chapter 11, section 3.1.   [44] See chapter 11, section 3.2.
[45] Decision 22/CP.7, Draft Decision – CMP.1 (Article 7), paragraph 3 (a)–(f).

submitted emissions, defined as aggregate submitted emissions of the
gases and from the sources listed in Annex A to the Kyoto Protocol, by
more than 7 per cent;

- If, at any time during the commitment period the sum of the numerical
  values of the percentages calculated in relation to the single year eligibility requirement (stated above) for all years of the commitment period for
  which the review has been conducted exceeds twenty; or

- If, an adjustment for any key source category (as defined in IPCC Good
  Practice Guidance) of the party concerned that accounted for 2 per cent
  or more of the Party's aggregate emissions of the gases from the sources
  listed in Annex A was calculated during the inventory review in three
  subsequent years, unless the Party concerned has requested assistance
  from the Facilitative Branch of the Compliance Committee in addressing
  this problem, prior to the beginning of the first commitment period, and
  assistance is being provided.[46]

The application of adjustments will be a critical element for many Annex I Parties,
especially some EITs, who continue to have capacity-related difficulties in submitting complete inventories.[47] If current inventory standards are anything to go by,
the application of adjustments to complete missing or inadequately justified emissions data is likely to be not an infrequent event. Where an adjustment is proposed
by an ERT and is disputed by an Annex I Party, the matter is to be determined by
the Enforcement Branch of the Compliance Committee.[48] COP-9 adopted technical guidance in the form of recommendations for COP/MOP on methodologies for
the application of adjustments by ERTs to ensure that the circumstances in which
these are proposed and applied are understood and acceptable to Annex I Parties in
the hope that this will limit the number of cases brought before the Enforcement
Committee concerning disputed adjustments.[49] Decision 20/CP.9 requests the Secretariat to establish a process to enable ERTs to gain experience with adjustments
in the inventory review process in 2003–2005 using real inventory data, subject to
the consent of the Party concerned.

The issue of guidance on how adjustments will be applied in respect of sinks
sources will be considered at COP-10, taking account of methodological work by
the IPCC (completed for COP-9 in accordance with a request from COP-7) to develop

---

[46] The reference to assistance from the Facilitative Branch is part of its 'early warning' and
proactive assistance functions designed to ensure it helps Parties fix problems to stop non-
compliance issues from arising.

[47] See chapter 11, section 3.3 and box 11.2.

[48] Chapter 11, section 3.3 explains the process for the application of adjustments to inventories.

[49] Decision 20/CP.9, Technical guidance on methodologies for adjustments under KP Article 5.2.

Good Practice Guidance for LULUCF.[50] It is important to note that the mechanism eligibility provisions make clear that, for the first commitment period, Parties will have to *submit* annual inventory data on sinks as part of their mechanism eligibility requirements. The quality of sinks data, however, will be immaterial because the quality assessment for determining eligibility is limited to the parts of the inventory pertaining to emissions of GHGs from sources/sectors listed in Annex A to the Protocol. The lack of a quality assessment of sinks data was a significant issue at Marrakesh because a number of Annex I Parties, particularly EITs, still find it difficult to provide accurate data on sinks. Parties that had wanted to link improvement of sinks data to mechanism eligibility had to be satisfied with the fact that Parties that fail to provide accurate data on sinks will only be allowed to issue RMUs in respect of sinks on which they have reported adequately – a provision which provides some degree of environmental integrity but which creates no incentives for general improvement of sinks data as a whole.[51]

4.7   *Supplemental information*

Submission of supplementary information on assigned amount pursuant to Article 7.1 by Annex I Parties and adherence to guidelines for accounting of assigned amount adopted pursuant to Article 7.4 are eligibility requirements for all three mechanisms. The supplemental information to be included is set out in the KP reporting guidelines in Decisions 22/CP.7 and 22/CP.8, and in Decision 19/CP.7, and is explained in chapter 11. Questions of implementation relating to information about how an Annex I Party is striving to implement its Article 3.14 commitments are not an eligibility condition for the mechanisms.[52]

4.8   *Commitment period reserve*

The requirement to establish and maintain a CPR is set out in Decision 18/CP.7 on emissions trading. Although it is not formally expressed as an eligibility requirement for all mechanisms, provisions relating to it must be adhered to if a Party is to engage in mechanisms transaction in conformity with Decision 18/CP.7. The CPR is discussed further below.

4.9   *Eligibility assessment, consequences and reinstatement*

Oversight of the mechanism eligibility conditions is to be provided by the Enforcement Branch of the Compliance Committee in accordance with Decision 24/CP.7.[53] Enforcement Branch procedures and timetables for how mechanism eligibility will be assessed are explained in chapter 12.

---

[50] Decision 21/CP.7, paragraphs 2–4.   [51] Decision 19/CP.7, Annex, paragraph 26.
[52] See chapters 5 and 9.   [53] See chapter 12.

A determination of non-eligibility by the Enforcement Branch leads automatically to the suspension of eligibility to use the flexibility mechanisms by the Party concerned.[54] Such a determination cannot be appealed to the COP/MOP in any circumstance.[55] The consequence of ineligibility is that the ineligible Annex I Party (and any legal entities it had authorised to participate in the mechanisms under its own authority) cannot undertake transactions dealing with Kyoto units. The range of transactions that an ineligible Party is barred from undertaking is mechanism-specific because Decision 24/CP.7 states that the suspension 'is to be in accordance with the relevant provisions' under Articles 6, 12 and 17. Thus an Annex I Party that does not meet the eligibility criteria for JI is still able to issue and transfer ERUs using the 'Track 2' procedure, provided it meets some of the eligibility criteria set forth in Decision 16/CP.7. For ET, a suspension of eligibility appears to mean that no transactions relating to any of the Kyoto units can be undertaken until eligibility is reinstated.[56]

Because the effects of being barred from use of mechanisms could be very significant for Parties that place high reliance on use of mechanisms to achieve their Article 3 commitments, special expedited procedures were included in two places to speed up the overall assessment of eligibility by the Enforcement Branch to enable it to make positive determinations of mechanism eligibility as speedily as possible.[57]

First, Section X of Decision 24/CP.7 itself defines expedited procedures for the consideration of mechanism eligibility by the Enforcement Branch.[58] And second, in the guidelines for the review of information under Article 8, expedited review procedures have been beefed up by COP-8 relating to review of inventory and other information requirements due under the Protocol to deal specifically with cases concerning reinstatement of mechanism eligibility.[59]

Notwithstanding these expedited provisions, the eligibility requirements for all three mechanisms state that an Annex I Party will be *deemed* to be eligible once sixteen months have elapsed from the date on which it submitted the information needed to establish its assigned amount and demonstrated its capacity to account for its emissions and assigned amount under Article 7.4 *unless* the Enforcement Branch finds that it does not meet eligibility conditions, or alternatively there is earlier confirmation by the Enforcement Branch that it does not meet these conditions or that it is not proceeding with any question of implementation with respect

---

[54] Decision 24/CP.7, Annex, Section XV, paragraph 4.   [55] See chapter 12, section 5.10.
[56] Decision 18/CP.7, Annex, paragraph 2.   [57] Decision 24/CP.7, Annex, Section X.
[58] See chapter 12.
[59] Decision 22/CP.8, Annex III, paragraph 19bis. See COP-8 report, part II, FCCC/CP/2002/7/Add.3, pp. 40–2. See also chapter 11.

to that Party, and has informed the Secretariat accordingly.[60] The rules further provide that an Annex I Party will continue to meet the eligibility criteria specified for each of the mechanisms 'unless and until the Enforcement Branch . . . decides that the Party does not meet one or more of the eligibility requirements, has suspended the Party's eligibility, and has transmitted this information to the Secretariat'.[61] The sixteen-month period was chosen to take into account the time-frame for the completion of the annual review inventories and supplementary information due under Kyoto – a process which is supposed to take approximately twelve to thirteen months, if everything proceeds according to schedule.[62] The availability of adequate funding and resources for the ERTs to complete their work on schedule is thus of critical importance.

Agreement that eligibility is to be presumed unless rebutted by an actual decision of the Enforcement Branch was a contentious issue in the mechanism negotiations. The approach that the 'green light is on unless switched red' by the Enforcement Branch was included because some Annex I Parties were concerned that bureaucratic delays in the Article 8 review processes might unduly limit their (and hence their legal entities') participation in the mechanisms. Other Parties were concerned that presumed eligibility potentially could allow participation in the mechanisms to proceed without any of the environmental integrity eligibility criteria being met, even when fundamental 'questions of implementation' have been raised by ERTs. These concerns arise from the fact that the decision-making procedures of the Compliance Committee relating to voting (which allow any two members of the Enforcement Branch from Annex I Parties, or any three overall, to veto a final determination being made by the Enforcement Branch) could be used to prevent a determination of ineligibility from ever being made.[63] The integrity of Enforcement Branch procedures and the ability of its members to act as independent experts are thus critical to the environmental integrity of the Protocol and are discussed in chapter 12.

4.10   *Acceptance of compliance procedures*

At Marrakesh, Parties agreed preambular language that 'environmental integrity is to be achieved through sound modalities, rules and guidelines for the mechanisms, sound and strong principles and rules governing land use, land use change and forestry activities and a strong compliance regime'.[64] But unresolved

---

[60] Decision 16/CP.7, Annex, paragraph 22 (a); Decision 17/CP.7, Annex, paragraph 32 (a) and Decision 18/CP.7, Annex, paragraph 3 (a).

[61] Decision 16/CP.7, Annex, paragraph 22 (b); Decision 17/CP.7, Annex, paragraph 32 (b) and Decision 18/CP.7, Annex, paragraph 3 (b).

[62] See chapter 11: figure 11.3 sets out these time-frames.   [63] See chapter 12, section 5.3.4.

[64] Decision 15/CP.7, paragraph 8 and Draft Decision – /CMP.1 (mechanisms), paragraph 7.

differences about the binding nature and form of the compliance procedures that should be adopted by the COP/MOP left a number of JUSCANNZ countries unwilling to agree acceptance of the compliance procedures as an eligibility condition for use of the mechanisms.[65]

The final wording agreed at Marrakesh provides that

> the eligibility to participate in the mechanisms by a Party included in Annex I shall be dependent on its compliance with methodological and reporting requirements under Articles 5.1 and 5.2 and Articles 7.1 and 7.4 of the Protocol. Oversight of this provision will be provided by the enforcement branch of the compliance committee, in accordance with the procedures and mechanisms relating to compliance as contained in decision 24/CP.7, assuming approval of such procedures and mechanisms by the [COP/MOP] in decision form in addition to any amendment entailing legally binding consequences, noting that it is the prerogative of the [COP/MOP] to decide on the legal form of the procedures and mechanisms to compliance.

It is important to emphasise that this wording was not intended to undermine or prejudice oversight of agreed eligibility conditions by the Enforcement Branch which all Parties agree is necessary.

5   Emissions trading

Article 17 requires the COP (not the COP/MOP) 'to define the relevant principles, modalities, rules and guidelines, in particular for verification, reporting and accountability for emissions trading' amongst Annex B Parties with the proviso that such trading shall be supplemental to domestic action for the purposes of meeting the quantified commitments under Article 3. Because more substantive provisions on trading threatened adoption of the Protocol, the three short sentences of Article 17 represent all that could be agreed in Kyoto. Four years of negotiations later, the ET modalities agreed at Marrakesh barely run to two pages – evidence enough that if foundational principles can be agreed, the conceptual simplicity of emissions trading is an alluring feature. But it is one which requires binding targets, robust reporting and a strong national and international infrastructure to monitor, track, verify and compel compliance to make good its promise. The following sections provide an overview of ET under the Protocol and set out the salient features of the trading modalities agreed at Marrakesh.

---

[65] See chapter 12, section 5.11.

5.1   Overview

The key feature of Article 17 trading is that it is confined to Annex B Parties – i.e. countries with binding targets under the Protocol.[66] These Parties will have access to units of 'assigned amount' and, subject to the modalities agreed at Marrakesh, and not otherwise, they will be able to transfer and acquire these units and the full range of Kyoto units (box 6.1) from each other to fulfil their Article 3.1 commitments.[67] The purpose of ET – to meet Article 3 commitments – is important to bear in mind because it means ET is a *means* to achieve a given environmental constraint. Article 17 trading is therefore a classic example of a cap-and-trade scheme of the kind first proposed by the US in the Protocol negotiations in 1996.[68]

As with the other mechanisms, the Marrakesh Accords provide that ET has to be undertaken in accordance with modalities agreed by the COP which will be endorsed by the COP/MOP. This is significant because at Kyoto a number of JUSSCANZ countries had argued that the provisions of the Protocol gave them a 'right to trade' without further reference to the COP. On the other hand, the need to develop further trading modalities quickly was one reason why Article 17 refers to the COP, and not the COP/MOP, as the body charged with defining further trading rules; the rationale being that the COP could provide institutional authority for interim trading which Parties thought might proceed even prior to the entry into force of the Protocol in a way that is now envisaged for the CDM. Another possible rationale was the US desire to remain engaged in the development of trading modalities as a Party to the Convention even if it did not ratify the Protocol.[69]

5.2   Principles and supplementarity

The reference in Article 17 to defining the relevant 'principles' for ET was a 'code word' referring to a range of moral and equity issues and environmental concerns that had been touched upon during the Protocol negotiations but which developing countries felt had not been adequately considered (box 6.1). Decision 15/CP.7 sets out the principles, nature and scope of all three mechanisms and addresses issues relating to equity, fungibility and supplementarity which are discussed above.

5.3   Participation requirements

The reference in Article 17 to 'modalities, rules and guidelines, in particular for verification, reporting and accountability for emissions trading' relates to concerns that the emissions trading could serve the purposes of helping Parties

---

[66] Chapter 5, section 5.1 explains the terms Annex I Parties and Annex B Parties.
[67] Decision 18/CP.7, Annex, paragraph 2.   [68] FCCC/TP/2000/2, pp. 82–6.   [69] See chapter 1.

meet their Article 3 commitments and not adversely affect the environmental integrity of the Protocol. These concerns are addressed through the participation and eligibility requirements, explained above, and through the commitment period reserve, explained below.

5.4   *Commitment period reserve*

Because selling Kyoto units through emissions trading is likely to prove profitable, Article 17 creates the possibility that an Annex I Party could find itself in non-compliance with its Article 3 commitments through calculated or inadvertent over-selling, particularly where there is weak international enforcement of compliance with international commitments.[70] The concept of a commitment period reserve emerged as a compromise to address large-scale selling by specifying the minimum quantity of Kyoto units a country must have in its national registry at any time and thus limiting the scope of non-compliance. One of the challenges was to set the CPR requirements so that they would protect against non-compliance yet not be so restrictive as to limit the liquidity of the market. The Bonn Agreement provided that 'each [Annex I] Party shall maintain . . . a commitment period reserve which should not fall below 90 per cent of [its] assigned amount . . . or 100 per cent of five times its most recently reviewed inventory, whichever is the lowest'.[71] The reserve can be made up of any Kyoto units valid for that commitment period. The limits adopted would prevent large-scale non-compliance.

At Marrakesh insistence by some Parties that the word 'should' did not make *maintenance* of the CPR at 90 per cent levels mandatory resulted in the CPR related text being shifted from the eligibility section of Decision 18/CP.7 into a later portion of the text. Because lack of a mandatory level would have provided no safeguard against overselling, and thus undermined the sense of the compromise agreed in Bonn, negotiators agreed to leave the Bonn wording intact but agreed that 'a Party shall not make a transfer which would result in these holdings [of ERUs, CERs, AAUs and/or RMUs] being below the required level of the commitment period reserve'.[72]

Decision 19/CP.7 requires an Annex I Party to calculate the level of its CPR as part of the process of establishing its assigned amount. The transaction procedures set out in this Decision also make it difficult for any Annex I Party to breach the minimum level of the CPR without attracting immediate attention because the transaction log to be maintained by the Secretariat will verify whether all transactions of Kyoto units are in conformity with the required rules.[73] If any transaction is found not to be in order, because for example it breaches the CPR limits, the log will notify the national registry concerned which is legally obliged to stop the transaction.

---

[70] Yamin et al., 2001.   [71] Decision 5/CP.6.   [72] Decision 18/CP.7, Annex, paragraph 8.
[73] Decision 19/CP.7, Annex, Section II.D.

The acquiring registry will also be notified. Any units already transferred in breach of CPR limits will be deemed invalid for compliance purposes until the level of the CPR is re-established, with Parties being given thirty days to return to the required level. All discrepancies must be forwarded to the Secretariat as part of the review process for the Party or Parties concerned under Article 8. Thus any Party that has dropped its CPR below required levels will have to address questions relating to this in the context of the review of supplementary information under Articles 7.1 and 7.4 which is conducted annually by ERTs.[74] Any Party that allows its CPR to fall below required limits without taking prompt corrective measures risks finding itself before the Enforcement Branch and in the meantime is not able to transfer Kyoto units (other than those issued and transferred under Track 2 JI explained below).

5.5   *Restraints and linkages*

Because participation in Article 17 is voluntary, an Annex I Party is free to impose restrictions on who it will trade with under Article 17 and with respect to what. For example, a Party may refuse to accept certain ERUs and CERs towards its commitments and is free to decide the amount of CERs its legal entities can acquire for use towards compliance with domestic obligations it may establish.[75] No trade law implications would appear to flow from these types of restraints because transfers of Kyoto units represent exchanges of sovereign commitments which are not covered by international trade law disciplines as these are concerned with trade restraints relating to traditional types of goods and services.[76]

Parties that can participate in Article 17 emissions trading may do so without establishing a national emissions trading scheme. They may grant authorisation to governmental bodies or authorise legal entities to participate even in the absence of a national trading scheme. Many Parties will, however, establish national trading schemes as one kind of domestic policy measure. Where such national trading schemes exist, the relationship between Kyoto units and the permit or allowance of the domestic scheme will need to be addressed.[77]

6   Clean Development Mechanism

6.1   *Overview*

Subject to meeting the participation requirements outlined above, the CDM modalities developed pursuant to Article 12 of the Protocol at Marrakesh

---

[74] See chapter 11, section 3.8.2.

[75] On CERs and ERUs generated by nuclear facilities, see validation and registration section below.

[76] Werksman, 1999c.

[77] On linking national and international trading schemes, see Haites and Mullins, 2002.

allow non-Annex I and Annex I Parties and their authorised entities to jointly undertake emission reduction and afforestation/reforestation *projects*, in non-Annex I Parties that contribute to sustainable development and result in CERs.[78] Article 12 of the Protocol therefore creates an innovative international 'baseline-and-credit' trading scheme with unprecedented levels of coverage in terms of activities and types of partnerships (box 6.1). By creating assets with market value, CERs, the CDM is intended to help channel private sector investment towards climate friendly projects that might not otherwise have taken place.

Lack of non-Annex I Parties' quantitative mitigation commitments in the CDM context creates incentives for those involved in CDM projects to inflate the amount of CERs claimed, through, for example, manipulation of counterfactual 'baseline' scenarios. Processes leading to CER issuance thus require multilateral oversight. This oversight is provided by the EB which itself draws on independent organisations to assess conformity of CDM project activities with internationally agreed modalities. An additional innovative aspect of the CDM is that a share of the proceeds from certified project activities, the CERs, is automatically deposited in the CDM Registry to fund adaptation in developing countries vulnerable to climate change and, in due course, to cover CDM associated administrative expenses.

Finally, apart from generating CERs, one strategic rationale for the CDM's inclusion in the Protocol was to provide a quantified means for non-Annex I Parties to contribute to mitigation commitments and to get a better understanding of trading mechanisms but without such Parties having to take on legally binding mitigation targets. Participation by developing countries in the CDM is thus part of their broader efforts to contribute to climate mitigation in a manner which provides for 'learning by doing' whilst respecting their sustainable development priorities.

6.2   *CDM project cycle*

Article 12 of the Protocol lacked operational details specifying various actors' roles in CDM project activities. Many project cycles with different implications for actors were possible and there were many competing visions and preferences. These included the 'classic' model where an Annex I Party or its legal

---

[78] Article 12 and Decision 17/CP.7 refer to CDM 'project activities' rather than to 'projects'. The former term is conceptually broader, as 'activities' could cover policies and measures unrelated to physical projects. For convenience, this chapter uses the two terms interchangeably as, presently, current proposals for the CDM seem only to involve projects.

entities invests in projects in partnership with a developing country Party (bilateral approach), a unilateral approach where a non-Annex I Party undertakes CDM activities without an Annex I Party counterpart (unilateral CDM) and where an international financial institution or other intermediary puts together a portfolio of CDM activities on behalf of others (multilateral or portfolio approach). Like Article 12 itself, the project cycle set out in the Marrakesh CDM modalities can be tailored to fit all these approaches provided that the project concerned follows the five stages of the CDM project cycle and conforms to all the substantive requirements therein. Only projects that do so will result in the issuance of CERs by the EB into the CDM Registry.

Before any particular project can commence its journey through the project cycle, the following preliminary steps are necessary:

- Designation of a national authority, called the *Designated National Authority (DNA)*, to provide written approval of the voluntary participation of *each Party* involved in the proposed project and to confirm the project's sustainable development credentials;
- Designation of one or more *Applicant Entities (AEs)* to carry out key functions in the project cycle by the EB on a provisional basis. Once confirmed by COP/MOP, these are known as *designated operational entities (DOEs)*. DOEs must be hired on a contractual basis by project participants to perform specific functions;
- Written clarification by *Project Participants (PPs)* of their respective roles, including crucially, how CERs arising from the project are to be distributed and the communication modalities necessary for PPs to liaise with the EB and the Secretariat. PPs can be Parties or private and/or public entities authorised by a Party to participate in the project under the responsibility of the Party; and[79]
- Establishment of a *CDM Registry* by the EB to ensure the accurate accounting of the issuance, holding, transfer and acquisition of CERs by Parties not included in Annex I.[80]

The project cycle is set out in figure 6.1 below which indicates the lead institutional actor with responsibility for steps needed to progress from one stage to the next stage of the CDM project cycle. This project cycle applies to all CDM activities except for CDM small-scale project activities for which a more streamlined cycle

---

[79] See section 4 above.   [80] Decision 17/CP.7, Annex, paragraphs 64–6, and Appendix D.

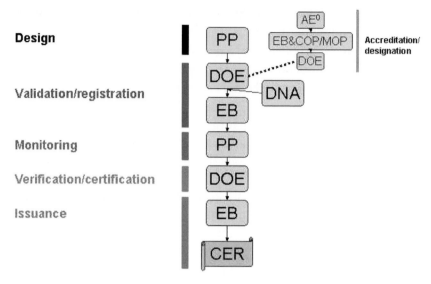

Source: UNFCCC Secretariat CDM website

Fig. 6.1   CDM project activity cycle

has been agreed (see below).[81] The five steps of the CDM project cycle are:

Step 1: Project design

A PP should design and submit information about a proposed project using a specific format. Appendix B of Decision 17/CP.7 outlines the key categories of information that 'shall' be included by PPs in the format of a document called the Project Design Document (PDD). This element of the PDD has been further refined by the Executive Board on the basis of Appendix B of the CDM modalities.[82] Submission of the PDD is necessary to commence the process for validation.[83]

Step 2: Validation and registration

Validation is the process of independent evaluation of a project activity by a DOE on the basis of the CDM-PDD to assess whether the proposed activity conforms to the CDM modalities.[84] Registration is the formal acceptance by the EB of a validated project

---

[81] Decision 21/CP.8, Annex II, Simplified modalities and procedures for small-scale CDM project activities.

[82] CDM-PDD, Version 01, in effect 29 August 2002, available at http://cdm.FCCC.int/Reference/ Documents/cdmpdd/ English/cdmpdd.doc.

[83] Decision 17/CP.7, Annex, paragraph 35.   [84] Decision 17/CP.7, Annex, paragraphs 35–52.

as a CDM project activity. Registration is the prerequisite for the verification, certification and issuance of CERs related to that project activity.

A 'pre-validation' stage is also envisaged where a project is based on a new baseline and/or monitoring methodology. In such pioneering cases, the new baseline methodology shall be submitted by the DOE to the Executive Board for review, prior to a validation and submission for registration of this project activity, with the draft PDD, including a description of the project and identification of PPs. Where methodologies previously agreed by the EB are being used, these methodologies must have been made publicly available along with any relevant guidance by the Board.

Step 3: Monitoring

Monitoring refers to the identification, collection and archiving of information necessary to design and implement a monitoring plan as required by CDM modalities. Implementation of the monitoring plan by the PP is a condition for the verification, certification and issuance of CERs.[85]

Step 4: Verification and certification

Verification refers to the periodic independent review and *ex post* determination by a DOE of the monitored reductions in anthropogenic GHG emissions by sources that have occurred as a result of a registered CDM project activity during the verification period.[86] Certification is the written assurance by the DOE that, during a specified time period, a project activity achieved the reductions in anthropogenic emissions by sources of GHGs as verified.

Step 5: Issuance of CERs

Certification results in a certification report by the DOE which forms the basis of a request by the DOE to the EB for issuance of CERs.[87] Issuance refers to the instruction by the EB to the CDM Registry Administrator to issue (i.e. create) a specified number of CERs into the pending account of the EB. The responsibility to forward CERs to the registry accounts of the PPs rests with the CDM Registry which must also forward the CERs to cover the share of the proceeds for administrative expenses and adaptation to the

---

[85] Decision 17/CP.7, Annex, paragraphs 53–60.
[86] Decision 17/CP.7, Annex, paragraphs 61–3.
[87] Decision 17/CP.7, Annex, paragraphs 64–6.

appropriate accounts. Thus the EB has no role in the final allocation of CERs to PPs as this is a purely technical act undertaken by
the CDM Registry Administrator.

6.3   *CDM institutions and procedures*

Article 12.4 provides that the 'CDM shall be subject to the authority and
guidance of the COP/MOP and be supervised by an executive board of the CDM'.
This section outlines the roles and responsibilities of various institutions and
actors in the overall oversight of the CDM, focusing on how the institutions, rules
and procedures of the CDM have given effect to Article 12.7 which requires the
COP/MOP 'to elaborate modalities and procedures with the objective of ensuring
transparency, efficiency and accountability through independent auditing and
verification of project activities'. Accordingly, apart from the actors involved in
the project cycle set out above, it describes how stakeholders and FCCC accredited
observers are involved in the CDM.[88]

6.3.1   Prompt start of CDM

Until the entry into force of the Kyoto Protocol, the COP will play a significant preparatory role on Protocol issues. The 'prompt start' of the CDM envisaged
in Article 12.10 has necessitated that, in relation to the CDM, the COP plays a
decision-making, rather than a preparatory, role. Decision 17/CP.7 at paragraphs 2
and 4, accordingly provides that the COP 'shall assume the responsibilities of the
COP/MOP' as set out in the CDM modalities and that the EB and any DOEs 'shall
operate in the same manner' as specified in the CDM modalities, i.e., as if the Protocol had entered into force. All the decisions taken by the COP, the EB and DOEs
are intended to be confirmed and given full retrospective effect by the COP/MOP
upon the Protocol's entry into force, including issuance of CERs. For clarity, the
remainder of this chapter refers to the role of the COP/MOP but readers should
bear in mind that presently the COP is acting as the COP/MOP.

6.3.2   COP/MOP

The COP/MOP has ultimate authority over the CDM as a whole. Other than
fundamental procedural matters of political relevance, such as amendment or
elaboration of the rules of procedure of the EB, over which the COP/MOP retains
decision-making powers, the CDM modalities confine the role of the COP/MOP
essentially to examining broader strategic issues relating to the CDM, such as the
geographical spread of projects and of DOEs and arranging funding of CDM project

---

[88] See chapter 3, section 3 and chapter 14, section 3.2.

activities for those in need of assistance (discussed under funding issues below). Because only the COP/MOP has the necessary legal authority, it also takes formal decisions involving external bodies, such as the designation of DOE.[89]

So far as the relationship between the COP/MOP and the EB is concerned, the COP/MOP shall give 'guidance' to the EB on recommendations made to the COP/MOP by the EB as well as on the basis of annual reports submitted from the EB.[90] This formulation means that the COP/MOP is not intended to be involved in the day-to-day administration of the CDM or to re-open matters which the CDM modalities define as functions to be exercised by the EB. This division of labour was not readily accepted by a number of developing countries, particularly oil-exporting developing countries, as they wanted the EB either to formulate recommendations which the COP/MOP should decide and/or allow matters decided by the EB to be appealed to the COP/MOP. These views did not prevail because the lack of majority-voting decision-making rules for the COP/MOP would have meant PPs could not be certain that any agreement would ever be reached by the COP/MOP, or even if it was, would have resulted in lengthy delays.

6.3.3   Executive Board

Apart from the mention in Article 12.4 stating that, subject to guidance from the COP/MOP, the Executive Board should supervise the CDM, Article 12 mentions only one other function for the EB: the provision of guidance on the involvement of private and/or public entities. Decision 17/CP.7 elaborates the functions, composition and rules of procedure for the EB. The creation of a limited membership body with substantive decision-making functions *and* majority voting was a breakthrough in the Bonn Agreements as until then Parties had been unable to agree composition and voting issues in relation to other bodies.[91] Because the EB is the first of the Marrakesh Accord bodies to commence operation, its rules of procedure and working practices are under greater scrutiny and will, in all probability, develop further with more experience. The iterative nature of the additional rules adopted by the Board is reflected in guidance provided by COP-8 which adopted the Board's rules of procedure but encouraged the Board 'to keep its rules of procedure under review, and if necessary, make recommendations . . . of any amendments or additions aimed at safeguarding its efficient, cost-effective and transparent functioning'.[92]

---

[89] See chapter 13.   [90] Decision 17/CP.7, Annex, paragraphs 2–4.

[91] The COP bureau, explained in chapter 13, section 2.1, and the CGE, explained in chapter 11, section 4.4, are advisory and/or procedurally orientated bodies.

[92] Decision 21/CP.8, paragraph 1.

Functions   The Board's main functions are to accept validated projects formally as CDM projects, issue CERs and accredit operational entities provisionally, pending their formal designation by the COP/MOP. These functions, however, are carried out on the basis of rules and guidelines approved by the COP/MOP. The Marrakesh Accords include a number of procedural rules relating to the operation of the Board which were supplemented through a full set of rules of procedure elaborated by the Board and adopted (with some amendments) by COP-8.[93]

The operational functions of the EB involve close and direct liaison not only with Parties and IGOs, but also with businesses, project developers, NGOs and other private entities involved in implementing CDM projects. To be effective, the EB has therefore had to adopt a more 'business-like' approach than that commonly seen in other intergovernmental organisations. The environmental integrity of the CDM, and potentially of the Protocol, could come to depend on the quality of decisions made by the Board. Finally, because its work involves financial investments worth millions of dollars, it must be seen to be acting in an impartial manner. For this reason special requirements have been built in to safeguard commercially confidential information that members of the EB come across during their duties as well as after their term has expired.[94]

Membership   The Board is composed of ten members from Parties to the Kyoto Protocol, including one from each regional group plus one from the small island developing states (mirroring the COP Bureau formula), along with two representatives of Annex I Parties and two of non-Annex I Parties. In addition, the Marrakesh Accords specify that the formula will be applied taking into account the current practice in the COP Bureau, an implicit reference to the representation of oil-exporting developing countries through one of the groups. Given that three of the five regional groups are almost exclusively composed of developing countries, this formula ensures a greater representation of developing countries in the EB. In an innovative move aimed at accommodating the high demand for representation on the EB, each full member is accompanied by an alternate from the same group. Alternates enjoy most of the rights of members, but not the right to vote. The addition of alternates has proved to be an especially useful resource to draw upon because the Board has established a number of specialist panels and liaison points and the intensity of meetings (six per year) means not all members have been able to attend all meetings. References to 'members' below therefore also apply to 'alternates', unless otherwise specified.

---

[93] Decision 21/CP.8, Annex I, Rules of Procedure of the EB, hereafter 'CDM Rules'.
[94] Decision 17/CP.7, Annex, paragraph 6.

Members are nominated by their groups and elected by the COP/MOP. As with other elected posts, Parties will be required to give active consideration to the nomination of women for the EB to improve the gender balance of FCCC and KP elected institutions.[95] The EB elects its own Chair and Vice-Chair at its first meeting each year, with one being from an Annex I Party and one from a non-Annex I Party, and the positions rotating annually between the two groups.[96] The Chair's functions inscribed in the EB's rules of procedure are very similar to those set out for the COP President in the COP's Rules of Procedure, described above. The Vice-Chair's main function is to replace the Chair, should s/he be absent.

Members of the EB are elected for a period of two years, and are eligible to serve for a maximum of two terms.[97] They must 'possess appropriate technical and/or policy expertise' (although the nature of such expertise is not specified). Importantly, they must act in their personal capacities, a departure from other bodies under the Convention where members of bodies act as government representatives. To ensure financial integrity and independence, EB members must not have any 'pecuniary or financial interest' in any CDM project or designated operational entity. Additionally, EB members are forbidden from disclosing any confidential or proprietary information relating to their work, including after their term of office has expired. All EB members must take a written oath of service confirming their adherence to the above-mentioned stipulations before assuming their duties.[98] In addition, the Board may suspend any member, and recommend to the COP/MOP that his/her service be terminated, if that member is found to be in breach of the above provisions, or fails to attend two consecutive EB meetings without proper justification.[99] However, the member concerned is given the right to a hearing, and the matter must be put to a vote within the EB.

---

[95] Decision 36/CP.7. See chapter 13, section 2.3.

[96] To enhance continuity, Decision 18/CP.9 adopted by COP-9 amended rules 4 and 12 of the CDM Rules to allow the Chair and Vice-Chair to be in office between the election of new members and alternates and the first meeting of the EB in a calendar year.

[97] Service as an alternate does not count, however, towards the term of office of a member. An alternate may, therefore, serve two consecutive terms and then be elected as a full member for a further two consecutive terms, and vice versa. This allows alternates to 'train up' as well as providing an important measure of continuity, although it does mean Parties not represented on the Board may have to wait longer to get a chance to be elected to the Board.

[98] CDM Rules, rule 10.2 for the text of the oath of service.

[99] This provision aims to ensure the effective functioning and full representation of the Board and to ensure that Board members know what is expected of them and are fully committed to their role from the start. It reflects problems encountered in other intergovernmental arenas (e.g. the IPCC), where Bureau/committee members have routinely failed to attend meetings.

Board meetings   The EB must meet at least three times a year, where possible in conjunction with sessions of the regime bodies. It actually met twelve times from 2001 to 2003 – six times per year (see below). The cost of participation by developing country members and their alternates as well as other Parties eligible under the FCCC is to be covered by the budget of the EB.[100] Details of these costs are provided in the EB second report to COP-9. Desire to reduce costs has led to innovate ways of the Board meeting 'virtually' and using the Internet to facilitate decision-making (see section below on voting).

The Chair, assisted by the Secretariat, drafts the provisional agenda for each meeting, which is agreed by the EB at its previous meeting. Members may, however, propose additional items up to four weeks before the start of the meeting, with the provisional agenda then circulated to members by the Secretariat at least three weeks before the meeting's opening. All documents for the EB are first sent to members two weeks before each meeting, and then posted on the Secretariat website, subject to confidentiality provisions. Before a meeting of the EB can start, a quorum must be present, consisting of at least two-thirds of the members (not alternates), including a majority of Annex I and non-Annex I Party members.[101] The working language of the Board is English but all decisions of the EB must be made publicly available in all six UN languages.[102]

The EB began its work as soon as the modalities and procedures for the CDM were decided upon through the Marrakesh Accords, with an organisational meeting held immediately after COP-7. Its work programme and decisions are set out in the two annual reports submitted by the EB to COP-8 and COP-9.[103] On the basis of these reports, COP-8 approved the rules of procedure of the EB and the simplified modalities and procedures for small-scale CDM projects (SCC) which are to be found at Annex I of Decision 21/CP.8. This Decision also provided further guidance on the EB's work, with additional guidance being provided by COP-9.[104]

Observers and stakeholders   According to both the Marrakesh Accords and the CDM rules of procedure, meetings of the EB are 'open to attendance, as observers, by all Parties and . . . FCCC accredited observers and stakeholders, except where otherwise decided'. In this regard, the CDM rules of procedure specify that Parties

---

[100] Decision 17.CP.7, paragraph 8 (c).

[101] Decision 17/CP.7, Annex, paragraph 14, and CDM rule 28.

[102] Decision 17/CP.7, Annex, paragraph 17, CDM rule 31.

[103] FCCC/CP/2003/2 and Add.1, Annual Report of the EB to COP (2001–2002) ('First CDM report'). FCCC/CP/2003/2, Annual Report of the EB to COP (2002–2003) ('Second CDM report').

[104] Decisions 18/CP/9 and 19/CP.9.

to the Convention that are not Parties to the Protocol may exercise the same rights as all other observers.[105]

To enhance the efficiency of the EB's work, the 'open to attendance by observers' rule has been interpreted in a novel, highly restrictive manner that runs contrary to the usual meaning given to the term 'attendance' which refers to physical presence at a meeting. In the CDM case, Parties and IGOs, along with representatives nominated by each NGO constituency, up to a maximum of fifty persons, are not permitted to enter the room where the EB is meeting but are allowed to observe the proceedings of the Board by sitting in a nearby room where the meeting is broadcast live. Observers are permitted to make presentations to the Board, on the invitation of its Chair. Meetings are, in addition, broadcast live over the Internet, without any viewing restrictions and, where EB meetings have coincided with subsidiary body sessions, the EB Chair has briefed observers after the meetings.

Voting Decisions of the EB are to be taken by consensus where possible but, if all efforts at reaching consensus have been exhausted, decisions may be taken by a three-fourths majority[106] of members present and voting; that is, members present at the meeting and casting an affirmative or negative vote.[107] The interaction of this rule with the quorum requirements described above means that in practice decisions can only be made by the Board if they have support from the majority of Annex I Parties and also from Parties not included in Annex I. Each member has one vote and alternates may not vote, unless they are acting for the member in his/her absence.[108] Interestingly, the CDM Rules go further in defining an operational meaning of consensus; that is, the Chair ascertains whether consensus has been reached, but is required to declare that there is no consensus 'if there is a stated objection to the proposed decision under consideration'.[109] This definition implies that one member can force the issue to a vote.

The CDM Rules include innovative procedures for electronic remote voting, if the Chair judges that a decision cannot wait until the next meeting.[110] A decision proposed by the Chair with an invitation to adopt it by consensus is transmitted to all members (and alternates for information), via the Board's electronic mailing list maintained by the Secretariat. A quorum of the board must confirm receipt of the message, after which point members have two weeks to formulate comments. Unless any objections are raised, the decision is deemed adopted after that time.

---

[105] CDM rule 2.14 and rules 26 and 27. The draft rules of procedure originally proposed by the EB to COP-8 were amended by the COP to add this point. This is, of course, of particular concern to the US.

[106] Decision 17/CP.7, Annex, paragraph 15, and CDM rule 29 paragraph 1.

[107] CDM rule 29, paragraph 3.   [108] CDM rule 29, paragraph 4.

[109] CDM rule 29, paragraph 2.   [110] CDM rule 30.

However, if an objection is made, the proposed decision is not adopted, and is included on the provisional agenda for the next meeting. The electronic voting procedures enable the EB to take decisions on a virtual basis, speeding up its work whilst keeping the operational costs of the Board low. These requirements also ensure that members do not prejudice the adoption of decisions by the Board by simply failing to turn up.

Panels and liaison with SBSTA   The EB is mandated to establish any 'committees, panels or working groups' that it deems necessary, and may draw on outside expertise, including from the FCCC roster of experts, taking into account the need for regional balance among the providers of such expertise.[111] A public call for experts is usually issued via the Internet to obtain a slate of candidates for the panels with 'demonstrated and recognized technical expertise',[112] and members are then appointed by the EB. The panels are served by a Chair and Vice-Chair (one each from an Annex I and non-Annex I Party) designated from among the EB members. Where the work involved is particularly technical or time-consuming, panel members are paid fees according to UN procedures.[113] The Board moved quickly to agree General Guidelines for Panels in March 2002.[114] The following panels have since been established:

- CDM Small Scale Project Activities (SCC Panel), April 2002;
- CDM Accreditation Panel (CDM-AP), June 2002, which is supported by CDM Assessment Teams (CDM-AT);
- CDM Methodologies for Baselines and Monitoring Plans (Meth Panel), June 2002.

The work of the EB is closely linked to that of the SBSTA in several areas, including, for example, the SBSTA's work on provisions for LULUCF projects. Interaction between the two bodies was called for in the CDM modalities, and has been ensured by the nomination of certain Board members to follow the work of the SBSTA in these areas, reporting to the EB on developments.[115]

6.3.4   Designated national authorities

The two main functions of a DNA are to:

- provide written approval of the voluntary participation of *each Party* involved in the project; and

---

[111] Decision 17/CP.7, Annex, paragraph 18; CDM rule 32.

[112] CDM rule 32, paragraph 2.   [113] See First CDM report, paragraphs 29 (c), 23 (a) and 21 (b).

[114] See First CDM report, section III.D.

[115] Decision 17/CP.7, paragraph 6 (e). See First CDM report, section III.D and Second CDM report, section III.F.

- obtain confirmation by the *host Party* DNA that the project activity assists it in achieving sustainable development.[116]

These requirements were drafted to take into account the fact that many Annex I Parties found the idea of approving individual projects unnecessary and laborious. Developing country Parties on the other hand insisted on formal approval of each project to ensure their officials would better be able to track and control CDM activities to conform to their national sustainable development priorities and strategies. The absence of such a requirement would have meant that private and/or public entities in the host country would have determined what was or was not sustainable development for the country as a whole. Letters of approval for each project activity by the host Party must be provided before registration of a CDM project activity by the Board.

6.3.5   Designated operational entities

The CDM project cycle makes DOEs primarily responsible for checking that CDM projects are in conformity with the CDM modalities by specifying that DOEs shall:

- validate proposed CDM project activities and put them forward for registration by the EB; and
- verify and certify reductions in emissions.[117]

Prior to anything being submitted to the EB, therefore, DOEs must be hired on a contractual basis by PPs to undertake one or other of these functions in relation to a particular project (because doing both might create conflicts of interests for a particular project, although in exceptional circumstances and upon request to the EB, a DOE can perform all these functions for a project).[118]

Although the CDM modalities contain provisions allowing the Board to review DOE actions relating to the execution of these functions, the CDM modalities envisage that in the vast majority of cases validation, verification and certification decisions taken by DOEs will be final, with the Board only getting involved in examining 'problem' CDM projects (box 6.2 explains the information and reviews relevant for such CDM projects).

Because the quality, consistency and transparency of the work done by DOEs is critical to the CDM, the modalities set out certain standards that must be met by any organisation that wants to become a DOE.[119] These standards are referred to as *accreditation standards* and are contained in Appendix A of the CDM modalities. Additional procedures specifying how applicant entities (AEs) should go about

---

[116] Decision 17/CP.7, Annex, paragraph 40 (a).   [117] Decision 17/CP.7, Annex, paragraph 27.
[118] Decision 17/CP.7, Annex, paragraph 27 (e).   [119] Decision 17/CP.7, Annex, paragraphs 20–5.

applying for DOE status have been agreed by the Board.[120] Designation of an AE can be made by the EB on a provisional basis, with COP/MOP reserving the right to confirm this status. Only once the COP/MOP has done so, is the entity actually called a DOE.

To maintain standards, the CDM modalities also specify procedures to suspend or withdraw the designation of a DOE if a review pursuant to paragraph 20 of the CDM modalities (which takes place once every three years or is triggered if a spot-check reveals relevant information) finds that the DOE no longer meets the accreditation standards. In such a case, the EB can make a status decision with immediate effect about the status of the DOE which remains in effect until a final decision is made by the COP/MOP. Projects that have been validated, verified or certified by a DOE that has subsequently been suspended are not affected unless 'significant deficiencies' in the DOE's work relating to these were found. In such cases, the EB can decide to appoint a different DOE to review those projects. If this review finds that excess CERs have already been issued, the original DOE shall acquire and transfer the equivalent amount of CERs to the CDM Registry within thirty days of the end of the review. These requirements, in particular, making DOEs liable for restoring CERs resulting from their 'bad work', are intended to keep DOEs on their toes.

Additional responsibilities and functions for DOEs are spelt out in the CDM modalities. These specify that a DOE shall:

- Be responsible for ensuring that the DOE complies with host country applicable laws when carrying out its functions;
- Demonstrate that it has no real or potential conflict of interest in the CDM project;
- Maintain a publicly available list of all CDM projects in which it is involved;
- Submit annual activity reports to the EB; and
- Make non-confidential information from CDM projects publicly available as required by the Board.

To assess whether these AEs meet the accreditation standards, the Board has set up a special panel, CDM-AP, which will go through each application, including conducting on-site visits by CDM Assessment Teams, to see if the requisite criteria

---

[120] Report of the Seventh Meeting of the EB, Annex 2, Procedures for accrediting operational entities by the EB, Version 03, January 2003, as clarified by the EB at its eleventh meeting which issued additional clarification regarding cost implications of changes to an application made by an applicant entity, set out in Annex 1 of the Report of the Eleventh Meeting of the EB, and clarification agreed by the Board regarding witnessing opportunities, set out in Annex II of the same Report.

are met. The Board has confirmed that once the CDM-AT has been undertaken for an AE, the AE can propose a new methodology for baselines which is the first step in getting CDM projects ready for validation (see below).

Box 6.2   Information and review provisions and stakeholders and observers in the CDM project cycle

Proposing projects will require resources and time and, while the CDM is in its start-up phase, a certain amount of dedication from the pioneers. Negotiators of CDM modalities had to balance the need for a project cycle that generated legal certainty and reduced transaction costs with the need to ensure that decisions taken by the Board and the DOEs are environmentally credible, of a consistently high quality and are made in a transparent and legitimate manner. The CDM modalities balance these needs in a number of ways. First, the modalities provide for *representation* of FCCC accredited observers, stakeholders (discussed under cross-cutting issues) and Parties not on the Board at meetings of the EB (discussed above), and of course, subject to FCCC accreditation procedures, at sessions of the COP (chapter 13).

Second, the CDM modalities mandate that certain kinds of *information* must be made publicly available to allow third parties to subject aspects of the EB to greater scrutiny than might be provided if such information was given only to fellow time-pressed government delegates who may lack expertise or first-hand knowledge about particular problems. Prior to the project cycle, information provided by an applicant entity to gain DOE status must include publicly available information about its internal procedures for carrying out DOE functions, including procedures for allocation of responsibility and for handling complaints.[121] This Accreditation Procedure adopted by the Board makes clear how others actors can help the Board determine whether an AE is qualified to be designated as a DOE. As part of the validation process, the PDD must show that comments by 'local stakeholders' have been invited and were duly taken into account in designing the project;[122] the PDD must contain information provided by stakeholders as well as show how it was taken into account.[123] The PDD and

---

[121] Decision 17/CP.7, Annex, Appendix A.

[122] The PP has to observe all relevant laws, domestic and international, that may generate such a requirement. Paragraph 27 (c) states that it is the responsibility of the DOE to check that a CMD project meets these legal requirements.

[123] Decision 17/CP.7, Annex, Appendix B.

other information provided by a PP related to validation of a particular project must also be made publicly available by a DOE except for those sections which are covered by legitimate confidentiality concerns (these cannot include matters relating to additionality and the environmental impacts).[124] The DOE must allow thirty days to receive comments from Parties, stakeholders and FCCC accredited observers, make such comments publicly available and report how its has taken them into account if it decides to go ahead with requesting registration of the project. After a project has been registered, another significant provision of information requirement is at the point of verification and certification when the DOE must make the monitoring report and the verification report, which together provide the basis for calculating the amount of CERs that the DOE will request the EB issue, publicly available, as well as the final certification report itself.[125]

The third element is the provision of two sets of *formal reviews* by the EB. NGOs and stakeholders do not have direct standing to trigger these two reviews but can, of course, provide information and lobby Parties involved in the project as well as Board Members. The first review relates to validation and registration of CDM projects and is set out in **paragraph 41** of the CDM modalities. This provides that registration of a CDM project validated by a DOE becomes final after eight weeks if no request for review has been made by a Party involved in the project or at least three members of the EB. The scope of the review must be related to the validation requirements and the Board must finalise its decision about the review no later than the second meeting following the request for review. The Board has recently adopted procedures which spell out how the review pursuant to paragraph 41 may be undertaken and these are being applied provisionally by the Board pending their adoption by the COP (COP/MOP).[126] The second review relates to issuance of CERs which will be considered final fifteen days after the DOE has submitted a certification report unless a review has been triggered by a Party involved in the project or at least three Board members in accordance with paragraph 65 of the CDM modalities. The scope of this review shall be limited to issues of fraud, malfeasance or incompetence of the DOE. The request for a review must be considered by the EB at its next meeting to determine if it has merits. If so, the review must be completed within thirty

---

[124] Decision 17/CP.7, Annex, paragraphs 6, 27 (h) and 40.

[125] Decision 17/CP.7, Annex, paragraphs 62–3.

[126] Decision 18/CP.9 contains a draft recommendation to COP/MOP setting out procedures for the reviews under paragraph 41. See also Second Report to the EB, FCCC/CP/2003/2, Annex.

days following the decision to perform the review. If the EB decides that excess CERs have been issued, it shall request the CDM Registry to transfer an equivalent sum of Kyoto units to its cancellation account and these may not be used or further transferred or used for compliance purposes.

6.4   *Validation and registration requirements*

This section describes *project level requirements* that must be met if a project is to be validated by a DOE and then registered by the Board. With the exception of small-scale projects and projects relating to afforestation and reforestation (discussed below), project level validation and registration requirements are the same for *all* types of CDM projects relating to *emission sources.*

Although some Parties wanted to exclude certain project activities, such as nuclear projects, based on their views about their inherently unsustainable development credentials, these views did not prevail and, in fact, no project types are excluded from the CDM. In the case of nuclear projects, the Preamble to Decision 17/CP.7 recognises that 'Annex I Parties are to refrain from *using* CERs generated from nuclear facilities to meet their commitments under Article 3.1'.[127] Parties agreed, however, that it is the host Party's prerogative to confirm whether a CDM project assists sustainable development. Annex I Parties also have choice over whether to authorise particular legal entities to engage in nuclear CDM projects. Additionally, Annex I Parties are to refrain from using CERs that might have been generated by nuclear facilities, thus removing the economic incentive for such projects that CERs might otherwise provide.

6.4.1   Standard CDM projects

It is important to remember that a Party and its legal entities can only participate in the CDM if the *government level participation requirements*, set out above, are met. In the case of the CDM, it is the responsibility of the DOE to check that PPs meet the participation requirements relating to designation of national authorities and that all PPs meet the 'Party to the Protocol' requirements. The latter requirement has been clarified by the Executive Board and, to avoid duplication, is discussed under the participation section in the cross-cutting issues.

In addition to these participation requirements, the DOE has responsibility to review the PDD and any supporting information to confirm that a project meets

---

[127] Similar language is found in JI modalities, see section 7.7.

the following requirements:

- Comments by local stakeholders have been invited, a summary of the comments received has been provided and a report to the DOE on how due account was taken of any comments has been received from the PP;
- PPs have submitted to the DOE documentation on the analysis of environmental impacts of the project activity, including transboundary impacts, and, if those impacts are considered significant by the PP or the host Party, have undertaken an environmental impact assessment in accordance with procedures required by the host Party;
- The project activity is expected to result in a reduction of anthropogenic emissions of GHGs from sources 'that are additional to any that would occur in the absence of the proposed activity' subject to paragraphs 43–52 of the CDM modalities (box 6.4);
- If the baseline and monitoring methodologies used for the project have previously been approved by the Board, they have been made publicly available along with any guidance provided by the Board. If new baseline and monitoring methodologies are proposed, the DOE has submitted these prior to the request for validation for review by the Board and these have been approved by the Board without subsequent COP/MOP revision (box 6.3);
- Provisions for monitoring, verification and reporting are in accordance with Decision 17/CP.7, its annex and relevant COP/MOP decisions; and
- The project activity conforms to all other requirements for CDM project activities contained in Decision 17/CP.7, its annex and relevant COP/MOP decisions.[128]

Box 6.3 CDM additionality, baselines and crediting

Additionality, baselines and choice of methodologies are highly technical issues upon which the environmental integrity of the CDM depends. Article 12.5 provides that CERs should be generated from a CDM project if the emission reductions can be certified on the basis of:

- real, measurable and long-term benefits related to the mitigation of climate change; and
- reductions are additional to any that would occur in the absence of the certified project activity.

---

[128] Decision 17/CP.7, Annex, paragraph 37.

Various 'additionality tests' were proposed during the Marrakesh negotiations to prevent CERs going to projects that would happen even without the CDM. Paragraph 43 provides that a project is considered to be additional if anthropogenic emissions by sources are reduced below those that would have occurred in the absence of the registered CDM project activity. Proposals that additionality requirements should include a financial test to ensure that funding for CDM projects is additional to ODA, including to GEF contributions, proved controversial, although a reference with this intent is set out in the Preamble to Decision 17/CP.7.[129]

Paragraph 44 provides guidance on construction of baselines (which refer to estimates of what future emissions would be within the project boundary *without* the CDM project intervention) as these are crucial to deciding how many CERs will be generated by a project. What happens to emissions outside the project boundary is crucial for environmental integrity as CERs can be generated but with increased emissions outside the project boundary – an issue known as 'leakage'. The CDM modalities provide that baselines shall be established in a 'bottom-up' manner by PPs working through DOEs to propose new methodologies for the Board's approval using the 'pre-validation' procedure. Baselines are meant to be transparent, conservative and importantly *project-specific*. They must take national circumstances into account, may include scenarios where projected emissions rise above current levels and must be defined so that CERs cannot be earned for decreases attributable to *force majeure*.

Project specific baselines increase transaction costs for PPs. Multi-project baselines, or several projects using the same baseline, would reduce these. The CDM modalities try to create some degree of standardisation of approach to baseline setting by requiring PPs to select from three approaches set out in paragraph 48 and also by defining how leakage issues should be addressed by PPs. The issue of the crediting period is linked to baselines because the length of time credits can be claimed for can 'freeze' the degree of technological and other developments that can be taken into account in constructing a 'reasonable' future. The CDM modalities state that the crediting period must be either a maximum of ten years with no renewal option or a maximum of seven years but which may be renewed twice provided that for each renewable the DOE informs the EB that the original baseline is still valid.

More detailed provisions on baseline methodologies proved difficult at Marrakesh due to lack of time, conceptual differences and lack of technical

---

[129] See section 6.7 on funding of CDM.

expertise. Additional elements were developed in the form of Appendix C to the CDM modalities but there was insufficient understanding of their full implications. Thus these elements are entitled 'terms of reference for establishing guidelines on baseline and monitoring methodologies' and, though included in the CDM modalities, are not actually mentioned therein. Appendix C is referred to, however, in the 'prompt start' part of Decision 17/CP.7 concerning the COP request to the EB to prepare recommendations on any 'other relevant matter', including, but not limited to, Appendix C. In response, the EB has undertaken an extensive body of work on baseline and monitoring methodologies.

It has provided guidance and clarification on this issue in four separate guidance/clarification notes.[130] At its eleventh meeting, the Board elaborated procedures for submission and consideration of proposed new baseline methodologies.[131] To date, some sixteen proposals for new baseline and monitoring methodologies have been submitted to the Board by PPs, of which two have been approved, nine not approved and the remaining five are to be reconsidered after suggested amendments are made.[132]

These substantive requirements for the DOE are accompanied by additional procedural rules the DOE itself must comply with if it is to transmit a validation report to the Executive Board that is itself in conformity with Decision 17/CP.7. These procedural requirements state that the DOE shall:

- Prior to the submission of the validation report, obtain written approval of the voluntary participation of all Parties involved in the project and, in addition, confirmation from the host Party that the project achieves sustainable development;
- Make the PDD publicly available whilst safeguarding information deemed confidential (box 6.3);
- Receive, within thirty days, comments on the validation requirement from Parties, stakeholders and FCCC accredited NGOs and make these publicly available;

---

[130] Eleventh Meeting of the EB, Annex I, Further clarifications on methodological issues; Ninth Meeting of the EB, Annex 3, Further clarifications on methodological issues; Eighth Meeting of the EB, Annex I, Clarifications on issues relating to baseline and monitoring methodologies; and Fifth Meeting of the EB, Annex 3, Guidance by EB to the Panel on guidelines for methodologies for baseline and monitoring plans.

[131] Eleventh Report of the EB, Annex, Version 04.

[132] Second Annual Report of the EB, FCCC/CP/2003/2, paragraphs 31–9.

- After the deadline for receipt of comments, make a determination as to whether, on the basis of the information provided and taking into account comments received, the DOE will validate the project;
- Inform PPs of the DOE's decision and date, including, if the project is rejected for validation, the reasons for its rejection; and
- Where it decides to validate a project, to make the validation report, comprising the PDD, approval of host Party and comments received, publicly available upon transmission to the Board.[133]

Any project that has been rejected for validation may be reconsidered, provided, after appropriate revisions, it goes through the validation and registration steps, including the public comment requirements.

In sum, to be validated and registered as a standard CDM project, the Parties involved in the project have to meet their participation requirements, the PP and the project itself must conform with the substantive requirements spelt out in the CDM modalities, including, in this early phase, prior acceptance of baseline and monitoring methodologies, and finally the DOE itself must adhere to certain procedural requirements relating to its preparation of the validation report before this can be transmitted to the EB to trigger a valid request for registration.

6.4.2   Small-scale projects

Because Parties realised that the complexity and transaction costs of the 'standard' CDM project cycle might deter small projects and skew the CDM in favour of large-scale projects, COP-7 agreed that, as part of the CDM 'prompt start', simplified modalities and procedures should be adopted for small-scale CDM project activities (SCC projects). Based on the Board's work, COP-8 adopted such modalities and procedures explained in box 6.4.[134]

Box 6.4   Simplified modalities and procedures for small-scale
CDM projects

Decision 17/CP.7 states that the following three small-scale project activities can take advantage of simplified modalities and procedures:

- Renewable energy project activities with a maximum output capacity equivalent to up to 15 megawatts (or appropriate equivalent);

---

[133] Decision 17/CP.7, Annex, paragraph 40.
[134] Decision 21/CP.8, Annex II, Simplified modalities and procedures for small-scale CDM project activities ('SCC M & P').

- Energy efficiency improvement project activities which reduce energy consumption, on the supply and/or demand side, by up to the equivalent of 15 gigawatt/hours per day;
- Other project activities that both reduce anthropogenic emissions by source and directly emit less than 15 kilotonnes of carbon dioxide equivalent annually.

COP-8 adopted the SCC M&P contained in Annex II of Decision 21/CP.8. The EB completed the SCC M&P by agreeing the three appendices envisaged in Annex II of Decision 21/CP.8 as follows: simplified PDD (Appendix A), indicative methodologies (Appendix B) and provisions for avoiding debundling (Appendix C). The completion by the Board of this work in early January 2003 gave the green light for submission of applications for potential SCC projects. The Board further stressed that PPs may propose new SCC project activity categories and amendments/ improvements to the SCC M&P which shall be reviewed at least once a year, and that the CDM Meth Panel will continue to work on Appendix B in consultation with experts.[135]

6.4.3   Afforestation/reforestation projects

Inclusion of sinks in the CDM was controversial at Marrakesh for many political and technical reasons.[136] The Bonn Agreements brokered a compromise that only afforestation and reforestation projects shall be included in the CDM for the first commitment period, with a decision on activities to be included in the second commitment period to be negotiated in the context of these negotiations. CDM sinks activities shall be subject to the forest principles set out in Decision11/CP.7.[137] For the first commitment period, additions of CERs from sinks projects by an Annex I Party are capped at 1 per cent of its base-year emissions (times five). The implications of this cap for each Annex I Party are set out in Appendix II to this book.

Because Article 12 of the Protocol and the CDM modalities themselves refer only to emission sources, and not to sinks, it was not clear how inclusion of afforestation/reforestation would fit into the CDM project cycle, particularly bearing in mind that inclusion of sinks brings in issues that are either unique or have different policy implications. These include issues regarding non-permanence, additionality, leakage, uncertainties and socio-economic and environmental impacts,

---

[135] Second Annual Report of the EB, FCCC/CP/2003/2, paragraphs 27–30.
[136] See chapter 5, sections 2.3, 4.5 and 5.11.   [137] See chapter 5, section 5.11.

including impacts on biodiversity and natural ecosystems. Because supporters of sinks inclusion tried at Marrakesh to resist negotiations of an entirely different and new project cycle for sinks, Decision 17/CP.7 specified that inclusion of CDM project activities covering afforestation and reforestation 'shall be in the form of an annex on modalities and procedures . . . reflecting *mutatis mutandis*, the annex to the present decision'.

Modalities for afforestation and reforestation projects under the CDM were adopted by COP-9 in December 2003 and are set out in Decision 19/CP.9. The rules for afforestation and reforestation projects under the CDM are identical to those for emission reduction projects with a few exceptions. A project must be implemented on land that was not forested on 1 January 1990. A project may choose a single crediting period of thirty years or a renewable crediting period of twenty years with up to two renewals for a total of sixty years. The project proponents must consider the socio-economic and environmental impacts of the proposed project in accordance with the procedures required by the host Party.

Projects may specify which of the carbon pools – above-ground biomass, below-ground biomass, litter, dead wood and soil organic carbon – are to be included in the project. Project participants may choose not to account for one or more carbon pools if they can provide transparent and verifiable information that the exclusion will not increase the quantity of reductions claimed. Thus if a pool is a sink, it need not be measured, but if a pool is a net source it must be measured, since failure to do so would overstate the reductions achieved by the project.[138] Greenhouse gas emissions from activities on the land prior to afforestation or reforestation are not included in the baseline.[139] But emissions associated with the project must be deducted from the increase in carbon stocks.

Since the carbon stored by the trees and soil can be released again by disease, fire, harvesting or other events, special provisions are included to address the non-permanence of these projects. The project proponents must choose one of the two options to address non-permanence. Both options verify and certify the net increase in the carbon stocks due to the project since its inception at regular intervals.

Under one option tCERs equal to the certified net increase in the carbon stocks *since the inception of the project* are issued after each verification. The tCERs expire at the end of the subsequent commitment period, so they can only be used for

---

[138] So project proponents may choose to exclude a pool that is a small sink that is costly to measure.

[139] This yields a conservative estimate of the reductions achieved. It also avoids the possibility of earning credits for reducing the emissions associated with displacing activities on the land prior to it being planted with trees. For example, if the land was used for cattle grazing prior to being planted, credits cannot be earned for reducing those emissions.

compliance with the commitments for the period in which they are issued. If the trees are still there when the project is next verified, new tCERs will be issued to replace the ones that have expired. No new tCERs can be issued after the end of the project's crediting period.

Under the other option lCERs equal to the certified net increase in the carbon stocks *since the previous verification of the project* are issued after each verification. If there has been an increase in the carbon stocks during the period, additional lCERs are issued. If there has been a partial or complete release of carbon since the previous verification, an appropriate share of the outstanding lCERs must be replaced by AAUs, CERs, ERUs, RMUs or lCERs from the same project. If a verification report is not received when required, the lCERs for that project must be replaced. The lCERs for a project expire and must be replaced at the end of the project's crediting period.

The rules define small-scale afforestation and reforestation project activities under the CDM as those that are expected to result in net removals by sinks of less than 8 kilotonnes of CO_2 per year and are developed or implemented by low-income communities and individuals as determined by the host Party. If a project is designated a small-scale afforestation or reforestation project activity and then achieves net removals greater than 8 kilotonnes of CO_2 per year, the excess removals will not be eligible for the issuance of tCERs or lCERs. Simplified rules for small-scale afforestation and reforestation projects are to be developed for adoption at COP-10 in December 2004.

6.5   *Monitoring and verification and certification requirements*

Monitoring refers to the identification, collection and archiving of information necessary to design and implement a monitoring plan as required by CDM modalities.[140] A monitoring plan for a proposed projected activity must be based on a previously approved monitoring methodology or, if it is new, one that has been submitted to the Board using the 'pre-validation' procedure set out in paragraphs 37 and 38 of the CDM modalities (described above in relation to methodologies for new baselines). The proposed plan must satisfy the DOE that it is appropriate and reflects good monitoring practice.

If approved, it becomes known as 'the *registered monitoring plan*'. Any revisions to this shall be justified and submitted for validation to the DOE. Implementation of the registered monitoring plan by the PP is a condition for the verification, certification and issuance of CERs. The PP shall provide a monitoring report to the DOE contracted to perform verification in accordance with the registered plan which will normally set out the frequency, content and timing of such information.

[140] Decision 17/CP.7, Annex, paragraphs 53–60.

Verification and certification are defined in the CDM project cycle section above.[141] A DOE is responsible for performing verification at regular intervals on the basis of the *monitoring report* which, subject to confidentiality provisions, it shall make publicly available. A DOE may conduct on-site visits, review performance records, talk with PPs and stakeholders, examine measurement equipment and use alternative sources of data with a view to establishing that monitoring methodologies have been correctly applied. It may make recommendations for future improvements. On the basis of the foregoing, it shall calculate the reductions in emissions that would not have occurred in the absence of the CDM project activity and inform the PP of any concerns it may have regarding the conformity of the actual project with the PDD, giving the PP an opportunity to address and correct these concerns.

The DOE's *verification report* shall be provided to the PP, the Parties involved and the Board, and shall be made publicly available. This report will give rise to a *certification report* by the DOE, certifying how many CERs the project has achieved during a specific time period which shall be transmitted to PPs, the EB and made publicly available.

6.6   *Issuance of CERs*

The DOE's certification forms the basis of a request by the DOE to the EB for issuance of CERs.[142] Issuance refers to the instruction by the EB to the CDM Registry Administrator to issue (i.e. create) a specified number of CERs into the pending account of the EB.

Issuance becomes final fifteen days after the date of receipt of the request for issuance, unless a Party or at least three members of the EB request a review of the proposed issuance of the project. The scope and procedures for this review are explained in box 6.3 above.

Upon being instructed by the EB to issue CERs, the responsibility to forward CERs to the registry accounts of the PPs rests with the CDM Registry which must also forward, at the same time, the relevant number of CERs to cover the share of the proceeds for administrative expenses (not yet determined) and adaptation (set at 2 per cent) to the appropriate accounts. Thus the EB has no role in the final allocation of CERs to PPs as this is a purely technical act undertaken by the CDM Registry Administrator. A particular merit of these provisions is that the CERs to cover adaptation (and at some future stage for administrative expenses) are collected automatically at the point of issuance, leaving no possibility of their non-payment by PPs.

---

[141] Decision 17/CP.7, Annex, paragraphs 61–3.
[142] Decision 17/CP.7, Annex, paragraphs 64–6.

The Executive Board has responsibility for the development, establishment and functioning of the CDM Registry, as defined in Appendix D of the CDM modalities.[143] This Registry creates accounts for non-Annex I Parties and thus allows the accurate tracking of issuance, holding, transfer and acquisition of CERs by non-Annex I Parties. The requirement for the EB to develop and maintain the CDM Registry not only makes possible various approaches to CDM (unilateral, bilateral and multilateral, explained above) but also ensures that non-Annex I Parties are not under an obligation to develop their own national registries. The structure and functioning of the CDM Registry is similar in substance to the national registries to be established by Annex I Parties, including public disclosure requirements.

Where a DOE's accreditation status has been withdrawn or suspended, any ERUs, CERs, AAUs and RMUs equal to the excess CERs issued, as determined by the EB, shall be placed in a cancellation account in the CDM Registry and cannot be further transferred or used for the purpose on compliance with Article 3.1 commitments.[144]

Given the work going on in SBSTA to develop Annex I Parties' national registries, the EB decided not to establish an interim CDM Registry in 2003.[145] It agreed instead to issue a public call to Parties and organisations for inputs relating to the development of the CDM Registry and to request the Secretariat to begin development of the CDM Registry with a timeline for continuing work.

6.7   *Funding issues*

6.7.1   ODA/public funds

The issue of whether donors can generate CERs on the back of public funds has given rise to friction between donors and developing countries. Developing countries have argued that ODA and public funds should not be used to fund CDM projects because doing so means resources earmarked for the sustainable development of developing countries are used instead to assist Annex II Parties (donors) meet their own climate mitigation commitments, and this has the potential to distort funding of developing countries' sustainable development as prioritised by them.

Accordingly, Decision 17/CP.7 states that 'public funding for CDM projects from Parties in Annex I is not to result in the diversion of official development assistance and is to be separate from and not counted towards the financial obligations

---

[143] Decision 17.CP.7, Annex, paragraphs 5 (l) and 66.
[144] Decision 17/CP.7, Annex, Appendix D, paragraph 8.
[145] Second Annual Report of the EB, paragraph 46.

of Parties included in Annex I'.[146] This reference, included in the Preamble to Decision 17/CP.7 to reflect its weakened legal status, is not included as a test of additionality to be examined by DOEs. Assessment of whether Annex I Parties are complying with it is a matter for the COP/MOP to review, following its mandate to 'assist in arranging funding of CDM projects activities, as necessary'.[147] It should be noted that tracking and separating out funding for sustainable development generally from 'new and additional' resources provided to the Convention's financial mechanism has historically proved problematic for reasons explained elsewhere.[148] Thus broader financial mechanism discussions, in particular whether public expenditures on CDM activities will be defined in non-climate regime institutions, such as the OECD DAC, as climate-related ODA, will have a bearing on monitoring adherence to the 'no diversion' stipulation set out in Decision 17/CP.7.

6.7.2   Assistance in funding and geographic imbalance

Private investment gravitates primarily towards a handful of the larger developing countries. Concerns that the bulk of developing countries would not benefit from the CDM led to inclusion of Article 12.6 in the Protocol. This states that the 'CDM shall assist in arranging funding of certified project activities as necessary'. The COP/MOP has an explicit function to review the regional and sub-regional distribution of CDM projects with a view to identifying systematic or systemic barriers to their equitable distribution and take appropriate decisions, based, inter alia, on a report by the EB.[149]

Concern that, due to lack of capacity and technical expertise, DOEs might be based only in developed countries, which might increase costs and reduce choice for developing country PPs, led to inclusion of a review function for the COP/MOP of this issue. In this case the EB does have an explicit mandate to report to the COP/MOP on the geographic and regional distribution of DOEs and has already endorsed corrective actions to make the financial payment of fees by developing country based DOEs less onerous (see below). Discussions are also under way regarding a 'phased' approach to accreditation that would allow more developing country DOEs to come forward as applicant entities.[150] Additionally, COP-9 has requested Parties and other organisations to assist with capacity-building to encourage a greater spread of DOEs from developing countries.[151]

---

[146] Decision 5/CP.1 on AIJ contains similar wording but the issue was nuanced because no credits could be gained in the pilot phase.

[147] Decision 17/CP/7, Annex, paragraph 3.   [148] See chapter 10.

[149] Decision 17/CP.7, Annex, paragraph 4. See also Second Annual Report of the EB.

[150] Second Annual Report of the EB.   [151] Decision 18/CP.9, paragraph 1.

6.7.3   Share of proceeds

Given the private sector nature of the CDM, Article 12.8 includes a unique international 'levy' on CDM activities by mandating that a 'share of the proceeds' of certified project activities is to be used for two purposes: to cover the CDM's administrative costs and to fund adaptation needs of developing country Parties vulnerable to the adverse effects of climate change. The wording of Article 12.8 creates no priority between these two uses. The Marrakesh Accords reached a political agreement that the share of the proceeds for adaptation 'shall be two per cent of the CERs issued for a CDM project activity'.[152] CERs will be collected by the EB at the point of issuance of CERs and, in due course, made available to the Adaptation Fund established under the Protocol.[153] It further agreed that CDM projects hosted by LDCs shall be exempt from the share of the proceeds related to adaptation.

So far as administrative expenses are concerned, Parties agreed that the share of the proceeds to cover these shall be determined by the COP upon recommendation of the EB.[154] The EB has in turn stated that it will not consider making a recommendation until 2004 when there is more information about CER prices.[155] Additionally, the Board has pointed out that requiring PPs to pay CDM administrative costs in the early stages of the prompt start phase in which costs are front-loaded due to the need for intensive development of additional rules and procedures, could penalise, rather than support, CDM pioneers.

Pending a recommendation by the EB and a decision by the COP, Parties have been invited to provide funding for the EB by contributing to the Trust Fund for Supplementary Activities, recognising that some basic funding for Secretariat support has come from the core budget. COP-7 called for contributions 'in the order of $6.8 million' to support the prompt start of the CDM,[156] on the understanding that, if requested, these would later be reimbursed. By COP-8, however, only a fraction of this total had been received.[157] This led to a revised budget for 2002–2003 amounting to US $4.32 million. Actual contributions to date amount to US $1.74 million.[158]

To lessen resource constraints, organisations applying for accreditation as operational entities must also pay a registration fee of US $15,000, with the option for applicants from developing countries paying this in two instalments.[159] This has raised a total of US $240,000 from the sixteen applicant entities to date.[160] In

---

[152] Decision 15/CP.7, paragraph 15.   [153] See chapter 10.
[154] Decision 15/CP.7, paragraph 15.   [155] Second Annual Report of the EB.
[156] Decision 38/CP.7, paragraph 14.   [157] First Annual Report of the EB, paragraph 34.
[158] Second Annual Report of the EB, paragraph 74.
[159] First Annual Report of the EB, paragraphs 19 (c) and 35.
[160] Second Annual Report of the EB, paragraph 69.

addition, the Board has recently agreed to a system of raising a registration fee as a down-payment until a share of the proceeds may be determined.[161] The fee will vary depending on the size of the project, ranging from a minimum of US $5,000 to a maximum of US $30,000, with these figures to be reviewed and revised in light of experience. The second report of the EB to COP-9 addresses the financial and budgetary issues in more detail. The costs of operating the CDM prior to the entry into force of the Protocol was part of the contentious negotiations on the budget that took place at COP-9 due to the US position to refuse to contribute towards Protocol-related activities (see chapter 16). This prompted COP-9 to invite Parties to make contributions urgently for funding the administrative expenses of the CDM.

7   Joint implementation (Article 6)

7.1   *Overview*

Article 6 of the Protocol allows Parties in Annex I to use 'emission reduction units' (ERUs) resulting from GHG abatement or sequestration projects in any other Annex I Party for the purposes of meeting their Article 3.1 commitments.[162] Joint implementation amongst Parties with binding quantitative commitments under the Protocol has been succinctly described 'as a specific form of emissions trading related to individual projects rather than a trading of assigned amounts from any source'.[163]

Delegates often find the concept of JI confusing because the term 'JI' straddles elements of emissions trading with project-based forms of trading. Accordingly, the 'hybrid' nature of JI, its history and its institutional implications are explained in more detail in box 6.5.

The Bonn Agreement provided limited guidance on how to institutionalise JI. It clarified that Annex I Parties' eligibility to participate in all mechanisms was dependent on meeting reporting and review requirements. It also recommended that the COP/MOP establish 'a supervisory committee to supervise, inter alia, the verification of ERUs generated by Article 6 projects activities' but without specifying its functions and composition.[164] Negotiations on Decision 16/CP.7 interpreted the Bonn guidance so as to create two 'tracks' for JI. Track 1 and Track 2 are available when a host Annex I Party is in conformity with its reporting and review

---

[161] Second Annual Report of the EB, paragraph 69.

[162] For convenience, we have used the term 'JI' and 'Article 6 projects' interchangeably in the main body of the text because the mechanism defined by Article 6 continues to be popularly known as 'joint implementation'.

[163] European Commission, 1998.   [164] Decision 5/CP.6, Section 2.

requirements and allow this Party to validate JI projects and issue and transfer ERUs without additional external scrutiny.[165] Where the host Annex I Party fails to meet its reporting and review eligibility requirements, it can only participate in JI projects under Track 2. This requires international oversight of JI activities provided by the Article 6 Supervisory Committee (A6SC) whose functions, powers and rules of procedures are very similar to those of the EB. The project cycle under Track 2 is also very similar to the CDM project cycle, incorporating reliance on 'independent entities' (IEs), rather than on DNAs. IEs are accredited third-party organisations that perform essentially the same functions as DNAs but in the context of a streamlined project cycle that merges the distinct steps of the CDM project cycle. Issues relating to, inter alia, participation, eligibility, fungibility, equity and supplementarity are addressed in the cross-cutting issues section.

Box 6.5   Joint implementation: history and characteristics

From Kyoto right through to Marrakesh, negotiators found it hard to address the particular challenge JI created: how to create institutional arrangements that would address simultaneously the environmental policy concerns arising from a cap-and-trade trading scheme with concerns arising from the operation of a baseline-and-credit one. Where the host Party has a binding target it does not have long-term incentives to give away ERUs. Although Article 6 provides that JI projects must generate ERUs additional to any that would otherwise occur, the zero-sum nature of Annex I Article 3 commitments means additionality is not critical for the environmental integrity of JI as a mechanism where all Parties are meeting their reporting and review commitments. By contrast, where reporting and review commitments are not being met, a host Party can easily underestimate its emissions and thus oversell its assigned amount through JI. In these circumstances, its participation in JI requires some form of external scrutiny if environmental integrity is to be secured.

   Article 6 of the Protocol did not help negotiators sort out responses to these distinct policy issues because its provisions included additionality and reporting and review commitments as conditions for JI participation. Finally, sound environmental reasons, cross-cutting concerns relating to supplementarity, fungibility, equity and the application of the 'adaptation levy' to JI and ET, led many developing countries to insist on 'institutional

---

[165] The reporting and review requirements for Annex I Parties mean that expert review teams will already have provided one layer of external scrutiny. See chapter 11.

parallelism' for Article 6 – meaning that JI should replicate as closely as possible the rules, institutional structures and procedures for the CDM.

Substantive progress was only possible at Marrakesh after modalities for the CDM and ET were finalised for three reasons. First without knowing the nature of its parentage, the CDM and ET, the 'hybrid' mechanism could not emerge. Second, mechanism negotiations, with complex linkages to simultaneous negotiations on compliance and Articles 5, 7 and 8, left delegates with little time to focus on JI, which was accorded the lowest priority out of the three mechanisms by JUSSCANNZ and developing countries. Finally, because EITs, the principal beneficiaries of JI, do not form a cohesive political bloc in negotiations and have capacity constraints, a coherent vision of JI modalities emerged relatively late on in the negotiations.[166]

7.2   JI institutions

7.2.1   COP–COP/MOP

The role of the COP/MOP is defined in the annex to Decision 16/CP.7 in one short sentence, stating that it 'shall provide guidance regarding the implementation of Article 6 and exercise authority over the Article 6 supervisory committee'.[167] The lack of specificity results from Annex I Parties' overall preference for bilateral approach project-based mechanisms. A number of specific tasks and functions for the COP/MOP are set out in, and/or implied from, the section on the A6SC. Additionally, the wide scope of this short reference combined with the general functions and power of the COP/MOP under Article 13 mean it could undertake a very wide of functions on any Protocol matter, including JI.[168]

7.2.2   Article 6 supervisory committee

The A6SC was not envisaged in the Kyoto Protocol, but established through the Marrakesh Accords when it became clear that some form of independent body was needed to supervise Track 2 JI (box 6.6).[169] The A6SC will be established at

---

166 See chapter 3, section 2.11.

167 The reference here to 'Article 6 Guidelines' is to the Annex to Draft Decision – /CMP.1 (Article 6), Guidelines for the Implementation of Article 6 of the Kyoto Protocol, which is appended to Decision 16/CP.7.

168 See chapter 13.

169 Decision 16/CP.7, Article 6 Guidelines, sets out the A6SC rules of procedure. Section C.

the first session of the COP/MOP. The Marrakesh Accords include provisions governing the institutional and procedural aspects of its operation but a fuller set of procedural rules for the A6SC functioning may be devised for consideration by the COP/MOP, as has happened with the EB.

Because JI projects cannot result in ERUs until 2008, no 'prompt start' or interim role has been envisaged for the COP prior to the entry into force of the Protocol or of the A6SC, notwithstanding that JI projects starting as of the year 2000 may be eligible as Article 6 projects.

When established, it will function under the authority and guidance of the COP/MOP, to which it will report annually.[170] The Marrakesh Accords include provisions governing the institutional and procedural aspects of its operation but a fuller set of procedural rules for the A6SC functioning may be devised by the A6SC itself for consideration by the COP/MOP.

The main function of the A6SC is to supervise the work of IEs who will be responsible for verification of emission reduction units generated through JI projects hosted by countries that are not fully in compliance with their reporting and review commitments under Track 2.[171] Thus, like the Executive Board, the A6SC's functions include responsibility for the following:

- Accreditation of IEs in accordance with standards and procedures contained in Appendix A of the Article 6 Guidelines;
- Review of standards and procedures for the accreditation of IEs, giving due consideration to the relevant work of the EB and making recommendations to the COP/MOP on revisions to these standards and procedures;
- Review and revision of reporting guidelines and criteria for baselines and monitoring in Appendix B of the Article 6 Guidelines for consideration by the COP/MOP;
- Elaboration of a PDD for Article 6 projects for consideration by the COP/MOP, taking into consideration Appendix B of the CDM modalities and giving consideration to relevant work of the EB as appropriate;
- Review of the validation determination made by an IE under paragraph 35 of the Article 6 Guidelines (JI validation review) and review of the verification/certification determination made by an IE under paragraph 39 of the Guidelines (JI verification/certification review); and
- Elaboration of additional rules of procedures for consideration by the COP/MOP.

---

[170] Article 6 Guidelines, Annex, paragraphs 2 and 3 (a).
[171] Article 6 Guidelines, Annex, paragraph 3.

Given that JI projects take place exclusively among Annex I Parties, the supervisory committee's composition is deliberately skewed to provide for greater representation of Annex I Parties, with EITs granted strong representation. The A6SC is composed of ten members, including three members from the Annex I Party EITs, three from Annex I Parties that are not EITs,[172] three from non-Annex I Parties, and one member from the small island developing states.[173] As with the EB, however, each member is accompanied by an alternate from the same region, and both members and alternates are nominated by their constituencies and formally elected by the COP/MOP.[174] As with other elected posts, Parties will be required to give active consideration to the nomination of women for the A6SC to improve the gender balance of FCCC and KP elected institutions.[175] The cost of participation of developing country members and those of other Parties eligible under FCCC practices are to be covered by the budget of the A6SC.[176]

The A6SC's procedures parallel those of the EB also in many other respects, including provisions for election of a Chairperson and Vice-Chairperson and the rotation between them, the terms of office for its members, the need for them to serve in their personal capacity, the financial interest and confidentiality provisions to which they are subject, and the role of alternates. Again, similar to the EB's procedures, the A6SC's members must have 'recognized competence relating to climate change issues and in relevant technical and policy fields'.

The A6SC is to meet 'at least two times a year, whenever possible in conjunction with the . . . subsidiary bodies'. As with the EB, two-thirds of members must be present to constitute a quorum, including a majority of Annex I and non-Annex I Parties, and meetings are 'open to attendance, as observers, by all Parties and FCCC accredited observers and stakeholders', unless the A6SC decides otherwise. Decisions are to be taken by consensus unless all such efforts have been exhausted, in which case they may, as a last resort, be taken by a three-fourths majority vote. The full texts of all decisions are made publicly available in all six UN languages. As noted above, the A6SC is expected to develop its additional rules of procedure, which are likely to draw heavily on those agreed for the EB.

JI lacks a 'share of the proceeds' provision to fund administrative costs. The issue of who should pay the administrative costs arising from the procedures contained in the Article 6 Guidelines proved too complex to negotiate in detail in the last days of Marrakesh. Accordingly, the Article 6 Guidelines reflect all that could be agreed in terms of principle, which is that such costs 'shall be borne by both the

---

[172] These include not only the Annex II Parties, but also Annex I Parties that are neither EIT nor included in Annex II (namely, Liechtenstein, Monaco and Turkey).

[173] Article 6 Guidelines, Annex, paragraph 4.   [174] Article 6 Guidelines, Annex, paragraph 5.

[175] Decision 36/CP.7.   [176] Paragraph 10 (a).

Parties included in Annex I and the project participants according to specifications set out in a decision by the COP/MOP at its first session'.[177]

7.2.3   Independent entities

IE functions are not spelt out in a specific section as for the CDM but have to be gleaned instead from the Article 6 Guidelines, Section E concerning the verification procedure set out in paragraphs 30–45 and from Appendix A which sets out standards and procedures for the accreditation of IEs.

Granting accreditation status to a potential IE rests with the A6SC, in contrast to the CDM (where the COP/MOP designates on the basis of EB recommendations and provisional designation). The standards and procedures set out in Appendix A are almost identical to those used for the CDM, in part because the actual tasks the IEs will undertake under Track 2 JI are functionally equivalent to those under the CDM.

The provisions for suspension and withdrawal of accreditation status of an IE who does not meet the accreditation standards set out in paragraphs 42 and 43 are also very similar to the CDM. They give any IE the opportunity of a hearing, provide for immediate effect of the A6SC's decision and that the suspension or withdrawal of an IE will not affect verified projects unless 'significant deficiencies' are found, in which case the IE concerned shall acquire an 'equivalent amount of AAUs and ERUs and place them in the holding account of the Party hosting the project within 30 days'.

7.3   *Participation/eligibility*

Participation and eligibility requirements are discussed in detail in the section on cross-cutting issues. For ease of reference, the differences between the eligibility criteria for Track 1 and Track 2 are summarised in table 6.2.

Article 6.4 provides that if a question of implementation of the provisions of Article 6 is identified by the in-depth review process (Article 8), transfers and acquisition of ERUs may continue to be made after the question has been identified, but these units may not be used by a Party to meet its commitments 'until any issue of compliance is resolved'. The Article 6 Guidelines adopted state at paragraph 25 that 'the provisions in Article 6.4 of the Protocol shall pertain, inter alia, to the requirements of paragraph 21 above', i.e. the paragraph defining the eligibility conditions for JI. Inclusion of this provision is intended to limit the kinds of questions that can give rise to the restriction of the use of ERUs to questions related to the specified eligibility requirements.

---

[177] Article 6 Guidelines, Annex, paragraph 7.

Table 6.2 *Difference between Track 1 and Track 2 JI*[178]

	JI Track 1	JI Track 2
Participation requirement to be met by the host country	1. Party to the Kyoto Protocol 2. has submitted a report for determining their initial assigned amounts 3. has a national system of evaluation of greenhouse gas emissions from sources and storage using sinks 4. has a computerised national registry compliant with the international requirements 5. annually submits a current inventory protocol fully compliant with the Kyoto Protocol requirements	1. Party to the Kyoto Protocol 2. has submitted a report for determining their initial assigned amounts 3. has a computerised national registry compliant with the international requirements
Verification	Host country performs the verification of greenhouse gas emissions	An independent entity performs the verification
Transfer of ERUs	The host country transfers the agreed amount of ERUs	Host country can transfer ERUs only if after verification by an independent entity

Paragraph 41 of the Article 6 Guidelines states that 'any provisions relating to the commitment period reserve or other limitation to transfer under Article 17 shall not apply to transfers by a Party of ERUs issued into its national registry that were verified in accordance with the verification procedure under the Article 6 supervisory committee'.

7.4   *Track 1 procedure*

Although paragraph 23 of the Article 6 Guidelines does not use the term 'Track 1', its contents create a streamlined procedure that has become popularly known by this name. The procedure stipulates that where the *host* Party is considered to meet the eligibility requirements in paragraph 21 of the Article 6 Guidelines it may verify reductions in anthropogenic emissions and removals by sinks from an Article 6 project 'as being additional to any that would otherwise occur,

---

[178] Source of table 6.2: Wollansky and Freidrich, 2003.

in accordance with Article 6.1 (b)'. Upon such verification, the host Party may issue the appropriate quantity of ERUs in accordance with Decision 19/CP.7. This is done by converting AAUs into ERUs and transferring them through the system of national registries.

Track 1 does not entail international scrutiny in respect of the JI project by the A6SC and IEs and appears to give discretion to the host Party to choose baseline and monitoring methodologies. Because the reference to Article 6.1 (b) of the Protocol refers to the additionality test which also applies in the CDM, it may be that choice of methodologies may, in practice, be influenced by international developments as to what is/is not a reasonable methodology.

A Party which can undertake Track 1 JI projects may at any time elect to use the Track 2 procedure instead. This might be done, for example, to provide greater credibility to the project and the Party than might be possible under Track 1.

7.5   *Track 2 verification procedure*

Track 2 applies when not all the eligibility criteria can be met by a host Party. As table 6.1 makes clear, at a minimum the host Party must have established its assigned amount and have in place a national registry which meets the requirements under Articles 5 and 7.[179] Such a host Party can then transfer ERUs, provided that an IE validates the project and it is subsequently verified by an IE according to the procedures set out below.

The validation part of the procedure is based on the validation/registration requirements of the CDM. For Article 6 projects, PPs must prepare a PDD (to be tailor-made by the A6SC on the basis of Appendix A) containing information to allow the IE to assess the following:

- Approval by Parties involved;
- Whether the project would result in reduction of anthropogenic emissions by sources or enhancement by sinks additional to any that would otherwise occur;
- Whether there is an appropriate baseline and monitoring plan in accordance with Appendix B; and
- Whether documentation has been submitted on the analysis of the environmental impacts of the project activity, including transboundary impacts in accordance with host Party procedures, and, if the environmental impacts of the project are considered by the PPs or the host Party to be significant, the PPs have undertaken an environmental impact assessment in accordance with host Party procedures.

---

[179] See section 4 above and chapter 11, section 3.

The PDD and supporting documentation submitted to the IE by PPs must be made publicly available for thirty days to enable the IE to receive public comments. The IE then makes its determination as to whether to validate a project and, in so doing, makes its decision, an explanation of its reasons and how the comments it received were taken into account publicly available. This determination becomes final unless a review is requested by a Party involved in the project or three members of A6SC request it in accordance with paragraph 35 of the Article 6 Guidelines.[180] The A6SC has a maximum of six months from the date of the request to conclude the review and its decision is final.

Once the project has commenced, PPs shall submit to 'an' accredited IE a report in accordance with the monitoring plan. The reference to 'an' (rather than to 'the') IE would appear to suggest that the IE undertaking verification must be different from 'the' IE that determined the project's validation, as would normally be the case under the CDM.[181]

Upon receipt of the report (which is functionally comparable to the monitoring report in the CDM project cycle), the IE shall make a determination of the reductions/enhancements reported by PPs and make its determination publicly available through the Secretariat, together with an explanation of its reasons. This determination shall be deemed final fifteen days after the date of it being made public unless a Party involved or three members of the A6SC request a review in accordance with the procedure specified in paragraph 39 of the Article 6 Guidelines.[182] When the final decision is made, the host Party is entitled to issue and transfer the ERUs but only if in compliance with its minimum JI eligibility criteria set out above.

7.6   *LULUCF projects*

Article 6 covers projects relating to sinks activities which are covered by the Kyoto Protocol as only specific categories may count towards an Annex I Party's Article 3.1 commitments.[183] Article 6 projects aimed at enhancing anthropogenic removals by sinks shall conform to definitions, accounting rules, modalities and guidelines under Articles 3.3 and 3.4.[184] Decision 19/CP.7 on accounting modalities governs how an Annex I Party may issue RMUs in relation to its (domestic) sinks which are being counted towards compliance under Articles 3.3 and 3.4.

---

[180] The comparable CDM procedure under paragraph 40 of the CDM modalities (see box 6.3).

[181] Decision 17/CP.7, Annex, paragraph 27 (e).

[182] This corresponds to the review at post-certification/pre-issuance stage of the CDM under paragraph 64 of the CDM modalities.

[183] See chapter 5, section 5.11.   [184] Decision 16/CP.7, Draft Decision, paragraph 4.

7.7   *Small-scale and nuclear projects*

The JI Guidelines allow all types of projects to be JI projects. There are no specific provisions to encourage small-scale projects under JI as is currently the case for the CDM. The Article 6 Guidelines stipulate that Annex I Parties are to refrain from using ERUs from nuclear facilities to meet their commitments under Article 3, as is the case for CERs under the CDM.

7

Research, systematic observation, education, training and public awareness

1   Introduction

This chapter describes the commitments relating to research and systematic observations, training and education and public awareness provisions. Accurate, timely and widely shared information is vital for understanding the climate system, whether changes are above normal variability and the consequent environmental, social and economic policy implications, including whether, when and who should take action to mitigate, adapt and provide financial support. Research will only feed effectively into policy processes if there is sufficient understanding of its implications by policy-makers, experts and the wider public. This has led to the inclusion of commitments in the Convention and the Protocol on education, training and public awareness. These have been developed in recent years, including through the New Delhi work programme on Article 6 of the Convention.

2   Research and systematic observation

2.1   *Convention and Protocol commitments*

FCCC: Commitments for scientific cooperation and exchange of information are necessary because there is no general international law duty compelling states to undertake research on the issue of climate change through international channels and to make the results of that research accessible to other countries. The broad thrust of the Convention and Protocol's commitments is to require all Parties to cooperate on scientific and technical research, in particular on the development and maintenance of systematic observation systems to reduce uncertainties related to the climate system and to promote exchange of information.

During the Convention's negotiations two annexes setting out detailed proposals on the priorities for research and systematic observation and for exchange of information respectively were deleted because some delegations had had insufficient time to consider them.[1] The remaining, somewhat disjointed provisions can be found in Articles 4.1 (g), 4.1 (h) and 5 of the Convention. Article 9 establishing SBSTA and Article 21 addressing the interim arrangements between the Convention and the IPCC and other scientific bodies are also relevant and are discussed in more detail in chapter 15. The Protocol incorporates the Convention's provisions and goes further than the Convention in formally recognising the role played by the IPCC in the climate regime by referring to it in several articles, but otherwise does not significantly add to the Convention's provisions on research, systematic observation and exchange of climate information.

Article 4.1 (g) of the Convention requires all Parties to 'promote and cooperate in scientific, technological, technical, socio-economic and other research, systematic observation and development of data archives related to the climate system and intended to further the understanding and to reduce or eliminate the remaining uncertainties regarding the causes, effects, magnitude and timing of climate change and the economic and social consequences of various response strategies'. The broad definitions of 'climate change' and 'climate system' in Article 1.3 mean the commitment in Article 4.1 (g) covers promotion and cooperation across a very broad range of matters involved in understanding climate change, its impacts and both mitigation and adaptation options. Article 4.1 (h) commits all Parties to promote exchange of information of this wide-ranging research by refering to 'the full, open and prompt exchange of relevant scientific, technological, technical, socio-economic and legal information related to the climate system and climate change, and to the economic and social consequences of various response strategies'.

Article 5 (a) adds more details to the commitments under Article 4.1 (g) by requiring Parties to support and further develop, as appropriate, international and intergovernmental programmes and networks or organisations aimed at defining, conducting, assessing and financing research, data collection and systematic observation, taking into account the need to minimise duplication of effort. Article 5 (b) also elaborates the commitments in Article 4.1 (h) on exchange of information by mandating Parties to support international and intergovernmental efforts to strengthen systematic observation and national scientific and technical research capacities and capabilities, particularly in developing countries, and to promote

---

[1] A/AC.237/15 (1992), INC-4 Report, Annex II on exchange of information, and A/AC.237/18, INC-5, Part I, Annex I on priorities for research/systematic observations. See Bodansky, 1993, text and notes at footnotes 354–8, p. 510.

access to, and the exchange of, data and analyses obtained from areas beyond national jurisdiction. Article 5 (c) calls on Parties to take into account the particular concerns and needs of developing countries and to cooperate in improving their endogenous capacities and capabilities to participate in efforts relating to research, systematic observation and exchange of information.

There is no mention of the IPCC or other existing scientific bodies and networks, such as the Global Climate Observing System, in Article 5 although much climate research was, and still is, being done in international and intergovernmental programmes and networks. Although Article 5 requires Parties to 'support' these bodies, this provision means it is up to each Party to determine when and whether it will finance the work of these bodies. Thus these bodies are not directly accountable to, nor funded by, the climate regime. Cooperation between these organisations and the Convention is thus of critical importance – in terms of ensuring both that the work of such bodies can support the policy needs of the Convention and that the 'support' mandated by the Convention in Article 5 is indeed provided to these bodies. Effective discharge of the liaison role played by SBSTA in acting as the interface between the Convention and these bodies is thus of particular significance to the overall scientific functioning of the climate regime.

Box 7.1   The Global Climate Observing System

GCOS was established to ensure that the observations and information needed to address climate-related issues are obtained and made available to all potential users. Discussions relating to the establishment of GCOS were contemporaneous with the negotiations on the Convention itself, with GCOS formally being established in 1992 through a joint agreement between the WMO, the Intergovernmental Oceanographic Commission (IOC) of UNESCO, UNEP and the International Council for Science (ICSU). GCOS is intended to be a 'long-term, user-driven operational system capable of providing the comprehensive observations required for monitoring the climate system, for detecting and attributing climate change, for assessing the impacts of climate variability and change, and for supporting research toward improved understanding, modelling and prediction of the climate system'. Its stated aim is to address the total climate system. GCOS does not itself directly make observations but stimulates and coordinates needed observations by national or international organisations in support of their own requirements as well as of common goals. Thus GCOS helps generate climate data for application to national economic development as well as international efforts to combat climate change. GCOS builds upon, and works in partnership with, other existing and developing observing systems such as the Global Ocean Observing System, the Global Terrestrial Observing System, and the Global Observing System and Global Atmospheric Watch of the World Meteorological Organization. Current GCOS priorities are: seasonal-to-interannual climate prediction; detection of climate trends and climate change due to human activities; reduction of the major uncertainties in long-term climate prediction; and improved data for impact analysis. GCOS is directed by a Steering Committee which provides guidance, coordination and oversight to the programme. The GCOS Secretariat, located at the WMO headquarters in Geneva, Switzerland, supports the activities of the Steering Committee, the panels and the GCOS programme as a whole. Three science panels, reporting to the Steering Committee, have been established to define the observations needed in each of the main global domains (atmosphere, oceans and land). These are the Atmospheric Observation Panel for Climate, the Ocean Observing Panel for Climate (OOPC) and the Terrestrial Observation Panel for Climate.

Kyoto: Article 10 (d) of the Protocol requires all Parties to

> cooperate in scientific and technical research and promote the maintenance and the development of systematic observation systems and development of data archives to reduce uncertainties related to the climate system, the adverse impacts of climate change and the economic and social consequences of various response strategies, and promote the development and strengthening of endogenous capacities and capabilities to participate in international and intergovernmental efforts, programmes and networks on research and systematic observation, taking into account Article 5 of the Convention.

This wording reiterates selected elements of Articles 4.1 (g) and 5 but without adding any new commitments. This reflects the fact that research issues were fairly low priority in the highly politicised, and rather overcrowded, AGBM agenda which was focused on strengthening Annex I Parties' mitigation commitments rather than strengthening the entire fabric of the climate change regime.

2.1.1   Rule development

Scientific and technical information on the certainty, magnitude and likely consequences of the impacts of climate change is of critical importance to the development of adaptation strategies as well as the timing of mitigation. The

IPCC 1996 SAR, and the work of other international bodies, highlighted, however, the inadequacy and further deterioration of the global system of observations. Accordingly, since COP-3 this issue has been considered as part of the COP's standing agenda item on cooperation with international organisations. Progress on rule development of a significant nature has been slowed down by the fact that the adequacy of research and systematic observations systems and options on how best to remedy deficiencies has been discussed without a clear definition of the long-term needs of the Convention. Additionally, to date Parties have not agreed on the short-term priorities because finance is limited and Parties' short-term needs do not coincide. For developing country Parties, for example, impacts-related observations are more critical than for Parties less vulnerable to climate change or better able to adapt to its consequences.

Decision 3/CP.3 urged Parties to provide the necessary financing to reverse the decline in existing observational networks and to support GCOS through appropriate funding mechanisms. COP-3 also requested SBSTA to consider the adequacy of global observational systems and to report to COP-4 on its conclusions. In response to this Decision, the GCOS Secretariat prepared a report that concluded that 'available observations often have major deficiencies with respect to climate needs', that observations in many parts of the world were inadequate to meet the needs of the Convention and these deficiencies were serious enough to undermine any decision made concerning the mitigation of, and adaptation to, climate change. COP-4 through Decision 14/CP.4 acted on these conclusions by agreeing that all Parties should undertake, inter alia, the following:

- programmes of systematic observations, including preparation of national action plans;
- free and unrestricted exchange of data to meet the needs of the Convention;
- support for capacity-building in developing countries to enable them to collect, exchange and utilise data to meet local, regional and international needs; and
- support for the work of atmospheric, oceanographic and terrestrial observing systems.

In addition to adoption of these guidelines, Decision 5/CP.5 requested the GCOS Secretariat, in consultation with relevant regional and international bodies, including the GEF, to organise regional workshops to identify the capacity-building needs of developing countries and to consider the need for an intergovernmental process on global observations. Parties agreed at SBSTA-12 that there was no need for such an intergovernmental process at this stage and existing processes should be more effective. Workshops were held in the South Pacific and Africa in 2000–2001 with a view to identifying the capacity-building needs of developing countries and funding options to collect, exchange and utilise data.[2] These regions and South America were previously identified as regions where the quality of atmospheric observations had deteriorated or where observations were no longer being made. Improvements in these regions were especially necessary because data from observations is needed to allow developing country Parties in these climatically vulnerable regions to assess how to cope with climate impacts.[3]

In considering follow-up on this agenda item, SBSTA-15, held in Marrakesh in 2001, endorsed plans by the GCOS Secretariat to prepare a second report on the adequacy of the global observing system, with an interim version of this Report to be provided to SBSTA-16 so that the final version of the Report could be considered by SBSTA-18, thus enabling COP-9 to undertake a substantive consideration of these issues.[4] A final version of the GCOS Report was presented to SBSTA-18, held in June 2003. Although noting improvements, the GCOS Report concluded that 'there remain serious deficiencies in the ability of the current global observing systems for climate to meet the observational needs of the FCCC' and thus stressed that further action was necessary if there is to be compliance with Article 5 of the Convention.[5] In considering the GCOS Report, SBSTA noted that work remains to be done to identify priorities for actions, to remedy deficiencies within the domain-based networks and to estimate the cost implications. On the basis of advice from SBSTA-19, COP-9 adopted Decision 11/CP.9 on GCOS which provides, inter alia, as follows:

- Parties recognise the need for a clear definition of long-term needs of the Convention and short-term priorities, particularly of developing countries, and welcome the work of the ad hoc Group on Earth Observations to develop a ten-year implementation plan for a comprehensive, coordinated and sustained Earth observing system or systems as well as the establishment of the Global Climate Observing System Cooperation Mechanism;
- GCOS, in consultation with other international bodies, is requested to develop a framework for preparation of guidance materials, standards and reporting guidelines for terrestrial observing systems and associated data and to submit a progress report on this issue to COP-11;

---

[2] FCCC/SBSTA/2000/5, SBSTA-12 Report, paragraph 59.

[3] FCCC/SBSTA/2003/9.

[4] FCCC/SBSTA/2001/8, SBSTA-15 Report, paragraph 41 (d)/; FCCC/SBSTA/2002/MISC.10, Interim GCOS Report.

[5] Second Report on the Adequacy of the Global Observing System for Climate in Support of the FCCC, GCOS-82 (ES), WT/TD No. 1143), April 2003. The findings are summarised by the FCCC Secretariat in FCCC/SBSTA/2003/9, paragraph 26.

- Parties are requested to review the second adequacy report within the context of their national capabilities and to take actions individually, bilaterally and multilaterally to maintain baseline stations and long-term climate records and make information available through digitisation and exchange;
- Under the guidance of the GCOS Steering Committee, the GCOS Secretariat is requested to coordinate the development of a phased five- to ten-year implementation plan for the integrated global observing systems for climate, using a mix of high-quality satellite and in situ measurements, dedicated infrastructure and targeted capacity-building, and to report on progress in the development of this plan to SBSTA-20, to hold a review of it by SBSTA-21 and to submit a final implementation plan to SBSTA-21;
- GCOS, in consultation with other international organisations, is requested to develop a framework for guidance materials, standards and reporting guidelines for terrestrial observing systems and to submit a progress report to COP-11;
- The GCOS Secretariat is to provide SBSTA-22 with a report on progress made towards funding the initial ocean climate observing systems;
- On the basis of these various reports, SBI, when next reviewing the guidelines for preparation of national communications, is to incorporate into the guidelines the supplementary reporting format developed by SBSTA-13; and
- With regard to the crucial issue of funding, Parties, particularly Annex I Parties, are encouraged to contribute to funding relevant mechanisms to the meet the high-priority needs, as identified in the Second GCOS Adequacy Report, in developing countries, in particular LDCs and SIDS, noting that filling the gaps in baseline atmospheric networks is an urgent need that should be met by 2006.

2.1.2   Reporting guidelines

An important strand of rule development relating to research and systematic observation is the formulation of additional guidelines for the preparation of national communications to ensure that Parties provide information about the implementation of their Article 4.1 (g) and 5 commitments. Decision 14/CP.4 kick started this process by requesting Annex I Parties to submit information on research and systematic observation as an element of their second national communications, with non-Annex I Parties requested to do likewise 'as appropriate' in their initial national communications.

Fuller guidelines were adopted by COP-5 which aim to assist Parties to report on their actions relating to Articles 4.1 (g) and (h) and 5 of the Convention.[6] The guidelines are mandatory for Annex I Parties. Non-Annex I Parties may use them 'as appropriate'. The guidelines aim to provide information that was not always reported consistently or at all to the GCOS Secretariat, including, for example, programmes on building capacity in developing countries and support for adaptation and technology transfer that had the indirect effect of supporting developing countries' participation in global research and systematic observations as this kind of support was not always in the realm of knowledge assessed by GCOS. The guidelines also show new areas of emerging agreement among Parties, for example in the use of space technology to substitute for direct observations in certain cases. The guidelines are framed in mandatory terms and non-mandatory terms (shall versus should) but it should be borne in mind that non-Annex I Parties can choose to use these guidelines 'as appropriate'.

Decision 4/CP.5 requested Annex I parties to provide a detailed report on their activities on research and systematic observation using the guidelines adopted pursuant to Decision 5/CP.5 in conjunction with their third national communications. Decision 5/CP.5 also mandated the Convention and GCOS Secretariats to develop a process to analyse and synthesise the information contained in the national communications. The first compilation and synthesis of national reports on the global observing systems was presented by the Convention Secretariat to SBSTA-17 and COP-8, with an additional report being presented by the GCOS Secretariat.[7] Decision 11/CP.9, described above, includes a timetable for improvement of reporting guidelines by SBI when it next reviews national communications guidelines.

2.1.3   Financing

Beyond the commitment in Article 5 of the Convention to 'support' international organisations, the Convention and the Protocol do not contain financial commitments that are sufficiently detailed enough to ensure that funding is available for research bodies and networks like GCOS that are engaged in servicing the climate regime.

Decision 5/CP.5 requested COP-5 to examine the resulting information, including the difficulties encountered by developing countries, and options for financial support to reverse the decline in observational networks, including the support

---

[6] Decision 5/CP.5 and FCCC/CP/1999/7, FCCC Guidelines on Reporting and Review, Section III, FCCC Reporting Guidelines on Global Climate Change Observing Systems, pp. 101–6.

[7] FCCC/SBSTA/2002/INF.15, FCCC Secretariat compilation and synthesis. FCCC/SBSTA/2002/MISC.10, GCOS Report.

provided to developing countries. It is important to recognise that rule development to support the participation of developing countries in research and systematic observations has also taken place under other agenda items, notably through COP decisions relating to adaptation, technology transfer and capacity-building. To ensure that non-Annex I Parties do not continue to lag behind in research and observation, Decision 5/CP.7 of the Marrakesh Accords, for example, states that the GEF shall provide financial resources for 'strengthening existing, and where needed, establishing national and regional systematic observation and monitoring networks' as well as 'national and regional centres and institutions for the provision of research, training, education and scientific and technical support in specialized fields relevant to climate change'.[8] Research and observation are also referred to in the COP's capacity-building framework.[9] Finally, the work of the EGTT on enabling environments addresses broader problems faced by developing countries in training and maintaining experts to identify research and technological needs. Recognising that the priority research and observation needs identified by non-Annex I Parties in their regional action plans require funding, COP-9 gave additional guidance to the Convention's financial mechanism, inviting the GEF to give appropriate considerations to these needs, whilst noting the existence of other bilateral and multilateral agencies and mechanisms that support global climate observing systems.[10]

3   Education, training and public awareness

Climate change mitigation and adaptation require governments to persuade a huge number of businesses, communities and individuals to adjust their behaviour. The complexity of climate science, the wide range of interests affected and long time-frames make this a challenging task requiring cooperation amongst national and international bodies, as well as the media and other elements of civil society. It is more challenging still for developing countries, where more immediate food, health, sanitation and poverty alleviation goals tend to eclipse global environmental concerns.

Education can facilitate behavioural changes as one purpose of education is to enable people to make choices. Technical training for policy-makers at all levels and for different target groups is needed to ensure that decisions incorporating climate considerations are made. Sensitisation of the public about climate change can both enhance public support for mitigation and adaptation policies

---

[8] Paragraph 7 (iv) and (v). Note that Decision 6/CP.7 does not quite give GEF this as 'guidance'.
[9] Decisions 2/CP.1 paragraph 15 (i), and 3/CP.7, paragraph 20 (e).
[10] Decision 4/CP.9, paragraph 3.

as well as induce changes in individual behaviour. Public access to information is a critical component in enhancing public participation in decision-making, as this enhances both the effectiveness and the legitimacy of decision-making. Education, training, public awareness and access to information are thus key components of strategies to change behaviour and sit alongside 'carrots and sticks' traditionally used by governments such as policies and measures and binding targets. The explicit inclusion of Articles 4.1 (i) and 6 in the Convention on education, training, public awareness and access to information signals the importance attached to these components since the earliest days of the climate regime.

This section explains commitments in the Convention and the Protocol on education, training, public awareness and access to information and the New Delhi Work Programme. Because this issue is cross-cutting in nature, this section highlights other aspects of the climate regime that are particularly important for the further implementation of activities relating to education, training, public awareness and access to information, including financing.

3.1   *Convention and Protocol commitments*

FCCC: Article 4.1 (i) establishes a commitment for all Parties to promote and cooperate in education, training and public awareness. It calls for the widest participation, including from NGOs, in this regard. Article 6 of the Convention expands upon this basic provision by requiring Parties to promote and facilitate this at the national, regional and sub-regional levels as well as through cooperation with relevant international bodies, bearing in mind their national laws, regulations and capacities. Article 6 mentions public access to information and public participation in climate decisions which are not mentioned in Article 4.1 (i). The key elements of Article 6 (a) are:

- development and implementation of educational and public awareness programmes on climate change and its effects;
- public access to information on climate change and its effects;
- public participation in addressing climate change and its effects and developing adequate responses; and
- training of scientific, technical and managerial personnel.

Article 6.2 (b) highlights the need for Parties to promote and cooperate at the international level, using existing bodies, where appropriate, in respect of:

- development and exchange of educational and public awareness material on climate change and its effects; and
- development and implementation of education and training programmes, including the strengthening of national institutions and the

exchange or secondment of personnel to train experts in this field, in particular for developing countries.

Kyoto: Article 10 (e) of the Protocol requires Parties to

cooperate in and promote at the international level, and, where appropriate, using existing bodies, the development and implementation of education and training programmes, including the strengthening of national capacity building, in particular human and institutional capacities and the exchange or secondment of personnel to train experts in this field, in particular for developing countries, and facilitate at the national level public awareness of, and public access to information on, climate change.

Article 10 (e) singles out the provisions of Article 6 relating to the role of international organisations in improving education and training and in strengthening the capacity of national institutions to undertake the commitments of Article 6, reflecting developing countries' underlying concern that they needed more international support and assistance with education and training with specialist personnel. Accordingly, Article 10 (i) contains a provision stating that 'suitable modalities should be developed to implement these activities through the relevant bodies of the Convention, taking into account Article 6 of the Convention'.

Rule development: Development of modalities to implement Article 6 further was taken up by SBSTA-8 in 1998 shortly after the adoption of the Protocol. Other aspects of the Convention and the need for completion of rules enabling Parties to ratify the Kyoto Protocol, however, left little time for the Parties and the COP to engage seriously with Article 6 issues until after the adoption of the Marrakesh Accords. Between 1998 and 2002, however, a number of workshops and initiatives took place which contributed to the approach and activities subsequently considered by COP-8.[11] These include a suggestion by SBSTA-8 to explore the establishment of a United Nations Climate Change Day to promote awareness and instructions to the Convention Secretariat to develop proposals to integrate Article 6 into the work programme of SBSTA.[12] The small number of submissions from Parties on these issues provided too limited an input and, accordingly, SBSTA-10 invited Parties to make further submissions.[13] SBSTA-12 recognised that, notwithstanding the lack of attention from SBSTA, many Parties, IGOs and NGOs had begun to develop information products envisaged in Article 6 and requested the

---

[11] Background paper prepared for the Workshop for the Development of a Work Programme 2002.

[12] FCCC/SBSTA1998/6, SBSTA-8 Report, paragraph 37.

[13] FCCC/SBSTA/1999/6, SBSTA-10 Report, paragraph 61.

Convention Secretariat to examine how to proceed further on the basis of examining experience to date and best practices.[14] Side events at SBSTA-12 and SBSTA-13 helped clarify approaches and priorities for a work programme on Article 6 that was further encouraged by SBSTA-14, held in July 2001, which also requested the Convention Secretariat to provide information on options concerning the establishment of a UN Climate Change Day.[15] The development of a broader website to serve as a clearing house for Parties' Article 6 needs and the convening of a workshop were mandated by SBSTA-15 held in Marrakesh, which also recognised that the CGE had addressed education, training and public awareness in its work and had stressed the importance of implementing a country-driven strategy for such activities.[16]

The adoption of Decision 11/CP.8, named the 'New Delhi Work Programme on Article 6 of the Convention' by COP-8, now provides a framework for consideration of these activities, which are necessarily of a cross-cutting nature, and thus has provided an important new focus for the work being undertaken by Parties, the Convention Secretariat and other intergovernmental and non-governmental organisations, as well as providing the COP with an opportunity to consider how international activities might best support that work. The approach and key elements of the Delhi Programme are explained below.

3.2   *New Delhi programme of work*

Decision 11/CP.8 comprises a Decision and an annex structured into four sections. This establishes a five-year programme of work by Parties, IGOs, NGOs and the Convention Secretariat, to be reviewed by the COP on an interim basis in 2004 and then in 2007.

Section A of the annex to Decision 11/CP.8, entitled 'observations', stresses the need for a country-driven approach to ensure that each country selects priority areas of greatest relevance to it and delivers these in a culturally appropriate manner consistent with their sustainable development priorities and capacities, and the need to learn from existing work on Article 6 being done by Parties, IGOs, NGOs, community-based organisations, as well as the private and public sector. Parties are requested to report on activities to implement Article 6, within their national communications where possible, and in other reports, on their accomplishments, lessons learned, experiences gained, and remaining gaps and barriers observed.

---

[14] FCCC/SBSTA/2000/5, SBSTA-12 Report, paragraph 64.

[15] FCCC/SBSTA/2001/2, SBSTA-14 Report, paragraph 27.

[16] FCCC/SBSTA/2001/6, SBSTA-15 Report, paragraphs 42–5.

Section B, entitled 'purposes and guiding principles', sets out the scope and basis for action for Article 6 activities, stressing the need for a flexible framework and the need for consistency with existing COP Decisions, including those adopted in Marrakesh, detailed above. Section B lists considerations that should guide Article 6 activities, such as the country-driven approach, cost-effectiveness, promotion of partnerships, networks and synergies, in particular synergies between conventions, and an interdisciplinary, holistic, systematic approach which accords with the principles of sustainable development.

Section C, entitled 'scope of the work programme', encourages Parties to undertake activities under the rubric of the six main elements of Article 6, tailored, as appropriate, to their national circumstances and capacities: (international cooperation, education, training, public awareness, participation and access to information).

Recognising the importance of partnerships, the role of Parties, IGOs and NGOs is mapped out in Section D. The section on Parties is the longest and encourages Parties to, inter alia:

- develop institutional and technical capacity to identify gaps and needs for the implementation of Article 6;
- designate and support a national focal point for Article 6 activities to identify areas for possible international cooperation, synergies with other conventions, and coordination of Article 6 matters in the national communication;
- develop a directory of competent organisations and individuals;
- develop criteria for identifying and disseminating information on good practices;
- increase availability of copyright-free and translated climate change materials in accordance with laws and standards related to the protection of copyrighted materials;
- integrate climate change issues at all educational levels and across disciplines;
- seek input and public participation from all stakeholders, including participation by youth, in the formulation and implementation of efforts to address climate change and encourage participation of representatives of all stakeholders and major groups in the climate change negotiation process;
- inform the public about causes of climate change and sources of greenhouse gas emissions, including through popular versions of the IPCC's work; and

- share the findings contained in their national communications and national action plans or domestic programmes on climate change with the general public and all stakeholders.

IGOs are invited to continue supporting efforts to implement activities under Article 6 through their regular programmes, and through provision of financial and technical support. NGOs are likewise encouraged to continue their activities and to consider ways to enhance cooperation between NGOs from Annex I and non-Annex I countries. The current work of IGOs and NGOs on Article 6 activities can be found on the Secretariat website.[17]

The role of the Convention's Secretariat is central in facilitating and coordinating the role of other bodies. The Secretariat is to prepare regular reports to SBSTA on progress achieved by Parties in implementing Article 6, based on information contained in national communications and other sources of information, particularly in time for the interim review in 2004 and the review in 2007. It is to facilitate coordination of Article 6 related inputs by IGOs and NGOs. More specifically, the Secretariat is to continue work on the structure and content of an information clearing house, including information on existing resources that could facilitate (i) the implementation of the work programme, and (ii) information exchange and cooperation between Parties, intergovernmental and non-governmental organisations working on Article 6 issues, and to identify institutions that could host and provide regular support for such a clearing house.

Since COP-8, the Secretariat has developed a proposal for an information network clearing house.[18] Subject to availability of supplementary funding, SBI-18 encouraged continuation of this work and requested a report on progress by SBI-19, including options for an institutional home of the coordinating entity of the clearing house and financial implications for its maintenance, and proposed development of a prototype of the clearing house by SBI-21 (before COP-10).[19] The Secretariat has also produced a compilation and synthesis of information on Article 6 activities contained in Annex I Parties' third national communications.[20] Parties have agreed not to add climate change to the forty-one theme days already observed within the UN system but to seek incorporation of climate change into one of the existing themes and to encourage Parties to organise an awareness day at the national level.

One important question which SBI-19 will address is whether the guidelines for Annex I Parties should contain guidance on how Article 6 activities should be reported. SBI-18 invited Parties to submit their views on this issue and asked the

---

[17] FCCC/WEB/2002/3.   [18] FCCC/SBI/2003/4.
[19] FCCC/SBI/2003/8, SBI-18 Report, paragraph 35.   [20] FCCC/SBI/2003/7/Add.4.

Secretariat to prepare a compilation and synthesis of these views for SBI-19 held in Milan.[21] SBI-19 provided guidance on these matters, including the exploration of institutions that could house the clearing house and develop a small-scale version of this, and the organisation of a workshop and an interim informal advisory group to facilitate future work in this area.[22]

3.3   *Financing and linkages*

Although undertaken by many Parties, including developing countries, Article 6 activities were not clearly featured in guidance given to the Convention's financial mechanism. The approaches and conclusions reached by SBSTA and various workshops convened to further Article 6 prior to COP-7 fed into COP decisions adopted as part of the Marrakesh Accords, in particular those relating to capacity-building,[23] technology transfer,[24] implementation of Articles 4.8 and 4.9[25] and training of reviewers of Annex I Parties' national communications under the Kyoto Protocol.[26] Because these Decisions already incorporate elements related to Article 6, Decision 11/CP.8 expressly mentions these linkages, acknowledging that Article 6 activities should be in accordance with previous COP Decisions.[27] SBI-19 also encouraged Parties to report on all six areas of Article 6 in their national communications, noting that additional and/or separate interim reports on implementation of the New Delhi Work Programme remain a voluntary initiative.

On funding, Decision 11/CP.8 emphasises the need for funding to help developing country Parties implement Article 6 and highlights Decision 6/CP.7, paragraph 1 (h), which states that the GEF, as an operating entity of the financial mechanism, 'should provide financial resources to developing country Parties, in particular the least developed and the small island developing States among them, for undertaking more in-depth public awareness and education activities and community involvement and participation in climate change issues', recalling the relevance of Decision 11/CP.1.[28] Although Parties are free to determine their own needs, Decision 11/CP.8 recognises that 'as initial priorities, the implementation of the work programme will require the strengthening of national institutions and capacities, in particular in developing countries, and the establishment of a mechanism to provide and exchange information'. Additionally, Decision 11/CP.8 recognises that whilst Article 6 activities can easily be reported in national communications or other reports, measuring or quantifying the impacts of these activities may be more challenging. This aspect has been highlighted to avoid an overly rigid

---

[21] FCCC/SBI/2003/17.   [22] FCCC/SBI/2003/8, SBI-18 Report.

[23] Decisions 2/CP.7 and 3/CP.7, chapter 10.   [24] Decision 4/CP.7, chapter 10.

[25] Decision 5/CP.7 and 6/CP.7, chapters 8 and 9.   [26] Decision 23/CP.7, chapter 10.

[27] Chapter 10.   [28] Chapter 8.

application of the concept of 'incremental costs' by the GEF in accordance with Article 4.3 to the financing of Article 6 activities. Multilateral and bilateral organisations are also encouraged to support Article 6 activities and relevant capacity-building in non-Annex I Parties, in particular the least developed countries and small island developing states among them. Decision 4/CP.9 adopted by COP-9 requested the GEF to continue its support for education, training and public awareness activities relating to climate change.

8

Adaptation

1 Introduction

Adaptation to the adverse effects of climate change has been recognised as an important element of the climate regime since its inception. Implementation of the Convention's adaptation provisions has been impeded, however, by three interlocking factors: lack of agreement about the meaning, scope and timing of adaptation; limited capacity in developing countries to undertake vulnerability assessments and planning; and bottlenecks in the availability of funding.[1] Rule development has also been constrained by procedural and political factors, notably the fragmentation of policy caused by the lack of a single COP agenda item to address adaptation issues and political complications in disentangling adaptation from the conceptually distinct potential problems facing energy exporting countries arising from implementation of response measures.

This chapter brings together the disparate Convention and Protocol provisions on adaptation and related rule development as follows. Section 2 explains the meaning, scope and timing of adaptation in the climate regime, setting out some of the underlying policy issues at stake.[2] Sections 3, 4 and 5 describe the Convention and Protocol adaptation provisions, and subsequent rule development concerning these, as follows:

- Adaptation preparation and planning commitments;
- Adaptation financing; and
- Special adaptation-related provisions for LDCs.

---

[1] See Huq et al., 2003. See also Sperling, Multi-Agency Report, 2003.
[2] See chapter 4, section 1.

2   Meaning, scope and timing of adaptation

2.1   *Definitions*

The Convention and the Protocol do not contain definitions of 'adaptation' nor related terms such as 'adaptive capacity' and 'vulnerability'. Various definitions have been used and have been refined over time to reflect improved understanding.[3] The IPCC's definitions, explained in box 8.1, are the most commonly deployed definitions. The Convention's definition of the 'adverse impacts of climate change' does have an important bearing on what can be considered as adaptation because it limits the scope of the Convention to human-induced climate change rather than natural climatic variability. This limitation was included to ensure that Annex II Parties undertaking commitments relating to adaptation financing did not bear responsibility for all climate-related adaptations and is discussed below.[4]

Because adaptation covers a very broad range of human activities and natural processes, many different typologies have been devised to conceptualise the different types and forms of adaptation. Concrete examples of planned adaptation concerning human societies include increasing the robustness of infrastructure designs and long-term investments, such as increasing the range of temperature and levels of precipitation that roads and buildings can withstand without failure, as well as devising financial, administrative or legal techniques to transfer risks away from vulnerable communities and/or to provide for collective loss-sharing mechanisms. Planned adaptation concerning ecosystems includes enhancing the adaptability of vulnerable natural systems, such as by the creation of eco-corridors, as well as reversal of trends that increase vulnerability through, for example, the introduction of set-backs for developments in vulnerable areas (e.g. floodplains, coastal zones).

Box 8.1   Adaptation: key concepts and definitions

The IPCC defines *adaptation* as 'adjustments in practices, processes, or structures [which] can moderate or offset the potential for damage or take advantage of opportunities created by a given change in climate'.[5]

---

[3] Smit et al., 2000. See also FCCC Secretariat, Technical Issues: Adaptation Technologies, FCCC/TP/1997/3.

[4] Section 4.1.

[5] IPCC, 2001a–d. The definition of adaptation used in the previous IPCC report, SAR, did not highlight opportunities created by a changing climate because adaptability was taken to

Sensitivity refers to 'the degree to which a system is affected, either adversely or beneficially, by climate-related stimuli'.[6] *Vulnerability* is defined by the IPCC as 'the degree to which a system is susceptible to, or unable to cope with, adverse effects of climate change, including climate variability and extremes. Vulnerability is a function of the character, magnitude, and rate of climate change and carious to which a system is exposed, its sensitivity, and its adaptative capacity'.[7] The IPCC definitions cover adaptation undertaken by human society as well as adaptation by ecosystems. Importantly the IPCC definitions do not distinguish between adaptation to natural variability and adaptation to human-induced climate change. Under the Convention, adaptation is referred to as adaptation to the 'adverse effects of climate change'. The Convention's definition of '*adverse effects of climate change*' covers a broad range of effects on natural systems and human societies caused by climate change.[8] The Convention's definition of climate change limits its scope to additional changes to the climate system attributed directly or indirectly to human activity.[9] However, even with this limitation, the broadness of the term 'adaptation' under the Convention presents problems so far as prioritisation of resources is concerned, necessitating continual dialogue between a wide range of stakeholders involved in understanding, responding and funding adaptation to climate impacts.

2.2   *Scope and timing*

How much adaptation should be undertaken and over what timescale are important policy issues raising fundamental choices, in particular about how the Parties should implement the precautionary and preventative approach set out in Article 3.3 taking cost-effectiveness into consideration.[10] An additional related

refer 'to the degree to which adjustments are possible in practices, processes or structures of systems to projected or actual changes on climate. Adaptation can be spontaneous or planned, and can be carried out in response to or in anticipation of changes in conditions.' IPCC, SAR, 1996, WG II.

[6] IPCC, TAR, 2001b, WG II, SMP, p. 6.   [7] IPCC, TAR, 2001b, WG II, SMP, p. 6.

[8] FCCC Article 1.1 states that 'adverse effects of climate change' means changes in the physical environment or biota resulting from climate change which have significant deleterious effects on the composition, resilience or productivity of natural and managed ecosystems or on the operation of socio-economic systems or on human health and welfare.

[9] FCCC Article 1.2 states that 'climate change' means a change of climate which is attributed directly or indirectly to human activity that alters the composition of the global atmosphere and which is in addition to natural climate variability observed over comparable time periods.

[10] See chapter 4, and section 2.5 Aldy et al., 2003, for an explanation of the significance of differences in aggregate and relative costs.

policy issue is who should bear the costs of climate impacts. Countries that are most vulnerable and contribute little to global emissions, such as LDCs and AOSIS, have tended to prioritise preventive approaches requiring polluters to make emissions cuts as well as requesting assistance from the main contributors to cope with impacts. The counterview, rarely espoused by any country but which is evident in the climate policy literature that is economics based, highlights that from a global perspective it may be more cost-effective to let the Earth adapt to climate change (with some form of assistance to particular countries to help them cope) than to undertake more costly mitigation, particularly in the short term. Such views, however, rarely take into account the costs of climate change and of adaptation which are either not quantified at all or generally poorly quantified.[11]

The Convention's commitments applicable to all Parties provide broad but significant guidance on the extent and timing of adaptation by mandating that Parties plan for and implement *both* mitigation and adaptation through their national programmes. This guidance is prescriptive but does not mandate a particular policy solution and timescale. The ultimate objective of the Convention stated in Article 2 also offers guidance by emphasising that the prevention of climate change is essential for achieving the ultimate objective of the Convention.[12] The second sentence of Article 2 implicitly accepts that some degree of adaptation is necessary because it states that the time-frame for achieving a safe level of atmospheric concentrations should 'allow ecosystems to adapt naturally to climate change, to ensure that food production is not threatened and to enable economic development to proceed in a sustainable manner'. This has led some to conclude that 'the Convention also has an important, but unstated objective, of establishing a vehicle to ensure that countries, particularly those most vulnerable, are able to prepare adequately for adaptation to the adverse effects of climate change'.[13] The principles referenced in Article 3 of the Convention lend some support to this view because Article 3.1 requires Annex I Parties to take the lead in 'combating climate change and the adverse effects thereof' and Article 3.2 requires that 'the specific needs and special circumstances of developing country Parties, especially those that are particularly vulnerable to the adverse effects of climate change', should be given full consideration. These principles are given effect by Articles 4.3 and 4.4 of the Convention mandating Annex II Parties to assist developing countries to cope with climate impacts.

---

[11] IPCC, TAR, 2001c, WG III.

[12] Chapter 4 discusses the nature, role and legal implications of Articles 2 and 3.

[13] Sands, 1995b: p. 274, who considers that the numerous references in the Convention to 'effects' and 'adverse effects' (twenty-two times) and to 'vulnerability' and 'impacts' (seven times) support this view.

It should be noted that whilst Article 3.3 explicitly mandates a precautionary basis for action to prevent climate change and reduce its adverse effects, in recent years this aspect has received less attention in climate policy due to much greater attention to short-term economic implications. This is also due, in part, to the importance attached in climate policy to cost-effectiveness considerations, articulated by fossil fuel interests, to rationalise deferment of mitigation action based on the questionable assumption that it is cheaper to deal with the costs of climate impacts and/or to mitigate in the future when cheaper mitigations options become available.

Estimating the costs of climate change, sometimes also known as the benefits of avoided climate change, is thus an important strand in adaptation-related policy discussions. Such costs encompass two interrelated elements: the costs of adaptation measures (such as building sea defences and strengthening buildings) and the costs of damage caused by climate change (such as decreased yields, increased deaths and diseases, and the costs of extreme events such as floods, etc.). Estimation of such costs presents scientific, technical and methodological challenges that have complicated rule development on adaptation.[14] This is because the future impacts of climate change are not as well known as the current costs of mitigation. In addition, producing a single figure to represent climate impact costs (to compare with mitigation costs) involves a number of problematic steps.[15] First it requires converting impacts that are qualitatively incomparable (ecosystem damage, human health and mortality, adaptation costs) into a common metric, usually money. But from a policy perspective a monetised metric has limitations because, in the real world, countries and people have moral and legal rights that cannot be abrogated to maximise the benefits accruing to other countries and groups. A second, related problem is that aggregation of impact costs at a global level can mask the uneven distribution of climate impacts and costs facing the most vulnerable countries and groups. For example, the economic contribution of subsistence farmers (at present the bulk of rural poor) are frequently left out of GDP calculations, so estimating climate damages in GDP terms may not pick up impacts on this highly vulnerable group. Finally, there is little prospect of including costs associated with either socially contingent effects (including risks of conflict) or non-linearities (step changes in the climate system, including Gulf Stream suppression, release of methane hydrates, or large-scale release of carbon dioxide or other greenhouse gases from the terrestrial biosphere).

These considerations make weighing the costs of mitigation against the costs imposed by climate change extremely difficult at all levels of decision.[16] Although Articles 4.3 and 4.4 mandate Annex II Parties to assist developing countries with the

---

[14] Smith and Hitz, 2003. See also chapter 4, section 2.5.   [15] OECD, 2003.   [16] OECD, 2003.

costs of adaptation to the adverse effects of climate change, these provisions do not spell out in sufficient detail the level and timing of the availability of funding and, as a result, they have been fiercely argued over since COP-1. An additional complication is that the legal mandate of the GEF, the international entity operating the Convention's financial mechanism, authorises it to fund activities which generate global environmental benefits that locally orientated forms of adaptation may not yield.[17] Notwithstanding these policy challenges, the Marrakesh Accords and the Delhi Ministerial Declaration adopted at COP-8 have underlined the importance of the implementation and financing of adaptation for all countries.

3   Preparation and planning commitments

The Convention sets out commitments applicable to *all* Parties to prepare, plan and implement adaptation-related activities as well as more detailed commitments for Annex I Parties.

3.1   *National programmes: adaptation measures*

FCCC: Article 4.1 (b) is the pivotal commitment in the Convention because it requires all Parties to formulate, implement, publish and update national and, as appropriate, regional programmes containing measures 'to facilitate adequate adaptation to climate change'. Such programmes should be integrated with economic and developmental planning which should take place within the framework of sustainable development.[18] Article 4.1 leaves each Party to determine the nature, time and content of what might constitute 'adequate adaptation'. Additionally, the chapeau of Article 4.1 of the Convention gives each Party discretion to determine adaptation measures appropriate for its circumstances. It is important to recognise that due, in part, to the varied circumstances of Parties, the commitment in Article 4.1 (b) does not mandate the pursuit of any particular adaptation policies by a Party. Thus, in that sense, Article 4.1 (b) can be seen as a procedural commitment, albeit one that is highly significant because it leads to establishment of processes charged with the important function of identifying, implementing and assessing adaptation options.

Article 12 of the Convention requires all Parties to report on their implementation of the Convention, including Article 4.1, through their national communications. The guidelines for the preparation of national communications provide for

---

[17] Chapter 10, section 2.4, explains the concept of global environmental benefits and the GEF's role.

[18] FCCC Article 3.4. See also Decision 17/CP.8, Annex, paragraph 38.

more detailed information to be submitted by Annex I Parties than by non-Annex I Parties, including in relation to adaptation, and are discussed in chapter 11.

Kyoto: Article 10 (b) requires Parties to formulate, implement, publish and update programmes containing 'measures to facilitate adequate adaptation to climate change', incorporating the chapeau of Article 4.1 of the Convention as discussed above. The only significant advancement in the Protocol from the Convention is that subparagraph (i) of Article 10 (b) specifies that adaptation technologies and methods for improving spatial planning would improve adaptation to climate change. The wording of Article 10 (b) (i), that national programmes 'would' involve use of adaptation technologies (rather than 'shall' or 'should') ensures that Article 10 (b) (i) does not create a new commitment additional to the Convention but gives Parties to the Protocol more specific guidance in how they may implement the existing commitment contained in Article 4.1 (b).

Article 10 (b) (ii) requires all Parties to report on the implementation of the Protocol, including on their national programmes, through their national communications. Annex I Parties must include information about national programmes in their national communications in accordance with Article 7 of the Protocol. Developing country Parties must 'seek to include in their national communications, as appropriate, information on programmes which contain measures that a Party believes contribute to addressing climate change and its adverse impacts including measures that contribute to mitigation, capacity building and *adaptation measures*' (emphasis added). This provision advances the communication commitment contained in the Convention. Developing countries had agreed to inclusion of similar wording in the guidelines for the preparation of national communications adopted at COP-2, paving the way for its subsequent inclusion in the Protocol.[19]

Rule development: Implementing Article 4.1 (b) of the Convention and Article 10 (b) of the Kyoto Protocol requires each Party to establish domestic policy processes with sufficient institutional, administrative and legal capacity to formulate and implement their national programmes, to have ongoing oversight of such programmes, and to ensure their integration with the broader range of economic and development planning. Although there is no legal obligation for them to do so, most Parties have undertaken, or are in the process of undertaking, a 'vulnerability and adaptation assessment' as a first step in formulating adaptation strategies defining specific policy options to prevent and minimise the adverse impacts of climate change which may then be 'mainstreamed' in broader policy processes.[20]

As with mitigation strategies, a number of intergovernmental agencies and UN bodies have devised methodologies, guidelines and technical resources to assist Parties undertake vulnerability assessments and adaptation strategies. These

---

[19] Decision 10/CP.2, paragraph 15 (e).   [20] Huq et al., 2003.

also provide some a degree of coherence and comparability of approaches. The use of these methodologies and tools is not mandatory for either Annex I or non-Annex I Parties. Currently, the most well-known adaptation methodologies are:

- *IPCC Technical Guidelines for Assessing Climate Change Impacts and Adaptations* (T. Carter, M. Parry, H. Harasawa and S. Nishioka, 1994);
- *UNEP Handbook on Methods for Climate Change Impact Assessment and Adaptation Strategies* (J. Feenstra, I. Burton, J. Smith and R. Tol, 1998);
- *International Handbook on Vulnerability and Adaptation Assessment* (R. Benioff, S. Guill and J. Lee, 1996);
- 'Compendium of Decision Tools to Evaluate Strategies for Adaptation to Climate Change' (prepared for FCCC Secretariat by Stratus Consulting, May 1999, available on the FCCC website). This is being updated by the Convention Secretariat and will be available in 2004 in the form of a Resource Book/Compendium on Methodologies to Assess Impacts, Vulnerability and Evaluate Strategies for Adaptation to Climate Change.

Current reporting guidelines for Annex I Parties specifically mention the IPCC and UNEP guidelines and 'encourage' Annex I Parties to use them.[21] Annex I Parties are to provide information on the expected impacts of climate change and 'an outline of the action taken to implement Article 4.1 (b) and Article 4.1 (e)'. Annex I Parties may also report on specific results of scientific research in the field of vulnerability assessment and adaptation. The reference to reporting 'action' did not exist in the previous guidelines adopted by COP-2. Information on vulnerability and assessment provided by Annex I Parties in their first national communications led the Secretariat to conclude: 'The relatively low degree of reporting about vulnerability and adaptation strategies suggests a high level of uncertainty in this regard, rather than a non-fulfillment of the current guidelines.'[22] Reporting on these matters has subsequently improved considerably. In their third national communications, more detailed information on 'actions' is provided but these refer on the whole to future programmes and research on potential adaptation options, with the Secretariat noting that many Annex I Parties do 'not

---

[21] Decision 9/CP.2, Annex, paragraph 41, which only mentions the IPCC 1994 guidelines and Decision 5/CP.5, Annex, paragraph 49 which refers to both the IPCC and UNEP guidelines. An additional tool called the Adaptation Policy Framework was developed by UNDP in 2003 but is currently not mentioned in the guidelines which were prepared before its completion (available from the UNDP website: www.undp.org/adp outline.htm).

[22] FCCC/CP/1996/12, paragraph 53.

provide a clear indication of the methods used to assess and analyze adaptation options', with the range of adaptation measures currently identified as 'very limited'.[23]

So far as reporting by non-Annex I Parties is concerned, the guidelines for preparation of national communications adopted at COP-2 did not contain much detail on how non-Annex I Parties were to prepare information on vulnerability and assessment, although Parties were encouraged to provide information they thought relevant to their ability to address climate change, particularly in view of their specific circumstances, such as those listed in Article 4.8, discussed below.[24]

The new guidelines for non-Annex I Parties adopted by COP-8 give greater guidance on the reporting of vulnerability and assessment.[25] The revised guidelines allow such Parties to use any 'appropriate methodologies and guidelines' provided they are 'consistent, transparent and well documented'. The guidelines and handbooks produced by the IPCC, UNEP and Beniof et al. are specifically mentioned but without a presumption that only these must be used.[26] The more detailed provisions in the COP-8 guidelines for second and subsequent national communications were designed to encourage a higher quality of information on vulnerability and adaptation options than submitted in initial national communications, which varied in their scope and detail, and to ensure that future requests for adaptation funding are based on information that is as sound as countries are capable of producing, bearing in mind their limited capacity and boundaries of current scientific knowledge. The Convention Secretariat is finalising a Manual for National Communications to support non-Annex I Parties' preparations of their second national communications.

3.2   *Planning and integration*

Background: Some adaptation to climate impacts – by natural systems and human societies – will take place autonomously without policy intervention. Anticipation of climate impacts and planned interventions will, however, play an important part, particularly in protecting already vulnerable ecosystems, communities and countries. Because of this, integration of adaptation activities has been recently recognised as important for achieving the Millennium Development Goals, particularly those relating to poverty, health and sustainable development.[27] Adaptation planning must be undertaken by the wide range of local, national and international organisations dealing with social, economic and

---

[23] FCCC/SBI/2003/7, paragraphs 52–3.   [24] Decision 10/CP.2.   [25] Decision 17/CP.8, Annex.
[26] Decision 17/CP.8, Annex, paragraph 30.   [27] Sperling, Multi-Agency Report, 2003.

development processes. Thus, integration and 'mainstreaming' of climate considerations by non-climate policy-makers working in a wide range of institutional
settings is an important element in the effective implementation of the Convention adaptation provisions.[28]

Planning

FCCC: The Convention provides for international cooperation, integration and
mainstreaming of adaptation activities. Article 4.1 (e) requires Parties to cooperate
with each other in preparing for adaptation to the impacts of climate change.
Along with other provisions of the Convention, such as Article 4.4, the commitment in Article 4.1 (e) underscores the acceptance by all Parties that adaptation to
climate impacts is a matter for international cooperation and not something to be
borne alone. Article 4.1 (e) spells out some specific adaptation-related actions Parties should develop and elaborate 'as appropriate' at a national and, where appropriate, regional level. These actions should cover integrated plans for coastal zone
management, water resources and agriculture, and for the protection and rehabilitation of areas, particularly in Africa, affected by drought and desertification,
as well as floods.

Article 4.1 (f) requires all Parties to

> take climate change considerations into account, to the extent feasible,
> in their relevant social, economic and environmental policies and
> actions, and employ appropriate methods, for example impact
> assessments, formulated and determined nationally, with a view to
> minimizing adverse effects on the economy, on public health and on the
> quality of the environment, of projects or measures undertaken by them
> to mitigate or adapt to climate change.

This procedural commitment is designed to ensure the integration of climate
change in all relevant fields of policy-making and of actions undertaken by Parties.
Article 4.1 (f) draws attention to the fact that, unless they are designed carefully,
policies and actions undertaken by Parties to adapt to climate change could generate adverse effects, sometimes known as *maladaption*. Article 4.1 (f) is not limited
to policy-making related to the domestic sphere but applies to all policies and
actions. The qualification of the term 'to the extent feasible' means it is essentially up to each Party to determine the nature and scope of the process of integration. Article 4.1 (f) requires Parties to employ 'appropriate methods' with a view to
minimising such adverse effects. As discussed in chapter 5, environmental impact
assessments (EIAs) are mentioned favourably in Article 4.1 (f), but their use is
not mandatory under the Convention. The phrase 'as formulated and determined

[28] For a detailed discussion of integration and mainstreaming, see chapter 5, section 4.4.

nationally' makes clear that each Party is to determine the scope and application of EIAs at the national level.[29]

Kyoto: There is no direct equivalent or advancement of Article 4.1 (e) and (f) which is applicable to all Parties in the Kyoto Protocol. The inclusion of Articles 2.3 and 3.14 does, however, require Annex I Parties to give consideration to the minimisation of the adverse effects of climate change and the impacts of response measures. These provisions, discussed in more detail below, may result in greater policy focus on integration of climate considerations in non-climate policy and in the greater use of tools such as EIAs.

Rule development: As with mitigation programmes, the COP has not adopted decisions to guide further how Parties might address implementation of Article 4.1 (e). Nor has it sought to highlight the importance of mainstreaming adaptation in the work of other international bodies, although some work is underway.[30]

Rule developments under the Convention are now beginning indirectly to emphasise the need for adaptation planning and to envisage increased use of specific tools such as EIAs, trying to strike a balance between inappropriate international prescriptiveness and the need to ensure that national actions, particularly those funded through the Convention's financial mechanisms, are based on sound information. Thus Decision 5/CP.7 on the implementation of Articles 4.8 and 4.9, adopted by COP-7 and discussed in more detail below, whilst confirming the importance of a 'country driven approach' to adaptation planning allowing 'specific activities most appropriate to their unique national circumstances', also insists that 'action related to adaptation follow an assessment and evaluation process, based on national communications and/or other relevant information, so as to prevent maladaptation and to ensure that adaptation actions are environmentally sound and will produce real benefits in support of sustainable development'.[31] Paragraph 7 (iii) of the same Decision instructs the GEF, as operator of the Convention's financial mechanism, to provide funding for training in specialised fields, including environmental impact assessment, as part of the measures to address the adverse effects of climate change.

Guidelines for national communications also provide some additional 'prompts' for Parties to consider in terms of their implementation of Article 4.1 (e). In their initial national communications, non-Annex I Parties must report on

---

[29] Decision 5/CP.7, paragraph 7 (iii), states that GEF is to fund training in, inter alia, EIAs.

[30] See, for example, the UNEP Financial Services Initiative which has been endorsed by many banks and insurance companies which have agreed to incorporate environmental considerations into their internal and external processes.

[31] Decision 5/CP.7, paragraphs 1 and 2.

general steps taken to implement Article 4.1 and are 'encouraged' to include information on:

- Policy options for adequate monitoring systems and response strategies for climate change impacts on terrestrial and marine ecosystems;
- Policy frameworks for implementing adaptation measures and response strategies in the context of coastal zone management, disaster preparedness, agriculture, fisheries and foresting, with a view to integrating climate change impact information, as appropriate, into national planning; and
- Capacity-building relating to integration of climate change concerns in medium and long-term planning.[32]

The new guidelines for second and subsequent communications agreed at COP-8 also mandate reporting of general steps to report on implementation of the Convention. But the guidelines also encourage non-Annex I Parties to provide more details on:

- Vulnerability and adaptation assessments;
- Approaches, methodologies and tools used, including scenarios for impact assessments and associated uncertainties;
- Vulnerability and adaptation options in key vulnerable areas, including, to the extent possible, priority areas, allowing for an 'integrated analysis' of the country's vulnerability to climate change.[33]

In addition, non-Annex I Parties may report on use of policy frameworks, such as NAPAs, discussed below.

By contrast, and in a reversal of the general pattern, the guidelines for Annex I Parties for reporting vulnerability assessment, climate impacts and adaptation measures are not as detailed: Annex I Parties are only required to report on the expected impacts of climate change and 'an outline of actions' as described in the section above on national programmes.

3.3   *Technology commitments and adaptation*

Background: Like mitigation, adaptation to the adverse impacts of climate change will require development of new technologies, techniques and know-how. The localised nature of climate impacts means that development of a diversity of adaptation technologies and approaches will be essential to combating the adverse effects of climate change.

---

[32] Decision 10/CP.2, Annex, paragraph 15 (b) (c) and (d). See also chapter 10.
[33] Decision 17/CP.8, Annex, paragraphs 32–6. See also chapter 11, section 4.

Technology

FCCC and Kyoto: Article 4.1 (c) of the Convention requires all Parties to cooperate in the development, diffusion and transfer of mitigation technologies. Article 10 (c) of the Protocol, which requires all Parties to cooperate in the promotion of effective modalities for the development, application and diffusion of environmentally sound technologies, covers both mitigation and adaptation technologies. These provisions are described in more detail in chapter 10.

Rule development: The COP looks at technology issues, including adaptation technologies, at each of its sessions as part of its review of Article 4.1 (c).[34] On adaptation specifically, COP-1 requested 'the preparation of an inventory and assessment of environmentally sound and economically viable technologies and know-how conducive to mitigating and adapting to climate change'.[35] COP-2 requested that this report be expedited.[36] Following that request, the Secretariat organised a meeting of technical experts on adaptation in conjunction with a meeting on adaptation held by the IPCC in Amsterdam in March 1997.

A follow-up overview paper, circulated to Parties by the Secretariat as a 'technical paper' in October 1997, focused on how appropriate adaptation technologies can be developed, assessed and made available to developing country Parties in the short, medium and long terms, including an examination of the conditions necessary for such efforts to succeed.[37] A programme of work to be undertaken by the Secretariat to support the development and consideration of adaptation technologies by Parties was agreed in the context of the Convention's budget for 1998–1999.[38] COP-3 requested the Convention Secretariat to continue its work on the synthesis and dissemination of information on environmentally sound mitigation and adaptation technologies.[39] This Decision specifically called for the acceleration of the 'development of methodologies for adaptation technologies, in particular decision tools to evaluate alternative adaptation strategies'.

SBSTA-8 in June 1998 encouraged the Secretariat to continue with its work on adaptation technologies, including addressing different topics identified in the expert/IPCC meeting held in 1997.[40] This led to a Secretariat technical paper on coastal zone management technologies.[41] The paper was welcomed by SBSTA-11 held in 1999, which noted that coastal adaptation strategies should incorporate soft engineering approaches, as well as planning and institutional measures, and that further work on such technologies should be considered as part of the transfer of technology consultative process, and requested the Secretariat to make new

---

[34] See chapter 10, section 6.   [35] Decision 13/CP.1.

[36] Decision 7/CP.2. This also instructed the Secretariat to undertake a survey of technology and information needs and to explore options for establishing 'one stop' databases of state-of-the-art technologies accessible to developing countries

[37] FCCC/TP/1997/3.   [38] FCCC/CP/1997/INF.1   [39] Decision 9/CP.3.   [40] FCCC/SBSTA/1998/6.

[41] FCCC/TP/1999/1.

information on adaptation technologies, including coastal adaptation technologies, available to Parties, as appropriate, via the Secretariat's website.[42] To facilitate policy-making by Parties on adaptation issues, a 'compendium of decision tools to evaluate strategies for adaptation to climate change' has been prepared.[43] The Expert Group on Technology Transfer created at COP-7 is intended to deal with technology-related issues, including those concerning adaptation, through its work programme, as explained in chapter 10. Its current work programme does not examine particular adaptation (or mitigation) technologies but relates to broader cross-cutting issues such as capacity-building and the creation of enabling environments.

3.4   *Adaptation and capacity-building*

Chapter 10 explains COP decisions taken to remedy the patchwork of Convention and Protocol related commitments on capacity-building and actions taken by the GEF, the entity operating the financial mechanism, to align its procedures for accessing funding accordingly. In May 2003, the GEF commenced development of an adaptation strategy for all its climate-related adaptation work to respond to rule development, particularly in terms of the Marrakesh Accords.[44]

To date the GEF has supported adaptation-related capacity-building largely in the context of 'enabling activities' for the preparation of initial national communications, which has provided a number of developing countries with financial support to undertake vulnerability and adaptation assessments.[45] This is described below in the section on GEF reporting.

3.5   *Special needs and circumstances*

3.5.1   Commitments applicable to all parties

Background: Articles 4.8 and 4.9 require *all* Parties to give special consideration to particular groups of countries, including in relation to funding, insurance and technology. Rule development relating to these articles has been complex for political and procedural reasons described in box 8.2 below. For clarity, this section is divided into two parts, the first explaining how Articles 4.8 and 4.9 must be considered by all Parties and the second focusing on the specific commitments on consideration of special needs and circumstances by Annex I Parties, including work on implementation of Articles 2.3 and 3.14 of the Kyoto Protocol.

---

[42] FCCC/SBSTA/1999/11. Parties' submissions on the paper are contained in FCCC/SBSTA/1999/MISC.11.

[43] 'Compendium of Decision Tools to Evaluate Strategies for Adaptation to Climate Change', prepared for the FCCC Secretariat, Stratus Consulting, May 1999. Available from FCCC website.

[44] GEF/C.21/Inf.10, A proposed GEF approach to Adaptation to Climate Change.

[45] See section 4.7 on GEF reporting and box 10.5.

FCCC: Articles 4.8 and 4.9 contain commitments applicable to *all* Parties to give special consideration to particular groups of developing country Parties. Article 4.9 provides that all 'Parties shall take full account of the specific needs and special situation of the least developed countries in their actions with regards to funding and transfer of technology.' Article 4.8 of the Convention mandates special consideration is given to nine categories of developing countries that may be vulnerable to the adverse effects of climate change and/or the impacts of the implementation of response measures.[46] It specifies that in their implementation of the Convention *all* Parties shall give 'full consideration to what actions are necessary under the Convention, including actions related to funding, insurance and the transfer of technology, to meet the specific needs and concerns' of such developing country Parties arising from the adverse effects of climate change. Article 4.8 specifies that the COP 'may take actions, as appropriate, with respect to this paragraph'. This provision does not mandate the provision of funding, insurance and technology transfer to developing countries but simply provides a procedural 'marker' for future consideration by the COP. The reference to 'insurance' in Article 4.8 is the only remaining trace of an international insurance pool submitted by AOSIS in 1991 to help finance adaptation costs, discussed below under 'funders' in adaptation financing.[47]

The legal import of Article 4.8 on the implementation of existing commitments is not clear, with some commentators highlighting that 'it may well have been included for purely political purposes so that particular categories could receive explicit recognition in the Convention'.[48] Others point out that whilst Article 4.8 is not a definition of who is 'particularly vulnerable', it is useful, nevertheless, in providing an agreed starting point defining the kinds of vulnerabilities relevant for considering the nature, scope and priority of assistance to be provided to developing countries.[49] The legal relationship between Article 4.8, which covers all developing countries, including LDCs, with the more specific provisions for LDCs in Article 4.9 has also proved difficult to pin down. Be that as it may, both Articles 4.8 and 4.9 have led to the adoption of a number of significant COP decisions relating to LDCs, adaptation and the implementation of response measures.

Kyoto: Article 10 (g) of the Protocol simply requires that all Parties 'give full consideration, in implementing the commitments under this Article, to Article 4, paragraph 8, of the Convention'. Article 11.1 of the Protocol specifies that all

---

[46] Chapter 9 discusses the impact of implementation of response measures.

[47] Bodansky, 1993: p. 528. See also proposal for an insurance mechanism submitted by Vanuatu on behalf of AOSIS, A/AC.237/WGII/CRP.8, 17 December 1991, and AOSIS International Insurance Pool, A/AC.237/Misc.1/Add.3 and A/AC.237/15.

[48] Bodansky, 1993, text at footnote 475, p. 531.   [49] Yamin, 1998b.

Parties must take Article 4.9 of the Convention into account in the implementation of Article 10 of the Protocol.

Rule development: As explained in box 8.2, up until COP-3 consideration of the implications of Articles 4.8 and 4.9 fed into other COP agenda items. COP-3 requested SBI to commence discussions of Articles 4.8 and 4.9 but Decision 3/CP.3 did not mention Articles 2.3 or 3.14 of the Kyoto Protocol. COP-4 agreed to include discussion of Article 2.3 as well as 3.14 in this process and made satisfactory completion of work related to this part of the BAPA with Decision 5/CP.4 setting out a two-year programme of work to identify further actions for the COP to consider. COP-5 tried to conceptualise this framework in a more coherent manner by separating out the three distinct strands of work encompassed by Articles 4.8 and 4.9 as follows: work related to adaptation to adverse impacts of climate change; work related to implementation of response measures; and work related to implementation of Article 3.14. A number of expert workshops were convened to support policy discussions in this area as follows: (a) a workshop on views and actions relating to Article 4.8/4.9 and 2.3/3.14 to follow up Decision 5/CP.4[50] held in 1999; and (b) two workshops held back-to-back on initial actions related to adverse impacts and on response measures held in March 2000.[51] The results of these workshops fed into COP-6 part II which reached broad political agreement about these issues with COP-7, resulting in a package of decisions on Articles 4.8 and 4.9 with specific provisions to meet the needs of LDCs and adaptation and agreement on how Article 3.14 should be further considered. The substantive contents of the Marrakesh Accords are discussed below, with Decision 5/CP.7 requesting the organisation of a number of meetings to further consideration of specific issues.

Thus, post-Marrakesh the programme of workshops has continued, mapping out various issues that might support rule development in the future, although current discussions relating to policy are at an early stage of understanding. A workshop on the status of modelling activities relating to adverse impacts and response measures was held in May 2002 and was reported to SBI-16.[52] More recently, two workshops were held in May 2003 prior to SBI-18: one on insurance and risk assessment in the context of climate change and extreme weather events and the other on insurance-related actions to address developing country needs in relation to the adverse impacts of climate change and from the impact of response measures.[53] And finally, workshops were convened on synergies and cooperation with other conventions in Finland in June 2003 and on economic diversification in Tehran in October 2003. These complete the workshops mandated by

---

[50] FCCC/SB/1999/9.   [51] FCCC/SB/2000/2.

[52] FCCC/SBI/2002/6, paragraphs 24–7, referring to an oral report of the workshop.

[53] FCCC/CP/2003/11.

Decision 5/CP.7. The future direction, time-frame and policy content of further rule development in this area now remain to be developed.

3.5.2   Commitments applicable to Annex I Parties

Kyoto: The Protocol contains specific commitments for Annex I Parties relating to the consideration of the needs and circumstances of developing country Parties covered by Articles 4.8 and 4.9 beyond those contained in the Convention. Article 2.3 of the Protocol requires Annex I Parties to strive to implement mitigation-related policies and measures so as to minimise adverse effects, including the adverse effects of climate change, effects on international trade and social, environmental and economic impacts on other Parties, especially developing country Parties, in particular those mentioned in Articles 4.8 and 4.9 of the Convention. In a similar vein, Article 3.14 of the Protocol requires Annex I Parties to implement their commitments under Article 3.1 of the Protocol in such as way as to minimise the adverse social, environmental and economic impacts on developing countries, particularly those identified in Articles 4.8 and 4.9 of the Convention. Article 3.14 states that the COP/MOP is required to consider what actions may be necessary to minimise such impacts as well as to consider the 'establishment of funding, insurance and transfer of technology'.

The commitments in Articles 2.3 and 3.14 are procedural in that they do not oblige Annex II Parties to provide funding, insurance or technology to developing countries for dealing with adverse impacts and/or response measures. But these provisions do require the COP/MOP to give consideration to these issues, with Article 3.14 setting up expectations that the first session of the COP/MOP will consider the establishment of funding, insurance and transfer of technology.

At COP-3, Parties did not agree to include consideration of Articles 2.3 and 3.14 as part of the 'prompt start' provisions accompanying the adoption of the Protocol. Consideration of Articles 2.3 and 3.14 came to be included as part of the BAPA at COP-4.[54] Decision 5/CP.7 of the Marrakesh Accords sets out a number of COP decisions that relate directly to Articles 4.8 and 4.9 of the Convention and Articles 2.3 and 3.14 of the Protocol. These are being discussed through the convening of workshops described above. In addition, because Article 2.3 concerns PAMs which all Parties agree support the implementation of the Convention as well as the Protocol, its impact on implementation by Annex I Parties is being considered under the Convention's work on Annex I PAMs described in chapter 5.[55] The substance of COP decisions related to adaptation adopted at Marrakesh is explained below in this chapter. Matters related to the impacts of

---

[54] Decisions 1/CP.4 and 5/CP.4.   [55] See chapter 5, section 5.3.

the implementation of response measures are set out separately in the following chapter.

Box 8.2   Adaptation and the COP agenda: a brief history

Newcomers to the climate regime find tracking adaptation rule development both difficult – because the rules are interspersed in various COP decisions – and perplexing – because an issue as widely supported as adaptation seems to be embroiled in procedural disputes about which Convention article is the relevant basis for action. Although the consideration of Articles 4.8 and 4.9 of the Convention by the COP as a separate agenda item only commenced at COP-4, many fundamental issues relating to adaptation were being addressed by earlier COPs on the basis of other Convention provisions. This is because rule development concerning the adverse impacts of climate change has revolved around making good commitments *already agreed* in the Convention under Articles 4.3 and 4.4. Thus, adaptation issues are discussed as part of the negotiations giving guidance to the GEF or other agenda items relating to technology. Adoption of Decision 3/CP.3 by COP-3 added a new dynamic because this Decision mandates the COP to consider actions related to Articles 4.8 and 4.9 at future sessions as a separate agenda item. An agenda item explicitly addressing developing countries' adaptation-related needs and circumstances has the potential advantage of highlighting a broader range of issues that might not have fitted well into other agenda items. But in the case of adaptation it also brought complications because Decision 3/CP.3 was critical to getting OPEC countries to withdraw their veto on the adoption of the Kyoto Protocol.[56] As noted by one commentator, 'a major political success of OPEC was to align its fears procedurally alongside those of other 'vulnerable groups' listed in Articles 4.8 and 4.9'.[57] This linkage was, and remains, legally and procedurally necessary for OPEC countries because, unlike adaptation, which is covered in Article 4.1 and supported by financial commitments agreed under Articles 4.3 and 4.4, the Convention contains no financial commitments in favour of developing countries affected by the implementation of response measures. This is also true of the Kyoto Protocol. OPEC countries have had to use Article 4.8 of the Convention as a legal basis to foment wider support for their demands for financial assistance and 'compensation' for potential economic 'injuries'. This means, however, that progress on adaptation issues has become

---

[56] Grubb et al., 1999: p. 140.   [57] Grubb et al., 1999: p. 140.

conditional upon equivalent progress on response measures. Since COP-5, mounting frustration at the pace of progress caused by this linkage has led to procedural moves to organise the COP agenda to separate out consideration of urgent LDC adaptation needs under Article 4.9 from broader adaptation/response measures issues covered by Article 4.8 as well as to differentiate between Convention commitments arising from Article 4.8/4.9 from Protocol-related issues arising from Article 3.14. These attempts are partly reflected in the structure of the Marrakesh Accords which carve out special work programmes for LDCs and set out work on Article 3.14 in a separate decision. The possibility, desirability and implications of a procedural separation between adaptation issues and implementation of response measures under Article 4.8 more generally is likely to continue at future COP sessions, reflecting the very different nature of adaptation and response measure concerns.

4   Adaptation financing

Background: The Convention's financial mechanism, the role of the GEF as the entity entrusted with its operation, and the financial commitments set out in the Convention are explained in chapter 10. This section explains rules, institutional and procedural features that have a particular bearing on adaptation financing. For ease of reference issues related to adaptation by LDCs are discussed in section 5 below. The issue of potential liability for damage caused by anthropogenic climate change on the basis of general principles of state responsibility has led some Parties to the Convention to make declarations to their instrument of ratification which are discussed in chapter 4.

4.1   *Resource providers*

FCCC: The obligation to provide funding for adaptation-related activities, set out in Articles 4.3 and 4.4 of the Convention, applies to the twenty-four Parties listed in Annex II.[58] Annex II Parties must provide sources to the Convention's financial mechanism but may also provide funding through bilateral, regional and other multilateral channels.[59]

Kyoto: The advancement of adaptation commitments set out in the Protocol must be funded by the Parties listed in Annex II of the Convention that choose to become Parties to the Protocol. The lack of ratification by the USA, the largest single contributor to the Convention and the GEF, has been an important consideration

---

[58] See chapter 10.   [59] Article 11.5

in designing the funding priorities of the new funds established by the Marrakesh Accords, as described below.

Declining ODA levels and frustration at the bottlenecks in the provision of adaptation funding through the Convention's financial mechanism led developing countries to consider sources of adaptation funding other than Annex II Parties during the Protocol's negotiations. An adaptation levy is to be paid by proponents of activities under the CDM.[60] Article 12.8 therefore provides another source of adaptation financing, although its exact scale will depend on the stringency of Annex I Parties' abatement efforts and the CDM's investment attractiveness.[61] It should be noted that, although participation in CDM activities is voluntary for Parties and their private entities, payment of the adaptation levy is mandatory in order for proponents to obtain CERs accruing from CDM projects.[62] To encourage CDM investments in LDCs, proponents of CDM projects undertaken in LDCs are exempt from the adaptation levy.[63]

Rule development: Changes to the list of countries included in Annex II, and the respective contribution made by each, are set out in chapter 10. Attempts by developing countries to extend the CDM adaptation levy to emissions trading under Article 17 and JI projects under Article 6 as part of the Marrakesh Accords did not succeed. Finally, discussions around insurance-based proposals as mandated by Decision 5/CP.7 on Articles 4.8 and 4.9 could conceivably result in the adoption of mechanisms that bring in other sources of finance, including from the private sector.[64] Discussions covering various types of insurance, risk transfer and collective loss-sharing mechanisms are at an early stage of discussion and it is unclear after COP-9 what process and time-frame will support policy gestation.[65]

4.2   Recipients

FCCC and Kyoto: The Convention and the Protocol mandate provisions of financial and technological assistance to 'developing countries'. The meaning of this term is explained in chapter 10. Current regime practices mean that all Parties that are not listed in Annex I of the Convention can receive funding relating to adaptation of measures covered by Article 4.1 pursuant to Article 4.3.

Article 4.4 of the Convention specifies that Annex II Parties shall assist '*developing countries that are particularly vulnerable to the adverse effects of climate change* in meeting costs of adaptation to those adverse effects' (emphasis added). Article 12.8

---

[60] See chapter 6, section 6.7.   [61] Haites and Yamin, 2000.   [62] See chapter 6, section 6.7.
[63] Decision 17/CP.7, paragraph 15 (b).   [64] Decision 5/CP.7, Annex, paragraph 9.
[65] FCCC Report of the workshop mandated by Decision 5/CP.7 on insurance-related actions and risk assessment. See also Linnerooth-Bayer et al., 2003.

of the Protocol and many COP decisions, particularly those providing guidance to the Convention's financial mechanism, also use this terminology.

The COP has not actually defined which countries are particularly vulnerable nor set out criteria to establish this. Instead, based on a variety of information, including the IPCC Reports and initial national communications, so far as financial and technological resources are concerned, the COP has highlighted the need to meet the adaptation needs of two particular groups of countries: LDCs and SIDS. This is reflected in the guidance to the Convention's financial mechanism adopted by COP-7 which states that 'the GEF . . . should provide financial resources to developing countries, in particular the least developed and the small island States among them'.[66] It is also reflected in recent COP decisions on capacity-building in Decision 2/CP.7 which states, for instance, that capacity-building is important for all developing countries, 'especially those that are particularly vulnerable', and specifically mentions LDCs and SIDS.[67] The same Decision calls on Annex II Parties to provide resources for implementing the capacity-building framework to developing countries, particularly LDCs and SIDS, and calls on Annex II Parties to give particular attention to the needs of LDCs and SIDS.[68]

The rationale for highlighting these two groups of countries is their limited adaptive capacity to cope with the adverse effects of climate change, and in the case of LDCs, their extreme low levels of economic development which, combined with high levels of poverty, makes them especially vulnerable to the adverse effects of climate change. It is important to note that highlighting the adaptation-related needs of LDCs and SIDS does not imply that other developing countries are not particularly vulnerable to climate change impacts. The aim of highlighting LDCs and SIDS is to signal some degree of sequential and institutional prioritisation rather than exclusion of other groups whose adaptation-related needs must also be met pursuant to Articles 4.3 and 4.4 of the Convention.

4.3   *Amount*

FCCC: The issue of *scope* refers to the range of adaptation activities that must be financed, with *amount* referring to the proportion of the cost to be funded.

Amount and scope are practically related because both limit Annex II Parties' financial responsibilities. Article 4.3 of the Convention obliges Annex II Parties to provide new and additional financial resources to the Convention's financial mechanism to cover the *agreed full incremental costs* incurred by developing country Parties of all measures covered by Article 4.1 and the *agreed full costs* incurred by developing countries in complying with their reporting obligations under

---

[66] Decision 6/CP.7, paragraph 1.   [67] Decision 2/CP.7, Annex, paragraph 17.
[68] Decision 2/CP.7, Annex, paragraph 20.

Article 12. These terms are explained in detail in chapter 10. Article 4.5 requires Annex II Parties to facilitate and finance the transfer of environmentally sound technologies and know-how to developing countries to implement commitments under the Convention.

Article 4.4 provides that Annex II Parties shall also assist the developing country Parties that are particularly vulnerable to the adverse effects of climate change in meeting *costs of adaptation* to those adverse effects. This commitment has been seen as potentially one of the costliest under the Convention, although others have questioned its significance given the lack of details set out in Article 4.4,[69] including the lack of reference to the concept of agreed full costs or incremental costs and the fact that Article 4.4 refers to 'costs of adaptation' and not 'the costs of adaptation'.[70] Article 4.4 also makes no mention of the Convention's financial mechanism, leaving open whether adaptation-related funding under Article 4.4 was to be provided through the Convention's financial mechanism or other channels such as bilateral and multilateral ones.[71] Finally, Article 4.4 does not actually say whether funding for Article 4.4 is to be 'new and additional' nor what the time-frame for it to be made available is.

Kyoto: As explained in chapter 10, guidance previously agreed by the COP for the Convention's financial mechanism applies to the Protocol on a *mutatis mutandis* basis.[72] Thus the concepts of agreed full and incremental costs in the COP guidance to the GEF concerning adaptation is carried over to the Protocol. The Protocol does not contain a provision which is directly comparable to Article 4.4 of the Convention, although Article 11.1 of the Protocol refers to the need to take Article 4.4 into account. Additionally, Article 12.8 of the Protocol, defining the CDM, can be seen an *one* means of giving concrete effect to Article 4.4, although Article 4.4 remains a legally distinct financial commitment.[73]

Rule development: As explained in chapter 10, adaptation activities generate local, rather than global, benefits, making it difficult to apply concepts such as 'incremental costs' as mandated by the Convention and the GEF's constituent Instrument of Establishment. This limitation explains why developing countries viewed the operation of the Convention's financial mechanism by the GEF as being inimical to the effective implementation of their adaptation-related Convention commitments. Negotiations on the Marrakesh Accords were viewed as an opportunity to remedy adaptation finance bottlenecks, including the lack of detail

---

[69] Sands, 1992, states that Article 4.4 'amounts to an implicit acceptance of responsibility for causing climate change [that is] likely to emerge as one of the unusual, and perhaps costly, commitments in the Convention. But see Bodansky, 1993: p. 528.

[70] Bodansky, 1993: footnote and text at note 466, points out that Article 4.4 uses the indefinite 'costs of adaptation' rather than 'the costs of adaption'.

[71] Bodansky, 1993: p. 528.   [72] KP Articles 10 and 11.   [73] See chapter 6, section 6.7.3.

on the timing, extent and institutional modalities of adaptation finance that had been experienced over the years. Adaptation under the three funds established by the Marrakesh Accords is discussed below.

4.4   Scope

FCCC and Kyoto: The range of activities that can be funded as adaptation activities under the Convention and the Protocol is very wide. Furthermore, the chapeau of Article 4.1 of the Convention and Article 10 of the Kyoto Protocol gives all Parties, developed and developing, a large measure of discretion to determine adaptation activities appropriate for its circumstances, bearing in mind its national circumstances, developmental priorities and objectives. These considerations are one reason why Annex II Parties remain hesitant about financing adaptation costs.

Rule development: Decision 5/CP.7 on the implementation of Articles 4.8 and 4.9 tries to balance the need for flexibility and diversity arising from differing national circumstances with the need for predictability and certainty. Decision 5/CP.7 confirms the importance of a 'country driven approach' to adaptation planning, allowing 'specific activities most appropriate to their unique national circumstances', but, at the same time, it also insists that 'action related to adaptation follow an assessment and evaluation process, based on national communications and/or other relevant information, so as to prevent maladaptation and to ensure that adaptation actions are environmentally sound and will produce real benefits in support of sustainable development'.[74] Although this is not strictly speaking a limitation on the scope of activities, the creation of a process to assess, filter and prioritise adaptation activities suitable for funding creates a temporal pipeline for advancing adaptation projects in a more transparent and manageable manner and provides some assurance that funding proposals are based on information that is as sound as possible. This conforms with the basic thrust of the three-staged approach to funding set out by COP-1 in Decision 11/CP.1, discussed in more detail below.

4.5   COP guidance

Background: This section sets out the guidance given to the Convention's financial mechanism, operated by the GEF, on adaptation funding. The thrust of rule development has been to enhance such resources and to simplify procedures enabling developing countries to build capacity, including through learning by doing and adaptation demonstration projects.

---

[74] Decision 5/CP.7, paragraphs 1 and 2.

FCCC and Kyoto: Article 11 of the Convention establishes the Convention's financial mechanism and states that it is for the COP to determine its policies, programme priorities and eligibility criteria. Article 11 of the Protocol incorporates use of the Convention's financial mechanism, stating that guidance provided by the COP will apply *mutatis mutandis* to the Protocol.[75] These provisions are explained in more detail in chapter 9.

Rule development: Decision 11/CP.1 sets out the initial guidance adopted by COP-1 to the GEF on the policies, programme priorities and eligibility criteria it should follow for Convention-related matters, including adaptation. This Decision remains the cornerstone of adaptation financing, although it has been refined and elaborated through COP decisions, particularly Decisions 5/CP.6 and 6/CP.7 adopted as part of the Marrakesh Accords.[76] Decision 11/CP.1 envisages that adaptation will require short-, medium- and long-term strategies which are to be 'cost-effective' and 'implemented on a stage-by-stage basis' as follows:

- Stage I: Planning. This covers studies of possible climate change impacts, identification of particularly vulnerable countries or regions and policy options for adaptation and capacity-building;
- Stage II: This covers measures, including further capacity-building, which may be taken to prepare for adaptation, as envisaged in Article 4.1 (e), but such measures are only fundable for particularly vulnerable countries/regions identified at Stage I;
- Stage III: This covers measures to facilitate adequate adaptation, including insurance, and other adaptation measures as envisaged by Articles 4.1 (b) and 4.4.

Decision 11/CP.1 made clear that the Convention's financial mechanism would only fund Stage I measures undertaken as enabling activities in the context of the formulation of national communications. Paragraph 1 (d) (iv) makes clear that the GEF is to meet the agreed full costs of relevant adaptation activities undertaken as part of activities required by Article 12.1. Such activities may include studies of possible impacts of climate change, identification of options for implementing adaptation provisions, especially the obligations in Article 4.1 (b) and (e), and relevant capacity-building.

Funding for Stages II and III would only be available if evidence from Stage I studies as well as other relevant scientific and technical studies, such as those of the IPCC, and any other evidence of the adverse effects of climate change is first

---

[75] KP Article 11.2.

[76] Decisions 5/CP.7 and 6/CP.7. Decision 2/CP.7 concerning capacity-building is also relevant, as are the Decisions dealing with LDCs, NAPA and the LEG discussed below.

considered by the COP which 'may decide that it has become necessary to imple-ment the measures envisaged in Stage II and III'.[77] In this eventuality, Annex II Parties are to provide funding to implement such measures under their obligation under Articles 4.3 and 4.4. Paragraph (iv) states that the COP should then decide on the channel or channels for funding for Stage II and III, anticipating that such funding may be provided by Annex II Parties directly through channels other than the Convention's financial mechanism.

COP 4 gave additional guidance to the GEF through Decision 2/CP.4 on Stage II activities. This invited the GEF to support developing countries that want to

> implement adaptation response measures under Article 4.1 of the Convention for adaptation activities envisaged in decision 11/CP.1, paragraph 1 (d) (ii) (Stage II activities) in particularly vulnerable countries and regions identified in Stage I activities, and especially in countries vulnerable to climate-related natural disasters, taking into account their preparatory adaptation planning frameworks in priority sectors, the completion of Stage I activities, and in the context of their national communications.

The practical implementation of Decisions 11/CP.1 and 2/CP.4 continued to give rise to a number of problems and these are now addressed in the Marrakesh Accords. The underlying policy issues were:

- Can vulnerability assessment and identification of adaptation options (Stage I activities) be undertaken outside the context of the formulation of national communications?
- When can Stage II and Stage III activities be supported, and what assess-ment and information gathering need to be undertaken to ensure funding through the Convention's financial mechanism?

Decisions 5/CP.7 and 6/CP.7 resolve these questions by providing more focused channels and procedures for adaptation financing for LDCs and by removing or clarifying constraints contained in Decision 11/CP.1. The key areas of rule devel-opment resulting from the Marrakesh Accords are:

- Identification and communication of LDC adaptation needs is no longer tied to the process of preparation and submission of national communications but linked instead to the preparation of NAPAs, which may constitute 'the first step in the preparation of national communica-tions', with funding for these to be provided by the LDC Fund.[78]

---

[77] Decision 11/CP.1, paragraph 1 (d) (iii).   [78] See chapter 10, section 4.1.

- Stage II measures can be implemented by developing country Parties provided work has been undertaken at the national level in the context *either* of national communications *or* of in-depth national studies, including NAPAs.[79] This means that funding for Stage II measures is not dependent on submission of national communications *per se* but still requires in-depth assessment at national level.

- Although Stage III measures are not mentioned as such, the Marrakesh Accords provide that 'pilot or demonstration projects to show how adaptation planning and assessment can be practically translated into projects' may receive funding 'on the basis of information provided in national communication *or* in-depth studies, including NAPAs, and of the staged approach endorsed . . . in Decision 11/CP.1'.[80] The reference to the 'staged approach' means that countries that want to undertake pilot or demonstration projects must have undertaken Stage I and Stage II activities.

- Funding for Stage I and Stage II activities and pilot/demonstration projects shall be provided by the Convention's financial mechanism and the new funds established by the Marrakesh Accords, and thus not left entirely to other channels.

- The SCCF and/or the Adaptation Fund can also fund adaptation activities 'where sufficient information is available to warrant such activities, inter alia, in the areas of water resources management, land management, agriculture, health, infrastructure development, fragile ecosystems, including mountainous ecosystems, and integrated coastal zone management'.[81]

Decision 6/CP.8 is also relevant as it requests GEF to provide expedited funding for non-Annex I Parties' national communications and for the prompt implementation of capacity-building measures.[82] Additional guidance for adaptation funding has been agreed at COP-9, guidance relating to the policies, programmes and eligibility criteria for the SCCF. Decision 5/CP.9 relating to the SCCF provides that adaptation activities 'shall have top priority for funding'. Implementation of adaptation activities is to be supported by the SCCF 'where sufficient information is available to warrant such activities' and taking into account national communications and/or NAPAs and other relevant information. The Preamble to Decision 5/CP.9 notes that the SCCF supports the implementation of the Convention as well as achievement of the WSSD and Millennium Development Goals, but without making the achievement of these a precondition for funding. Finally, COP-9 agreed

---

[79] Decision 6/CP.7, paragraph 1 (a).

[80] Decision 6/CP.7, paragraph 1 (b) and Decision 5/CP.7, paragraph 7 (b) (v).

[81] Decision 5/CP.7, paragraph 8, Decision 7/CP.7, paragraph 2, and Decision 10/CP.7, paragraph 1.

[82] See chapter 10, section 7.4.

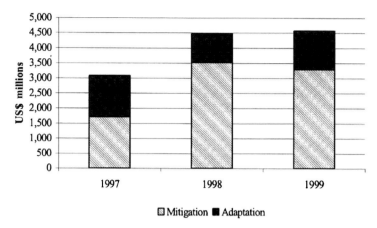

Fig. 8.1   Bilateral contributions to adaptation projects in NC3s of Annex II Parties[83]

that adaptation activities under the SCCF can relate to water resource management, land management, agriculture, health, infrastructure development, fragile ecosystems, including mountainous ecosystems and integrated coastal zone
management, improvement in the monitoring of diseases/vectors and related
forecasting and early warning systems, capacity-building for preventative measures and disaster preparedness and strengthening or establishing national and
regional centres for rapid responses to extreme weather events.[84] In addition to
Decision 5/CP.9, COP-9 also adopted Decision 4/CP.9 providing guidance to the GEF
as discussed below.

4.6   *Funds and channels*

Funding for adaptation is to be channelled through four different funds,
all of which are operated by the GEF subject to guidance from the COP:

- GEF Trust Fund for Climate Change;
- LDC Fund;
- Special Climate Change Fund; and
- Adaptation Fund.

Chapter 10 describes in detail how these funds operate or will operate. The Convention and the Protocol also allow Annex II Parties to provide, and developing
country Parties to avail themselves of, financial resources for the implementation
of their commitments through bilateral, regional and multilateral channels. A
recent study of such channels underlined the significance of these other channels
of funding as shown in figure 8.1, but concluded that, based on Annex I Parties'

[83] FCCC/TP/2003/2, figure 5.   [84] Decision 5/CP.9, paragraphs 1–2.

third national communications, adaptation has received a much smaller share of bilateral contributions.[85]

4.7   *GEF reporting on adaptation*

GEF annual reports to the COP are an important source of information on the status of adaptation activities undertaken by Parties, whether supported by Convention mandated funding or otherwise. The GEF activities related to adaptation can be grouped under three headings:

- GEF support for adaptation under the climate change area;
- GEF support for adaptation under other focal areas; and
- Other developments.

In its report to COP-8, for example, the GEF reported that 132 countries have received financial support and technical guidance to assist them in preparing their first national communications, amounting to some $86.97 million, with some countries undertaking Stage I activities such as voluntary vulnerability and adaptation assessments. The GEF has also financed two regional Stage I enabling activity projects relating to adaptation, one in the Caribbean and the other in the Pacific.[86] All of these were funded on an agreed full cost basis. Many countries have also conducted independent impact studies aimed at the identification of vulnerable regions and sectors, and adaptation options with support from sources such as the US Country Studies Program, the Netherlands, the European Union and others. The GEF reported these studies were carried out using the 1994 IPCC Technical Guidelines, with the results being communicated in some instances through non-Annex I Parties' initial national communications.[87]

The GEF noted, however, that many Parties have not yet completed their analysis of vulnerability and that only a few have identified policy options for adaptation.[88] Under Convention guidelines, support for Stage II and Stage III activities is conditional upon Stage I adaptation activities having been completed, whether the assessments are undertaken in the context of national communications or otherwise. Some Stage II activities have already commenced. The GEF has also provided funding for Stage II in response to six country requests, again in the context of enabling activities related to national communications, which means such activities are supported on an agreed full cost basis.[89]

The GEF is also beginning to support adaptation to climate change in the context of its other focal areas, in particular, biodiversity, land degradation and

---

[85] FCCC/TP/2003/2, paragraph 55.   [86] FCCC/CP/2002/4, paragraph 35.
[87] FCCC/CP/2002/4, paragraph 34.   [88] FCCC/CP/2002/4, paragraph 13.
[89] FCCC/CP/2002/4, paragraph 37.

international waters, demonstrating that it can use a multi-focal area approach to integrate adaptation into other activities.[90] Finally, to respond to the evolution of COP guidance on adaptation, in particular the establishment of new funds, the GEF is currently preparing a comprehensive Adaptation Strategy.[91] To advance work on this, the GEF Scientific and Technical Advisory Panel has established an Expert Group.[92] This met in Nairobi to elaborate elements of the GEF Adaptation Strategy.[93] A proposed approach for the GEF Adaptation Strategy was circulated for information in May 2003 and forms the background for the new strategic priority in the climate change focal area (Piloting an Operational Approach to Adaptation) which COP-9 has encouraged the GEF to operationalise as soon as possible in its Decision 4/CP.9.[94]

5   LDCs and adaptation

Background: The LDCs form a bloc of forty-nine countries with approximately 10.97 per cent of the world's population.[95] Although LDCs' special needs for finance and technology have been recognised since the earliest days of the climate regime, and are reflected in Article 4.9 of the Convention, LDC adaptation needs were only explicitly highlighted at COP-6 when the COP adopted Resolution 2/CP.6 as an input to the Third UN Conference on LDCs, held in May 2001.[96] The Resolution recognises that low levels of human, institutional and technological development limit LDCs' adaptive capacity, making them vulnerable to natural and economic shocks, and thus among the most vulnerable to the adverse impacts of climate change. COP-6 agreed to examine how NAPAs could assist LDCs to meet their adaptation needs. As part of the negotiations on Articles 4.8 and 4.9, COP-7 formalised a work programme for LDCs to prepare NAPAs with institutional support from the LDC Expert Group and financial resources from a dedicated fund – the LDC Fund.

5.1   *LDC work programme*

Article 4.9 of the Convention requires Parties to take 'full account of the specific needs and special situation of the least developed countries in their action with regard to funding and transfer of technology'. Decision 5/CP.7

---

[90] FCCC/CP/2002/4, paragraphs 38–40.   [91] See GEF Report to COP-9, FCCC/CP/2003/3.

[92] GEF/C.19/Inf.12, Report of the STAP Expert Group Workshop on Adaptation, 18–20 February 2002, Nairobi, Kenya.

[93] GEF/C.19/Inf.12.

[94] GEC/C.21/Inf.10, 29 April 2003, A proposed GEF approach to Adaptation to Climate Change. For a summary of this paper, see GEF Report to COP-9, FCCC/CP/2003/3.

[95] See chapter 3, section 2.6.   [96] Resolution 2/CP.6.

contains sections specifically addressing LDC needs. This work programme covers support for the following activities:

- strengthening existing or establishing, where needed, new national climate change secretariats and/or focal points in LDCs to enable effective implementation of the Convention and the Protocol;
- training in negotiating skills and language to develop capacity of LDC negotiators to participate effectively in the climate change process; and
- preparation of NAPAs which can serve as a simplified and direct channel of communication of information relating to LDC vulnerabilities and adaptation.

The first two activities are not limited to adaptation but intended to strengthen LDC capacity to deal with all aspects of climate change. The preparation of NAPAs is, however, central to implementation of the other two elements of the work programme because NAPA preparation is intended to facilitate the development of capacity which will assist achievement of the other two activities.

5.2   *NAPAs*

Initial guidelines for the preparation of NAPAs are set out in Decision 28/CP.7. Although Parties agreed to review and, if needed, to improve these guidelines at COP-8, they decided that a revision of the guidelines was not necessary.[97] This was confirmed by COP-9.[98] Thus, at present, LDCs have been invited to use the NAPA guidelines adopted at COP-7, referring, where appropriate, to the work of the LEG if there is need for their further clarification.[99]

The guidelines for NAPAs are divided into six sections. Sections A and B set out the rationale and objective of NAPAs. The rationale for NAPAs was recognition of the fact that many LDCs simply do not have the capacity to prepare and submit national communications in the foreseeable future and their low adaptive capacity renders them in need of immediate and urgent support to start adaptation to climate change. The objective of NAPAs is to serve as simplified and direct channels of communication for information relating to urgent and immediate adaptation needs of the LDCs. As stated above, preparation of NAPAs also benefits capacity-building and could constitute the first step in the preparation of initial national communications.

Sections C and D of the guidelines set out the characteristics and guiding elements for NAPAs. Although not explicitly stated, an important principle of NAPAs is that countries should use existing information, including traditional knowledge, and that there should be no new studies. The NAPAs should set

---

[97] Decision 9/CP.8.   [98] Decision 8/CP.9.   [99] Decision 9/CP.8, paragraphs 1 and 2.

clear priorities for urgent and immediate action in an easy-to-understand, action-orientated manner. NAPAs should be prepared through a participatory process involving stakeholders, particularly local communities, be based on a multidisciplinary approach, build upon existing plans and studies such as national action plans under the UNCCD, national biodiversity strategies, poverty reduction strategy papers (PRSPs) and national sectoral policies. In addition, NAPAs should be guided by sustainable development, gender equality, a country-driven approach, sound environmental management, cost-effectiveness, simplicity and flexibility to suit individual country circumstances.

Section E of the NAPA guidelines defines a process that may be used for the preparation of NAPAs. Although LDCs do not have to follow this process, something similar is likely to be needed to incorporate the various elements in the NAPA guidelines. Additionally, the GEF has described the process set out in Section E as 'logical', stating that it 'attaches great significance to this holistic, multidisciplinary and cross-sectoral approach, openness and transparency of the process, and the participation of a wide range of stakeholders in the preparation of the NAPAs'.[100] For these reasons, in providing financial assistance for NAPAs, the GEF will seek information about how each of the requirements of Section E is being met. The key elements of the process set out in Section E are:

- Establishment of a national multidisciplinary NAPA team, composed of government agencies and civil society, by the national climate change focal point through an open, flexible, inclusive and transparent process;
- Responsibility for preparation of NAPAs to rest with the NAPA team;
- NAPA team to synthesise *available* information and conduct a participatory assessment of vulnerability to climate change, identifying key climate change adaptation measures based on the vulnerability assessment and identification and prioritisation of country-driven criteria for the selection of priority activities;
- Development and prioritisation of actual proposals based on the criteria above in the format required by the COP;
- Public review and revision of the NAPA document;
- Final review by a team of government and civil society representatives, including the private sector, with any advice solicited by the LEG;
- National government endorsement and public dissemination of the final NAPA document.

---

[100] GEF Operational Guidelines for Expedited Funding for Preparation of NAPAs by LDCs, April 2002, paragraph 9.

The structure and format of NAPAs is set out in Section F. This also provides some guidance for the criteria to be used for selecting priority activities and requires the development of a set of 'profiles' for selected priority activities to facilitate the funding process. Thus, following a rigorous process for NAPA preparation is likely to increase the chances for funding from the GEF and other sources for implementation of NAPAs.

5.3   *LDC Expert Group*

The LEG was established at COP-7.[101] It is an important element in the package of decisions adopted under the Marrakesh Accords following negotiations on the implementation of Articles 4.8 and 4.9 of the Convention.[102]

The LEG's main purpose is to advise LDC Parties themselves on the preparation and implementation strategy for NAPAs. In so doing, the LEG is mandated to coordinate its work with other adaptation initiatives which are ongoing in the intergovernmental arena. Unlike the other limited membership bodies under the Convention, whose work all passes through the subsidiary bodies, the LEG communicates directly with LDC Parties, circulating documentation to help such Parties prepare NAPAs, including through web-based tools intended to speed up the preparation of NAPAs, as adaptation is essentially a country-driven issue which LDC experts are best equipped to assist with. A special LDC website has been developed by the climate change Secretariat to facilitate this direct communication, and the structure and form of this is in keeping with its primary mandate which is to assist LDCs (rather than to assist the COP).

The LEG is expert-based, with its members required to have 'recognized competence and appropriate expertise to assist in the development of NAPAs', including expertise in 'vulnerability and adaptation assessment'. The LEG consists of nine members from LDCs, including five from Africa and two each from Asia and the small island states. There is no representation for Latin America and the Caribbean as a region because Haiti is the only LDC in that region and is represented through members elected by small island states. The three remaining members come from Annex II Parties. Unlike the other expert groups, therefore, the LEG's membership is not representative of the full spectrum of Party groups: developing countries that are not LDCs cannot serve on the LEG, nor can EITs as none are currently listed in Annex II of the Convention.

The experts are selected by the groups of Parties themselves, but once they have been appointed, they must act in their personal capacity, that is, not as governmental negotiators, and not have any 'financial or pecuniary interest' in the work of the group.[103] The Decision, however, does not require these experts

---

[101] Decision 29/CP.7.   [102] Decision 5/CP.7.   [103] Decision 29/CP.7, Annex, paragraph 4.

to be drawn from the regime's roster of experts. The LEG may also draw upon additional expertise, if needed,[104] although this must be approved by the LEG Chairperson and done 'judiciously'.[105]

In order to forge links with the CGE's work on adaptation issues, two members of the LDC Expert Group – including one from an LDC and one from an Annex II Party – must also be members of the CGE.[106] In addition, to ensure coordination with the climate change negotiations themselves, the Chair or other representative of the LEG is required to attend meetings of the COP and subsidiary bodies.[107] The LEG annually elects a Chair, Vice-Chair and two rapporteurs – one Anglophone and one Francophone – from among its *LDC members*,[108] each of which is assigned specific functions[109] (the Annex II Party members cannot, therefore, serve as officers of the LEG). The functions of the Chair include outreach activities and ensuring that members fulfil their commitments within the specific time-frames; those of the Vice-Chair include fundraising; and those of the rapporteurs include liaising with Anglophone and Francophone members respectively and, for the Francophone rapporteur, accessing French-language literature for use by the group.

The LEG reports to the SBI, which also approves its programme of work.[110] In establishing the LEG, Parties sought to make clear that this decision responded to the 'unique circumstances' of LDCs, and did not set a precedent for the formation of any other groups for other categories of countries.[111] This concern also explains, in part, why the LEG's original mandate extended only until COP-9.[112] Because NAPA preparation is still in its early phase, with the majority due for completion in 2004/2005, Parties agreed at COP-9 to extend the LEG's mandate until COP-11 when the COP will again review its need for continuation and terms of reference.[113]

The first meeting of the LEG, in Tanzania in February 2002, developed a programme of work that was approved by SBI-16 in June 2002.[114] The second meeting in June 2002 developed more detailed guidance for users of the NAPA guidelines adopted by COP-7 in the form of annotations.[115] These annotations were considered by SBI-17, which agreed with the LEG's recommendation that the NAPA guidelines adopted by COP-7 should not be formally amended but the annotations

---

[104] Decision 29/CP.7, Annex, paragraph 2.
[105] FCCC/SBI/2002/5, Report on the first meeting of the LEG, and paragraph 17.
[106] COP 7 adopted a mirror provision to this effect in its Decision 31/CP.7 on the CGE (paragraph 2).
[107] Decision 29/CP.7, Annex, paragraph 6.   [108] Decision 29/CP.7, Annex, paragraph 5.
[109] FCCC/SBI/2002/5, Report on the first meeting of the LEG, paragraphs 6–9.
[110] Decision 29/CP.7, Annex paragraphs 7 and 8.   [111] Decision 29/CP.7, paragraph 2.
[112] Decision 29/CP.7, paragraph 4 and Annex, paragraph 3.
[113] Decision 7/CP.9, paragraphs 1 and 5.   [114] FCCC/SBI/2002/6 and FCCC/SBI/2002/5.
[115] FCCC/SBI/2002/INF.14.

made by the LEG should be made widely available to users and funders.[116] The SBI's conclusions were then endorsed by COP-8, which agreed to review the guidelines in the light of Parties' experience and in the context of the outcome of the LEG's work, including its terms of reference, at COP-9. The third meeting of the LEG in Samoa in March 2003 discussed how LEG members would service requests from LDCs, agreeing that LEG members would not travel to particular countries as members but would provide assistance in other ways and that further work on a model service agreement had to be agreed.[117] The LEG also considered requests from COP-7 that it provide its views on the LDC Fund and the SCCF and forwarded these views to SBI-18.[118] Apart from this work, the LEG has played an important role in organising the four regional workshops on NAPAs mentioned in Decision 8/CP.8 which have been held in Bangladesh, Samoa, Ethiopia and Bhutan.[119]

5.4   *LDC work programme funding*

COP-7 adopted the LDC Fund under the Convention to support the LDC work programme referred to in Decision 5/CP.7. The LDC Fund supports the preparation of NAPAs on the basis of guidance provided by COP-7 and COP-8. Further guidance for the LDC Fund was agreed at COP-9 which supported the implementation of NAPA.[120] Details of the LDC Fund are discussed in chapter 10.

The attendance of LDC delegates within the climate change process is funded through the supplementary fund discussed in chapter 16. The declining levels of funding for participation are likely to affect adversely the ability of LDCs to participate effectively in the climate change process, contrary to expectations established by Decision 5/CP.7 that stress the need for increased levels of participation by LDCs in international processes as part of the implementation of the LDC Work Programme.

---

[116] SBI-17 report, FCCC/SBI/2002/17, paragraphs 40–1.   [117] FCCC/SBI/2003/6, paragraph 7.
[118] FCCC/SBI/2003/INF.12 and Add.1.   [119] Decision 8/CP.8, paragraph 3.
[120] Decision 9/CP.9.

9

Impacts of response measures

1   Introduction

The term 'impacts of response measures' is not defined in the Convention and the Protocol but refers generally to the negative economic impacts resulting from the implementation of climate mitigation policies. These economic impacts arise from efforts to *prevent* climate change and thus have nothing to do with adaptation to the adverse impacts of climate change. The issue of impacts of response measures is focused on estimating the costs and benefits of mitigation, in particular with estimating spillover effects and welfare impacts resulting from actions to prevent climate change taken by one country, or set of countries, on other countries. Although the IPCC points out that most economic models tend to overstate their costs, and none can accurately predict these impacts on a country basis, it is widely agreed that a reduction in the demand for all forms of carbon-based fossil fuels is one of the consequences of efforts to mitigate climate change.[1] The effects of response measures on energy demand, however, will vary according to fuel type, and the impacts of this on energy exports will vary considerably among energy exporting countries. Additionally, development and use of carbon sequestration technologies could potentially deflect the need to reduce demand for fossil fuels depending on whether such technologies prove economic and environmentally viable.[2]

Because the world's economies are linked through international trade and capital flows, the issue of impacts resulting from the implementation of response

---

[1] IPCC, 2001a. See also Barnett et al., 2004, which explains the merits and shortcomings of energy-economic models predicting economic impacts; and Bartsch and Müller, 2000.

[2] See chapter 5 on sinks and reservoirs, section 4.5.

measures is of interest to all countries. In the climate change regime, however, it has been highlighted principally by energy exporting developing countries, particularly by some of OPEC's eleven members.[3] Tables 9.1, 9.2 and 9.3 at the end of this chapter set out some key data explaining the positions of various energy dependent countries in terms of fossil fuel revenues, oil and gas reserves, as well as current and future demands. Figure 9.1 indicates the relative size of price fluctuations projected as arising from the Kyoto Protocol compared with historical variations in oil prices.[4]

This chapter explains how the Convention and the Protocol address issues arising from the impacts of response measures.[5] Rule development has, however, been particularly protracted because of demands made by some OPEC members for 'compensation for economic injuries' and the procedural linkage fostered by OPEC members between this issue and adaptation, as explained in chapter 8. This chapter provides an overview of the key provisions in the Convention and Protocol that relate to the impacts of response measures and includes some background information on the situation of energy exporting/producing countries. Section 3 explains rule development in relation to significant policy issues encapsulated in the Convention's provisions of particular interest to countries interested in impacts of response measures. Section 4 explains the finance, technology and insurance-related actions agreed pursuant to Article 4.8 of the Convention as well as developments agreed as part of the Marrakesh Accords concerning the implementation of Articles 2.3 and 3.14 of the Kyoto Protocol.

2   Convention and Protocol provisions

Articles 4.8 and 4.10 of the Convention and Articles 2.3 and 3.14 of the Protocol are the key provisions on impacts of response measures. The Convention's definitions and principles contained in Articles 2 and 3, discussed in chapter 4, are also relevant. Article 4.2 of the Convention, which covers the commitments of Annex I Parties, including their PAMs and coordination of these to address specific issues such as subsidies, is also of relevance and is discussed in chapter 5.

2.1   *Definitions and scope*

The Convention does not define the impacts of the implementation of response measures in the way that it sets out a definition of the 'adverse impacts of climate change' in Article 1.1. Thus the scope and nature of the kinds of 'impacts' to be considered and 'response measures' that give rise to them are not

---

[3] See chapter 3, section 2.7.   [4] Pershing, 2002. See also Michaelowa, 2003.
[5] Barnett and Dessai, 2002.

defined in the Convention and COP decisions. The Convention mentions the term 'response strategies' in Article 4.1 (g) concerning cooperation in research and again in Article 4.1 (h) concerning exchange of information, referring in both cases to the 'economic and social consequences of various response strategies'. To date the focus of attention in climate negotiations has been on the economic impacts.

Finally, for clarity it should be noted that under the Convention the term 'adverse impacts of climate change' intentionally excludes consideration of the impacts of response measures.[6] Accordingly, the numerous provisions of the Convention addressing the adverse impacts of climate change do not create any substantive commitments relating to reducing the impacts of response measures. Thus, unlike adaptation which is covered extensively – albeit in a piecemeal fashion – in the Convention and the Protocol and backed by commitments relating to the provision of finance by Annex II countries, there are no financial commitments for Annex II Parties concerning impacts of response measures in the Convention. Importantly, because they only cover adaptation and mitigation to climate change, the financial commitments in Articles 4.3 and 4.4 do not extend to economic impacts resulting from the implementation of response measures.[7]

2.2   *Principles*

Article 3 does not expressly mention the impact of response measures but a number of the listed principles are of significance for countries affected by the impact of response measures.[8] Article 3.2 requires that full consideration be given to the needs and circumstances of developing country Parties that would 'have to bear a disproportionate or abnormal burden under the Convention'. Article 3.3 on the precautionary approach mentions the need to take cost-effectiveness into account and states that PAMs should be 'comprehensive, cover all relevant sources, sinks and reservoirs of greenhouse gases and adaptation, and comprise all economic sectors'. These provisions are often cited by energy exporting Parties as policy justification for inclusion of sinks and arguing against PAMs targeting fossil-fuel related emissions to the exclusion of other sources of GHGs. The reference to cost-effectiveness also speaks in favour of use of flexibility mechanisms which economic models indicate tend to reduce the impact of response measures on oil exporting countries.

Article 3.4 concerns the right of Parties to promote sustainable development. In this regard the Marrakesh Accords stated that 'minimising the impact of the

---

[6] Bodansky, 1993: text and footnote 272, p. 497.
[7] Bodansky, 1993: commentary, text and footnote 477, p. 531.
[8] Chapter 4 discusses the nature, scope and legal status of these principles.

implementation of Article 3.1 of the Protocol is a development concern affecting both the industrialised and developing countries'. Article 3.5 of the Convention promotes a supportive and open international economic system leading to sustainable economic growth and development in all Parties, particularly developing country Parties, and states that measures to combat climate change, including unilateral ones, should not constitute a means of arbitrary or unjustifiable discrimination or a disguised restriction on international trade.[9] Article 3.5 appears neither to endorse nor to prohibit using trade measures of the sort contained in the Montreal Protocol as a means of increasing the effectiveness of the Convention in terms of compliance and enforcement.[10] Chapter 17 discusses the institutional linkages between the climate change and trading regimes and current efforts to foster greater understanding and synergies.

Finally, it is important to note that demands for compensation for economic injuries persistently made by some OPEC members up until Marrakesh are deemed by many developed and developing countries to be inconsistent with the Convention's principle of common but differentiated responsibility enshrined in Article 3.1, because such compensation demands are based on the view that developing countries have a right to pollute and any curtailment of this right deserves compensation from developed countries.[11]

2.3   *Commitments*

2.3.1   Developed countries

Article 4.10 is the clearest provision in the Convention addressing impacts of response measures. This states that *all* Parties shall 'take into consideration in the implementation of the commitments of the Convention the situation of Parties, particularly developing country Parties, with economies that are vulnerable to the adverse effects of the implementation of measures to respond to climate change'. Article 4.10 states that 'this applies notably to Parties with economies that are highly dependent on income generated from the production, processing and export, and/or consumption of fossil fuels and associated energy-intensive products and/or the use of fossil fuels for which such Parties have serious difficulties in switching to alternatives'. Article 4.10 is essentially procedural and requires each Party to take the considerations mentioned therein into account at the national level. Because the circumstances

---

[9] See chapter 4, section 2.7.   [10] Bodansky, 1993: text and footnotes 327–9.

[11] Speech by HE Dr Alí Rodríguez Araque, Secretary General, OPEC, 'Challenges facing the oil-producing countries in the 21st century', Second International Oil Summit, Paris, 25 April 2001, which confirms that many observers perceive OPEC's position in climate change as being based on the right to pollute.

of developing countries affected by the impacts of response measures are covered in Article 4.8, discussed below, Article 4.10 was included in the Convention essentially to give due recognition to developed countries with economies significantly dependent on energy production/consumption, such as Australia, the Russian Federation and the US.[12] For this reason Article 4.10 does not require Parties to address how international forms of financial and technological assistance might assist Parties affected by response measures. Although Article 4.10 is an obvious legal base for the COP to consider the issue of response measures, there has been little rule development based on Article 4.10.

2.3.2   Developing countries

Article 4.8 requires all Parties to give consideration to actions, including actions related to funding, insurance and technology transfer for the nine categories of developing countries listed in paragraphs (a)–(h), arising from the adverse impacts of climate change and/or the impacts of the implementation of response measures. Article 4.8 (h) is the most relevant for impacts of response measures as it highlights 'countries whose economies are highly dependent on income generated from the production, processing and export, and/or on consumption of fossil fuels and associated energy-intensive products'.

Article 4.8 is essentially procedural in that it requires all Parties to give 'full consideration to what actions are necessary under the Convention, including actions related to funding, insurance and the transfer of technology, to meet the specific needs and concerns' of such developing country Parties arising from the adverse effects of climate change. Unlike Article 4.10, however, Article 4.8 specifies that the COP 'may take actions, as appropriate, with respect to this paragraph'. This provision does not mandate the provision of funding, insurance and technology transfer to developing countries but has provided a procedural 'marker' for further consideration of these issues by the COP, discussed below.

2.3.3   Other provisions

The incorporation of climate considerations in other policies, and the minimisation of adverse effects, including through use of EIAs, is mentioned in Article 4.1 (f).[13] The Convention also mentions the term 'response strategies' in Article 4.1 (g) concerning cooperation in research and again in Article 4.1 (h) concerning exchange of information, referring in both cases to the 'economic and social consequences of various response strategies'. These provisions are discussed in chapter 7. Articles 7.2 (e) and 9.2 (b) concerning the COP and SBSTA

---

[12] Bodansky, 1993: text and footnotes 476–7, p. 531.

[13] Chapter 8, section 3.2 discusses this in more detail.

also mention assessment of the 'effects' of measures taken in the implementation of the Convention which could cover impacts of implementation of response measures.

2.3.4   Kyoto Protocol provisions

Article 10 (g) of the Protocol requires that all Parties 'give full consideration, in implementing the commitments under this Article, to Article 4, paragraph 8, of the Convention'. There is no equivalent to Article 4.10 of the Convention in the Protocol. There is also no direct equivalent or advancement of Article 4.1 (e) and (f) in the Kyoto Protocol.[14]

Article 2.3 of the Protocol requires Annex I Parties to strive to implement mitigation-related policies and measures so as to minimise adverse effects, including the adverse effects of climate change, effects on international trade and social, environmental and economic impacts on other Parties, especially developing country Parties, in particular those mentioned in Articles 4.8 and 4.9 of the Convention. The commitment to strive to *minimise* goes beyond what is contained in Articles 4.8 and 4.9 of the Convention which just require due account be given to the needs and circumstances of the Parties affected by impacts of response measures.

Article 3.14 requires Annex I Parties to implement their commitments under Article 3.1 of the Protocol in such as way as to minimise the adverse social, environmental and economic impacts on developing countries, particularly those identified in Articles 4.8 and 4.9 of the Convention. Article 3.14 states that the COP/MOP is required to consider what actions may be necessary to *minimise* such impacts as well as to consider the 'establishment of funding, insurance and transfer of technology'. Again the commitment in Article 3.14 goes beyond what is contained in the Convention.

Although Articles 2.3 and 3.14 both mention the adverse impacts of climate change, this was included against the inclinations of some OPEC members who had wanted these provisions to refer only to the impacts of response measures. Annex I Parties and the majority of developing countries felt, however, that singling out impacts of response measures for special consideration would not do justice to the range of impacts and countries contained in Article 4.8 and might be construed as prioritising the needs of countries identified in Article 4.8 (h). Although Articles 2.3 and 3.14 go beyond what is contained in the Convention, these commitments are still procedural in nature in that they do not oblige Annex II Parties to provide funding, insurance or technology to developing countries for dealing with adverse impacts and/or response measures. But these provisions do require the

---

[14] See chapters 5 and 8.

COP/MOP to give consideration to these issues, with Article 3.14 setting up expectations that the first session of the COP/MOP will consider the establishment of
funding, insurance and transfer of technology.

3   Rule development

Like adaptation, many aspects of the issue of impacts of response measures
are considered by the COP through the lens of other agenda items. This section
tries to bring together these disparate elements in terms of salient policy issues
encapsulated in the Convention's provisions on response measures as follows:

- Minimisation of impacts of response measures;
- Coordination of Annex I Parties' PAMs; and
- Decreasing economic vulnerability to impacts of response measures.

The process of rule development on impacts of response measures has taken place
in tandem with negotiations on adaptation issues on the basis of Decisions 3/CP.3,
5/CP.4 and 12/CP.5. This process, including the workshops held on Articles 4.8, 2.3
and 3.14, took place alongside workshops examining adaptation and is described
in more detail in box 8.2 in chapter 8. In tracking future rule development, it
is important to understand that in the foreseeable future the COP's work on
impacts of response measures will be undertaken under two strands: as a follow-
up to Decision 5/CP.7 on Article 4.8 which concerns Convention-related commitments, including under the COP agenda item addressing Annex I Parties' PAMs
and 'best practices'; and in relation to response measures and related commitments under the Protocol and work to be undertaken in the future on the basis of
Decision 9/CP.7 on Article 3.14.

3.1   *Minimisation of impacts of response measures*

Articles 4.8 and 4.10 of the Convention only require Parties to give due
consideration to the needs and circumstances of developing country Parties potentially affected by impacts of response measures and contain no commitments
regarding the minimisation of such impacts. Furthermore, because there is no
agreed methodology to assess the effectiveness of how Parties should give 'due
consideration' and because the current guidelines for Annex I Parties to prepare
their third national communications were adopted in 1999 prior to COP-7, these
guidelines do not require any reporting of how Annex I Parties are implementing
Articles 4.8 and 4.10. Recognising this, SBSTA-16 in June 2002 requested the Secretariat in their compilation and synthesis of the third national communications to
look out for reporting by Annex I Parties on response measures under Article 2.3.
However, because the national communication guidelines were adopted prior to

the SBSTA request, the latest national communications contain little information on the subject of response measures.[15]

Because Parties have agreed that implementation of PAMs under Article 2 of the Protocol will also support the implementation of the Convention, the question arises whether consideration of the issue of response measures could also feature in the information-sharing work relating to PAMs and good practices, discussed in more detail in chapter 5. The issue of whether impacts of response measures will be handled in this work was further discussed at COP-9 by SBSTA, but there was no agreement on how this work should progress. Accordingly, SBSTA agreed to discuss this at future sessions.[16] Issues relating to the implementation of Article 2.3 were addressed by SBSTA-19 in Milan but Parties also disagreed on how further work could be advanced and this item was also deferred for further consideration at future SBSTA sessions.[17]

As far as rule development relating to Article 3.14 of the Protocol is concerned, these commitments requiring Annex I Parties to strive to minimise impacts of response measures go beyond those contained in the Convention. And this has been accompanied by a greater interest, particularly among some OPEC countries, as to how Annex I Parties will strive, in practice, to implement their Article 2.3 and 3.14 commitments. Article 7 of the Protocol requires Annex I Parties to incorporate supplementary information demonstrating compliance with their commitments under the Protocol. Decisions 22/CP.7 and 22/CP.8 elaborate guidelines for the preparation of supplemental information in the context of national communications (submitted approximately every three years), including on minimisation of impacts under Article 2.3.[18]

Additionally, Decision 9/CP.7 on the implementation of Article 3.14 requests each Annex I Party to provide supplementary information as part of its inventory report (submitted annually) relating to how it is striving to minimise impacts mentioned in Article 3.14 and to incorporate information on actions to minimise these impacts. These actions are to be identified on the basis of methodologies to be developed at a workshop to be held prior to the second session of the COP/MOP.[19] The development of methodologies to determine if Annex I Parties are striving to minimise adverse effects, including the adverse effects of climate change, is to be set in motion prior to COP/MOP-2.[20] These steps are part of the process established by Decision 9/CP.7 for the implementation of Article 3.14 which is to include consideration of establishment of funding, insurance and technology transfer. The results of this process, including actions taken by Annex I Parties, is to be

---

[15] FCCC/SBSTA/2002/INF.13   [16] SBSTA-19 report, FCCC/SBSTA/2003/15.
[17] SBSTA-19 report, FCCC/SBSTA/2003/15.   [18] See chapter 11.
[19] Decision 9/CP.7, paragraphs 3 and 10.   [20] Decision 9/CP.7, paragraph 6.

reviewed at COP/MOP-3, which shall also consider the establishment of funding, insurance and technology transfer pursuant to Article 3.14. Decision 9/CP.7 also states that Parties not included in Annex I are invited to provide information on their specific needs and concerns related to the adverse social, environmental and economic impacts arising from the implementation of Article 3.1 and Annex II Parties are requested to provide funding for this purpose.

During the Marrakesh Accord negotiations, one of the aims of OPEC countries was to make submission of information about minimisation of impacts of response measures by Annex I Parties a matter that could be examined by the Enforcement Branch of the Compliance Committee. This was not agreed and paragraph 4 of Decision 9/CP.7 confirms that information submitted by Annex I Parties relating to implementation of Article 3.14 shall be considered only by the Facilitative Branch of the Compliance Committee.[21]

3.2   *Coordination of PAMs*

Removal of subsidies that distort markets (rather than correct market failures) and coordination of economic instruments such as carbon/energy taxes and emissions trading can lessen impacts of implementation of response measures as well as reduce overall compliance costs.[22] Article 4.2 (e) and Article 7.2 (c) of the Convention require Annex I Parties to enhance the individual and joint effectiveness of PAMs and refer rather obliquely to removal of subsidies. The issue of whether and how this work will integrate consideration of response measures was considered at COP-9 by SBSTA-19 but no agreement could be reached and thus SBSTA will examine this issue at future sessions.[23]

As explained in chapter 5, although Article 2.1 (a) (v) of the Protocol gives Annex I Parties discretion to decide what PAMs they will undertake to meet their Article 3 commitments, it is much more explicit in mandating Annex I Parties progressively to reduce or phase out a broad range of subsidies. Decision 9/CP.7 amplifies these provisions by calling Annex II (not Annex I) Parties to the following actions:

- Progressive reduction or phasing out of market imperfection, fiscal incentives, tax and duty exemptions and subsidies in all GHG emitting sectors, taking into account the need for energy price reforms to reflect market prices and externalities; and
- Removing subsidies associated with environmentally unsound and unsafe technologies (this is an oblique reference to coal and nuclear power).

---

[21] See chapter 12, section 5.4.   [22] IPCC, TAR, WG II, Mitigation,
[23] Chapter 5, section 5.3; FCCC/SBSTA/2003/15.

Reporting on phasing out of market imperfections, fiscal incentives, tax and duty exemptions and subsidies on an annual basis through Annex I Parties' national inventories will be mandatory under Article 3.14 of the Protocol.[24] This is significant because, according to the OECD, environmentally harmful subsidies in OECD countries were estimated at $400 billion in 2000, with energy production subsidies accounting for $20–30 billion per annum (of which one-third goes to supporting coal production).[25]

The issue of subsidies favouring the coal, nuclear and renewables sector has been raised by Saudi Arabia in the WTO's Committee on Trade and Environment (CTE) which is considering the relationship between trade and the environment as mandated by paragraph 31 (i) of the Doha Declaration.[26] Because the submissions made by Saudi Arabia and other WTO members relate to regime linkages, they are discussed in chapter 17.[27] Discussions at SBSTA-18 evidence growing awareness that the relationship between trade and environment generally, and the climate change regime and the WTO in particular, would benefit from further examination in terms both of enhancing synergies between the two regimes and avoiding conflicts.[28] Key issues include: in what circumstances would unilateral trade restrictive measures enacted by individual countries be justified, and in what circumstances would multilaterally agreed trade measures pursuant to the FCCC and the Protocol be deemed compatible with the WTO if such measures are designed to (a) offset the competitive advantage enjoyed by non-compliers, and (b) impose sanctions on non-compliers as a way of building a broader coalition of countries participating in the MEA?

3.3   *Decreasing vulnerability to impacts of response measures*

Proposals to provide compensation to developing countries have not commanded sufficient support from developed and developing countries for various reasons. Consequently, rule development has focused on other kinds of policy interventions to reduce the vulnerability of developing country Parties potentially affected by impacts of response measures. These are spelt out in Decision 5/CP.7 which does not use mandatory language but focuses on encouraging parties to undertake the activities therein. Paragraph 20, for example, states that Annex II Parties are encouraged to provide information 'in their national communications

---

[24] Decision 22/CP.7, Section H.   [25] Van Beers and de Moor, 2001.

[26] Doha Declaration, World Trade Organization, WT/MIN(01)/DEC/1, para. 31 (i). Saudi Arabia's submission can be found in TN/TE/W/9.

[27] FCCC/SBSTA/2003/INF.7.

[28] Chapter 17 discusses the relationship between the climate change regime and the WTO in more detail. See also chapter 4, section 2.7, Charnovitz, 2003, and Brack and Gray, 2003.

and/or any other relevant report' of their existing and planned support programmes to meet the specific needs of developing country Parties arising from
the impact of the implementation of response measures. Paragraph 21 provides
that non-Annex I Parties can also provide information in their national communications or any other relevant report on their specific needs and concerns arising
from impacts of response measures.

The activities set out in paragraphs 22–9 are to be supported through the GEF,
the SCCF (in accordance with Decisions 6/CP.7 and 7/CP.7) and other bilateral and
multilateral sources. These activities are:

- Cooperation between Annex I and non-Annex I Parties in creating
  favourable conditions for investment for economic diversification (paragraph 22);
- Assistance by Annex II Parties to developing countries, in particular those
  most vulnerable to the impacts of the implementation of response measures, in meeting their capacity-building needs (paragraph 23);
- Consideration of appropriate technological options in addressing the
  impacts of response measures, consistent with national priorities and
  indigenous resources (paragraph 24);
- Cooperation in technological development of non-energy uses of fossil
  fuels, with Annex II Parties providing support (paragraph 25);
- Cooperation in the development, diffusion and transfer of less greenhouse gas-emitting advanced fossil-fuel technologies, and/or technologies
  relating to fossil fuels, that capture and store greenhouse gases, with
  Annex II Parties facilitating the participation of the least developed countries and other non-Annex I Parties to this end (paragraph 26);
- Provision of financial and technological support by Annex II Parties for
  strengthening the capacity of developing country Parties identified in
  Article 4.8 for improving efficiency in upstream and downstream activities, taking into account the need to improve the environmental efficiency
  of these (paragraph 27);
- Promotion of investment in, and support and cooperation with, developing country Parties by Annex II Parties in the development, production,
  distribution and transport of indigenous, less greenhouse gas-emitting,
  environmentally sound, energy sources, including natural gas, according to the national circumstances of each of the Parties (paragraph 28);
  and
- Support for research into, and the development and use of, renewable
  energy, including solar and wind energy, by Annex II Parties in developing
  country Parties.

Paragraph 30 mandates the convening of an expert workshop on insurance-related issues to meet the specific needs and concerns of developing countries arising from the impacts of the implementation of response measures. This workshop was held in Bonn in June 2003 due to budget constraints in 2002.[29] Decision 5/CP.7 requests SBSTA and SBI to assess the response by Parties to the actions listed in paragraphs 22–9 above. The implementation of Decision 5/CP.7 was examined by SBI-19 in December 2003 under its agenda item dealing with Articles 4.8 and 4.9 of the Convention. Although a draft COP decision was prepared defining a process for follow-up on issues relating to economic impacts and diversification, no conclusions could be agreed in relation to issues relating to impacts of response measures. Accordingly, SBI agreed to invite Parties to submit information on adaptation-related issues and to consider the draft COP decision at future sessions.[30]

The above activities fall under the Convention. So far as the Protocol is concerned, Decision 9/CP.7 sets out a process to determine how Annex I Parties will implement their Article 3.14 commitments, including the development of appropriate methodologies to facilitate identification of impacts and of actions to minimise these.

Paragraph 7 of Decision 9/CP.7 also invites the IPCC to prepare a technical paper on geological carbon storage technologies, covering current information, and to report to COP/MOP-2. Paragraph 8 of Decision 9/CP.7 sets out a similar list of activities to that contained in paragraphs 22–9 which Annex II Parties, and other Parties included in Annex I in a position to do so, should give priority. The remainder of this Decision concerns minimisation of impacts of response measures described above, relating to establishment of a process for devising, adopting and using agreed methodologies to assess whether Annex I parties are striving to implement their Article 3.14 commitments.

4   Financing

4.1   *Convention and Kyoto*

Article 4.1 of the Convention covers implementation of mitigation and adaptation-related commitments and does not contain any obligations for developing countries relating to impacts of response measures. The financial commitments in Articles 4.3 and 4.4 of the Convention do not extend to economic impacts resulting from the implementation of response measures. Article 10 of the Protocol does not break any ground on the financing of impacts of response measures.

---

[29] Michaelowa, 2003.   [30] SBI-19 report, FCCC/SBI/2003/19.

4.2   *Rule development*

The financing of activities by developing country Parties that might be affected by the impacts of response measures is dealt with in the following decisions:

- Decision 5/CP.7 on Articles 4.8 and 4.9;
- Decision 6/CP.7 giving guidance to the GEF as operator of the Convention's financial mechanism;
- Decision 7/CP.7 establishing the SCCF as a new fund under the Convention and Decisions 7/CP.8 and 5/CP.9 setting out guidance for what it can fund; and
- Decision 9/CP.7 which defines a process to address funding, technology and insurance issues arising from Article 3.14.

It is important to note that this package of decisions does not yet extend the Convention's finances to cover the costs of the impacts of response measures in a mandatory fashion. Instead, these Decisions signal that certain activities that might help developing country Parties address the issue of how impacts of response measures are, in principle, to be funded.

The kind of activities that could be covered are those listed in paragraphs 22–9 of Decision 5/CP.7, described above, which include activities that build capacity, assist assessment and planning, and activities aimed at reducing the vulnerability of developing countries to response measures, such as economic diversification. Because the activities mentioned in paragraphs 22–9 are not explicitly included in Decision 6/CP.7, which serves as guidance to the GEF, funding for these activities will not necessarily come through the GEF but can come through the SCCF, by Annex II Parties directly on a bilateral basis or through other multilateral channels as recognised in paragraph 19 of Decision 5/CP.7 itself.

As discussed in more detail in chapter 10, COP-7 agreed to establish the SCCF under the Convention to finance activities that are complementary to those currently funded by the GEF, including activities to assist developing country Parties referred to under Article 4.8 (h) in diversifying their economies in accordance with Decisions 5/CP.7 and 7/CP.7. COP-8 agreed to define further the prioritised activities, programmes and measures to be funded out of the SCCF by COP-9.[31] Decision 5/CP.9 set out the guidance that COP-9 could agree for the SCCF. Because the demands for compensation by OPEC countries remain extensive and because the EU and a large number of developing countries remain opposed to the very limited resources of the SCCF being used for economic diversification when

---

[31] Decision 7/CP.8, paragraph 2.

there are other pressing needs, such as adaptation needs of vulnerable countries, COP-9 could not agree on guidance that would address funding for activities under paragraph 2 (c) and (d) of Decision 7/CP.7.[32] COP-9 agreed that such activities are also to be funded by the SCCF and invited Parties to submit views on activities, programmes and measures in these areas to SBI-21 in order for COP-10 to take a decision on these matters.[33]

So far as Decision 9/CP.7 concerning Article 3.14 of the Protocol is concerned, this sets up a discussion process to advance thinking on what actions related to funding, technology and insurance might be established by the COP/MOP in the future, with expectations that this issue will be considered at the third session of the COP/MOP.[34]

---

[32] Paragraph 2 (c) refers to energy, transport, industry, agriculture, forestry and waste management activities, and paragraph 2 (d) refers to activities to assist developing countries referred to in Article 4.8 (h) in diversifying their economies, in accordance with Decision 5/CP.7.

[33] Decision 5/CP.9, paragraph 4.   [34] Decision 9/CP.7, paragraph 10.

Table 9.1 *Regional distribution of fossil fuel reserves and exports (at end of 1998)*

Region	Gas (billion cubic metres)			Oil (million barrels)			Coal (million tons)	
					Exports			
	Reserves	Exports	LNG	Reserves	Crude	Product	Reserves	Exports
N. America	8,400	90.5	1.8	85,100	156.8	59.1	256,500	104.7
S. America	6,200	3.6		89,500	115.1	44.4	21,600	36.0
Europe	5,200	87.4		20,700	39.9	40.2	122,000	45.8
Middle East	49,500	0.5	20	673,700	817	109.8	200	
FSU	56,700	122		65,400	123	52.3	230,000	18.7
Africa	10,200	27.5	25.8	75,400	253	34.4	61,400	67.1
Asia-Pacific	10,200	1.5	65.4	43,100	70.4	56.3	292,000	246.9
Unidentified					9	13		
World	146,400	333.1	113	1,052,900	1584.9	409.5	984,000	519.2

Source: Pershing, 2002

Table 9.2 *Change in demand for fossil fuels 1990–2010 (million tonnes oil equivalent)*

Region	Gas demand			Oil demand			Coal demand			GNP
	1990	2010	%	1990	2010	%	1990	2010	%	%
N. America (excl. Mexico)	493.6	704.6	1.8%	837.6	1025	1%	551.8	736.6	1.5%	2.3%
S. America	74.8	185.1	4.6%	248.9	243.8	2.7%	20.3	44.2	−13.7%	3.4%
OECD Europe	243.3	506.1	3.7%	617.1	779.1	1.2%	398	371.5	−0.3%	2.1%
Middle East	79.9	164.2	3.7%	151.3	218.8	1.9%	3.4	12.7	6.7%	2.4%
FSU	614.1	646.7	0.3%	473.2	329	−1.8%	411.6	357	−0.7%	−0.5%
Africa	31.9	70.5	4.0%	87.8	145.4	2.6%	74.7	111.7	2%	2.1%
Asia-Pacific	140.4	444.1	5.9%	661.4	1372	3.7%	829.3	1635	3.5%	5.0%
Bunkers				119	175	1.9%				
World	1678	2721	2.5%	3196	4468	1.7%	2289.1	3269	1.8%	3.1%

Source: Pershing, 2002

Table 9.3   *Oil-exporting country revenues*

Country (ranked by oil exports as share of % of GDP)[35]	Economic rents from oil			
	Gross[36] (million $ 1998)	% of GNP	Share from export to OECD	Share from export to non-OECD
1. Oman	5,406	40.4%	47.8%	52.2%
2. Qatar	3,053	33.0%	96.2%	3.8%
3. Saudi Arabia	42,857	32.0%	81.2%	18.8%
4. UAE	13,479	29.9%	87.4%	12.6%
5. Angola	2,495	29.3%	74.5%	25.5%
6. Kuwait	7,626	25.2%	82.2%	17.8%
7. Iraq	4,071	13.8%	71.5%	28.5%
8. Venezuela	10,959	12.1%	87.4%	12.6%
9. Nigeria	7,600	11.6%	83.2%	16.8%
10. Libya	4,258	9.2%	96.2%	3.8%

Source: Pershing, 2002

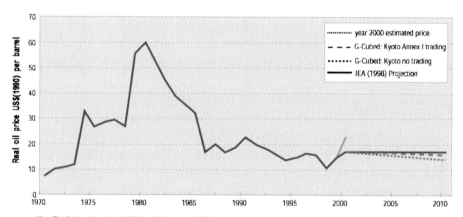

Note: The oil price shown is that of UK Brent deflated by the US GDP deflator. The year 2000 estimated price is based on actual prices January to August and futures prices September to December.
Sources: IMF, International Financial Statistics, August 2000 and various earlier issues. IEA (1998b) and McKibbin *et al.* (1999).

Fig. 9.1   Real oil price 1970–2010

[35] The ranking is based only on the top twenty oil exporting countries by volume.
[36] Calculated as the difference between production costs and spot market prices multiplied by quantity of exports.

10

Finance, technology and capacity-building

1   Introduction

Countries' contribution to climate change and their capacity to prevent and cope with its consequences vary enormously. The Convention and the Protocol therefore mandate financial and technological transfers from Parties with more resources to those less well endowed and more vulnerable. Limited human and institutional capacity can also cause bottlenecks in policy formation and implementation. Accordingly, in recent years, the COP has adopted a number of decisions to strengthen capacity-building in developing countries as well as EITs.

This chapter describes rules relating to resources – financial, technological and human and institutional – relevant for achieving the substantive commitments contained in the FCCC and the Protocol. This chapter focuses on the Convention's financial mechanism, operated by the Global Environment Facility (GEF), which also serves the Protocol. Section 2 describes resource commitments under the Convention and the Protocol, defining who provides financial and technological assistance, to whom, for what and for how much. This section thus explains legal concepts such as 'new and additional' resources, 'incremental costs' and 'agreed full costs'. Section 3 describes how the Convention's financial mechanism works. This explains the relationship between the COP and the GEF and how guidance provided by the COP in terms of the policies, programme priorities and eligibility criteria is taken into account by the GEF. Section 4 explains the purpose, governance and operation of the three new funds established by the Marrakesh Accords – the LDC Fund, the Adaptation Fund and the Special Climate Change Fund – which will be operated by the GEF. Section 5 describes how GEF funding can be accessed, which requires an understanding of its governance, operational strategy and project cycle. Sections 6 and 7 examine in more detail the framework decisions adopted by the COP on two key cross-cutting resource issues: development and transfer of technology and capacity-building. For those unfamiliar with MEA finances, a brief history of the GEF is provided in box 10.1.

2   **Resource commitments**

   Background: The rules contained in the Convention and the Protocol on financial and technological flows appear to divide Parties into two camps: those that provide resources, listed in Annex II of the Convention, and those that receive resources, developing countries. Reality is more complex than this simple division. In recent years, climate policy has had to become more responsive to requests for financial, technological and capacity-building assistance from Parties that are not developing countries. Despite resistance from developing countries, assistance for EITs and for Parties not listed in Annex I but who do not consider themselves to be developing countries, such as the CACAM countries, has moved higher up the policy agenda.[1] Pressure to consider who should be included in Annex II – the donors – has been more limited but could increase if significant contributors continue to decrease levels of financial support to the financial mechanism.

Box 10.1   The GEF: a brief history

At Rio, the institutional mechanism(s) for channelling funding to developing countries to meet global environmental objectives divided countries. To avoid proliferation of funds and resultant conflicts/overlaps in mandates, developed countries wanted to use the GEF to service the then four focal areas relating to the global environment: ozone, biodiversity, climate change and international waters.[2] The GEF had been set up in 1991 as a joint pilot project by the World Bank, UNDP and UNEP, who are known as its Implementing Agencies (IAs). Developing countries objected to the GEF because of its donor dominated governance structure and lack of transparency. They preferred new funds directly under the control of each respective COP to be established as had happened under the Montreal Protocol. The compromise reached under the FCCC and the CBD turns on the distinction between the 'financial mechanism' defined by, and governed by, the COP of each Convention, and the existing international entity (or

---

[1] See Decision 35/CP.7, Request from a group of countries of Central Asia, Caucasus, Albania and Moldova on their status under the Convention. See also chapter 3, section 2.7.

[2] Two others were added in 2002 by the GEF Assembly: land degradation and POPs.

entities) designated to operate it on a day-to-day basis. The GEF was designated as the entity to operate the financial mechanism – but only on an interim basis.[3] A decision about its future designation was deferred until it was restructured to respond to developing country concerns. The restructuring was completed in March 1994, ensuring that the GEF had an equitable, balanced and transparent governance structure as required by Article 11.2 of the FCCC. The GEF's interim status ended at COP-4 which designated it as 'an entity entrusted with the operation of the financial mechanism'.[4] Since then, relations between the COP and the GEF have been more constructive and less politically confrontational. Increased demand for the GEF's services from other conventions and resolution of 'teething' problems contributed to COP-8's conclusions about the second review of the financial mechanism in 2002 which noted that the GEF had performed its role as an entity operating the financial mechanism 'effectively'.[5] The third review will take place at COP-12 to be held in 2006.

2.1   *Resource providers*

2.1.1   Annex II parties

FCCC: Three provisions in the Convention mandate provision of resources: Article 4.3 which covers financial resources to cover implementation of general commitments and reporting, Article 4.4 which deals with adaptation costs and Article 4.5 which addresses technology transfer. The providers, or donors, of these resources are 'the developed country Parties' and 'other developed Parties' listed in Annex II of the Convention. The phrase 'other developed Party' refers to the EU.[6]

Kyoto: The Protocol's financial provisions, covered in Article 11, are also applicable only to Parties included in Annex II of the Convention. It should be noted, however, that Article 12 of the Protocol mandates the collection of a share of the proceeds from CERs towards the cost of adaptation of developing countries which are particularly vulnerable to the adverse effects of climate change. Because investments under the CDM can be undertaken by Parties included in Annex I, the share of the proceeds will come from a broader group of Parties, and their private investors, than just those listed in Annex II. This broadening was resisted by the private sector, many EITs and some developing countries as it marks a fundamental shift away from reliance on ODA funding from OECD countries.

---

[3] Article 21.3 and Decision 9/CP.1   [4] Decision 3/CP.4.

[5] Decision 5/CP.8, Preamble, paragraph 5.

[6] Annex II refers to the European Community. On the difference between the EU and the EC, see chapter 3, section 2.8.

Rule development: Article 4.2 (f) of the Convention mandated a review of the lists included in Annex I and Annex II not later than 31 December 1998. COP-7 agreed to amend the Convention to remove the name of Turkey from Annex II.[7] This amendment entered into force on 28 June 2002 and accordingly there are now twenty-four Annex II Parties to the Convention.

Under the Convention and the Protocol, the legal obligation to provide resources remains limited to Annex II Parties. In practice, however, contributions to the Convention's financial mechanism are provided by a broader range of countries than those included in Annex II. For the third GEF replenishment, for instance, as set out in box 10.2 below, nine countries not listed in Annex II of the Convention have pledged contributions.

2.1.2   Adequacy, predictability and burden sharing

FCCC and Kyoto: The Convention and the Protocol do not specify the level of resources to be provided by Annex II Parties nor the burden-sharing arrangements amongst them. Article 4.3 of the Convention and Article 11.2 of the Protocol refer instead to 'the need for adequacy and predictability in the flow of funds and the importance of appropriate burden-sharing among developed country Parties'. Article 11.3 (d) requires the COP to work with the GEF to allow 'determination in a predictable and identifiable manner of the amount of funding necessary and the conditions under which that amount shall be periodically reviewed'.

Rule development: Adequacy and predictability of financial resources are important for planning for long-term problems such as climate change. In the early years of the climate change regime, developing countries attempted to ensure that adequate resources would be provided in a predictable manner by Annex II Parties. Further to Article 11.3 (d), they sought, in particular, that the COP (rather than the GEF or donors) should assess the amount needed by developing countries to implement their Convention commitments. Institutionally and politically, most donors resist being legally bound by specific sums and timetables, particularly where costs are large, uncertain and extend beyond electoral cycles – as is the case with climate change. The compromise reached is set out in Paragraph 9 of the Memorandum of Understanding (MOU) between the COP and the GEF, adopted by COP-2, which defines their legal relationship.[8] Paragraph 9 of the MOU provides that 'the COP and the [GEF] Council shall jointly determine the aggregate GEF funding requirements for the purpose of the Convention'.

An Annex to the MOU defining procedures to facilitate such a joint determination was adopted a year later at COP-3.[9] The Annex contains procedures, found in

---

[7] Decision 26/CP.7.

[8] Decision 12/CP.2. The legal character of the MOU is explained below in section 3.1.

[9] Decision 12/CP.3.

the Report of SBI-4 rather than Decision 12/CP.3 itself, which is part of the MOU.[10] These procedures reiterate that the COP and the GEF Council will jointly determine the aggregate GEF funding needed for the Convention. In anticipation of each GEF replenishment, explained in box 10.2, the COP is to make an assessment of the amount of funds necessary to assist developing countries, taking into account the following: their agreed full costs of preparing national communications; their agreed full incremental costs of implementing other commitments; information from the GEF on the number of eligible programmes and projects approved, as well as those turned down owing to lack of resources, and other sources of funding available for the implementation of the Convention.[11] On the occasion of each replenishment, the GEF is to report to the COP on how it has taken the COP's previous assessment into account, providing the COP with an opportunity to consider the adequacy of the resources available. The Annex envisages that the reiteration of this process will present an opportunity for the COP and the GEF to review the amount of funding necessary and available in accordance with Article 11.3 (d).

In practice what happens is that the GEF Secretariat and the Trustee of its funds jointly prepare 'assessments/funding scenarios' of future funding needs for each of the mechanism's focal areas. These assessments are then submitted for the consideration of potential donors during replenishment negotiations and one is ultimately agreed upon as the level of the replenishment of the financial mechanism for a period of four years. The GEF also effectively determines the amount of resources that will flow through the Convention's financial mechanism and the amount of resources available outside the financial mechanism for climate-related activities (to cover, for example, funding needs of eligible EITs).

For many years, the decisions taken by the GEF on these issues have obviated the practical need for the COP to assess the level of funding in the manner anticipated in the Annex to the MOU – which many acknowledge would in any case have been difficult given the diversity of interests represented in the COP. At COP-8, Parties mandated the Convention Secretariat, in consultation with the GEF Secretariat, to prepare for SBI-20 (to be held immediately before COP-12) a report 'on the implementation of 12/CP.2 and 12/CP.3, in accordance with Article 11 on the determination of funding necessary and available for the implementation of the Convention'.[12] This report will be examined by SBI-20 prior to COP-12 in time for input to the GEF replenishment negotiations in 2006.

So far as *predictability* of finances is concerned, the GEF replenishment cycle has provided a measure of financial predictability for the climate change regime.

---

[10] FCCC/SBI/1996/14.   [11] FCCC/SBI/1996/14, MOU, Annex, paragraph 1 (a)–(d).

[12] Decision 5/CP.8, paragraph 3.

While no donor agrees to a specific amount for climate change, each pledges a specified amount towards the agreed target of the GEF replenishment, and subsequently enters into a commitment through the Trustee to pay that amount during a specified period. For example, the US has agreed to pay the sum of US $300 million into the GEF Trust Fund during the current phase of GEF III.

Because funding for climate change can flow outside the Convention's financial mechanism, it has been difficult to track *ex post*, let alone to predict in advance, the overall sums of resources available for climate change. Delays between amounts pledged by countries and amounts actually transferred also affect predictability. Two recent developments should improve this situation. First, although designed to 'firewall' the GEF from complications resulting from the US position of no-financing of activities relating to the Kyoto Protocol, the joint political declaration made at COP-7 by the EU and its member states, together with Canada, Iceland, New Zealand, Norway and Switzerland, announces their preparedness to contribute collectively €450 million/US $410 million annually by 2005 to climate change, with this level to be reviewed by 2008.[13] Although assessing the 'new and additionality' character of these funds, and other kinds of funds, remains problematic, as discussed below, such announcements enhance predictability.

The second development which might have positive impacts on tracking of resources is a COP-7 agreed requirement for Annex II Parties to report annually on the provision of finances and technological resources through their national communications listing contributions to the GEF and other multilateral institutions and programmes separately, and broken down on a year-by-year basis.[14] Annex II Parties' contributions to the Adaptation Fund must be reported on an annual basis allowing a faster assessment of funding trends by the COP than the three-year *ex post* reporting through national communications for other types of funding.[15]

So far as *financial burden-sharing* is concerned, COP-7 agreed that 'appropriate modalities for burden sharing among the Parties included in Annex II need to be developed'.[16] No time-frame for the development of such modalities is specified. The reference to the need to develop burden-sharing modalities in the COP-7 decision is all that remains of proposals put forward by the President of COP-6,

---

[13] Decision 7/CP.7 and FCCC/CP/2001/MISC.4. The text of the declaration clarified that funding can include contributions to GEF climate-change-related activities; bilateral and multilateral funding additional to current levels; funding for the special climate change funds, the Kyoto Protocol Adaptation Fund and the LDC Fund; and funding deriving from the share of proceeds of the CDM following entry into force of the Kyoto Protocol.

[14] Decision 7/CP.7, paragraph 1 (e) and (f). Note FCCC/CP/1999/7, FCCC guidelines on reporting and review of Annex I Parties, Section VIII, does not take this into account yet. See chapter 11.

[15] Decision 10/CP.7, paragraph 6.   [16] Decision 7/CP.7, paragraph 1 (d).

Jan Pronk, that would have initiated financial burden-sharing among Annex I Parties based on their share of CO_2 emissions in 1990 (with a 50 per cent reduction for EITs). This proposal was rejected by EITs as it would have amounted to renegotiating their Convention commitments.

Apart from this proposal, issues relating to financial burden-sharing have taken place largely in the GEF, particularly during replenishment negotiations, rather than in the COP. Contributions to the Convention's finances and the GEF are explained in box 10.2. Although not made explicit in GEF documentation, the contributions of different countries to previous GEF replenishments have been roughly based on their shares in the International Development Association.[17] This approach to burden-sharing cannot be described as a binding rule but it guides expectations and provides a common reference point for subsequent political negotiations.

A final consideration with regard to burden-sharing is the decision by the US and Australia not to proceed with ratification of the Protocol, which means they will not be Annex II Parties for the purposes of funding the Protocol. What impacts this has on overall levels of resources available through the Convention's financial mechanism and the new funds established by the Marrakesh Accords remains to be seen.

Box 10.2   GEF replenishments, Annex II Parties and contributors

Funding for the GEF comes from its members who now include 175 developed and developing countries. Every four years these countries decide how much money to pledge towards the next period of funding. This process is called replenishment. Apart from the pilot phase, there have been three replenishments. The dates and total amount pledged are:

- Pilot Phase (1990–1994) – US $1.13 billion
- First Replenishment (1995–1998) US $2 billion
- Second Replenishment (1998–2002) US $2.75 billion
- Third Replenishment (2002–2006) US $3 billion

For the third replenishment, thirty-two countries have pledged contributions. This includes all the Parties listed in Annex II except the EU which does not contribute to the GEF in its own right because its members states undertake this responsibility. Five developing countries (China, Côte

---

[17] Instrument Establishing the GEF, 16 March 1994, Annex C, Contributions, Explanatory Note.

d'Ivoire, India, Nigeria and Pakistan), two countries listed in Annex I (Slovenia and Turkey) and two countries that are OECD members but are not listed in Annex I (Mexico and the Republic of Korea) have also pledged contributions to the third replenishment. Since 1991, the GEF has allocated $4 billion in grants across its focal areas and leveraged an additional $12 billion in co-financing from other sources to support more than 1,000 projects in over 140 developing nations and countries with economies in transition. The 'leveraging' of other resources is an important feature, with the GEF claming that each $1 leverages three to five times that amount from other sources. The GEF is now the main funding channel for climate change projects in developing countries.

From 1991 to June 2003, GEF grants to climate change activities totalled US $1.6 billion (out of a total of $4.4 billion for all focal areas), with an additional $9 billion contributed through co-financing.[18] Over the most recent reporting period (July 2001–May 2002), total project financing for climate change activities exceeded US $901 million, of which the GEF provided US $136 million in grant financing. The climate change allocation in the period 1998–2002 for enabling activities (national communications) was 3 per cent.[19] It is important to note, however, that not all climate-related funding goes through the GEF as some is provided through bilateral, regional and other multilateral channels. An assessment in 2001 by the CGE of GEF and non-GEF funding for national communications showed that the GEF provided $79.6 million with non-GEF sources providing $54 million, a ratio of 60:40.[20] Thus, assessing the total amount of climate-related funding provided by Annex II Parties, and other Parties not so listed, is more complex than totalling GEF contributions. Recent work by the OECD DAC has concluded that, in general, bilateral ODA activities targeting the objectives of the FCCC are few and represent a small share of total bilateral aid – an annual average of 7.2 per cent of OECD members' total bilateral ODA commitments in 1998–2000 which amounted to some US $2.7 billion *annually*.[21] Of course, the 7.2 per cent represents quite a sizeable sum when compared to the US $2.97 billion in total pledged to the GEF to cover 2002–2006 for all six focal areas.

---

[18] FCCC/CP/2003/3, GEF annual report to COP-9. See also FCCC/CP/2002/8, GEF annual report to COP-8.

[19] FCCC/SBI/2001/15, CGE Report, p. 23 provides more details of funding of national communications.

[20] FCCC/SBI/2001/15, CGE Report, p. 25 and table 1.

[21] FCCC/TP/2003/2, paragraph 53 and OECD, 2002b.

2.2   *Resource beneficiaries*

2.2.1   Developing countries and non-Annex I parties

FCCC and Kyoto: Parties listed in Annex I of the Convention are explicitly described as having 'developed country' status. The term 'developing country' is not, however, defined in the Convention, the Protocol or in subsequent COP decisions.[22] Thus the question arises which of the current 154 Parties to the Convention that are not listed as Annex I Parties should be considered as 'developing countries'.[23] This is important because Articles 4.3, 4.4 and 4.5 of the Convention specify that Annex II Parties are to provide resources to *developing countries*. Other resource-related provisions which single out developing countries are Article 4.7, which states that the extent to which *developing countries* will implement their commitments will depend on the effective implementation of developed country Parties of their financial and technological commitments; Article 4.8 which requires all Parties to give consideration to the specific needs and circumstances of *developing countries*; and Articles 12.4 and 12.5 which give developing countries longer lead times to prepare national communications and allow them to propose projects for financing. The Convention also singles out LDCs for special consideration in Articles 4.9 and 12.5. The Convention's provisions on developing countries are imported into the Protocol by virtue of Articles 10 and 11 and references in Articles 2.3 and 3.14.

Rule development: Guidance adopted by COP-1 expressly stated that 'only developing countries would be eligible to receive funding through the financial mechanism, in accordance with Article 4.3'.[24] Guidance to the GEF from COP-2, COP-4 and COP-5 at times used the terms 'developing countries' and 'non-Annex I Parties' interchangeably.[25] Finally, for funding and representation purposes, parts of the Marrakesh Accords placed countries into groups neither found in the Convention nor used consistently across the package of decisions adopted by COP-7.[26] The need

---

[22] The use of per capita thresholds to define which delegations get funding from the supplementary fund to assist participation in the FCCC is discussed in chapter 16, section 2.3.

[23] See chapter 3, and Appendix I for details of which regional, economic and political groups individual Parties belong to.

[24] Decision 11/CP.1, paragraph 1 (c) (i).   [25] See e.g. Decision 11/CP.2, paragraph 1 (c) and (e).

[26] Decision 2/CP.7, for example, is entitled 'capacity building in developing country (non-Annex I Parties)' although its substantive provisions then speak of developing countries. Decision 4/CP.7 on technology refers, in parts, to 'Parties other than developed country Parties and other developed Parties not included in Annex II'. This term was intended to ensure that developed countries such as the CACAM countries that were not listed in either Annex I or Annex II were covered. Finally, Decision 6/CP.7 providing guidance to the GEF stated that the GEF should provide funding 'to developing country Parties, in particular the least developed and small island developing states among them'.

for a clear definition of 'developing countries' was brought onto the formal policy agenda by Parties from the CACAM group at COP-7.[27] As explained in box 10.3, no formal definition of 'developing country' has been reached by the COP in response to the CACAM request which relates to a much wider set of commitments than resource transfer.

In practice, so far as access to finances is concerned, all non-Annex I Parties are eligible for funding by the GEF based on Paragraph 9 (a) of its Instrument of Establishment, explained in box 10.3. The GEF has funded all non-Annex I Parties for climate activities without reference to whether such Parties qualify for lending by the World Bank or technical assistance from UNDP as specified in Paragraph 9 (b) of its Instrument. Thus, although the Convention and the Protocol legally limit entitlement to funding to 'developing countries', in practice all Parties not listed in Annex I of the Convention are eligible for funding under the Convention's financial mechanism. The GEF's practice has been endorsed by the COP which discussed this issue at COP-8.[28]

It is important to note that a number of non-Annex I Parties have actually not sought funding from the GEF even though in theory they are eligible in terms of the COP guidance. These countries include the Republic of Korea and Singapore. In the following chapter, the term 'developing country' will continue to be used as it is consistent with the language of the Convention and the Protocol, although it should be taken as read that other Parties not listed in Annex I are also eligible for GEF funds.

Priority setting amongst those eligible for funding is a sensitive political issue and one on which the COP has only been able to make limited inroads. Guidance provided by COP-7 to the GEF on funding matters related to the Convention states that the GEF should provide funding 'to developing country Parties, in particular the least developed and small island developing states among them' in respect of activities covered by that guidance.[29] In view of their special vulnerabilities and needs, the GEF has already prioritised LDCs and SIDS by offering them additional financial assistance (up to $25,000) to prepare proposals for projects to enhance capacity-building.[30] The provision of new funds, the LDC Fund, the Adaptation Fund and the SCCF could also prioritise activities favoured by particular groups of Parties.

---

[27] FCCC/CP/2001/12.

[28] Decision 6/CP.8, paragraphs 1 (c) and (d) mandate the GEF to 'provide financial resources to non-Annex I Parties, in particular the least developed country Parties and small island states among them'.

[29] Decision 6/CP.7, paragraph 1. Decision 6/CP.8 reaffirms this but substitutes 'non-Annex I Parties' for the term 'developing country Parties'.

[30] GEF, 2001a.

Box 10.3   Recipients: developing countries and non-Annex I Parties

The Convention and the Kyoto Protocol limit the obligation of Annex II Parties to provide financial resources exclusively to 'developing countries'. Currently, of the 194 Parties to the FCCC, 154 are not listed in Annex I. Of these, 130 are members of the G-77.[31] Parties such as Mexico, the Republic of Korea, Malta and Cyprus, Israel and a number of Parties from Central Asia and Central/Eastern Europe are not considered or do not consider themselves to be developing countries and do not associate politically with the G-77. At COP-7, the CACAM group submitted a request to clarify their status, as they wanted to benefit from the Convention's financial provisions and be represented on the limited membership bodies established by the Marrakesh Accords (such as EGTT and LEG) whose membership is defined in terms of developed/developing countries. This request has not resulted in the adoption of a definition of 'developing country' because Parties cannot agree on fundamental policy issues about when and according to what measure countries ought to be classified as developing countries. At SBI-17, which took place alongside COP-8, Parties agreed that all countries that are not listed as Annex I Parties were eligible to receive funding from the Convention's financial mechanism.[32] Draft conclusions confirming this could not be formally adopted by the SBI or COP-8, which simply mandated SBI to continue its discussion of the issues at future sessions. No substantive progress was made at SBI–18 held in June 2003 or at COP-9.

It is important to note that there is no common definition of 'developing countries' across the United Nations and different international organisations use different definitions and thresholds.[33] In the field of environmental governance, Paragraph 9 of the Instrument Establishing the Global Environment Facility is an important reference point. Paragraph 9 (a) of the Instrument states that the GEF can provide funding to countries if it is in accordance with the guidance provided by the COPs of the conventions it services. The ozone regime defines per capita thresholds for consumption of ODSs which, if exceeded, bar a country from taking advantage of the Protocol's grace periods and financial assistance provisions.[34] In climate change, the COP has approved all countries that have ratified the Convention

---

[31] See chapter 3 and Appendix 1 showing the political, regional and UN groupings of all Parties.
[32] FCCC/SBI/2002/L.14, Draft conclusions proposed by Chair.   [33] See chapter 3, section 2.2.
[34] Article 5, 1987 Montreal Protocol. A developing country must have an annual consumption of no more than 0.3 kg per capita of CFCs and no more than 0.2 kg per capita of halons to take advantage of the Protocol's grace periods.

and are not listed in Annex I as being eligible for funding, even if this is not stated consistently in all COP guidance to the GEF.[35] Parties to the CBD have not been able to define the term 'developing countries' either and thus far have not provided practical clarification to the GEF.[36] Paragraph 9 (b) of the GEF Instrument states that all other types of GEF grants (i.e. all those not covered by the guidance from the COPs of the various conventions) must conform with any eligibility criteria set by the GEF Council *and* are available only if a country 'is eligible to borrow from the World Bank (IBRD and/or IDA) or if it is an eligible recipient of UNDP technical assistance through its country Indicative Planning Figure (IPE)' (currently around US $4,000 per capita). The thresholds used by the World Bank group and UNDP differ and are revised periodically. Apart from being difficult to track down by environmental policy-makers, these thresholds depend on a country's economic fortunes which fluctuate and do not necessarily coincide with its capacity to address long-term environmental problems.

2.2.2   Parties with economies in transition

FCCC and Kyoto: Annex I of the Convention and Annex B of the Protocol refer to 'countries that are undergoing the process of transition to a market economy'. So far as being recipients of financial resources under the Convention and the Protocol is concerned, the position of EITs is as follows. Parties that consider themselves to be EITs but are not formally listed as Annex I Parties to the Convention can obtain funding from the Convention's financial mechanism because they are non-Annex I Parties. Parties that are EITs and are listed as Annex I Parties, such as Russia, cannot be recipients of finances under the Convention's financial mechanism as the financial mechanism is only available to 'developing countries'. Such EITs can still receive funding for climate activities from the GEF but outside its role as the financial mechanism to the Convention. The availability of financial resources to Annex I Party EITs under the GEF outside the framework of the Convention's financial mechanism is still subject to conditions stated in Paragraph 9 of its Instrument of Establishment and/or adopted by the GEF Council (box 10.3). These conditions make clear that Annex I EITs can only receive funding for climate change if they are Parties to the Convention. Furthermore, when the GEF finances

---

[35] Decision 6/CP.8 and related discussions at COP-8.

[36] In response to a 1997 request from the CBD COP to the UN Office of Legal Affairs requesting clarification of the term 'developing country', UNOLA confirmed that only the COP of the CBD can provide such a definition and that definitions used by other bodies cannot be considered as binding for the various environmental conventions serviced by the GEF.

EITs outside the Convention's financial mechanism, the approach it takes is in all other respects consistent with guidance given by the COP. Annex I Parties that are EITs that exceed the World Bank and UNDP thresholds cannot qualify for GEF funding.

As with developing countries, EITs can obtain funding for environment activities through bilateral, regional and multilateral channels outside the GEF. One of the most notable trends of the last decade has been the shift in proportional terms of ODA funding from developing countries to countries from Central and Eastern Europe. Thus limits on availability of funding for EITs under the Convention and the GEF are only one part of the overall picture of resource flows available to such countries. The split between the funding provided to EITs and non-Annex I Parties by the GEF is usually reported in the GEF Report to the COP.

2.3   *New and additional resources*

FCCC and Kyoto: Article 4.3 of the Convention and Article 11.2 of the Protocol specify that Annex II Parties shall provide 'new and additional financial resources' to developing country Parties. Article 4.4 of the Convention states that Annex II Parties 'shall also assist developing countries that are particularly vulnerable to the adverse effects of climate change in meeting the costs of adaptation to those adverse effects'. Article 4.4 makes no reference to 'new and additional resources' or 'incremental costs' because, during the Convention's negotiations, donors considered these matters would be met outside of GEF resources based on the widely shared assumption that such resources would also be new and additional.[37]

Rule development: The 'new and additional' requirements were intended to ensure that existing, scarce ODA funds would not be diverted by Annex II Parties to fund their obligations under the new conventions agreed at Rio. Measuring what is 'new and additional' has been technically difficult and politically challenging for two reasons. The first, more conceptual, reason relates to defining the baseline. The second, more technical, reason relates to difficulties of collecting financial data from numerous government departments and international organisations. For both reasons, the COP has not been able to provide detailed guidance on what should count as 'new and additional'. Current reporting guidelines leave matters largely in the hands of Annex II Parties: these state that Annex II Parties 'shall indicate what "new and additional" financial resources they have provided pursuant to Article 4.3' and require such Parties to clarify how they have determined that such resources are 'new and additional'.[38] Nine (out of a possible twenty-four)

---

[37] See chapter 8.   [38] FCCC/CP/1999/7, Section VII.

Annex II Parties reported on 'new and additional' resources in their third national communications using a variety of approaches but generally counting contributions to GEF as 'new and additional'.[39] This is important because the Instrument Establishing the GEF, explained below, states that the GEF shall provide 'new and additional grant and concessional funding'.[40]

Because the concept of 'new and additional' resources is part of the broader sustainable agenda and the cost-sharing principles agreed at UNCED, other international institutions have also undertaken work on defining 'new and additional' – all beset by the same definitional and technical problems. For example, the UN Commission on Sustainable Development (CSD), as part of its 1995 work developing 134 voluntary indicators of sustainable development, piloted an indicator measuring 'new and additional' which tried to capture the amount of new or additional funding for sustainable development given/received since 1992.[41] This indicator is not part of the final set of fifty-eight indicators currently available from the CSD because conceptual differences hampered establishment of a 'baseline' that could be agreed by all. Other linked indicators, such as environmental protection expenditure, or total ODA, given as a percentage of GDP and the ratio of net resource transfers to GDP were justifiably deemed as useful, or potentially more useful, as indicators than whether resources were additional to their historic 1992 values.

The issue of 'new and additional' funding is closely linked to the technical problems of tracking finances from Annex II Parties through various bilateral and multilateral channels. Current FCCC guidelines which require Annex II Parties to separate out reporting of financial resources provided to the GEF from resources provided through bilateral, regional and multilateral channels increase accessibility and comparability.[42] This requirement has made it easier to analyse the trend of contributions paid by Annex II Parties to the GEF in recent years. This information, however, does not always tally with the information reported by the GEF, as the latter reports in Special Drawing Rights (SDRs) rather than US dollars, and over a July–June financial period. Inconsistencies such as this demonstrate that rules to help donor and recipient Parties track the most basic financial information are still at an early stage of development.[43] This is despite the fact that COP-1 mandated the Convention Secretariat to 'collect information from multilateral and regional financial institutions on activities undertaken in implementation of Article 4.1 and Article 12 of the Convention [without] introducing new forms

---

[39] FCCC/SBI/2003/7/Add.1, paragraph 30.   [40] Instrument Establishing the GEF, Article 1.2.

[41] Indicators of Sustainable Development: Guidelines and Methodologies, available from CSD or online at www.un.org/esa/sustdev/natlinfo/indicators/indisd/indisd_mg2001.pdf.

[42] FCCC/CP/1999/7, Section VII and p. 269.   [43] FCCC/SBI/2003/7/Add.1, paragraph 124.

of conditionalities'.[44] A recent pilot initiative to track bilateral ODA from OECD countries targeting the Rio Conventions between 1998 and 2000, conducted by the Development Assistance Committee of the OECD (OECD DAC), could spur further developments relating to bilateral as well as multilateral channels.[45]

2.4   Incremental and full costs

FCCC and Kyoto: The Convention and the Protocol provide that new and additional resources are to be provided to meet 'the agreed full costs' incurred by developing country Parties in complying with their obligations under Article 12.1 of the Convention and Article 10.1 (a) of the Protocol. These provisions relate to the preparation of national communications, including preparation of inventories and national mitigation and adaptation programmes, mandated by Article 4.1 (a) of the Convention.

So far as developing country commitments under Article 4.1 (b)–(i) are concerned, Annex II Parties must provide resources covering the 'agreed full incremental costs' of implementation of these other commitments. The distinction in levels of funding developing countries are entitled to receive in terms of implementation of their commitments under Article 4.1 (a) and those arising from Article 4.1 (b)–(i) is based on the concept of 'incremental costs' and 'global environmental benefits'. It is difficult to understand the ramifications of the terms 'full' and 'agreed' without first understand the concept of 'incremental costs' as this is critical in determining how much funding GEF will actually provide for particular projects. The rationale and meaning of 'incremental costs' is explained in detail in box 10.4 below.

Rule development: Although appearing technical in nature, the issue of incremental costs raises politically sensitive issues about the sustainable development pathways developing countries can or should follow. The subjectivity inherent in the complex calculation of incremental costs, and the frustration this has generated amongst recipients, has meant that since the Convention's adoption, the COP, and the GEF, have been engaged in a continuing round of rule development to clarify the basic concept of incremental costs and to simplify its application.

The initial guidance provided by COP-1 stated that 'the application of . . . incremental costs should be flexible, pragmatic and on a case-by-case basis'.[46] This was intended to correct the somewhat rigid, formulaic approaches being put

---

[44] Decision 11/CP.1, paragraph 2 (a).
[45] OECD, 2002a. Note, with the exception of Iceland, membership of the OECD DAC coincides with Parties listed in Annex II.
[46] Decision 11/CP.1, paragraph 1 (e).

forward by theoretical economists working on GEF issues at the time.[47] The guidance from COP-1 advised caution, stating that 'the various issues of incremental
costs are complex and difficult and further discussion on the subject is therefore
needed' and concluding that further guidelines 'will be developed by the COP at a
later stage on the basis of experience'. COP-2 requested the GEF to report on experience gained in the application of the concept of agreed full incremental costs.[48]
This report, submitted to COP-3, was acted on by COP-4.[49] The COP was then also
able to consider the recommendations made by an independent assessment of
the GEF, the First Study of the GEF's Overall Performance (OPS-1), which had been
presented to the First GEF Assembly in Delhi in 1998 and had been critical of
the complexity of the incremental cost calculations.[50] Bearing in mind that the
GEF had already taken action to respond to OPS-1 recommendations, the resulting guidance provided by COP-4 encouraged the GEF 'to make the process for the
determination of incremental costs more transparent and its application more
pragmatic'.[51]

Negotiations at COP-5, COP-6 and COP-7 on financial issues did not focus explicitly on incremental costs but were heavily influenced by developing countries'
experiences of what could (and could not be) funded by the GEF, bearing in mind
its mandate to achieve global environmental benefits. The experience of countries vulnerable to the adverse effects of climate change in seeking GEF funding
for adaptation activities beyond planning generated support for the creation of
new funding arrangements at COP-7 that might prioritise adaptation and other
developmental needs – whether or not these maximised global environmental
benefits.[52] The most recent guidance adopted at COP-8 has focused largely on the
operational modalities of these funds. However, in view of the concerns and recommendations made by OPS-2 about incremental costs, COP-8 invited the GEF 'to
continue to make the concept of agreed incremental costs and global benefits
more understandable, recognising that the process for determining incremental
costs should be transparent, flexible and pragmatic, consistent with the [Second
GEF Assembly] Beijing Declaration'.[53]

Legally, the term 'agreed' means agreed between the developing country
incurring the cost and the GEF – in practice the Implementing Agency or Agencies in charge of a particular GEF project. As noted in OPS-1 and OPS-2, in many
instances, particularly in the early learning phase of the climate regime, costs were

---

[47] GEF background documents on incremental costs include GEF/C.7/Inf.5 and GEF/C.14/5 documentation. See also the GEF Programme for Measuring Incremental Costs for the Environment
(PRINCE), available from the GEF website.
[48] Decision 11/CP.2, paragraph 3.   [49] FCCC/CP/1997/3.
[50] Porter et al., 1997 (hereafter OPS-1).   [51] Decision 2/CP.4   [52] See chapter 8.
[53] Decision 5/CP.8, paragraph 4 (c).

largely determined by the GEF's Implementing Agencies based on complex estimates generated by international consultants, rather than agreed by developing
country officials on the basis of their informed understanding.[54] Thus, although
developing country officials formally 'agreed' GEF funded costs, there was little
understanding and consequently reduced levels of country 'ownership' of GEF
projects. Because of general confusion about what the GEF can and cannot fund,
similar problems have arisen about the meaning of the word 'full' as used in Article 4.3 of the Convention, albeit to a lesser extent. In principle, the term 'full'
means that all significant costs are to identified and that the GEF funding is not
to be reduced by subtracting either any additional domestic benefit or share of
the global benefit the recipient country will enjoy.[55]

Box 10.4   Incremental costs and global environmental benefits

The FCCC and CBD were negotiated in the run-up to the 1992 Earth Summit
at Rio de Janeiro. Faced with other pressing developmental priorities,
developing countries insisted at Rio that developed countries provide new
and additional financial and technological resources to defray the costs of
meeting their new global environmental commitments. Because integration
of environmental protection is central to sustainable development, and
brings national benefits, developed countries argued that they should
provide only part of such costs – specifically the part generating 'global
environmental benefits' – as had happened in the case of the Montreal
Protocol where developed countries agreed to meet the 'incremental costs'
incurred by developing countries in switching to ozone-friendly substances.
Accordingly, the FCCC, the CBD and Agenda 21 all mandate developed
countries to provide developing countries with the 'incremental costs' of
meeting their environmental commitments. Although the FCCC does not
actually mention the term 'global environmental benefits' (GEB), the
Instrument Establishing the GEF states that the GEF's purpose is provide new
and additional resources for the 'agreed incremental costs of measures to
achieve green global environmental benefits'.[56]
   As explained by the GEF to COP-3, incremental cost is the difference
between the costs of one way of achieving certain objectives (the baseline)

---

[54] OPS-1. See also Christoffersen et al., 2002 (hereafter OPS-2).
[55] FCCC/CP/1997/3, Report of the GEF to COP-3, Annex A, Experience of the GEF in the Application
of Agreed Full Incremental Costs, paragraph 12.
[56] Instrument Establishing the GEF, 1994.

and another way of achieving the same objective along with some additional objective or constraint.[57] Specifically, the incremental costs of a project are the difference in costs between doing a project that achieves national goals but does not give global environmental benefits and doing one that does. In cases where the baseline involves 'no national action', the total costs of a project equal the incremental costs. For example, without the FCCC, countries would not need to prepare GHG inventories or submit national communications so the baseline is simply 'no inventory'. Because the incremental cost of the inventory/NC is actually the total cost, the Convention mandates that Annex II Parties meet the total costs of inventory and national communications in full. In other cases, however, countries will incur incremental costs in order to realise GEBs. For example, a coal-powered power station with pollution control might provide national benefits at lower costs than use of advanced solar energy that provides the same developmental objectives (clean power) but also results in GEB. Because solar technology is currently more costly than coal, it imposes an incremental cost on the country and it is this increment, rather than the total project costs, which can be funded by the GEF.

Although simple in theory, the practical determination of incremental cost can be subjective, complicated, time-consuming and requires a high level of expertise. As a result, lengthy delays in the submission and approval of GEF projects have occurred. Clarification of the incremental cost concept and its practical application were an important part of the follow-up to OPS-2, considered by the Second GEF Assembly, held in Beijing in October 2002. The GEF will report on the Action Plan it has formulated in response to OPS-2 recommendations through its report to the COP.[58]

2.5   *Grant and concessional funding*

FCCC and Kyoto: Article 11.2 of the Convention states that the provision of financial resources through the financial mechanism shall be 'on a grant or concessional basis, including for the transfer of technology'. Article 11 of the Protocol incorporates this provision into the financing provisions of the Protocol.

Rule development: COP-1 provided guidance to the GEF on development of the GEF's long-term Operational Strategy.[59] This Operational Strategy was

---

[57] FCCC/CP/1997/3.
[58] See GEF/C.21/Inf.4, Action Plan to respond to the Recommendations of the Second GEF Assembly, the Policy Recommendations of the Third Replenishment, the Second Overall Performance Study of the GEF and the WSSD.
[59] Decision 12/CP.1.

subsequently approved by the GEF in 1995 and a new Strategy is currently under preparation. The existing Strategy envisages that the GEF will provide funding mainly in the form of grants but that the GEF could play an even larger catalytic role through other forms of financing such as 'concessional and contingent lending, trusts and revolving funds and loan guarantees against specified mitigation-related risks and temporary equity participation'. It states that 'until the Council approves revisions, modifications, or additional financing modalities, project support will be restricted to grants for incremental costs'.[60]

The issue of co-financing, including the ratio of money leveraged by the GEF through use of its resources, has recently become an important issue as evidenced by new guidance accepted by the GEF Council which stresses the need to increase co-financing of GEF projects.[61] Although important definitional and methodological problems remain, the GEF Council is in the process of providing more guidance which may require future achievement of minimum levels of co-financing by all GEF projects, with some developing countries suggesting ratios in the order of 12:1, rather than the 12:3 to 12:5 as currently leveraged by the GEF.

2.6   Other sources of financing

FCCC and Kyoto: Article 11.5 of the Convention and Article 11.3 of the Protocol contain a substantively identical provision stating that Annex II Parties 'may also provide and developing country Parties avail themselves of, financial resources related to the implementation of the Convention through other bilateral, regional and multilateral channels'.

Rule development: The overall size of funds flowing outside the Convention's financial mechanism has recently been estimated by the OECD DAC, as described in box 10.2. Sensitivities from donors and recipients about control over, and conditionalities attached to, resource flows outside the Convention, combined with problems relating to 'mainstreaming' environmental concerns into sectoral policy, mean that there has been little rule development beyond reporting, as explained in section 2.3. This is reflected in the lack of COP follow-up to COP-1's request to the Convention Secretariat to 'collect information from multilateral and regional financial institutions on activities undertaken in implementation of Article 4.1 and Article 12 of the Convention [without] introducing new forms of conditionalities'.[62] The national communication reporting guidelines require Annex II Parties to report on their climate-related contributions to the GEF and bilateral, regional and multilateral channels and provide an important source of

---

[60] Operational Strategy, 1995, p. 5.   [61] GEC/C.20/6, Co-financing, September 2002.
[62] Decision 11/CP.1, paragraph 2 (a).

information.[63] The initiative undertaken by the OECD DAC to track financial flows for the Rio Conventions could lead to further developments in this area.

3   Financial mechanism

3.1   *Overview*

FCCC: Article 11.1 of the Convention defines, rather than establishes, a 'financial mechanism', stating that 'its operation shall be entrusted to one or more existing international entities'. Article 11.2 states that the financial mechanism 'shall have an equitable and balanced representation of all Parties within a transparent system of governance'. The financial mechanism functions 'under the guidance of and [is] accountable to the COP, which shall decide on its policies, programme priorities and eligibility criteria related to this Convention'. The day-to- day operation of the financial mechanism is entrusted to the GEF which has an independent governance structure. Article 11.3 mandates the GEF and the COP to agree upon arrangements to give effect to Articles 11.1 and 11.2.

Although the term 'financial mechanism' and the GEF are sometimes used interchangeably, 'financial mechanism' correctly refers to the totality of legal, institutional and procedural arrangements that regulate and make possible the flow of financial resources mandated by the Convention. The purpose of the financial mechanism is to give effect to the resource commitments set out in Articles 4.3, 4.4 and 4.5 of the Convention, explained in section 2 above. The purpose of the GEF is broader – it supports the Convention but it can also fund climate activities outside of the Convention's framework as well as its other focal areas.[64] Reliance on the GEF to operate the financial mechanisms adds a layer of institutional complexity to understanding, and accessing, Convention resources but it also improves efficiency and consolidation of global environmental coherence.[65] This is because, at the end of the day, the sources of the money pledged to the GEF are the same and the GEF plays a large role in deciding how much is to be allocated to each convention and how much goes 'outside' this. The Marrakesh Accords have compounded the complexity by establishing two additional funds under the Convention, both of which will be operated by the GEF.

Kyoto: Article 11 of the Protocol incorporates the Convention's financial provisions into the Protocol's legal framework. Thus the financial mechanism of the

---

[63] FCCC/CP/1999/7, Section VII; see also section 2.3.

[64] The GEF's other focal areas are biodiversity, ozone, international waters, land degradation and persistent organic pollutants.

[65] Sjoberg, 1996

Convention is available for use under the Protocol to finance the advancement by developing countries of their Article 4.1 Convention commitments as elaborated by Article 10 of the Protocol. The Protocol, like the Convention, acknowledges that implementation of commitments by developing countries is subject to the provision of financial and other resources by stating in Article 11.1 that Parties to the Protocol 'shall take into account the provisions of Article 4, paragraphs 4, 5, 7, 8 and 9, of the Convention'.

Article 11.2 states that the 'guidance to the [GEF] in relevant decisions of the COP, including those agreed before the adoption of this Protocol, shall apply *mutatis mutandis* to the provisions of [Article 11.2]'. The term '*mutatis mutandis*' simply means in all relevant respects. The use of the words 'shall apply', rather than the weaker form 'take into account', is intended to avoid inconsistent advice being provided to the GEF by the COP and the COP/MOP, bearing in mind that decisions relating to the Protocol will be made only by Parties to the Protocol as stated in Article 13.2. The Marrrakesh Accords established the Adaptation Fund under the Protocol, to be operated by the GEF.

Rule development: Negotiations between the COP and the GEF on the arrangements called for by Article 11.3 of the Convention commenced prior to COP-1.[66] These negotiations involved sensitive political issues which divided developed and developing countries as well as raised novel legal issues on account of the GEF's unique institutional structure. The final arrangements are spelt out in the MOU between the COP and the Council of the GEF agreed at COP-2, and the Annex to the MOU agreed by COP-3.[67] The MOU took legal effect on 1 July 1994. The exact legal nature of the MOU remains a matter of legal speculation because different views are held about the legal nature of the COP itself.[68] The MOU is in substance, if not in name, akin to a legal treaty defining the roles and responsibilities of the COP and the GEF. The MOU can only be modified in writing by agreement between the COP and the GEF Council and can be terminated at six months' notice by either side. The following section describes the key elements of the MOU.

3.2   *COP guidance: scope, frequency and form*

Article 11.3 (a) required the COP and the GEF to agree on modalities to ensure that projects funded by the GEF are in conformity with COP guidance on policies, programme priorities and eligibility criteria. Paragraph 2 of the MOU

---

[66] Decision 10/CP.1

[67] Decision 12/CP.2. sets out the MOU. See Decision 12/CP.3 and FCCC/SBI/1996/14 for the Annex to the MOU.

[68] See chapter 13 on legal capacity of the COP and the GEF.

reaffirms that the COP will decide on the 'policies, programme priorities and eligibility criteria related to the Convention for the financial mechanism which shall function under the guidance of and be accountable to the COP'. In the Convention and the MOU, the phrase 'under the guidance of and be accountable to the COP' was used in preference to the stronger language 'under the authority of' proposed by developing countries because donors considered the stronger language might unduly limit the GEF's operational freedom.

In terms of frequency, Paragraph 2 of the MOU states that the 'COP will, after each of its sessions, communicate to the Council of the GEF any policy guidance approved by the COP concerning the financial mechanism'. Because the MOU also provides that the GEF will report to the COP annually, guidance from the COP has, more or less, also been given on an annual basis. Guidance usually takes the form of COP decisions explicitly titled 'guidance' or 'additional guidance' to the operating entity of the financial mechanism. But this is not always the case. COP decisions on national communications from non-Annex I Parties, as well as decisions adopted at Marrakesh covering capacity-building, adaptation and technology transfer, sometimes contain guidance for the GEF. In practice, the GEF tends only to 'listen' to COP decisions that have the formal title of 'guidance to the GEF'. For clarity, each annual report of the GEF provides a useful list of the 'main' COP decisions the GEF considers as containing COP guidance.

The ten-year accumulation of broad guidance in various COP decisions is increasingly difficult to track down and for the GEF to operationalise because the COP guidance can be too general, based as it is on the need to forge agreement among nearly 200 Parties and because the COP has tended to add, rather than prioritise, additional activities for funding.[69] As part of its second review of the financial mechanism, these considerations led COP-8 to request

> the GEF secretariat, in consultation with the Convention secretariat, to initiate a dialogue in order to implement more effectively the guidance provided by the COP [to the GEF], drawing upon the experience gained and lessons learned from the projects and programmes funded by the GEF, and to explore opportunities for streamlining guidance, and to report on the outcome of this dialogue in its report to [COP-10].[70]

3.3   *Reconsideration of particular decisions*

In FCCC Article 11, the word 'projects' was deliberately omitted from the list of things the COP decides to ensure a clean division of labour, giving the GEF operational responsibility for particular funding decisions with the COP

---

[69] OPS-2, p. 47.   [70] Decision 5/CP.8, paragraph 2.

retaining broader policy guidance functions. However, Article 11.3 (b) requires the COP and the GEF to agree modalities to allow the COP to reconsider 'a particular funding decision' in the light of the COP's policies, programmes and eligibility criteria. Paragraph 5 of the MOU clarifies that the COP's mandate does not extend to the routine consideration of projects but is limited to responding to concerns expressed by a Party dissatisfied with a particular GEF decision where this results from the GEF's interpretation of COP guidance. The MOU provides that the COP cannot make a decision about the project concerned. Rather, it 'may ask the Council of the GEF for further clarification on the specific project decision and in due time may ask for a reconsideration of that decision'.[71]

The manner in which a Party may bring its 'observations' is not specified. At SBI-18, for example, one Party made a recent decision outlining how, in its view, the GEF had not applied COP guidance on national communications in response to a specific request from the SBI-17 for Parties to share their experiences with the GEF.[72]

3.4   *GEF reporting and accountability*

The MOU contains modalities giving effect to Article 11.3 (c) concerning reporting and accountability of the GEF.[73] There are three main types of provisions: those relating to annual reporting, those relating to representation and attendance of GEF officials and those relating to a periodic, more fundamental review and evaluation of the financial mechanism.

3.4.1   Annual reporting

The MOU provides that the GEF must report annually to the COP. The Annual Report should set out all GEF-financed activities (including those undertaken by GEF Implementing Agencies) during its financial year which runs from July to June. The Annual Report of the GEF, its consideration by the COP and subsequent formulation of a COP guidance on the GEF's Report thus forms the backbone of the formal cycle of communication, and means of accountability, between the COP and the GEF. There are three broad areas that must be reported by the GEF in the Annual Report:

- Substantive information on how the GEF has 'applied the guidance and decisions of the COP in its work related to the Convention', including an analysis of how the GEF has implemented the policies, programme priorities and eligibility criteria established by the COP;

---

[71] Decision 12/CP2, paragraph 5.   [72] FCCC/SBI/2003/MISC.8
[73] Decision 12.CP.2, paragraphs 6–8.

- A synthesis of GEF climate projects under implementation and a listing of projects approved by the GEF Council, with an indication of the financial resources required for those projects; and
- Relevant monitoring and evaluation (M & E) reports undertaken by the GEF in the climate change focal area, in particular an annual review of implementation of GEF projects.

All other official public documentation of the GEF, in particular major reviews of its operations, is also made available to the COP. The GEF Council may seek guidance from the COP on any matters it considers relevant to the operation of the financial mechanism, as happened, for instance, at COP-1 when the GEF requested COP guidance on the development of its operational strategy.[74]

It is important to note that the GEF does not report directly to the COP the amount of resources provided to it by Annex II Parties. Consequently this has to be worked out on the basis of information submitted by each Annex II Party to the Convention through its national communication. GEF recipient countries report on GEF-funded activities to the GEF. As noted by OPS-2, 'under the [FCCC and CBD] conventions, the individual countries are not required to report on GEF-funded activities' in their national reporting and communications to the COPs'.[75] The lack of readily accessible information indicating how much donors have provided annually, and – from the recipient side – the lack of information on the impact and significance of GEF-funded projects, makes assessment of the GEF's performance more difficult to pin down.

3.4.2   Representation of officials

The formal submission of documents and reports from the GEF to the COP is complemented by more informal means of communications. Opportunities for dialogue between the COP and the GEF are provided in the MOU through the reciprocal attendance of representatives of the GEF and the Convention Secretariat at meetings of their respective bodies.[76] The Chair/CEO of the GEF reports, for example, in person at COP meetings. Such face-to-face meetings allow political coalitions, Parties, particularly those not on the GEF Council, as well as stakeholders not able to follow GEF proceedings, opportunities for a mutual exchange of views which enhances accountability but at the expense of raising travel costs.[77] It also allows them to raise items of concern. For example, at COP-9 Cuba raised its concern over being denied visas to the US to attend GEF Council meetings despite being the Caribbean countries' representative.

---

[74] Decision 12/CP.1.   [75] OPS-2, p. 48.   [76] Decision 12/CP.2, MOU, paragraph 11.
[77] FCCC/CP/2002/8.

3.4.3   Periodic review and evaluation

Article 11.4 of the Convention mandated COP-1 to review the interim designation of the GEF as an entity operating the financial mechanism as provided for in Article 21 of the Convention, and within four years thereafter to review the financial mechanism and to take appropriate action. COP-1 confirmed the GEF's interim status but agreed to make a determination of its definitive status within four years and this was reaffirmed by COP-2 and COP-3.[78] Box 10.1 explains why the GEF was accorded this interim status and the process leading to its definitive designation as an entity operating the Convention's financial mechanism at COP-4 in 1998.

So far as review of the financial mechanism is concerned, COP-2 requested the SBI to undertake the first review of the financial mechanism.[79] During 1997, SBI-5 worked out guidelines defining the objectives, methodology and criteria for reviewing the financial mechanism.[80] COP-3 endorsed these guidelines and mandated continuation of the review.[81] At COP-4 in 1998, FCCC Parties finally concluded their review and ended the GEF's interim status, by designating it as 'an entity entrusted with the operation of the financial mechanism'.[82] A second review of the financial mechanism was concluded by COP-8 held in 2002.[83] The third review will take place in 2006 by COP-12. This four-year interval allows the COP utilise information from any overall evaluation reports undertaken by the GEF itself as part of its four-year replenishment cycle.

Both reviews to date were based on guidelines adopted by SBI-5, as subsequently endorsed by COP-4, and which COP-8 confirmed should, subject to any amendments, be used as a basis for future reviews.[84] These guidelines state that the objective of the review is to assess: conformity of the financial mechanism with Article 11 and COP guidance, the effectiveness of funded activities in implementing the Convention and the effectiveness in the provision of resources to developing countries by Annex II Parties.[85] The review is to draw upon a wide range of inputs: GEF Reports, information provided by Parties on their experiences, annual reviews of the GEF by the COP, reports from the GEF's monitoring and evaluation programme, reports from the UNCSD and relevant bilateral and multilateral funding institutions, and relevant information provided by IGOs and NGOs.[86] The effectiveness of the financial mechanism is to be judged by taking into

---

[78] Decision 9/CP.1, Decision 12/CP.2 and Decision 11/CP.3.   [79] Decision 11/CP.2, paragraph 4.
[80] SBI-5 report, FCCC/SBI/1997/6, Annex II.   [81] Decision 11/CP.3.
[82] Decision 3/CP.4. This decision formally incorporates the guidelines for the review of the financial mechanism adopted by the SBI in 1997.
[83] Decision 5/CP.8.   [84] Decision 5/CP.8, paragraph 5.
[85] Decision 3/CP.4, Annex, section A.   [86] Decision 3/CP.4, Annex, section B.

account: transparency of decision-making, adequacy, predictability and timely disbursement of funds for developing countries, the responsiveness and efficiency of the GEF project cycle and expedited procedures, including its operational strategy, the amount of resources provided to developing countries, including amounts leveraged, and finally, the sustainability of funded projects.[87]

The consistency, coherence and operational clarity of COP guidance to the financial mechanism is not mentioned in the guidelines but is likely to form an element of the next review given the conclusion of OPS-2 and COP-8 that thought be given to this issue.[88] Other matters agreed by COP-8 as part of the second review include requiring GEF to report on its plan of action in response to OPS-2, the need for further review of its project cycle, increasing administrative efficiency and cost-effectiveness of GEF operations, simplification of incremental costs and more extensive integration of GEF activities with national priorities through, for example, national sustainable development strategies and poverty reduction strategies.[89]

It is important to note that the MOU between the COP and the GEF falls short of obliging the GEF to take into account the conclusions of any review and evaluation undertaken by the COP. Paragraph 12 of the MOU maintains the GEF's legal independence by stating that 'such evaluations will be taken into account by the COP in its decisions, pursuant to Article 11.4, on arrangements for the financial mechanism'. Of course, in practice, the GEF has demonstrated its responsiveness to COP guidance as confirmed by OPS-2 and by COP-8 which concluded that 'the GEF has effectively performed its role as an entity operating the financial mechanism of the Convention'.[90] Nevertheless, COP-8 requested the GEF to report to COP-9 on 'how it has taken into consideration the recommendations of the second review of the effectiveness of the financial mechanism by the COP'.[91]

4   Marrakesh Accords funds

Background: Negotiations for the Kyoto Protocol, and the subsequent intense period of rule development on matters essential for its ratification, meant that resource issues related to the implementation of developing country commitments received less attention than would otherwise have been the case. Additionally, developing country frustration that the financial mechanism funded a limited range of activities, particularly in relation to adaptation and capacity-building, led to a review of the regime's finances. At COP-7 Parties agreed there was

---

[87] Decision 3/CP.4, Annex, section C.   [88] Decision 5/CP.8, paragraph 2.
[89] Decision 5/CP.8, paragraphs 1 and 4 (a)–(d).
[90] OPS-2, p. 46 and Decision 5/CP.8, Preamble.   [91] Decision 5/CP.8, paragraph 1.

a need for new and additional funding beyond contributions which are allocated to the climate change focal area of the GEF and to multilateral and bilateral funding for the implementation of the Convention.[92] COP-7 agreed that institutional arrangements separate from the existing GEF Trust Fund for climate change activities were necessary. Additionally, COP-7 agreed to expand the scope of activities eligible for funding by establishing three new funds.

Two of these funds – the LDC Fund and the SCCF – are established pursuant to the Convention and therefore subject to guidance from the COP. The third fund, the Adaptation Fund, is to be established under the Kyoto Protocol. It would initially be subject to COP guidance and subsequently to COP/MOP guidance upon entry into force of the Kyoto Protocol.[93] All three funds are to be operated by the GEF on the basis that each fund remains distinct from the existing GEF Trust Fund used for climate change activities which shall remain in operation.

In its report to COP-8 on arrangements for the establishment of the new climate change funds, the GEF has noted that 'the respective roles and responsibilities of the COP and the GEF provided for in the MOU will be applied, *mutatis mutandis*, for the purposes of the [new] funds'. Additionally, the GEF has stated that 'in operating the funds, operational policies and procedures and governance structure of the GEF will apply to the operation of all the funds, unless the COP determines through guidance concerning the modalities for operating the funds that other arrangements should be made'.[94] Thus when these funds are fully operational, the GEF will operate four funds – potentially on the basis of four different sets of guidance provided by the COP.

4.1   *Least Developed Countries Fund*

Article 4.9 of the Convention requires Parties to give special consideration to LDCs in their action with regard to funding and transfer of technology. Decision 5/CP.7 contains sections specifically addressing LDC needs. COP-7 also adopted a specific fund under the Convention, the purpose of which is 'to support a work programme for the least developed countries' as referred to in Decision 5/CP.7. This work programme covers support, inter alia, for the following activities:

- Strengthening existing or establishing, where needed, national climate change secretariats and/or focal points in LDCs to enable effective implementation of the Convention and the Protocol;
- Training in negotiating skills and language to develop capacity of LDC negotiators to participate effectively in the climate change process;

---

[92] Decision 7/CP.7, paragraph 1.   [93] Decision 10/CP.7, paragraph 4.   [94] GEF/C.19/6.

- Preparation of NAPAs which can serve as a simplified and direct channel of communication of urgent and immediate needs of LDCs relating to their vulnerabilities and adaptation; and
- Support for the LEG established by Decision 29/CP.7.

The substantive aspects of the LDC work programme, including NAPAs and the role of the LEG, are set out in more detail in chapter 8 on adaptation.

In terms of funding, COP-7 agreed that the LDC Fund should fund the preparation of NAPAs as signalled in Decision 27/CP.7 and instructed the GEF accordingly.[95] Funding for the preparation of NAPAs is to cover their 'agreed full costs'.[96] To support the NAPA process further, COP-8 gave additional guidance to the GEF requesting funding from the LDC Fund, to the extent sufficient bilateral resources were unavailable, for the organisation of four regional workshops in 2003, under the guidance of the LEG.[97] Decision 5/CP.7 sets out the scope of activities, beyond NAPAs, that are to be funded from the LDC Fund. The issue of where funding for the *implementation* of NAPAs would be covered by the LDC Fund was left to COP-9. At Milan, after much disagreement, Parties agreed that the LDC Fund should provide financial support for implementation of NAPAs 'as soon as possible after their completion'.[98] COP-9 requested the GEF to develop operational guidelines to this end, taking into account an array of considerations such as national priorities, cost-effectiveness, complementarity with other funding sources, equitable access by LDCs to funding of NAPAs, urgency and immediacy of adapting and prioritisation of activities. Importantly, the GEF is also to take into account 'criteria for supporting activities on an agreed full-cost basis, taking into account the level of funds available'. The effect of these conditions on funding means the GEF will have considerable discretion in providing LDCs with funding for implementation of NAPAs. The Adaptation Fund and the SCCF can also fund adaptation activities by LDCs and are discussed below.

Given the priority attached by COP-7 to the establishment of the LDC Fund, the GEF made swift arrangements for the Fund's operation which were reported to COP-8 and completed by COP-9.[99] In accordance with guidance from COP-7, these arrangements provide for the World Bank to act as Trustee of a multi-donor Trust Fund that is separate and distinct from the regular GEF Trust Fund – both in terms of charging of administrative costs and for purposes of operations. To maintain financial distinctness, separate reports and work programmes will have to be prepared by the GEF on the LDC Fund. In terms of resources mobilisation, after

---

[95] Operation of the LDC Trust Fund for Climate Change, GEF/C.21/5/Rev.1, April 2003.
[96] Decision 27/CP.7, paragraph 1 (a).   [97] Decision 8/CP.8, paragraph 3.   [98] Decision 9/CP.9.
[99] See FCCC/CP/2002/4, GEF/C.19/6, GEF/C.21/5/Rev.1, paragraph 3 and FCCC/CP/2003/3.

consultation with the Convention Secretariat and the IAs, the GEF's assessment of total funding requirements for NAPA preparation is US $12 million. By June 2003, total contributions received for the Fund amounted to US $9 million with a total of US $16 million pledged.[100] To assist disbursement, in consultation with experts from the LEG, the Convention Secretariat and IAs, the GEF has prepared Operational Guidelines for the Expedited Funding for the preparation of NAPAs, which were presented to the GEF Council for information in May 2002.[101] These allow projects of up to US $200,000 per LDC to be approved through GEF's expedited procedures.

4.2   *Special Climate Change Fund*

COP-7 agreed to establish the SCCF under the Convention to finance the following activities that are complementary to those currently funded by the GEF:

- Adaptation, in accordance with paragraph 8 of Decision 5/CP.7;[102]
- Transfer of technologies, in accordance with Decision 4/CP.7;[103]
- Energy, transport, industry, agriculture, forestry and waste management projects; and
- Activities to assist developing country Parties referred to under Article 4.8 (h) in diversifying their economies in accordance with Decision 5/CP.7.[104]

Currently, the GEF Trust Fund is used to support enabling activities and projects that fall within GEF's four climate-related operational programmes, described in box 10.5. The GEF also funds short-term projects in areas that fall outside the operational programmes, provided they are cost-effective. The addition of categories that can be funded by the SCCF, listed above, generally expands what can be funded, in particular for adaptation and for activities to assist fossil-fuel dependent developing country Parties diversify their economies.[105]

COP-7 agreed 'to provide guidance to the [GEF] on the modalities for operating this fund, including expedited access' but requested the GEF to report on making the necessary arrangements for establishment of this fund. In terms of institutional modalities, on the basis of information submitted by the GEF in its Annual Report to COP-8, the COP was able to confirm that the GEF should:

- Promote complementarity of funding between the SCCF and other funds operated by the GEF;

---

[100] GEF/C.21/5/Rev.1, Annex II. See also FCCC/CP/2003/3.   [101] GEF/C.19/Inf.7.
[102] See chapter 8.   [103] See section 6.   [104] See chapter 9.   [105] See chapters 8 and 9.

- Ensure financial separation of the SCCF from other GEF-operated funds;
- Ensure transparency in the operation of the SCCF;
- Adopt streamlined procedures for SCCF while ensuring sound financial management.[106]

COP-8 agreed further to define the prioritised activities, programmes and measures to be funded out of the SCCF and to finalise these by COP-9, taking into account views submitted by Parties and by the LEG and the Expert Group on Technology Transfer in time.[107] At SBI-18, held in June 2003, discussions took place on the basis of views submitted by Parties, the LEG, the EGTT and a Secretariat summary and synthesis of these various views.[108] The finalisation of guidance for operationalisation of the SCCF was one of the major achievements of COP-9. Parties confirmed that the SCCF should serve as a catalyst to leverage additional resources from other sources. Activities are to be country-driven, cost-effective and integrated into national sustainable development and poverty-reduction strategies. The recognition that the SCCF should support activities that contribute to the achievement of the WSSD and the MDGs as well as to integration of climate change considerations into development activities is emphasised in the Preamble but does not form a condition for SCCF funding. Funding shall be provided taking into account national communications or NAPAs and other relevant information provided by the applicant Party – making clear that funding is not dependent on submission of national communications alone. In terms of priorities, COP-9 agreed that adaptation is to have 'top priority' but there is an inference that applicants to the Fund will include sufficient information to warrant funding of such activities.[109] Technology transfer and capacity-building are also essential areas to receive SCCF funding, particularly in the following four priority areas: implementation of the results of technology needs assessment, technology information, capacity-building for technology transfer and enabling environments.

Because the demands for recompense by some OPEC countries remain extensive and because the EU and a large number of developing countries remain opposed to the limited resources of the SCCF (estimated at US $50 million annually) being used for economic diversification in the face of other pressing needs, COP-9 could not reach a conclusion about what activities, programmes and measures, if any, should be supported by the SCCF for activities under paragraph 2 (c) and (d) of

---

[106] Decision 7/CP.8, paragraph 1.   [107] Decision 7/CP.8, paragraph 2.
[108] FCCC/SBI/2003/MISC.1 and Add.1, FCCC/SBI/2003/INF.12 and Add.1, and FCCC/SBI/2003/INF.3.
[109] See chapter 8 for more detailed discussion of adaptation activities under the SCCF.

Decision 7/CP.7.[110] COP-9 invited Parties to submit views on this issue to SBI-21 in order for COP-10 to take a decision on these matters.[111] Notwithstanding the deferment of this issue to COP-10, Decision 5/CP.9 means that the GEF will finally be able to operationalise the SCCF which Parties had agreed to set up three years earlier.

4.3   *Adaptation Fund*

Article 12.8 on the CDM provides that a share of the proceeds from certified project activities undertaken by Annex I Parties to the Protocol is to be used to fund adaptation in vulnerable developing country Parties. The Protocol also contains adaptation and finance-related commitments under Articles 10 and 11. Because the Kyoto Protocol is a separate legal instrument from the Convention, an adaptation fund that was legally and administratively distinct from those established under the Convention had to be created. Accordingly, COP-7 agreed to establish an Adaptation Fund 'to finance concrete adaptation projects and programmes in developing country Parties that are Parties to the Protocol, as well as activities identified in paragraph 8 of Decision 5/CP.7'.[112] Paragraph 8 (a)–(d) of Decision 5/CP.7 provides that the following activities are to be supported through the SCCF and/or the Adaptation Fund, and other bilateral and multilateral sources:

- Prompt implementation of adaptation activities, where sufficient information is available to warrant such activities, inter alia in the areas of water resources management, land management, agriculture, health, infrastructure development, fragile ecosystems, including mountainous ecosystems, and integrated coastal zone management;
- Improving the monitoring of diseases and vectors affected by climate change, and related forecasting and early-warning systems, and in this context improving disease control and prevention;
- Supporting capacity-building, including institutional capacity, for preventive measures, planning, preparedness and management of disasters relating to climate change, including contingency planning, in particular for droughts and floods in areas prone to extreme weather events; and
- Strengthening existing and, where needed, establishing national and regional centres and information networks for rapid response to extreme weather events, utilising information technology as much as possible.

---

[110] Paragraph 2 (c) refers to energy, transport, industry, agriculture, forestry and waste management activities and paragraph 2 (d) refers to activities to assist developing countries referred to in Article 4.8 (h) in diversifying their economies in accordance with Decision 5/CP.7.

[111] Decision 5/CP.9, paragraph 4.   [112] Decision 10/CP.7, paragraph 1.

Financing for the Fund will be generated by the share of the proceeds on CDM project activities as well as other sources of funding. COP-7 agreed that the share of the proceeds 'shall be two per cent of the CERs issued' for all CDM project activities except for activities registered in LDCs which are exempt from this.[113] Modalities allowing the GEF to collect and transfer the share of the proceeds have yet to be agreed. Because the amount of financing from the CDM is uncertain and may not be sufficient to meet needs, financing for the Adaptation Fund will also come from other resources, such as the US $410 million annually by 2005 announced by a group of Annex II Parties at COP-7. All developing countries will be eligible for funding under the Adaptation Fund, including LDCs as the LDC Fund only covers their 'urgent and immediate' adaptation needs and thus there is no expectation of their exclusion from the SCCF or Adaptation Fund for other needs. Although paragraph 1 of Decision 10/CP.7 states that the Fund will provide funding in developing country Parties that are Parties to the Protocol, there is some ambiguity as to whether ratification of the Protocol is a condition to receiving funding for all kinds of activities covered by the Decisions. This is because Decision 10/CP.7 also refers to funding of adaptation activities identified in paragraph 8 of Decision 5/CP.7 which does not contain a Protocol ratification requirement. This ambiguity may need to be addressed through further COP guidance.

The Adaptation Fund will be operated and managed by the GEF with guidance to be provided by the COP until the entry into force of the Protocol when the Fund will function according to guidance provided by the COP/MOP. Because CDM projects can be undertaken by Annex I Parties from 2000, COP-7 agreed that such Parties shall report on their financial contributions to the Adaptation Fund on an annual basis.[114] These reports will be reviewed by the COP (and in future by the COP/MOP) on an annual basis.[115] This provision will ensure sound financial management and let the COP keep a close eye on how much funding is being generated for adaptation by the CDM through the share of proceeds. Any revision of the 2 per cent figure will not have retroactive effect as it will not affect projects already registered under the CDM. Annex I Parties that intend to ratify the Protocol are invited to provide funding additional to the share of the proceeds on CDM activities.

As the Protocol has not yet entered into force, the COP has not yet prioritised providing guidance on the Adaptation Fund, thus it has not been possible for the GEF to mobilise resources for either of these funds or to make them operational.[116] In principle, the Adaptation Fund will be managed by the World Bank acting as a

---

[113] Decision 17/CP.7, paragraph 15.   [114] Decision 10/CP.7, paragraph 6.
[115] Decision 10/CP.7, paragraph 7.   [116] GEF/C.21.Rev.1, paragraph 2.

Trustee, the Fund will be kept operationally and in management terms separate from other GEF-operated funds, and until the COP (COP/MOP) determines otherwise, will be subject to existing GEF policies, principles, eligibility criteria and operational strategies.

5   Accessing GEF resources

The GEF is an integral component of the climate change regime yet insufficiently understood by many in FCCC negotiations who do not attend its meetings, as these are generally covered by finance/aid, rather than environment, ministries. An understanding of its governance structure, operational policies, principles and institutional procedures is helpful in accessing funds from the GEF and, in the long term, enhancing the quality of policy guidance provided by the COP. Accordingly, this section explains how the GEF works.

5.1   *GEF mission*

The GEF's mission is to forge international cooperation and finance actions to address six critical threats to the global environment: biodiversity loss, climate change, degradation of international waters, ozone depletion, land degradation and persistent organic pollutants.[117]

5.2   *GEF governance structure*

The GEF's governance structure is laid out in the Instrument for the Establishment of the Restructured Global Environmental Facility (GEF Instrument), agreed in 1994, which entered into force on 31 July 1994 through subsequent adoption by the governing bodies of UNDP, the World Bank and UNEP.[118] The GEF governance structure is unique in that it comprises several components – some established through the GEF Instrument and others with their own independent legal authority. These components are:

- GEF Assembly
- GEF Council
- COPs of international conventions serviced by GEF
- Implementing and Executing Agencies
- GEF Secretariat
- World Bank as Trustee of GEF Trust Fund

---

[117] On the background and purpose of the GEF establishment, see Sand, 1994, and Werksman, 1995.

[118] UNDP, 1994; UNEP, 1994; World Bank, Executive Directors, 1994; and World Bank, Board of Governors, 1994.

- GEF Scientific and Technical Advisory Panel (STAP)
- Host Country GEF Focal Points.

The **GEF Assembly**, composed of 175 states, meets every three years to review and approve general policies, operations and amendments to the founding GEF Instrument. Any country can become a member by simply depositing an instrument in accordance with Annex A of its Instrument. Decisions at the Assembly must be taken by consensus. The Assembly has met twice: in 1998 in Delhi and in 2002 in Beijing.

Decision-making in the GEF is centred on the **GEF Council** which functions as an independent board of directors, with primary responsibility for developing, adopting, and evaluating GEF programmes. The Council is composed of thirty-two representatives from its member states who are grouped together for representation purposes in thirty-two constituencies unique to the GEF. The Council meets twice a year, for three days at a time, to review, comment upon, and reject or accept each GEF project, future business plans, work programmes and policies.[119] All decisions are by consensus but, if this is not possible, any member can request a formal vote. A decision will only be taken by a double-weighted majority, that is, an affirmative vote representing both a 60 per cent majority of the total number of participants and a 60 per cent majority of the total contributions. This gives donors and recipients a veto but neither side can, on their own, take a decision. Each GEF Council meeting is preceded by a meeting with NGOs.

The **international conventions** provide guidance to the GEF Council. Relations between the GEF and the respective COPs of the FCCC and CBD are governed by Memoranda of Understanding.[120] These MOU will also apply, *mutatis mutandis*, to the COP/MOPs established by the protocols to these Conventions: the 1997 Cartagena Biosafety Protocol and the 1997 Kyoto Protocol.

GEF Operations are carried out by a tripartite partnership composed of the UNDP, the World Bank and UNEP, which are referred to as the three **Implementing Agencies**. Relations between the GEF and IAs are governed by interagency agreements pursuant to Annex D of the GEF Instrument. The IAs report to the GEF Council, not the Conventions, for their Convention-related work. The key function of IAs is to help countries develop and implement GEF projects and programmes that receive GEF co-financing. Any governmental agency, non-governmental organisation, educational institution or private sector company in an eligible country may propose a project to one of the GEF Implementing Agencies at any time. There is de facto specialisation among the IAs: UNDP is favoured for building human

---

[119] GEF Council Rules of Procedure, available at www.gefweb.org/public/Rules%20of%20Procedures%20Eng.pdf.

[120] See sections 3.1 and 3.2 above on COP guidance and the MOU.

and institutional capacities; the World Bank is mainly responsible for investment projects; and UNEP provides assistance to certain global initiatives and to the STAP.

Until 1999, every GEF project had to be developed and implemented with one of the three IAs. To speed up the project cycle, and to ensure the service provided by IAs remains responsive and competitive, the GEF Council has recently allowed other agencies to perform some functions undertaken by the three IAs. Such agencies are designated as **Executing Agencies with Expanded Opportunities (EAEOs)**.[121] The following seven organisations now have EAEO status: since May 1999, African Development Bank, Asian Development Bank, European Bank for Reconstruction and Development and Inter-American Development Bank; since May 2000, UNIDO and FAO; and, as of April 2001, the International Fund for Agriculture.

The World Bank acts as **Trustee of the GEF Trust Fund**, i.e. the Bank manages the funding the GEF uses to fulfil its mission. This is because the GEF Instrument does not provide the GEF with the necessary formal independent legal status of an international organisation.[122] The Bank's role as Trustee is quite separate from the role the Bank plays as an IA. GEF operations are coordinated by a **Secretariat** of around forty people based in the World Bank in Washington, DC but which is functionally independent of the Bank. The Secretariat is headed by the GEF Chief Executive Office.

The **Scientific and Technical Advisory Panel** was established as an independent body to review projects and provide sound scientific and technical advice regarding GEF policies, operational strategies and programmes. STAP conducts reviews of selected, not all, projects in certain circumstances and at specific points in the GEF project cycle and maintains a roster of experts whose work feeds into the GEF's monitoring and evaluation work. STAP's twelve members are selected by the Executive Director of UNEP, in consultation with UNDP, the World Bank and the GEF Secretariat, with UNEP providing the STAP Secretariat and acting as its liaison. The **GEF Operations Committee** is a forum used by the GEF Secretariat to discuss major policy issues with other members of the GEF 'family' – including, when appropriate, representatives from the various convention secretariats.

Finally, most countries receiving GEF assistance have designated government officials to take responsibility for GEF activities as follows: a **Political/National focal point** who coordinates matters related to GEF governance and an **Operational focal point** who oversees individual project-related matters. These focal points help ensure that GEF projects conform to their country's own priorities. Without such confirmation, a project will not satisfy the GEF criterion of being 'country-driven'.

---

[121] GEF Instrument 1994.   [122] See section 3.1 above.

5.3   *GEF operations*

The GEF finances activities in the six 'focal areas' described in the GEF's mission statement on the basis of the Operational Strategy (OS). The OS has been described as an overall strategic 'road map' – rather than a rulebook – and sets out the direction of GEF funding on the basis of frameworks provided by the Conventions as well as STAP and other stakeholders.[123] The OS was approved by the GEF Council in October 1995.[124] A new operational strategy is being prepared to reflect the addition of two new focal areas, land degradation and persistent organic pollutants, approved by the GEF Assembly in October 2002. The current OS is organised in three parts:

- A policy framework, comprising key operational principles and strategic considerations, applicable to all GEF activities;
- A general description of the programming of GEF operations which establishes three kinds of GEF activities: operational programmes, enabling activities and short-term response measures; and
- A separate operational strategy for each of the six focal areas, incorporating where available, guidance from conventions.

5.3.1   Principles and strategic considerations

The operational principles and strategic considerations applicable to all GEF activities must be consistent with core principles, such as consistency with COP guidance, and provide global environmental benefits whilst being country-driven, with involvement from stakeholders. Strategic considerations include complementing development funding, not generating negative environmental impacts and reducing risks caused by uncertainty.

5.3.2   Programming

The term 'programming' refers to the policy framework and sequencing of funded activities relevant for achieving global environmental objectives. The GEF requested guidance from COP-1 on the approach to be followed in developing its operational strategy as this influences programming.[125] Three approaches were presented by the GEF to the COP: (a) a strategy of maximising short-term cost-effectiveness – basically securing the cheapest and greatest GHG reductions available; (b) a strategy of maximising long-term cost-effectiveness – which would have favoured expensive, zero-carbon technologies such as renewables with a view to lowering their long-term cost; (c) a mixed strategy wherein projects would

---

[123] Mertens, 1996, and Burgiel and Cohen, 1997.   [124] GEFDOC #12.
[125] FCCC/CP/1995/4, paragraphs 5–10.

be selected in accordance with a double set of programme priorities – if they met either one of the long-term programme priorities or one of the short-term priorities.

Predictably, the COP picked the middle way – the mixed strategy – perhaps because this fits better with the political need not to exclude particular kinds of projects and to maximise geographic balance in the spread of projects.[126] The OS is based on this mixed approach which means that GEF operations are programmed in three broad, interrelated categories, known as operational programmes, enabling activities and short-term response measures.

1 Operational programmes   An operational programme is simply a conceptual and planning framework for the design, implementation and coordination of a set of projects to achieve a global environmental objective in a particular focal area. The opposite of a programme – 'the let a hundred flowers bloom' approach – would make long-term planning and coordination among IAs and other actors difficult and mean less strategic use of scarce GEF funds. The operational programmes relevant to climate change have been developed largely by the GEF but with guidance and endorsement by the COP. The GEF currently has thirteen Operational Programmes (OPs) which are evolving and details of which are available from the GEF. The climate change focal area has had four programmes:

- OP#5: Removal of barriers to energy efficiency and energy conservation
- OP#6: Promoting the adoption of renewable energy and reducing implementation costs
- OP#7: Reducing the long-term costs of low greenhouse gas emitting energy technologies
- OP#11: Promoting environmentally sustainable transport.

Projects falling under these OPs will be eligible for funding but it is important to bear in mind what the GEF does not fund under these programmes:

- Total cost of mitigation (the GEF only funds 'full agreed incremental costs');[127]
- Research and studies in these areas;
- Change from a renewable fuel to a fossil fuel even if more efficient; and
- Investment under OP#5 and OP#6 (because these programmes are about encouraging what should be happening anyway).

There is currently no GEF operational programme for adaptation activities, although, as discussed in chapter 8, the GEF is developing a framework for adaptation. Additionally, mitigation activities in the agriculture, forestry, waste

---

[126] Decision 12/CP.1, paragraph 2.   [127] Section 2.2.

management, transport and energy sectors and carbon sequestration, and other activities to help oil-producing countries diversify their economies, do not have corresponding operational programmes – although some activities in these areas can be covered if they fall under the four OPs or under short-term measures, explained below. COP-10 will decide if the SCCF could potentially fund some of these additional activities.

     2 Short-term measures   The mixed approach adopted by the COP recognised that country-driven projects could emerge that could not be placed within an existing GEF operational programme but could still be worthy of funding. Such projects could be in new areas that might form the basis of future programmes or just be 'too good to miss' in view of their GHG reduction benefits and costs. To provide flexibility, the Operational Strategy allows the GEF to fund such projects outside the framework of an operational programme under the heading 'support under short-term response measures'. Because such projects would not be expected to yield significant strategic or programmatic objectives, they must demonstrate clear short-term benefits and be highly cost-effective. For example, climate change projects aimed solely at reducing the net emissions of GHGs or urgent measures to conserve an extremely endangered species could be eligible for funding under this category.

     3 Enabling activities   The term 'enabling activities' is currently used by the GEF to refer to activities which help countries either fulfil essential communication requirements related to a convention, such as the preparation of national GHG inventories and initial national communications, or else provide a basic and essential level of information to enable policy and strategic decisions to be made as well as assisting planning that identifies priority activities within a country. Such activities normally qualify for full cost funding and are linked to the broader discussions on capacity-building, discussed in section 7.

5.3.3   Funding modalities

     If an activity appears to conform to the policies, programme priorities and eligibility criteria described above, and has formal country approval, it can be submitted to the GEF for funding, but these proposals must be endorsed by GEF focal points and also be prepared with the assistance of the IAs or EAEOs.[128] The IAs and EAEOs have detailed guides to help project proponents access GEF funding. In brief, the format in which projects are submitted and the procedures applicable for their subsequent consideration depend essentially on how much money the GEF is being asked to provide. The largest projects require GEF Council

---

[128] GEF/C.13/Inf.7, Pipeline of the Implementing Agencies, April 1999.

approval. Other kinds of activities can be approved by the GEF CEO under authority delegated to him by the Council, whilst some of the smallest grants are decided by the IAs without reference to the GEF Council. The different kinds of GEF projects and applicable procedures are as follows:

- **Full-Sized Projects** (FSPs) refer to projects where the grant provided by the GEF exceeds US $1 million. Such projects must be endorsed as eligible by the GEF Council using standard GEF project cycle procedures which involve review by STAP experts.

- **Medium-Sized Projects** (MSPs) refer to projects where the GEF grant is less than US $1 million. Medium-sized projects take between six and twelve months to develop and receive Council approval; however, if the GEF portion of the budget is under $750,000, projects do not require a technical review or Council approval.

- **Project Preparation and Development Facility** (PDF). This supports preparatory work for submission of MSPs, FSPs or Block B grants. Funding for project preparation is available in three tranches or 'blocks'. **Block A** grants (up to US $25,000) fund the initial stages of project or programme identification. Such grants are approved through the IAs and EAEOs which can take between four and six months. **Block B** grants (up to US $350,000) fund further information gathering necessary to complete FSP proposals and provide necessary supporting documentation. These normally take twelve months. These grants are approved by the GEF CEO with input from GEF OP. Medium-sized projects are not eligible for PDF Block B grants, though they are eligible for Block A grants. **Block C** grants (up to US $1 million) are normally made available after a project proposal is approved by the GEF Council but where additional financing is required for larger projects to complete technical design and feasibility work.

- **Small Grants Programme** (SGP) offers grants up to $50,000 for eligible projects that represent local contributions to preservation of the global environment. Each country participating in the SGP has its own National Coordinator, National Selection Committee and National Strategy. Project selection occurs at the national level and does not require GEF Council approval. The SGP is managed solely by UNDP and is not available from UNEP or the World Bank. SGP proposals may only be accepted from participating countries. To date, over 1,100 community-based projects have been funded under the SGP.

- **Small and Medium Enterprise (SME) Programme**. This programme is a partnership with the International Finance Corporation (IFC), a World Bank affiliate. The SME programme finances projects that demonstrate a positive environmental impact and have basic financial viability, thus promoting private sector investment opportunities in developing countries.

- **Enabling Activities**. Grants for enabling activities which help countries undertake essential planning and/or fulfil convention reporting are explained in section 7.

Once a project has been approved, it moves into the 'project execution' or implementation phase and becomes subject to a number of monitoring and evaluation mechanisms, the principal one being the annual Project Implementation Review (PIR). With other information, this feeds into the production of an annual Project Performance Report (PPR) which is summarised in the GEF Annual Report to the COP.

6   Technology

6.1   Background

The development, application and diffusion of low/zero carbon technologies, as well as necessary changes in lifestyles and removal of barriers to allow existing carbon-reducing technologies to compete fairly on the market, is of critical importance in preventing climate change.[129] Adaptation technologies are also important for minimising adverse impacts. This section explains the Convention and Protocol provisions to promote research and development (R & D) as well as on transfer of such technology, including through use of financial resources under the Convention's financial mechanism. It then explains the comprehensive framework of actions to implement these commitments, adopted as part of the Marrakesh Accords which also established the Expert Group on Technology Transfer.[130]

Technology, and its transfer, is a politically charged issue. Negotiations have taken place during the 1990s which saw a broad change in the types and magnitude of international financial flows that drive technology transfer, resulting in declining levels of ODA (in both absolute terms and as a percentage of funding for projects) and a dramatic increase in opportunities for obtaining private sector financing for technology acquisition – at least for some countries.[131] These changes altered dramatically the relative capacities and roles of various stakeholders. The 1990s emphasis on markets and globalisation to deliver developmental gains means that rule development in this area has therefore focused on fostering mechanisms and developing tools to help Parties implement their existing

---

[129] IPCC, 2000. See also OECD, 2003.   [130] Decision 4/CP.7.   [131] UNEP, 2001.

technology-related commitments better, rather than on laying down new, more stringent commitments for governments. Transfer of technology will also take place through initiatives taken outside the climate change regime, as evidenced by the announcement by the US of an international framework for cooperation for research and development of carbon capture and storage technologies, discussed in chapter 5, and more directly through the Kyoto Mechanisms, discussed in chapter 6.

6.2   *Technology-related commitments*

FCCC: The three most important provisions in the Convention on technology are Articles 4.1 (c), 4.3 and 4.5. Article 4.1 (c) requires all Parties to 'promote and cooperate in the development, application and diffusion, including transfer, of technologies, practices and processes that control, reduce or prevent anthropogenic emissions of greenhouse gases not controlled by the Montreal Protocol in all relevant sectors, including the energy, transport, industry, agriculture, forestry and waste management sectors'. For non-Annex I Parties implementation of Article 4.1 (c) is closely linked to Articles 4.3 and 4.5 of the Convention which define the obligations of Annex II Parties in relation to technology transfer.

Article 4.3 mandates Annex II Parties to provide new and additional financial resources, emphasising 'including for the transfer of technology', to developing countries to implement Article 4.1 of the Convention.[132] Article 4.5 requires Annex II Parties to

> take all practicable steps to promote, facilitate and finance, as appropriate, the transfer of, or access to, environmentally sound technologies and know-how to other Parties, particularly developing country Parties, to enable them to implement the provisions of the Convention. In this process, the developed country Parties shall support the development and enhancement of endogenous capacities and technologies of developing country Parties. Other Parties and organisations in a position to do so may also assist in facilitating the transfer of such technologies.

These provisions are linked to the functions of the Subsidiary Bodies and to the reporting of information in national communications.[133]

---

[132] Section 2.
[133] Article 9.2 (c) on SBSTA, Article 10 on SBI discussed in chapter 13, and Article 12, reporting, discussed in chapter 11.

Article 4.1 (c) singles out mitigation technologies and does not mention adaptation technologies. The references to 'practices and processes' refers to behavioural and lifestyle changes, ensuring that Article 4.1 (c) strikes a balance between two polar views regarding the role of technology in the climate debate: one giving prominence to carbon-free technologies that would permit life to proceed as 'normal', the other giving greater prominence to changes in behaviour as a necessary complement to development of new technologies.[134]

Article 4.1 (c) is the only explicit obligation in the Convention requiring all Parties to promote and cooperate in the development, application and diffusion of clean technologies and mitigation-related behavioural practices and processes. Annex I Parties report on their implementation of Article 4.1 (c) in the context of information provided by them in their national communications, mainly under the section on PAMs as there is no other section in the guidelines explicitly dealing with technology *per se*.[135] To date, Annex I Parties have tended to report on national technology and R & D related PAMs because international cooperative mitigation technology efforts, such as pooling of R & D budgets, have not been planned or implemented. The most recent analysis of Annex I Parties' national communications concludes that 'it does not seem that so far the environment or climate change in particular, have been principal areas of corporate or technological emphasis'.[136] The analysis also concluded that there was little information on how existing policies could persuade markets to ensure optimal uptake of new efficient technologies close to economic viability and what new policies are needed to stimulate technologies in the medium and long term.[137] Reporting on Article 4.1 (c) by non-Annex I Parties also takes place through their national communications but few countries have used these to report in any detail on their technology-related needs and projects.

So far as reporting on Articles 4.3 and 4.5 is concerned, FCCC Reporting Guidelines contain a mandatory requirement for Annex II Parties to provide in their national communications information relating to private/public sector technology transfer.[138] Annex II Parties should provide information, where feasible, on technology transfer activities using a standard table to report on technology transfer success and failure stories.[139] Additionally, Annex II Parties should report on activities for financing access by developing countries to 'hard' and 'soft' environmentally sound technologies and actions taken by Annex II governments to promote, facilitate and finance technology transfer, and support endogenous

---

[134] OECD 2003 paper.   [135] See chapters 5 and 11.

[136] FCCC/SBI/2003/7/Add.2, 29 May 2003.

[137] FCCC/SBI/2003/7/Add.2, paragraph 252.   [138] See table 11.3.   [139] See table 11.3.

capacities and technologies of developing countries. Parties may also report how they have encouraged private sector technology transfer activities.[140]

Kyoto: Articles 10 and 11 of the Protocol incorporate the provisions of Articles 4.1, 4.3 and 4.5. The Protocol negotiations were, however, influenced by decisions relating to technology development and transfer adopted at previous COP sessions. Some of these decisions elaborated and made good gaps and limitations in Article 4.1 (c) and were thus incorporated into the technology provisions of the Protocol.

Article 10 (c), for example, clarifies, strengthens and expands the scope of the commitment in Article 4.1 (c) of the Convention. Article 10 (g) provides that all Parties shall

> cooperate in the promotion of effective modalities for the development, application and diffusion of, and take all practicable steps to promote, facilitate and finance, as appropriate, the transfer of, or access to, environmentally sound technologies, know-how, practices and processes pertinent to climate change, in particular to developing countries, including the formulation of policies and programmes for the effective transfer of environmentally sound technologies that are publicly owned or in the public domain and the creation of an enabling environment for the private sector, to promote and enhance the transfer of, and access to, environmentally sound technologies'.

Unlike Article 4.1 (c), Article 10 (c) clearly covers adaptation as well as mitigation technologies as it refers to technologies 'pertinent to climate change, particularly to developing countries'. Because adaptation concerns are likely to foreshadow mitigation for many vulnerable developing countries, a clear commitment to developing, financing and transferring adaptation technologies by all Parties advances the provision of Article 4.1. This commitment is qualified by 'as appropriate' and acknowledges that developing countries have a role in developing, financing and transferring climate technologies, and not just as recipients of technology transfers.

A second, clear change from the Convention is the inclusion of the concept of 'environmentally sound technologies' (ESTs) in lieu of the word 'technologies'. The concept of ESTs was used in Decision 13/CP.1 and reflects agreed language on ESTs in Chapter 34 of Agenda 21. ESTs encompass technologies that have the potential for significantly improved environmental performance relative to other technologies. Broadly speaking, these technologies protect the environment, are less polluting, use resources in a sustainable manner, recycle more of their wastes and products, and handle all residual wastes in a more environmentally acceptable

---

[140] See table 11.3.

way than the technologies for which they are substitutes. Furthermore, as argued in Chapter 34 of Agenda 21, ESTs are not just 'individual technologies, but total systems which include know-how, procedures, goods and services, and equipment as well as organisational and managerial procedures'. Thus the incorporation of ESTs into the Protocol emphasises a more rounded approach to technology issues than signalled in the Convention which seemed to focus on 'hardware'.

A third aspect in which the Protocol language on technology differs from the Convention is the distinction drawn between public and privately owned technologies. The Protocol recognises that governments can take a leading role in transferring publicly owned technologies but that, in relation to technologies held by the private sector, the creation of 'an enabling environment' is much more significant. This marks a shift in thinking by developing countries who until then had emphasised the role of developed countries as transferors rather than their own role as creators of an environment conducive to market-led technology transfer. Thus the provisions on technology mark an area where the Protocol clearly advances the implementation of existing commitments, rather than simply reiterating them.

Rule development: At COP-1, Parties agreed to place the issue of technology on the agenda of each COP in order to provide continuous advice to improve the operational modalities of technology transfer.[141] Each COP has therefore taken decisions on technology. Decision 4/CP.7, adopted as part of the Marrakesh Accords, sets out a framework for implementation of Article 4.5 which subsumes the most significant elements set forth in previous COP Decisions. Decisions adopted by prior COPs are now of lesser practical importance but provide useful background to understanding the Marrakesh Accords and are, for that reason, summarised below.

The remainder of this section focuses on the role and current work programme of the EGTT. COP-1 agreed to review the implementation of Articles 4.5 and 4.1 (c) of the Convention as a separate agenda item at each COP session. Decision 13/CP.1 requested the Convention Secretariat to collect information from Annex II Parties on their implementation of Article 4.4 and from other international bodies on concrete measures taken on the transfer of ESTs and know-how to mitigate as well as to facilitate adequate adaptation to climate change. The Secretariat was mandated to prepare a progress report and an inventory and assessment of economically viable ESTs for COP-2 and to update these documents for each COP session. In view of the wide range of technologies and Parties' varied economic and environmental needs and circumstances, and the limited expertise and resources available within the Secretariat, this 'cataloguing' exercise did not prove easy. COP-2 expressed concern over the slow progress in the implementation of Decision 13/CP.1. Decision 7/CP. 2 reaffirmed the full text of Decision 13/CP.1 but also requested the Secretariat to

---

[141] Decision 13/CP.1, paragraphs 4 and 5.

give high priority to completion of a survey of the initial technology needs of non-Annex I Parties. Recognising that much work on technology was being done by other bodies, COP-2 also requested the Secretariat to consult with UN bodies and other IGOs to identify existing technology information activities and needs to assist in the task of developing 'one-stop' technology centres and database(s) of state-of-the- art ESTs. COP-2 also requested the Secretariat to expedite the preparation of reports on adaptation technology and for the SBI to evaluate and report on the transfer of technologies from Annex II Parties to other Parties. COP-2 could not agree on the need for an expert group, along the lines of the Assessment Panels used in the Montreal Protocol, because of disagreements about the political/regional balance in its membership, but requested SBSTA to revert to this issue at a future session, in the light of any experience gained from the operation of any future expert roster (see chapter 15).

Decision 9/CP.3 adopted by COP-3 reaffirmed previous Decisions, requesting the Secretariat to continue its work and consult with the GEF and other bodies on their capabilities and abilities to support work on (an) international technology information centre(s), as well as national and regional centres. The Secretariat was requested to consider specific case studies, drawing on the experience of Parties, with the aim of evaluating barriers to introduction and implementation of ESTs, and Parties accepted that they should create an enabling environment to stimulate private sector investment in, and transfer of, ESTs.

By COP-4, it was clear that lack of capacity in developing countries to assess their own technology needs was a significant bottleneck and the provision of EST inventories would make more policy sense if developing countries better understood their technology needs. Accordingly, the central thrust of Decision 4/CP.4 requested Annex II Parties to support capacity-building and institutional strengthening in developing countries to enable the transfer of ESTs and urged non-Annex I Parties to submit their prioritised technology needs. Because many of these issues were discussed in a politicised atmosphere, COP-4 also agreed that the Chairman of the SBSTA should establish 'a consultative process', comprising a limited number of Party representatives with technology- related expertise, to make recommendations on how significant policy issues could be addressed to achieve agreement on 'a framework for meaningful and effective actions to enhance implementation of Article 4.5 of the Convention'.[142] The informality and limited time-frame for the small group of Parties invited to be part of the consultative process avoided the

---

[142] COP-4 encourages all relevant international organisations to mobilise and facilitate efforts to provide resources needed by developing country Parties to meet their agreed incremental costs, including development and transfer of technologies, in preparing for adaptation to adverse effects of climate change.

problem encountered by proposals to establish more formal Assessment Panels and the initiative proved fruitful. Accordingly, COP-5 agreed to extend the consultative process referred to in Decision 4/CP.5 to allow completion of a series of regional workshops initiated by the SBSTA Chairman as part of the consultative process. These workshops provided a less politicised forum for countries to agree a framework of actions to implement Article 4.5, and Decision 9/CP.5 allowed the SBSTA Chairman working with the Secretariat to prepare a draft decision for COP-6 on the basis of the outcomes of the consultative process. Much of the framework was agreed prior to the adoption of the Bonn Agreements, but Decision 5/CP.6 ended almost a decade of disagreement about the political/regional balance of representation by resolving to establish the twenty-member EGTT, discussed below.

6.3   *Marrakesh Accords: a framework for Article 4.5*

Although previous COP Decisions led to much constructive work by the Convention Secretariat, the GEF and other international organisations, effective rule development remained largely stalemated. Developing countries emphasised repeatedly that Annex II Parties were not implementing their technology transfer commitments effectively, leading developed countries to retort, with some justification, that developing countries should first articulate clearly their technology needs and/or create conditions conducive to technology transfer by the private sector. Realisation that capacity-building was essential to ensure that technology-related information could be provided, understood and acted upon, resulted in a greater policy emphasis on the resources and mechanisms needed to build such capacity.

Decision 4/CP.7 balances and integrates these elements. Expressed to be a 'framework', the Decision states that its purpose 'is to develop meaningful and effective actions to enhance the implementation of Article 4.5 of the Convention by increasing and improving the transfer of ESTs and know-how'.[143] The overall approach emphasises that the successful development and transfer of ESTs requires a country-driven, integrated approach, at a national and sectoral level, that involves cooperation among various stakeholders, and covers the following five key activities: technology needs assessments, technology information, enabling environments, capacity-building and mechanisms for technology transfer.[144] The substantive part of Decision 4/CP.7 (hereinafter the Framework Decision) defines what is meant by each of these elements, identifying a key purpose and elaborating on how it could be implemented.

---

[143] Decision 4/CP.7, paragraph 1.   [144] Decision 4/CP.7, paragraph 2.

- Technology needs and needs assessment

Technology needs and needs assessment are a set of country-driven activities to determine mitigation and adaptation technology priorities.[145] Although Article 4.5 only refers to technology transfer to developing countries, the Framework Decision covers all non-Annex I Parties.[146] The activities mentioned in paragraph 1 should involve stakeholders, address barriers to technology transfer and regulatory options, capacity-building and financial incentives. The objective of needs assessment is to facilitate the transfer of, and access to, ESTs under Article 4.5. Needs assessment should be undertaken subject to the provision of resources from Annex II Parties and any other assistance offered by other Parties and organisations. This information is to be made available through non-Annex I Parties' national communications and other reports and channels (e.g. clearing houses) to be considered by SBSTA on a regular basis.

- Technology information

Technology information defines the means, including hardware, software and networking, to facilitate the flow of information between relevant stakeholders.[147] The scope of information includes economic, environmental and technical parameters as well as information about the availability of ESTs. Such information underpins other activities related to Article 4.5. To further implementation, the Framework Decision mandates the Convention Secretariat to develop a new search engine on the Internet to allow quick access to existing inventories of ESTs relevant to climate mitigation and adaptation. This should build on its current work, including that undertaken by the Climate Technology Initiative (CTI) and other organisations. The Secretariat is mandated to identify gaps in existing EST inventories and to update and develop these as needed. The Secretariat is also mandated to establish 'an information clearing house', including a network of technology information centres, by COP-8.

- Enabling environments

The term 'enabling environment' is used to describe government policies that focus on creating and maintaining an overall macroeconomic environment allowing technology suppliers and consumers to cooperate.[148] Enabling environments include government actions, such as fair trade policies, removal of technical, legal

---

[145] Decision 4/CP.7, paragraphs 3–7.

[146] Decision 4/CP.7 does not use the term 'non-Annex I Parties', referring instead to 'Parties other than developed country Parties, and other developed Parties not included in Annex II, particularly developing countries'. See section 2.2, box 10.3 and pp. 272–4.

[147] Decision 4/CP.7, paragraphs 8–11.   [148] IPCC, 2001c. See also FCCC/TP/2003/2.

and administrative barriers to technology transfer, sound economic policy, regulatory frameworks and transparency, all of which create an environment conducive to private and public sector technology transfer.[149] Parties agree that implementation should focus on identification and removal of barriers to a conducive environment, including, inter alia, ensuring fair trade policies, utilising tax preferences, preferential government procurement and export credit programmes to promote transfer of ESTs as well as protecting IPRs and improving access and transfer of publicly funded technologies, including through joint R & D.

- Capacity-building

For the purposes of Article 4.5, capacity-building is defined as 'a process which seeks to build, develop, strengthen, enhance and improve existing scientific and technical skills, capabilities and institutions in NAIP [non-Annex I Parties] to enable them to assess, adapt, manage and develop ESTs'.[150] It should be primarily undertaken by and in developing countries and should be guided by the principles established in Decisions 2/CP.7 and 3/CP.7.[151] The scope of activities to be covered by capacity-building is set out in paragraph 18 which covers a broad range of sectors, institutions and stakeholders involved in transfer of ESTs. Paragraph 19 sets out the initial scope of needs and areas for enhancing non-Annex I Parties' endogenous capacities and technologies. Implementation involves Annex II Parties making available resources to enable developing countries to undertake needs assessments, giving particular attention to the needs of LDCs and SIDs.

- Mechanisms for technology transfer

Mechanisms for technology transfer include enhanced coordination among stakeholders to engage them in efforts to accelerate the development, diffusion, transfer of and access to ESTs through technology cooperation and partnerships (public/public, private/public and private/private) and the development of projects and programmes to support such ends. Implementation also involves the EGTT, discussed below, whose role is to provide scientific and technical advice on the advancement of activities relating to Article 4.5, including the preparation of an action plan.

6.4   *Expert Group on Technology Transfer*

6.4.1   Terms of reference

The EGTT was established as part of the Framework Decision. Its terms of reference are included in the Appendix to Decision 4/CP.7. The EGTT's principal mandate is to enhance the implementation of FCCC Article 4.5, including 'by

---

[149] Decision 4/CP.7, Annex, paragraphs 12–14.
[150] Decision 4/CP.7, Annex, paragraphs 15–21.   [151] Section 7 below.

analysing and identifying ways to facilitate and advance technology transfer activities', and to make recommendations to the SBSTA in this regard.[152] Recently, it has also been asked by COP-8 to provide views on funding of technology, signalling a willingness to interpret the terms of reference in a practical manner.[153]

The EGTT comprises twenty members: three members each from Africa, Asia and Latin America and the Caribbean, and one member from the small island developing states, plus seven members from Annex I Parties and (like the CGE) three from 'relevant international organisations'.[154] As with the CGE above, the language used in this formula unintentionally excludes non-Annex I Parties that are part of the Central and Eastern European group.[155] The EGTT's members are nominated by Parties[156] – that is, by their groups – but serve on the EGTT in their personal capacity, confirming its technical and expert nature.[157] Members must have expertise in one of several specified areas – greenhouse gas mitigation and adaptation technologies, technology assessments, information technology, resource economics, social development. Thus the EGTT's membership is based on expertise balanced with the need to provide broad geographic representation. Members are elected for two years and are eligible to serve two consecutive terms, while the members from international organisations serve on an 'issue-oriented basis' only.[158]

Decision 4/CP.7 mandates the EGTT to meet twice a year in conjunction with sessions of the SBs and to report annually to the SBSTA, which also approves its programme of work for the following year.[159] Each year, the EGTT elects a Chair and Vice-Chair, one from an Annex I and one from a non-Annex I Party, with the positions of Chair and Vice-Chair rotating annually between the two sets of Parties. The EGTT's mandate extends to COP-12 when its continuation and terms of reference will be reviewed.[160]

6.4.2   EGTT work programme

At its preparatory meeting in Seoul, Republic of Korea, April 2002, the EGTT drafted a programme of work for 2002–2003 which was approved by SBSTA-16.[161] The programme is based on actions that advance the five key themes and areas identified in the 'framework for meaningful and effective actions', plus

---

[152] Decision 4/CP.7, paragraph 2 and Appendix, paragraphs 1 and 2.

[153] Decision 7/CP.8, paragraph 2.   [154] Decision 4/CP.7, Annex, paragraph 26.

[155] Section 2, box 10.3.

[156] Decision 4/CP.7, paragraph 2 and Appendix, paragraph 4.

[157] Decision 4/CP.7, Appendix, paragraph 7.   [158] Decision 4/CP.7, Appendix, paragraph 4.

[159] Decision 4/CP.7, Appendix, paragraph 3.   [160] Decision 4/CP.7, paragraph 2.

[161] See SBSTA-16 report, FCCC/SBSTA/2002/2, Annex II.

a sixth cross-cutting area analysing information from national communications relevant to the EGTT's work.

The first EGTT meeting took place in Bonn, Germany, in June 2002, at which the EGTT invited representatives of the UNDP, UNEP and the International Energy Agency, represented by the Climate Technology Initiative, to fill the three IGO membership slots.[162] The EGTT's Annual Report was presented to SBSTA-17.[163] This Report and other aspects of the EGTT's work fed into the Secretariat's progress report on the implementation of activities under the Framework Decision which was discussed at SBSTA-17 in October 2002 and which provides a useful summary of the many different workshops held to further the Framework Decision.[164]

A second meeting of the EGTT was held in Delhi in October 2002. At this the EGTT discussed support for the UNDP-GEF programme to complete a handbook for assessing technology needs, subsequent workshops to assess the use of the handbook for assessing technology needs and improved access to technology information in existing global and regional/thematic networks and clearing houses, and a request to the Chair of SBSTA to organise a workshop to explore the various facets of enabling environments and to report on this workshop to SBSTA-18.[165]

In its annual consideration of the agenda item on technology, COP-8 encouraged the EGTT to continue its good work.[166] It requested the Chair of SBSTA to conduct consultations and facilitate collaboration among expert groups established under the Convention on their work programmes on cross-cutting issues, including those relating to technology transfer and capacity-building initiatives, and to take into account, when examining the work of the EGTT, innovative ways to address the outcomes of technology needs assessment already completed by developing country parties and parties with economies in transition. It also requested the Secretariat to assist the Chair of SBSTA to facilitate consultations among expert groups.

The EGTT's third meeting in Bonn, in May 2003, considered a technical paper on enabling environments for technology transfer prepared by the Secretariat under the guidance of the EGTT.[167] It also discussed the outcomes of the workshop on enabling environments held in Ghent, Belgium in April 2003.[168] In his oral report to SBSTA-18, the EGTT Chair reported that the EGTT would hold three workshops on advancing work on technology needs assessments, in collaboration with CTI, in 2003–2004 and would turn its attention to producing a technical

---

[162] COP-7 report FCCC/CP/2001/13/Add.1.

[163] FCCC/SBSTA/2002/9.   [164] FCCC/SBSTA/2002/10.   [165] FCCC/SBSTA/2002/CRP.7

[166] Decision 10/CP.8.   [167] FCCC/TP/2003/2.   [168] FCCC/SBSTA/2003/INF.4.

paper on capacity-building and development and transfer of technology which would feed into the COP-9 comprehensive review of the implementation of the capacity-building framework annexed to Decisions 2/CP.7 and 3/CP.7.[169]

SBSTA-19 agreed the EGTT's work programme for 2004 but noted that this would require additional supplementary budget resources.[170] The Secretariat also expressed support for the work done by the Secretariat on the FCCC technology information clearing house (TT: CLEAR) and, subject to funding, requested it to organise a workshop on innovative options for financing the development and transfer of technologies and to prepare a paper on the high-level round table discussions held at COP-9 for consideration by SBSTA-20.

6.5   *Funding*

The extent to which the technology transfer provisions in the Convention, the Protocol and the Framework Decision are implemented by developing countries is linked to the provision of financial resources.[171] Accordingly, COP-7 requested the GEF to provide financial support for the implementation of Decision 4/CP.7 through its climate change focal area and the SCCF established under Decision7/CP.7. COP-7 also urged developed country Parties to provide technical and financial assistance through existing bilateral and multilateral cooperative programme to support the efforts of the Parties to support the annexed framework.

The provision of financial support for technology-related activities, such as those described in Decision 4/CP.7, is already funded by the Convention's financial mechanism on the basis of the GEF's Operational Strategy.[172] There is no separate operational programme earmarked 'technology' because the GEF's entire approach to financing is based on integrating the development, application, diffusion and demonstration of ESTs into almost all of its projects. For this reason, the GEF has tended to resist narrowly defined COP guidance on funding of technology transfer which it sees as overly specific and an intrusion on operational matters.[173] The Report to COP-8 puts it thus: 'GEF climate projects often address technology assessments, information systems, capacity building elements, and mechanisms for technology transfer as defined in [Decision 4/CP.7]...the GEF strategy and operational programmes provide support for these activities within the context of broader actions and commitments to reduce greenhouse gas emissions.'[174]

To help refine priorities, COP-8 requested the EGTT to submit its views on what technology-related activities, programmes and measures should be funded out of

---

[169] FCCC/SBSTA/2003/10, paragraphs 30–3.   [170] SBSTA-19 report, FCCC/SBSTA/2003/15.
[171] Sections 2.2.   [172] Section 5.3.   [173] Lusthaus et al., 2000.
[174] FCCC/CP/2002/4, paragraph 20.

the SCCF to allow COP-9 to take a decision on the SCCF.[175] The EGTT's response emphasised technology-needs assessment and the development and transfer of adaptation technologies but also covered a broad range of activities set out in the Framework Decision.[176] This has fed into Decision 5/CP.9 adopted by Parties at COP-9 on the funding priorities for the SCCF, discussed above, which will as a result fund a range of technology-related activities.

7   Capacity-building

7.1   *Background*

Capacity-building is a significant cross-cutting issue which now features prominently in the climate regime, implementation of which is supported by a wide range of actors, including the Convention Secretariat, the CGE and numerous IGOs and NGOs. The term 'capacity-building' is not, however, defined in the Convention, the Protocol or COP decisions.[177] No common definition exists across the UN, but it is widely defined as the process of creating or enhancing capacities within a country to perform specific tasks on an on-going basis in order to attain a given developmental objective.[178] The following three aspects are generally stressed:

- Human resource development (e.g. training and education);
- Institutional strengthening (e.g. improved organisational methods and procedures); and
- Creation of a receptive environment, sometimes called systemic capacity (e.g. increased public awareness, enactment of rules and regulations conducive to development).[179]

Although both the Convention and the Protocol contain some references to 'endogenous capacities', there is no general provision on capacity-building in its broad sense in either instrument. This is somewhat surprising given the centrality and cross-cutting nature of capacity-building to implementation efforts by developing countries in a highly complex and new policy area such as climate change. This section describes the capacity-building related commitments in the Convention and Protocol but then focuses mainly on the package of decisions taken on capacity- building since the mid-1990s which culminated in the adoption by COP-7 of two 'framework' decisions to guide capacity-building activities – now

---

[175] Decision 7/CP.8.   [176] FCCC/SBI/2003/INF.12/Add.1, Annex, p. 2.

[177] Decision 4/CP.7, Annex, paragraph 15 provides a definition of capacity-building in relation to technology transfer, discussed at p. 311 above.

[178] GEF, 1997.   [179] GEF, 1997

supported by a wide range of bilateral and multilateral channels as well as IGOs and NGOs. The concept of 'enabling activities', which refers to a subset of capacity-building activities funded by the GEF that relate to the implementation of Convention, is also explained in box 10.5 below.

7.2   *Capacity-building-related commitments*

FCCC: The Convention lacks a general provision on capacity-building but mentions it in three separate provisions:

- Article 4.5 which states the need to develop and enhance 'endogenous capacities' in the context of technology transfer;[180]
- Article 5 (c) which provides for cooperation to improve endogenous capacities relating to research and systemic observation;[181] and
- Article 9.2 (d) which requires SBSTA, in the context of scientific programmes and international research, to provide advice on 'ways and means of supporting endogenous capacity-building in developing countries'.[182]

Kyoto: The Convention's provisions are imported into the Protocol as a result of Articles 10, 11 and 15. Like the Convention, the Protocol lacks a general provision on capacity-building. Article 10 (c), which requires all Parties to cooperate to promote technology transfer and know-how, contains an implicit reference to developing technology-related capacities. Article 10 (d) of the Protocol simply reaffirms Article 5 (c) of the Convention requiring Parties to strengthen and develop endogenous capacities and capabilities to participate in international research and networks on research and systematic observations.[183] Article 10 (e), which requires all Parties to cooperate in strengthening national capacity-building, in particular human and institutional capacities, relating to the issues of education, training and public awareness, placed a significant new emphasis on capacity-building which has led COP-8 to adopt a programme of work in this area, discussed further in chapter 7.

The final reference in the Protocol to capacity-building is Article 10 (b) (ii). This requires non-Annex I Parties to report on capacity-building measures they believe are contributing to addressing climate change in their national communications. This reporting requirement is a new commitment as it is not included in the Convention. Its inclusion was not as heavily resisted by developing countries as other new commitments were.[184] This is because it aims at helping non-Annex I

---

[180] Section 6.   [181] See chapter 7.   [182] See chapter 13.   [183] See chapter 7.
[184] FCCC/TP/2000/2, paragraph 340.

Parties communicate their circumstances and capacity needs better to the COP and had, in any case, already been agreed by developing countries, albeit in a non-legally binding form of Decision 10/CP.2.[185]

Rule development: The necessity of rule development on capacity-building was recognised by the COP, and other international bodies, including the GEF, early on in the regime. The cross-cutting nature of capacity-building prompted the adoption of around twenty COP decisions directly on or related to capacity-building and/or enabling activities and funding by the GEF. Two broad phases of rule development are evident. The first, from COP-1 to COP-4, saw capacity-building issues being dealt with in a discrete manner under other relevant agenda items. This approach had merits in linking capacity-building clearly to specific Convention commitments, such as timely submission of initial national communications, capacity-building for which was supported by the CGE.[186] The drawbacks were fragmentation of capacity-building efforts with a consequent lack of coherence, coordination and prioritisation in their funding and implementation. The second phase of rule development, initiated by COP-5, has seen capacity-building being addressed as a cross-cutting, foundational issue meriting its own agenda item.[187] This approach has led to the adoption at COP-7 of two frameworks for capacity-building, one for developing countries and the other for Parties with economies in transition, with each framework defining the scope, purpose, principles and respective roles different agents should play in capacity- building.[188] Reflecting its greater political priority, since the adoption of the Marrakesh Accords, capacity-building has become an SBI and COP agenda item (previously it was a joint SB agenda item).

The alignment of the Convention's rules on financial and technical resources to support the framework for capacity-building in developing countries adopted at Marrakesh has yet to be completed and is likely to end when the COP finalises decisions relating to the new funds established by the Marrakesh Accords undertaken at COP-9, and when it completes its reviews of the implementation of the capacity-building frameworks, expected at COP-10. Capacity-related COP decisions adopted prior to Marrakesh remain significant either because they provide more detailed information about capacity-building needs than included in the Marrakesh capacity-building decisions, and/or they contain

---

[185] See chapter 11.   [186] Chapter 11, section 4.4 discusses the role of the CGE.

[187] Decisions 10/CP.5 and 11/CP.5.

[188] Decision 2/CP.7, Capacity building in developing countries (non-Annex I Parties), (hereinafter DC/CB Decision), and Decision 3/CP.7, Capacity building in countries with economies in transition (hereinafter EIT/CB Decision).

specific guidance to the financial mechanism which is still applied by GEF to determine funding for capacity-building activities. The following section explains the DC/CB and EIT/CB Decisions, using the structure provided by the Decisions themselves and highlighting, as appropriate, elements from other relevant COP decisions.

7.3   *Marrakesh Accords: frameworks for capacity-building*

7.3.1   Purpose

Because of its cross-cutting nature and the need to provide an overarching guidance for the various means in which capacity-building work can be supported, the DC/CB and the EIT/CB Decisions adopted at COP-7 establish 'frameworks' to address capacity-building needs relevant both to the implementation of the FCCC and for the effective participation of Parties in the Kyoto Protocol process.[189] Both Decisions include a recommendation that the first session of the COP/MOP adopt a decision reaffirming these frameworks and with additional reference to priority areas for capacity-building relating to the Protocol.[190] Both Decisions are stated to have 'immediate effect'. This means they are intended to guide capacity-building efforts undertaken by Parties and agencies working on climate change subsequent to COP-7. The use of the word 'should' in preference to the more mandatory 'shall' throughout these Decisions, and the annual oversight of the substantive provisions by the COP, means that Parties view these decisions in a different legal light from other parts of the Marrakesh Accord 'package'.[191]

In terms of content, the two Decisions are very similar, with some linguistic differences due essentially to their respective drafting histories. There are two important conceptual differences between the two, reflecting the specific interests, needs and legal commitments of each group. The first is that EITs have quantified commitments under the Convention and the Protocol. The other is that EITs are mostly highly developed countries with strong scientific, technological and administrative institutions and no entitlement to financial support under the Convention. The capacity-building needs of developing countries are more extensive, must be met within the broader context of development and must take into account that a disproportionate amount of their capacities will be needed to cope with the adverse impacts of climate change for which financial support is available under the Convention.

---

[189] Decision 2/CP.7, paragraph 1; Decision 3/CP.7, paragraph 1.
[190] Decision 2/CP.7, paragraph 13; Decision 3/CP.7, paragraph 8.
[191] Chapter 1 explains the legal character of COP Decisions. See also box 13.2.

7.3.2   Guiding principles and approaches

Because capacity-building is cross-cutting in nature, both Decisions confirm that they build upon provisions of the FCCC, the Protocol and previous COP Decisions. The principles and approaches outlined in the DC/CB Decision stress that capacity-building should:[192]

- Be country-driven and tailored to meet the specific needs and circumstances of each country rather than being guided by a 'one size fits all' approach;
- Recognise that capacity-building is an ongoing iterative process, i.e. not something that starts and stops with particular projects;
- Be undertaken in an 'effective, efficient, integrated and programmatic manner' and maximise synergies between the climate regime and other MEAs. This provision was included to discourage donor-driven, uncoordinated, ad hoc activities, particularly without consideration of the multiple MEA reporting obligations;
- Pay particular attention to LDCs and SIDS in view of their special circumstances and vulnerabilities – these are listed in the Decision;
- Be led, wherever possible, by existing national bodies, in particular national coordinating mechanisms and focal points. This contributes to long-term sustainability and enhances integration and awareness of initiatives at the national level;
- Involve 'learning by doing' and utilise 'demonstration projects' to identify capacities in need of further development.

With the exception of the reference to LDCs and SIDS, the EIT/CB Decision stresses essentially similar principles and approaches to those described above – albeit in slightly different language. To meet their specific concerns, EIT capacity-related activities should recognise that, as Parties included in Annex I, EITs have quantified commitments which challenge their existing capacities and which must be enhanced to prepare EITs for their effective participation in the Protocol.

7.3.3   Objective and scope of capacity-building

Paragraph 14 of the DC/CB Decision states that the objective of capacity-building is 'to assist developing countries build, develop, strengthen and enhance their capacities to achieve the objective of the Convention through the implementation of the provisions of the Convention and the preparation for their effective participation in the Kyoto Protocol'. This provision was included to address what

---

[192] Decision 2/CP.7, paragraphs 7–14.

many developing countries perceived as donor prioritisation of capacity-building related to submission of national communications and/or mitigation activities and to ensure these did not crowd out activities relating to other concerns such as research and systematic observations and vulnerability assessment.

To operationalise this point, paragraph 15 contains fifteen subparagraphs scoping out capacity-building needs and areas relating to all aspects of implementing the Convention. Paragraph 16 contains a 'catch-all' provision stating that other capacity-building activities and responses identified in the future, for example on the basis of national capacity-building assessments, 'should continue to inform the scope and implementation of this framework' to ensure that the list remains dynamic and responsive to country-driven needs. The list of needs identified in paragraph 15 is based on the Annex to Decision 10/CP.5 and related submissions from Parties.[193] Paragraph 4 notes that capacity-building needs identified in previous COP decisions, and activities to meet them that commenced prior to COP-7, should continue to be promptly addressed. These other decisions include Decision 4/CP.7 concerning technology transfer which contains technology-transfer-related capacity-building.[194]

It should be noted that the process of identifying and prioritising capacity needs was advanced by the GEF through the 'Capacity Development Initiative' (CDI). Launched in May 1999, this eighteen-month consultative process made a broad assessment of capacity-building needs, undertaken on a regional basis, particularly in the areas of biodiversity, climate change and land degradation. The CDI also examined the effectiveness of existing bilateral and multilateral efforts to meet those needs as well the need for a longer-term strategy and GEF action plan for enhancing those efforts. This was complemented by a survey of capacity-building needs of developing countries in relation to the Kyoto Protocol undertaken by UNITAR.[195] The findings and recommendations of the CDI were reported in September 2001 and played a part in the development of the capacity-building frameworks adopted by COP-7. Because it was not clear to Parties whether these prior initiatives conformed fully to the capacity-building frameworks later adopted by COP-7, the CDI is referred to in both Decisions as one source of information about capacity-building needs and activities.[196]

7.3.4   Implementation and review

Developing countries' responsibilities for implementation of the framework are set out in paragraph 19 and require them 'to continue to identify their

---

[193] FCCC/SB/2000/INF.1, Annex, and FCCC/SB/2000/INF.5.   [194] See section 6.
[195] UNITAR, 2001.
[196] Decision 2/CP.7, Annex, paragraph 27 and Decision 3/CP.7, paragraph 21. A list of capacity-building needs of developing country Parties is provided in FCCC/SBI/2002/INF.15 and FCCC/SBI/2003/14.

specific needs, options and priorities … on a country driven basis taking into account existing capacities and past and current activities'. Funding for this is now available from the GEF as explained below. Developing countries should also promote South–South cooperation by utilising institutions in developing countries and information sharing, ensure participation of a wide range of stakeholders and promote coordination and sustainability of capacity-building efforts of national institutions. Annex II Parties should provide additional resources to developing countries to implement the framework and to enable them to undertake 'country-level needs assessments'. Countries which have completed these should be able to implement capacity-building activities promptly under the framework. Funding for LDCs' and SIDS' 'immediate priority needs' is to be addressed urgently. Both developing country and Annex II Parties should improve the coordination and effectiveness of capacity-building efforts through dialogue between and among each other.[197] Except for the references to LDCs and SIDs, the EIT/CB Decision contains provisions that place broadly similar responsibilities on EITs and on Annex II Parties.

The coordination of capacity-building initiatives – avoiding 'turf fights' and enhancing synergies among and between various international organisations and MEAs – has provided the rationale for enhanced implementation responsibilities for the Convention Secretariat.[198] In both Decisions, the Secretariat is requested to cooperate with the GEF and IAs and other entities to facilitate the implementation of the capacity-building framework. It will also deal with the information needs of the COP and SBs necessary to review the frameworks. The Convention Secretariat's programmes of work on capacity-building, and the work of other bodies, are summarised in documentation presented to COP-8 and SBI-18.[199] It is important to note that the work of the CGE on developing countries' national communications plays an important role in supporting related capacity-building.[200]

The review provisions set out in paragraph 31 of the Annex to the DC/CB Decision provide for regular monitoring and review of progress to be undertaken by the COP, with the SBI taking the lead on making recommendations. A 'comprehensive review' was mandated at COP-9 and every five years thereafter.[201] The GEF is requested to report on its progress in support of the implementation of the framework in its annual report to the COP, discussed below. The EIT/CB Decision provides for 'regular' review but without a date for the first review. Parties at SB-18 decided that they would recommend to adopt a decision at COP-9 stating that the EIT review will be based on the review of national communications. In addition,

---

[197] Decision 2/CP.7, Annex, paragraph 18.

[198] Decision 2/CP.7, paragraph 33; Decision 3/CP.7, paragraph 29.

[199] FCCC/SBI/2002/INF.15 and FCCC/SBI/2003/MISC.2.   [200] See chapter 11, pp. 367–9.

[201] Decision 2/CP.7, paragraphs 10 and 11.

it only 'invites' institutions involved in supporting EITs, such as the GEF, to provide information to the COP. After considering the scope, timing and inputs to be used for these reviews at SBI-17 and SBI-18, Parties have agreed to take decisions at COP-10 in relation to the review of the implementation of and the effectiveness of both the non-Annex I Parties and EIT capacity-building frameworks.[202] Decision 9/CP.9 adopted by COP-9 confirms this. It requires the first review to be undertaken by COP-10, with further reviews at five-yearly intervals for non-Annex I Parties and based on the frequency reviews of EITs' national communications.

Box 10.5   Defining capacity-building and enabling activities

The term 'enabling activities' is not actually defined in the FCCC or subsequently by the COP or by the GEF, although the GEF and the COP have both indicated the kinds of activities it should cover. For the GEF, the term refers to activities which help countries either fulfil essential communication requirements related to a convention, such as the preparation of national GHG inventories and initial national communications, or else provide a basic and essential level of information to enable policy and strategic decisions to be made as well as assisting planning that identifies priority activities within a country.[203] Because the GEF views capacity-building as a means towards more substantive programme ends, the GEF has relied on particular projects as vehicles to transfer resources in support of capacity development. However, as noted by the GEF evaluation unit, 'project interventions are generally narrow, disconnected and short term' and thus do not allow sufficiently for long-term, strategic development of capacity-supporting broad environmental objectives.[204] In the FCCC, Parties place more emphasis on longer-term capacity-building which meets broad environmental goals. This is difficult to fund through individual projects and does not fit well with the GEF 'enabling activities' programme which funds specific capacity needs linked to international conventions.[205] These differences of approach were highlighted by the initial guidance provided by COP-1 on funding priorities. Decision 11/CP.1 stated that 'priority should be given to the funding of agreed full costs (or agreed incremental costs as appropriate) incurred by developing country Parties in

---

[202] SBI-18 report, FCCC/SBI/2003/8, paragraph 23.

[203] FCCC/CP/2002/3/Add.1, Section II, Review by the GEF of its Climate Change Enabling Activities.

[204] Lusthaus et al., 2000.   [205] Section 5 explains GEF's Operational Strategy and programmes.

complying with their obligations under Article 12.1 and other relevant commitments under the Convention'. This broad guidance led many developing countries to believe many more capacity-related activities would be covered by the GEF's enabling activities guidelines than were subsequently funded by the GEF. Decisions 10/CP.2 and 11/CP.2 clarified some aspects but did not map out a long-term approach to funding of capacity-building in its broad sense. Decisions 2/CP.7 and 6/CP.7 adopted in Marrakesh, particularly when read with the list of capacity-building needs set out in paragraphs 14 and 15 of Decision 2/CP.7, serve to emphasise to the GEF, and other funding agencies, the importance attached by developing countries to funding a much broader range of capacity-building activities than has been supported in the past and the need for this to be done in a more strategic manner.[206] Some of these concerns and conclusions were echoed in the recommendations of a study of the GEF's 'enabling activities' in the area of climate change undertaken by the GEF's monitoring and evaluation unit, mandated by the GEF Council in October 1998, which reported its findings in 2000 to COP-6, in accordance with Decision 10/CP.5.[207] The Study pointed out the long-term sustainability limitations of linking capacity-building to the fulfilment of discrete, time-bound Convention commitments, such as submission of national communications. It also pointed out that 'removing ambiguities associated with the definition and finality of some terms (e.g. enabling activity, capacity building, etc.)' could help in a uniform application of the GEF guidelines and that a 'more systematic strategy aimed at ensuring the establishment of a sustainable enabling activity process should be defined by COP and operationalised by the GEF'.[208] The preparation of a longer-term strategy for capacity-building was put in hand by the GEF in 2000, and is referred to in Decision 2/CP.7. Finalisation has been delayed to accommodate further guidance being provided by COP-9 in relation to capacity-building funding priorities for the SCCF which COP-9 agreed in Decision 5/CP.9 discussed above.

7.4   *Funding*

Both the DC/CB and EIT/CB Decisions provide a cooperative framework to help Parties make the best use of their resources as well as providing an internationally agreed framework to facilitate the work of donors, international agencies

---

[206] FCCC/CP/2000/3/Add.1, paragraphs 33–4.   [207] FCCC/CP/2000/3/Add.1.
[208] FCCC/CP/2003/3/Add.1.

and other organisations involved in capacity-building. Both Decisions therefore encourage multilateral and bilateral agencies to coordinate their activities in support of their respective frameworks through the provision of financial and technical resources.

In terms of substantive provision of financial resources, the two Decisions are quite different. Because EITs that are Annex I Parties are not entitled to funding from the Convention's financial mechanism (although they can, and do, obtain funding from the GEF outside the Convention's framework) the EIT/CB Decision explicitly notes that the provision of resources for capacity-building from the GEF must be 'within its mandate'.[209] Parties who consider themselves to be EITs but are not formally included in Annex I of the Convention are eligible for funding from the GEF, as explained in box 10.3 above.

The DC/CB Decision explicitly states that '[this Decision] should serve as a guide for the GEF . . . and be considered by multilateral and bilateral organisations in their capacity building activities'.[210] It also states that financial and technical resources should be made available through the GEF and, as appropriate, through multilateral and bilateral agencies and the private sector, to assist developing countries, in particular the LDCs and SIDS. Additional guidance to the GEF on funding of capacity-building is set out in paragraphs 3, 4 and 5 of Decision 6/CP.7. As operator of the financial mechanism, the GEF is requested to 'provide financial assistance to implement the capacity building framework [in Decision 2/CP.7] and further to support, enhance and implement its activities in accordance with this framework'.[211] Paragraphs 3 and 4 request the GEF 'to adopt a streamlined and expedited approach to financing activities within the framework for capacity building . . . contained in Decision 2/CP.7' and to report to COP-8 on the how it has implemented this guidance and its support for the implementation of Decision 2/CP.7.

Decision 2/CP.7 requests the GEF to 'elaborate a country-driven strategy for its capacity-building activities'.[212] Because the development of such a strategy was also part of the conclusions of the CDI, the DC/CB Decision states that the result of activities conducted by the GEF, including the CDI, as well as activities conducted by other multilateral, bilateral and private sector entities, may be considered in further developing a long-term funding framework.[213] In response to these requests, the GEF's report to COP-8 diplomatically states that the GEF has 'attempted to keep pace with [COP's] emerging decisions and guidance'.[214] It notes that a revised GEF paper on 'Elements of strategic collaboration and a framework

[209] Section 2.2.   [210] Decision 2/CP.7, Annex, paragraph 1.
[211] Decision 6/CP.7, paragraph 5.   [212] Decision 2/CP.7, Annex, paragraphs 21 and 22.
[213] Decision 2/CP.7, paragraph 27.   [214] FCCC/CP/2002/4, paragraph 21.

for GEF actions for capacity building for the global environment' was scheduled to be presented to the Council in 2003.[215] This GEF Elements paper is intended to respond to the COP's guidance on capacity-building, and will factor in guidance from COP-9 about the capacity-building activities to be funded by the SCCF set out in Decisions 5/CP.9 and 4/CP.9. Until the completion of its strategic approach, GEF support for capacity-building will be provided through a diversity of GEF programmes and procedures as follows:

- As a component of all standard GEF projects (FSPs, MSPs, PDFs, etc.), provided the projects fall within the four GEF climate-related Operational Programmes and meet other project eligibility criteria such as generating global environmental benefits.[216]
- As part of its 'enabling activities' programme to assist countries to undertake essential planning and/or fulfil convention-mandated reporting and planning obligations. The following kinds of enabling activities, explained more fully below, are fundable:
  - preparation of initial national communications;
  - capacity-building in priority areas; and
  - national self-assessments of capacity-building needs.
- For LDCs, support for preparations of NAPAs funded from the LDC Fund.[217]
- Public awareness and education capacity-building needs are addressed through integration with enabling activities and/or standard GEF projects.[218]

Grants for enabling activities relating to non-Annex I Parties' initial national communications for less than US $350,000 per eligible country can be approved by the GEF CEO under expedited procedures, without expert review by STAP or the Council, but only if the enabling activities necessary for their preparation fall within the scope of the GEF operational guidelines.[219] This covers some preparatory and planning measures called 'Stage I adaptation activities'.[220] Enabling activities that go beyond the measures included in GEF operational guidelines for initial national communications must be submitted as standard GEF projects and subject to standard approval procedures. This is also the case where the total costs of enabling activities involve 'significant deviations' from the typical cost ranges for enabling activities covered by expedited procedures. An additional US $100,000 per country

---

[215] FCCC/CP/2002/4, paragraph 23.   [216] Section 2.2.   [217] Section 4.1 and chapter 8.
[218] FCCC/CP/2002/4, paragraphs 29–30.
[219] GEF, 1997, Part I (these replace earlier GEF guidelines contained in the February 1996 document GEF/C.7/Inf.10).
[220] See chapter 8.

is available as a 'top-up' to maintain capacity in priority areas built as a result of previous enabling activities, also using expedited procedures, including capacity-building relating to technology-needs assessment and climate observation systems.[221] These procedures are currently being revised to take into account the revised guidelines for submission of non-Annex I Parties' second national communications adopted by COP-8. The GEF also funds up to $200,000 for countries undertaking national self-assessments of capacity-building needs (NCSAs), again through expedited procedures.[222] These procedures were adopted in response to the recommendations of CDI that GEF support countries to identify and prioritise capacity-building needs on a country-driven basis. Because COP-7 guidance and previous COP decisions recognise the special needs and vulnerabilities of LDCs and SIDS, these Parties are entitled to additional financial assistance (up to $25,000) to prepare proposals for capacity-building projects.[223]

Details of all GEF projects, including enabling activities, are reported by the GEF to the Convention Secretariat and then to COP on an annual basis in accordance with Decision 10/CP.2 and can also be found in the annual document, the GEF Operational Report on GEF Programmes. It should be noted that although the GEF remains the most significant channel for funding of national communications, and is mandated to cover the 'full costs' of these, other sources of bilateral and multilateral funding have made a significant contribution, as set out in box 10.2, providing in many cases funding for activities such as research which do not appear to be adequately funded by the GEF in the context of national communications.[224]

[221] GEF, 1999.   [222] GEF, 2001a and b. See also Decision 2/CP.4 and chapter 11.
[223] Decision 6/CP.7, paragraph 1 and GEF, 2001b.   [224] FCCC/SBI/2001/15.

11

Reporting and review

1   Introduction

Regular reporting by Parties according to common guidelines, and the systematic review of those reports, makes up the backbone of the climate change regime. This reporting and review process supplies valuable information on, among other things, the GHG emissions of Parties and their sources, the actions being taken to combat climate change and their effectiveness, and the local impacts of climate change. Reporting and review has taken on added importance under the Kyoto Protocol, providing the basis for assessing compliance with legally binding targets and for ensuring the validity of transactions under the Kyoto mechanisms. Rigorous reporting and review is thus critical to ensuring the environmental integrity of the climate change regime and, linked to this, to securing the transparency needed to reassure Parties that the burden of implementation is being shared as agreed. The basis for reporting and review under the climate change regime is established in the Convention, which requires all Parties to 'make available to the Conference of the Parties' emission inventories,[1] and to submit regular 'communications'.[2] In their communications, all Parties are required to include an inventory of national GHG emissions and removals, and a general description of the steps they are taking or envisaging to implement the Convention, along with other information relevant to achieving the Convention's

---

[1] FCCC Article 4.1 (a).

[2] FCCC Articles 4.1 (j) and 12. The term 'communication' stems from objections raised during the negotiation of the Convention that the term 'reporting' 'suggested an intrusive, interventionist process' (Bodansky, 1993: p. 544).

objective.[3] The timetable, specific content and review process for these, however, differ between Annex I and non-Annex I Parties, in line with the differentiated nature of their climate change mitigation commitments. Another key feature of the reporting and review process under the climate change regime is the close integration between the rules under the Convention and the Kyoto Protocol, comprising a streamlined process that seeks to minimise the reporting burden on Parties and the resources needed for the review process.

This chapter begins by considering the rules in place for reporting and review by Annex I Parties under the Convention and the Protocol, before moving on to rules in force for non-Annex I Parties. The key elements of the complex reporting and review process of the climate change regime are explained in box 11.1 below.

Box 11.1   Key elements of the reporting and review process

Accounting guidelines: Rules adopted by the COP for Annex I Parties to monitor and record transactions in emission/removal units under the KP, including setting up a **national registry.**

Common reporting format: A component of the **FCCC/KP reporting guidelines** for Annex I Parties setting out standard tables to report aggregate GHG data.

Compilation and accounting report: An annual report prepared by the Secretariat under the Kyoto Protocol recording the emissions data reported by Annex I Parties in their annual inventories and their transactions in emission/removal units. The report will draw on the *compilation and accounting database* maintained by the Secretariat, which will continuously update the record of Annex I Parties' transactions in emission/removal units.

FCCC/KP reporting guidelines: Rules on how to prepare and submit GHG inventories and national communications under the FCCC and KP, including on their contents, periodicity and presentation. For Annex I Parties, separate guidelines are in place for national communications and GHG inventories under the FCCC, with further guidelines for reporting *supplementary information* required under the KP. For non-Annex I Parties, there is only one set of reporting guidelines for both national communications and GHG

---

[3] FCCC Article 12.1. The Convention permits any group of Parties to make a joint communication, provided that it includes information on the fulfilment by each individual Party of its obligations (FCCC Article 12.8), but no group has yet sought to avail itself of this provision.

inventories under the FCCC and none have yet been devised for reporting under the KP.

GHG inventory: Data submitted by a Party on its GHG emissions, which Annex I Parties must submit annually. Annex I Parties to the KP submit a single annual inventory incorporating that under the FCCC and including *supplementary information* to demonstrate compliance with KP obligations. Non-Annex I Parties do not submit an annual inventory, but include emissions data in their national communications.

IPCC methodological guidelines: Officially the *IPCC 1996 Revised Guidelines for National Greenhouse Gas Inventories*, these are common methodologies and reporting formats devised by the IPCC and endorsed by the COP for calculating emissions data and compiling GHG inventories.

IPCC Good Practice Guidance: An elaboration of the IPCC methodological guidelines setting out how to address uncertainty to help ensure that inventories are not over/underestimated.

National communication: Report submitted by Annex I and non-Annex I Parties detailing the action they are taking to meet their commitments. For Annex I Parties to the KP, the national communication under the KP must include *supplementary information* to demonstrate compliance with KP obligations and it also incorporates their FCCC national communication.

National inventory report: A component of the **FCCC/KP reporting guidelines** for Annex I Parties to report disaggregated qualitative/quantitative information on their GHG inventories.

National registry: The procedures set up by an Annex I Party to ensure the accurate tracking of transactions under the KP mechanisms and LULUCF projects, including the issuance, transfer, cancellation and retirement of emission/removal units. The Marrakesh Accords require Annex I Parties to set up a national registry as part of their **accounting guidelines**.

National system/National system guidelines: A KP provision referring to the institutional, legal and procedural arrangements put in place by an Annex I Party to ensure that it can adequately estimate, report and archive emissions data. The Marrakesh Accords include guidelines for national systems.

Post-commitment period report: The report submitted by each Annex I Party under the KP after the additional period for fulfilling commitments at the end of the commitment period. This report is used as a basis for assessing compliance with emission targets.

Pre-commitment period report: The report submitted by each Annex I Party under the KP prior to the start of the commitment period, providing the data needed to establish its assigned amount and prove its ability to monitor its emissions accurately.

Review/Review guidelines: The detailed analysis of an Annex I Party's national communication and GHG inventory under the FCCC and KP by a team of experts, led by the Secretariat. Under the FCCC, the review is termed an *in-depth review* for national communications and a *technical review* for inventories. Under the KP, the **pre-commitment period** and **post-commitment period reports** are also reviewed. Guidelines are in place for conducting reviews under the KP.

2   The Convention rules: Annex I Parties

The reporting and review process for Annex I Parties under the Convention is summarised in figure 11.1. Each of its elements is discussed in more detail below.

2.1   *National communications*

Under the Convention, all Annex I Parties are required to submit a *national communication*, including a detailed description of the policies and measures they are taking to mitigate climate change, and a specific estimate of the effects these are projected to have on GHG emissions.[4] Moreover, the reporting of this information is bound up with the specific commitment of Annex I Parties to 'aim' to return their GHG emissions to 1990 levels by 2000.[5] The Convention also requires Annex II Parties to include details of the financial assistance they are providing to developing countries, along with the measures they are taking to promote the transfer of environmentally sound technologies to developing countries and EITs.[6] These basic requirements included in the Convention have been elaborated considerably through reporting guidelines adopted by the COP.

At the time of writing, most Annex I Parties had already submitted three national communications (see table 11.1). In accordance with the Convention,

---

[4] FCCC Article 12.2.   [5] See FCCC Article 4.2 (b), and chapter 5.   [6] FCCC Article 12.3.

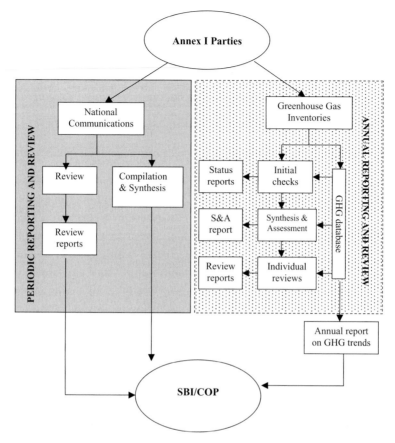

Fig. 11.1   The reporting and review system under the Convention[7]

national communications are made publicly available,[8] on the Secretariat's website. Timeliness of submission of national communications has been a problem,[9] with only thirteen Annex I Parties submitting their third national communications on time, and twenty submitting theirs over three months late.

2.1.1   FCCC reporting guidelines for national communications

National communications must be prepared according to common *reporting guidelines* agreed by the COP. These 'FCCC reporting guidelines' for national communications have been revised three times, each time specifying in more detail the information that Parties must include in their reports and how this should be presented, with the aim of improving the comprehensiveness, accuracy,

---

[7] The authors wish to thank the FCCC Secretariat for its help in producing this figure.
[8] FCCC Article 12.10.   [9] See SBI-16 report, paragraphs 11 (c) and (d).

Table 11.1 *Periodicity of national communications under the Convention*

Communication	Deadline
First[10]	Within six months of entry into force of the Convention for the Party[11]
Second[12]	15 April 1997[13] (15 April 1998 for EITs)
Third[14]	30 November 2001
Fourth[15]	1 January 2006

transparency and comparability of the data provided. The guidelines used for the most recent third national communications were agreed at COP-5.[16] On some specific topics, Annex I Parties are encouraged to use guidelines contained in other publications, notably the IPCC Technical Guidelines for Assessment of Climate Change Impacts and Adaptations.[17] Table 11.3 appended to this chapter summarises the contents of the current FCCC reporting guidelines for Annex I Party national communications, organising these into mandatory requirements (phrased in terms of 'Parties shall ...'), recommended elements ('Parties should ...') and optional, indicative elements ('Parties may ...').

A separate set of guidelines for reporting on research and systematic observation activities was agreed at COP-5.[18] For more on this issue, see chapter 7.

The quality of reporting in the climate change regime is generally good, even if Parties do not always follow the guidelines to the letter, making comparison of information difficult. Developing countries have been particularly critical of reporting by Annex II Parties on their technology transfer and financial assistance programmes, viewing this as incomplete and insufficiently detailed.

---

[10] FCCC Articles 4.2 (b) and 12.5.

[11] Or within six months of entry into force of the amendment to Annex I for those Parties added to Annex I by Decision 4/CP.3 (see box 5.4 in chapter 5).

[12] Decision 9/CP.2, Communications from Parties included in Annex I to the Convention: Guidelines, schedule and process for consideration.

[13] Update only required from those Parties whose first communications were due in 1996.

[14] Decision 11/CP.4, National communications from Parties included in Annex I to the Convention.

[15] Decision 4/CP.8, National communications from Parties included in Annex I to the Convention.

[16] Decision 4/CP.5. The guidelines themselves are contained in document FCCC/CP/1999/7. See Decision 9/CP.2 for the guidelines used for the second national communications, and INC Decision 9/2, Annex I, for those used for the first national communications.

[17] IPCC, 1994.

[18] Decision 5/CP.5, Research and systematic observation, with the guidelines in FCCC/CP/1999/7.

2.2   *Greenhouse gas inventories*

The Convention requires all Parties to provide a national inventory of their GHG emissions by sources and removals by sinks.[19] In the case of Annex I Parties, an annual GHG inventory must be submitted on 15 April each year, including emissions data from 1990 up to the last but one year prior to the date of submission.[20] GHG inventories for 2003 should therefore include data from the base year up to 2001. This requirement aims to ensure that the most up-to-date data is available to track emission trends, supplementing the full national communications, which are submitted less regularly.

From a shaky start, the timeliness of submission of annual GHG inventories has shown considerable improvement. Twenty-two Annex I Parties had submitted their inventories by the due date in 2002, compared with just four in 1998. Each round of inventories has also seen progress in the completeness of data,[21] suggesting that the regular reporting process has pushed Annex I Parties into improving their GHG data collection systems. Despite this, however, data sets are still not complete, with few Parties having yet supplied complete data for all years since 1990. EITs have faced particular problems in this regard, including in the timely submission of their inventories, reflecting their generally more limited capacity and resources.

2.2.1   IPCC methodological guidelines

The Convention requires GHG inventories to be compiled 'using comparable methodologies . . . agreed upon by the COP'.[22] The Convention further calls on the COP to 'consider and agree on methodologies' for calculating GHG emissions and removals by sinks at its first session.[23] The methodologies used pursuant to this requirement are those developed by the IPCC. The first set of guidelines was finalised in 1994, published in 1995, and duly agreed upon by COP-1.[24] These were subsequently revised in 1996 to form the *Revised 1996 IPCC Guidelines for National Greenhouse Gas Inventories* ('IPCC methodological guidelines').

The IPCC methodological guidelines provide step-by-step directions to help countries calculate their emissions and compile their GHG inventories.[25] The

---

[19] FCCC Article 12.1 (a).

[20] See Decision 3/CP.1, Preparation and submission of national communications from the Parties included in Annex I to the Convention.

[21] See, for example, FCCC/SB/2002/INF.2, paragraph 8.   [22] FCCC Articles 4.1 (a) and 12.1 (a).

[23] FCCC Article 4.1 (c).

[24] See Decision 4/CP.1. This decision also makes reference to the IPCC Technical Guidelines for Assessing Climate Change Impacts and Adaptations, which are discussed in chapter 8.

[25] The IPCC 1996 Revised Guidelines (IPCC, 1996b) consist of three volumes: Reporting Instructions (vol. 1); Workbook (vol. 2); and Reference Manual (vol. 3).

guidelines include different methods (or 'tiers') that Parties may use to calculate their emissions at varying levels of detail, depending on their capacity to do so. They also provide 'default' *activity data* and *emission factors* (see box 11.2 for an explanation of these terms) that can be used to calculate emissions to a minimum degree of accuracy in countries that lack national data and have little experience in preparing inventories. However, the guidelines encourage the use of country-specific methodologies wherever possible, so long as these are compatible with the IPCC system. The guidelines also incorporate a common reporting framework for countries to compile their GHG inventories, whatever the methodology they have used. This framework, including standard reporting tables, aims to secure transparency and allow for comparison between inventories. The IPCC has developed computer software to assist Parties with the compilation and reporting of their inventories.

At the request of the SBSTA, the IPCC, through its National Greenhouse Gas Inventories Programme (NGGIP), has also prepared 'Good Practice Guidance',[26] which elaborates on, and complements, the IPCC methodological guidelines. The aim of this IPCC good practice guidance, completed in 2000 for all sectors other than LULUCF, is to help national experts deal with data uncertainties, to ensure that inventories are neither over nor underestimated as far as can be judged, and that any uncertainties are minimised. It includes, for example, decision trees to help experts select which method to use to calculate their emissions from individual source categories, including key source categories (those which contribute most to overall emissions and trends). The IPCC good practice guidance also greatly extends advice on the estimation of uncertainties and on quality assurance/quality control (see box 11.2 for an explanation of these terms).

Again at the request of the SBSTA, the IPCC subsequently developed a further report on 'Good Practice Guidance' relating specifically to the LULUCF sector, to serve the needs of Annex I and non-Annex I Parties to both the Convention and the Kyoto Protocol. This was finalised by the IPCC in 2003.[27]

These three products – the IPCC methodological guidelines, the IPCC good practice guidance and most recently the IPCC LULUCF good practice guidance[28] – together make up the basis for the compilation of GHG inventories by Annex I Parties. The IPCC is now updating the IPCC methodological guidelines, at the

---

[26] IPCC, 2000b.

[27] IPCC, 2004. See Decision 11/CP.7, Land use, land-use change and forestry, paragraph 3, and Decision 13/CP.9, Good practice guidance for LULUCF in the preparation of national greenhouse gas inventories under the Convention; also IPCC-21 report, section 4. The good practice guidance is available from http://www.ipcc-nggip.iges.or.jp/.

[28] As it has only recently been adopted, Annex I Parties are required to use the IPCC LULUCF good practice guidance for their inventories only from 2005. See Decision 13/CP.9.

SBSTA's request, with the aim of completing work by early 2006.[29] This work will merge and update the inventory guidelines and the good practice guidance.

2.2.2   FCCC inventory reporting guidelines

Until 1999, FCCC reporting guidelines for GHG inventories, based on the IPCC methodological guidelines, were incorporated within the reporting guidelines for national communications (see section 2.1.1 above). At COP-5, however, separate FCCC reporting guidelines for GHG inventories were adopted.[30] These were subsequently revised at COP-8, based on Parties' experience in using the first set, and taking into account the IPCC good practice guidance.

The two sets of guidelines – FCCC and IPCC – should not be confused. While the IPCC's *methodological* guidelines explain in technical detail how emission totals should be calculated based on activity data and emission factors, the FCCC inventory *reporting* guidelines set out the reporting framework that Parties must use when submitting information on their GHG emissions under the Convention, how this information should be presented, and what additional supporting information should be provided.

According to the FCCC inventory reporting guidelines, the annual inventories of Annex I Parties should consist of two components:

- A **common reporting format** (CRF), which provides standard tables for Parties to complete and submit electronically, including aggregate emissions data, activity data and other relevant information, thereby facilitating data analysis and comparison across inventories and different years. A complete CRF, including all the required GHG data, should be submitted annually for the latest inventory year, as well as for any previous years where data has been recalculated.

- A **national inventory report** (NIR), in which Parties report qualitative and disaggregated quantitative information, such as an explanation of methodologies used, the rationale for selecting specific emission factors, and explanations of data gaps and uncertainties. An updated NIR must be submitted electronically each year.

The emissions data to be included in the CRF cover carbon dioxide (CO_2), methane (CH_4), nitrous oxide (N_2O), hydrofluorocarbons (HFCs), perfluorocarbons (PFCs) and sulphur hexafluoride (SF_6), presented gas-by-gas and disaggregated as completely

---

[29] See SBSTA-17 report, paragraph 14 (f).

[30] Decision 3/CP.5, Guidelines for the preparation of national communications by Parties included in Annex I to the Convention, Part I: FCCC reporting guidelines on annual inventories. The guidelines themselves are contained in document FCCC/CP/1999/7.

as possible by source and sink. Aggregate emissions data should also be provided, using global warming potentials (GWPs) for a 100-year time period, as set out in the IPCC SAR[31] (on GWPs, see box 11.2 and also chapter 5). Data on HFCs and PFCs should be disaggregated by chemical,[32] with data provided for actual emissions where this is available, and also for potential emissions where relevant.[33]

Parties must also report the contributions of emissions from key sources to their national totals, in terms of both absolute emission levels and emission trends. In addition, Parties should provide emissions data on the indirect GHGs carbon monoxide (CO), nitrogen oxides (NOx), non-methane volatile organic compounds (NMVOCs) and sulphur oxides (SOx), and also on any other GHGs for which 100-year GWPs may be determined in the future by the IPCC and adopted by the COP.

Any data gaps should be clearly indicated using standard notation keys (e.g. 'NO' for 'not occurring', 'IE' for 'included elsewhere') and justified, while Parties should also provide a quantitative estimate of the uncertainty associated with data and underlying assumptions. Data that is deemed to be confidential (e.g. for military reasons) may be reported at a higher level of aggregation to prevent disclosure of sensitive information.[34] Any *adjustments* (see box 11.2 for an explanation of this term in this context) that have been made to the data should be reported separately. In line with the IPCC's methodological guidelines, and also COP Decision 2/CP.3, emissions from international aviation and maritime transport (bunker fuels) should also be reported separately from national emission totals.[35] For verification purposes, CO_2 emissions from fuel combustion should be reported using both the IPCC reference and sectoral approaches.[36]

---

[31] See IPCC, 1995a, Technical Summary, table 4.

[32] The IPCC SAR lists thirteen HFCs and seven PFCs, with GWPs ranging from 140 to 11,700 for HFCs, and from 6,500 to 9,200 for PFCs: IPCC, 1995a.

[33] This is also in accordance with Decision 2/CP.3, Methodological issues related to the Kyoto Protocol, paragraph 2. The difference between 'actual' and 'potential' emissions occurs because there is often a considerable time lag between the consumption of a chemical and the release of emissions into the atmosphere. A new refrigerator, for example, may release small amounts of HFCs through leakage and servicing over its working life, but the bulk will be released when it is disposed of. 'Potential emissions' thus refers to the amount of emissions that will eventually be released from a chemical, while 'actual emissions' refers to the amount of emissions released on an annual basis. Actual emissions data are therefore more representative, where they are available. See IPCC, 1996b, vol. 3, section 2.17.2.

[34] The protection of confidential data is provided for in the Convention itself (Article 12.9).

[35] See chapter 5.

[36] While the IPCC methodological guidelines are based on a sectoral approach, that is, estimating emissions from different economic sectors (e.g. transport, industry), they also include a 'reference approach' for estimating CO_2 emissions from fuel combustion, using aggregate data on a country's fossil fuel supply and the carbon content of those fuels. Comparing estimates of CO_2 emissions from fuel combustion resulting from the two approaches can provide

The NIR, for its part, is aimed at enhancing transparency and facilitating the review of the inventory by expert review teams (see section 2.3 below). In their NIR, Annex I Parties should explain the methodologies, assumptions, emission factors and activity data they have used to estimate emissions in each sector, and also describe the institutional arrangements and procedures in place for preparing GHG inventories. A description of the key source categories should be provided, as well as a discussion of emission trends by gas, source and in aggregate. The NIR must include an evaluation of uncertainties in the inventory and an assessment of the completeness of data, and should also give justifications for any recalculation of data for previous years (according to the IPCC good practice guidance, it is considered good practice to recalculate historical emissions where methods have improved, new source categories have been incorporated, or errors corrected). In addition, the FCCC reporting guidelines require Parties to elaborate a plan for quality assurance/quality control aimed at monitoring the quality of the inventory; information on this should be provided in the NIR. The FCCC reporting guidelines set out a common structure to be followed when drafting the NIR.

Box 11.2   Key terms in GHG inventories[37]

Activity data: Data on the magnitude of human activities resulting in emissions/removals of GHGs taking place during a given period of time. For the energy sector, for example, the annual activity data for fuel combustion sources is the total amount of fuel burned annually. Estimates of GHG emissions are developed on the basis of activity data and **emission factors**.

Adjustment: This term has two different meanings. Under the FCCC reporting guidelines, an adjustment refers to a case where a Party has modified its emissions data to take account of unusual conditions in a particular year, such as fluctuations in the electricity trade.

Under the KP reporting and review guidelines, however, expert review teams have a mandate to apply adjustments – in other words, make changes – to an Annex I Party's reported emissions data, if the data is found to be incomplete or inconsistent with the IPCC methodological guidelines as elaborated by the IPCC good practice guidance. The aim of applying

---

a basic means of verifying a GHG inventory, with any large differences meriting further investigation and explanation.

[37] See IPCC, 1996b, vol. 1, glossary; and glossary of terms used in the IPCC TAR, available at www.ipcc.ch.

adjustments in this way is to correct problems to ensure that, as far as possible, emissions are not underestimated and removals/base year emissions not overestimated.

Emission factor: A coefficient reflecting the amount of emissions that each activity generates. Emission factors are often based on sample measurement data to develop a representative rate of emissions for a given activity level under a given set of operating conditions. The emission factors for activities in different countries will vary according to national circumstances (e.g. efficiency of fuel combustion). The IPCC methodological guidelines, however, include default emission factors for countries that have not yet developed their own. Estimates of GHG emissions and removals are developed on the basis of **activity data** and emission factors.

Global warming potential (GWP): A measure of the relative effectiveness of different GHGs in absorbing infrared radiation (and therefore contributing to global warming) over a period of time, as compared with CO_2, whose value is taken to be 1 (e.g. the GWP of methane over 100 years is 21, that of nitrous oxide is 310, and that of SF_6 is 23,900).[38] The concept of GWPs, developed by the IPCC for use within a policy context, thus allows the total impact of the well-mixed GHGs to be evaluated together as a basket, which is fundamental to the Kyoto Protocol system.

Quality control (QC): A system of routine technical activities to measure and control the quality of GHG inventories as they are being developed, e.g. accuracy checks and the use of approved standardised procedures.

Quality assurance (QA): Review procedures conducted by personnel not directly involved in the inventory compilation process to verify that data quality objectives were met.

2.3   *Review process*

The Convention calls on the COP to 'assess, on the basis of all information made available to it . . . the implementation of the Convention by the Parties, the overall effects of the measures taken pursuant to the Convention . . . and the extent

---

[38] IPCC, 1995a, Technical Summary, table 4. These are the GWPs used in the Kyoto Protocol system (see chapter 5) although they have subsequently been updated in the TAR.

to which progress towards the objective of the Convention is being achieved'.[39] The COP's review function[40] also extends to other mandates, including to 'periodically examine the obligations of the Parties and the institutional arrangements under the Convention, in the light of . . . the experience gained in its implementation', to 'keep under regular review the implementation of the Convention', as well as to 'review the adequacy' of the commitments of Annex I Parties under Article 4.2 (a) and (b).[41] The national communications submitted by Parties provide the core information needed by the COP to fulfil these review functions. To assist the COP, the SBI is mandated to 'consider the information communicated [by Parties], to assess the overall aggregated effect of the steps taken by the Parties' and to 'consider the information communicated [by Annex I Parties]' for the COP's review of the adequacy of Article 4.2 (a) and (b).[42] It is on the basis of these provisions that the COP has adopted procedures for considering and reviewing the national communications and GHG inventories submitted by Annex I Parties. These procedures are discussed below.

2.3.1   National communications

2.3.1.1 Compilation and synthesis   A *compilation and synthesis* of each set of national communications is prepared by the Secretariat and presented to the COP, via the SBI.[43] These compilation and synthesis documents summarise and consolidate the information provided by Annex I Parties under each heading of the FCCC reporting guidelines, identifying key patterns and trends. Annex I Parties' reports on research and systematic observation (see chapter 7), prepared according to the guidelines agreed at COP-5, are subject to a separate compilation and synthesis.[44]

2.3.1.2 In-depth review and expert review teams   The national communications of Annex I Parties are also subject to in-depth review (IDR) by expert review teams, which are conducted according to procedures adopted at COP-1 in 1995.[45] The stated purpose of the in-depth review process is to review Annex I Party national communications 'in a facilitative, non-confrontational, open and transparent manner' in order to 'provide a thorough and comprehensive technical assessment of the implementation of the Convention by individual Annex I Parties and Annex I

---

[39] FCCC Article 7.2 (e).   [40] See chapter 13.

[41] FCCC Articles 7.2 (a), 7.2 and 4.2 (d), respectively.   [42] FCCC Article 10.2 (a) and (b).

[43] See A/AC.237/81 and Corr.1; FCCC/CP/1996/12 and Adds.1–2; FCCC/SBI/1997/19 and Add.1; FCCC/CP/1998/11 and Adds.1–2; FCCC/SBI/2003/7 and Adds.1–4.

[44] See FCCC/SBSTA/2002/INF.15.

[45] Decision 2/CP.1, Review of first communications from the Parties included in Annex I to the Convention.

Parties as a whole'.[46] The in-depth review process does not, therefore, involve any political assessment of the measures taken by Parties, nor does it provide policy recommendations.

According to the IDR procedures, expert review teams are coordinated by a representative of the Secretariat, and may include representatives of relevant IGOs (such as the OECD or IEA), as well as experts nominated by Parties, who should make up the majority of any team and participate in their personal capacity. The Secretariat must try to ensure regional balance in each team, including from developing countries, as well as balance in skills and expertise. A roster of experts, based on nominations by Parties, is held with the Secretariat,[47] and the Secretariat selects four to five experts from the roster for each review.

The in-depth review process involves a preparatory stage during which the experts consider the national communication and other documentary information provided by Parties to identify any issues they feel would merit further discussion. These might include, for example, lack of clarity over how estimates of the effects of climate change policies were arrived at. An in-country visit to the Party itself will then follow, with its prior approval (the use of in-country visits was expanded following the adoption of Decision 6/CP.3, which stated that these should take place 'as a general rule'[48]). A typical in-country visit will last a working week, and include meetings with the national experts who were involved in preparing the communication. Expert review team members will typically bring up issues identified through the preparatory stage, while the national experts have an opportunity to supply updated or additional information. In some cases, the considerable time lag between the submission of the national communication and the in-country visit means that the in-depth review report serves as an interim report to the next national communication. The in-country visit is an uncontroversial, facilitative process, aimed at expanding and clarifying the information already contained in the national communication, rather than questioning or criticising it. It plays an important role in helping Parties to enhance the quality of their next national communication, and also helps build capacity among the experts themselves, many of whom are involved in preparing the national communication of their own countries, both in Annex I and non-Annex I Parties. The process thus promotes the exchange of information among countries, stimulating debate on different climate policies and their relative effectiveness.

Following the in-country visit, the expert review team prepares a report under its own authority, assisted by the Secretariat. The Party is provided with an

---

[46] Decision 2/CP.1, Annex I, paragraph 1.
[47] See chapter 15.
[48] Decision 6/CP.3, Communications from Parties included in Annex I to the Convention.

opportunity to comment on a draft of the report within eight weeks of its receipt (the introduction of a suggested time-frame was another elaboration to the procedures introduced by Decision 6/CP.3). If the expert review team feels unable to accept any comment, then the Party's view will be included in a separate section of the report. In-depth review reports are published as official FCCC documents.

The in-depth review process is financed through the Secretariat's core budget. Funding is only provided, however, to cover the travel and subsistence costs of experts from developing countries and EITs that are eligible for funding under the wider FCCC rules,[49] and not for any work carried out for the preparation stage or the drafting of the report, which must be covered by the expert's own institution. Experts from Parties that are not eligible for funding must be supported by their own institutions.

The in-depth review reports are formally subject to consideration by the SBI, which develops recommendations for the COP. They are rarely discussed in any depth, however, and very rarely on an individual basis. Instead, the SBI focuses its attention primarily on procedural aspects, with the Secretariat reporting regularly on progress in the conduct of the reviews and any issues arising. Although the IDRs do not have a high profile in the negotiations, they do perform a vital function in enhancing the transparency of the climate change process and the accountability of Parties. Through the IDRs, individual Parties, NGOs and the media have access to independently reviewed information, allowing them to scrutinise a Party's climate change policies and their effectiveness.

2.3.2   Greenhouse gas inventories

2.3.2.1 Compilation   The Secretariat maintains a database of *GHG emissions and removals*, which is regularly updated and made publicly available on the Secretariat website.[50] In addition, the Secretariat publishes an *annual report* on GHG inventory data submitted by Annex I Parties, including graphs depicting emission trends and an assessment of the overall conformity of Annex I Parties with their reporting obligations.[51]

2.3.2.2 Technical review   At COP-8, Parties launched a *technical review process* for annual inventories.[52] As its name suggests, this review process consists of a technical exercise aimed at verifying the data supplied and the consistency of inventory reporting with the guidelines, while helping Parties to improve the

---

[49] See chapter 16.   [50] See http://ghg.unfccc.int.

[51] See, for example, FCCC/SB/2002/INF.2 and FCCC/WEB/2002/10.

[52] Decision 19/CP.8, FCCC guidelines for the technical review of greenhouse gas inventories from Annex I Parties.

quality of their inventories. The design of this technical review process was based on experience gained from a trial period established at COP-5.[53]

The technical review process involves three stages. First, an *initial check* of each annual inventory is carried out by the Secretariat, involving a rapid assessment of the completeness of the information provided and its conformity with the required reporting format. The Secretariat prepares a status report for each Annex I Party based on this initial check and posts it on the FCCC website within seven weeks of receipt of the annual inventory and after the Party has been given the opportunity to comment on a draft.

Secondly, the Secretariat prepares a *synthesis and assessment* of all the Annex I Party inventories.[54] This consists of two parts. Part I provides synthesised data and information allowing comparisons across Parties, identifying common method-ological issues and key sources of emissions for each Annex I Party. Part II serves as input for the next stage of the review process – individual reviews of inventories – by providing a preliminary analysis of issues requiring the attention of the expert review teams. Again, the Party has the opportunity to comment on a draft of the synthesis and assessment and the preliminary analysis.

Thirdly, each inventory is subject to an *individual review* by an expert review team, involving a 'detailed examination of the inventory estimates, procedures and methodologies used in the preparation of inventories'.[55] Individual reviews are conducted through three different approaches:

- *Desk-based review*, where experts review information sent to them by the Secretariat in their home country or country of residence;
- *Centralised review*, where experts meet in a single location to review the information; and
- *In-country review*, where a scheduled visit to the country under review takes place.

Most inventories are subject to desk-based or centralised review on an annual basis, with each Annex I Party subject to an in-country review once every five years. Priority is given to centralised reviews, with desk-based reviews conducted only in the two subsequent years following an in-country visit. The Secretariat manages the reviews, and all reports are placed on its website.[56]

---

[53] Decision 6/CP.5, Guidelines for the technical review of greenhouse gas inventories from Annex I Parties.

[54] A first synthesis and assessment report covers inventories submitted within ten weeks of the due date (15 April each year). Inventories submitted later than this are covered by addenda to the report.

[55] Decision 19/CP.8, Annex, paragraph 17.

[56] See http://unfccc.int/program/mis/ghg/index.html.

Mirroring the practice for the in-depth review of national communications (see above), experts for all three approaches are drawn from the FCCC roster of experts, serve in their personal capacity, and must reflect regional balance. Funding is available only for eligible developing countries and EITs. Beyond this, however, individual review procedures for inventories are more detailed than for national communications. Two lead reviewers 'with substantial inventory review experience'[57] are appointed – one each from an Annex I and non-Annex I Party – and the team as a whole must encompass expertise in all IPCC sectors (e.g. energy, industrial processes, agriculture, land use change and forestry, and waste). Lead reviewers play a particularly important role, being responsible for monitoring the progress of the review and ensuring its conformity with the guidelines. Expert review teams for in-country visits are generally composed of six members, and teams for desk-based and centralised reviews of twelve members. The guidelines set out a tight timetable for the reviews, which should be completed within twenty or twenty-five weeks for desk-based and centralised reviews, respectively, and within fourteen weeks for in-country reviews.[58] The expert review team then prepares an individual review report on each inventory, which the guidelines specifically state 'should not contain any political judgement'.[59] A code of practice is in place for the treatment of confidential information.[60] Once again, the Party is allowed to comment on a draft, before the final report is officially published.

The competence of experts is critical to the effectiveness of the review process. To secure that competence, the SBSTA has developed a training programme for members of expert review teams, including an examination, which must be successfully completed by prospective reviewers.[61] Expert reviewers will also be required to sign an 'agreement on expert review services', including an obligation to disclose any conflict of interest, protect confidential information and perform duties in an objective and neutral manner.[62]

3   The Kyoto Protocol rules: Annex I Parties

Given the legally binding nature of its targets and the need to safeguard the integrity of the Kyoto mechanisms, accurate reporting is particularly important under the Kyoto Protocol. The reporting requirements under the Kyoto Protocol are therefore more elaborate than those under the Convention, although

---

[57] Decision 19/CP.8, Annex, paragraph 36.   [58] Decision 19/CP.8, Annex, paragraph 41.

[59] Decision 19/CP.8, Annex, paragraph 39.

[60] See Decision 12/CP.9, Issues relating to the technical review of greenhouse gas inventories from Parties included in Annex I to the Convention, Annex II.

[61] See Decision 12/CP.9, Annex I.   [62] See Decision 12/CP.9, Annex III.

they are founded on the same basic elements of annual GHG inventories and periodic national communications.

The Kyoto Protocol thus requires each Annex I Party to incorporate 'the necessary supplementary information for the purposes of ensuring compliance' with its mitigation commitments in its annual emissions inventory submitted under the Convention.[63] Similarly, each Annex I Party must incorporate 'the necessary supplementary information to demonstrate compliance' with its Protocol commitments in its national communication submitted under the Convention.[64] Detailed guidelines for reporting this supplementary information for both inventories and national communications were agreed in a single document as part of the Marrakesh Accords and an additional COP-8 decision[65] ('KP reporting guidelines').

Annex I Parties that are Parties to the Protocol will only have to submit a single emissions inventory and national communication, with the more extensive specifications mandated under the Kyoto Protocol superseding those required under the Convention. Conversely, Annex I Parties that do not become Parties to the Kyoto Protocol will only be subject to reporting requirements under the Convention.

In addition to their regular national communications and GHG inventories, the Marrakesh Accords require Annex I Parties to submit three 'one-off' reports: a report before the start of the commitment period to facilitate the establishment of their assigned amounts (*'pre-commitment period report'*); a report at the end of the commitment period to help assess compliance with their mitigation commitments (*'post-commitment period report'*);[66] and a separate report on their achievement of *'demonstrable progress'* under Article 3.2 of the Kyoto Protocol.

Annex I Parties' reporting commitments, combined with provisions for the review of those reports, are key components of what can be termed the Kyoto Protocol's 'accountability mechanisms'. These accountability mechanisms aim to secure the integrity of the Kyoto Protocol and its emission targets by ensuring that emissions data and information supplied by Parties are as complete and accurate as possible. Two further components of these accountability mechanisms include the requirement under the Kyoto Protocol for Annex I Parties to develop a *national*

---

[63] KP Article 7.1.   [64] KP Article 7.2.

[65] Decision 22/CP.7, Guidelines for the preparation of the information required under Article 7 of the Kyoto Protocol, and Draft Decision -/CMP.1 of the same title; with pending sections completed by Decision 22/CP.8, Additional sections to be incorporated in the guidelines for the preparation of the information required under Article 7, and in the guidelines for the review of information under Article 8 of the Kyoto Protocol.

[66] The terms 'pre-commitment period report' and 'post-commitment period report' are used for explanatory purposes in this book only, and not in the official texts of the climate change regime.

system for estimating their emissions,[67] and the obligation under the Marrakesh Accords for Annex I Parties to set up a *national registry* for tracking transactions in emission/removal units.[68] Given that national systems and national registries, as additional accountability mechanisms, are closely linked to the Kyoto Protocol's reporting requirements, they are also discussed in this chapter.

All these elements of the Kyoto Protocol reporting system are summarized in table 11.2 and discussed below.

3.1   *National systems*

The Kyoto Protocol requires Annex I Parties to have in place, no later than one year prior to the start of the first commitment period (2007), a national system for the estimation of GHG emissions and removals. A national system is defined by the Marrakesh Accords as 'all institutional, legal and procedural arrangements' made within an Annex I Party 'for estimating anthropogenic emissions by sources and removals by sinks . . . and for reporting and archiving inventory information'.[69] The requirement to establish a national system aims to ensure that all Annex I Parties develop sufficient capacity to monitor accurately and report on their emissions by the time the first commitment period kicks in. This is particularly important for many of the EITs, whose capabilities to estimate emissions remain weak. In this respect, the Marrakesh Accords urge Annex II Parties to provide assistance to EITs in setting up their national systems.[70]

The Kyoto Protocol establishes that guidelines for preparing national systems must incorporate the methodologies accepted by the IPCC and agreed upon by the COP,[71] that is, the IPCC methodological guidelines (see box 11.1). As IPCC good practice guidance is defined as an elaboration of the IPCC methodological guidelines (see below), it is also incorporated in the detailed guidelines for national systems.

The detailed national system guidelines, adopted as part of the Marrakesh Accords,[72] require Annex I Parties to establish institutional procedures for compiling their emissions inventories, including the designation of a single entity with overall responsibility for the inventory, the allocation of specific responsibilities

---

[67] KP Article 5.1.

[68] See Decision 19/CP.7, Modalities for the accounting of assigned amounts under Article 7.4 of the Kyoto Protocol, and Draft Decision -/CMP.1 of the same title, Annex.

[69] Decision 20/CP.7, Guidelines for national systems under Article 5, paragraph 1, of the Kyoto Protocol, and Draft Decision -/CMP.1 of the same title, Annex, paragraph 2.

[70] Decision 20/CP.7.

[71] KP Article 5.1 and Decision 2/CP.3, Methodological issues related to the Kyoto Protocol.

[72] Decision 20/CP.7, Guidelines for national systems under Article 5, paragraph 1, of the Kyoto Protocol, and Draft Decision -/CMP.1 of the same title, and Annex.

Table 11.2 *Summary of elements of KP reporting process for Annex I Parties*

Element	Time-frame	Purpose
National system	Establish by 2007	Ensure accurate monitoring/reporting of emissions
National registry	Establish in time to be reported in pre-commitment period report	Record all transactions in emission/removal units, e.g. under the Kyoto mechanisms and LULUCF projects
Pre-commitment period report	Before 1 January 2007 or one year after entry into force of Protocol for Party	Establish a Party's assigned amount and demonstrate its capacity to monitor/report its emissions accurately
GHG inventory	First due April 2010 (including data for 2008), yearly thereafter	Report GHG data, including all information required under the Convention, plus supplementary information to demonstrate compliance with KP
National communication	First due 1 January 2006, periodically thereafter. (every three to five years, to be decided by COP/MOP)	Provide information on actions to implement commitments, including all information required under the Convention, plus supplementary information to demonstrate compliance with KP
Post-commitment period report	Around July 2015, that is, 100 days after expert review (lasting up to one year) of last inventory for commitment period (to be submitted by 15 April 2014)	Basis for assessment of compliance
Report on demonstrable progress	1 January 2006	Basis for reviewing how Party has made 'demonstrable progress' in meeting its commitments by 2005, as required by KP Article 3.2

among government agencies and other organisations, and a process for officially approving the inventory and responding to any issues raised by the expert review process. Annex I Parties must also develop and implement quality assurance and quality control procedures including, for example, a basic review of the inventory by personnel who have not been involved in its development, preferably an independent third party, as well as a more extensive review of data for key sources. In addition, Annex I Parties must systematically archive inventory information for each year, including all disaggregated emission factors, activity data and supporting information, as well as details of quality assurance and quality control procedures.

3.2   *National registries*

Under the accounting guidelines agreed as part of the Marrakesh Accords, Annex I Parties must each establish and maintain a *national registry*. National registries are intended to act like a banking system, recording all transactions in emission/removal units (AAUs, CERs, ERUs and RMUs), including their issuance, transfer, cancellation and retirement.[73] According to the Marrakesh Accords, an organisation must be designated to serve as 'administrator'[74] of the national registry, which must consist of a standardised electronic database, incorporating various accounts designated by a unique number. These accounts include a 'holding account' for the Party and one for each legal entity authorised by the Party to hold units, along with 'cancellation accounts' for cancelled units and a 'retirement account' for those units that have been retired.[75] All non-confidential data (on confidentiality, see also below) is to be made publicly available via the Internet, including up-to-date information on the status of the various accounts and a list of legal entities authorised to hold emission units.

The national registries are part of a broader accounting system, also including a separate *CDM registry* and an independent *transaction log* maintained by the Secretariat. General design requirements for technical standards[76] were adopted at COP-8 to ensure the accurate, transparent and efficient exchange of data between individual national registries, the CDM registry and the transaction log. More detailed technical and functional specifications fleshing out these general design requirements are due to be adopted at COP-10.

---

[73] Decision 19/CP.7, Draft Decision -/CMP.1, Annex, section II B and C.

[74] Two or more Annex I Parties may manage their registries together, so long as each national registry remains distinct.

[75] Decision 19/CP.7, Draft Decision -/CMP.1, Annex, section II C.

[76] Decision 24/CP.8, Technical standards for data exchange between registry systems under the Kyoto Protocol.

3.3   *Greenhouse gas inventories and supplementary information*

The first annual GHG inventory under the Kyoto Protocol is scheduled for submission with the first inventory due under the Convention for the first year of the commitment period after the Protocol has entered into force for a Party.[77] For the Annex I Parties that have already ratified the Kyoto Protocol, therefore, the first annual inventory under the Protocol would be due in April 2010, providing data for the year 2008.

3.3.1   IPCC methodological guidelines and adjustments

As with the Convention, the Kyoto Protocol's negotiators deemed it necessary that Parties should use common methodologies for estimating their GHG emissions. Moreover, they considered that such methodologies should remain in place for the duration of the commitment period, so that Parties would not face uncertainty over the extent of their emission targets and whether methodological developments (e.g. possible future agreement on how to allocate bunker fuel emissions) might modify these. At the same time, however, negotiators had to balance the need for certainty with the desirability of applying improved methodologies that could more accurately estimate emissions, as these are updated over time.

The Kyoto Protocol[78] and its accompanying Decision 2/CP.3 thus reaffirm that Parties should use the IPCC methodological guidelines as the methodological basis for estimating their emissions, as they do under the Convention. If Parties fail to use the IPCC's methodologies, *adjustments* (see box 11.2 for an explanation of this term in this context) must be applied to their GHG inventories to ensure that any data problems are corrected. Although the Kyoto Protocol calls on the COP/MOP regularly to review and revise the methodologies used, based on input from the IPCC and the SBSTA, any such revision can only be used to ascertain compliance with emission targets *adopted after the revision*. A similar approach is used with regard to the GWPs that Parties must use to calculate their emission totals.[79] The Kyoto Protocol and its accompanying Decision 2/CP.3 specify that these must be the IPCC's 1995 GWPs for a 100-year time period; any revision will only apply to emission targets adopted subsequent to that revision.

The Marrakesh Accords flesh out these provisions in more detail.[80] They establish that IPCC good practice guidance constitutes an elaboration of the IPCC methodological guidelines, and hence that Annex I Parties are obliged to use this guidance when preparing their GHG inventories under the Kyoto Protocol.[81]

---

[77] KP Article 7.3.   [78] KP Article 5.2.   [79] KP Article 5.3.

[80] See Decision 21/CP.7, Good practice guidance and adjustments under Article 5, paragraph 2, of the Kyoto Protocol, and Draft Decision -/CMP.1 of the same title.

[81] Decision 21/CP.7, Draft Decision -/CMP.1, paragraph 1.

By designating the good practice guidance as an elaboration (rather than a revision) of the IPCC methodological guidelines, this methodological development could be incorporated into the Kyoto Protocol system, without contravening its provisions. Adjustments to data shall be applied only if inventory data submitted by Annex I Parties is found to be incomplete or inconsistent with the IPCC methodological guidelines and the agreed good practice guidance. These adjustments must be conservative, to ensure that emissions are not underestimated and removals or base-year emissions overestimated, and can only be calculated after a Party has had the opportunity to correct any data deficiencies. Expert review teams have the task of identifying any need for adjustments, and calculating what those adjustments should be (see also section 3.8.1 below). More detailed technical guidance on methodologies for adjustments was adopted at COP-9.[82] Methodologies for adjustments relating to the LULUCF sector will be developed in time for COP-10.[83]

3.3.2   KP reporting guidelines

The KP reporting guidelines require annual GHG inventories under the Kyoto Protocol to include all the information already incorporated in annual inventories under the Convention, notably GHG data supplied according to the common reporting format and a national inventory report.

The additional supplementary information that Parties must report on an annual basis, in accordance with the KP reporting guidelines, includes the following:[84]

- Detailed information on activities in the LULUCF sector, and emissions/removals resulting from these;
- Detailed information on the total quantities of emission units (AAUs, CERs, ERUs and RMUs) in each account of a Party's national registry at the beginning and end of the year, along with detailed information on the total volume of different transactions (issuance, transfer, cancellation, retirement) that took place throughout the year;
- Information on any discrepancies identified by the Secretariat's 'transaction log', and efforts made to correct these;

---

[82] Decision 20/CP.9, Technical guidance on methodologies for adjustments under Article 5, paragraph 2, of the Kyoto Protocol.

[83] Decision 21/CP.7, paragraph 4.

[84] Unless otherwise stated, all references in this section are to the KP reporting guidelines contained in Decision 22/CP.7, Draft Decision -/CMP.1, Annex, with pending sections completed by Decision 22/CP.8.

- A calculation of the Party's current commitment period reserve under emissions trading;[85]
- A description of any changes to national systems or national registries;
- Information on how the Party is striving to implement its commitments in such a way as to minimise adverse impacts on developing countries, in accordance with KP Article 3.14.[86] Annex II Parties must, in addition, provide information on how they are giving priority to certain actions, such as the phasing out of market imperfections, cooperating in the technological development of non-energy uses of fossil fuels, and assisting developing countries that are highly dependent on fossil fuel income to diversify their economies.

3.4   *National communications and supplementary information*

According to the Kyoto Protocol, supplementary information relating to the Kyoto Protocol should be submitted with the first national communication that is due under the Convention when the Kyoto Protocol enters into force for a Party.[87] For almost all Annex I Parties, this is likely to be the fourth national communication, due on 1 January 2006. The periodicity of subsequent national communications will be determined by the COP/MOP, taking into account the timetable for national communications under the Convention, but will probably be every three to five years, as it is already under the Convention.

3.4.1   KP reporting guidelines

Similar to annual GHG inventories, national communications under the Kyoto Protocol must incorporate all the information currently supplied in national communications under the Convention, plus supplementary information needed for Annex I Parties to demonstrate compliance with their obligations under the Protocol. According to the KP reporting guidelines, this supplementary information includes the following:

- Detailed information on national systems and national registries;
- Information to demonstrate that use of the mechanisms is supplemental to domestic action, and how domestic action thus constitutes a significant element of the effort made to meet emission targets;
- A description of policies and measures implemented to tackle climate change under KP Article 2. This includes steps taken to promote and/or implement decisions of ICAO and IMO to reduce GHG emissions from bunker fuels (KP Article 2.2), along with information on how Annex I

---

[85] See chapter 6.   [86] See chapter 9.   [87] KP Article 7.3.

Parties are striving to implement policies and measures in such a way as to minimise adverse effects (KP Article 2.3);

- Information on legislative, enforcement and administrative procedures put in place at the domestic or regional levels to promote compliance with the Kyoto Protocol's targets;
- A report of activities undertaken in fulfilment of the Protocol's general commitments under Article 10, for example on scientific research and education and training, including assistance to developing countries for technology transfer and capacity-building;
- For Annex II Parties, a report on new and additional financial resources provided to non-Annex I Parties to help them meet their obligations under the Kyoto Protocol.

3.5   *Pre-commitment period report*

According to the accounting guidelines, each Annex I Party must submit a report to 'facilitate the calculation of its assigned amount'[88] ('pre-commitment period report') to the Secretariat before the start of the commitment period, that is, prior to 1 January 2007, or one year after the entry into force of the Protocol for the Party, whichever is the latest. The purpose of this pre-commitment period report is twofold. First, it is a vehicle for Parties to supply the information needed to establish their assigned amounts. In several instances under the Kyoto Protocol and Marrakesh Accords, Parties are given a choice on the elements to be included as part of their emission targets. The pre-commitment period report is the place where they must declare their choice. These elements include the following:[89]

- Selected base year for HFCs, PFCs and SF_6 (1990 or 1995);
- Elected permissible activities in the LULUCF sector to be counted under Article 3.4 and a statement of whether each LULUCF activity (under both Articles 3.3 and 3.4) is to be accounted annually or for the entire commitment period;
- Selected single minimum values for tree crown cover, land area and tree height for the accounting of LULUCF activities and a justification for these;
- Any agreement under Article 4 (joint fulfilment of commitments).

Parties must also submit their own calculation of their assigned amount, and of their 'commitment period reserve' under emissions trading.[90]

---

[88] Decision 19/CP.7, Draft Decision -/CMP.1, Annex, paragraph 6.
[89] See chapter 5.   [90] See chapter 6.

The second purpose of the pre-commitment period report is for each Party to demonstrate its capacity to monitor its emissions, notably by providing a description of its national system and national registry, as well as complete inventories of its GHG emissions.

3.6   *Post-commitment period report*

The accounting guidelines require each Annex I Party to provide a report to the Secretariat[91] after the end of the commitment period (more precisely, after the additional period granted for fulfilling commitments, that is, 100 days after the deadline for completion of the expert review process for the last year of the commitment period).[92] Given that the annual GHG inventory for the last year of the commitment period, that is, 2012, will be due on 15 April 2014, and that, according to the review guidelines, the expert review process for inventories is to be completed within a year (see figure 11.3), the 'post-commitment period' report would be due from 24 July 2015. This 'post-commitment period report' must include information on the total quantities of emission/removal units in the Party's national registry and their status (e.g. retired, cancelled, etc.). It is on the basis of this post-commitment period report, combined with the *compilation and accounting report* (see section below) prepared by the Secretariat for the last year of the commitment period, that compliance will be assessed.

3.7   *Report on 'demonstrable progress'*

The Kyoto Protocol requires Annex I Parties to have made 'demonstrable progress' in meeting their commitments under the Protocol by 2005.[93] The Marrakesh Accords subsequently 'urge[d]' each Annex I Party that is also a Party to the Kyoto Protocol to submit, by 1 January 2006, a report to the COP/MOP with the basis for reviewing the demonstration of progress.[94] The use of the term 'urge' is considerably weaker than the 'shall' requiring the submission of annual inventories, national communications and the establishment of national systems and national registries. An additional decision, adopted at COP-8, sets out the required contents and format of the report.[95]

According to these brief guidelines, the report on demonstrable progress must include a description of domestic measures aimed at preparing for the implementation of mitigation commitments under the Protocol, including legal and

---

[91] Decision 19/CP.7, Draft Decision -/CMP.1, Annex, section III.A.

[92] Decision 24/CP.7, Procedures and mechanisms relating to compliance under the Kyoto Protocol, section XIII. See chapter 12.

[93] KP Article 3.2. See also chapter 5.   [94] Decision 22/CP.7, paragraph 4.

[95] Decision 25/CP.8, Demonstrable progress under Article 3, paragraph 2, of the Kyoto Protocol.

institutional steps and programmes for domestic compliance and enforcement. The report must also include trends in, and projections of, GHG emissions, along with an evaluation of how the described domestic measures will contribute to the achievement of a Party's emission commitments, in the light of these trends and projections. In addition, the report must incorporate a description of the activities, actions and programmes taken by the Party to fulfil its general commitments and financial obligations. The report is to be prepared in accordance with the broader FCCC and KP reporting guidelines, and incorporate any 'relevant contribution' arising from the SBSTA's ongoing work on 'good practices' in policies and measures.[96] The information contained in the report, which Annex I Parties are requested to submit as a single document, should be consistent with that contained in the Party's fourth national communication under the Convention, which is due at the same time (see table 11.1) and, as noted above, is likely also to be the first national communication under the Kyoto Protocol.

3.8   *Review process*

The Kyoto Protocol establishes that the information submitted by Annex I Parties will be reviewed by expert review teams.[97] The review process holds particular significance under the Kyoto Protocol, given that the review reports provide the basis for the decision-making process under the compliance regime, and that compliance with reporting obligations constitutes an eligibility criterion for participating in the Kyoto mechanisms.[98] Moreover, similar to the COP procedures under the Convention, the COP/MOP has the task of reviewing the implementation of the Kyoto Protocol,[99] with national communications, GHG inventories and other information submitted under the Protocol providing the fundamental basis for that review. All the reports submitted under the Kyoto Protocol and described above are subject to review. In addition, an *expedited review* procedure is in place whereby a Party whose eligibility to participate in the Kyoto mechanisms has been suspended due to problems in meeting its reporting obligations may request the reinstatement of its eligibility if it feels it has corrected those problems.

Reviews under the Kyoto Protocol are based on the same general approach as that for the Convention, that is, involving both the *expert review* of information submitted by individual Parties, and the *compilation* of that information by the Secretariat. This chapter considers each type of review in turn.

---

[96] This work on improving 'transparency, effectiveness and comparability of policies and measures' is aimed, among other things, at elaborating 'elements for reporting information on demonstrable progress', possibly including 'criteria and quantitative parameters' (Decision 13/CP.7, 'Good practices' in policies and measures among Parties included in Annex I to the Convention). For a more in-depth discussion, see chapter 5.

[97] KP Article 8.1.   [98] See chapter 6.   [99] KP Article 13.4 (a) and (b).

3.8.1   Expert review teams

The Marrakesh Accords, and a subsequent COP-8 decision,[100] set out detailed guidelines for the conduct of all expert reviews ('KP review guidelines').[101] These are founded on the procedures followed under the Convention,[102] sharing many similarities, especially with the technical review of annual inventories under the Convention, as both were developed in parallel and often by the same negotiators. The mandates given to the expert review teams under the Kyoto Protocol, however, are stronger, and many aspects of the guidelines are more detailed and extensive. Mirroring the Convention procedures, the Kyoto Protocol characterises the review process as consisting of 'a thorough and comprehensive technical assessment of all aspects' of a Party's implementation of the Protocol. Under the Kyoto Protocol, however, expert review teams also have the mandate to identify 'potential problems in, and factors influencing' the fulfilment of those commitments. Expert review teams are mandated to put questions to Annex I Parties regarding these potential problems and offer advice on how to correct them. If a Party does not subsequently correct the problem within the given time-frame (see figure 11.3 below), the expert review team may list the problem as a 'question of implementation' in its report, and it will then be considered by the Compliance Committee.[103] The review guidelines specify, however, that only problems concerning commitments of a mandatory nature may be listed as questions of implementation. As noted above, the expert review teams also have the mandate to calculate 'adjustments' to a Party's emissions data, if there is concern that IPCC methodologies or good practice guidance have not been adhered to. The Marrakesh Accords do specify, however, that the expert review teams 'shall refrain from making any political judgement'. The role of the expert review teams remains that of making a technical assessment, not a judgement on the performance of Parties, which remains the purview of the COP/MOP and the Compliance Committee.

The code of practice for the treatment of confidential information developed for the technical review of greenhouse gas inventories under the Convention (see

---

[100] Decision 23/CP.7, Guidelines for review under Article 8 of the Kyoto Protocol, and Draft Decision -/CMP.1 of the same title; with pending sections completed by Decision 22/CP.8, Additional sections to be incorporated in the guidelines for the preparation of the information required under Article 7, and in the guidelines for the review of information under Article 8 of the Kyoto Protocol.

[101] Unless otherwise specified, all references in the remainder of this section are to the KP review guidelines, as contained in the above-cited decisions.

[102] Decision 3/CP.1, elaborated by Decision 6/CP.3. Interestingly, however, the guidelines under the Kyoto Protocol refer simply to 'review' and not to 'in-depth review', as the Convention procedures do.

[103] See chapter 12.

above) will also apply under the Kyoto Protocol.[104] To recall, the Convention itself provides for the protection of confidential data.[105] Instances of confidential information are likely to be rare, involving issues of commercial sensitivity rather than national security.[106]

Following the broad practice under the Convention, the review guidelines provide for expert review teams to be coordinated by the Secretariat, composed of experts selected from the FCCC roster of experts (including experts from IGOs) who participate in their personal capacity, with funding provided for travel expenses only to developing country and EIT experts. The reference to the FCCC roster of experts means that experts from Parties that do not ratify the Kyoto Protocol may also serve on these teams. This was explicitly agreed upon the drafting of the review guidelines, in consideration of the technical nature of the reviews, and, no doubt, concerns about losing the strong expertise of the US in such technical matters. Mirroring the practice for annual inventory technical reviews under the Convention, expert review teams under the Kyoto Protocol are led by 'lead reviewers'. Given the importance of these individuals to the review process, COP-9 adopted criteria for their selection, such as extensive technical expertise and experience.[107] As part of their responsibilities, lead reviewers are required to prepare an annual report to the SBSTA with suggestions on how to improve the review process. Lead reviewers will remain based in their home institutions, travelling to regular meetings associated with the review.[108] All experts will be required to sign the agreement for expert review services agreed under the Convention (see above).

Training is provided to all experts, who are subsequently assessed for their competence to conduct reviews, and additional training may be offered to lead reviewers. In this regard, a specific training programme has been agreed for experts participating in the review of the 'pre-commitment period report', which is the first review to take place under the Kyoto Protocol.[109] As it is also required to do under the Convention, the Secretariat must ensure a good spread of expertise among the experts on a review team, along with balance between Annex I and non-Annex I experts. In addition, it is required to submit an annual report to the SBSTA on the composition of expert review teams for the Kyoto Protocol (e.g. on the nationalities of the experts).

All the reports of the expert review teams will be made publicly available, and forwarded by the Secretariat, together with any written comments by the Party

---

[104] Decision 21/CP.9, Issues relating to the implementation of Article 8 of the Kyoto Protocol, and Draft Decision -/CMP.1 of the same title.

[105] FCCC Article 12.9.   [106] See Anderson, 2002.   [107] Decision 21/CP.9, Annex II.

[108] Decision 23/CP.8, Terms of service for lead reviewers, and Draft Decision -/CMP.1 of the same title.

[109] Decision 21/CP.9, Annex I.

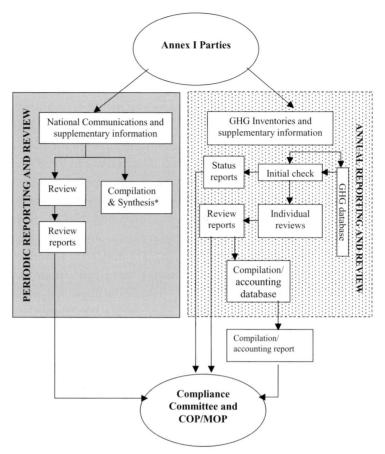

* The Marrakesh Accords do not state how the compilation and synthesis report will
be considered, with the COP/MOP expected to take further decisions in this regard.

Fig. 11.2   The reporting and review system under the Kyoto Protocol[110]

that is the subject of the report, to the COP/MOP, the Compliance Committee and
the Party concerned.

The regular review process for annual inventories and national communications is summarised in figure 11.2.

3.8.2   Review of greenhouse gas inventories

According to the KP review guidelines, the annual inventories and
accompanying supplementary information must be reviewed on an annual basis.
This annual review follows a similar process to that under the Convention (compare figures 11.1 and 11.2), albeit a more detailed one.

---

[110] The authors wish to thank the FCCC Secretariat for help in producing this figure.

The review of annual inventories includes two elements. First, the expert review team conducts an *initial check* on receipt of the inventory, aimed at verifying whether the information is complete and consistent, and structured according to the reporting guidelines. This initial check, though basic, is important. If a Party fails to submit an annual inventory, including the common reporting format and national inventory report, within six weeks of the submission date, or if it fails to provide an emissions estimate for source categories that individually accounted for 7 per cent or more of its aggregate emissions, the Party may lose its eligibility to participate in the Kyoto mechanisms. This initial check is conducted through a desk-based or centralised study, resulting in a status report.

Secondly, the review team conducts a full *individual inventory review* to examine the emissions inventory and other supplementary information in more depth. This review is carried out through a desk-based or centralised review, with one in-country visit per Party during the commitment period, which will involve a more in-depth examination. If the expert review team deems it necessary, however, it may request an additional in-country visit to clarify any apparent problems.

The expert review team examines the extent to which the Party has followed the KP reporting guidelines and IPCC methodological guidelines (including IPCC good practice guidance), and identifies any digressions. It compares emission estimates with those provided in previous submissions to spot any irregularities, and, where possible, also compares activity data with other independent, authoritative sources. The expert review team assesses how any issues that it has raised in previous reviews have been addressed, and makes recommendations on how to improve future inventories.

The inventory review results in a review report, which may identify problems that require adjustments to be made to the emissions data. These could include, for example, gaps in the emissions dataset or failure to apply IPCC good practice guidance. The Party concerned is given an opportunity to correct the problem before any adjustment is applied. If the problem is not corrected, the expert review team will recommend an adjustment, together with a justification for that recommendation. If the Party refuses to accept the recommended adjustment, the matter will be forwarded to the Compliance Committee. The application of adjustments is not merely a technical exercise; if it proves necessary, for example, to apply an adjustment to any key source category that accounted for 2 per cent or more of a Party's aggregate emissions covered by the Kyoto Protocol for three consecutive years, the Party may lose its eligibility to participate in the mechanisms (unless it sought assistance from the Compliance Committee in resolving the problem prior to the start of the first commitment period, and assistance is being provided). A Party may also lose its eligibility if its aggregate *adjusted* emissions exceed its aggregate *submitted* emissions by more than 7 per cent for any single year during the commitment period, or if at any time during the commitment period, the sum of the percentages by which its submitted emissions have exceeded its adjusted emissions for all years of the commitment period for which a review has been conducted is greater than twenty.

The annual review will also evaluate the supplementary information provided by the Party, including:

- Information on transactions in emission/removal units. The expert review team will check that the information supplied is consistent with data in national registries, the Secretariat's transaction log and the CDM registry, and will evaluate any discrepancies and their causes. It will also verify that the level of the commitment period reserve has been correctly calculated and that any double-counting in the LULUCF sector has been avoided.
- Any changes to national systems and national registries. If the annual review identifies any significant problems relating to a Party's national registry, the expert review team may recommend an additional 'thorough review' of the registry, including the use of standardised tests.
- Information on the minimisation of adverse impacts on developing countries under Article 3.14. The information submitted by Annex I Parties on this issue will be compiled into a separate document by the Secretariat. Its special treatment reflects the particular importance placed on this issue by fossil fuel exporting developing countries, and their determination that the information provided will be duly brought to light and considered (see also chapter 9).

In all cases, the expert review team will check whether the supplementary information has been provided in accordance with the reporting guidelines, assess the extent to which any previous questions have been resolved, identify any potential problems relating to the transparency, completeness and timeliness of information provided, and recommend possible ways of improving the reporting of information.

Tight timetables are in place for the annual review, which must be completed within one year of the date when the information was due for submission and include an opportunity for the Party to comment on a draft of the review report. The mandated timetable for both the initial check and the full inventory review is illustrated in figure 11.3.

3.8.2.1 Compilation and accounting database and annual report   As required by the accounting guidelines,[111] the Secretariat will maintain a so-called *compilation*

---

[111] Decision 19/CP.7, Draft Decision -/CMP.1, Annex, Part III, sections B and C.

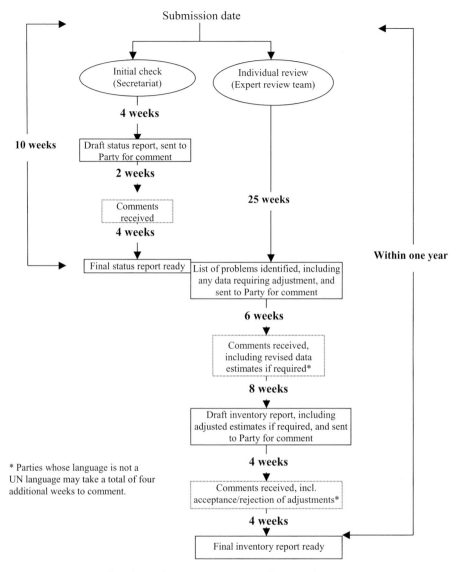

Fig. 11.3   Time-frame for the annual review of inventories and supplementary information under the Kyoto Protocol

and accounting database, that is, a database recording the emissions of Annex I Parties and their transactions in emission/removal units, as reported in their annual inventories. A separate record will be kept for each Annex I Party. The database, which will be updated each year following the expert review of annual inventories and the resolution of any outstanding questions, will also include data on a Party's activities in the LULUCF sector, any adjustments applied by the expert review teams, and the updated level of the commitment period reserve for emissions trading. Each year, the Secretariat will issue a *compilation and accounting report* for each Party, incorporating the most up-to-date information relating to it contained in the database.

At the end of the commitment period and the additional period for fulfilling commitments, the Secretariat will issue a final compilation and accounting report for each Party. Combined with each Party's post-commitment period review report (see below), the information contained in this final compilation and accounting report will form the basis for assessing the Party's compliance with its emissions target.

3.8.3   Review of national communications

Each national communication is subject to individual review, conducted through a desk or centralised review, followed by an in-country visit. The individual review provides an assessment of the completeness of the national communication, along with a detailed examination of each of its sections and how the information presented therein was arrived at. The review will thus consider, for example, information on 'supplementarity' in the context of the flexibility mechanisms, policies and measures implemented under KP Article 2, emission projections and the effects of policies and measures, information on the implementation of the Protocol's general commitments, and financial and technology transfer initiatives.

The guidelines for the review of national communications under the Kyoto Protocol are particularly stringent as regards timeliness of submission of national communications. Annex I Parties are requested to inform the Secretariat before the submission deadline of any likely delay and, if the national communication is more than six weeks late, the delay will be made public and brought to the attention of the COP/MOP and Compliance Committee. Such measures aim to address the problems of late reporting experienced under the Convention. Once a national communication has been submitted, the review process should be complete within two years. Again, Annex I Parties have an opportunity to comment on a draft of the review report.

According to the KP review guidelines, the Secretariat will also prepare a report on the *compilation and synthesis* of the national communications submitted by Parties under the Kyoto Protocol. The COP/MOP is likely to take further decisions on the nature, structure and process for consideration of this report.

In addition, the KP reporting guidelines request the Secretariat to prepare a report 'relating to' the commitment of Annex I Parties 'to implement domestic action . . . with a view to reducing emissions in a manner conducive to narrowing per capita differences between developed and developing country Parties while working towards achievement of the ultimate objective of the Convention'. This commitment is part of the principles, nature and scope of the Kyoto mechanisms, adopted as part of the Bonn Agreements.[112] What this Secretariat report will cover is as yet unclear, but it is likely, at a minimum, to include a discussion of the per capita emissions of both Annex I and non-Annex I Parties (see chapter 6 for a more in-depth discussion of this issue).

3.8.4   Review of pre-commitment period report

The review of the pre-commitment period report – the report that Annex I Parties must submit prior to the first commitment period to facilitate the establishment of their assigned amounts – includes an in-country visit, where experts evaluate the base year GHG data supplied by the Annex I Party, along with the calculation of its assigned amount and information on its national system and national registry.

This 'initial review' is of particular significance, with the purpose of ensuring that the basic data and methodological foundations are in place for the commitment period, and to avoid any data recalculations for the base year during the commitment period itself. In their 2002 inventories, for example, twenty-six Parties reported revised base year emission estimates, due to improved figures or an updated methodology. The changes for aggregate emissions ranged from −6 per cent to +16 per cent, although for twenty Parties the change was within the range of +/−2 per cent.[113]

Upon completion of the review and application of any adjustments, the base year GHG data will be fixed and remain unchanged for the first commitment period. The expert review team will also corroborate that the assigned amount calculated by the Party, which provides the foundation for the whole Kyoto Protocol system, stands up to scrutiny. In addition, it will confirm that the national system and national registry established by the Annex I Party are credible, conform to guidelines for their establishment, and are adequate for the purposes of monitoring emissions and conducting transactions in emissions units. Particular emphasis is placed in the guidelines on a 'thorough review' of each Party's national registry as part of the review of the pre-commitment period report, which will include testing of the registry using standard electronic tests and sample data to assess its capacity to perform its functions.

---

[112] Decision 5/CP.6, The Bonn Agreements on the Implementation of the Buenos Aires Plan of Action.

[113] FCCC/SB/2002/INF.2, paragraph 14.

3.8.5   Review of post-commitment period report

According to the KP review guidelines, the post-commitment period report submitted by Annex I Parties upon expiration of the additional period for fulfilling commitments will also be subject to review. This review is, of course, very important given that the post-commitment period report provides the basis for assessing a Party's compliance with its emission targets. This final review will be desk-based or centralised, and will cover the same scope as the review of annual inventories and supplementary information. It will assess whether the information provided is complete and conforms to the reporting guidelines, and identify any problems or inconsistencies, also drawing on information in the compilation and accounting database and annual report. Once the review is complete and, if possible, any problems resolved, the expert review team will assess whether a Party's emissions for its commitment period exceed those in the retirement account of its national registry,[114] in other words, whether or not a Party has met its emission target, and will prepare a report to that effect.

3.8.6   Review of report on 'demonstrable progress'

The Secretariat is requested to prepare a synthesis – or summary – of reports on demonstrable progress submitted by Annex I Parties, to be considered by the SBI at its first session in 2006. The SBI will use this synthesis as the basis for reviewing the demonstration of progress by Annex I Parties, with a view to providing advice on how to proceed to the subsequent session of the COP/MOP.[115]

3.8.7   Expedited review

As noted above, failure to adhere to the KP reporting guidelines may result in the suspension of a Party's eligibility to participate in the flexibility mechanisms. If a Party that has been suspended in this way feels it has corrected the problem (e.g. by improving its national system), it may request an *expedited review* aimed at reinstating its eligibility, without waiting for the next scheduled review. Although the review is expedited, the guidelines state that this 'shall not compromise the thoroughness of the examination by the expert review team'.

To do so, the Party may submit a request either through an expert review team or directly to the Compliance Committee's enforcement branch, and then provide additional information on how it has corrected the problem previously identified. The expert review team charged with evaluating the request to reinstate eligibility will not be composed of the same experts that conducted the review leading to the original suspension. Depending on the issue that led to the suspension, the

---

[114] See section 3.2 above.   [115] Decision 25/CP.8.

expedited review will be performed either as a centralised or an in-country review, as deemed appropriate by the Secretariat. The time-frame for the expedited review is accelerated compared to the review of annual inventories, potentially taking ten weeks or less, akin to that for an initial check (see figure 11.3). A Party should give the Secretariat at least six weeks' notice before submitting information in support of its request for reinstatement of eligibility, to give the Secretariat time to ensure that an expert review team is ready to start work within two weeks of receiving the information. The expert review team then has five weeks to prepare a draft review report, and the Party has three weeks to comment upon it. If no comments are provided, or if the Party notifies the expert review team that it will not provide comments, then the draft report automatically becomes the final report of the expert review team.

4   The Convention rules: non-Annex I Parties

4.1   *National communications*

The Convention commits each non-Annex I Party to submitting an initial national communication within three years of the entry into force of the Convention for it, or of the 'availability of financial resources' to cover the costs of its preparation. LDCs, however, may submit their initial national communication at their discretion.[116] Non-Annex I Parties must include an emissions inventory as part of their national communication,[117] but there is no requirement for an annual inventory to be submitted.

A first set of FCCC reporting guidelines for non-Annex I Party national communications was agreed at COP-2 in 1996,[118] with a revised set adopted at COP-8.[119] These revised guidelines should be used by non-Annex I Parties to prepare their second national communications, unless they have already started to prepare these and received funding to cover their costs.[120] As summarised in table 11.4 appended to this chapter, the guidelines include fewer mandatory obligations couched in terms of 'shall' and are more general in nature than those of Annex I Parties, allowing leeway according to the extent of Parties' capacities. Non-Annex I Parties that wish to do so are invited to use elements from the Annex I Party FCCC reporting guidelines when preparing their national communications,[121] while guidelines for reporting on global climate observing systems that were adopted at COP-5 may

---

[116] FCCC Article 12.5.   [117] FCCC Article 12.1 (a).

[118] Decision 10/CP.2, Communications from Parties not included in Annex I to the Convention: Guidelines, facilitation and process for consideration.

[119] Decision 17/CP.8 and Annex, Guidelines for the preparation of national communications from Parties not included in Annex I to the Convention.

[120] Decision 17/CP.8, paragraph 1 (a).   [121] Decision 17/CP.8, paragraph 2.

also be used by non-Annex I Parties on a voluntary basis.[122] In their national communications, developing countries may also, on a voluntary basis, propose projects for financing, including, if possible, an estimate of the associated incremental costs and benefits of any project, and of the emission reductions and increments of removals of GHGs. Parties may specify the technologies, material, equipment, techniques or practices that would be needed to implement such projects.[123] The list of projects proposed by non-Annex I Parties in their national communications is regularly compiled and published by the Secretariat, and submitted to the GEF for consideration.[124]

At the time of writing, 115 non-Annex I Parties had submitted their initial communications, with most submissions made in the years 2000, 2001 and 2002. Some of the largest emitters, however, were not among them, or had only very recently submitted their initial national communications. A table on the status of preparation of non-Annex I Party national communications, including information provided by Parties on the expected date of submission, is regularly updated by the Secretariat.[125] No time-frame has yet been set for the preparation of second national communications. Although COP-9 was requested to make a decision on this long-deferred issue,[126] it was unable to do so. Some non-Annex I Parties, however, have already started working on their second communications. At the time of writing, three non-Annex I Parties had submitted their second national communications.

Clearly, the submission of national communications by non-Annex I Parties has lagged behind that of Annex I Parties. Ten years after the Convention's entry into force, initial national communications – and therefore official emissions data – from some major developing country emitters are still lacking, or have only just been received. Procedural hurdles encountered in the disbursement of financial assistance by the GEF and its implementing agencies has contributed to this delay. Debates on non-Annex I national communications in the SBI are routinely punctuated by accusations from developing countries that problems with GEF funding have hindered the submission of their national communications.

Part of the problem also lies in the high degree of politicisation of this issue compared with its Annex I Party equivalent. This is because the question of non-Annex I Party national communications has become embroiled – at least beneath the surface – with the extremely sensitive issue of developing country commitments and access to funding for climate projects. Non-Annex I Parties were anxious, for example, that revised guidelines for second national communications should not include any reporting requirements that might introduce new climate

---

[122] Decision 5/CP.5, paragraph 8.   [123] FCCC Article 12.4.   [124] See e.g. FCCC/WEB/2002/8.
[125] See e.g. FCCC/WEB/2003/4.   [126] Decision 17/CP.8, paragraph 1 (f).

change mitigation commitments 'through the backdoor'. Similarly, at COP-9, the G-77 and China did not accept discussion of any timetable for the frequency of sub-mission of non-Annex I Party national communications, on the grounds that this could constitute an additional commitment for developing countries. At a funda-mental level, especially for the larger developing country emitters, declaration of a GHG inventory and therefore total amount of emissions has important strategic consequences, as any negotiation on developing country emission commitments will almost certainly be based on those figures declared in the national commu-nication. Moreover, non-Annex I Parties are eligible for GEF funding to cover only the 'incremental costs' of climate mitigation and other measures to implement the Convention and the Kyoto Protocol.[127] Similarly, the only emission reductions that qualify under the CDM are those additional to any that would have occurred in the absence of the CDM project. Some non-Annex I Parties therefore fear that declaring climate policies in their national communications could prejudice their access to funding both through the GEF and the CDM in the future, as it may be concluded that activities would have happened anyway, as part of national climate policy.

4.2   *National adaptation programmes of action*

COP-7 launched a new type of report – national adaptation program-mes of action (NAPAs) – to provide LDCs with a framework for simplified and tar-geted reporting on their vulnerability and urgent adaptation needs.[128] For more on NAPAs and the LDC Expert Group, see chapter 8.

4.3   *Financial and technical support*

Financial resources to support developing countries in meeting their reporting commitments are mandated by the climate regime and are discussed in detail in chapter 10. By 30 June 2002, the GEF had disbursed US $87.6 million to fund, or part fund, the preparation of initial national communications for 133 individual non-Annex I Parties, amounting to just under 6 per cent of the US $1.5 billion allocated to the climate change focal area. The amount granted to individ-ual non-Annex I Parties for the preparation of their initial national communica-tions has varied between US $0.09 million (Zimbabwe) to US $3.5 million (China), with the vast majority of grants amounting to under US $0.5 million.[129] The GEF

---

[127] See chapter 10.
[128] Decision 5/CP.7, Implementation of Article 4, paragraphs 8 and 9 of the Convention (Deci-sion 3/CP.3 and Article 2, paragraph 3, and Article 3, paragraph 14, of the Kyoto Protocol).
[129] See FCCC/SBI/2002/15 and FCCC/SBI/2003/INF.15 on GEF funding for national communica-tions.

works through its implementing agencies to provide support to non-Annex I Parties in the preparation of their national communications. To date, 80 per cent of activities relating to national communications have been implemented by the UNDP.[130]

Non-Annex I Parties that have submitted their initial national communications may submit proposals to the GEF for further funding (so-called 'top-up projects') to ensure that capacities gained through the national communication preparation process are not lost, but rather enhanced through capacity-building activities in priority areas.[131] Non-Annex I Parties may also apply for funding to prepare their second national communications based on the revised FCCC reporting guidelines, and additional guidance was given to the GEF at COP-8 confirming this.[132]

The Secretariat of the Convention facilitates the provision of financial and technical assistance to developing countries for the preparation of their national communications.[133] The Secretariat reports to the SBI on a regular basis on its activities relating to financial and technical assistance.[134] In the early years of the climate change regime, the Secretariat's activities in support of non-Annex I Parties were conducted under the rubric of the CC:INFO, CC:FORUM and CC:SUPPORT programmes.[135] These programmes, however, have now been largely mothballed, although the Secretariat activities have themselves continued. The Secretariat's support activities have also involved partnership with other IGOs, notably through the UNDP-based National Communication Support Unit (NCSU), which superseded the National Communication Support Programme (NCSP).[136] Launched in 1998, the NCSP was a joint initiative of the climate change Secretariat, UNDP, UNEP and the GEF, aimed at enhancing Parties' capacity to prepare good quality national communications, and ensuring the timely and cost-effective implementation of GEF projects in this regard. Regional workshops, preparation of technical manuals and a dedicated electronic mailing list and website are all in place to help achieve these aims.[137] The NCSP has assisted 130 non-Annex I Parties, through funding from the GEF ($2.1 million) and bilateral programmes ($1.3 million).

Another important initiative for the preparation of first national communications was CC:TRAIN. This was a UNDP programme, executed by UNITAR in

---

[130] NAI newsletter, edition 1.

[131] Decision 2/CP.4, paragraph 1 (d); see also GEF, 1999, paragraph 7.

[132] See Decision 6/CP.8, Additional guidance to an operating entity of the financial mechanism. Non-Annex I Parties whose funding proposals for second national communications have already been approved based on the initial guidelines will continue to receive funding.

[133] FCCC Article 8.2 (c).   [134] See, for example, FCCC/SBI/1999/INF.11.

[135] See Decision 3/CP.2, Secretariat activities relating to technical and financial support to Parties; and FCCC/SBI/1996/10.

[136] See www.undp.org/cc.   [137] See also FCCC/SBI/2002/15.

cooperation with the FCCC Secretariat, which was launched in 1994 and funded by the GEF with support from several Annex II Parties.[138] The programme disbursed just under $4 million[139] to fund workshops and other training packages, along with short courses on vulnerability and adaptation assessment at a small number of developing country universities. UNITAR is now establishing a follow-up programme to CC:TRAIN.[140]

Several Annex II Parties have also been particularly active in providing *bilateral* support to non-Annex I Parties for the preparation of their national communications. The Consultative Group of Experts on Non-Annex I Party national communications (CGE) highlighted several of these in its report to COP-7,[141] including the US Country Studies Programme, which has allocated approximately US $30 million to support over forty non-Annex I Parties.

4.4   *Review process*

Non-Annex I Party national communications are compiled and synthesised by the Secretariat in the same way as national communications from Annex I Parties, but are not subject to in-depth review. As national communications from non-Annex I Parties have come in gradually, the Secretariat has prepared a number of compilation and synthesis documents for initial national communications, each time providing updates based on new communications received.[142] The compilation and synthesis documents are considered by the SBI and the COP.[143]

4.5   *Consultative group of experts*

At COP-5 in 1999, Parties launched the Consultative Group of Experts on National Communications from Non-Annex I Parties (CGE), with the general objective of 'improving national communications from non-Annex I Parties'.[144] The CGE, which is composed of twenty-four experts drawn from the roster of experts, has the distinction of being the first specialised body set up under the climate change regime. Its representation is deliberately skewed in favour of developing countries, including five experts from each of the three predominantly non-Annex I Party regions and six from Annex I Parties including one from EITs. This formula unintentionally excludes non-Annex I Parties that are part of the Central and Eastern European group, such as Albania, Armenia and Georgia. Three experts from international organisations, selected by the Secretariat, also serve on the CGE; at

---

[138] FCCC/SBI/1999/INF.11.   [139] FCCC/SBI/2001/15.

[140] See www.unitar.org/ccp.   [141] FCCC/SBI/2001/15, section VIII.

[142] See, for example, FCCC/SBI/2002/16 (summary in FCCC/SBI/2002/8) and FCCC/SBI/2003/13.

[143] See, for example, Decisions 30/CP.7 and 2/CP.9.

[144] Decision 8/CP.5, Other matters relating to communications from Parties not included in Annex I, paragraph 3.

the time of writing, these included representatives of the NCSU and the IPCC Task Force on Inventories. Experts serve for two years, and for a maximum of two terms. Additional experts may also be drawn from the roster on an ad hoc basis when required, in consultation with the SBI Chair. The positions of Chair and rapporteur of the CGE rotate each year among the three *non-Annex I* regions, with the rapporteur succeeding as Chair. The Annex I Parties serving on the CGE cannot, therefore, serve as Chair or rapporteur. As of 2004, funding for meetings of the CGE, that is, to finance the participation of delegates from eligible developing countries and EITs, will be provided in the core programme budget.[145]

In accordance with its mandate and terms of reference, which were further elaborated at COP-7 and revised at COP-8,[146] the CGE provides a forum for experts, especially from developing countries, to exchange experiences with the national communication process and discuss ways of improving it. For the first two years of its work, it organised itself into six task groups, each responsible for examining a specific aspect of national communications (e.g. national circumstances, abatement options). The CGE has considered methodological issues, such as the difficulties faced by many non-Annex I Parties in using the IPCC methodological guidelines, as well as problems in developing emission factors and activity data appropriate for developing country situations. It has also reviewed existing financial and technical support activities and identified gaps, as well as opportunities for better coordination. In addition, the CGE has identified and assessed problems faced by non-Annex I Parties that have not yet submitted their initial national communications, and provided input to the development of the revised guidelines. The CGE has submitted recommendations to the SBI on such issues.[147] The CGE is continuing its work to improve national communications as most non-Annex I Parties start to prepare their second communications, with a mandate to provide technical advice and support to those Parties, including through regional workshops and training on the use of the revised FCCC reporting guidelines.

The CGE is institutionally linked to the LDC Expert Group, with at least two of its members – including one from an LDC and one from an Annex II Party – participating in both groups in order to ensure coordination on adaptation issues.[148]

---

[145] Decision 3/CP.8, Consultative Group of Experts on National Communications from Parties not included in Annex I to the Convention, paragraph 4.

[146] See Decision 8/CP.5, Annex; Decision 31/CP.7, Consultative Group of Experts on National Communications from non-Annex I Parties; and Decision 3/CP.8.

[147] For more details, see reports on the CGE's meetings: FCCC/SBI/2000/16 (first meeting), FCCC/SBI/2001/2 (second meeting), FCCC/SBI/2001/3 (third meeting), FCCC/SBI/2002/2 (fourth meeting) and FCCC/SBI/2002/15 (fifth meeting).

[148] Decision 31/CP.7, paragraph 2.

The CGE reports to the SBI on its work,[149] and its mandate and terms of reference are reviewed periodically by the COP. The next review is scheduled for COP-13 (2007).[150]

5   The Kyoto Protocol rules: non-Annex I Parties

Non-Annex I Parties also have reporting obligations under the Kyoto Protocol, which are incorporated in the set of general commitments for *all* Parties included in Article 10 (while these also apply to Annex I Parties, they are largely eclipsed by the more detailed obligations in Articles 5, 7 and 8). In general terms, non-Annex I Parties are thus committed to including information in their national communications on programmes and activities undertaken pursuant to Article 10[151] (see chapter 5).

Provisions in Article 10 relating to reporting of GHG inventories draw on the Convention and the initial FCCC reporting guidelines for non-Annex I Parties (and now also the revised guidelines). Non-Annex I Parties that are Parties to the Kyoto Protocol are thus required to formulate, where relevant and to the extent possible, cost-effective programmes to improve the quality of local emission factors, activity data and/or models that reflect the Party's specific socio-economic conditions. The Kyoto Protocol similarly draws on the initial FCCC reporting guidelines to require non-Annex I Parties to include in their national communications information on programmes containing measures that the Party believes contribute to addressing climate change and its adverse impacts, including the abatement of increases in GHG emissions, enhancement of removals by sinks, capacity-building and adaptation measures.[152]

The question of how reporting by non-Annex I Parties under the Kyoto Protocol will be conducted, and how this will be coordinated with reporting under the Convention, has not yet been addressed.

---

[149] Decision 3/CP.8, Annex, paragraph 11.   [150] Decision 3/CP.8, paragraph 3.

[151] KP Article 10.1 (f).

[152] Compare KP Article 10 (b) (ii) with Decision 10/CP.2, initial FCCC reporting guidelines for non-Annex I Parties, paragraph 15 (e).

Table 11.3 *Summary of FCCC reporting guidelines for Annex I Party national communications*[153]

Section	'Shall' include	'Should' include	'May' include
National circumstances	How national circumstances affect GHGs over time Any request for consideration under Article 4.6 or 4.10[154]	Relationship between national circumstances and GHGs, including disaggregated indicators	'Whatever information best describes national circumstances', e.g. population profile, energy resources, travel distances
GHG inventory	Summary information	Factors underlying emission trends	
Policies and measures ('PAMs')	PAMs in place to achieve commitments (not necessarily with GHG mitigation as primary objective) Reporting on PAMs by sector, subdivided by GHG Description of each principal PAM under standard headings, including: objectives of policy; type of instrument; implementation status How PAMs are modifying longer-term GHG trends	Distinction between adopted, planned and implemented PAMs Action under Article 4.2 e (ii)[155] Information on: energy, transport, industry, agriculture, forestry, waste, overall policy context How progress in mitigating emissions is monitored/evaluated Quantitative estimate of impacts of PAMs for a particular year	PAMs that are: innovative and/or replicable; adopted through regional/international efforts; cross-sectoral Strategies for sustainable development/other relevant policy objectives Inter-ministerial decision-making processes/bodies Costs and side-benefits Interaction with other national PAMs Any discontinued PAMs
Projections and total effects	'At a minimum', projection of future emissions 'with measures', including currently implemented and adopted PAMs Gas-by-gas projections for CO_2, CH_4, N_2O, PFCs/HFCs, SF_6 Aggregate projections for each sector and national total using GWPs Separate reporting of bunker fuel emissions Estimated *total* effect of *adopted and implemented* PAMs in terms of GHGs avoided/sequestered in 1995 and 2000	Quantitative projections for 2005, 2010, 2015, 2020 Brief explanation of model/approach used with references to detailed information, and any differences since previous communications Sensitivity of projections to assumptions Standard table on key underlying assumptions/variables (e.g. GDP)	'Without measures' and 'with additional measures' projections Projections of indirect GHGs and sulphur oxides Total expected effect of *planned* PAMs
Vulnerability assessment, impacts, adaptation	Expected impacts of climate change Outline of action under FCCC	'Encouraged to use' IPCC 1994 Technical Guidelines, UNEP Handbook 1998[156]	Coastal zone management plans, water resources, agriculture Research results on adaptation/vulnerability assessment
Financial resources and technology transfer	Details of measures under FCCC Indication of 'new and additional' resources provided and how determined as such Standard table on GEF contributions Details of assistance to particularly vulnerable DCs	Standard tables on multilateral (other than GEF), bilateral and regional contributions	How private sector technology transfer activities have been encouraged, and how these help meet commitments

	Bilateral/regional/other multilateral financial contributions
	Distinction between private/public sector technology transfer
	Standard table, where feasible, on technology transfer activities, including success/failure stories
	Activities for financing DC access to environmentally sound technologies
	Steps taken by governments to promote/facilitate/finance technology transfer, and support endogenous capacities/technologies of DCs
Research and systematic observation	Information on actions, addressing domestic/international activities, and capacity-building in developing countries
	General policy/funding
	Opportunities for/barriers to international data/information exchange, action to overcome barriers
	Information on highlights/innovations/significant efforts in climate research
	Summary of support for climate observing systems
Education, training and public awareness	Information on actions
	Information on: public information/education materials; resource/information centres; training programmes; participation in international activities
	Information on: public participation in preparation/domestic review of national communication; education; public information campaigns

153 See FCCC/CP/1999/7, p. 80–100.

154 Under Article 4.6, EITs are allowed 'a certain degree of flexibility' in the implementation of their commitments, including with regard to the selection of their base year (see chapter 5). Under Article 4.10, the situation of Parties with economies that are vulnerable to the adverse effects of the implementation of measures to respond to climate change is to be taken into consideration.

155 Article 4.2 (e) (ii) requires each Annex I Party to identify and periodically review its own policies/practices which encourage activities leading to greater GHG emissions than would otherwise occur.

156 IPCC, 1994, and UNEP, 1998.

Table 11.4 *Summary of FCCC reporting guidelines for non-Annex I Party national communications*[157]

Section	'Shall':	'Should':	'Are encouraged to':	'May':	Other
National circumstances		Description of development priorities/objectives/circumstances forming basis to address climate change and adverse impacts	Provide summary in tabular form	Features of geography/climate/economy affecting ability to address climate change Specific needs/concerns over adverse effects of climate change/impact of response measures Existing institutional arrangements for preparing NCs on a continuous basis	
National GHG inventory	Communicate GHG inventory to extent capacities permit For initial NC, for 1994 or 1990 For 2nd NC, for 2000 As appropriate and to extent possible, provide gas-by-gas estimates of CO_2, CH_4 and N_2O by sources/sinks	Use IPCC methodological guidelines If Party wishes to report aggregate emissions, use IPCC 100 year GWPs To extent possible, report bunker fuel emissions separately	Use country-specific/regional emission factors/activity data for key sources, or propose plans to develop them Formulate cost-effective programmes to develop/improve emission factors/activity data Use tables in Guidelines and apply IPCC good practice guidance	Other gases, e.g. SOx, in IPCC Guidelines Use different methods (tiers) from IPCC Guidelines to produce most accurate estimate	LDCs 'could' estimate their GHG inventory for years at their discretion

Describe procedures to
collect/archive data

As appropriate, information on
HFCs, PFCs, SF_6 and on CO, NOx,
NMVOCs

Report CO_2 fuel combustion
emissions using sectoral and
reference approaches

Explain any large differences

Information on: methodologies to
estimate emissions;
capacity-building needs;
uncertainty and methodologies
to estimate uncertainties

Include IPCC sectoral
tables/worksheets in both
electronic and hard copy

(cont.)

157 See Decision 17/CP.8, Guidelines for the preparation of national communications from Parties not included in Annex I to the Convention, Annex.

Table 11.4 (cont.)

Section	'Shall':	'Should':	'Are encouraged to':	'May':	Other
General description of steps taken/ envisaged to implement FCCC	Information on general description of steps taken/envisaged to implement FCCC, taking into account common but differentiated responsibilities, specific development priorities/objectives/ circumstances *Adaptation:* Information on general description of steps to formulate/ implement/ publish/ regularly update programmes with measures to facilitate adequate adaptation	*Adaptation:* Information on vulnerability and adaptation measures to meet specific needs/concerns	*Adaptation:* Use appropriate methodologies for evaluating adaptation strategies/measures to reflect national situation (e.g. FCCC decision tool compendium) Information on: scope of vulnerability/adaptation assessment, identifying most critical vulnerable areas; approaches/tools/ methodologies/scenarios to assess impacts/ vulnerability/adaptation and uncertainties Information on and, to extent possible, evaluation of, adaptation in key areas	Information on programmes containing measures to mitigate climate change/facilitate adequate adaptation *Adaptation:* Use appropriate guidelines/ methodologies to assess vulnerability/ adaptation to reflect national situation[158] Where relevant, report on use of policy frameworks (e.g. NAPAs) for developing/ implementing adaptation strategies/ measures	The extent to which developing countries will effectively implement their commitment to communicate this information will depend on the effective implementation by developed countries of their commitments on financial resources/ technology transfer

(cont.)

Mitigation: Information on general description of steps to formulate/ implement/publish/ regularly update programmes with mitigation measures

Any other information Party considers relevant

Mitigation: Use available/ appropriate methods to formulate/prioritise programmes containing mitigation measures

Should be done in framework of sustainable development objectives, including social/economic/ environmental factors

To extent capacities allow, information on measures/programmes contributing to mitigation, including, as appropriate, by key sectors on methodologies/ scenarios/results/ measures/ institutional arrangements

Mitigation: Use appropriate technical resources (e.g. IPCC reports) to assess mitigation programmes on various economic sectors

[158] E.g. IPCC, 1994, and UNEP, 1998.

Table 11.4 *(cont.)*

Section	'Shall':	'Should':	'Are encouraged to':	'May':	Other
Other information considered relevant to achievement of FCCC objective			As appropriate, information on steps to integrate climate change considerations into social/economic/ environmental policies Information on: technology transfer activities; research/systematic observation; research on programmes containing mitigation/adaptation measures & development of emission factors/ activity data; implementation of capacity-building activities (Decision 2/ CP.7); efforts to promote information sharing among/within countries/regions		Invited to provide information on activities relating to education, training, public awareness

Constraints/gaps, and related financial/ technical/ capacity needs	In accordance with national circumstances/ development priorities, describe: constraints/gaps and financial/ technical/capacity needs; activities to overcome gaps/ constraints to FCCC implementation and to preparing/ improving NCs on continuous basis / Provide information on financial/ technical support for NC preparation provided by themselves/GEF/ Annex II Parties and bilateral/ multilateral institutions	To extent capacities permit, list projects for financing (Article 12.4) / Information on: country-specific technology needs/assistance received from developed countries and financial mechanism; how assistance is used to support endogenous capacities/ technologies/ know-how; other relevant needs/ areas for capacity-building	Information on: opportunities for implementation of adaptation measures, including pilot/ demonstration projects; barriers to implementation of adaptation measures; how support programmes from Annex II Parties are meeting specific needs/concerns relating to vulnerability/ adaptation

12

Compliance

1   Introduction

This chapter explains provisions in the climate regime that facilitate compliance by Parties with their international commitments and, where necessary, correct cases of non-compliance. These provisions encompass traditional dispute settlement procedures and newer non-compliance procedures and mechanisms. Traditional dispute settlement provisions tend to be adversarial and bilateral in nature in that one state takes proceedings against another (or else suspends performance of its commitments), usually after an international obligation has been breached and damage to the environment has already occurred. For reasons explained in box 12.1, no Party to an MEA has actually used traditional dispute settlement procedures to correct non-compliance. Thus, since the earliest days of the negotiations on the Convention, the main emphasis in the climate regime, as with other MEAs, has been on the development of specialised non-compliance procedures.[1] After several years of intense negotiations, these efforts resulted in the adoption of procedures and mechanisms relating to compliance under the Kyoto Protocol at COP-7 which many observers regard as the most advanced compliance system in international environmental law.[2]

The essence of modern non-compliance approaches is that procedures to address compliance in a proactive, non-confrontational and preventative manner are established by the treaty body (such as the COP) which are then overseen by a specialised institution comprising state representatives from across the political spectrum. The emphasis is shifted from individual states seeking recourse to legal

[1] Werksman, forthcoming; Oberthür and Ott, 1999.
[2] UNEP, 2002; Wang and Wiser, 2002; Nollkaemper, 2002; and Lefeber, 2001.

proceedings to the multilateral oversight of compliance problems by international institutions which seek to facilitate compliance by providing incentives, such as the provision of advice and financial assistance, and, where non-compliance occurs, to enforce commitments by imposing consequences aimed at bringing the state concerned back into compliance. As explained in box 12.1, theoretical and practical developments from a broad range of disciplines and international agreements have supported the trend towards multilateral compliance procedures by generating valuable insights as to why states fail to comply with their international environmental commitments.[3] An additional motivation for deployment of new non-compliance techniques in climate change is that significant or persistent non-compliance would undermine confidence in the regime and have negative environmental consequences. Non-compliance in the climate change regime would also have broader negative social, economic and political impacts because the climate regime is an integral part of the UNCED agreements and failure to tackle climate change could undermine achievement of the Millennium Development Goals.[4] These considerations are particularly relevant in the case of the Protocol because of its binding quantitative commitments for Annex I Parties and because use of Kyoto's flexibility mechanisms must be underpinned by legal certainty.

This chapter is structured as follows. Section 2 explains key elements relevant to compliance, including the role of national compliance systems as well as aspects of international compliance systems such as reporting, review and verification. Section 3 explains the traditional dispute settlement provisions contained in the Convention and the Protocol. Section 4 explains non-compliance provisions developed pursuant to Article 13 of the Convention concerning the multilateral consultative process. Section 5 examines Decision 24/CP.7, which contains the procedures and mechanisms relating to compliance under the Kyoto Protocol in the form of an annex to this COP decision.

Box 12.1   Non-compliance procedures in other regimes

The traditional machinery of dispute settlement provides one way in which states can be held to account but it has never been used in an MEA to enforce compliance as its use in the environmental context raises many problems. Typically the obligation breached is not owed to a single state but to the international community as a whole because it addresses a 'global concern'

---

[3] Chayes and Chayes, 1995; Brown Weiss and Jabobson, 1998; and Mitchell, 1996.
[4] See chapter 17.

such as climate change. Additionally, dispute resolution may involve complex causation issues, such as disentangling natural from anthropogenically induced variability. Deciding who is responsible given that all countries emit GHG emissions is also difficult, as is assessing the nature of damages that might be awarded. Even if a case is 'won', legal remedies are often environmentally defective. They may result in an order of cessation (which may or may not be obeyed) and/or provide compensatory payments but these may not make good the damage that has already occurred. This is particularly problematic in climate change because damage could turn out to be significant, irreversible and is likely to be imposed on those least able to cope, including future generations.

To address these shortcomings, around a dozen MEAs now have specialised non-compliance procedures or are in the process of agreeing them.[5] A range of non-environmental instruments, principally the ILO, WTO, international human rights regimes, arms control agreements and the World Bank Panel, also provide examples of specialised procedures designed to promote and enforce compliance through non-judicial means. The non-compliance procedure adopted pursuant to the 1987 Montreal Protocol was particularly influential in the climate regime as it had already dealt with a number of 'cases' by the time the Protocol was adopted, particularly relating to EITs who are expected to face technical and capacity-related problems in meeting their Kyoto quantified commitments. These considerations and examples served as the backdrop to negotiations on Article 13 which called on COP-1 to design a multilateral consultative process (see box 12.2). The adoption of UNEP guidelines on compliance with, and enforcement of, MEAs in 2002 supports the further development of effective non-compliance procedures by MEAs. Given the advancements made by other MEAs, the failure to adopt the Multilateral Consultative Committee ten years after the adoption of the Convention will put the Convention in an almost unique position among modern MEAs in *not* having a non-compliance procedure.

2   Key concepts

Non-compliance is a broad term. In the climate change regime it could cover failure to meet a wide range of commitments. These commitments can be of a *substantive character* (e.g. keeping emissions below a certain limit) or of a *procedural*

[5] For an overview of compliance procedures in other regimes, see Holtwisch, 2003; Wiser, 1999b.

character (e.g. reporting or undertaking an environmental impact assessment).[6] It is also useful to think of a third category, *institutional obligations*, which refers to obligations implemented through the regime's institutions (e.g. the obligation of the COP to review the adequacy of commitments).[7]

Efforts to enforce compliance with substantive and procedural commitments can take place both at the national level and at the international level. Compliance at the national level concerns efforts a Party makes to ensure adherence of its legal entities and individuals to a Party's international commitments. This is often done by a Party enacting national environmental legislation and enforcing this domestically. This book does not address national compliance but it should be noted that national courts may increasingly be implicated in the implementation and resolution of international environmental law.[8] States do not themselves undertake many of the activities that give rise to GHG emissions which are linked to vital economic interests and reduction of which could potentially result in high compliance costs. Additionally, although responsibility to ensure national compliance with such legislation rests with each government, in practice many states allow 'citizen suits', encouraging private enforcement of their national legislation through national courts. Like most other MEAs, the Convention and the Protocol do not create provisions that would require Parties to develop national compliance systems. The rules on the Kyoto mechanisms do provide, however, that legal entities who participate in the mechanisms must do so under the authority of the Party concerned which must ensure the adherence of such entities to the rules agreed pursuant to the Protocol.[9]

This chapter does not address the relationship between governments and their citizens but is focused instead on the international level of the climate change regime which aims to secure compliance by Parties with their commitments under the FCCC and the Kyoto Protocol. At the international level, modern compliance procedures encompass three main components.[10] These are (i) reporting obligations, such as those relating to national inventories and national communications; (ii) verification of information provided, for example in climate change through review processes known as in-depth reviews undertaken by expert review teams (ERTs); and (iii) the assessment of compliance and deliberation of responses to non-compliance by specialised institutions, such as the Compliance Committee established under the procedures and mechanisms established by the Marrakesh Accords. The climate regime has probably the most advanced reporting and review provisions of any MEA and these are explained in detail in chapter 11. This chapter

---

[6] Sands, 1995b.   [7] Chapter 13 discusses obligations of the COP and COP/MOP.
[8] Nollkaemper, 2002; Bodansky and Brunnee, 1998.   [9] See chapter 6, section 4.
[10] Wang and Wiser, 2002.

focuses on the third component. It should be noted, however, that ERTs form a critical link between the verification aspects of the regime and the practical functioning of the compliance regime established under the Protocol.

3   Dispute settlement

3.1   *Scope and purpose*

Rules without institutions and procedures to enforce them create legal uncertainty. A foundational rule of international law is that states have an obligation to make reparations for breach of an international obligation.[11] To give practical effect to this rule, the international legal order establishes a number of general and issue-specific international legal and administrative bodies to provide states who consider their rights to have been breached with means of legal redress, such as arbitration and judicial settlement. Thus, although traditional dispute settlement techniques have certain disadvantages in the area of international environmental law, they do provide one way in which states can hold each other to account. Facilitative and preventative means of securing non-compliance are thus a useful corrective and supplement to traditional techniques, not a substitute. And in some cases, involving, for example, non-compliance by a rich state that remains unresponsive to 'facilitative' approaches, resource to traditional dispute settlement may, in fact, provide a more appropriate means of response. Article 14 of the Convention and Article 19 of the Protocol contain provisions allowing recourse to traditional means of dispute settlement.[12] Both instruments also include 'enabling provisions' prompting the adoption of non-traditional means of promoting compliance by their respective institutional bodies, the COP and the COP/MOP, which are set out in Article 13 of the Convention and in Article 18 of the Protocol, discussed in more detail below.

3.2   *Article 14 of the FCCC and Article 19 of the Protocol*

Article 19 of the Protocol states that 'the provisions of Article 14 of the Convention on settlement of disputes shall apply, *mutatis mutandis*, to this Protocol'. This reference means the essential features of Article 14 are incorporated into the Protocol. Such incorporation was envisaged in the Convention, which provides in Article 14.8 that Article 14 shall apply to any related legal instrument adopted by the COP unless the instrument provides otherwise.

UNFCCC   Article 14.1 provides that in the event of a dispute between any two or more Parties concerning the interpretation or application of the Convention, the Parties

---

[11]   See chapter 1, section 3.

[12]   Chapter 1, section 5.3 explains the role of the ICJ in international dispute settlement.

concerned shall seek a settlement of the dispute through negotiation or any other peaceful means of their own choice. This means a Party must first notify and try to 'iron out' its concerns with the other Party concerned before it becomes entitled to use more adversarial dispute settlement techniques. In many cases, this may result in differences being resolved, obviating the need for any further steps.

Article 14.2 gives a Party (with the exception of the EU as a REIO) a choice when ratifying, accepting, approving or acceding to the Convention, to declare to the Depository that in respect of any dispute concerning the interpretation or application of the Convention, it recognises as compulsory *ipso facto* and without special agreement, in relation to any Party accepting the same obligation, whether to accept the jurisdiction of the ICJ and/or arbitration in accordance with procedures to be adopted by the COP 'as soon as practicable'. A REIO may make a declaration with like effect in relation to arbitration. Articles 14.3 and 14.4 contain provisions concerning the ongoing legal validity and revocation of such declarations.

[handwritten margin note: Choice of: Accept JD of ICJ or arbitration]

If a Party is not going to use Article 14.2, twelve months have elapsed since its notification to the other Party that a dispute exists between them, and the Parties concerned have not been able to settle their dispute through negotiations or other peaceful means, Article 14.3 provides that the dispute 'shall be submitted, at the request of any of the parties to the dispute, to conciliation'. Article 14.6 provides that in this event

[handwritten margin note: Conciliation committe (not legally binding)]

> a conciliation commission shall be created upon the request of one of the parties to the dispute. The commission shall be composed of an equal number of members appointed by each party concerned and a chairman chosen jointly by the members appointed by each party. The commission shall render a recommendatory award, which the parties shall consider in good faith.

This means that the result of the conciliation would not be legally binding but it has to be considered by the Parties. Article 14.7 provides that 'additional procedures relating to conciliation shall be adopted by the COP as soon as practicable, in an annex on conciliation'. In sum, Article 14 provides for optional recourse to the ICJ and/or arbitration but for *mandatory* recourse, at the request of *one* Party to a dispute, to non-binding conciliation.[13]

Because the focus has been on development of specialised compliance procedures, the COP has not adopted the annexes setting out procedures for arbitration mentioned in Article 14.2 (b) nor the one on conciliation mentioned in Article 14.6. It should be noted, however, that because the conciliation procedure is already set out in the Convention, it can be invoked without 'additional procedures' being

---

[13] Bodansky, 1993: p. 549.

adopted. In the absence of the adoption of the multilateral consultative process (MCP) elaborated under Article 13 (discussed below), the conciliation procedure provides one way Parties can raise concerns about compliance with Convention commitments. The 'state-to-state' nature of the traditional means of dispute settlement means that non-state actors cannot trigger any of the means of redress listed in Article 14.

4   Non-compliance procedures under the Convention

4.1   *Multilateral consultative process*

Article 13 of the Convention required the first session of the COP to 'consider the establishment of a multilateral consultative process, available to Parties on their request, for the resolution of questions regarding the implementation of the Convention'.

This provision was included because negotiators agreed that a forward-looking, non-adversarial, facilitative rather than punitive procedure, similar to the one adopted by the ozone regime, would be a helpful feature of the climate regime. Inclusion of Article 13 provided comfort to delegations who had accepted the gradual whittling down of the oversight functions and mandates of the COP and SBI that a dedicated procedure, involving a specialised group with more technical resources and time to assess the compliance of individual Parties, would soon emerge. As expected, COP-1 established an ad hoc group (AG13) to design the MCP. This group met six times in 1995–1998, culminating in COP-4 approving the text of the MCP prepared by AG13 with the exception of two paragraphs.[14] Although the MCP has not been adopted by the COP and is thus not formally part of the rules, institutions and procedures of the climate regime, all of the text containing its mandate and modalities has been agreed by Parties except for two paragraphs relating to representation. Box 12.2 provides a brief history of the MCP and disputed paragraphs. The key features of the agreed text on the MCP are:

- The establishment of a Multilateral Consultative Committee (MCC) as a standing committee meeting not less than once a year;
- The objective of the MCC is provision of advice or assistance, promotion of understanding of the Convention and prevention of disputes on request to those entitled to 'trigger' its mandate;
- The process is to be facilitative, cooperative, non-confrontational, transparent, timely and non-judicial;

---

[14] Decision 10/CP.4. See also FCCC/AG13/1998/2, Report of AG13 on its sixth session.

- Questions of implementation can be 'triggered' by a Party or Parties concerning their own implementation, or that of others, and by the COP (not by the Secretariat or in-depth review teams);
- Outcomes are to be conclusions and recommendations for the Party(ies) to consider and could include measures the MCC thinks are necessary for effective implementation; and
- Due process requirements are to give opportunities for comment to the Party concerned.

Box 12.2   The development of the Multilateral Consultative Process

After its establishment by COP-1, AG13 generated wide-ranging discussions and insights, including from organisations and experts with experience of other non-compliance procedures.[15] Parallel negotiations on the Kyoto Protocol compliance procedures were a complicating factor because the design of the MCP would differ quite markedly if Parties agreed to binding targets and if these were to be adopted through an amendment of the Convention or, as it turned out, a protocol. To ensure dialogue between these two processes, COP-2 invited AG13 to continue its work but to respond to any advice sought by the AGBM on MCP-related issues.[16] Although the AG13 continued its work in the run up to COP-3, by 1997 Parties' views had shifted to focusing on the possible design of compliance procedures under the Kyoto Protocol. COP-3 requested AG13 to complete its work by COP-4.[17] At its final meeting in June 1998, AG13 was able to agree all outstanding aspects of its work except for the question of representation on the proposed Multilateral Consultative Committee. The disagreement turned on G-77/China arguing for 'equitable geographic representation', which would have given developing countries more say, and developed countries wanting a politically equal balance between Annex I and non-Annex I Parties. COP-4 approved the text of the MCP prepared by AG13 with the exception of bracketed text about representation.[18] COP-5 was asked to review these issues with a view to adopting an MCP 'when those issues' have been resolved, but this has never happened due to lack of interest in view of more pressing interest in developing compliance procedures under the Protocol.

---

[15] Decision 20/CP.1.   [16] Decisions 4/CP.2 and 5/CP.2.   [17] Decision 14/CP.3.
[18] Decision 10/CP.4. See also FCCC/AG13/1998/2, Report of AG13 on its sixth session.

4.2   *Compliance assessment by the COP*

The Convention's substantive rules, and its institutional machinery, are structured to limit the extent to which international scrutiny can be exercised by regime institutions over a Party's observance of its Convention commitments and, absent the MCC, there are no dedicated procedures now in place for the COP to examine individual cases of non-compliance.

Article 7.2 (e), for example, requires the COP to 'assess, on the basis of all information made available to it . . . the implementation of the Convention by the Parties, the overall effects of the measures taken pursuant to the Convention, in particular environmental, economic and social effects as well as their cumulative impacts and the extent to which progress towards the objective of the Convention is being achieved'. This use of 'softer' words such as the replacement of 'monitor' by 'assess' and 'implementation' in place of 'compliance' was intended to check international oversight of individual Parties' fulfilment of commitments.[19] Notwithstanding this softer wording, Article 7.2 (e) can support greater international scrutiny by the COP over each Party's compliance, should this be agreed.[20]

To date, however, Article 7.2 (e) has formed the basis for the COP's rather general consideration of Parties' inventory data and national communications. In practice, the SBI has only had time to subject national communications to a brief and general debate in an open SBI plenary faced with a heavy agenda.[21] Thus, the extent to which the COP has actually reviewed Parties' compliance track records has been limited. Should it decide to play a greater role in assessing compliance by Parties (which it must do essentially by agreement of all Parties as majority-voting on this issue is not possible), Article 7.2 (g) makes clear that the COP can make 'recommendations' on any matter necessary for the implementation of the Convention.[22]

5   Compliance procedures and mechanisms under the Kyoto Protocol

5.1   *Overview*

The 'procedures and mechanisms relating to compliance under the Kyoto Protocol' annexed to Decision 24/CP.7 (hereinafter the 'Kyoto compliance procedures') are probably the strongest and institutionally most sophisticated non-compliance procedures adopted by any MEA to date. The quasi-judicial character of the Enforcement Branch of the Compliance Committee is markedly different in character from the kind of assistance and early warning functions that will be

---

[19] Bodansky, 1993: pp. 547–8.   [20] Bodansky, 1993: p. 547.
[21] See chapters 11 and 13.   [22] See chapter 13, section 2.1.

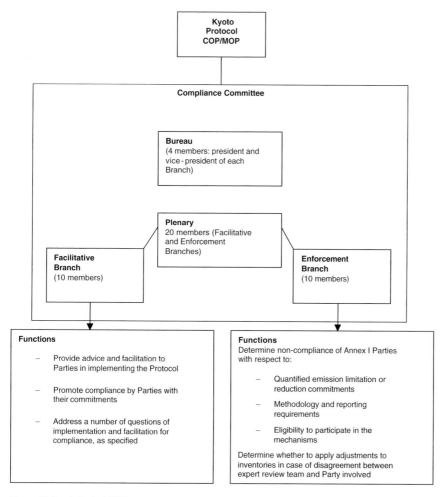

Source: McKenzie R. et al. 2003.

Fig. 12.1   Structure and functions of the Compliance Committee

undertaken by the Facilitative Branch. The acceptance of these compliance procedures by all Parties is thus a remarkable achievement for the climate change
regime. Figure 12.1 provides an overview of the structure and functions of the
Compliance Committee that will oversee the Kyoto compliance procedures.

The development of the Kyoto compliance procedures in the light of the mandates provided by Articles 16 and 18 of the Protocol is set out in box 12.3, which
also touches on the legally binding character of consequences, an issue which is
explained further at the end of this section. Because the assessment of compliance
with Article 3.1 will actually take place some time after 2015, and accounting rules
relating to adjustments, for example, have yet to be tested, the focus of attention

here is on the functions which need to be executed earlier in time, particularly those relating to assessment of eligibility for the Kyoto mechanisms. This section is structured to follow as closely as possible the structure of Decision 24/CP.7.

5.2   *Objective*

The objective of the Kyoto compliance procedures 'is to facilitate, promote and enforce compliance with the commitments under the Protocol'. This objective signals clearly the desire to provide proactive, assistance-based forms as well as the intent to hold Parties to account through enforcement. The use of the word 'under' is highly significant because it is intended to capture legally rules agreed pursuant to commitments defined in the Protocol by way of COP decisions, such as those set out in the Marrakesh Accords.

Box 12.3 Development of compliance procedures under the Kyoto Protocol[23]

The Kyoto Protocol was based on the assumption that the work of AG13 would result in the establishment of an MCP under Article 13 of the Convention. Article 16 of the Protocol accordingly provides that the COP/MOP shall 'consider the application of, and modify as appropriate' the MCP established by the COP and that the MCP will 'operate without prejudice to the procedures and mechanisms established in accordance with Article 18 [of the Protocol]'. Article 18 provides that COP/MOP-1 shall

> approve appropriate and effective procedures and mechanisms to determine and to address cases of non-compliance with the provisions of this Protocol, including through the development of an indicative list of consequences, taking into account the cause, type, degree and frequency of non-compliance. Any procedures and mechanisms under this Article entailing binding consequences shall be adopted by means of an amendment to this Protocol.

Inclusion of Articles 16 and 18 gives clues about Parties' thinking in 1997, reflecting basic agreement that mechanisms and procedures that might be appropriate for the Protocol would need to be radically different in character from those likely to be provided by the proposed MCC under the Convention. Inclusion of the second sentence in Article 18 requiring binding

---

[23] On the history of the development of these procedures, see Lefeber, 2001; Wang and Wiser, 2002; Werksman, 1998; Australian Department of Foreign Affairs and Trade, 2000.

consequences to be adopted in the form of an amendment signalled, however, that Parties were unwilling to concede at Kyoto whether such procedures and mechanisms *should* entail binding consequences and, even to the extent this was agreed, would still wish to reserve their individual rights as sovereign states on whether such consequences should be of potential application to them.

By 1998, the agreement at COP-4 to wind up AG13 and to establish a joint working group (JWG) to prepare procedures and mechanisms relating to compliance under the Protocol was premised on the fact that all Parties to the Convention would become Parties to the Protocol and therefore political effort need not be expended on completing the outstanding issues that prevented establishment of the MCC under the Convention.[24] In hindsight this assumption has proved too optimistic and means that there is now no dedicated compliance procedure in place to hold Parties to the Convention that are not going to ratify the Protocol to account.

5.3   *Compliance Committee*

The Compliance Committee will be established pursuant to the procedures and mechanisms relating to compliance under the Kyoto Protocol adopted under the Marrakesh Accords.[25] Establishment of the Compliance Committee will take place at COP/MOP-1. The Committee is a standing body. It has the authority to take a range of decisions applicable to individual Parties, including a range of consequences to be applied to Parties found in non-compliance. It is likely to meet at least twice each year, probably together with the SBs. The Committee itself is composed of four bodies: a plenary, bureau, Facilitative Branch and Enforcement Branch.

5.3.1   Plenary

The plenary's functions include reporting to the COP/MOP on the Committee's activities, applying the general policy guidance received from the COP/MOP and submitting administrative and budgetary matters to the COP/MOP. Additionally, the plenary is responsible for developing any further rules of procedure that may be needed, including on confidentiality, conflict of interest and submission of information by IGOs and NGOs, and translation. The plenary of the Compliance

---

[24] Decision 8/CP.4.
[25] Decision 24/CP.7. Unless otherwise stated, all references relate to the Annex to this Decision, which sets out the compliance procedures and mechanisms.

Committee is made up of twenty members, ten from each Branch (accompanied by their alternates), with the Chair of each Branch serving as Co-Chairs of the plenary.

5.3.2   Bureau

The bureau of the Committee comprises four persons: the Chair and Vice-Chair of each of the two Branches. The two Branches are called upon to 'interact and cooperate in their functioning', and the bureau may designate one or more members of one Branch to contribute to the work of the other (on a non-voting basis). The tasks of the bureau are likely to be akin to those of the COP and subsidiary body bureaux in terms of being restricted to organisational and procedural matters, the most important being deciding to which of the two Branches to allocate questions of implementation upon their receipt by the Committee (see below).

5.3.3   Election of members/Chairs

The members of the Compliance Committee are to be formally elected by the COP/MOP. As with the other two Kyoto Protocol bodies, each member can be accompanied by an alternate, elected from the same group. The addition of alternates provides the opportunity for a wider group of Parties to learn about, and possibly be involved in, the Committee's work, especially if the workload mounts, as has happened in the work of the CDM where a membership of ten was simply too small a number to handle all the tasks given to the Board.

The two Branches are each made up of ten members, using the same membership formula as the EB/CDM (that is, one member from each of the regional groups plus the small island developing states, plus two each from Annex I and non-Annex I Parties). This means that there is a majority of non-Annex I Parties, which was the cause of deep concern for Annex I Parties, given that the work of the Enforcement Branch of the Compliance Committee will be focused on their commitments and not those of non-Annex I Parties.[26] The view that all Parties to a multilateral environmental treaty are entitled to be represented in bodies assessing compliance with the treaty prevailed, not least because developing countries are the most vulnerable to the impacts of climate change and thus have as much stake as the Annex I Parties in ensuring impartial adherence by all Parties to the Protocol.

A Chair and Vice-Chair are elected annually, one from an Annex I Party and one from a non-Annex I Party, with the chairing of each Branch rotating annually

---

[26] The US was particularly opposed to granting a majority to non-Annex I Parties in the Compliance Committee, and it is unlikely that this formula would have been adopted had the US been intending to become a Party to the Kyoto Protocol and actively participated in negotiations on the Bonn Agreements and Marrakesh Accords.

between these two groups of Parties. Committee members and alternates are required to serve in their 'individual capacities' and have 'recognized competence relating to climate change and in relevant fields such as the scientific, technical, socio-economic or legal fields'. These criteria are essential for safeguarding the independence and integrity of the compliance bodies. In electing the members of the Facilitative Branch, the COP/MOP is called upon to seek to ensure that these various fields are reflected among its members in a balanced manner. With regard to the Enforcement Branch, the COP/MOP must be satisfied that the members have legal experience. As with other elected posts, Parties will be required to give active consideration to the nomination of women for the Compliance Committee to improve the gender balance of FCCC and KP elected institutions.[27]

Members may not serve for more than two terms of four years; this longer term of office than for the other two limited membership bodies under the Kyoto Protocol is aimed at building up institutional experience in dealing with compliance issues.

5.3.4   Compliance Committee procedures and voting

The basic procedures of the Compliance Committee are set out in the Kyoto compliance procedures and include rules concerning a quorum, the adoption of decisions and frequency of meetings. A quorum of three-fourths is required, specifically for the 'adoption of decisions'; the rules are silent on whether such a quorum also applies to the *convening* of meetings.

The voting rule for the Compliance Committee incorporates the concept of a double majority. If all efforts at reaching consensus have been exhausted, decisions may be adopted by a three-fourths majority of members present and voting, but decisions of the Enforcement Branch require, in addition, a majority of Annex I and non-Annex I Parties. The safeguard of double majority voting for the Enforcement Branch was included to allay concerns of some Annex I Parties that they might be subject to unfair or politically motivated decisions, given that its membership is based on equitable geographic representation which provides a simple majority for developing countries.[28] Although taking decisions (called determinations in the Kyoto compliance procedures) is important, so is the ability to block decisions. In this respect it should be borne in mind that, so far as the Enforcement Branch is concerned, any two Annex I Party members could, in theory, block a decision from being taken. The ability to block a decision is especially relevant in the context of mechanisms eligibility where eligibility is initially *presumed* unless a (positive) determination is made otherwise.[29] The only safeguard against one set of Parties

---

[27] Decision 36/CP.7, and chapter 13, p. 451.   [28] Wang and Wiser, 2002: p. 190.

[29] See chapter 6, sections 3.3 to 4.10.

using their voting right in a political manner is the ability of all members to act in their individual capacity as mandated by the Committee's rules to ensure its integrity as a quasi-judicial body.

5.4   *Facilitative Branch*

The Facilitative Branch is responsible for providing advice and facilitation to Parties in implementing the Protocol. In addition, the Facilitative Branch serves to promote compliance with the Kyoto Protocol and provides an early warning system for potential non-compliance. The mandate of the Facilitative Branch basically covers everything that is not expressly assigned to the Enforcement Branch. Because matters relating to Article 3.14 (impacts of response measures) had been particularly contested, for extra clarity the mandate of the Facilitative Branch states that they are within its mandate;[30] likewise, information demonstrating supplementarity in relation to the use of the Kyoto mechanisms.[31]

As part of its 'early warning function' the Facilitative Branch will be responsible for providing advice and facilitation for compliance with:

- Commitments under Article 3, paragraph 1, of the Protocol, prior to the beginning of the relevant commitment period and during that commitment period;
- Commitments under Article 5, paragraphs 1 and 2, of the Protocol, prior to the beginning of the first commitment period; and
- Commitments under Article 7, paragraphs 1 and 4, of the Protocol prior to the beginning of the first commitment period.

Because it applies to developed and developing country Parties, the Facilitative Branch is required to take into account the principle of common but differentiated responsibilities and respective capabilities in the application of one or more of the following consequences:

- Provision of advice and facilitation of assistance to individual Parties regarding the implementation of the Protocol;
- Facilitation of financial and technical assistance to any Party concerned, including technology transfer and capacity-building from sources other than those established under the Convention and the Protocol for the developing countries;
- Facilitation of financial and technical assistance, including technology transfer and capacity-building, taking into account Article 4, paragraphs 3, 4 and 5, of the Convention; and

---

[30] See chapter 9, section 3.1.   [31] See chapter 6, section 3.3.

- Formulation of recommendations to the Party concerned, taking into account Article 4, paragraph 7, of the Convention.

In the early years of the regime it is very likely that much of the Facilitative Branch's work will focus on ensuring that Annex I Parties that are EITs are able to meet their reporting and review requirements. This may mean the Facilitative Branch having to consider how to arrange 'facilitation' of financial resources 'outside' the financial mechanism of the regime which, of course, will have impacts for developing countries.[32]

5.5   *Enforcement Branch*

The Enforcement Branch, for its part, is responsible for determining whether each Annex I Party is in compliance with:

- Its quantified emission limitation or reduction commitment under Article 3;
- The methodological and reporting requirements under Articles 5.1, 7.1 and 7.4; and
- The eligibility requirements for the flexible mechanisms under Articles 6, 12 and 17.

It is also responsible for authorising the application of adjustments to Annex I inventories in the event of a dispute between a Party and the ERT.[33] The compilation and accounting databases for accounting of the assigned amount, which is to be maintained by the Secretariat according to Decision 19/CP.7, will take into account any corrections to be made as a resolution of questions of implementation raised by ERTs once these have been determined by the Enforcement Branch.

The degree of discretion given to the Enforcement Branch to impose consequences has been limited to ensure legal certainty and decrease the chance of political interference.[34] Thus, the consequences to be 'automatically' applied by the Enforcement Branch are defined tightly to suit the type of commitment that has not been fulfilled. Failure to meet Article 5.1, 5.2 and 7.1 requirements will lead to a declaration of non-compliance and a requirement to submit an action plan indicating how and by when a Party intends to remedy the failing. Failure to meet mechanisms eligibility means a general suspension from mechanisms eligibility but the precise limitation on what kinds of transactions are not allowed depends on the eligibility requirement for particular mechanisms.[35] Non-compliance with

---

[32] See chapter 10, section 2.2.   [33] See chapters 5 and 11.   [34] Werksman, forthcoming.
[35] See chapter 6.

Article 3.1 will require the following: deduction of 1.3 tonnes for every tonne over-emitted from a Party's assigned amount for the next commitment period, plus a detailed compliance plan indicating how the Party will meet its new target and inability to transfer under Article 17 emissions trading. The application of all such consequences must be aimed at the restoration of compliance to ensure environmental integrity and to provide an incentive to comply.

5.6   *Submissions*

The question of submissions relates to who has standing before the Compliance Committee in respect of enforcement and the kind of information that must be supplied to trigger action. The most significant trigger source is likely to be reports containing questions of implementation raised by ERTs which have the right to send these to the Compliance Committee without political intervention from a Party. The procedures provide that the Committee shall receive through the Secretariat, questions of implementation indicated in reports of ERTs under Article 8 of the Protocol,[36] together with any written comments by the Party which is subject to the report. Additionally, questions of implementation can also be submitted by:

- Any Party with respect to itself; or
- Any Party with respect to another Party, supported by corroborating information.

The Committee shall also receive all other final ERT reports. Although NGOs cannot be 'triggers' of enforcement action in their own right, they are likely to be critical to the effective functioning of the compliance procedures as they will scrutinise self-reported data by Parties and will send discrepant information to the relevant branch as well as make such information public. The Secretariat is not allowed to 'trigger' enforcement because some Parties thought this might undermine its role as an independent and neutral body at the service of all Parties.

5.7   *Allocation and preliminary examination*

This important function will be undertaken by the bureau to ensure that a question of implementation is supported by 'sufficient information', is not *de minimi* or ill-founded and is based on Protocol requirements. These thresholds permit a certain degree of subjectivity: thus the preliminary examination and allocation stage is likely to be of great significance, especially in mechanisms eligibility cases, where eligibility is presumed till withdrawn. There seems to be no procedural check of any kind on the bureau's decisions on these issues (the plenary

---

[36] See chapter 11.

hears reports from each branch but not from the bureau about the latter's decisions). Because the general procedures which contain provision on transparency apply *after* this preliminary stage, it is not clear how the integrity of this stage will be secured, suggesting this may be an area for the Committee, acting perhaps on the basis of COP/MOP guidance, to elaborate additional procedural rules requiring, inter alia, the bureau to list questions they have not decided to proceed with as well as to give reasons for their decisions.

5.8   *General procedures*

These set out general requirements designed to secure due process, transparency and legal certainty, including by defining, inter alia, upon what basis a branch may make a determination, allow a Party to be represented and given opportunities to comment, allow competent NGOs/IGOs with relevant information to make factual and technical information available, and make information available to it publicly available, bearing in mind any confidentiality rules.

5.9   *Procedures for the Enforcement Branch*

Because of the gravity of the commitments it is dealing with, and the consequential need for efficiency and timeliness, time-bound general procedures have been developed for the Enforcement Branch. In addition, to make things speedier still, expedited procedures have been included where questions of implementation relate to mechanisms eligibility requirements.

Depending on resources and workload, these time constraints may set difficult challenges for the Enforcement Branch.[37] The procedures allow a Party that has been suspended to speed up restoration of its mechanisms eligibility status. Such a Party can reapply directly to the Committee or to an ERT. COP-8 agreed more detailed rules relating to reporting and review of information to enable this to happen.[38]

5.10   *Appeals*

To shield the Committee's work from political interference, appeals to the COP/MOP can only be made on the grounds of due process in relation to the work of the Enforcement Branch. Should the COP/MOP decide to override the decision of the Enforcement Branch, it would require a three-fourths majority of Parties present and voting. A decision of the Branch still stands until overridden. Even if an appeal is successful, the COP/MOP can only refer the decision back to the Enforcement Branch for reconsideration.

[37] See chapter 6, sections 4.7 to 4.10.   [38] See chapter 11.

5.11   *Role of COP/MOP*

The COP/MOP's role is confined to considering the reports of the Compliance Committee on its work, providing general policy guidance to the Committee, and adopting decisions on administrative and budgetary matters. It may, in limited cases, hear appeals (discussed above) but it otherwise cannot intervene in individual cases.

5.12   *Additional period for fulfilling commitments*

Often called 'true-up', the additional period for fulfilling Article 3.1 commitments is intended to give Annex I Parties a final chance of ensuring they meet their quantitative commitments on the basis of the final set of checks and figures completed by the ERTs.[39] The additional period lasts until 'the hundredth day after the date set by the Conference of the Parties serving as the meeting of the Parties to the Protocol for the completion of the expert review process under Article 8 of the Protocol for the last year of the commitment period'. A Party can only be found out of compliance with its Article 3.1 commitments after that 100th day (which is likely to be mid-2015), i.e. some eighteen years after Kyoto was adopted.

5.13   *Legally binding nature and mode of adoption*

Decision 24/CP.7 contains the procedures and mechanisms relating to compliance under the Kyoto Protocol in the form of an Annex to this COP decision which recommends their adoption to the first session of the COP/MOP. Thus, entry into force of the Kyoto Protocol is required before COP/MOP-1 can take up the issue of whether the Kyoto compliance procedures entail legally binding consequences, and if so, whether these need to be agreed in the form of an amendment, as stipulated in Article 18 of the Protocol, or whether the COP/MOP will consider another way of adopting the Kyoto compliance procedures. The legally binding character of consequences to be applied by the Enforcement Branch, and the related issue of mode of adoption of the package of procedures, held up acceptance of the Bonn Agreements at COP-6 and then the Marrakesh Accords at COP-7.

Due to concerns expressed by a small number of JUSCANNZ Parties, Decision 24/CP.7 reiterates that it is the prerogative of the COP/MOP to decide on the legal form of the procedures and mechanism relating to compliance. Decision 15/CP.7 concerning the Kyoto Protocol's flexibility mechanisms now requires all Parties to accept the authority of the Enforcement Branch to provide oversight of the eligibility conditions for the mechanisms.

---

[39] See chapter 11.

Adopting the Kyoto compliance procedures in the form of an amendment to the Protocol would generate the highest legal certainty but only if the amendment were to be ratified by all Parties more or less contemporaneously, thus providing a uniform legal regime. But if ratification proceeds on different timescales or some choose never to ratify, some Parties may be legally bound by the amendment and others not. Such a differentiated regime is difficult to reconcile with Annex I Parties being bound by legally binding targets defined for 2008–2012 which also require enforcement mechanisms of comparable legal robustness to be available on equivalent timescales. Additionally, because accounting of transfers and acquisition under the Protocol involves all Annex I Parties, all must adhere to uniform accounting modalities which must be strictly and consistently enforced to guarantee environmental integrity.[40]

The adoption of Kyoto compliance procedures by way of a COP/MOP decision until such time as an amendment enters into force might be one way to address some of these concerns, because a COP/MOP decision could have immediate effect and be applicable to all Protocol Parties. Because a COP/MOP decision may not be regarded as legally binding, the legal character of the consequences might be considered to be political. In this context, however, it should be noted that the extent to which something is considered 'legally binding' in international law is ultimately an expression of political will. Thus it will be up to Parties whether or not they choose to regard a COP/MOP decision as having only political consequences or legally binding consequences.

---

[40] See chapter 6, section 4.

13

Institutions

1   Introduction

International oversight of the implementation and development of treaty rules takes places through a set of institutions established by the climate change regime. The Conference of the Parties, the supreme body of the Convention, sits at the apex. It is supported by two subsidiary bodies (SBs): the Subsidiary Body for Scientific and Technological Advice (SBSTA) and the Subsidiary Body for Implementation (SBI). Influenced by concerns of sovereignty and institutional economy, Parties decided that the COP would serve as the meeting of the Parties to the Kyoto Protocol – the COP/MOP – while the two subsidiary bodies would also serve the Protocol. A striking feature of the climate change regime since the adoption of the Marrakesh Accords has been the development of an increasingly dense institutional network, with the designation of several specialised bodies with limited membership mandated to work on specific issues under both the Convention and the Kyoto Protocol. This chapter explains the institutions of the climate change regime (illustrated in figures 13.1 (Convention) and 13.2 (Kyoto Protocol)), including their composition, mandates, modus operandi, and likely operation under the Kyoto Protocol. In some cases, notably the specialised bodies, readers are referred to a more detailed discussion in other chapters of this book. It should be noted that the Secretariat, another body established by the Convention, plays a vitally important role in ensuring the smooth functioning of the regime's institutional machinery as discussed in this chapter. Its role, however, which is essentially supportive rather than policy-making, is taken up in chapter 15.

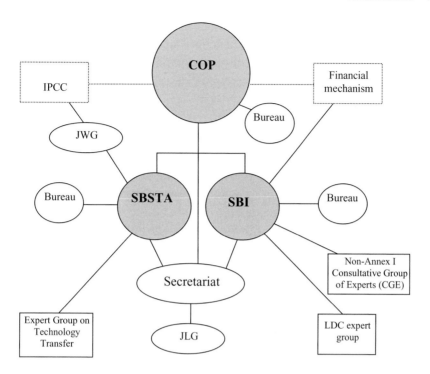

.... Independent bodies that provide services to the climate change process

JLG: Joint Liaison Group (FCCC, CBD, UNCCD) (officers and secretariats)
JWG: Joint Working Group (officers and secretariats)

Fig. 13.1   FCCC institutions

2   **FCCC institutions**

2.1   *The Conference of the Parties*

The establishment of an international institution by states signals acceptance that the pursuit of a shared goal is better achieved through a permanent
mechanism to facilitate cooperation. The way in which the mandate, functions
and modalities of an international institution are defined is critical for determining the kinds of actions that institution can undertake, whether or not its
actions create binding obligations for the creating states, and the nature of the
legal relations it can enter into. This section deals with the mandate, functions and
operational modalities of the Convention COP. It is important to note that these
elements are interrelated and must be assessed together, in the light of current
practices, to deduce the legal ambit of the COP vis-à-vis the rights and obligations

incumbent on Parties and other actors and institutions involved in the climate change regime. Much of the explanatory analysis below is also of relevance to understanding the institutions created by the Kyoto Protocol, although for the purposes of clarity these are addressed in a separate section later in this chapter.

2.1.1   Mandate and functions

Article 7.1 of the Convention states that 'A Conference of the Parties is hereby established.' According to the chapeau of Article 7.2, as the 'supreme body of this Convention' the COP has overall responsibility to keep under regular review the implementation of the Convention and any related legal instruments adopted by the COP. The chapeau further provides that the COP is entitled to make, within its mandate, decisions necessary to promote the effective implementation of the Convention. The following subparagraphs (a) to (m) of Article 7.2 list specific functions the COP should undertake to fulfil its role thus defined. This list is not exhaustive, with the COP required to undertake other functions specified elsewhere in the Convention. Additionally, a very important 'catch-all' or 'savings' clause has been included at Article 7.2 (m), enabling the COP to exercise any other functions required for the achievement of the Convention. This clause gives the COP broad legal powers ensuring the COP's legal authority will not be vulnerable to *ultra vires* type challenges.[1] This is important because the Convention's Rules of Procedure[2] provide that Parties have the right to challenge its competence.[3] The savings clause enables the COP to take up new functions as needs arise, limiting greatly the circumstances justifying recourse to the right to challenge provided for in the Rules.

Article 7.2 (a) requires the COP to 'periodically examine the obligations of the Parties and the institutional arrangements under the Convention, in the light of the objective of the Convention, the experience gained in its implementation and the evolution of scientific and technological knowledge'. No time-frame for the frequency of such reviews is specified in this general provision. However, several specific, time-bound reviews were also built into the Convention for the COP to undertake, including review of the obligations of Annex I Parties, and review of the lists of Parties contained in the Convention's two annexes.[4]

Article 7.2 (b) and (c) assigns to the COP two specific tasks of 'promot[ing] and facilitat[ing] the exchange of information on measures adopted by the Parties to address climate change and its effects' and 'facilitat[ing], at the request of two or more Parties, the coordination of measures adopted by them to address climate change and its effects'. In both cases, the COP must do so 'taking into account

---

[1] Bodansky, 1993: p 534.   [2] FCCC/CP/1996/2: see chapter 14.   [3] Rule 35.
[4] FCCC Article 4.2 (d) and (f) respectively. For more on these reviews, see chapter 18

the differing circumstances, responsibilities and capabilities of the Parties and their respective commitments under the Convention'. The COP has acted upon Article 7.2 (b) in the context of work on policies and measures[5] but, to date, there has been no request under Article 7.2 (c).

Article 7.2 (d) mandates the COP to 'promote and guide . . . the development and periodic refinement of comparable methodologies . . . inter alia, for preparing inventories of greenhouse gas emissions . . . and removals . . . and for evaluating the effectiveness of measures to limit the emissions and enhance the removals of these gases'. This is an area on which the COP regularly takes decisions, including the endorsement of methodological guidelines developed by the IPCC.[6]

Article 7.2 (e) requires the COP to 'assess, on the basis of all information made available to it . . . the implementation of the Convention . . . , the overall effects of the measures taken pursuant to the Convention, in particular environmental, economic and social effects as well as their cumulative impacts and the extent to which progress towards the objective of the Convention is being achieved'. This forms the basis for the COP's regular consideration of Parties' inventory data and national communications, as well as other types of information, such as GEF and IPCC reports. The extent to which the COP has actually reviewed the effects of Parties' implementation has been greatly restricted by political disagreements. Article 7.2 (g) makes clear that the COP can make 'recommendations' on any matter necessary for the implementation of the Convention, while Article 7.2 (i) allows the COP to establish any new type of subsidiary body as it sees fit.

The remaining subparagraphs of Article 7.2 specify more routine functions, which are largely self-explanatory. These include trying to mobilise financial resources[7] (h), reviewing reports submitted by the subsidiary bodies and providing guidance to them (j), adopting rules of procedure and financial rules[8] (k), and considering, adopting and publishing regular reports on the implementation of the Convention (f). Regarding the latter function, at COP-1, Parties called on the Secretariat to prepare a first 'report on implementation' as a 'public information document'.[9] This report, however, was never prioritised and has never been published. The COP can also 'seek and utilize' the services and cooperation of, and information provided by, competent international organisations, IGOs and NGOs (l).[10]

2.1.2   Legal nature

What is the legal nature of the body established by Article 7.1? Does it exist on the international legal plane in its own right or is the term 'COP' shorthand for describing an agreed legal and political space in which Parties meet from

---

[5] See chapter 5.   [6] See chapter 11.   [7] See chapter 10.   [8] See chapters 14 and 16.
[9] Decision 7/CP.1.   [10] See chapter 17.

time to time? International legal personality is *one* element defining the scope of action of an international organisation. Other elements include the functions entrusted to the organisation, whether decisions are to be made by consensus or by majority voting and also whether the decisions themselves are of a binding nature.[11] Legal personality may even be inferred from these elements on the basis of the legal doctrine of 'implied powers' whereby legal personality is conferred because without it the organisation could not effectively achieve its object and purpose.[12] Together these elements determine the fundamentally important issue of the degree of autonomy the COP has in the development of climate policy and the extent of its authority in the subsequent enforcement of COP rules. The legal nature of the COP also has a direct practical bearing on the form and nature of guidance given by the COP to external bodies such as the GEF,[13] as well as the establishment and functioning of the Secretariat in the host country, Germany, an issue which also involves the United Nations.[14]

The Parties to the FCCC have not *expressly* confirmed or rejected whether the COP exists on the international legal plane as an international organisation. Nor have they confirmed or rejected the view that the COP is in essence a series of intergovernmental meetings, in other words, a rolling conference. Both strands of thinking exist side by side and can find some support in the three opinions expressed by the United Nations Office of Legal Affairs (UNOLA) in response to requests for legal advice on the nature of FCCC institutional arrangements (see box 13.1 below). These opinions are not binding on Parties but provide an independent source of advice, and have been supplemented by subsequent practice by the Parties.

Box 13.1   The legal nature of the FCCC: UNOLA opinions

The first UNOLA opinion in 1993 clearly stated that, once the FCCC was in force, it would 'establish an international entity/organization with its own separate legal personality, statement of principles, organs and a supportive structure in the form of a Secretariat'.[15]

UNOLA provided a second opinion in 1994 following the FCCC's entry into force. This confirmed that the COP had international legal personality because it could enter into a legally binding treaty with the World Bank with regard to the financial mechanism operated by the GEF.[16]

---

[11] Churchill and Ulfstein, 2000; Werksman, 1995.   [12] Churchill and Ulfstein, 2000, note 59.
[13] See chapter 10.   [14] See chapter 16.   [15] UNOLA, 1993.
[16] A/AC.237/74. The opinion noted by contrast that 'the founders of the GEF did not provide it with the legal capacity to enter into legally binding arrangements or agreements', paragraph 18.

The third UNOLA opinion in 1995 was more nuanced, perhaps because the issue at hand was the juridical personality of the Convention Secretariat, not the COP.[17] This opinion noted that, whilst 'none of the ... bodies of the Convention has been duly vested by the Parties with a clear juridical personality on the international plane' and none of the 'entities established by the Parties have been accorded the appropriate privileges and immunities, including immunity from legal process', the analysis undertaken by UNOLA 'of both the legal nature and functions of [FCCC bodies] indicates that they have certain distinctive elements attributable to international organizations'.[18]

Subsequent practice by the Parties confirms that, so far as the COP is concerned, Parties broadly accept it has presence on the international legal plane. This lends support to views expressed by legal academics suggesting that whatever its formal designation, the COP should be regarded as a self-governing treaty-based institution which can be considered to be an international organisation, albeit of a less formal, more ad hoc nature than traditional international organisations.[19] According to this view, 'international institutional law should apply to [it] and supplement the law of treaties when it comes to assessing [its] powers'.[20]

What legal consequences flow from these seemingly arcane considerations? The reluctance to delineate clearly the legal nature of the COP signals the constant need for Parties to 'sign off' on virtually all aspects of climate policy. This, coupled with the failure of the COP to agree rules of procedure that would allow majority decision-making,[21] evidences the reluctance of Parties to surrender sovereignty to the COP in anything other than an ad hoc, piecemeal and incremental fashion. The COP may be an international organisation, but it is one that presently enjoys a fairly limited degree of actual autonomy from the will of its Parties. This reality confirms the importance of the caveat expressed by distinguished legal academics that, whilst the body of law governing international institutions is relevant to bodies such as the COP, 'one should not lose sight of the special characteristics of these arrangements and that, accordingly, the powers of [bodies such as the COP] are not necessarily identical to those of formal IGOs in all respects'.[22] Thus the designation of the COP as an international body, or the absence of such a designation, will not in and of itself explain the nature and extent of the COP's powers. To understand this, one must constantly evaluate the legal provisions

---

[17] FCCC/SBI/1996/7. See also chapter 16.   [18] FCCC/SBI/1996/7.
[19] Churchill and Ulfstein, 2000, p. 26.   [20] Churchill and Ulfstein, 2000, p. 26.
[21] See chapter 14.   [22] Churchill and Ulfstein, 2000, p. 27.

adopted pursuant to the FCCC in the light of Parties' actual practices, recognising that these are shaped by the need to solve individual issues, rather than a once and for all abrogation of sovereignty.

Regarding its relationship with external bodies, the 1994 UNOLA opinion makes clear that 'the Conference of the Parties to the Convention (COP) has an independent legal character and is not a subsidiary of the General Assembly or of any other body'. Thus, the COP is a self-governing autonomous body and no other international body has the power to instruct the COP or its SBs.[23] An obvious concomitant is that the COP cannot instruct other international organisations, and must frame any guidance it may wish to provide in the form of requests.

So far as internal matters are concerned, the COP is expressly stipulated to be the 'supreme' body to ensure that other bodies established by the FCCC do not interpret their own mandates in a way that might usurp or challenge the COP's overall legal authority. Accordingly, the deliberations of the SBs are expressed as 'recommendations' or 'conclusions' and submitted to the COP for action. One practical consequence is that no initiative under the FCCC, however worthy or beneficial for the climate, can proceed without agreement from the Parties.[24] It also means that Parties are generally reluctant to delegate tasks to limited membership bodies because these would not directly involve all Parties as the COP does. This reluctance hampers consideration of specialised areas, as in-depth technical work is not possible in an intergovernmental forum open to more than 180 Parties. The establishment of limited membership bodies in recent years (see below) reflects growing recognition that the COP's supremacy will be better served by a more sophisticated institutional division of labour.

Another significant consequence of the supremacy of the COP, and the application of insights from the law of international organisations, is that COP decisions in relation to internal matters, i.e. those of an organisational and procedural nature such as adoption of rules of procedure, admission of observers, financial and budgetary issues and instructions to the Secretariat, can be considered to be of a legally binding character.[25]

Finally, the supremacy of the COP is reflected in the fact that it is the authoritative source of general guidance for Parties not only for implementation issues, but also for resolving any general ambiguities regarding interpretation of treaty terms. In all areas of law, interpretation can be so far-reaching that it comes close to rewriting the rules. Policy-making by the COP is no different, and it has been suggested that action by the COP which has this effect 'might be better regarded

---

[23] The situation is different for the Secretariat. Because it is institutionally linked to the UN, the UN retains certain powers over the functioning of the Secretariat. See chapter 16.

[24] Note that 'agreement' does not necessarily equate to 'consensus'. See chapter 14.

[25] Churchill and Ulfstein, 2000, text at note 71.

as an agreement *inter partes* modifying or supplementing the multilateral environmental agreement within the meaning of Article 39 or Article 41 (1) (b) of the Vienna Convention rather than subsequent practice within the meaning of Article 31 (3) (b) or the practice of an organ under international institutional law'.[26] This might be a more accurate legal characterisation of certain COP decisions, such as the Marrakesh Accords, which have significant implications for the interpretation of binding rules set out in the FCCC.[27] Nonetheless, many Parties would view the main role of the COP as a political one, with its decisions being primarily of a political rather than legal nature (except, of course, for the legally binding instruments that it may adopt, such as protocols – see box 13.2 below).

2.1.3   COP outputs

Each COP session results in a report summarising the COP's proceedings and its actions. While the COP can adopt legally binding instruments (such as amendments, annexes and protocols[28]), its actions more commonly take the form of decisions, resolutions or declarations, or else are reported as 'other actions'. From a legal point of view, there is little difference between the terms 'decisions', 'resolutions' and 'declarations'. All bear the stamp of COP authority and all are circumscribed by the legal mandate of the COP. Nevertheless, a number of procedural practices and a certain mindset have emerged in the climate change regime to differentiate between these outputs. These are summarised in box 13.2. Of course, the COP's so-called 'non-decisions' – issues on which there is no agreed output or only output of a largely symbolic nature – are equally important to understanding the dynamics and politics of the climate change regime.[29]

The outputs of the COP have been prolific. At the time of writing, meeting in nine full sessions plus a resumed sixth session, the COP has adopted the Kyoto Protocol,[30] two amendments to the lists of Parties in the Convention's Annexes I and II,[31] 189 decisions, twelve resolutions and two declarations, with a third declaration being 'noted' rather than adopted due to lack of consensus. At recent sessions, many of the decisions adopted by the COP have contained draft decisions relating to the Kyoto Protocol that the COP recommends be adopted by the first session of the Protocol's principal body, the COP/MOP. In so doing the COP acts, in effect, as a precursor to the COP/MOP.[32]

---

[26] Churchill and Ulfstein, 2000, text and references prior to footnote 117.

[27] This contrasts with seeing them as 'soft law'. See chapter 1.

[28] FCCC Articles 15, 16 and 17. See chapter 18.   [29] On 'non-decisions', see Gupta, 1997.

[30] See Decision 1/CP.3.   [31] See Decisions 4/CP.3 and 26/CP.7.

[32] A similar approach was followed prior to the entry into force of the FCCC when the final sessions of the INC adopted recommendations for decisions that were subsequently formally adopted by COP-1. INC-11 report, part II.

Box 13.2   COP outputs

Legally binding instruments
Amendments, annexes, amendments to annexes, and protocols are the COP's
most important outputs. Protocols and amendments to the Convention
require ratification by Parties before they can enter into force, but new
annexes and amendments to annexes enter into force automatically, except
for Parties that specifically reject them.[33]

Decisions
Decisions provide authoritative statements by the COP to guide Parties'
future conduct and implementation. Decisions concerning internal,
procedural and administrative matters, while not legally binding, are
observed as general principles of international law. COP decisions touching
the commitments of Parties are not considered to be legally binding in the
way that treaties, formal amendments and new protocols are, and they are
not required to be ratified. Decisions can, however, become binding in
particular circumstances, such as when they evidence customary
international law.[34] Their precise legal status and legal implications at any
time will depend therefore on their content and on Parties' conduct and
legal expectations. The Marrakesh Accords contain many decisions with
significant legal implications for the interpretation and implementation of
binding rules contained in the FCCC and KP. The legal status of these
particular decisions is likely to be subject to differing views in coming years.

Declarations
In the climate regime, the term 'declaration' has been reserved for political
agreements, often drafted at the ministerial level. Typically, these provide
high-level political guidance on the direction of the regime rather than
detailed technical input. The *Geneva Ministerial Declaration*, negotiated among
some ministers at COP-2, injected political momentum into the Protocol
negotiations. It was not, however, adopted by the COP due to lack of
consensus. The Declaration was instead 'noted' by the COP and reproduced
in the COP-2 report together with the objections raised by Parties.[35] The
Marrakesh Ministerial Declaration, serving as input for the 2002 World Summit
on Sustainable Development (WSSD), was adopted by COP-7 in the form of a

---

[33] See chapter 18.   [34] On customary international law, see chapter 1.
[35] See COP-2 report, part II, Annex, and COP-2 report, part I, Annex IV.

decision after lengthy negotiations.[36] This was also the case for the *Delhi Ministerial Declaration on Climate Change and Sustainable Development* adopted at COP-8.[37] To underscore their political importance, such declarations are numbered as the first decision of the COP session at which they are adopted (1/CP.x), and placed in the COP report accordingly.

Resolutions

In the climate regime, resolutions have been used to express the sense of the COP on matters of a ceremonial nature, such as expressions of gratitude to the host country of the COP and, at COP-7, to the retiring Executive Secretary, along with, at COPs 4 and 6, expressions of solidarity with regions affected by severe weather events. A further resolution, adopted at COP-6, provided input to the Third United Nations Conference on Least Developed Countries.[38]

COP Report

Part I records the procedural and organisational elements of the COP such as the election of officers, documents presented, and a summary of the opening statements. Proposals for items which failed to be included on the formal COP agenda, or which result in no agreement, are also recorded in Part I, as are any grievances or concerns raised by Parties which they insist be put on official record. **Part II** contains decisions, resolutions and declarations adopted at that session, along with a 'catch-all' section titled 'Other action taken by the COP'. This section often encompasses both the least controversial (e.g. calendar of meetings) and most controversial of issues. The latter include 'non-decisions', i.e. issues on which the COP cannot agree but is considering further. Examples include the proposal by Brazil concerning a possible formula for allocating responsibility for climate change (COP-3 report), and the proposal by Canada at COP-6 Part II on the potential of clean energy (COP-6 Part II report).

2.1.4   Timing and venue

Article 7.4 specifies that the COP must meet on an annual basis, unless Parties decide otherwise.[39] Although anecdotal evidence suggests that many delegations find the annual cycle of COP sessions unnecessarily exhausting,

---

[36] Decision 1/CP.7.   [37] Decision 1/CP.8.

[38] See part II of the reports on COP-1, COP-2, COP-3, COP-4, COP-6 and COP-7.

[39] Rule 4.1.

Parties have been quite rigid in insisting on an annual COP.[40] The COP typically meets for ten or twelve days, usually during the last three months of the calendar year. The calendar of meetings for COP (and SB) sessions, that is, their approximate dates, is decided by the COP far in advance, sometimes four or five years ahead, given the need to secure conference facilities and avoid clashes with other intergovernmental meetings. The COP is required to decide, at each session, on the exact date and duration of its next session.[41] In doing so, it should endeavour not to hold a session at a time that would make the attendance of a significant number of delegations difficult.[42] This is an implicit reference to religious observances, including Ramadan, which the sessional periods of the COP and SBs have therefore sought to avoid, if possible.

Extraordinary COP sessions may be held at other times if the COP deems it necessary.[43] A Party may submit a written request for an extraordinary session, which, in order to be actioned, must receive support from at least one-third of the Parties within six months of the request being communicated to the Parties by the Secretariat.[44] No extraordinary session, however, has ever been held, although the ordinary session of COP-6 was 'resumed' eight months later.[45] This course of action was followed rather than convening an extraordinary session in order to avoid formalising the failure of COP-6. A similar strategy was used at INC-5, the deadline for negotiations on the Convention, with the resumption of that session – and the adoption of the FCCC – taking place three months after INC-5 failed to reach agreement.[46] The Secretariat must notify all Parties of the dates and venue of a session – whether ordinary or extraordinary – at least two months before it is held.[47]

Sessions of the COP take place at the seat of the Secretariat, unless the COP decides otherwise or the Secretariat makes other arrangements in consultation with the Parties.[48] Hosting sessions in Bonn causes least disruption to the Secretariat, is the cheapest option and contributes to consolidating the institutional basis of the regime. Parties, however, have offered to host COP sessions, with the attendant prestige serving as an important motivation. Changing venues in this way also has the benefit of promoting awareness, and encouraging a sense of

---

[40] The US sought, for example, to postpone the date of COP-6 until after the entry into office of its new administration following the 2000 presidential elections. This was opposed by many countries on the grounds of the 'annual' rule, which perhaps masked fears that postponement could derail negotiations on the Kyoto Protocol. Another proposal was made at COP-9 to schedule COP-10 in 2005, in order to seek a higher profile for that session, which would then coincide with the launch of negotiations on second period commitments under the Kyoto Protocol, along with the scheduled review of demonstrable progress in the implementation of the Protocol.

[41] Rule 4.2   [42] Rule 4.2   [43] FCCC Article 7.5 and Rule 4.3.   [44] Rule 4.4
[45] Decision 1/CP.6.   [46] See chapter 2.   [47] Rule 5.   [48] Rule 3.

ownership, of the climate change process across different geographical regions. Although any Party may offer to host the COP, a practice has developed whereby the venue of the COP often rotates together with the position of COP President among the five UN regions[49] (see section 2.1.5 below). Before any offer is formally accepted, the Secretariat will usually conduct a fact-finding mission to the prospective host venue to ensure that suitable facilities are available. An offer to host the COP may be formally accepted by the COP or SBI, or by the COP Bureau, on the COP's behalf, depending on the timing involved.[50]

Diplomatic courtesy, and the fact that the host country bears the incremental additional costs of holding the COP away from the seat of the Secretariat, means that offers to host the COP have never been refused.[51] Depending on the venue, the cost of hosting a COP amounts to a rough average of US $1 million, including the costs of transporting the Secretariat and its equipment from Bonn. Where no offer is received to host a COP session, it is held at Secretariat headquarters (e.g. see COP-5 in table 13.1 below).

In addition to supplying appropriate logistical facilities, the host country is expected to show leadership at the applicable COP session and promote a successful outcome, with its actions in this regard extending beyond those of the COP President (see below). The general expectation is that the host country will also host an intersessional meeting of the COP Bureau or Expanded Bureau,[52] and consult informally with key Parties prior to the COP. Although not specified in any rule, a widely shared expectation is that the host country will take the lead in advancing progressive outcomes and fostering cooperation among Parties rather than, or at least in addition to, defending its own interests.

The dates and venues of COP sessions to date and their Presidents are shown in table 13.1.

2.1.5   Bureau

Rule 22 provides that the COP shall elect eleven officers at the start of each of its ordinary sessions to serve for the remainder of that session. These

---

[49] The rotation of the Presidency, however, takes precedence, as this is required by the Rules of Procedure. Italy, for example, hosted COP-9, but the Central and Eastern European group nominated the Hungarian President, in accordance with regional rotation. Alternatively, where this is politically possible, the order of regional rotation may be modified so that the host can also preside (e.g. the case of Argentina for COP-4).

[50] The COP Bureau, for example, was mandated to decide on Argentina's offer to host COP-10. See Decision 14/CP.9, Date and venue of the tenth session of the Conference of the Parties.

[51] Although Jordan's offer to host COP-5 (see report on COP-4, part I, paragraphs 31–2) was withdrawn following a technical mission and concerns on the part of the Jordanian government over the costs involved.

[52] On the Expanded Bureau and other 'friends' groups, see chapter 14.

Table 13.1 *Dates, venues and Presidents of COP sessions*[53]

COP	Dates	Venue	President	Country	UN Region
COP-1	28 Mar–7 April 1995	Berlin	Merkel	Germany	WEOG
COP-2	8–19 July 1996	Geneva	Chimutengwende	Zimbabwe	Africa
COP-3	1–11 Dec 1997	Kyoto	Ohki	Japan	Asia
COP-4	2–14 Nov 1998	Buenos Aires	Alsogaray	Argentina	LAC
COP-5	25 Oct–5 Nov 1999	Bonn	Szyszko	Poland	CEE
COP-6	16–24 Nov 2000	The Hague	Pronk	Netherlands	WEOG
Part II	13–27 July 2001	Bonn			
COP-7	29 Oct–9 Nov 2001	Marrakesh	Elyazghi	Morocco	Africa
COP-8	23 Oct–1 Nov 2002	New Delhi	Baalu	India	Asia
COP-9	1–12 Dec 2003	Milan	Persányi	Hungary	CEE

officers serve as the Bureau of the session,[54] and consist of a President, seven Vice-Presidents, a Rapporteur and the Chairs of the two subsidiary bodies.

The offices of President and Rapporteur are normally subject to rotation among the five regional groups,[55] as a general rule in alphabetical order. Where there is an offer to host the COP, however, the alphabetical order may be modified to allow the host country to preside (see note 49). Each of the five UN regional groups[56] is represented on the Bureau by two officers and, in an innovation tailored especially to the climate change regime, an additional post is reserved for the small island developing states.[57] This additional post was disputed at COP-1, with some oil-exporting developing Parties claiming that a dedicated seat on the Bureau should also be granted to developing countries referred to in Article 4.8 (h).[58] Although these Parties declared their opposition to Rule 22 on this basis, the Rule has since been consistently applied without objection.[59] This is because of an informal understanding that such oil exporters will be accommodated within the existing formula, by ensuring they are represented through one of the regional groups, often Asia.

The representation of other interests is also ensured on an informal basis. Within the WEOG group, for example, one seat will be occupied by an EU member,

[53] Adapted from UNFCCC Secretariat 2002.   [54] On Bureaux, see Széll, 1993; Lang, 1989.

[55] Rule 22.1.

[56] Africa, Asia, Central and Eastern Europe, Latin America and the Caribbean, Western Europe and Others. See chapter 3.

[57] Rule 22.1.

[58] Countries whose economies are highly dependent on income generated from the production, processing and export, and/or on consumption of fossil fuels and associated energy-intensive products.

[59] See report on COP-1, part I, paragraphs 9–14.

and the other by a non-EU member. Similarly, among Central and Eastern Europe, one seat has traditionally been occupied by a member of the CG-11, and the other by either the Russian Federation or the Ukraine, who are members of the Umbrella Group.[60] A representative of the host country of the next COP is usually also invited to attend COP Bureau meetings and thus serves as an *ex officio* participant. *Ex officio* means 'by virtue of one's office' and confers participation rights to officials who otherwise are not members.

Serving on the Bureau confers prestige and influence, and membership is considered an honour. Bureau members have access to useful information, often in advance of others. They also have more contact with Secretariat staff and others working with the COP President. For eligible countries,[61] having a member on the COP Bureau means funding is available, upon request, for an extra delegate to attend negotiating sessions.

Bureau members are elected from among the representatives of the Parties present at the session,[62] Rules 51, 52 and 53 set out detailed procedures for conducting such elections. Elections, however, have never been held, mirroring the practice in many international fora whereby UN regional groups have traditionally put forward agreed nominations for posts, which are then simply rubber stamped in the opening COP plenary. In practice, therefore, Parties only have a say over the nomination of their regional representative, not over the overall composition of the Bureau, nor any of its other individual members.

It is not uncommon for regional groups to have trouble reaching agreement on their representatives, and it has, at times, proved impossible to elect the Bureau at the start of the COP session. In such circumstances, the existing Bureau has continued to meet because the Rules of Procedure specify that Bureau members stay in office until their successors are elected.[63] If an officer resigns, then the Party holding the position is required to nominate another representative of the same Party to fill the post.[64] Officers may be re-elected, but may not serve for more than two terms.[65] Because of the regional rotation rule, COP Presidents have always served for only one term.

A striking feature of the COP Bureau is that, to date, only seven women have served on it. Of these, two were ministers elected to serve as COP Presidents for

---

[60] See chapter 3 on political negotiating groups.   [61] See chapter 16.   [62] Rule 22.1.

[63] Rule 22. On occasion, when the full slate of members has been agreed with the exception of one nomination, the remainder of the Bureau has been elected and met, pending the election of its final member (see report on COP-6, part I, paragraphs 41–4).

[64] Rule 25.

[65] Rule 22.2. This rule was waived at COP-6, when a Bureau member was elected for a third term, to permit him to serve for a (permitted) second term as SBI Chair (report on COP-6, part I, paragraph 43). The rotation requirement, however, means that COP Presidents have never been re-elected.

a term of just one year. The anomaly in gender distribution led to a decision at COP-7 aimed at improving the representation of women on the regime bodies. Parties are now invited to 'give active consideration to the nomination of women for elective posts in any body established under the Convention or the Kyoto Protocol'.[66]

    2.1.5.1 Functions of the Bureau   The functions of the Bureau are not defined in the Convention or Rules of Procedure. Instead, the Bureau's role and operational procedures have evolved organically over the years, taking into account practices of similar bodies in other international regimes and the needs and expectations of the COP.

    The Bureau typically meets daily during COP sessions, once during SB sessions, and once intersessionally. The meetings of the Bureau are closed to everyone except its members and supporting Secretariat staff. In practice, however, Bureau members can be accompanied by an advisor, as this ensures continuity and a greater pool of expertise. The Bureau agenda is not publicly available and neither are the informal records of Bureau proceedings kept by the Secretariat. Bureau members are expected to brief their respective regional or nominating groups, while NGOs and others have to glean intelligence by lobbying delegates.

    The Bureau's principal task is dealing with procedural issues relating to the organisation of the work of the COP. Given its limited membership, it is not a negotiating forum for substantive issues. However, Bureau meetings provide an informal point of contact for delegates to exchange views on substantive matters, although these discussions remain strictly off the record.

    The functioning of the Bureau tends to vary from session to session, depending on the personalities of its members and the approach of the COP President. Usually, it assumes an advisory role, providing informal guidance to the President on how best to conduct negotiations in order to reach agreement. As many Presidents are ministers with little experience of chairing complex international bodies like the COP, this is a particularly important function. Bureau members (with the exception of the President – see below) serve as representatives of their regional groups with whom they are supposed to consult, and can therefore often provide 'advance warning' of how certain proposals might be received. The Bureau may, for example, advise the President on how a particularly sensitive agenda item should be dealt with.

---

[66] Decision 36/CP.7, Improving the participation of women in the representation of Parties in bodies established under the United Nations Framework Convention on Climate Change and the Kyoto Protocol.

In addition to its informal advisory role, the COP Bureau performs some standard procedural functions, such as examining the credentials of Party representatives and reviewing requests for admission by NGOs and IGOs, once these have been screened by the Secretariat.[67] The Bureau is also involved in the selection of the Executive Secretary.[68] In addition, Bureau members often serve as chairs of contact groups and other informal negotiating forums,[69] given that their endorsement by the respective regional groups already endows them with a position of authority.

    2.1.5.2 President   The President is formally elected immediately after the opening of each COP session, at which point s/he takes over from the previous President.[70] The COP President is always elected on the first day of the COP, even if there is no agreement on the remaining officers, to ensure someone can manage the conduct of COP business.

The position of COP President is typically held by the environment minister of the presiding country. As with other international conferences, the duties of the President to ensure an orderly conduct of business are absolutely vital.[71] In the words of one legal academic, 'an incompetent presiding officer can, single-handedly, create procedural chaos if he does not understand the Rules, or does not enforce them, or acts in a dictatorial or partisan manner'.[72] However, unlike many other conferences where states can exercise control over the appointment of the presiding officer, the COP has no real choice because, as discussed above, the position of President usually goes hand in hand with that of the host country (or a regional nominee). One comforting fact is that a country which has chosen to put itself forward to preside over a COP is likely to have a strong interest in the final outcome, to which the reputation of the minister concerned will become attached. The Secretariat also plays a very important role in guiding the COP President, especially in situations where s/he lacks experience of complex intergovernmental negotiating arenas such as the climate change regime.

The formal functions and powers of the COP President are set out in the Rules of Procedure. Even if these Rules did not exist, many of the powers they confer could be justifiably regarded as customary international law, so ingrained are they in the international legal fabric.[73] The Rules of Procedure thus provide that the President 'shall have complete control over proceedings and over the maintenance of order thereat'. To ensure s/he does not act in a dictatorial or partisan manner, the Rules make clear that the President 'remains under the authority of the Conference

---

[67] See chapter 14.   [68] Decision 14/CP.1, paragraph 7. See chapter 16.
[69] See chapter 14.   [70] Rule 26.   [71] Sabel, 1997: p. 52.   [72] Bailey, 1984: p. 111.
[73] Sabel, 1997: p. 420.

of the Parties'[74] and that he or she must remain impartial, and not exercise the rights of the representative of a Party.[75] Within this broad circumscription, the President is assigned several specific tasks by the Rules, including the following:

- Declare the opening and closing of sessions, preside over meetings and ensure the observance of procedural rules;[76]
- Accord the right to speak;[77]
- Put questions to the vote and announce decisions;[78]
- Rule on points of order (with the possibility of challenge);[79]
- Propose to the COP to close the list of speakers, or otherwise curtail the debate;[80] and
- Agree the provisional agenda for each session drafted by the Secretariat.[81]

The COP President also has a much broader, informal role in bringing the diverse interests of Parties to consensus. The President is thus expected to exercise leadership, putting forward compromise proposals and texts, and holding consultations with Parties, often at ministerial level. Each President has considerable discretion in terms of the use s/he makes of the Bureau or other means of consultations, such as a 'friends' group,[82] to promote agreement. The President's role is a delicate one in this respect as proactive approaches, whilst important for generating political momentum, can also raise concerns about the impartiality and accountability of the President.

To date, each President has struck a different balance between protecting the rights of Parties enshrined in the Rules and seeking to direct the COP to a successful political outcome, inevitably with varying degrees of success. Some have kept a relatively low political profile, fulfilling their formal duties and holding general consultations, but delegating the actual conduct of negotiations to others. Others have adopted a hands-on approach and become involved in most aspects of the process, including chairing negotiations and supervising the drafting of COP decisions. Still others have chosen a mix of approaches.

2.1.5.3 Vice-Presidents and Rapporteur　　Rule 24 provides that, if the President must absent him/herself for any reason, s/he will designate one of the Vice-Presidents to serve in his/her place, who will then assume the same functions and responsibilities. The Vice-Presidents, for example, routinely preside over the high-level segment speeches, while the President is engaged in the negotiations themselves.

---

[74] Rules 23.1 and 23.3, respectively.　　[75] Rule 22.3.　　[76] Rule 23.1.　　[77] Rules 6, 23, 32.
[78] Rule 23.1.　　[79] Rules 23.1, 34.　　[80] Rule 23.2.　　[81] Rule 9.　　[82] See chapter 14.

Although not stated in the Rules, the post of Rapporteur has the task of supervising the preparation of the report on the COP session by the Secretariat, and presenting the draft report, which is issued under his/her name, to the COP plenary. Unless the Rapporteur shows unusually high interest in the drafting process, his/her contribution to the report is largely confined to formally approving the Secretariat's work. Like that of COP President, the position of Rapporteur is normally subject to rotation among the five regional groups.[83] Rotation has not been so closely adhered to, however, because formal responsibility for the report, and the tradition within the UN system whereby the Rapporteur is seen as a more junior post, means this position is rarely sought after.

2.2   *The subsidiary bodies*

Articles 9 and 10 of the Convention provide for two permanent subsidiary bodies to advise and assist the COP: the SBSTA and the SBI.

2.2.1   Mandate

Both the SBSTA and SBI are open-ended bodies composed of Party representatives, reflecting the reluctance of Parties to involve independent, non-governmental, experts in formulating guidance for the COP or examining the implementation of commitments.[84] The basic function of both bodies is to provide assistance and advice to the COP on their respective spheres of responsibility. In addition to developing recommendations for the COP, usually in the form of draft decisions, the SBs also adopt conclusions on their agenda items. These are usually procedural in nature, for example elaborating on their programme of work, requesting a background document from the Secretariat or inviting Parties to submit views on an issue. Sometimes, the conclusions will set out the negotiated approach of the SB to addressing an issue, which may serve as the prelude for a later COP decision. Although SB conclusions do not have the legal or political significance of COP decisions, they may still be very contentious and hotly negotiated. Both bodies operate 'under the guidance' of the COP and must report regularly to it.[85]

2.2.1.1 SBSTA   The SBSTA's main task, as set out in Article 9.1, is to provide the COP and other SBs with 'timely information and advice on scientific and

---

[83] Rule 22.1.   [84] Bodansky, 1993.

[85] Early sessions of the SBI also adopted 'decisions' (see SBI-1 and SBI-4 reports), but this practice has been discontinued, presumably to avoid inconsistent policy-making at different levels of the climate regime's institutional hierarchy.

technological matters relating to the Convention'. The SBSTA's role is in fact not confined to the scientific and technological domains but encompasses other disciplines. The Convention accordingly requires the SBSTA to be 'multidisciplinary' and mandates representation by 'government representatives competent in the relevant field of expertise'. In practice, however, there is no monitoring of the expertise of delegates.

The SBSTA is mandated by Article 9.2 to draw upon 'existing competent international bodies' in its tasks. These include providing assessments of 'the state of scientific knowledge relating to climate change and its effects' and 'the effects of measures taken in the implementation of the Convention'.[86] Hence, a central role for the SBSTA is serving as the principal interface between the regime on the one hand, and the scientific, technical and technological input provided by outside bodies, primarily the IPCC, on the other. This role is discussed in more detail in chapter 15.

In a similar vein, the SBSTA is charged with providing advice 'on scientific programmes, international cooperation in research and development related to climate change, as well as on ways and means of supporting endogenous capacity-building in developing countries'.[87] Building on this mandate, the SBSTA is responsible for the Convention's work on its Article 5, Research and Systematic Observation, acting as a liaison point with scientific research programmes such as the Global Climate Observing System of WMO. For more on this role, see chapter 7.

Another task for the SBSTA is to 'identify innovative, efficient and state-of-the-art technologies and know-how and advise on the ways and means of promoting development and/or transferring such technologies'.[88] On this basis, the SBSTA bears primary responsibility for the Convention's work on the development and transfer of technologies.[89] Finally, the SBSTA is given the general mandate of responding 'to scientific, technological and methodological questions' from the COP and other SBs.[90] As part of this catch-all category, the SBSTA is responsible for all the Convention's work on methodological issues.[91]

An important challenge for the SBSTA is achieving a balance between its necessary and useful engagement with intergovernmental politics (thereby enabling the IPCC to remain scientifically focused and as free of politics as possible[92]), and excessive politicisation, which can hamper its ability to provide scientific and technical advice. The SBSTA's role and stature as a policy-oriented negotiating forum dealing with scientific and technical issues has indeed grown in importance with

---

[86] FCCC Article 9.2 (a) and (b) respectively.   [87] FCCC Article 9.2 (d).
[88] FCCC Article 9.2 (c).   [89] See chapter 10.   [90] FCCC Article 9.2 (e).
[91] See chapter 11.
[92] For a more in-depth discussion of the relative roles of the SBSTA and IPCC, see chapter 15.

the adoption of the Kyoto Protocol and the concurrent mushrooming of issues requiring detailed technical work (e.g. on rules for the LULUCF sector, detailed reporting guidelines and the registry system).

   2.2.1.2 SBI   According to Article 10.1, the role of the SBI is to assist the COP 'in the assessment and review of the effective implementation of the Convention'. Akin to the SBSTA, representation is by government delegates who should be 'experts on matters related to climate change'. The SBI has the specific task of assisting the COP 'in the preparation and implementation of its decisions'.[93] The other functions of the SBI outlined in the Convention involve the review of national communications. Pursuant to this, the SBI is requested to assist the COP in carrying out the review of Annex I Party obligations envisaged under Article 4.2 (d).[94]

   Despite the 'implementation' focus of its title, the SBI's mandate to examine the implementation by individual Parties is curtailed by the limitation that it 'assess the *overall aggregated effect* of the steps taken by the Parties'[95] (emphasis added). This limitation was included in response to sovereignty concerns expressed during negotiations on the Convention. Parties did not want the SBI to evolve into a similar animal to the (highly effective) Implementation Committee under the Montreal Protocol, which considers, and adopts recommendations on, cases of potential and actual non-compliance with the Montreal Protocol's ODS phase-out schedules.[96]

2.2.2   Division of labour

   While the Convention states that the 'functions and terms of reference' of the SBSTA 'may be further elaborated' by the COP,[97] this provision is not included for the SBI (reflecting concern to curb the potential scope of the SBI's powers, as discussed above). Nevertheless, the mandates for both SBs set out in the Convention have been elaborated upon in the same way by subsequent COP decisions, notably Decisions 6/CP.1 and 13/CP.3.[98] The early years of the climate change regime experienced protracted procedural debates over the appropriate division of labour between the two bodies. With experience, however, the SBs have matured and their respective areas of work have become more clearly demarcated, with increasing continuity in representation on the part of many delegations, thereby contributing to the gradual development of technical expertise and specialisation.

---

[93] FCCC Article 10.2 (c).   [94] FCCC Article 10.2 (a) and (b). See also chapter 18.
[95] FCCC Article 10.2 (a).   [96] See also chapter 12.   [97] FCCC Article 9.3.
[98] Decision 6/CP.1, The subsidiary bodies established by the Convention, and Decision 13/CP.3, Division of labour between the Subsidiary Body for Implementation and Subsidiary Body for Scientific and Technological Advice.

The allocation of new issues to one SB or another can be a significant procedural matter because of the way in which the two bodies are perceived. The SBI is seen as the more political body, and issues are therefore sometimes assigned to the SBSTA precisely to downplay their political element and dampen the controversy surrounding them. This happened, for example, to the Brazilian proposal on a new method for estimating the contribution of Parties to climate change, the Canadian proposal on cleaner energy, and the issue of policies and measures.

Pursuant to Decisions 6/CP.1 and 13/CP.3, some issues fall under the purview of both SBs, such as the development of guidelines for national communications and the transfer of technology, for which the SBSTA is supposed to provide technical input to the SBI's work. Providing input from one body to another in this way is, to a large extent, a procedural fiction, given that the same Parties – and sometimes the same individuals – are members of both bodies, and the degree of expert specialisation within the SBSTA and SBI is still limited. In practice, therefore, one SB or the other has, over time, typically assumed *de facto* overall responsibility in the case of most agenda items. This division of labour that has evolved for the main agenda items of the climate change regime is summarised in table 13.2 below.

During the post-Kyoto negotiations leading to the Marrakesh Accords, the climate change regime experimented with the convening of joint meetings of the SBs on most issues under the Buenos Aires Plan of Action, including the flexibility mechanisms, implementation of Articles 4.8 and 4.9, capacity-building and AIJ. These meetings were chaired alternately by the two SB Chairs, with both usually seated at the podium. This was a pragmatic solution to bypass time-wasting procedural discussions over the division of labour between the SBs on these highly complex issues, all of which were rightly seen as having both political and technical dimensions.

2.2.3   Timing and venue

Unlike the mandated annual sessions of the COP, there is no schedule set out in the Convention for SB sessions. Rule 27.4 provides that it is up to the COP to determine the schedule of meetings of the SBs. This is done about four years in advance through the adoption of the periodic calendar of meetings. The current practice is that the SBs meet twice a year for about one week, with one session held in conjunction with the COP. When the SBs meet on their own, they almost always do so in Bonn, as it is rare for a Party to seek to host these lower profile meetings. The only exception to date was the first part of the thirteenth SB sessions (September 2000), an additional session aimed at promoting agreement at COP-6, hosted by France.

Table 13.2 *SB division of labour*

Agenda item	Body
Guidelines for Annex I Party inventories and national communications	SBSTA (SBI)[99]
Review of Annex I Party inventories and national communications	SBI
Non-Annex I Party national communications, including the CGE	SBI[100]
Development and transfer of technologies	SBSTA[101]
Financial mechanism	SBI
Methodological issues	SBSTA
Work relating to the IPCC (e.g. consideration of Assessment Reports)	SBSTA
Scientific, technical and socio-economic aspects of impacts of, and vulnerability and adaptation to, climate change	SBSTA
Scientific, technical and socio-economic aspects of mitigation	SBSTA
Matters relating to least developed countries	SBI
Education, training and public awareness	SBSTA
Research and systematic observation	SBSTA
Cooperation with relevant international organisations	SBSTA
Activities implemented jointly	SBSTA[102]
Technical examination of proposals (e.g. Brazilian proposal, Canadian proposal)	SBSTA
Interpretation of the Convention (e.g. request by the CACAM group)	SBI
Proposed amendments to the Convention or its annexes	SBI
Administrative and financial matters	SBI
Arrangements for intergovernmental meetings	SBI
Policies and measures	SBSTA

[99] The SBSTA and SBI should, in theory, both be involved in the preparation of guidelines for Annex I Party reports, with revised guidelines developed by the SBSTA being approved by the SBI before they are recommended to the COP. The SBSTA, however, has adopted an increasingly dominant role in the development of guidelines. See, for example, report on SBI-16, paragraph 52, whereby it is agreed that the revised guidelines for the reporting and review of greenhouse gas inventories will be forwarded directly to the COP without going to the SBI.

[100] Although the SBSTA is supposed to provide methodological input to the development of guidelines for non-Annex I national communications, it has not done so for many years (see SBSTA-8 report, paragraphs 32–3). Its work in this respect has to some extent been supplanted by the establishment of the CGE.

[101] The SBI has not considered this issue since its seventh session, where it did so together with the SBSTA through a joint working group. The launch of the 'consultative process' under the SBSTA at COP-4 and the subsequent establishment of the EGTT placed this issue more squarely under the remit of the SBSTA. See chapter 10.

[102] Since the completion of negotiations under the Buenos Aires Plan of Action, this issue has been dealt with only by the SBSTA.

Table 13.3 *Past and present subsidiary body Chairs*

Term of office	SBSTA	SBI
Elected at COP-1 Served SB 1–7	Tibor Farago (Hungary)	Mahmoud Ould El Ghaouth (Mauritania)
Elected at COP-3 Served SB 8–10	Chow Kok Kee (Malaysia)	Bakary Kanté (Senegal)
Elected at COP-5 Served SB 11–15	Harald Dovland (Norway)	John Ashe (Antigua and Barbuda)
Elected at COP-7 Served SB 16–17	Halldor Thorgeirsson (Iceland)	Raúl Estrada-Oyuela (Argentina)
Elected at COP-8 Served SB 18–19	Halldor Thorgeirsson (Iceland)	Daniela Stoycheva (Bulgaria)

2.2.4   Officers

The Rules of Procedure provide for each SB to elect a three-person Bureau, comprising a Chair, Vice-Chair and Rapporteur.[103] In practice, SB Chairs are usually elected as part of the overall slate of COP Bureau officers, given that they serve *ex officio* on the COP Bureau. The Vice-Chairs and Rapporteurs of the SBs, however, are elected by the SBs themselves.[104] This has sometimes proved difficult, and the SBs have, on occasion, found themselves without Vice-Chairs or Rapporteurs. Although no specific regional formula is set out in the Rules, the Chairs, Vice-Chairs and Rapporteurs must be elected 'with due regard to the principle of equitable geographic representation', and may serve for two terms only.[105] The position of SB Chair is held at the technical level, that is, by civil servant delegates, not ministers. The SB Chairs that have served to date are listed in table 13.3.

SB Vice-Chairs and Rapporteurs perform similar functions to their counterparts on the COP Bureau although, given the more technical nature of the SBs' work, they tend to have rather less work to do. They do not sit on the COP Bureau, but usually meet with the SB Chair on the eve of the session and during the session itself if this proves necessary.

All the powers and functions assigned to the President apply also to the SB Chairs, who therefore have complete control over their respective institutions and their organisation of work. As with COP Presidents, the particular personalities and approaches of the SB Chairs can impact considerably on the dynamic of negotiations. Because they are not of ministerial rank, the SB Chairs are typically more intimately involved in the actual negotiations and in overseeing the development

---

[103] Rules 22 and 27.   [104] Rule 27.6.   [105] Rule 27.5.

of draft text. This is helpful because SB chairs are usually senior delegates, with long-standing experience of the climate process, and therefore understand political dynamics and issues. They usually continue negotiating as delegates once their term of office has expired, providing much-needed institutional memory for the regime.

2.3   *Temporary subsidiary bodies*

To date, the COP has established three open-ended subsidiary bodies in addition to the SBSTA and SBI, all on an ad hoc basis with a specific mandate and time-frame.

The first was the Ad hoc Group on the Berlin Mandate (AGBM), established at COP-1 in 1995 to conduct the negotiations under the Berlin Mandate that led to the adoption of the Kyoto Protocol.[106] It met eight times and was disbanded on the eve of COP-3. The AGBM functioned largely like one of the permanent SBs, differing only in the composition of its Bureau. The highly political nature of the AGBM's work meant it was unable to agree on a three-person Bureau for itself, as this would have excluded half the groups competing for a seat. The impasse was breached by appointing a Vice-Chair and Rapporteur, plus the Chairs of the permanent SBs and six 'advisers', making a total of eleven persons, to which the standard COP Bureau formula could be applied.[107] The AGBM was chaired by Raúl Estrada-Oyuela (Argentina).

The Ad hoc Group on Article 13 (AG13) was also established at COP-1 in 1995, to conduct negotiations on the multilateral consultative process (MCP) envisaged under FCCC Article 13.[108] The AG13 functioned in the same way as the other SBs, including in the structure of its Bureau, and was chaired by Patrick Széll (UK). The AG13 met six times. It agreed all the components of the MCP except for the issue of composition of its multilateral consultative committee. It was disbanded at COP-4, with its work relegated to informal consultations under the COP President.[109]

The Joint Working Group on compliance (JWG) was established at COP-4 in 1998 to conduct negotiations on designing a compliance system under Article 18 of the Kyoto Protocol.[110] Unlike the AGBM and AG13, the JWG was not, strictly speaking, a subsidiary body in its own right, having been established under the SBSTA and the SBI. It functioned rather as a hybrid between a subsidiary body and an informal contact group.[111] The JWG enjoyed continuity from session to session under the same Chairs,[112] adhered to the Rules of Procedure (e.g. concerning interpretation),

---

[106] Decision 1/CP.1, paragraph 6.   [107] Report on AGBM 2 and 3.   [108] Decision 20/CP.1.
[109] Decision 10/CP.4. For more on the AG13, see chapter 12.   [110] Decision 8/CP.4.
[111] On contact groups, see chapter 14.
[112] Although one of the Co-Chairs (Espen Ronnenberg – Marshall Islands) resigned and was replaced by another (Tuiloma Neroni Slade – Samoa), who continued to serve with Harald Dovland (Norway).

convened intersessional meetings and produced written reports. Like a contact group, however, the JWG was led by Co-Chairs without a Bureau and reported to the SBSTA and SBI. The JWG was disbanded after COP-6 part I, having forwarded a text reflecting the status of negotiations on compliance to the subsidiary bodies.

2.4   Specialised bodies

Since 1999, a set of specialised bodies has been established to address specific areas relating to the implementation of the Convention. These are:

- The Consultative Group of Experts on National Communications from Parties not included in Annex I to the Convention (Consultative Group of Experts, or CGE);
- The Expert Group on Technology Transfer (EGTT); and
- The Least Developed Countries Expert Group (LEG).

These bodies, which have a limited membership corresponding to the execution of the expert tasks entrusted to them, have been created on an ad hoc and temporary basis. This is due to sovereignty concerns and a desire to make use of existing institutions in the interests of financial and administrative efficiency.

The first specialised body set up under the Convention was the CGE in 1999. Prior to that time, the establishment of proposed limited membership bodies – notably the multilateral consultative committee and intergovernmental technical advisory panels[113] – had been stymied by disagreement over their composition.

The establishment of the specialised bodies thus marks a new sophistication in the institutional arrangements of the COP. Their mandate, and formula for selection of membership, is highly specific, with each serving a particular process within the climate change regime. The terms of reference, and eventual continuation of each group, are subject to review by the COP. A common feature of all three is the technical nature of their work. Any conclusions and recommendations they reach must be reported either to the SBSTA or the SBI.

The three bodies all meet twice a year, usually in conjunction with the SBs, and also hold their own intersessional meetings and workshops. All three bodies draw on Internet technology to facilitate their work and communication among their members. There has been some attempt to enhance collaboration between the three bodies on issues that cut across their spheres of responsibility, notably technology transfer and capacity-building, with the COP requesting the SBSTA Chair to ensure such coordination.[114]

---

[113] See chapters 12 and 15.
[114] Decision 10/CP.8, paragraphs 2(a) and 3. See also SBI-18 report, paragraph 10.

Table 13.4 *Composition and officers of specialised bodies under the Convention*

Body (Total)	UN Regional group*			Small island	Annex I			Officers	Rotation
	Africa	Asia	LAC		All AI	AII	IGO		
CGE (24)	5	5	5	–	6	–	3	Chair and Rapporteur	DCs only
LEG (12)	5	2	–	2	–	3	–	Chair, Vice-Chair, two Rapporteurs (Anglo, Franco)	LDCs only
EGTT (20)	3	3	3	1	7	–	3	Chair and Vice-Chair	AI/NAI

LAC – Latin America and the Caribbean; AI – Annex I; AII – Annex II; NAI – non-Annex I; IGO – international organisations

* Central and Eastern Europe and Western Europe and Others regional groups are not included in the formula

In terms of their status within the climate change regime, these bodies appear to fall under the category referred to in the Rules of Procedure as 'committees or working groups', and therefore to be defined therein also as 'subsidiary bodies'.[115] Given that the Rules of Procedure apply *mutatis mutandis* to the SBs, it follows that they also apply to the specialised bodies (unless the COP agrees alternative rules for them), taking into account the specific composition and mandate of the body concerned. In practice, these bodies have assumed their own ways of working, but on a largely informal basis, adopting only a small number of rules for themselves, concerning, for example, the election of officers and schedule of meetings. The respective compositions of the specialised bodies and their officers is summarised and compared in table 13.4. Each specialised body is also discussed in more detail in the relevant chapters of this book: the CGE in chapter 11; the LEG in chapter 8; and the EGTT in chapter 10.

3   Kyoto Protocol institutions

The institutional design of the Kyoto Protocol balances three fundamental, and sometimes potentially competing, considerations. First, the Protocol was adopted to strengthen the FCCC, not to replace it. Second, FCCC Parties sought to avoid proliferation of new institutions wherever possible to promote efficiency and enhance synergy, a concern known as 'institutional economy'. Third, as a multilateral treaty in its own right, Parties to the Protocol form a legally autonomous regime, even though the Protocol shares the Convention's underlying structure

[115] Rule 2.8.

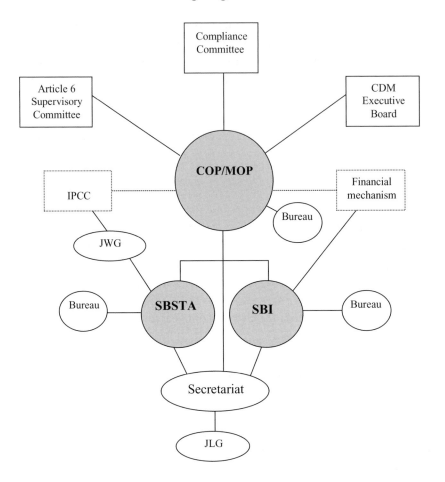

.... Independent bodies that provide services to the climate change process

JLG: Joint Liaison Group (FCCC, CBD, UNCCD) (officers and secretariats)
JWG: Joint Working Group (officers and secretariats)
Note: The work of these two more informal groups is likely to encompass both Convention and Kyoto Protocol matters.

Fig. 13.2   Institutions of the Kyoto Protocol

and ultimate objective, and all of the Convention's rules and principles must be observed by Protocol Parties.[116]

The institutional machinery of the Kyoto Protocol (see figure 13.2) rests upon the institutional infrastructure created under the FCCC. The Protocol deploys the COP to serve as 'the meeting of the Parties' – the COP/MOP – as well as drawing upon

---

[116] FCCC Articles 17.4 and 17.5 and KP Article 13.2.

the Convention's SBs, Secretariat and financial mechanism. These institutions have been modified, where necessary, to ensure the legal distinctness of Protocol institutions. New, specialised institutions have been created only where these serve needs specific to the Protocol that cannot be met by existing institutions. These are the Executive Board of the CDM, the Article 6 Supervisory Committee and the Compliance Committee.

Deploying existing institutions to serve the Protocol remains a novel approach to institutional design. The 2000 Cartagena Protocol on Biosafety, negotiated in parallel to the Kyoto Protocol, is the only other international agreement that establishes similar institutional arrangements to those found in the Kyoto Protocol. Whether such institutional arrangements prove workable in practice, given the different sets of Parties to the Protocol and the FCCC, remains to be seen.[117] Experience with the first COP/MOP, and the positions of those Parties that do not intend to ratify the Kyoto Protocol, notably the US and Australia, will influence institutional developments, in particular the degree of procedural separateness deemed practical or necessary to cater for the evolving political, legal and budgetary concerns raised by the two sets of Parties.

3.1   *COP/MOP*

Article 13.1 of the Kyoto Protocol states that 'the COP, as the supreme body of the Convention, shall serve as the meeting of the Parties to this Protocol' (COP/MOP). This section addresses the mandate of the COP/MOP, its legal relationship to the COP, and the operational modalities defining how the COP/MOP will function, recognising that some matters will be agreed definitively only when the COP/MOP meets, and even thereafter will be subject to refinement.

3.1.1   Mandate

Failure to use an upper case 'M' in 'meeting of the Parties', and the factually correct recognition that the COP *is* the supreme body of the Convention, does not detract from the fact that Article 13.1 of the Protocol creates a 'legally distinct' body, termed the COP/MOP, to oversee implementation of the Protocol.[118] The legal nature of the COP/MOP – whether it should be regarded, for example, as an organisation – depends on the factors and considerations discussed above dealing with the legal nature of the COP. The case for regarding the COP/MOP as an international organisation is even more compelling because, for example, the COP/MOP is served by permanent bodies (e.g. the CDM Executive Board) to implement specialised functions on its behalf.

---

[117] Arrangements for the first COP/MOP are discussed in FCCC/SBI/2002/12 and FCCC/SBI/2003/3.

[118] See, for example, SBI-18 report, paragraph 44 (a).

The formulation of Article 13.1 means that the COP/MOP cannot, without its consent, be subject to the COP. Attempts during the Kyoto Protocol negotiations to elevate the COP to a position of hierarchical superiority over the COP/MOP failed.[119] This is because the Convention states at Article 17.5 that 'decisions under any protocol shall only be taken by the Parties to the protocol concerned', which is reiterated in Article 13.2 of the Kyoto Protocol itself. It was agreed, however, that the COP/MOP should be 'functionally integrated [with the COP but] legally distinct'.[120] Protocol provisions dealing with the functions of the COP/MOP, as well as the timing and venue of its sessions, were subsequently defined to maximise cooperation between the two bodies and to minimise logistical and administrative inconvenience, preserving at the same time the legal and procedural distinctness of the Protocol institutions.

One caveat to the foregoing concerns emissions trading under Article 17 of the Protocol. This Article, drafted in haste on the last night at Kyoto, requires the COP, and not the COP/MOP, to define the relevant principles, modalities, rules and guidelines for emissions trading. The use of the COP to fulfil this function was agreed because it was believed this would 'fast track' negotiations on emissions trading whilst maintaining the involvement of all FCCC Parties.[121] The result is that, in this specific area, the COP will exercise a function that relates to the Kyoto Protocol, and not to the Convention. Post-Kyoto, Parties appear to have accepted, however, that to have proper legal effect, decisions adopted by the COP on emissions trading would need to be affirmed by the COP/MOP.[122] Whether Parties to the Convention who are not Parties to the Protocol will consider it necessary, or diplomatically politic, to make decisions *relating to the Protocol* remains to be seen.[123]

3.1.2   Functions

The Kyoto Protocol assigns several specific functions to the COP/MOP. Article 7.4, in particular subparagraphs (a)–(j), replicates for the COP/MOP, on a *mutatis mutandis* basis, the functions of the COP set out in FCCC Article 7.2 (a)–(m) explained above. There are three fewer subparagraphs under the Protocol because it was deemed not essential to carry over subparagraphs (f) and (j) of FCCC Article 7.2, dealing respectively with reports on implementation of the Convention and guidance to SBs. Likewise, subparagraph (k) of FCCC Article 7.2 relating to rules of procedure is dealt with in Article 7.5 of the Protocol. These minor discrepancies aside, express inclusion of these wide-ranging functions signifies clearly the legally

---

[119] Oberthür and Ott, 1999: pp. 241–2.   [120] FCCC/TP/2000/2, paragraph 365.

[121] See chapter 6; FCCC/TP/2000/2, paragraphs 380–95; Oberthür and Ott, 1999: p. 193.

[122] Decision 18/CP.7 and accompanying Draft Decision -/CMP.   [123] See chapter 1.

autonomous nature of the COP/MOP and its ability to undertake a wide range of actions to promote implementation of the Protocol. The need for functional integration is, however, stressed in Article 7 of the Protocol and elsewhere. For example, the COP/MOP is required to take decisions adopted by the COP fully into account, signalling the need for it to base its decisions upon a thorough deliberation of existing rules and the results of experience gained under the Convention.[124]

Additional functions for the COP/MOP are embedded in other provisions of the Protocol, with a number expressly requiring the COP/MOP to adopt decisions at its first session. A number of these issues, termed the 'unfinished business' of Kyoto, were deemed by some Parties to be of such significance that they were unwilling to ratify the Protocol until political negotiations on these were fully resolved.[125] These matters were covered by the Buenos Aires Plan of Action, which was effectively brought to a close with the adoption of the Marrakesh Accords. In resolving this 'unfinished business', the COP served as a transitional body for the COP/MOP pending the Protocol's entry into force.

The Kyoto Protocol provides for the COP/MOP to meet every year in conjunction with sessions of the COP, unless the COP/MOP decides otherwise. Procedures for convening extraordinary sessions of the COP/MOP are identical to those applicable to the COP.[126] Aside from these provisions, the Kyoto Protocol does not address how sessions of the COP/MOP should be organised. Important considerations in this regard will be ensuring the procedural and legal distinctness required by the Protocol bodies, and minimising the additional workload generated by these bodies in the face of an already overcrowded agenda.

The SBI has made recommendations to this effect, which the Executive Secretary is asked to take into account when preparing the provisional agendas of the COP, COP/MOP and SBs.[127] These include convening the COP and COP/MOP-1 separately but within the same sessional period, with separate agendas. Similar or related items, however, which concern both the Convention and Protocol (e.g. methodological issues, capacity-building), would be dealt with 'in proximity' (i.e. in sequential meetings) or jointly, in the interests of efficiency. A joint COP and COP/MOP high-level segment – that is, including debates/roundtables with ministerial participation[128] – would be convened, with only one speaker's list. No decisions, however, would be taken during such joint meetings. Interestingly, seating arrangements for the COP would also be used for the COP/MOP, sparing non-Parties to the Kyoto Protocol the inconvenience – and indeed embarrassment – of moving to observer seating at the opening of a COP/MOP meeting. The experience

---

[124] E.g. Article 7.4 (a) and (e).   [125] See chapter 2.
[126] KP Articles 13.6 and 13.7, respectively.   [127] See SBI-18 report, paragraph 44.
[128] See chapter 14.

with such arrangements at COP/MOP-1 will be evaluated by the SBI before modalities are discussed for subsequent sessions.[129]

3.1.3   Officers

The Kyoto Protocol implies that the COP Bureau will also serve the COP/MOP. However, when Kyoto Protocol issues under the purview of the COP/MOP are being discussed, any member of the COP Bureau representing a non-Party to the Kyoto Protocol will be replaced by an additional member from a Kyoto Protocol Party, elected by the Protocol Parties themselves.[130] The term of office of any replacement officer elected by and from among Parties to the Protocol shall expire at the same time as that of the officer being replaced.[131]

The Protocol does not give express guidance on the most important official: the President. It can be implicitly inferred, however, that the COP President, as a Bureau member, will also serve as the President of the COP/MOP, unless he or she is a representative of a Party that is not a Party to the Protocol. Electing the same person to serve simultaneously as President of both the COP and the COP/MOP is logistically convenient and ensures clarity in terms of leadership and responsibility for the overall smooth running of negotiating sessions.

3.2   *Subsidiary bodies and their Bureaux*

Article 15 of the Protocol provides that the SBSTA and the SBI will also serve the Kyoto Protocol, and the provisions relating to them under the Convention will apply *mutatis mutandis*. As with the COP Bureau, any member of the SBSTA and SBI Bureaux representing a non-Party to the Protocol will be replaced by the representative of a Protocol Party when the subsidiary bodies are exercising their functions under the Kyoto Protocol.[132]

Sessions of the SBSTA and SBI under the Kyoto Protocol will be held in conjunction with meetings of the SBs under the Convention. As discussed above for the COP and COP/MOP-1, the SBI has recommended that separate agendas be drawn up for the SBs acting under the Convention and under the Kyoto Protocol the first time they convene, with joint meetings held on items of common concern. This approach will then be evaluated for subsequent sessions.

3.3   *Specialised bodies*

There are three specialised bodies established under the Kyoto Protocol, one of which, the CDM executive board (EB/CDM), was provided for in the Protocol

---

[129] Decision 17/CP.9, Arrangements for the first session of the Conference of the Parties serving as the meeting of the Parties to the Kyoto Protocol.

[130] KP Article 13.3.   [131] Decision 17/CP.9.   [132] KP Article 15.2.

Table 13.5 *Composition and officers of specialised bodies under the Kyoto Protocol*

Body (total)	UN Regional group					Small island	Annex I		NAI	Officers
	Africa	Asia	LAC	CEE	WEOG		AI	EIT		
EB/CDM (10 + alternates)	1	1	1	1	1	1	2		2	All have a Chair and Vice-Chair, rotating between Annex I and non-Annex I members
A6SC (10 + alternates)	–	–	–	–	–	1	3[133]	3	3	
Compliance Committee (10 + alternates for each branch)	1	1	1	1	1	1	2		2	

LAC – Latin America and the Caribbean; CEE – Central and Eastern Europe; WEOG – Western Europe and Others; AI – Annex I; EIT – economies in transition; NAI – non-Annex I

[133] Including all Parties included in Annex I that are not EITs.

itself. The other two, the Compliance Committee and the Article 6 Supervisory Committee (A6SC), were set up by the Marrakesh Accords.

The Kyoto Protocol specialised bodies are different in character to those under the Convention. All three operate directly under the COP/MOP (rather than the SBs), and all three have authority to take decisions with which Parties are expected to comply. Their respective membership formulae and arrangements for officers are summarised and compared in table 13.5. The similarity between many aspects of these reflects the common negotiating history of the bodies, although their mandates and functions differ considerably. Each body is discussed in more detail in the relevant chapter of this book: the EB/CDM and A6SC in chapter 6; and the Compliance Committee in chapter 12 .

14

The negotiation process

1   Introduction

Parties to the climate change regime are engaged in a continuous round of negotiations, reviewing the implementation of commitments, adjusting existing rules and developing new rules to respond to evolving knowledge and changing circumstances. This negotiation process has become increasingly complex over the past decade, as the number of Parties has risen, the issues on the table have multiplied, and the political profile of climate change has grown. The twice-yearly sessions of the COP/subsidiary bodies, around which the climate change negotiations revolve, are regularly attended by more than 1,000 delegates for subsidiary body sessions, 3–4,000 for COP sessions, and over 5,000 for high profile sessions.[1] These meetings are structured around a crowded agenda, dozens of documents, a plethora of negotiating forums, late nights, and an array of activities on the side by NGOs, IGOs and governments. Moreover, the negotiation process is increasingly spilling out beyond the formal sessions, with a proliferation of workshops and meetings throughout the year.

The formal rules for the conduct of the climate change negotiations are set out in the Convention's Rules of Procedure.[2] A small number of procedural rules are also included in the text of the Convention itself, including rules specifying voting majorities in certain circumstances (e.g. for the adoption of

---

[1] By way of comparison, attendance at recent CBD COPs, which are held only every two years, has been around the 2,000 mark and, at sessions of the CBD's Subsidiary Body for Scientific, Technical and Technological Advice, around 500. Recent MOPs to the ozone regime have been attended by fewer than 700 participants, and meetings of its Open-Ended Working Group by fewer than 300.

[2] FCCC/CP/1996/2.

amendments).[3] Further procedural rules have been elaborated through COP decisions, including some applying to the negotiation process in general, and others relating to the specialised bodies.[4] In addition, unwritten practices have developed over time both in the UN system in general and specifically in the climate change regime, while the negotiation process is also shaped by the individual views and actions of the COP President, SB Chairs and Bureaux, who devote considerable effort to the strategic procedural management of the negotiations. In this regard, a critical dimension to the negotiations is the pivotal – albeit often unseen – role played by the Secretariat in promoting a smooth process and successful outcome; this role, which permeates all of the elements discussed in this chapter, is discussed more fully in chapter 16. Overall, few of the rules and practices that govern the climate change negotiation process are set in stone, but rather have evolved pragmatically out of the combined experience of the delegates and the Secretariat, greatly influenced by United Nations precedent and practice.[5]

This chapter explains the Rules of Procedure that underpin negotiations, before discussing various key aspects, such as decision-making, agendas, documentation and participation by observers. The chapter discusses formal and informal forums in which negotiations are conducted, including participation by ministers. Finally, the chapter examines activities that take place 'on the side' of the formal negotiations, along with the growing trend towards intersessional work in between sessions of the COP and SBs.

2   The Rules of Procedure

2.1   The Convention

FCCC Article 7.2 (k), in tandem with Article 7.3, mandated the COP, at its first session, to agree upon and adopt, by consensus, rules of procedure (and financial rules[6]) for itself and for any subsidiary bodies.

The rules of procedure to be adopted were drafted in the run-up to COP-1. They broadly mirrored the rules used in the UN General Assembly[7] and in other MEAs.[8] These draft rules, however, could not be adopted at COP-1 due to disagreements relating to the decision-making procedures set out in draft Rule 42, including the specified voting majorities required for adoption of particular decisions (see

---

[3] See chapter 18.

[4] The latter are discussed in the respective chapters of this book relating to the specialised bodies.

[5] The authors are indebted to Michael Zammit Cutajar for making this point.

[6] See chapter 16.   [7] A/520/Rev.15, Rules of procedure of the General Assembly.

[8] In particular the rules of the Basel Convention; see also the rules of procedure for the Montreal Protocol (see Ozone Secretariat, 2003) and the CBD (CBD COP-1 report, Annex III).

box 14.1 below).[9] The composition of the COP Bureau set out in Rule 22 constituted another, though lesser, bone of contention, with some oil-exporting developing countries arguing for a dedicated seat on the COP Bureau for countries referred to in FCCC Article 4.8 (h), that is, those whose economies are highly dependent on income generated from fossil fuels.[10]

In the absence of any consensus, the draft Rules of Procedure were 'applied' rather than adopted, with the exception of the disputed draft Rule 42.[11] Since then, in the face of continued lack of consensus, the fifty-nine draft rules have been 'applied' at all COP sessions, with the exception of Rule 42 on voting.[12] Successive COP Presidents have conducted informal consultations to try to break the deadlock, but to no avail.[13] Great importance was attached to resolving this issue during the Kyoto Protocol negotiations, given that, in the absence of any agreed majority voting rule for the adoption of protocols, the Protocol would have to be adopted by consensus. Since the successful adoption of the Kyoto Protocol by consensus, however, interest in securing formal adoption of the rules has diminished and the consultations of COP Presidents on this issue in recent years have been largely perfunctory or not taken place at all.[14]

The rules of procedure that are applied are those presented to COP-2.[15] We refer to these as the 'Rules of Procedure', because there is no disagreement to the now decade-old practice regarding their application except, of course, the voting rule.[16] Thus, the fact that they are 'applied' rather than 'adopted' is of little practical consequence, although the distinction continues to be highlighted by particular delegations to underline their insistence on consensus decision-making. Most of these Rules in fact reflect procedural practices that are so pervasive across international institutions that many are regarded as having the status of customary international law.[17]

The Rules of Procedure cover all aspects of the negotiation process under the climate change regime aiming, on the one hand, to secure the orderly conduct of business and adoption of decisions and, on the other hand, to safeguard the

---

[9] See COP-1 report, part I, paragraphs 9 and 10.   [10] See chapter 13.

[11] See COP 1-report, part I, paragraphs 9 and 10.

[12] See, for example, COP-2 report, part I, paragraph 12 and COP 7 report, part I, paragraph 22.

[13] For the most concerted attempt to resolve the dispute, see FCCC/CP/1997/5, where the COP-2 President put forward two options for consideration, a three-fourths or seven-eighths majority for all matters of substance.

[14] See, for example, COP-7 report, part I, paragraph 23.   [15] FCCC/CP/1996/2.

[16] Given their non-adopted status, the formal title of the rules is 'Draft rules of procedure as applied'. We have simply used the term 'Rules of Procedure' to refer to those rules contained in FCCC/CP/1996/2 to distinguish these clearly from other rules contained in the Convention, or derived from other sources such as COP decisions, which get a lower case.

[17] Sabel, 1997.

rights of delegations to explain their positions, submit proposals and participate in decision-making.[18] They apply to any session of the COP and SBs, can only be amended by consensus and, in the event of a conflict between the Rules of Procedure and the Convention, the Convention prevails.[19]

2.2   *The Kyoto Protocol*

KP Article 13.5 states that the COP/MOP shall apply the Rules of Procedure of the Convention *mutatis mutandis*, unless otherwise decided by consensus by the COP/MOP.

The three specialised bodies serving the Protocol – the Article 6 supervisory committee, the Executive Board of the CDM and the Compliance Committee – all have detailed rules of procedure spelt out in their constituent Decisions.[20] Each body is mandated to elaborate its rules of procedure further, with approval of these rules to be granted by the COP/MOP.[21]

3   Delegations

3.1   *Parties*

The Rules of Procedure provide for Parties attending sessions to be represented by a delegation consisting of a head of delegation, and any other individuals as may be required.[22] Alternate representatives may also be designated.[23] The credentials of representatives must be submitted to the Secretariat, if possible not later than twenty-four hours after the opening of a session of the COP,[24] although many Parties do not adhere to this time-frame. These credentials, which attest to the representatives' authority to take decisions, must be issued by either the Head of State or government, or by the Minister of Foreign Affairs of each country (or, in the case of regional economic integration organisations, the relevant competent authority). The Bureau examines the credentials of each Party and submits a report to the COP,[25] with delegates permitted to participate in the session on a

---

[18] Sabel, 1997.   [19] Rules 1, 27.1, 58 and 59, respectively

[20] See Decision 16/CP.7, Guidelines for the implementation of Article 6 of the Kyoto Protocol and Draft Decision -/CMP.1 of the same title. Annex Decision 17/CP.7, Modalities and procedures for a clean development mechanism as defined in Article 12 of the Kyoto Protocol and Draft Decision -/CMP.1 of the same title. Annex and Decision 24/CP.7, Procedures and mechanisms relating to compliance under the Kyoto Protocol, Annex. These specific rules are discussed in the relevant chapters of this book.

[21] The rules of procedure of the EB/CDM are to be approved by the COP to ensure its interim functioning.

[22] Rule 17.   [23] Rule 18.   [24] Rule 19.   [25] Rule 20.

provisional basis pending the COP's acceptance of their credentials.[26] The acceptance of credentials is typically a formality. No credentials are required for participation in SB sessions, the practice being that credentials submitted to the COP
carry through to the next COP session. Credentials from Parties to the Kyoto Protocol will apply for the participation of their representatives in both the COP and
the COP/MOP. A single report on credentials will be submitted for approval by the
COP Bureau to both the COP and the COP/MOP.[27]

3.2   *Observers*

3.2.1   Non-governmental organisations

In order to be represented at sessions of the regime bodies, non-
governmental *organisations* (rather than individuals) must be formally admitted.[28]
To pass through a first screening by the Secretariat, NGOs must fulfil two criteria. First, they must be 'qualified in matters covered by the Convention'.[29] This
requirement to demonstrate expertise or knowledge of the issue at hand is common in MEAs and is also part of the screening criteria for accreditation of NGOs
to the UN's Economic and Social Council (ECOSOC).[30] Secondly, they must supply proof of their non-profit, tax-exempt status, a requirement that again follows the rules for NGO accreditation to ECOSOC and has become established
practice in the climate change regime. The effect of this criterion is to require
businesses to group together in non-profit coalitions, rather than representing
themselves.

The Secretariat compiles a list of screened applicants for consideration by the
COP Bureau. The list of cleared applicant organisations is then put to the COP for
formal admission. Due to the large number of NGOs seeking admission, applications received between sessions of the COP that have passed through the Secretariat and Bureau may be presented to the next SB session for provisional
admission, pending formal action by the COP. The Convention, Kyoto Protocol
and Rules of Procedure state that observers may be admitted 'unless at least
one third of the Parties present at the session object', another clause that is
standard in MEAs.[31] A single admission procedure will apply upon entry into

---

[26] Rule 21.

[27] See Decision 17/CP.9, Arrangements for the first session of the Conference of the Parties
serving as the meeting of the Parties to the Kyoto Protocol, and Draft Decision -/CMP.1 of the
same title.

[28] On the admission process, see http://unfccc.int/resource/ngo/adm_proc.pdf.

[29] FCCC Article 7.6.   [30] See www.un.org/esa/coordination/ngo.

[31] FCCC Article 7.2, KP Article 13.8 and Rule 7.1.

force of the Kyoto Protocol, with the COP admitting observer organisations, who are then admitted to both the COP and the COP/MOP.[32]

In a new development for the climate change regime, a set of guidelines[33] has been prepared by the Secretariat, in consultation with NGO constituencies, establishing a 'code of conduct' for NGOs at climate change meetings. These guidelines are in line with those governing NGO participation in the wider UN system, and require, for example, that NGOs refrain from using meeting venues for unauthorised demonstrations, and that they respect other participants' 'social, cultural, religious or other opinions' in written materials while refraining from 'personal attacks'. This development was prompted by a small number of disruptive incidents involving individuals admitted as environmental NGOs.

3.2.2   Intergovernmental organisations, UN bodies and specialised agencies

Procedures for the admission of IGOs to the climate change regime parallel those described above for NGOs.[34] The Convention, Kyoto Protocol and Rules of Procedure, however, do not impose restrictions on attendance by *UN bodies and specialised agencies*, stating simply that these 'may be represented' at sessions of the COP, and by extension the SBs.

4   The agenda

A provisional agenda for each COP and SB session is drafted by the Secretariat, in agreement with the President.[35] It is circulated to Parties at least six weeks before the session in all six UN languages.[36] In practice, the Secretariat has little leeway in drawing up the provisional agenda, and each item must be justified according to the permissible categories specified in the Rules of Procedure.[37] These comprise:

- Items arising from the Convention, including COP functions specified in FCCC Article 7 (e.g. for the COP to review the national communications of Parties);

---

[32] See Decision 17/CP.9, Arrangements for the first session of the Conference of the Parties serving as the meeting of the Parties to the Kyoto Protocol, and Draft Decision -/CMP.1 of the same title.

[33] Guidelines for the participation of representatives of non-governmental organisations at meetings of the bodies of the United Nations Framework Convention on Climate Change, March 2003. Available at www.unfccc.int.

[34] FCCC Article 7.6, KP Article 13.8 and Rule 7.

[35] Rule 9.   [36] Rule 11.   [37] Rules 10, 12 and 16.

- Items that a previous session decided to include on the provisional agenda. Many decisions, for example, mandate the COP to consider a particular issue at a future date;
- Any item on the agenda of a previous session whose consideration was not completed at that session;
- Items proposed by a Party and received by the Secretariat before the provisional agenda is circulated; and
- Budgetary and administrative implications of matters arising from the substantive agenda.[38]

The COP Bureau has also been known to propose items for inclusion on the provisional agenda of the COP.[39]

The adoption of the agenda is a procedural matter. As with other decisions, the practice of the COP (and SBs) to date has been to adopt the agenda on the basis of consensus, although this is not specifically required by either the Convention or the Rules of Procedure.

Parties can, and often do, request additions, deletions or changes in the wording of items when the provisional agenda is proposed for adoption on the first day of the session,[40] although items may only be added if the COP or SB agrees these are urgent and important.[41] The presiding officer or Executive Secretary may also propose changes in response to concerns raised informally by Parties. This means that not all items, whether proposed by Parties or otherwise, make it onto the final agenda.

Refusing to allow an item onto the agenda is the surest way of blocking any future discussion of an unwelcome issue, thereby obviating the need to veto decisions at some future date. The corollary is refusal to remove an item from the agenda; just as consensus is needed to agree items, consensus is also needed to remove them. A Party can thus insist that its proposed item remains on the provisional agenda from session to session, even if it never makes it onto the agenda itself. A variant of this strategy is to hold items hostage to one another, accepting one only if the other is also agreed. Moreover, the requirement that items that have not been completed be carried over to the next session (unless there is consensus to do otherwise) means that deadlocked items can drag on from provisional agenda to provisional agenda.

Recent COP and SB sessions have seen growing controversy over the adoption of the agenda. A dramatic example was the item on voluntary commitments, which

---

[38] See also chapter 16.
[39] The Bureau proposed an item on 'Procedure for the appointment of the Executive Secretary' for the COP-8 provisional agenda. see FCCC/CP/2002/1.
[40] Rule 13.   [41] Rule 13

was placed on the provisional agenda at COP-4 by Argentina with the (Argentinian) President's support, but without significant prior consultations with Parties. Developing countries blocked its inclusion on the final agenda.[42] A strategy used to enable adoption of the agenda and the start of business in the face of controversial agenda items has been to place those items 'in abeyance', meaning that they are neither discussed at the session nor struck off the agenda, and are typically then carried over to the provisional agenda for the next session. The number of items 'in abeyance' has grown, with three dealt with in this way at COP-8 and COP-9; among these, the item on the second review of adequacy of Article 4.2 (a) and (b) has now been held in abeyance for five consecutive COPs.[43] Insights from the study of international regimes suggest that, as regimes confront politically sensitive issues, there will indeed be a rise in the number of 'non-decisions',[44] that is, items that do not make it onto the formal agenda, are held in abeyance, or result only in symbolic conclusions.

5   Conduct of business

The COP President or SB Chair is responsible for declaring the opening and closing of sessions and presiding over meetings.[45] Each two-week 'session' (or 'sessional period') of the COP and SBs comprises several individual 'meetings', lasting anything from a few minutes to many hours. The presiding officer must determine whether a quorum of one-third of the Parties is present before a meeting can start, and this rises to two-thirds for the taking of decisions.[46] Although it is rare for the quorum to be formally verified, the President and Secretariat will scan the room to check that sufficient delegates appear to be present and, in particular, that the main negotiating coalitions (e.g. the G-77, the EU)[47] are represented.

5.1   *Speaking: 'taking the floor'*

Parties may only speak at meetings if they have previously obtained permission to do so from the presiding officer.[48] Delegates seek permission to speak by placing their country flags[49] in a vertical position. The Rules of Procedure require the presiding officer to call upon speakers in the order in which they do so,[50] although the Chair or Rapporteur of an SB may be accorded precedence to explain the conclusions of that body.[51] The Secretariat maintains a list of speakers to help

---

[42] COP-4 report, part I, paragraph 14.   [43] See COP-9 report, part I.   [44] Gupta, 1997.
[45] Rule 23.1. For more on the role of the presiding officer, see chapter 13.
[46] Rule 31.   [47] See chapter 3   [48] Rule 32.
[49] So-called country 'flags' are, in practice, cardboard signs bearing the Party's name.
[50] Rule 32.   [51] Rule 33.

the presiding officer.[52] In practice, the presiding officer will often use his/her discretion to decide on the order in which s/he calls upon Parties.

The Rules of Procedure allow the presiding officer to call a speaker to order if his/her remarks are not relevant to the subject.[53] The presiding officer may also propose that the time allowed to each speaker be limited, along with the number of times that a delegate may speak on a particular issue. Before the meeting takes such action, two representatives may speak in favour and two against.[54] As far as can be ascertained, this Rule has only been invoked in the uncontroversial context of the high-level segment (see below) where the COP has placed a limitation on the length of policy statements delivered by ministers and heads of delegations during the general debate.

Parties may raise points of order, which, according to the Rules of Procedure, must be decided upon immediately by the presiding officer.[55] A delegate may appeal against the ruling. Any appeal must be put to the vote immediately, and the ruling stands, unless it is overruled by a majority of Parties present and voting.[56] Points of order are raised frequently in COP meetings but have always been resolved without voting.

The Rules also set out procedures for raising procedural motions, for example questioning the competence of the COP to discuss any matter or adopt a proposal, and calling for the suspension or adjournment of a meeting, or the adjournment or closure of the debate on a particular issue.[57] Such motions must be put to the vote before substantive discussion can continue. Although Parties have often called for debate to be adjourned, or a meeting suspended, no procedural motion questioning the competence of the COP has ever been formally raised, confirming the wide scope of its legal mandate.[58]

5.2   *Making proposals*

Any proposed text, or amendment to a proposed text, should normally be introduced in writing by a Party and handed to the Secretariat, which will then circulate copies to delegations. If submitted intersessionally in response to a request from the SBs, such proposals from Parties will typically be reproduced in 'MISC' documents, discussed below. Proposals submitted during sessions, however, will often be circulated simply as 'non-papers', in order to save time and paper.

Although, as a general rule, no proposal should be discussed unless copies have been circulated not later than the previous day, the presiding officer may waive this Rule.[59] In the fast-moving climate change negotiations, requiring written proposals to be circulated a day in advance would certainly place an impossible

---

[52] Rule 32.   [53] Rule 32.   [54] Rule 32.   [55] Rule 34.   [56] Rule 34.   [57] Rules 35 and 38.
[58] See chapter 13.   [59] Rule 36.

brake on the negotiation process. The spirit of this Rule is therefore adhered to rather than its letter, with the Secretariat making every effort to distribute new proposals as quickly as possible, to give delegations the maximum amount of time to consider them.

The text of any proposed amendment, annex or protocol to the Convention, however, along with any proposed amendment to an annex, must be communicated to the Parties by the Secretariat at least six months before the session at which it is proposed for adoption. This requirement, which is set out in the Convention as well as the Rules of Procedure,[60] is strictly adhered to.

Any proposal (or procedural motion) may be withdrawn by its proposer at any time before a decision on it is taken, provided that it has not been amended.[61] A proposal that has been withdrawn may be reintroduced by another Party, but once a proposal has been adopted or rejected, it may not be reconsidered at the same session, unless a two-thirds majority of the Parties decide otherwise.[62] This Rule has also never been invoked because Parties use informal channels to assess the political viability of proposals within the limits imposed by consensus decision-making.

In practice, the process of making proposals takes place in a more fluid manner than that suggested by the above Rules. Many different proposals and amendments to proposals are put forward, both in writing and orally, with little advance notice, and these are often withdrawn or reconsidered without invoking the formal rules. Regarding 'the rules of procedure as the creature of the conference and not as its master'[63] certainly provides flexibility and opportunities for procedural creativity for the Parties. There is danger, however, in the increased tendency of the COP to jettison procedural requirements clearly spelt out in the Rules. Smaller, less well-resourced and non-anglophone delegations, for example, are at a considerable disadvantage when Rules relating to advance circulation of documents and use of UN languages are waived in the interests of speed and expediency. This also increases the risk that mistakes will be made, including in the translated versions of documents, or problematic text adopted.

5.3   *Participation of observers*

The Convention and Rules of Procedure permit admitted observers to participate (in other words, to speak) in meetings of the COP and SBs upon invitation of the presiding officer and without the right to vote, unless at least one-third of the Parties present at the session object.[64] An added restriction is placed on representatives of NGOs and IGOs (but not UN bodies and specialised agencies),

---

[60] Rule 37 and FCCC Articles 15, 16 and 17.   [61] Rule 39.   [62] Rules 39 and 40.
[63] Sabel, 1997: p. 417.   [64] Rules 6 and 7.

who may only speak on 'matters of direct concern to the body or agency they represent'.[65] This restriction, however, has never been acted upon and, as far as can be ascertained, no Party has ever objected to an observer taking the floor.

The regime has seen considerable variation in the speaking slots granted to NGOs,[66] both over time and between the different bodies, depending on the approach of the presiding officer. While some have taken a minimalist approach, allowing only one general statement per constituency,[67] others have been more expansive, allowing individual NGOs to intervene on specific issues throughout the session. The AG13,[68] for example, was particularly liberal in this regard, allowing NGOs to intervene and make proposals on specific issues. Recent years have seen a trend towards the more expansive approach in the SBs, although it is still unusual for there to be more than half a dozen or so NGO interventions per two-week negotiating session. To some extent, this reflects the recognition on the part of many NGOs that delivering a statement in plenary is not necessarily the most effective way of getting their message across. In the more strictly choreographed proceedings of the COP, speaking slots for NGOs (along with IGOs and UN agencies) are typically limited to general statements on behalf of constituencies during the high-level segment involving ministers. In all cases, statements by NGOs are taken after those of Parties.

Written proposals or views from NGOs are not issued in MISC documents. The Secretariat has, however, introduced a new practice of issuing written submissions from NGOs, usually through the constituencies, on specific agenda items as Web-only documents and placing these on its website.[69] Such submissions have been referenced in the formal reports of the SBs, thereby providing an important opportunity for NGOs to provide input into the negotiations in a more structured way.

6   Decision-making

Rules for taking decisions lie at the heart of any intergovernmental process. The Convention itself specifies procedures for adopting certain kinds of decisions, including amendments, new annexes and amendments to annexes.

---

[65] Rule 7.

[66] Because IGOs and UN bodies do not assume an advocacy role, they rarely seek to take the floor in debates. These organisations, however, (especially UN bodies) may be formally invited to report on their work of relevance to the climate change regime under the SBSTA item on cooperation with relevant international organisations (see chapter 17).

[67] On the NGO constituencies, see chapter 3.   [68] See chapter 13.

[69] See, for example, the submission by the Climate Action Network in FCCC/WEB/2002/13.

For these decisions, in the absence of consensus, the Convention specifies three-fourths of Parties present and voting as the majority necessary for adoption.[70]

Lack of agreement on draft Rule 42 of the Rules of Procedure (see box 14.1 below), as discussed above, leaves a vacuum in respect of how substantive decisions are to be adopted. This vacuum cannot entirely be filled by customary rules because there is no agreed international norm concerning the majority required to approve substantive decisions. As noted by Sabel, 'customary rules exist only in regard to conduct of business', and the 'lack of consistency as to rules concerning the majority required to approve decisions' means that no customary rule can be said to have evolved regarding majority decision-making.[71] In the absence of any specified majority voting rule, there is currently a broad understanding in the climate change regime that substantive decisions should be adopted *by consensus*.[72]

Box 14.1   Draft Rule 42

Rule 42 comprises five paragraphs. The first deals with voting on matters of *substance*. There are two proposed alternatives. Alternative A calls for decisions to be taken by a two-thirds majority vote of the Parties present and voting, if consensus proves impossible, except for:

- The adoption of financial rules and the rules of procedure themselves, which the Convention states must be adopted by consensus;
- A decision to adopt a protocol, for which there are two further disputed alternatives: adoption by consensus, or by a three-fourths majority;
- Decisions relating to the financial mechanism and the financial obligations of Annex II Parties towards developing countries, which are to be taken by consensus.

Alternative B calls for all decisions to be taken by consensus, except for decisions on financial matters, which may be taken by a two-thirds majority. Paragraph 2 addresses voting on *procedural* matters, stating that these shall be taken by a majority vote. The disputed part of this paragraph sets out a proposed exception for a decision to close/limit debate or the list of speakers, requiring a two-thirds majority vote for this.

---

[70] FCCC Articles 15 and 16. The Kyoto Protocol includes the same provisions in its Articles 20 and 21. See chapter 18.

[71] Sabel, 1997: p. 420.   [72] Sabel, 1997: p. 420.

The remaining paragraphs are not disputed and no alternatives are presented, but they have been bracketed as a whole to reflect clearly that Rule 42 is under dispute.

Paragraph 3 provides for the President to rule on whether a matter is procedural or substantive, with any appeal against this ruling being put to the vote immediately. The President's ruling stands unless overruled by a majority.

Paragraph 4 addresses situations where a vote is equally divided, in which case a second vote is taken (except for the election of officers) and, if this is also equally divided, the proposal is rejected. Paragraph 5 defines 'Parties present and voting' as 'Parties present at the meeting at which voting takes place and casting an affirmative or negative vote', with abstentions not counted as votes.

The operational meaning of consensus is not defined in the Convention or the Rules of Procedure. Across a wide spectrum of intergovernmental processes, however, consensus is seen as distinct from unanimity, and is generally defined negatively to mean that there are no stated objections to a decision.[73] This is also the case in the climate context. In practical terms, this means that a small group of Parties, or arguably even a single Party, can, in principle, raise a formal objection to a particular decision, thus preventing its adoption, as happened at COP-2.[74] Considerable political efforts are therefore expended to accommodate the concerns of all Parties, either by changing the wording of a particular decision or through trade-offs on other issues.

Determining whether consensus exists and a decision can be adopted is one of the most significant tasks for a COP President or SB Chair, who is mandated by the Rules of Procedure to 'announce decisions'.[75] Charm, cunning, humour, daring and a range of other techniques are deployed by such officers to generate consensus. Often a presiding officer will rely upon the reluctance of Parties to be seen as standing in the way, especially at a high profile meeting under scrutiny from NGOs and the media. In this regard, the opportunity for a Party to make a statement registering its concerns, and for that statement to be recorded in the formal report on the session,[76] serves as a useful 'safety valve' that can enable reluctant Parties to join the consensus, while still safeguarding their national positions.[77] However, this does not always work and more behind-the-scenes work

---

[73] Sabel, 1997; Yefimov, 1989; Schermers and Blokker, 1995; Werksman, 1999a.

[74] See box 13.1 on COP outputs in chapter 13.   [75] Rule 23.1.   [76] See Werksman, 1999a.

[77] See, for example, statements made on adoption of the Berlin Mandate (Decision 1/CP.1) in COP-1 report, part I, paragraphs 58–60.

may be needed to defuse opposition. As a last resort, the presiding officer can make a ruling, which, if challenged, leads to a vote. The vote is called pursuant to the powers conferred on the presiding officer by the Rules of Procedure to make rulings and to have complete control over the meeting they are presiding over. This is backed by customary international law.[78] A memorable occasion in the climate regime when a presiding officer's ruling was challenged and the possibility of a vote was raised occurred during the Kyoto Protocol negotiations. At the negotiating session before Kyoto, Chairman Estrada ruled there was consensus to move forward with one of the negotiating options, although three Parties had expressed their objection to the option under consideration.[79] In the face of objections from these and several other delegations, Chairman Estrada stated his resolve to put his ruling to a vote. Recognising that a precedent could be set, and that the substantive issue at hand was of minor political consequence, the objectors withdrew their challenge, no vote was called and the Chairman's ruling stood.

If voting were to take place, it would normally be by show of hands.[80] A secret ballot, or a roll-call vote where each Party's vote is recorded in the relevant documents of the session, would be taken if a Party requested this.[81] Each Party has one vote, except for regional economic integration organisations (of which the EU is currently the only example), which do not have a vote separate from that of their members. If its members do not exercise their right to vote, however, a regional economic integration organisation may vote with a number of votes equal to that of its members.[82] Voting, once it has started, cannot be interrupted, except on a point of order concerning the actual conduct of the vote. Parties (except for the proposer) may explain their vote, either before or after the voting, but the presiding officer may set a time limit for this.[83] A further set of rules governs the order in which votes must be taken, along with voting on separate parts of proposals and on amendments to proposals.[84] The practical headache, and time-consuming nature, of organising voting in an intergovernmental forum as large and public as the COP deters challenges that might lead to voting.

At a more fundamental level, consensus is the preferred norm in international fora because such decisions command greater legitimacy and are more likely to be adhered to. Additionally, diplomatic and political considerations make states reluctant to engage in the open displays of disagreement that voting implies, even when rules allow this. However, although the 'consensus rule' has the advantage

---

[78] See e.g. Rules 23, 34, 42.2 and 42.3; Sabel, 1997.

[79] AGBM-8, October 1997. Tape recordings of the meeting held with the Secretariat (tape number 8:0459).

[80] Rule 48.   [81] Rules 48, 49 and 51.   [82] FCCC Article 18 and Rule 41.   [83] Rule 50.

[84] Rules 43, 44, 45, 46 and 47.

of promoting an inclusive regime where small minorities cannot be marginalised, it also promotes lowest common denominator solutions.[85] As Széll puts it, 'consensus respects the doctrine of sovereign equality of states but, by placing a veto in the hands of each party, it effectively ensures that the convoy advances at the pace of the slowest vessel'.[86] This can generate considerable frustration among the vast majority of Parties whose wishes are then thwarted.

6.1   *Decision-making under the Kyoto Protocol*

Given that the Rules of Procedure of the Convention will be applied *mutatis mutandis* to the Kyoto Protocol, decision-making under the Protocol is likely also to proceed on the basis of consensus, unless Parties to the Protocol decide to engage in efforts to resolve the dispute over Rule 42. Interestingly, the individual rules of procedure of the three specialised bodies serving the Protocol do allow for the adoption of decisions by majority-voting.

Another important aspect of decision-making under the Kyoto Protocol relates to the role of non-Parties in proceedings and elected bodies which is discussed further in Chapters 1 and 13.

7   Documents

The Rules prescribe that supporting documents for a session of the COP must be distributed to the Parties by the Secretariat at least six weeks before its opening.[87] All official Secretariat documents must be issued in the six official UN languages, namely, Arabic, Chinese, English, French, Russian and Spanish.[88] Along with most other conference servicing functions for the climate change regime, the processing and translation of documents is carried out by the UN Office at Geneva (UNOG).[89]

The strict implementation of the 'six-week' and translation rules, however, is impracticable, given the shortness of time between sessions, the time needed to draft a document (especially when it is based on submissions to be sent in by Parties), the large number of documents requested, and the resources needed to issue and translate these. Translation into all six languages of the UN is expensive, amounting to some US $950 per page.[90] It is therefore not unusual for some documents to be circulated only at the session itself, while not all documents are translated, especially those produced during the session.

[85] Werksman, 1996: p. 60.   [86] Széll, 1996: p. 212.   [87] Rule 11.   [88] Rule 54.
[89] See chapter 16.   [90] Figure supplied by the FCCC Secretariat.

The climate change regime is by no means unique in this regard. The UNGA itself, referring to the UN as a whole, has expressed 'deep concern' at the 'low rate of compliance with the six-week rule for the issuance of documentation' and at the fact that some official documents are not translated into all official languages.[91] The lack of timely translation certainly raises problems for delegates, especially for speakers of UN languages other than English. Late issuance or translation of documents has, at times, delayed the climate change process as delegates have asked for more time to consider a document or insisted on waiting for translations before proceeding with the debates. The Secretariat does, however, try to ensure that the most important documentation for a session, negotiating texts for example, are available on time and in all languages.

The documentation prepared for the climate change negotiations is voluminous. More than sixty documents, for example, were prepared for COP-7 in 2001, and over fifty for SB-16 in 2002. The cost implications of this were addressed by the COP as early as its second session,[92] following a recommendation to do so by the UN's Advisory Committee on Administrative and Budgetary Questions in light of general economy measures being implemented by the UN Secretariat.[93] Decision 17/CP.2, and a follow-up decision at COP-3,[94] urged the Executive Secretary to limit the length of documents prepared by the Secretariat, and delegates to curb the length of their submissions and demands for documents. The Executive Secretary was also requested to explore possibilities for making translated versions of documents available on the Secretariat website, which has now been implemented. Despite these decisions, however, the volume of documentation remains high, although not unusually so compared with other UN negotiation processes.

A summary of the main document types in the climate change regime, and the symbols that they bear, is presented in table 14.1. All official documents are made publicly accessible through posting on the Secretariat website, including, where relevant, translated versions.

7.1   Negotiating texts

Much of this documentation is intended to support the COP's cycle of policy-making, which results ultimately in the adoption of one or other types of outputs, such as COP decisions, resolutions, declarations and other legal

---

[91] UNGA resolution 56/242, Pattern of conferences, Section III, paragraphs 1 and 2, and Section IV, paragraphs 7 and 8.

[92] Decision 17/CP.2, Volume of documentation.   [93] A/50/7/Add.15.

[94] Decision 18/CP.3, Volume of documentation. See also proposals by the Secretariat in this regard in FCCC/SBI/1997/12.

Table 14.1   *Document types*[95]

Document type	Typical content	Symbol	Usual language
Regular	Session reports, provisional agendas, most Secretariat background documents, negotiating texts	-	All six UN languages
Information	Logistical data (e.g. list of participants at a COP session), more substantive information (e.g. a scoping study), or workshop reports	INF	English
Miscellaneous	Proposals or views submitted by Parties. No formal editing	MISC	Language of submission (usually English)
Technical papers	Detailed background papers on technical issues	TP	English
Limited distribution	Draft decisions or conclusions presented to the COP or SBs for adoption	L	All six UN languages
Conference room papers	New proposals or negotiating text prepared during a negotiation session to reflect the status of discussion on a particular issue. Occasionally draft decisions/conclusions presented to the COP or SBs for adoption, where there has been no time for translation and issuance as a limited distribution document (see above)	CRP	English
In-depth review report	Report on the in-depth review of an Annex I Party national communication	IDR	English
WEB-only	Issued only on the Secretariat website (available from the Secretariat in hard copy on request). Used for data/information that will be updated, and to circulate submissions by NGOs. Also used to publish review reports during the	WEB	English

(Cont.)

---

[95] Based on UNFCCC Secretariat, 2002.

Table 14.1   (cont.)

Document type	Typical content	Symbol	Usual language
	trial period for the technical review of Annex I annual inventories		
Daily programme	Issued every day during sessions of the COP and SBs to inform delegates of meeting times and venues for that day	OD	English, sometimes also in the host country language
Addendum	Subsequent addition to any of the above documents	Add	According to the original document
Revision	Subsequent revision to any of the above documents	Rev	
Corrigendum	Subsequent correction to any of the above documents	Corr	
Advance unedited version	Early version of a final document that has not yet been edited or translated, and is often not yet formatted according to the Secretariat's document template. Changes may therefore be included before the final version is released	–	English
Non-paper	Informal text circulated by the Secretariat or Parties with neither a symbol nor a Secretariat logo. Non-papers are used in the interests of speed, or to float preliminary proposals. They have no official status and are not posted on the website	–	Usually English

instruments.[96] The final form and content of these outputs is determined by negotiations based on a variety of negotiating texts. The section below provides a basic orientation to these.

For major negotiating rounds, such as those that led to the Kyoto Protocol and the Marrakesh Accords, Parties are first invited to submit their views in writing on particular issues. Such proposals are published in MISC documents (see table 14.1

---

[96] See chapter 13.

above). Parties use MISC documents to explain and exchange information about their respective positions. The COP President, or more frequently the Chair of the SB directly responsible for the negotiations, will, at a certain stage, seek a mandate to put all proposals together into a single document. The first step might be for this presiding officer to prepare a *synthesis of proposals*, that is, a text simply collating all proposals into a single document in some kind of streamlined and logical order. The second step is then often the preparation of a *consolidated text*, whereby similar proposals are merged and square brackets are introduced to indicate areas of disagreement. The key step is when the presiding officer gains a mandate from the Parties to prepare a *Chair's text*,[97] which presents a coherent version of a text that it is hoped could command widespread support from Parties. How far a presiding officer is prepared to go – creating an entirely new text or drawing faithfully on existing proposals – is a matter of judgement. As the text is intended to move delegations closer to agreement, it must strike a delicate political balance between taking risks to propel the negotiations forwards, and not going so far as to impose an unwanted solution that is then rejected.

In the case of less complex or politically sensitive COP decisions and SB conclusions, the process of generating agreement is much the same. In these cases, however, negotiating texts will be developed over the course of just one or two sessions, and will often be prepared by the relevant presiding officer on the basis of views expressed orally by Parties during debates, rather than written submissions.

8   Negotiating forums and techniques

Negotiations take place in a variety of forums. Although the basic types of negotiating forums – formal plenary meetings, working bodies of the COP, contact groups, informal consultations, 'friends' of the presiding officer, all of which are discussed further below – are common to most intergovernmental negotiations, different regimes tend to develop their own organisational practices that correspond to their particular political dynamics. The climate change regime has been procedurally creative in this regard, spawning a variety of approaches to the organisation of negotiating forums, reflecting the technical complexity of the subject matter, as well as the need for high-level political guidance from ministers.

8.1   *Plenary*

Formal plenary meetings of the COP and SBs lie at the heart of the climate change negotiations. It is only in plenary meetings that the COP may adopt its decisions (or other outputs) and the SBs their conclusions, whether of a procedural

---

[97] Or a President's text, as relevant.

or substantive character. Rule 30 provides that COP plenary meetings be held in public unless the COP decides otherwise, which it has never done. Although the same rule states that meetings of the SBs should be held in private (albeit with accredited observers still permitted to attend), the COP may decide otherwise, and such meetings have in fact always been held in public. Media representatives are often present for high-profile meetings. Plenary meetings of the COP and SBs are also broadcast live on the Internet and stored in a web archive by the Secretariat.

Seating for formal meetings is arranged in an amphitheatre style, with at least two seats, usually four, for each delegation. Delegations are sat in alphabetical order of their country names in English, except when a meeting is held in a francophone country, in which case French alphabetical order is used. Statements made in one official UN language must be interpreted into the others,[98] while the Secretariat must keep sound recordings of the COP, and wherever possible the SBs.[99]

In accordance with UN practice, official meeting hours run in three-hour time slots, from 10 a.m. to 1 p.m. and from 3 p.m. to 6 p.m. Evening or night meetings may also be held. These depend on the availability of interpretation services in line with UN rules governing interpreters' working hours, which are quite rigid. It is not uncommon for plenary meetings to have to adjourn before the conclusion of their business because the allotted interpretation time has run out. A contributing factor in this regard is the unpredictability of the negotiation process, making it difficult to plan when and for how long a plenary meeting will be needed, and also the almost routine delay in the start of formal plenary meetings as informal negotiations drag on. Valuable interpretation time is thus wasted, which can have repercussions on the substantive negotiations as some delegations may refuse to negotiate if no interpretation services are available. Like translation of documents, interpretation is also expensive. Although it has not been applied to the climate change regime, a recent UNGA resolution has in fact sought to limit the duration of meetings to the official hours, with the aim of discouraging additional meetings for budgetary reasons.[100]

Real negotiations, however, rarely take place in plenary. The large size of plenary meetings, their openness to the public and the formality imposed by strict adherence to the Rules of Procedure inhibit in-depth and frank discussion. Plenary meetings, especially those of the COP, are tightly choreographed by the presiding officer and Secretariat who seek to maximise use of the limited time available

---

[98] Rule 55. Parties may provide for interpretation of other languages into an official language. Host countries of COP sessions whose language is not one of the six official UN languages have sometimes covered the costs of doing so (e.g. Japan at COP-3).

[99] Rule 57.   [100] Resolution 56/242, section II, paragraph 1 and Annex.

by avoiding surprises and minimising unplanned debate. Proceedings of plenary meetings, again especially those of the COP, are generally confined to organisational and procedural matters (such as adoption of the agenda and allocation of items to other working bodies), prepared speeches, ceremonial events, and the formal adoption of decisions and conclusions. Plenary meetings also serve as an important forum for delegations to deliver statements staking out their official positions. These include, for example, expressions of concern over an adopted decision or putting on record a particular interpretation of a decision.[101] Parties may also use plenary meetings to formally raise concerns regarding procedural matters,[102] while the presiding officer may report on the state of play of negotiations, using such opportunities to voice concerns about the timing or direction in which they are proceeding.

8.2   *Working bodies*

The predominantly ceremonial nature of the COP means that the COP plenary assigns almost all of its agenda items to other working bodies, which meet in parallel with it. The task of these bodies is to finalise a decision or text for adoption by the plenary. COP sessions have differed in the working bodies used to conduct negotiations on behalf of the plenary, depending on the nature of the work at hand and the approach taken by the President.

The most common approach has been for the COP plenary to allocate most of its work to the Convention's SBs, when these meet in parallel with it (usually the first week of the COP session). Alternatively, in the final stages of a major negotiating round, the COP has sometimes convened a *Committee of the Whole*. Such a Committee of the Whole has essentially consisted of an informal COP plenary. That is, it has usually been convened in a smaller room, chaired by a delegate other than the President, and with more flexibility surrounding the application of the Rules. Interpretation, for example, has not always been provided, allowing meetings also to be held outside official meeting hours. Most meetings of such bodies have been held in public, and sound recordings have been kept. Other variations on this approach have been used. At COP-6 part I, for example, the President convened a so-called *informal high-level plenary* as the working body of the COP. This, in effect, was a Committee of the Whole in all but name, and was chaired by the President himself. At COP-6 part II and COP-7, the President dispensed with an intermediate

---

[101] At COP-7, for example, the delegate from the Republic of Korea stated his understanding that Decision 17/CP.7 (Modalities and procedures for a clean development mechanism) did not exclude the pursuit of unilateral CDM projects (COP-7 report, part I, paragraph 103).

[102] At COP-4, for example, Switzerland 'register[ed] a protest at the exclusion of many countries from the informal ministerial consultations convened by the President' (COP-4 report, part I, paragraph 78).

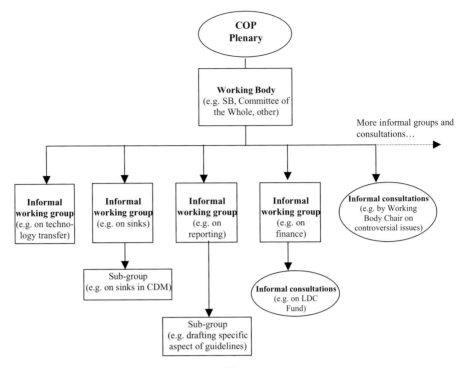

Fig. 14.1   Negotiating forums for a generic COP session

working body and convened a small number of *informal negotiating groups*, each charged with conducting negotiations on a cluster of issues.

The working body – whether the SBs, the Committee of the Whole, or a variation – typically refers the negotiation of specific issues, sometimes particular paragraphs or parts of sentences, to *informal working groups* (e.g. contact groups, negotiating groups – see below), which themselves may in turn convene spin-off groups or informal consultations. These informal groups report back on the results of their negotiations, hopefully with agreed text that can be agreed by the working body and then forwarded to the COP plenary for formal adoption. A clear understanding of how the chain of small informal groups reports to the larger working bodies which themselves report to the COP plenary is essential for participating successfully in the negotiations.

The SBSTA and SBI, when meeting outside of COP sessions, also convene numerous informal working groups and informal consultations to work on draft text, which is then forwarded to the SBs meeting in plenary for formal adoption. A generic 'chain of command' for a COP session is illustrated in figure 14.1, this would be the same for an SB session, without the COP at its head.

8.3   *Informal working groups*

The bulk of negotiations in the climate change regime takes place in informal working groups. Many different names are used for such groups (see box 14.2). They are open-ended, that is, any Party may attend, but vary considerably in their size, because only delegates with a particular interest in an issue tend to participate. Meetings are advertised in the daily programme and electronic notice boards, but no official written or audio records are kept and documents are rarely translated, with proposals circulated instead as 'non-papers'. The advantage of informal working groups is that meeting times are more flexible and delegates are able to talk more freely, knowing no decisions can be taken. Meetings typically take place in smaller, more intimate surroundings, without the use of prescribed seating arrangements and country flags.

Box 14.2   Names of informal working groups

Informal working groups are known by different names depending on their task and the stage of negotiations.

When they are convened by the SBs, they are typically known as *contact groups*. *Joint contact groups*, whose work straddles the mandates of both the SBSTA and SBI, may also be convened by both SBs.

At COP-3, COP-6 part II and COP-7, however, informal working groups were known as *negotiating groups*, to emphasise the urgency of their task in producing text. Conversely, during early negotiations on the Kyoto Protocol under the AGBM, they were termed *non-groups*, to emphasise their informal nature and the fact that no negotiations were taking place.

At COP-6 part I, the President convened four so-called *cluster groups* chaired by ministers, each dealing with a group of related issues (see also 'ministerial participation' below).

The term *drafting group* may be used when the group is engaged in intensive drafting on a negotiating text, usually in the final stages of a negotiation.

The basic nature of all these groups, however, is the same, and so the term 'informal working group' is used generically here.

The Chairs of informal working groups are designated by the presiding officer of their convening body. A practice has emerged post-Kyoto of appointing Co-Chairs, one each from an Annex I and non-Annex I Party, rather than a single Chair. This has the advantage of instilling confidence that the concerns of all Parties will be addressed in a balanced manner. In some cases, the Annex I and non-Annex I Parties (the latter usually through the G-77) themselves nominate the Co-Chair from their group. The informal working group (Co-)Chair(s) may decide to convene *sub-groups* on particular issues, or they may request individual delegates to conduct *informal consultations* on specific matters. These spin-off groups, which are usually not advertised, hold discussions and then report back to the main informal working group.

The COP has decided that representatives of IGOs and NGOs may attend 'any open-ended contact group' as observers, unless at least one-third of Parties raise an objection when the contact group is established.[103] On setting up a contact group, the presiding officer will formally extend an invitation to NGOs and IGOs to attend, and ask if there are any objections. The Chair of the contact group, however, retains the right to close the group to observers at any time, which frequently occurs in the final stages of negotiations. Whether an NGO/IGO is allowed to speak depends on the willingness of the contact group Chair. Moreover, informal working groups are often set up under names other than 'contact group' (see box 14.2), and vary in the degree of formality that they retain. Attendance by NGOs and IGOs at informal group meetings therefore remains discretionary and is often still decided on an ad hoc basis.

Informal working group discussions are traditionally conducted in English only, although exceptions have been made on rare occasions where warranted by the political stakes involved. Disquiet over the conduct of almost all informal negotiations in English only is a recurring concern of non-anglophone delegations, not just in the climate change regime, but throughout the UN system.

Established practice in the climate change process, derived from the wider UN system, demands that only two informal working group (or plenary) meetings be held at any one time, in the interests of fairness to small delegations and maintaining transparency in the negotiation process. Honouring this practice, however, has become increasingly difficult because the volume and pace of work has necessitated a proliferation of informal groups. Insistence on this practice has also, at times, been used as a blocking tactic, even by large delegations.

Combining a high demand for informal groups with the practice of no more than two meetings, along with the need for groups dealing with related issues not to meet in parallel, has led to the partial abandonment of traditional UN meeting hours, with time slots squeezed from three hours to two or even one and a half, and the working day expanded to start earlier in the morning and finish later at night. Night meetings are a strain on all delegates, but impact disproportionately on smaller, usually developing country, delegations, as discussed further below in the context of the 'last night' of negotiations.

---

[103] Decision 18/CP.4.

8.3.1   Informal consultations

Informal consultations differ from informal working groups in that advertised meetings are generally not held. Instead, a delegate is simply charged by the presiding officer to consult informally – in other words, hold a discussion – with interested Parties to try to reach agreement on a particular issue or draft text. This can be over a cup of coffee or in a small meeting room. There are two main types of informal consultations: those convened to deal with more technical issues that interest a relatively small number of Parties and do not warrant a full informal working group meeting; and those convened, on the contrary, to address more sensitive issues where private, behind-the-scenes discussion is likely to prove more productive. In some cases, the presiding officer may choose to conduct consultations him/herself, especially on particularly delicate matters.

Confusingly, the term informal consultations is also used to describe more general, high-level meetings convened by the COP President (or sometimes other presiding officers or appointed delegates) with a limited number of key Parties to help advance the broader negotiations and break political deadlocks. Also known as 'friends' groups, these are discussed below.

The 'no more than two meetings' practice does not generally apply to informal consultations, nor are these covered by Decision 18/CP.4, so that observers do not have the right to attend meetings (although they may, of course, lobby the consulting delegate in the corridors). This makes the informal consultation process a much more private one and one more suited to the final, most politically sensitive stages of a negotiation process.

The daily programme lists ongoing informal consultations and the delegate charged with conducting these, but any meeting places and times are generally not advertised. It is up to the consulting delegate to ensure that all interested Parties are duly consulted, and to Parties that are interested in an issue to make themselves known to the consulting delegate and turn up at any meetings.

8.4   'Friends' groups

In addition to the negotiating forums outlined above, many COP Presidents have also brought together a small group of 'friends' meeting in private to engage in more substantive discussions than possible in the COP Bureau.[104] Such 'friends' meetings take place at the COP session itself, and sometimes also prior to the session. Organising a 'friends' group remains entirely at the discretion of the presiding officer. No formal rules exist on whether, and if so how and when, to convene such a group, and what its purpose and membership should be. The

---

[104] As discussed in chapter 13, the Bureau deals almost exclusively with procedural and organisational matters.

name given to a 'friends' group may vary. In the climate context, such groups have sometimes been referred to as the *Expanded Bureau* as their core membership has comprised Bureau members plus additional Party representatives regarded as key by the President. When 'friends' groups are convened in the final stages of negotiations, the representation is often at ministerial level. Representatives of IGOs and NGOs are never admitted to 'friends' groups, and English serves as the lingua franca. The meetings are by invitation only and rarely formally publicised.

A 'friends' group can serve as an informal sounding board for the President and thus play a purely advisory role. Alternatively, such a group can actually play a negotiating role, whereby the 'friends' negotiate on behalf of the interests that they represent. When convened by SB Chairs, they can also provide technical expertise on a specific topic. The type of 'friends' group established, and the expectations about its role, has an enormous impact on the negotiations, including on transparency and accountability, which impacts on the legitimacy of end results.

Selecting the delegates to serve on a 'friends' group is a highly sensitive task. This is especially so if the group is intended to play a negotiating role, because large numbers of Parties are in effect being asked to give up their right to be directly involved in negotiations *and* to accept the final results reached by them. It is even more fraught when ministers attending the COP find out only some of them will be invited.

At COP-6 part II, the President devised a formula which involved the designation of a certain number of seats at the central negotiating table for each of the political negotiating coalitions.[105] These coalitions were allowed to select their own representatives plus an accompanying advisor and to rotate them depending on the issue being discussed. Other Parties were allowed to observe the proceedings. This formula, used again at COP-7, was made possible by the formation of new negotiating coalitions since COP-3 because almost all Parties to the Convention are now part of one kind of coalition or another. These coalitions can be readily accommodated provided the group is capable of agreeing a group representative, which is easier for some negotiating coalitions than others. Negotiations on the Delhi Declaration at COP-8 were also facilitated by the President meeting with representatives of the negotiating coalitions, first separately, then as a group.

From an administrative point of view, using the negotiating coalitions has made it easier for COP Presidents to engage in informal consultations by reducing the number of Parties s/he should involve, and devolving the headache of who should be chosen onto the Chairs or co-ordinator of the main coalitions. However, experience to date with 'friends' groups raises questions about their effectiveness

---

[105] See chapter 3.

in generating consensus on thorny substantive issues in a timely and transparent fashion.

First, with forty or so Parties round the table, 'friends' groups tend to replicate, rather than reduce, the diversity of political interests found in the wider negotiations. Second, the flexibility demonstrated by coalitions is not necessarily greater, and sometimes much less, than in closed contact groups because representatives sit behind a group flag and must therefore articulate group positions. They are rarely able to respond meaningfully, or with legitimacy, once the group's preferred options and fall-back positions are superseded. This 'group lock-in' effect is particularly pronounced for the G-77 because of the diversity of interests of its members. One potential repercussion is thus to accentuate, rather than diminish, the North/South dimension. Third, the size of the group is simply too large to allow for the mutual exchange of final concessions and compromises. These exchanges, and the delicate understandings that accompany them, unlock the sticking points in the final stages, but cannot be made in front of such a large, politically diverse audience without fear of losing political face. Finally, and for all these reasons, the use of 'friends' groups to negotiate substance in the final stages of a COP appears to have gone hand in hand with an increased number of bilaterals between key Parties, and between key Parties and the President, many occurring simultaneously with meetings of the 'friends' group.[106] In general, it is the smaller, politically less powerful delegations that are marginalised most by bilaterals on the final night.

It is less common for SB Chairs to convene a group of 'friends', to discuss either process or substance. The SB Chairs have, however, occasionally done so, sometimes delegating the chairing of such groups to a different delegate. The 'friends' groups convened by the SB Chairs to date have also generally had a more technical or specialised nature. For example, a 'friends' group was convened on the review of the financial mechanism at SBI-16 and technology transfer at SBSTA-12.

9   Ministerial participation

The presence of ministers lends prestige to COP proceedings and signals the acceptance of climate change as an issue worthy of high-level attention. Ministers also provide leadership and are able take policy decisions that lie beyond the mandate of their officials. For these reasons each COP session to date has included a segment with participation by ministers. This segment has usually taken place in the last two to three days of the COP session, with the aim of bringing the

---

[106] Grubb and Yamin, 2001.

influence of ministers to bear on the final stages of negotiations.[107] Ministers do not normally attend SB sessions, given their more technical nature.

While most countries send ministers to the major COP sessions, in practice many developing country ministers do not participate directly in the negotiations, preferring to limit their input to giving guidance to their delegations behind the scenes. Many developing country delegations thus continue to be represented by experts or diplomats in the negotiations themselves. The reasons for this are varied and complex, including language barriers, lack of capacity, and lower priority assigned to climate change at the domestic level. Developing country unease with focusing exclusively on ministerial input in the final stages of negotiations is reflected in the use, since COP-3, of the term 'high-level' rather than 'ministerial' segment.

9.1   *Traditional general debate*

A traditional general debate was held at each COP session up to and including COP-7, in line with established practice for ministerial participation in UN forums. The term 'general debate' is in fact largely a misnomer. Ministers and other heads of delegation register with the Secretariat to deliver speeches outlining their national positions, usually from the front podium in the main plenary room. These speeches, limited to three to four minutes, are pre-prepared and delivered to a tight schedule drawn up by the Secretariat. Some 100 statements have typically been made at each COP, sometimes going into the night. On occasion, such speeches have provided valuable input into the negotiations. An example is the opening of the high-level segment at COP-3, which was addressed by the Prime Minister of Japan, the Presidents of Costa Rica and Nauru, and the then-US Vice-President Al Gore, whose signal that the US would show added flexibility in the negotiations fostered a positive start to the session. In this regard, reporting on a minister's speech at a COP provides a valuable 'hook' for domestic media. This is especially significant for developing countries where public awareness of climate change is often low. Nonetheless, the traditional general debate is viewed by many as a poor use of time, with ministers often making speeches to nearly empty conference halls. Since COP-8, therefore, high-level segments have centred instead on roundtable discussions, as discussed below.

9.2   *Roundtable discussions*

Roundtable discussions have served as a more interactive means of involving ministers in the climate change process. Aimed at promoting a more lively and

---

[107] The exception was COP-6 part II, where ministers were invited to attend at the mid-point of negotiations.

spontaneous exchange of views on broad topics relating to the climate change process, roundtables chaired by ministers have been convened at COP-2, COP-5, COP-8 and COP-9.[108] The characters of these roundtables have evolved over time. The roundtable at COP-2 was exclusively ministerial and closed to observers, except for heads of UN agencies, resembling a 'friends' group. The objections raised by delegations not represented at ministerial level, however, led to a much more open formula for participation at COP-5, along with a change in name to 'informal exchange of views'. All heads of delegation were invited to participate, and a limited number of observers allowed to attend. Three half-day 'roundtable discussions' were held at COP-8, again with an open invitation to heads of delegation, and representatives of NGO constituencies permitted to contribute to the debate. Each half-day roundtable was co-chaired by an Annex I and non-Annex I minister. A similar approach was followed at COP-9. The roundtables have not produced any formal decisions or conclusions. An informal summary of discussions, however, has been included in the COP report.[109] Such roundtable discussions are generally seen as more open and constructive than the general debate, even though speeches still tend to be pre-prepared, spontaneity is limited, and the actual impact on negotiations doubtful.

9.3   *Direct participation*

The direct participation of ministers in the climate change negotiations has varied at different COP sessions. At COP-3, ministers focused their efforts on participating in the 'friends' group and conducted behind-the-scenes talks with counterparts. They were not involved in the day-to-day negotiations on the development of the text in the Committee of the Whole or the negotiating groups, which continued to be led by officials familiar with the text and UN procedures. Much greater emphasis, however, was placed on the role of ministers in the final stages of negotiations under the Buenos Aires Plan of Action, with ministers expected to participate not only in the 'friends' group, but also in the working bodies of the COP. At COP-6 part I, for example, the informal *high-level* plenary was intended primarily for participation by ministers, as were the four 'cluster groups', with each co-chaired by ministers.

Disparities in rank between industrialised and developing country delegates, however, can present diplomatic challenges. In the final hours, ministers from Annex I Parties often have to negotiate with officials from non-Annex I Parties.

---

[108] An additional ministerial roundtable, on the specific topic of technology transfer, was convened at COP-3.

[109] See COP-2 report, part I, Annex III; COP-5 report, part I, section IX.C; and COP-8 report, part I, section XI.B.

Both sides find this somewhat uncomfortable because politicians and officials have different strengths and approaches. Officials conversant in details can out-manoeuvre ministers not so experienced in technical and textual minutiae, while the lack of power of officials to agree to compromises can frustrate ministers. The ministerial cluster groups at COP-6 part I, for example, proved ineffective because ministers wanted to negotiate issues whilst officials wanted to draft text.[110] Because many of the issues straddled political and technical boundaries, with complex trade-offs between unrelated issues, the contribution of both was equally necessary, and finally achieved at COP-6 part II. Armed with sufficient political guidance from ministers, officials, by and large, returned centre stage to complete the complex matter of producing COP decisions that would actually be adopted by consensus.

10   The last night

The last nights of major negotiating rounds, whether conducted within a 'friends' group or other body, have acquired a momentum of their own in the climate change process, reflecting a similar trend in intergovernmental negotiations more broadly. Round-the-clock talks on the last night usually come at the close of an intensive week of negotiations, which may have already gone on through the night. Such 'negotiation by exhaustion', which impacts on the presiding officers and Secretariat as well as Parties, can have repercussions on the quality of the resultant agreement, with mistakes being made, sloppy language agreed, or controversial clauses slipped through. Participants may be too tired to monitor the agreement with the necessary care, if they have not already left to catch flights, as is frequently the case for developing country delegates with cheaper, fixed tickets. Working through the last night – or indeed sometimes the last two nights, as happened at COP-3 – thus has significant procedural equity considerations, which clearly impact disproportionately on smaller and less well-resourced delegations who do not have the capacity to rotate their representatives. It is not unusual to find well-rested delegates (usually from large industrialised country delegations) coming to the conference centre early in the morning to replace their weary colleagues who have negotiated throughout the night, while representatives from smaller delegations struggle to stay awake for the final hours of negotiations without reinforcements.

Despite these serious shortcomings, the dynamic of the last night has become an almost routine finale to COP proceedings – even if not strictly justified by the amount and significance of outstanding issues. The expectation that there

---

[110] See Grubb and Yamin, 2001.

will be a 'last night' which can overrun engenders brinkmanship because Parties simply push back the process of compromising and striking deals until the last possible moment. Certainly, late night negotiations provide a sense of drama and give delegates – officials with bosses at home, or ministers accountable to their electorate – ample opportunity to demonstrate that they made every effort to maintain their position before being forced to compromise.

11   On the side

The official negotiation process is surrounded by an immense jamboree of side events and exhibits, organised mostly by NGOs but also by UN bodies, other IGOs, the Secretariat and Parties themselves.

Side events cover a range of activities, from panel discussions to seminars and video presentations. Side events must be registered with the Secretariat, which assigns their time slots. Two side events usually take place in parallel, but up to four have sometimes been convened in response to particularly high demand, and where sufficient space has been available. The number of side events taking place has risen, with around 100 convened at COP-9. Some side events are now broadcast live on the Internet by the Secretariat, and are also covered by the independent *Earth Negotiations Bulletin*.[111] Space for exhibits is also allocated by the Secretariat to NGOs, IGOs and Parties on request, with the amount available depending on the venue. Additional events often take place at these exhibits, including the now established 'fossil of the day' award.[112]

Another important area of activity on the side of the official negotiations is that of the media, especially for the more high-profile sessions. Official press briefings are called by the Secretariat two or three times during a session of the regime bodies, with attendance by the Executive Secretary and the presiding officers. Briefings are also regularly called by Parties and NGOs, with the larger, more media savvy delegations, such as the EU and the US, sometimes holding press briefings twice a day at the higher profile negotiating sessions. The subsequent media attention raises awareness of climate change in domestic politics and, for media conscious ministers, can exert great pressure on them to agree a deal.

12   Intersessional workshops and presessional consultations

Intersessional workshops (which, when held immediately prior to a negotiating session, are called 'presessional consultations') are organised by the

---

[111] See www.iisd.ca/linkages.   [112] See section on 'Environmental NGOs' in chapter 3.

Secretariat at the request of the SBs, and less frequently the COP. The aim of workshops is to advance understanding of the technical components of an issue, or to discuss approaches and options relevant to the formal negotiations. Participation is by invitation only, with the invitation list drawn up by the presiding officer of the convening body. The fact that workshops have only limited participation inevitably raises concerns, although they are now widely accepted by Parties, provided their conclusions do not appear to pre-empt negotiations in the formal bodies. There have been several occasions where Parties, meeting in the formal SBs, were reluctant to accept the outcomes of a workshop as a basis for their work.

It is common for a Party to offer to host a workshop, especially if it has a particular interest in the issue under discussion. Presessional consultations are held immediately prior to a SB or COP session, at the venue of that session. Funding for the workshop/consultation, in particular to cover the costs of attendance by eligible developing countries and EITs, is provided by voluntary contributions to the Trust Fund for Participation, mostly from Annex II Parties.[113] The growing popularity of presessional consultations is itself partly a cost-effectiveness exercise, whereby it is cheaper to fly in delegates, who would be funded to attend the forthcoming SB/COP session anyway, a few days earlier, rather than pay for a round trip to a separate destination in between sessions. The Chair of the SB convening the workshop will often serve as its Chair, or invite another delegate to serve in his/her place.

Given their limited participation, workshops do not have a formal mandate to negotiate. They may, however, prepare draft texts for the consideration of the SBs, or informal negotiations may take place on the margins. Input from IGO or NGO experts is often sought to provoke discussion and elicit new ideas. The output of workshops is typically a Chair's report, which is then presented at the next formal session of the convening regime body.

A small number of places are often allocated to NGO observers, depending on the approach taken by the SB and workshop Chair. Invitations are typically issued through the constituency coordinators: three for ENGOs and BINGOs, and one each for the other constituencies. Each must pay their own expenses, causing particular problems for developing country NGOs. The issuance of such invitations causes problems when demand exceeds supply. There have consequently been complaints from NGOs (as well as supportive Parties, notably the US) demanding greater representation at workshops.[114] In response, the SBI has requested the SB and workshop Chairs, and the Secretariat, to make additional

---

[113] See chapter 16.   [114] See FCCC/SBI/2002/13.

efforts to promote transparency and the participation of observers, while safe-guarding the effectiveness of workshops.[115]

The growing number of workshops – thirteen in 2003 and fifteen in 2002, com-pared with seven each year from 1999 to 2001 – can be attributed in part to the increasingly overloaded agenda of the climate change regime, along with the more technical nature of some issues (such as revising guidelines for emission invento-ries) which require more time than can be allocated at a formal SB or COP session. The more restricted attendance at workshops can also provide for a more efficient work environment. Furthermore, in some cases, convening a workshop can serve as a politically feasible means of moving ahead on a particularly difficult issue. The proliferation of workshops, however, also has costs, with concerns raised over difficulties in identifying suitable time slots in an increasingly packed agenda, problems in obtaining sufficient funding, and the growing burden of work on Parties (especially small delegations). Delegates attending presessional consulta-tions followed by the formal sessions, for example, often find themselves spending up to three consecutive weeks away from home.

[115] See SBI-17 report, paragraph 50.

15

Scientific and technical input

1   Introduction

Access to the best available, most up-to-date scientific and technical information is of critical importance to the climate change regime.[1] The IPCC plays a vital role in the climate change regime by providing important scientific and technical input. The demand for such input has grown as the regime has matured, especially with the adoption of the Kyoto Protocol and the new issues that it introduced. This chapter examines the institutional channels through which the climate change regime receives scientific and technical input, and how this input is then considered in the negotiations.[2] It begins with a brief overview of the role of the SBSTA as the regime's scientific and technical body, before focusing on the IPCC as the regime's predominant source of scientific and technical information. The chapter then touches upon the contribution of the regime's roster of experts, the Secretariat, other IGOs and NGOs.

2   The Subsidiary Body for Scientific and Technological Advice

The main institutional channel for transmitting scientific input to the climate change regime is through the SBSTA, whose mandate is to 'provide the

---

[1] For the purposes of this chapter, scientific information is broadly defined as encompassing both the natural and social sciences.

[2] This chapter does not explore the commitments of Parties with respect to scientific research and systematic observation programmes, including the role of the Global Climate Observing System (GCOS). These are addressed in chapter 7.

COP with timely information and advice on scientific and technological matters relating to the Convention'.[3] The SBSTA, however, consists of an open-ended body of government delegates representing national interests, rather than a select group of impartial experts.[4] It therefore serves as a political negotiating forum on issues with significant scientific and technical content rather than a scientific assessment body. In this way, the climate change regime differs from several other environmental regimes[5] in not having limited membership expert bodies within the regime itself to provide or assess information on the science of climate change. Instead, information is provided by 'existing competent international bodies'[6] from outside the regime and processed by the SBSTA. The SBSTA thus serves as the 'link between ... assessments and ... information provided by competent international bodies and the policy-oriented needs of the COP',[7] that is, as a conduit between science from outside the regime, and the political negotiations within it.[8] In this role, the SBSTA is also mandated to 'formulate requests [for information] to competent international scientific and technical bodies'.[9]

The Convention does not state which bodies the SBSTA should draw on in its work. Article 21, however, which sets out interim arrangements that applied pending entry into force of the Convention, suggests a role for the IPCC, by calling on the head of the interim secretariat to 'cooperate closely' with the Panel 'to ensure that [it] can respond to the need for objective scientific and technical advice'. The inclusion of only a rather oblique reference to the IPCC was partly due to early concerns on the part of many developing countries who felt excluded from the IPCC and did not want official recognition of it in the Convention text.[10] Decisions taken at COP-1, however, expanded on the IPCC's role, citing it as a source of 'the latest international scientific, technical, socio-economic and other information',[11] as well as input on methodological issues.[12] Since then, the IPCC has become the predominant source of scientific and technical information and analysis to the climate change regime, with both COP decisions and the Kyoto Protocol referring to the IPCC and its work.[13]

[3] FCCC Article 9.1.   [4] See chapter 13.

[5] The ozone regime, for example, has three Assessment Panels, on Science, Environmental Effects, and Technology and Economics, which bring together experts nominated by governments but acting in their personal capacity.

[6] FCCC Article 9.2.   [7] Decision 6/CP.1, Preamble, subparagraph (a).

[8] See discussion in FCCC/SBSTA/1996/6.   [9] Decision 6/CP.1, Annex I, paragraph 1 (b).

[10] See Estrada, 1999.   [11] Decision 6/CP.1, Annex I, paragraph 1(a).

[12] Decisions 4/CP.1 and 6/CP.1.   [13] See KP Articles 3.4 and 5.

3   **The Intergovernmental Panel on Climate Change**

3.1   *Role, organisation and products*

3.1.1   Role

The IPCC and the climate change regime have been closely entwined since their inception. The establishment of the IPCC in 1988 as a joint initiative of WMO and UNEP was a clear, if implicit, forerunner to the launch of a political process on climate change. This approach was modelled on that used in the ozone regime, where intergovernmental, independent scientific research served as a precursor to the negotiations that led to the Vienna Convention. The establishment of the IPCC was subsequently endorsed by the UN General Assembly.[14]

The IPCC's role, as set out in the latest set of principles governing its work,[15] is to 'assess on a comprehensive, objective, open and transparent basis the scientific, technical and socio-economic information relevant to understanding the risk of human-induced climate change, its potential impacts and options for adaptation and mitigation'. These principles further establish that the IPCC 'shall concentrate its activities on the tasks allotted to it by the relevant WMO Executive Council and UNEP Governing Council resolutions ... *as well as on actions in support of the UN Framework Convention on Climate Change*'[16] (emphasis added). Hence, while the IPCC is an independent body, it has a clear role in providing support to the climate change regime.

It is often wrongly assumed that the IPCC carries out scientific research. Rather, the IPCC conducts what amounts to a massive review of climate change research published mostly in peer-reviewed journals by government bodies, universities, IGOs or individual researchers around the world. The IPCC is not mandated to make policy recommendations, but rather to provide the objective analysis needed for policy-makers to make informed decisions. A key tenet for the IPCC is thus to be 'policy relevant, but not policy prescriptive',[17] while striving 'to serve the policy community ... in a pro-active fashion'.[18]

3.1.2   Organisation

To carry out its role, the IPCC is organised into three *Working Groups*, each responsible for a specific area of climate change. The precise mandates of the three

---

[14] See UNGA Resolution A/RES/43/53.   [15] IPCC, 1998, paragraph 2.

[16] IPCC, 1998, paragraph 1.   [17] See IPCC-18 report, Appendix 2, paragraph 2 (a).

[18] See IPCC-20 report, decision 2, paragraph 4.4.

Working Groups have changed over time. Their current respective areas of work, which will extend until at least 2007,[19] are as follows:

- Working Group I: The science of climate change
- Working Group 2: Impacts, vulnerability and adaptation
- Working Group 3: Mitigation options.

An additional *Task Force on National Greenhouse Gas Inventories* (TFI) was established in 1996. This Task Force manages the IPCC's National Greenhouse Gas Inventories Programme (NGGIP), which carries out methodological work, including the development and improvement of guidelines for calculating and compiling emissions data.[20] The IPCC has also convened ad hoc groups or teams on specific issues with defined mandates (e.g. on financial issues and its outreach strategy).

3.1.3   Products

3.1.3.1 Assessment reports   The most high-profile products of the IPCC are its comprehensive Assessment Reports that present the status of knowledge on climate change, including separate reports from each of the three Working Groups.

Three such Assessment Reports have been prepared so far: the First Assessment Report (FAR) was issued in 1990, the Second Assessment Report (SAR) in 1995, and the Third Assessment Report (TAR) in 2000. The deadline for the Fourth Assessment Report (4AR) has been set as 2007.[21]

Each Working Group report included in the Assessment incorporates a sixty to seventy page *Technical Summary*, along with a ten to fifteen page *Summary for Policy-Makers* (SPM), which sets out the 'headline' conclusions of the Working Group report in a language intended to be accessible to policy-makers and the media. Given the political significance of the SPMs, the final draft is subject to political negotiation among the IPCC's member governments with the lead authors present to ensure scientific rigour, veracity and consistency with the other underlying report. In addition to the three Working Group reports, the TAR also incorporated a *Synthesis Report* (including its own SPM), which aimed to synthesise and integrate the main findings of the three Working Groups in order to address a set of policy-relevant questions devised by the IPCC with input from the SBSTA. Whether a synthesis report will be prepared for the 4AR had not yet been decided at the time of writing, although a scoping exercise on the form that a synthesis report might take was underway.

---

[19] See IPCC, 1997, The IPCC Third Assessment Report, Decision Paper (Adopted at the thirteenth session, Maldives, 22 and 25–28 September 1997), paragraph 2 (ii) and IPCC-18 report, Appendix 2, decision 8.

[20] See chapter 11.   [21] See IPCC-19 report, decision 6.1.

The preparation of these Assessment Reports constitutes the core of the IPCC's activities, with the five to six year 'assessment cycle' governing the IPCC's programme of work.

3.1.3.2 Special reports and technical papers   The IPCC also publishes shorter special reports and technical papers on specific issues.

- *Special reports* may contain new information and usually amount to several hundred pages. They are based on the same structure (with an SPM and technical summary), and prepared according to the same procedures, as full assessment reports (see 'assessment process' below).
- *Technical papers*, however, may include only information already contained in previous IPCC assessment reports and special reports, and follow an expedited preparation process (see 'assessment process' below). These are usually shorter documents, around forty to ninety pages.

These shorter reports are usually prepared at the request of the SBSTA, although some have been initiated by the IPCC itself, or at the request of other regimes, including the International Civil Aviation Organization, the Meeting of the Parties to the Montreal Protocol and the Conference of the Parties to the CBD. Individual Parties may propose the preparation of special reports and technical papers in the IPCC. At the IPCC's twenty-first session in 2003, for example, Germany proposed to prepare a special report on renewable energy sources.[22] The proliferation of requests to the IPCC for these shorter reports has led the Panel to adopt a framework and set of criteria for establishing priorities during the preparation period of the 4AR. The IPCC decided to continue considering requests to produce special reports, technical papers and methodological work on a case-by-base basis, but with priority given to the preparation of the 4AR, and also to requests from the climate change regime.[23] In evaluating proposals, the IPCC decided to take into account the availability of scientific information and experts, along with resource constraints and the relevance of the request to climate change and policy-makers.

3.1.3.3 Methodological work   One of the most important contributions of the IPCC to the climate change regime is its methodological work, carried out through the NGGIP and managed by the TFI. The IPCC has developed methodological guidelines for estimating and calculating GHG inventories, which have been endorsed by the SBSTA and COP for use by both Annex I Parties and non-Annex Parties.[24] In

---

[22] IPCC-21 report, section 14.1.   [23] IPCC-20 report, decision 2.   [24] IPCC, 1996b.

addition, it has developed good practice guidance to help Parties address uncertainties in the estimation of emissions/removals, which has again been endorsed by the SBSTA and COP, including, most recently, for the LULUCF sector under the Kyoto Protocol.[25] The NGGIP has also launched a database intended to help developing countries estimate their GHG emissions and removals.[26] Another important contribution of the IPCC is the concept of GWPs, which was introduced to the political community by the IPCC assessment process and is explained in chapter 5.[27]

3.1.3.4 Workshops and participation of developing countries   To help develop all of these products, the IPCC frequently sponsors or co-sponsors workshops and expert meetings. These are essential for experts to exchange views, develop text and scope future work, especially on issues that have received relatively little attention in previous assessments or in the literature.

A particularly important dimension to the IPCC is ensuring the participation of experts from developing countries (also EITs) in its work.[28] Indeed, part of the motivation behind the establishment of the IPCC with its intergovernmental membership was the mistrust felt by many developing countries at the emerging science of climate change which, at that time, was emanating almost exclusively from a handful of industrialised countries.[29] A Special Committee for the Participation of Developing Countries was therefore convened from 1989 to 1992. The IPCC now seeks to ensure that developing country and EIT experts are well represented in its institutions and preparation of its reports (see 'assessment process' below), while covering the costs of their attendance at meetings. In addition, regional workshops are held to gather unpublished information from developing country experts, while efforts are also made to consider non-English language literature.

3.2   *Procedures, institutions and budget*

3.2.1   Procedures

The IPCC has detailed rules in place governing the preparation and endorsement of its reports[30] (see 'assessment process' below). It does not, however, have a comprehensive set of rules of procedure for its meetings. Its proceedings are instead governed by its general principles,[31] which have been supplemented by further plenary decisions. On several important issues, such as voting on procedural matters and the election of officers, these principles invoke the broader

---

[25] IPCC, 2000b, and IPCC, 2004. See chapter 11, section 2.2.

[26] See http://www.ipcc-nggip.iges.or.jp/EFDB/main.php.

[27] On the genesis of the GWP concept, see Skodvin, 1999a.

[28] See Shackley, 1997.   [29] See Agrawala, 1998.   [30] IPCC, 1999.   [31] See IPCC, 1998.

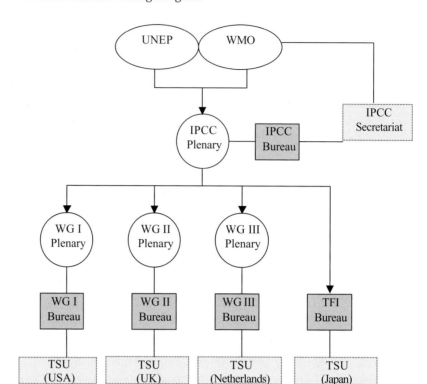

Notes: UNEP – United Nations Environment Programme; WMO – World Meteorological Organisation; WG – Working Group; TFI – Task Force on Inventories; TSU – Technical Support Unit; (country name) – current host of TSU (up to at least 2007).

Fig. 15.1   Institutional structure of the IPCC

General Regulations of the WMO.[32] In some cases, the IPCC has developed informal customary practices that, while well established, are not recorded in text. The IPCC's principles are reviewed every five years. The latest review, at the twenty-first session of the Panel in late 2003, decided that only editorial changes were needed to the current principles, notably to reflect the inclusion of methodological reports under the scope of the assessment process and procedures.[33]

3.2.2   Institutions

The IPCC is open to membership by any member of WMO and UNEP and counted 192 members in 2004. Its parent bodies, the UNEP Governing Council and WMO Executive Council, exercise broad oversight of the IPCC, whose institutional structure is depicted in figure 15.1.

---

[32] WMO, 1991.   [33] See IPCC-21 report, section 11.

3.2.2.1 IPCC and Working Group plenaries   The IPCC's main decision-making body, the IPCC plenary, meets approximately once a year, bringing together governmental representatives. These representatives frequently possess scientific or technical expertise, but there is no requirement for them to do so. The plenary is responsible for defining the overall work programme of the IPCC, determining the scope and structure of its major reports, approving its budget, revising its procedures, considering requests for scientific inputs from other bodies, and giving final approval or endorsement to its reports. The plenary's work is presided over by a Chair, assisted by three Vice-Chairs.[34] Three IPCC Chairs have served to date: Bert Bolin (Sweden) from the establishment of the IPCC until 1997; Robert Watson (USA) from 1997 to 2002; and Rajendra Kumar Pachauri (India) from 2002 to date.

The Working Groups have their own Working Group plenaries, which are also composed of government delegates. Typically, however, the scientific expertise and specialisation of these delegates is greater than in the wider IPCC plenary, while their level of seniority is lower. Plenary functions for the TFI are provided by the full IPCC plenary. NGOs and IGOs are welcome to attend sessions of the IPCC and Working Group plenaries. Other meetings, however, are by invitation only.[35]

According to the IPCC principles, delegates to the IPCC and Working Group plenaries are called upon to 'use all best endeavours to reach consensus'.[36] However, if this is not possible, decisions on procedural issues (e.g. election of officers) are taken according to WMO General Regulations, that is, they are subject to a vote. Except for the election of officers, where the decision is carried by a simple majority, other procedural decisions are carried by a two-thirds majority of votes cast for and against.[37] Separate procedures apply to the endorsement of IPCC reports and are discussed further below.

3.2.2.2 Bureaux   Each Working Group is co-chaired by two representatives (one each from a developed and developing country), and assisted by six Vice-Chairs, which together make up the Working Group Bureau.[38] The TFI Bureau has fourteen members, including two Co-Chairs, also from a developed and a developing country.[39]

The IPCC Bureau itself consists of thirty members, including the IPCC Chair and three Vice-Chairs, the Co-Chairs and six Vice-Chairs of each Working Group, and the Co-Chairs of the TFI.[40] The Bureau is tasked with assisting the IPCC Chair in taking

---

[34] See IPCC-18 report, Appendix 2, decision 11.

[35] See http://www.ipcc.ch/meet/meet.htm.   [36] IPCC, 1998, paragraph 10.

[37] See WMO, 1991.   [38] IPCC-18 report, Appendix 2, decision 11.

[39] IPCC-18 report, Appendix 2, decision 10.

[40] This composition was changed for the election of the most recent Bureau. Compare IPCC, 1997, paragraph 14, and IPCC-18 report, Appendix 2, decision 11.

decisions, and generally monitoring the progress of the IPCC and coordinating its work.[41] To this end, it meets up to three times a year, as well as during sessions of the IPCC plenary. According to the IPCC's principles, the IPCC and Working Group Bureaux, along with the TFI's members, must reflect 'balanced geographic representation, with due consideration for scientific and technical requirements'.[42] Although this is not stated in the principles, IPCC plenary decisions[43] have interpreted 'balanced geographic representation' according to the six WMO regions, comprising Africa, Asia, South America, North and Central America, South West Pacific and Europe.[44]

No set formula exists for the appointment of the Chair and three Vice-Chairs of the IPCC. The six Working Group Vice-Chairs, however, should between them represent the WMO regions not covered by the Co-Chairs 'wherever possible', while the developing country Co-Chairs of the three Working Groups should cover the three regions of Africa, Asia and Latin America/Caribbean.[45] The Task Force's twelve members include two from each of the WMO regions.[46] Each government seated on the Bureau is permitted to send another representative to Bureau meetings.[47] Other individuals invited by the Chair may also attend, and these typically include officials from the Technical Support Units (see below), along with a representative of the FCCC Secretariat.

The various WMO regions may nominate candidates for posts on the Bureaux, 'taking into account the relevant expertise/qualifications needed'.[48] Despite this provision, it is typically individual countries, rather than regions, that submit nominations for particular posts. There is no formal specification of the terms of office of Bureau members. To date, and in the interests of continuity, the practice has been to mirror the assessment cycle, with a new Bureau elected at the launch of work on each new Assessment Report and serving through to its completion. All Bureau members are eligible for re-election,[49] with no stipulation of any limit. The IPCC has since decided to review these procedures following the 2002 Bureau elections, where a particularly protracted process, complicated by the absence of clear formal rules for electing the IPCC Chair, led to a secret ballot being held to choose between three candidates for the post of Chair.[50]

[41] IPCC-8 report, paragraph 6.14.1.   [42] IPCC, 1998, paragraph 5.

[43] See, for example, IPCC, 1997.

[44] Under WMO General Regulations (WMO, 1991), countries may belong to more than one region, if their territories cross regional limits (which are set according to precise degrees of longitude and latitude) or by virtue of their overseas territories.

[45] IPCC, 1997, paragraph 14 (v).   [46] IPCC-18 report, Appendix 2, decision 10.

[47] IPCC-8 report, paragraph 6.13.   [48] IPCC, 1997, paragraph 14 (vii).

[49] IPCC-8 report, paragraph 6.15.3.

[50] See IPCC-19 report, paragraph 3a, and decision 1.

3.2.2.3 Secretariat and Technical Support Units   The IPCC is serviced by a small secretariat, housed at WMO's Geneva headquarters.[51] N. Sundararaman (India) served as Executive Secretary from the inception of the IPCC until 2000, when he was replaced by Renate Christ (Austria). Key tasks for the IPCC Secretariat are to organise plenary meetings, manage the Trust Fund (see below), oversee public information activities, disseminate reports and coordinate with member governments.

In addition, the Working Groups and TFI are each serviced by their own small secretariats, known as Technical Support Units (TSUs). These are hosted and resourced by the developed country holding the position of Co-Chair (see figure 15.1). The TSUs are responsible for coordinating the preparation of their respective reports, and organising expert meetings/workshops. In doing so, they receive support and guidance from the main IPCC Secretariat.

3.2.3   Budget

Under the IPCC's financial procedures,[52] the IPCC budget is managed by a joint WMO/UNEP IPCC Trust Fund, administered 'by mutual agreement' between the two parent organisations, under WMO financial regulations. The budget for the forthcoming year is adopted annually by the IPCC plenary, together with a forecast budget for the following year and an indicative budget for the third year. Since 1997, a small financial task team made up of Bureau members, co-chaired by a developed country and a developing country or EIT representative, has helped prepare the draft budget.[53] The accounts and financial management are audited according to WMO procedures.

The IPCC's annual budget covers the costs of the Secretariat, convening of plenary and Bureau meetings (including support for attendance by developing countries and EITs), outreach initiatives, and financial support for the developing country Co-Chairs of the Working Groups and TFI. The IPCC Chair may also request support, when this post is held by a developing country representative.

The annual budget fluctuates according to the assessment cycle. The forecast annual budgets between 2004 and 2007,[54] for example, range from under CHF 5 million (around US $3.8 million) for 2006, when the focus will be on drafting the 4AR by scientists working in their home institutions, to over CHF 8 million (around US $6 million) for 2007, when the Working Groups and full IPCC will meet in plenary to consider the 4AR, which will then be published.

---

[51] See www.ipcc.ch.   [52] IPCC, 1996a.   [53] IPCC, 1997, paragraph 16.

[54] See IPCC-20 report. The IPCC budget is calculated in Swiss francs. At the time of writing, 1 CHF = 0.76 US $.

Table 15.1   *Government contributions to the IPCC Trust Fund in 2002*[55]

Party	Amount (CHF)
Australia	91,795
Canada	547,627
China	14,900
EU	194,225
France	44,301
Germany	245,388
Iceland	10,000
Japan	180,000
Mauritius	1,480
Netherlands	50,000
New Zealand	29,026
Norway	38,200
Spain	133,125
UK	228,415
US	1,520,715

The IPCC budget is funded by grants from UNEP, WMO and the FCCC core budget (the latter amounting to US $350,000 per year for the biennium 2002–2003[56]), along with *voluntary* contributions from governments. Unlike the FCCC, the IPCC does not have an indicative scale of contributions for all its members. By way of illustration, table 15.1 shows the spread of contributions among different governments received in 2002. The voluntary nature of government contributions to the IPCC's core budget has led to financial uncertainty, and the IPCC has started to face financial constraints as a result of reduced contributions combined with growing requests for work.[57]

3.3   *The assessment process*

The IPCC has detailed procedures in place for the preparation of its Assessment Reports.[58] The first set of these procedures was adopted in 1993,[59] with the current, revised set adopted in 1999. Prior to 1993, the IPCC had prepared its

---

[55] Data from IPCC-XXI, Doc. 4, table 1. The figure for the US excludes an additional contribution of CHF 1,986,285 to translate and publish IPCC good practice guidance.

[56] See FCCC/SBI/2001/17/Add.1, table B.1.1.

[57] See Decision 19/CP.5, and SBSTA-11 report, paragraph 90 (c).

[58] IPCC, 1999. Unless otherwise specified, citations throughout this section refer to these procedures.

[59] IPCC, 1993.

reports through a more informal process. Concerns raised during the preparation of the FAR, however, pointed to the need for formal guidelines.

The IPCC's assessment process (summarised in figure 15.2 below) is unique in the intergovernmental arena in its combination of expert scientific analysis with government review and negotiation. The preparation of an Assessment Report begins with a decision taken by the IPCC plenary – that is, by government delegates – on the scope, structure and timing of the overall report. The real scientific assessment work is then launched in the Working Groups, where teams of experts are tasked with drafting each chapter of the respective Working Group report. These experts, who are largely nominated by governments but serve in their personal capacity, make up the 'scientific core'[60] of the IPCC. Others may also be invited by the Co-Chairs to participate.

The Working Group Bureaux have the responsibility of identifying coordinating lead authors (usually two) and lead authors (typically from four up to a dozen) for each chapter of the Working Group report, drawn from a list of experts nominated by governments or IPCC Bureau members. The group of coordinating lead authors and lead authors must 'reflect the need to aim for a range of views, expertise and geographical representation', with 'at least one and normally two or more' from developing countries. Lead authors, usually working in small groups, are responsible for the development of certain sections of the chapter, while coordinating lead authors have overall responsibility for the production of the chapter as a whole. The coordinating lead authors and lead authors may also enlist the help of additional contributing authors to prepare specific text, graphs or data. Governments are requested to nominate possible contributing authors, but lead authors may seek other contributions and consider unsolicited work.

The Working Group authors mentioned above remain based in their home institutions, fitting their IPCC responsibilities around their regular work. The authors thus make up a loosely knit, dispersed virtual network of scientists and research institutions. Occasional face-to-face meetings of authors are convened, but authors will generally keep in touch on a day-to-day basis via e-mail and the telephone. It is difficult to imagine how the IPCC could function in the absence of modern telecommunications. The authors do not receive any remuneration from the IPCC for their work, and it is expected that their home institutions and/or governments will support them in the discharge of their IPCC functions. The IPCC's work is therefore dependent on the goodwill of individual scientists and their employers. Authors from developing countries and EITs, however, do receive funding from the IPCC Trust Fund to cover the costs of attendance at meetings that are part of the assessment process.

[60] Skodvin, 1999b.

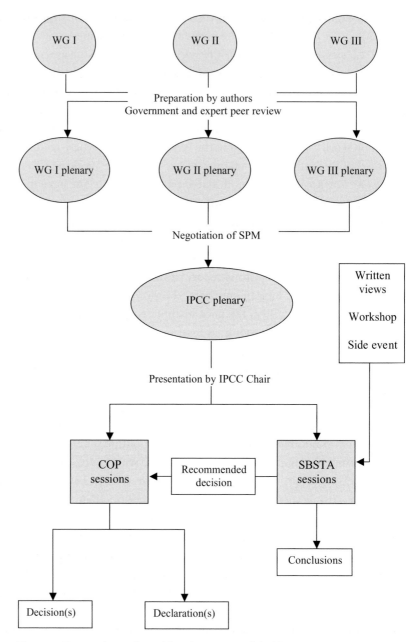

Fig. 15.2 Preparation and consideration process of the TAR

The principal task of the authors is to collect, review, summarise and assess the internationally available peer-reviewed literature on the issues covered by their particular chapter. Recognising that some important sources of information are not published in the academic literature or peer-reviewed, the IPCC introduced measures for using unpublished/non-peer reviewed literature in its revised 1999 procedures. The main thrust of these procedures is to ensure that the unpublished/non-peer reviewed material is archived by the IPCC, and made available to reviewers of the draft reports. The Working Group may also convene expert meetings or workshops in support of the assessment process on areas where existing analysis is lacking or discussion between the Working Groups is needed. For the 4AR, for example, the IPCC has identified a number of 'cross-cutting themes', which involve more than one working group. These have been explored through workshops and expert meetings.

3.3.1   Review

Chapter drafts are subject to a two-stage review process. First, the drafts are sent for expert review to experts nominated by governments, 'appropriate organisations', or the Working Group Bureau. Based on the review comments, the authors then prepare a revised draft, which is sent out for a second review, this time by both governments and experts. The IPCC's procedures state that eight weeks should normally be allowed for each stage of the review. The procedures place great importance on the need for objectivity, openness and transparency in the review process, calling for 'a wide circulation process' that involves 'as many experts as possible' from all regions. All written review comments are archived by the IPCC Secretariat for at least five years following the completion of the report.

The SPM of each Working Group report is prepared under the responsibility of the Working Group Co-Chairs and the technical summaries under the authority of the Working Group Bureaux. The TAR's Synthesis Report, for its part, was drafted directly under the IPCC Chair by a team of authors, who were also involved in the preparation of other aspects of the TAR. The SPMs, technical summaries and Synthesis Report are all subject to a simultaneous expert/government review.

Independent review editors, usually two per chapter, are appointed by the Working Group Bureaux to help oversee the review process. The review editors should normally consist of a member of the Working Group Bureau, plus an independent expert. Again, balance in geographical representation and 'scientific, technical and socio-economic views' is required. The review editors help identify reviewers for the expert review process and ensure that all comments are 'afforded appropriate consideration' by the chapter's authors.

In preparing the chapter drafts, the authors must seek to present the internationally accepted state of knowledge on the area in question. Where no consensus view is apparent, it is incumbent on the lead authors to clearly identify differing views that are nevertheless scientifically and technically justified. The review editors have an important role in this regard in providing advice 'on how to handle contentious/controversial issues and ensure genuine controversies are reflected adequately in the ... Report'. Given that scientific research itself is driven by dissent, and given the underlying contentious nature of the climate change issue, it is unsurprising that considerable debate often takes place within the chapter author teams. As far as possible, however, the process within the author teams is one of scientific dialogue, ostensibly untainted by politics.

3.3.2   Plenary endorsement

Following the two-stage review, the assessment process moves to the Working Group plenaries and their governmental representatives. The key task of the Working Group plenary is to formally 'approve' the SPM of the Working Group report through 'detailed, line by line discussion and agreement', to ensure that 'it is consistent with the factual material' contained in the underlying report. Unsurprisingly, heated debates typically erupt over the precise wording of SPMs, with governments seeking to emphasise or play down certain elements. As part of the debate, however, the chapter's lead authors and Working Group Co-Chairs may provide their expert opinion on whether or not a proposed change of wording is scientifically justified. The authority of these experts helps to ensure that the SPM retains its integrity, as does the fact that divergent politically polarized requests for wording changes often cancel each other out. Skodvin (1999b), for example, points out how, after almost three days of negotiation, one of the most controversial statements in the Working Group I SPM of the SAR changed from the original draft 'Taken together, these results point towards a detectable human influence on global climate' to the remarkably similar phrase 'the balance of evidence suggests a discernible human influence on global climate'.

In the event that disagreement remains, the IPCC's principles provide for differing views to be 'explained and, upon request, recorded'. In practice, the small number of disagreements that have not been resolved in the Working Group plenaries have been reflected through the use of footnotes to the text. The end product is therefore a political–scientific hybrid – the SPM is undeniably a politically negotiated document, but one that retains scientific rigour. The political involvement of governments in the SPMs helps to secure governmental 'buy in' to the science, while ensuring that IPCC reports are policy relevant and accessible to non-specialists, to an extent that would be hard to achieve in a purely scientific report.[61]

The technical summaries and underlying full reports are not discussed in detail but are simply subject to overall 'acceptance' by the plenary signifying the Working Group's concurrence that they present 'a comprehensive, objective and balanced view of the subject matter'. Changes called for by delegates as part of this acceptance process are typically minor in nature.

The three Working Group reports do not officially become IPCC products until they are endorsed by the full IPCC plenary, although this is usually a formality. The

---

[61] For an alternative view, see Boehmer Christiansen, 1994a and b.

IPCC plenary is not authorised to make changes to the Working Group reports, but nevertheless it must give the reports its formal acceptance, and 'note any substantial disagreements', according to the decision-making principles outlined above.

Some reports, however, are subject to formal approval by the IPCC plenary, as they cut across Working Group areas. This was the case, for example, with the TAR Synthesis Report, whose SPM was approved line by line, with the underlying report subject to a new process of section-by-section 'adoption', 'i.e. roughly one page or less at a time'.

3.3.3   Special reports and technical papers

The procedures outlined above also apply to the preparation of special reports. Technical papers, for their part, do not require approval/acceptance at a plenary meeting, as they may only contain pre-existing IPCC material. They are prepared under the responsibility of the relevant Working Group Bureau, and are subject to simultaneous expert/government review, before being sent to governments once again for final review.

3.3.4   Methodological work

Until recently, the IPCC's methodological work was not covered by the IPCC's procedures. The need to formalise the process for preparing and endorsing the IPCC's methodological work, however, became apparent with its growing political importance in relation to the Kyoto Protocol's methodological rules, especially on the LULUCF sector. The IPCC's procedures have now been provisionally amended[62] to apply also to the IPCC's methodological work. In essence, the procedures relating to special reports apply to the IPCC's methodological work, except that an overview chapter, rather than an SPM, will be prepared. This overview is subject to 'adoption', that is, section-by-section endorsement (like the underlying TAR Synthesis Report), rather than line-by-line approval.

3.4   *Institutional channels for input to the climate change regime*

In contrast to the MOU agreed between the COP and the GEF,[63] no formal arrangements are in place governing interaction between the IPCC and the climate change regime. Accepted practices for such interaction, however, have evolved over time.

The Joint Working Group (JWG) of the IPCC and the climate change regime serves as an important institutional channel for coordination between the two bodies. The JWG, which was established in 1995 at the request of the SBSTA,[64]

---

[62] See IPCC-20 report, decision 4 and Annex to paragraph 6.1.3.   [63] See chapter 10.
[64] See SBSTA-1 report, paragraph 24.

is composed of the Chair and Working Group/TFI Co-Chairs of the IPCC, the Chairs of the FCCC SBs, and key staff from both Secretariats. The purpose of the JWG, which has no formal mandate, is to exchange information and ensure coordination between the political regime and the IPCC, notably on process and administrative issues. It cannot take decisions, and functions on a purely informal and advisory basis. Meetings are usually held in private at each session of the SBs.

Links between the IPCC and the climate change regime are strengthened by the substantial overlap between the government delegates that attend plenary meetings of the IPCC and its Working Groups, and those represented on the SBSTA. IPCC officers routinely attend sessions of the climate change regime, while senior FCCC Secretariat staff similarly attend IPCC meetings.

The IPCC Chair regularly addresses the SBSTA under its item on 'Cooperation with relevant international organizations' to provide information on the IPCC's work programme and report on progress in its activities. The SBSTA is thus kept informed of the IPCC's work and, although it has no authority over it, the SBSTA can, and does, provide comments and underscore the key areas of interest for the climate change Parties (even if there is rarely consensus among delegates in this regard). The IPCC Chair also addresses the COP during its high-level segment, where he has traditionally offered a more personal assessment of the status of knowledge on climate change and its threat.[65]

IPCC representatives do not officially participate in debates or negotiations, but sometimes speak at the invitation of the Chair in response to technical questions. The channels available to other IGOs to input into the process (see below) are also open to, and used by, IPCC representatives. In addition, IPCC representatives may be called upon, by Parties or the Secretariat, to provide an *informal* opinion on technical issues in the negotiations as part of behind-the-scenes discussions. In the official negotiating forums, however, IPCC representatives must always sustain the political objectivity required of the Panel.

3.4.1   Assessment Reports

Recognising the link between scientific assessment and political negotiation, the SBSTA provided input to the IPCC at an early stage on the planned structure and content of the TAR.[66] It did so by eliciting and publishing written comments from Parties and convening an informal meeting between Parties and IPCC representatives. Given the differences of views among Parties, however, the

---

[65] See statements available at http://www.ipcc.ch/press/speech.htm.

[66] To recall, the SAR was planned and drafted before the Convention came into force and before the SBSTA met.

guidance given by the SBSTA to the IPCC could only be of a general and rather unfocused nature, and the process of developing the guidance evoked considerable controversy, especially over the regime's inputs on the Synthesis Report.[67] It is sobering that no such process of eliciting input from the SBSTA is planned for the 4AR, suggesting that its value was deemed limited.

According to its 'conduit' function, the Assessment Reports, once completed, are formally considered in the SBSTA. The SBSTA's tasks in this regard are to 'summarize and, where necessary, convert' the information provided 'into forms appropriate to the needs of the Conference of the Parties', and also to 'compile and synthesize' that information 'to the extent possible, and assess the implications thereof for the implementation of the Convention'.[68] A typical process of consideration for IPCC Assessment Reports in the climate change regime is summarised in figure 15.2 above.

The consideration of the IPCC's Assessment Reports in the SBSTA has been as much a political as a scientific process. Unlike the IPCC, the SBSTA does have a mandate to supply 'advice' to the COP, and can therefore make policy recommendations based on the IPCC's findings. Delegates have therefore sought to highlight aspects of the report that match their concerns or support their positions. The SBSTA's consideration of the SAR in 1996 was an acrimonious process as it sought, and failed, to select key findings from the report and couch these as recommendations for the Kyoto Protocol negotiations.[69] The eventual COP decision on the SAR simply thanked the IPCC for its work, and recognised the SAR as 'currently the most comprehensive and authoritative assessment now available of the scientific and technical information regarding global climate change'.[70] The Geneva Ministerial Declaration, drafted at COP-2,[71] did provide a much stronger endorsement of the SAR, but it could not be adopted, partly because of opposition by a small minority of Parties to its strong language on climate change science.[72]

Mindful of this difficult experience, the SBSTA took an alternative approach to its consideration of the TAR, eschewing any attempt to make policy recommendations. Although this was not to the liking of all Parties,[73] the SBSTA steered clear of the future of the climate change regime and the commitments of Parties,

---

[67] See SBSTA-7 report, paragraph 14, also FCCC/SBSTA/1997/MISC.4 and FCCC/SBSTA/1998/MISC.1.

[68] Decision 6/CP.1, Annex I, paragraph 1 (a) and (b).   [69] See SBSTA-3 report, Annex II.

[70] Decision 6/CP.2.   [71] See Report on COP-2, part II, Annex.   [72] See chapter 13, box 13.2.

[73] New Zealand, for example, 'expressed regret' that the conclusions adopted by SBSTA-16 'did not explicitly request the SBSTA . . . to begin to consider information . . . relevant to the future development of the Convention and the achievement of its objective' (SBSTA-16 report, paragraph 14).

focusing instead on technical information and further research, seeking to learn from TAR, explore how its mass of information could best be used, and identify issues for further consideration.[74] The SBSTA did so through workshops, informal side events and calls for written comments from Parties, as well as formal debate (see figure 15.2 above).

The result was agreement in the SBSTA that the TAR 'should be used routinely as a useful reference' for the deliberations of the COP and SBs,[75] and a decision to establish two new agenda items for the SBSTA:

- Scientific, technical and socio-economic aspects of impacts of, and vulnerability and adaptation to, climate change; and
- Scientific, technical and socio-economic aspects of mitigation.

Work under these two agenda items, which commenced at SBSTA-20 in 2004, is focused on exchanging information and sharing experiences on 'practical opportunities and solutions to facilitate the implementation of the Convention'.[76] The only COP decision on the TAR, taken at COP-7, was purely procedural, thanking the IPCC, encouraging Parties to make full use of the information in the TAR, and urging Parties to support the Panel.[77] The TAR was also acknowledged in the Delhi Ministerial Declaration on Climate Change and Sustainable Development, but only in its Preamble. The text 'recognizes with concern the findings of the [TAR], which confirm that significant cuts in global greenhouse gas emissions will be necessary to meet the overall objective of the Convention'.[78]

Unlike the FAR and the SAR – which informed the negotiations on the Convention and the Kyoto Protocol, respectively – the impact of the TAR on the regime has not been so clear. Open consideration of the TAR has certainly been stifled by the fear of developing countries that examination of the Report's findings could somehow provoke a discussion of their future commitments. Nonetheless, the SBSTA's work on the TAR has helped to promote a somewhat more wide-ranging debate on the international community's response to climate change. The two new agenda items could similarly facilitate more expansive thinking on vulnerability/adaptation and mitigation than would otherwise be possible under the existing specific items on the SBs' agendas.

---

[74] See SBSTA-16 report, paragraph 15.   [75] See SBSTA-16 report, paragraph 15 (c).

[76] See Decision 10/CP.9, Scientific, technical and socio-economic aspects of impacts of, and vulnerability and adaptation to, climate change, and scientific, technical and socio-economic aspects of mitigation.

[77] Decision 25/CP.7, Third Assessment Report of the Intergovernmental Panel on Climate Change.

[78] Decision 1/CP.8.

3.4.2   Specific requests: special reports, technical papers
           and methodological work

As noted above, the SBSTA usually makes requests for special reports and technical papers to the IPCC on behalf of the climate change regime.[79] The process of issuing and accepting these requests is an iterative one between the SBSTA and IPCC, and in particular between the more politically derived requests of Parties articulated in the SBSTA, and the more scientifically based considerations of the IPCC regarding the feasibility of a particular request. As an independent body, the IPCC is at liberty to refuse a request or call for a change in its terms of reference. Hence, the IPCC has, on occasion, suggested an alternative approach to a requested study, or referred back to the SBSTA when an initial request proved unclear or impractical. The IPCC plenary has, for example, converted requests for technical papers into special reports, on the grounds that the issue in question merited a full IPCC expert review.[80] Likewise, the SBSTA provides ongoing guidance and oversight on the production of requested IPCC reports, with the IPCC Chair reporting on progress in their preparation at each SBSTA session. Once a report is published, it is typically presented to the SBSTA by an IPCC officer, distributed to delegations, and then subject to consideration in both formal SBSTA sessions and informal settings, such as side events.

The methodological work of the IPCC is carried out both on its own initiative and in response to requests from the SBSTA. Illustrating the importance of the IPCC's methodological work to the climate change regime, the SBSTA has now formally requested the IPCC to update its methodological guidelines, with the aim of completing work by 2006.

4   Other sources of scientific and technical input

4.1   *FCCC roster of experts*

The FCCC roster of experts is used as a means of drawing on the knowledge and experience of individual climate change experts. Consisting of a list of individuals, nominated by Parties, who have expertise in various fields (e.g. methodologies, technology transfer), the roster is maintained by the Secretariat and published on its website.[81] It is used by the Secretariat to identify experts for a range of tasks, including preparing and reviewing draft papers requested by the SBSTA, participating in expert workshops and serving on teams for the in-depth review of Annex I Party national communications. The roster of experts is,

---

[79] During the Kyoto Protocol negotiations, the AGBM also issued requests to the IPCC.
[80] See, for example, IPCC-XX/Doc.19, regarding a proposed Special Report on Carbon Storage and Capture.
[81] See http://unfccc.int/program/mis/roster/index.html.

therefore, a reactive, rather than a proactive, channel for inputting scientific and technical information to the regime, whereby experts are called upon on an ad hoc basis to carry out specific pieces of work, rather than having a role in identifying emerging issues or formulating analysis on their own initiative.

The origins of the roster of experts, which was first launched in 1996, lie in failed attempts to launch more formal Intergovernmental Technical Advisory Panels under the SBSTA, similar to those deployed in the ozone regime.[82] Disagreement over the membership of these Panels meant that plans for their establishment were shelved at COP-2.[83] Devising a roster to which all Parties could nominate experts proved a more politically acceptable means of harnessing expertise. Until 1999, the Secretariat maintained three separate rosters, on technologies, methodologies and in-depth review. These rosters were then consolidated and the process for nomination to the roster formalised.[84]

To be included on the roster, prospective experts must complete an application form, identifying their areas of expertise from among listed categories, their language proficiency and experience. The form must be signed by the nominating government, which can specify the particular task for which the expert is suitable. Secretariat guidance[85] encourages Parties to nominate up to ten candidates, although some large countries have nominated many more than this. Experts participate on the roster in their personal capacity, and may come from the public, private or NGO sectors. The Secretariat periodically reports to the SBSTA on the use of the roster of experts, including on the regional distribution of experts selected for tasks.

4.2   Secretariat

The Secretariat itself is an important supplier of scientific and technical input for the regime. In addition to the compilations of Party submissions and reports on procedural matters that the Secretariat routinely publishes, the SBs will, on occasion, request the Secretariat to prepare substantive background papers to inform their deliberations. Such requests will usually concern technical issues that are specific to the climate change regime (e.g. use of registries for the flexibility mechanisms), and therefore on which analysis is sparse in the broader literature. The outcome of the Secretariat's work will typically be issued in the form of technical papers.[86] In preparing such papers, the Secretariat will often call on external consultants, sometimes drawing these from the roster of experts.

---

[82] See Decision 6/CP.1, paragraph 3.   [83] See COP-2 report, part-II, section III, paragraph 2.

[84] SBSTA-11 report, paragraph 108.

[85] Guidance to Parties: Updating of the FCCC roster of experts, available at http://unfccc.int/program/mis/roster/index.html.

[86] E.g. document FCCC/TP/2002/2 analysed the treatment of confidential information by international treaty bodies and organisations, as input into the SBSTA's debates on this matter. A FCCC technical paper should not be confused with an IPCC technical paper.

The main strength of the Secretariat is its ability to produce input in a timely manner and closely tailored to Parties' needs, without being beholden to a protracted intergovernmental review process. Moreover, the Secretariat is a prime source of expertise on the regime's rules, and is therefore very well placed to present targeted analysis on issues that are specific to the negotiations, such as the treatment of confidential data under the reporting guidelines. The Secretariat, however, is limited in the analysis that it can present by its mandate to remain objective and not advocate any particular approach.

4.3   Intergovernmental organisations

IGOs are another source of scientific and technical input for the climate change regime. Such input may be requested by the SBs or may come unsolicited as IGOs carry out research on climate change that is relevant to their field and communicate the results to the climate change regime. IGOs may request to address the SBSTA under the item 'Cooperation with relevant international organizations' in order to present their input, and perhaps circulate any written material to Parties. IGOs may also avail themselves of the opportunity open to all observers (and Parties) to run a stall exhibiting the information they have to impart, or host a side event to promote a more in-depth discussion of that information.[87]

There are many examples that could be cited of scientific and technical input prepared by IGOs and presented to the climate change regime. One of the key IGOs involved in 'hard' scientific research on the climate system is the GCOS which is explained in chapter 7. UNEP has prepared guidelines for reporting on vulnerability and adaptation, which are now referenced in the broader FCCC reporting guidelines, and UNDP is now advancing an adaptation capacity-building framework.[88] The FAO has supplemented the IPCC's work in serving as a source of expertise, solicited by the SBSTA, on the LULUCF sector.[89] The WHO has prepared reports on climate change and health, which have also been presented to the SBSTA.[90] The role of ICAO and IMO is examined in chapter 5, with chapter 17 discussing linkages with the Secretariats of other MEAs.

4.4   Non-governmental organisations

The hundreds of NGOs that are active in the climate change regime include many research bodies that serve as the regime's intellectual engine. The contribution of these research NGOs is particularly important on socio-economic issues and for policy analysis, with researchers active in following the negotiation process, evaluating negotiating outcomes, and examining possible approaches

---

[87] See also chapter 14.   [88] See chapters 10 and 11.
[89] See, for example, SBSTA-16 report, paragraph 29.
[90] See, for example, SBSTA-12 report, section IX.

for the future. A major strength of research NGOs is that they can put forward their own policy judgements and recommendations, as well as hard-hitting analysis, and can respond quickly to developments in the negotiations. The business and industry community also have an informational role to play in the climate change regime, with some possessing expertise in particular areas, such as the fluorocarbon sector and aviation emissions. The role of these actors in the regime is examined further in chapter 3. While not strictly speaking NGOs, research institutions that are run or funded by national governments, such as the UK's Hadley Centre for Climate Prediction and Research or the Dutch National Institute for Public Health and the Environment (RIVM), also supply important scientific input to the regime.[91] As with any form of information, the extent to which delegates pay credence to publications and other forms of advice from these various sources depends on the perceived objectivity and expertise of the source.

[91] See www.metoffice.com/research/hadleycentre/index.html and www.rivm.nl.

16

Administering the regime

1 Introduction

The administrative basis of the climate change regime was established in February 1991, when the UN Secretary-General called upon an UNCTAD official to head a team of a dozen seconded staff, working in borrowed offices and on a shoestring budget, to manage the negotiation of what became the FCCC. The administration of the climate change regime has since evolved into a complex enterprise, involving a Secretariat of over 160 staff members and a total annual budget, including several trust funds, of more than US $20 million. This chapter explores how the climate change regime is administered, focusing on its finances and the role of the Secretariat.

2 The programme budget

2.1 *Financial procedures*

In its Article 7.2 (k), the Convention calls upon the COP to 'agree upon and adopt . . . financial rules for itself and for any subsidiary bodies'. This was done at COP-1, with Decision 15/CP.1[1] establishing the financial basis for the operation of the COP, the SBs and the Secretariat. These financial procedures are founded on the wider Financial Regulations and Rules of the United Nations, which apply where Decision 15/CP.1 is silent.[2]

---

[1] Decision 15/CP.1, Financial procedures, and Annex I, Financial procedures for the Conference of the Parties to the United Nations Framework Convention on Climate Change, its subsidiary bodies and its permanent secretariat. Unless otherwise specified, the rules contained in this section are set out in the Financial procedures.

[2] Decision 15/CP.1, Annex I, paragraph 1. See also COP-1 report, part I, paragraph 98.

According to the financial procedures, the Executive Secretary prepares a draft *programme budget* every two years for the next biennium. This draft, which is circulated to Parties at least ninety days before the opening of the COP where it is due for adoption, is negotiated in the SBI and adopted by the COP by consensus.

2.1.1   Indicative scale of contributions

The core budget is primarily made up of annual contributions from all Parties on the basis of an *indicative scale*, adopted by consensus by the COP. The term 'indicative' conveys the notion that contributions are essentially voluntary in nature. While voluntary, however, contributing to the core budget is considered integral to a Party's obligations in the climate change regime, unlike contributions to the two explicitly voluntary trust funds discussed below.

The indicative scale of contributions for the climate change regime is determined on the basis of the UN scale of assessments. The UN scale itself is approved by the UN General Assembly and revised periodically. It is based primarily on capacity to pay, with contributions determined according to relative shares of total GNP, specified maximum and minimum thresholds, and other factors.[3] The indicative scale of contributions for the climate change regime incorporates the thresholds in the UN scale of assessments whereby no Party contributes less than 0.001 per cent of the total, and no contribution from an LDC Party exceeds 0.01 per cent.[4] These thresholds differ from those in the original financial procedures, following revisions to the UN scale of assessments introduced by the UN General Assembly in 1997.[5] The financial procedures of the climate change regime were themselves formally amended in 1998[6] to leave open the possibility of future changes to these thresholds following any further modifications to the UN scale of assessments. The UN scale was indeed further modified, in 2000, to lower the maximum contribution – that of the US – to 22 per cent (from 25 per cent).[7] This change has been incorporated into successive indicative scales of contributions to the climate change regime, but without the adoption of a specific decision in this regard.

It is worth noting that the scale of assessments has become a bone of contention in the wider UN system, notably in the context of the arrears of the US, the largest contributor. Several countries were unhappy with the lowering of the maximum

---

[3] See, for example, UNGA resolution 55/5, Scale of assessments for the apportionment of the expenses of the UN, 23 December 2000, paragraph 1.

[4] See Decision 17/CP.4, Administrative and financial matters, paragraph 15.

[5] See UNGA resolution 52/215, Scale of assessments, 22 December 1997.

[6] Decision 17/CP.4, paragraph 16.   [7] See UNGA resolution 55/5.

contribution as it raised their own budget contributions,[8] and have made their feelings clear also in the climate change regime.[9]

The indicative scale of contributions for the climate change regime differs slightly from the UN scale of assessments as the Parties to the Convention do not exactly match the members of the UN. Overall, there are fewer Parties to the Convention than UN members, while some Parties are not UN members. These include, until recently, Switzerland, as well as the EC, which stated, at COP-1, its intention to contribute 2.5 per cent of the programme budget, in addition to the contributions of its member states.[10]

2.1.2   The Trust Funds

The climate change regime operates through four main funds:

- The *Trust Fund for the Core Budget of the FCCC*, which receives the indicative contributions from Parties discussed above;
- The *Trust Fund for Participation in the FCCC Process*, which receives voluntary contributions to support the participation of eligible developing country and EIT Parties in the COP and its SBs;[11]
- The *Trust Fund for Supplementary Activities*, which receives additional voluntary contributions, usually for specific initiatives;[12] and
- The *Trust Fund for the Special Annual Contribution from the Government of Germany*, known as the *Bonn Fund*, which manages an annual contribution from Germany, the host of the Secretariat.[13]

2.2   *The core budget*

The core programme budget[14] of the Secretariat, as approved by the COP, has risen every year, as illustrated in figure 16.1 below, with the total core budget for the fifth biennium 2004–2005 exceeding that for 1996–1997 by over 85 per cent.

The core budget for the climate change regime contrasts with that for other global MEAs, such as the CBD and Montreal Protocol. At US $10,049,000, for example, the core budget of the CBD was around one-third less than that of the climate

---

[8] See UNGA Press release, 2000.   [9] See SBI-18 report, paragraph 52(f).

[10] See COP-1 report, part I, paragraph 97.

[11] In addition to the Financial procedures, see also Decision 18/CP.1, Other voluntary funding for the biennium 1996–1997.

[12] Although the financial procedures do not make specific reference to this fund, they do permit the UN Secretary-General, subject to the approval of the COP, to establish further trust funds (paragraph 16). Decision 18/CP.1 also makes reference to 'other voluntary funding' (paragraph 2).

[13] Decision 16/CP.3, Financial performance of the Convention in the biennium 1996–1997, paragraph 2.

[14] See Decisions 17/CP.1, 15/CP.3, 20/CP.5, 38/CP.7 and 16/CP.9 ('Programme budgets').

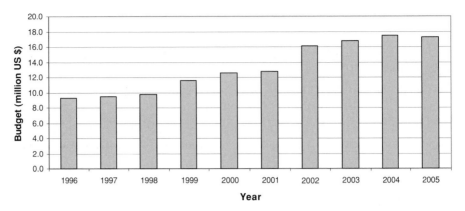

Fig. 16.1   Core budget of the Secretariat approved by the COP 1996–2005

change regime in 2002, while that of the Montreal Protocol, at US $3,907,646, was under a quarter for that year.[15] The relatively large climate change core budget reflects the particular stage of the climate change process, which is currently in full development with numerous activities under implementation and well-attended negotiating sessions, in turn requiring a comparatively sizeable Secretariat. It also reflects the high profile of the regime and the support that it enjoys among most members of the international community. Fierce debates over the level of the programme budget for 2004–2005, however, suggest that the steep and steady rise in the regime's budget has come to an end. Taking into account the increase in staff costs and fluctuations in the value of the dollar, the budget rise for 2004–2005 in fact represents a cut in funding compared to the previous biennium, with the Secretariat estimating that an extra US $2.5 million would have been needed simply to maintain Secretariat activities.[16] Given this shortage of funds, the decision adopting the 2004–2005 programme budget requests the Executive Secretary to provide the SBs with an indication of the administrative and budgetary implications of COP decisions under development, where these cannot be met from existing core budget resources. While the provision of such information is called for in the Rules of Procedure,[17] it is explicitly specified in the 2004–2005 programme budget decision for the first time, reflecting Secretariat concern over its ability to deliver in the face of budgetary constraints.

The contributions of Parties that are needed to make up the regime's core budget may be reduced by carry-over from unspent balances for previous financial periods, which usually accrue when very late payment of some contributions

---

[15] See CBD Decision V/22, Budget for the programme of work for the biennium 2001–2002; and MP Decision XIII/30, Financial matters: Financial reports and budgets.

[16] See FCCC/SBI/2003/15, note 1.   [17] See Rule 15.

makes it impossible to spend them in the intended biennium. In addition, the core budget enjoys a regular payment from the government of Germany (in addition to the 'Bonn Fund'), which also offsets the contributions of Parties. This totals €766,938 annually.[18]

The core budget does not fully fund the conference servicing costs of holding sessions of the COP and SBs (such as interpretation and translation). As part of the institutional linkage of the Secretariat to the UN (see section 3.1 below), these are covered by the UN's regular budget.[19] However, each programme budget to date has included an extra contingency amount (nearly US $6 million for 2004–2005), in the event that the UNGA decides no longer to fund climate change meetings from its regular budget.

According to the financial procedures, the Executive Secretary is required to maintain a 'working capital reserve' of 8.3 per cent of the total core budget in the core fund in order to 'ensure continuity of operations in the event of a temporary shortfall of cash', and must pay 13 per cent of the budget to the UN as 'overhead costs' for administrative support. Although these specific percentages were not set by the financial procedures, they have remained static since the first biennium (1996–1997).

In addition to setting a total amount of funds, the programme budget fixes the number of posts for each Secretariat programme (department) at various staff grades. Once the budget is adopted, the Executive Secretary is authorised to make transfers between the main appropriation lines for expenditure by the programmes. The financial procedures do not set any limits on such transfers. When adopting each programme budget, however, the COP has set an aggregate limit of 15 per cent of total estimated expenditure, including a maximum of minus 25 per cent for each appropriation line.

2.2.1   Contributions

The largest contributor to the climate change regime core budget is the US, which paid just over 21 per cent in 2002, an amount for that year of US $3,477,640.[20] Forty-four countries (mostly, but not all, LDCs and SIDS) each pay the smallest contribution, 0.001 per cent, amounting to some US $163 each in 2002. For 2003, the ten largest contributions added up to 76 per cent of the total, with the twenty largest adding up to 89 per cent (see table 16.1 below).

---

[18] Amounting, in September 2003, to around US $831,820.

[19] By its Decision 14/CP.1, Institutional linkage of the Convention Secretariat to the United Nations, the COP requested the UN General Assembly to decide to finance conference-servicing costs from the regular UN programme budget (paragraph 5).

[20] See FCCC/SBI/2002/INF.13, table 1.

Table 16.1   *Twenty largest contributors to the*
2003 FCCC core budget and their shares

	Party	% of core budget (2003)
1	US	21.311
2	Japan	18.904
3	Germany	9.463
4	France	6.263
5	UK	5.363
6	Italy	4.906
7	EC	2.5
8	Canada	2.478
9	Spain	2.440
10	Brazil	2.315
11	Republic of Korea	1.793
12	Netherlands	1.684
13	Australia	1.576
14	China	1.484
15	Switzerland	1.234
16	Russian Federation	1.162
17	Argentina	1.113
18	Belgium	1.094
19	Mexico	1.052
20	Sweden	0.995

In 1998, following the change to the UN scale of assessments whereby the minimum contribution was reduced to 0.001 per cent (see above), the Secretariat proposed to the SBI that Parties whose contributions would amount to less than 0.01 per cent should be exempt, as the cost of collecting these small amounts might exceed the contribution itself.[21] Parties however, including LDCs, indicated their wish to retain full participation in the budget, with contributions from all.[22]

Parties are required to pay their contributions on 1 January each year,[23] with notifications of the exact amount due sent out by the Secretariat by 30 September of the preceding year. For this reason, agreement on each new programme budget is usually reached at the mid-year SBI before the end-of-year COP where it is formally adopted, allowing the Secretariat to send out notification of contributions due. Very few Parties, however, pay their contributions on the due date.[24] By

---

[21] See FCCC/SBI/1998/4, Section IV.   [22] See Decision 17/CP.4, paragraphs 14 and 15.
[23] Decision 15/CP.1, paragraph 8(a).
[24] The following examples are taken from FCCC/SBI/2003/12.

30 June 2003, for example, 117 Parties had not yet made their contributions for 2003 and 74 had not made any contribution for 2002–2003. Twenty-two Parties, all of them developing countries whose maximum individual contribution currently amounts to 0.015 per cent of the budget, have never made any contribution since 1996 when the Trust Fund was established. Of particular concern, however, is late payment by major contributors. By 30 June 2003, ten of the top twenty contributors, and four of the top ten, had not yet submitted their contributions for that year. Such late and non-payment of contributions is, of course, not uncommon among international organisations.[25]

There are several reasons for late payment, over and above financial constraints for some countries.[26] These include differing financial periods, lengthy internal approval procedures, disjuncture between the ministry responsible for the climate change negotiations and that responsible for paying the contribution, administrative error, the desire to await a more favourable exchange rate – and sometimes simple foot-dragging. Although the regime's core operations have not, to date, been seriously affected, late payment of contributions, especially from major contributors, has, at times, caused cash flow problems for the Secretariat, requiring it to draw on the working capital reserve and unspent balances from previous years. It has meant delays in incurring expenditures, such as launching activities or recruiting staff, because, according to the financial procedures, commitments may be entered into only on the basis of paid contributions.[27] Late, and indeed non-, payment of contributions also goes against the principle of full financial participation in the regime.

The Secretariat has taken several initiatives to respond to the problem,[28] including sending reminders to the top twenty contributors if contributions are not received by mid-year, and publishing a report on the status of contributions at each negotiating session, in the hope of 'naming and shaming'. In addition, until the practice was suspended on the request of the SBI after COP-9, funding for participation at sessions of the COP and the SBs was not offered to Parties who would otherwise have been eligible for such funding (see below) if their contributions were more than one year in arrears, although LDCs and SIDS were exempt.[29] This did not, however, affect industrialised country contributors who are not, in any case, eligible for funding. The SBI has considered possible additional sanctions, following an expression of concern by Parties at COP-5 'at the continuing trend towards late payment of contributions'.[30] However, although the COP has

---

[25] For a commentary, see Jacob, 2003.   [26] See FCCC/SBI/2000/2.
[27] Decision 15/CP.1, paragraph 5; FCCC/SBI/2000/2, paragraph 3.
[28] See FCCC/SBI/2000/2.   [29] FCCC/SBI/2003/12, paragraph 16.
[30] Decision 21/CP.5, Income and budget performance in the biennium 1998–1999 and arrangements for administrative support to the Convention, paragraph 3.

continued to express concern at late contributions,[31] Parties have been reluctant to agree to any stronger measures beyond the Secretariat's above-mentioned initiatives. Indeed, as noted above, even the withholding of funding for participation from Parties in arrears proved controversial, and has now been suspended until COP-10, after which time the SBI will reconsider the issue. Other regimes have been more active in chasing up pending contributions. Parties to the CBD with contributions in arrears for more than two years, for example, may only send two delegates to meetings of the Convention bodies.[32]

2.3   Trust Fund for Participation

Through the Trust Fund for Participation, funding is provided for one delegate from eligible developing country and EIT Parties to attend sessions of the COP and SBs. Where sufficient funds are available, support is also provided to fund a second delegate from LDCs and SIDS at COP sessions. In addition, the Trust Fund supports the participation of Bureau members from eligible Parties at intersessional Bureau meetings, consultations or other official meetings related to the Convention process.[33] The provision of such funding reflects the limited financial resources of many Parties to cover the costs of sending delegates to participate in negotiation sessions. It is a common practice throughout the international environmental arena.

Eligibility for funding is determined according to GDP per capita. The current threshold in the climate change regime is that GDP per capita must not have exceeded US $6,500 in 2000 according to the Data Management Service of UNCTAD, rising to US $10,000 for SIDS and Parties providing Bureau members.[34] The funding thresholds have generated some isolated problems in the case of certain SIDS, whose per capita GDP is over the threshold, but their total GDP is low, making it difficult for them to afford participation in the climate change process.[35]

The amount requested by the COP in each of its programme budgets for the Trust Fund for Participation is shown in table 16.2 below.

Contributions to the Trust Fund for Participation, however, are made on an explicitly voluntary basis, primarily by OECD countries (see table 16.3 below). The amount received is therefore unpredictable. At COP-7 and COP-9, for example, there was insufficient funding to finance a second delegate from LDCs and SIDS, while at SB-18 in June 2003 the Secretariat was only able to fund a limited number

---

[31] See, for example, Decision 16/CP.8, Administrative and financial matters.
[32] See CBD Decision VI/29, Administration of the Convention and the budget for the programme of work for the biennium 2003–2004.
[33] See Decision 16/CP.2, Income and budget performance, and resource deployment for 1997.
[34] FCCC/SBI/2003/12, paragraph 16.
[35] The Bahamas, for example, has faced problems in this regard.

Table 16.2 *Trust Fund for Participation*

Biennium	Year	Requested in the programme budget (US $)
1	1996	2,770,990
	1997	2,049,590
2	1998	2,256,100
	1999	2,324,400
3	2000	1,845,900
	2001	1,845,900
4	2002	1,678,100
	2003	1,678,100
5	2004	1,678,100
	2005	1,678,100

of eligible Parties (eighty-five), prompting an official statement of 'deep concern' by the G-77 and China.[36]

Financial support for participation covers an economy class air ticket, purchased by the Secretariat for the eligible Party, according to the most direct, least costly route. Financial support also covers a daily subsistence allowance (DSA) for each day of the meeting plus travel days, according to the standard UN rate. These procedures follow those of the broader UN system. There are inevitably complaints about the financial support provided, with the most common being its general insufficiency. Small delegations frequently point out that funding a one-person delegation, or increasing a one-person delegation to two people, is not enough to ensure equitable participation by the Party in the process, especially when the delegate concerned may have only limited resources or expertise at his/her disposal. There are also concerns about the mode of financial support, with the 'least costly' rule often taking supremacy, so that funded delegates sometimes find themselves on time-consuming and tiring itineraries. LDCs made a formal complaint about such issues at SBI-15 in 2001.[37]

2.4   *Trust Fund for Supplementary Activities*

The Trust Fund for Supplementary Activities receives funding donated by Parties in addition to their indicative contributions to the core budget and voluntary contributions to the Trust Fund for Participation. The programme budget outlines proposed supplementary activities for the biennium, and an estimate

---

[36] See FCCC/SBI/2003/12, paragraph 15, also SBI-18 report, paragraph 49(b).
[37] See SBI-15 report, paragraphs 66–7.

Table 16.3   *Trust Fund for Participation: Contributors since 1996 (as of 31 October 2003)*
(US $)[38]

	1996/7	1998/9	2000/1	2002/3[39]
Australia	–	–	–	13,240
Austria	25,000	–	–	5,000
Canada	35,826	–	103,306	31,328
Denmark	115,000	40,000	63,686	–
EC	395,637	82,734	218,545	–
Finland	–	–	29,812	54,010
France	–	–	56,650	–
Germany	465,507	246,132	100,000	200,000
Greece	10,000	20,000	–	20,007
Iceland	–	–	–	1,973
Ireland	43,596	–	–	57,818
Italy	163,226	–	–	–
Japan	405,555	–	360,000	–
Netherlands	171,065	–	464,888	–
New Zealand	23,710	8,604	–	19,982
Norway	44,763	73,497	87,456	194,098
St Lucia	761	–	–	–
Portugal	–	–	10,000	19,978
Sweden	115,000	60,000	94,819	90,692
Switzerland	84,317	21,898	48,632	–
UK	161,290	326,745	393,640	306,761
US	375,000	1,064,000	825,000	752,395
TOTAL	2,635,253	1,943,610	2,856,434	1,767,282

of their cost. Such activities are generally in the field of public awareness, out-reach and information products, capacity-building and convening of intersessional workshops. In addition, the Trust Fund has been used as a channel to fund activities relating to the Kyoto Protocol. As the biennium progresses, additional activities, such as new workshops, may emerge in response to requests from the SBs or initiatives by the Secretariat. Parties will often earmark donated funds for specific purposes, and the Secretariat will seek to raise additional finance where a particular activity lacks funding. As shown in table 16.4, the amount of funds

[38] Data for 1996–2001 from Auditors' reports: Documents FCCC/CP/1998/9; FCCC/SBI/2000/9; FCCC/SBI/2002/10/add.1; data for 2002–2003 from FCCC/SBI/2003/INF.18.

[39] Includes contributions only up to 31 October 2003.

Table 16.4   *Trust Fund for Supplementary Activities*

Biennium	Year	Requested by the COP in the programme budget (US $)
1	1996	1,310,460
	1997	1,451,370
2	1998	2,062,600
	1999	2,086,200
3	2000	3,200,000
	2001	2,978,900
4	2002	7,050,000[40]
	2003	7,050,000
5	2004	8,995,100[41]
	2005	8,995,100

estimated in the programme budget as needed for supplementary activities has risen, reflecting the greater variety of activities underway in the climate change regime, especially with the adoption of the Kyoto Protocol. Table 16.5 lists contributors to the fund since 1996.

2.5   *The 'Bonn Fund'*

The 'Bonn Fund' administers the special contribution from the government of Germany, which amounts to around €1,789, 522 (previously DM 3.5 million) annually. (This is in addition to Germany's regular payment to the core budget – see above.) These funds are used primarily to offset the costs of organising conferences and other meetings in Bonn.

2.6   *Financial procedures under the Kyoto Protocol*

The Kyoto Protocol provides for the Convention's financial procedures to apply to it *mutatis mutandis*, unless otherwise decided by the COP/MOP.[42]

There is no explicit provision in the Kyoto Protocol requiring the separation of costs of supporting the Convention and the Protocol. Indeed, a proposal to do so

---

[40] Includes US $6.8 million over the biennium for the prompt start of the CDM.

[41] The 2004–2005 programme budget requests funds for the whole biennium (US $17,990,200), without dividing the sum between 2004 and 2005. In this table, the total sum is split equally between both years.

[42] KP Article 13.5.

Table 16.5 *Trust Fund for Supplementary Activities: contributors since 1996 (as of 31 October 2003) (US $)*[43]

	1996/7	1998/9	2000/1	2002/3[44]
Australia	–	19,173	59,260	5,292
Austria	–	38,168	–	–
Bahrain	–	1,026	1,857	–
Belgium	–	–	–	37,075
Canada	7,791	67,231	213,285	740,470
Denmark	–	60,000	115,000	125,950
EC	94,313	–	–	–
Finland	–	–	134,271	24,543
France	–	11,365	–	145,990
Germany[45]	–	129,932	–	375,118
Iceland	–	–	30,000	2,975
Ireland	10,300	24,939	5,150	20,000
Italy	9,000	–	–	1,229,626
Japan	232,821	235,000	200,000	526,573
Monaco	–	1,000	883	930
Netherlands	–	93,898	479,882	438,575
New Zealand	21,166	10,500	–	44,957
Norway	23,314	50,000	123,685	566,734
Portugal	–	–	–	52,810
Spain	–	–	–	5,714
Sweden	33,940	24,545	100,000	21,579
Switzerland	185,517	159,914	29,103	179,915
UK	–	57,339	171,580	461,889
US	944,600	2,278,651	3,791,829	300,000
Gaz de France[46]	–	–	–	50,000
TOTAL	1,562,762	3,262,681	5,455,785	5,356,715

that was put forward during the Protocol negotiations was not accepted, on the grounds that such a separation of costs would be impractical, and calculating the

[43] Data from Auditors' reports and FCCC/SBI/2003/INF.18.

[44] Includes contributions only up to 31 October 2003.

[45] Germany's special contribution, administered from January 1998 under the 'Bonn Fund', was managed as part of the Trust Fund for Supplementary Activities during the biennium 1996–1997.

[46] The contribution from this NGO was made in 1999, but only identified in 2002.

different contributions of Kyoto Protocol Parties and non-Parties would probably be more expensive than the savings achieved.[47] However, the repudiation of the Kyoto Protocol by the US – the largest financial contributor to the regime – and that country's decision not to fund Protocol-related activities, means that Convention and Kyoto Protocol costs have had to be separated out. The US made its position in this respect clear by withholding its proportionate share for the prompt start of the CDM from its contribution to the 2002–2003 core budget.[48]

Given the US position and the fact that the Kyoto Protocol could enter into force during 2004–2005, negotiations over the programme budget for that biennium were particularly difficult. The 2004–2005 programme budget eventually adopted at COP-9 includes the following provisions relating to the Kyoto Protocol:[49]

- An estimate of the proportion of the 2004–2005 core budget involving Kyoto Protocol 'preparatory activities', amounting to 9.51 per cent, which it is understood the US will withhold from its contribution.
- An 'interim allocation' of funds in the event that the Kyoto Protocol enters into force during the biennium. This amounts to a maximum of US $5,455,783 if the Protocol comes into force before 1 January 2005, or a pro rata amount if it enters into force later that year.
- An additional indicative scale of contributions for 2005 for the above-mentioned interim allocation, including only Parties that have ratified the Kyoto Protocol (to be revised as additional Parties ratify). The absence of the US means that other Parties pay a larger proportion of this interim allocation than they do of the core budget. Japan, for example, becomes the largest contributor, with a share of 22 per cent (as capped by the procedures governing the UN scale of contributions) compared with 18.938 per cent for the FCCC core budget. Similarly, China's contribution for the Kyoto Protocol interim allocation amounts to 2.187 per cent, compared with 1.487 per cent for the FCCC core budget. (These shares will, of course, change as additional Parties ratify.)
- A separation of resource requirements for the Trust Fund for Supplementary Activities between Convention and Kyoto Protocol related initiatives. At nearly US $8.6 million, the amount requested under the Kyoto Protocol is about 15 per cent greater than that under the Convention. It is notable that activities that are central to the functioning of the Kyoto Protocol – including support for the EB/CDM, the A6SC and the development of

---

[47] See FCCC/TP/2000/2, paragraphs 370–4. Also Werksman, 1999a, section 6.
[48] See FCCC/SBI/2003/INF.18, table 1, entry for United States of America.
[49] See Decision 16/CP.9, Programme budget for the biennium 2004–2005.

registries – are to be financed through the Trust Fund for Supplementary Activities, that is, depending on ad hoc, voluntary contributions from interested Parties, rather than core funds.

3   Secretariat

Article 8 of the Convention establishes a Secretariat charged with performing a variety of functions in support of the COP, the SBs and the Parties. The Secretariat to the Convention will also serve as the Secretariat to the Kyoto Protocol, applying the same provisions as under the Convention.[50]

At COP-1, two key decisions were taken with respect to the Secretariat. First, the Secretariat's headquarters were moved from Geneva to Bonn. This move followed an offer by the German government to host the Secretariat and an 'informal confidential survey' among Parties – in effect, a secret ballot – that eliminated other bids from Geneva, Toronto and Montevideo.[51] Secondly, it was decided that the Secretariat would be 'institutionally linked' to the wider UN system, 'while not being fully integrated in the work programme and management structure of any particular department or programme'.[52] This contrasts, for example, with the biodiversity and ozone secretariats, whose secretariat functions are carried out by UNEP. The permanent Secretariat came formally into being on this basis in January 1996, and opened its offices in Bonn later that year on 15 August.

3.1   *Institutional linkage with the UN system*

The institutional linkage of the Secretariat to the UN permeates every aspect of its work. Personnel procedures, including salary scales and entitlements, follow Staff Rules and Regulations of the UN.[53] Secretariat staff are recruited on behalf of the UN Secretary-General, although their appointment is limited to service within the Convention Secretariat, that is, they are not considered as internal candidates for posts elsewhere in the UN system. This institutional linkage provides the basis on which the UN funds conference servicing for the climate change regime from its regular budget (see above). Conference services (interpretation, document production and translation) are thus supplied primarily by staff from the UN Office at Geneva (UNOG). The Executive Secretary of the Secretariat reports to the UN Secretary-General. S/he does so through the UN's Department of Management on administrative and financial issues, in order to keep the Secretariat within the UN's administrative and financial framework, and through the UN's Department for Economic and Social Affairs, in order to integrate the climate change regime with the UN's work on sustainable development. The functioning

---

[50] KP Article 14.   [51] See COP-1 report, part 1, paragraphs 102–13.
[52] Decision 14/CP.1, paragraph 2.   [53] ST/SGB/2002/1, rules 100.1 to 112.8, 1 January 2002.

of the institutional linkage was reviewed in 1999 and again in 2001, but no changes were deemed necessary.[54] A further review will be held in 2006.

3.1.1 Juridical personality

As part of the headquarters agreement[55] signed with the government of Germany and the UN on its relocation to Bonn, the Secretariat was vested with juridical personality in Germany to enable the effective discharge of its functions. In accordance with the 1946 General Convention on Privileges and Immunities of the United Nations, the agreement includes the legal capacity of the Secretariat to contract, acquire and dispose of property, and institute legal proceedings, as well as the granting of privileges and immunities to staff and representatives of Parties and observers. In this context, the question was raised as to whether the Secretariat needed to be endowed with juridical personality also on the broader international plane. Despite advice from the UN Office of Legal Affairs that this would indeed be desirable, the Parties did not take any action at that time, but decided to reconsider the issue as part of the above-mentioned review of the institutional linkage with the UN system.[56] At each such review, however, the Parties have concluded that the absence of juridical personality on the international plane has not hindered the Secretariat in the effective discharge of its functions.[57] The issue may be reopened in the future if necessary.[58]

3.1.2 Administrative arrangements

Arrangements for administrative support to the Secretariat (funded through the 13 per cent overhead costs levied on the core budget – see above) are governed by a proposal from the UN Secretary-General that was accepted at COP-1.[59] This establishes, among other things, the authority of the Executive Secretary to appoint, promote, transfer and separate staff and to incur expenditures according to COP decisions. In turn, it establishes the responsibility of the UN Secretary-General to invest monies not immediately required, and that of the UN

---

[54] Decisions 22/CP.5 and 6/CP.6, Institutional linkage of the Convention Secretariat to the United Nations, subsequently endorsed by UNGA resolutions 50/115 of 20 December 1995, 54/222 of 22 December 1999, and 56/199 of 21 December 2001, all entitled Protection of global climate for present and future generations of mankind.

[55] See Headquarters Agreement signed on 20 June 1996, contained in FCCC/CP/1996/MISC.1. The agreement applies *mutatis mutandis* that already concluded between the UN and Germany in 1995 with regard to the location of the United Nations Volunteers in Bonn.

[56] Decision 15/CP.2, Agreement concerning the headquarters of the Convention Secretariat.

[57] For a fuller discussion of the juridical personality of the Secretariat, see Churchill and Ulfstein, 2000; also Werksman, 1999a.

[58] See FCCC/SBI/2001/9, paragraph 58.   [59] Decision 14/CP.1, paragraph 3.

Office of Internal Oversight Services to conduct an internal audit of the Convention financial system.

Since the move to Bonn, the administration of the Secretariat has become increasingly independent from its previous centre at UNOG.[60] The Secretariat is now responsible for all aspects of administration, except for certain functions that lie outside the delegation of authority to the Executive Secretary, including issuance of permits to travel and auditing. This has led, in turn, to the reimbursement to the Secretariat of some of the 13 per cent of the core budget levied by the UN for overhead costs to finance its own administration department. The Executive Secretary regularly reports to both the COP and SBI on developments on administrative issues.

3.1.3   Oversight and auditing

In accordance with the financial procedures, the Executive Secretary prepares a report twice a year on the financial and budgetary performance of the Secretariat, including the status of contributions from Parties and a description of how funds have been spent. In addition to this report, the Secretariat is subject to auditing by the UN at the close of each biennium. The conduct of such audits is contracted out by UN headquarters to member states, with the UN Board of Auditors composed of the heads of the national audit authorities of three member states. In 2002, for example, the Board of Auditors consisted of South Africa, the Philippines and France.[61] The auditor's reports present the certified financial statements for the biennium, along with the Board's opinion on the financial management of the Secretariat and recommendations for its improvement. So far, the Board has always certified that the 'financial statements present fairly, in all material respects, the financial position' of the Secretariat, and that 'transactions ... have, in all significant respects, been in accordance with the Financial Regulations [of the UN] and legislative authority'.[62] Recommendations made by the Board have included improving record-keeping of expenditures and obligations, strengthening budget planning and increasing value for money obtained by the Secretariat. The Board follows up on the implementation of past recommendations as part of its audit for the next biennium.

Overall, it is notable that, so far, the Parties to the climate change regime have not sought to be actively involved in the detailed management of the Secretariat, or to review its financial activities in any depth. While the reports from the Executive Secretary and auditors are formally considered by the COP and SBI, this consideration rarely generates much debate and amounts to a general overview rather than detailed monitoring. There are signs that this 'hands off' approach is starting

---

[60] See FCCC/CP/1998/8/Add.1.   [61] See FCCC/SBI/2002/10.   [62] See Auditors' reports.

to wane, however, reflecting the continued politicisation of climate change and the differences among the Parties. The programme budget decision for 2004–2005 is notable in including a request to the Executive Secretary to 'specify' how COP decisions relating to Article 4.8 – that is, the adverse effects of climate change and response measures on developing countries – are reflected in the work programme, along with a further request to conduct an 'internal review' to evaluate the Secretariat's activities and report thereon to COP-11. In a related move, Saudi Arabia, speaking for the G-77 and China, requested that an item be placed on the provisional agenda of SBI-20 and future sessions providing for a continuing review of the 'function and operations of the Secretariat'. This suggests that the work of the Secretariat may be subject to closer scrutiny by the Parties than previously. While constructive scrutiny of the Secretariat's work would, of course, be welcome, using the Secretariat as another tool for pursuing political ends would be a worrying new development for the regime.

3.1.4   Headquarters agreement

Another issue commanding the attention of the SBI is the headquarters agreement between the Secretariat and the government of Germany. The location of the Secretariat in Bonn has had many implications, both for the Secretariat itself, and for the Parties. The move of most embassies from Bonn to Berlin after the switch in the location of Germany's capital from January 1999 means that very few governments have liaison offices in Bonn to ensure regular interaction with the Secretariat, as they do in the major UN centres. The absence of any dedicated conference venue has led to negotiating sessions being held in a hotel which, while tolerable, is not a venue endowed with the facilities or gravitas that delegates to UN meetings expect. Germany's lack of experience with hosting intergovernmental organisations has also raised difficulties with such matters as the issuance of visas for conference delegates, and the granting of work permits and residence status for families of Secretariat staff. As the Secretariat has expanded and the UNCCD Secretariat has joined the UN premises in Bonn, office space has also become scarce. The Executive Secretary typically reports to each session of the SBI on the implementation of the headquarters agreement, and, on occasion, has made strong statements about the difficulties faced.

The government of Germany has responded to these difficulties, including by reviewing its visa/work permit practices, and developing plans to establish a UN campus on the site of the former parliamentary complex, comprising space for all UN offices hosted in Bonn and dedicated conference facilities. Completion of this conference centre is expected in 2006–2007. In addition, Germany's Foreign Affairs Ministry has appointed a 'Special Representative in Bonn' to help with practical problems faced by UN agencies. These initiatives, combined with the dedication of the local government of Bonn and the increase in UN staff in the city, promise to accelerate Bonn's transformation into an international city.

3.2   *Nature and structure of the Secretariat*

In June 2003, the number of approved posts in the Secretariat amounted to 168.5, including 93 professional staff[63] (although not all posts were filled at that time – see below). This is more than three times the number of staff employed when the permanent Secretariat first came into being seven years before. This figure also excludes consultants and contract staff, as well as temporary staff hired for sessions of the COP and SBs. The 2004–2005 programme budget provides for an additional twenty-four staff in the Kyoto Protocol interim allocation, including seventeen professionals. Overall, staffing accounts for around 70 per cent of the core budget.

The Secretariat's staff are international civil servants, who sign an oath to the UN Secretary-General on their appointment.[64] Professional staff are recruited from all over the world, with efforts made to maintain geographic balance. This is in accordance with the UN Charter, which states: 'The paramount consideration in the employment of staff … shall be the necessity of securing the highest standards of efficiency, competence and integrity. Due regard shall be paid to the importance of recruiting the staff on as wide a geographical basis as possible.'[65] Table 16.6 below shows that there is a predominance of professional staff from the Western Europe and Others group,[66] especially among managerial grades, although other groups are also well represented. The distribution of professional staff between Annex I and non-Annex I countries is relatively balanced, although, given the larger number of countries in the non-Annex I group, there is room for improvement.[67] The Secretariat also strives to promote gender equality in its recruitment, publishing information on the gender distribution of staff (see also table 16.6). Parties have recently begun to pay greater attention to the profile of the Secretariat, with the G-77 and China, for example, calling for greater geographical and gender balance during discussions at COP-9.

General service (junior administrative, secretarial and clerical) staff are recruited locally and not subject to nationality considerations, nor are consultants

---

[63] This includes staff financed by the Trust Funds and the Bonn Fund, as well as the core budget. See FCCC/SBI/2003/12.

[64] UN Charter Article 100 and ST/SGB/2002/1, regulation 1.1.

[65] UN Charter Article 101.3. See also ST/SGB/2002/1, regulation 4.2.

[66] Including most of the developed Western countries, except Japan (see chapter 3).

[67] By way of comparison, the regional distribution of CBD Secretariat professional staff at the time of writing was: Africa 33 per cent; Asia 11 per cent; LAC 11 per cent; CEE 3 per cent; WEOG 42 per cent. Data from www.biodiv.org.

Table 16.6[68] *Distribution of employed professional staff in the Secretariat by region and gender (as at 30 June 2003)*

Grade[69]	Africa	Asia	LAC	CEE	WEOG	AI	NAI	Male	Female
Managerial (16)	3	2	3	2	6	8	8	10	6
Professional (59)	7	10	10	6	26	32	27	36	23
Total (75)	10 (13%)	12 (16%)	13 (17%)	8 (11%)	32 (43%)	40 (53%)	35 (47%)	46 (61%)	29 (39%)

hired on the basis of short-term contracts.[70] In the first six months of 2003, 74 per cent of the seventy-four consultants hired by the Secretariat came from Annex I Parties, due largely to the advantages of geographical proximity.[71] The Secretariat relies heavily on consultants, both for specialised tasks and to cover for vacant posts, pending recruitment. The rapid growth of the Secretariat, structural changes introduced at each programme budget, late payment of contributions and a rather cumbersome recruitment process mean that a significant number of posts often remain unfilled for considerable periods of time. Six months into the 2002–2003 biennium, for example, a quarter of all posts and nearly a third of professional posts were vacant.[72]

In accordance with UN Staff Rules and Regulations, all Secretariat staff share a duty of impartiality, being required to serve the Parties in an unbiased manner.[73] The Secretariat's mandatory impartiality towards the Parties, however, is matched by its duty to uphold the ultimate objective of the climate change regime, as set out in the Convention. In this sense, the Secretariat is impartial but not neutral, acting as the 'permanent force' or 'guardian'[74] of the regime. While these two duties are, in principle, complimentary, the contrasting views of Parties and, frequently, the absence of any common 'will' among them, means that the two masters do not always speak with one voice.[75] This underlying potential tension is a central

---

[68] From FCCC/SBI/2003/12, tables 10(a) and (b). LAC: Latin America and the Caribbean; CEE: Central and Eastern Europe; WEOG: Western Europe and Others; AI: Annex I; NAI: Non-Annex I.

[69] Managerial: Assistant-Secretary-General (ASG), D-1 and 2 (Director level), and P-5; Other professional: P-2 to P-4.

[70] ST/SGB/2002/1, rules 104.5 and 100.1.   [71] FCCC/SBI/2003/12, paragraph 77.

[72] FCCC/SBI/2002/11, section IV.A.   [73] See ST/SGB/2002/1, regulation 1.2.

[74] See Honkanen et al., 1999.

[75] See Sandford, 1994; Depledge, 2001b; and Andresen and Skjaerseth, 1999.

dynamic in the Secretariat's work, and threatens to come to the surface in the context of the Secretariat's support for the Kyoto Protocol. While nearly two-thirds of Parties have ratified the Protocol, the few that do not intend to do so are powerful, and have raised questions about the extent to which the Secretariat, as the servant of all the Parties – but also the legal texts of the regime – should be seeking to uphold a Protocol that is not yet in force.

3.2.1   The Executive Secretary

The Rules of Procedure require the 'head of the Secretariat' to act in that capacity at all sessions of the COP and SBs, where s/he must provide, manage and direct the staff and services required by the COP and the SBs, within available resources.[76]

Since the establishment of the permanent Secretariat, the Executive Secretary has been appointed at the level of Assistant-Secretary-General. Prior to that time, the post held the D-2 rank (one lower). The first Executive Secretary, Michael Zammit Cutajar (Malta), served for over eleven years from the inception of the interim Secretariat, and earned great respect for his service to the climate change process.[77] The second Executive Secretary, Joke Waller Hunter (Netherlands), took office in May 2002.

According to Decision 14/CP.1, it is the responsibility of the Secretary-General to appoint the Executive Secretary, after consultation 'with the Conference of the Parties through its Bureau'.[78] Ms Waller Hunter was indeed appointed by the Secretary-General, on the basis of advice from senior UN and political figures. The extent of consultation with the COP Bureau, however, was brought into question by the Bureau itself, some of whose members thought this had been insufficient. The procedure for appointing the Executive Secretary is now under consideration by the COP.[79]

3.2.2   Role and functions of the Secretariat

Article 8 sets out the functions of the Secretariat. The specific tasks that it mentions are to:

- 'Make arrangements for sessions of the COP and its subsidiary bodies . . . and provide them with services as required';
- 'Compile and transmit reports submitted to it';
- 'Facilitate assistance . . . particularly [to] developing country Parties, on request, in the compilation and communication of information required [by] the Convention';

---

[76] Rule 28.   [77] See Resolution 2/CP.7, Expression of gratitude to the Executive Secretary.
[78] Paragraph 7.   [79] COP-8 report, part I, paragraph 127.

- 'Ensure the necessary coordination with the secretariats of other relevant international bodies'; and
- Enter into the 'administrative and contractual arrangements . . . required for the effective discharge of its functions'.

The Secretariat must also report on its activities to the COP, and perform any other functions specified in the Convention or its protocols, or requested by the COP. These functions are considerably expanded upon and specified in more detail in each programme budget. The adoption of the Kyoto Protocol and the subsequent Marrakesh Accords have greatly added to the workload of the Secretariat and taken it in an increasingly technical direction. In practice, the main roles of the Secretariat can be categorised as follows:

Logistical and strategic support for the COP, SBs, Bureaux and workshops: This is a core role of the Secretariat, which is specified in the Rules of Procedure.[80] As noted above, UNOG supplies interpretation, translation and distribution of documents and some assistance with conference servicing, and the Secretariat coordinates with UNOG staff for this purpose. Other areas of logistical support provided by the Secretariat include: the supply of appropriate meeting facilities; making available financial support and travel arrangements to eligible delegations; registration of, and liaison with, Parties and observers; arranging for sound recordings of sessions;[81] and coordination of side events on the margins of the formal meetings. Ensuring security, including monitoring the registration of participants and managing access to the meeting site, is another Secretariat function that has become increasingly important over recent years. The Secretariat draws on services provided by UN security in this regard. The frequency and sheer size of climate change meetings renders this logistical role of the Secretariat a highly complex and demanding one.[82]

In addition, the Secretariat has an important, informal role to play in the provision of strategic advice to the COP President, SB Chairs and their Bureaux on how best to conduct the negotiations. Indeed, the Rules of Procedure require the Executive Secretary to provide such advice.[83] Depending on the degree of proactiveness, experience and indeed competence of these officers, the role of the Secretariat in this respect can be absolutely crucial in steering the negotiations towards a successful outcome. In all cases, however, decision-making on, and responsibility for, the strategic conduct of negotiations rests with the officers, and not the Secretariat.

---

[80] Rule 29.   [81] See also Rule 57.   [82] See chapters 3, 13 and 14.   [83] Rule 28.2.

Support for negotiations/processes on specific issues: A second key role of the Secretariat is to provide support to the Parties in their negotiations on specific issues. Different Secretariat departments thus hold responsibility for negotiations on, for example, technology transfer, the flexibility mechanisms, methodological issues, capacity-building, and so on. Such support includes preparation of background documents and negotiating texts, running of workshops, liaison with delegations, briefing the presiding officers, and coordination with other bodies, such as the GEF. Once again, the Secretariat has a significant strategic role to play in thinking ahead on how issues could, or should, develop over time, and in advising the presiding officers. The Secretariat must always, however, remain objective in its dealings with the Parties.

Servicing the specialised bodies: The adoption of the Marrakesh Accords introduced important additional tasks for the Secretariat in servicing the new specialised bodies of the climate change regime. Servicing the three specialised bodies under the Kyoto Protocol, in particular, involves new, in some cases unprecedented, tasks for the Secretariat, including liasing more closely with the private sector in managing the CDM and JI project cycles, dealing with complex legal questions in support of the Compliance Committee, managing confidentiality issues, and serving as the main interface between Parties, other stakeholders (including businesses and NGOs) and these bodies on a day-to-day basis.

Compilation and review of data and information: An increasingly central element of the Secretariat's responsibilities is its work in compiling, reviewing and making available data and information.[84] This includes the Secretariat's long-standing task of coordinating the reviews of national communications and annual GHG inventory data, which will intensify under the Kyoto Protocol. Moreover, the Marrakesh Accords added a number of additional related tasks to the Secretariat's mandate, including, for example, the establishment and maintenance of a transaction log and a compilation and accounting database.[85]

Public outreach: Outreach is critical to the public face of the Secretariat and is enjoying a higher profile as the agenda item on education, training and public awareness gathers momentum.[86] The Secretariat maintains a website[87] including access to all official documentation, and develops public information products, such as guides to climate change, often in cooperation with UNEP. The Secretariat also issues press releases and manages relations with the media, while running a comprehensive library and a climate change documentation search facility.

---

[84] FCCC Article 8.2(b).   [85] See chapter 11.   [86] See chapter 7.
[87] See www.unfccc.int.

17

Linkages

1 Introduction

The all-encompassing nature of climate change means that it cuts across a broad range of issue areas on the international agenda, including other environmental problems, as well as developmental, economic and trade concerns. As a result, the climate change regime intersects with many different parts of the international system, including the following, which are the focus of this chapter:[1]

- Environmental regimes established by MEAs;
- The international trading regime under the WTO; and
- The broader work of the UN in the field of the environment, development and sustainable development.

Awareness of linkages between climate change and other issues, and the importance of tackling these in a coherent manner, has grown over the lifetime of the climate change regime. This awareness has led to moves to promote greater institutional cooperation across related regimes. These have emerged both through the forging of direct institutional links between the climate change regime and others, and as part of wider initiatives in the UN system. In broad terms, the twin aims of institutional cooperation have been to avoid conflicts and reap synergies, that is, to ensure that actions taken under one regime reinforce, and do not conflict

---

[1] This chapter does not address the implementation support functions carried out for the climate change regime by such UN bodies as UNDP, UNEP, UNCTAD and UNIDO. An overview of these functions is given in chapter 3, while specific functions (e.g. capacity-building) are dealt with in the relevant chapters.

with, actions under another. Such cooperation has taken many forms, including the following:

- **Promoting coherence of rules**, aimed at ensuring that the rules of the regimes reinforce, or at least do not contradict, each other;
- **Promoting coherence of national implementation**, aimed at ensuring that the implementation of the regimes' rules by Parties brings mutual benefits, or at least does not generate conflict;
- **Implementation support through international cooperation**, to maximise efficient use of resources and achieve common goals (e.g. in implementation projects, capacity-building, technology transfer, public awareness);
- **Joint or coordinated research and assessment**, including:
  - *Scientific* research/assessment to improve understanding of the relationship between issues and to encourage the development of compatible data collection and management initiatives;
  - Assessment of overlapping *technical and policy options* and good practices.
- **Exchange of information and experience** between regimes on their respective issue areas and activities.

This chapter begins with an overview of the channels in place under the Convention and Kyoto Protocol that provide for cooperation between the climate change regime and other parts of the international system. It then considers cooperative initiatives currently underway between the climate change regime and others. Finally, the chapter considers the broader agendas and governance initiatives of the UN system relating to environment, development and sustainable development, and how the climate change regime is linked into these.

2   **Channels for institutional cooperation under the Convention and Kyoto Protocol**

The need for institutional cooperation is recognised in the FCCC. The Convention mandates the COP to 'seek and utilize, where appropriate, the services and cooperation of, and information provided by, competent international organizations and intergovernmental . . . bodies'.[2] The SBSTA serves as the main arena for debates on such cooperation, based on its mandate to draw 'upon existing

---

[2] FCCC Article 7.2 (l)

competent international bodies'.[3] The standing item on 'Cooperation with relevant international organizations' on the SBSTA's agenda provides the main vehicle for Parties to discuss, and take action on, linkages and interaction with other
regimes and international bodies. Specific interconnections are also taken up
under relevant individual agenda items (e.g. LULUCF). The Convention calls on
the Secretariat to play a supporting role in institutional cooperation by ensuring
'the necessary coordination with the secretariats of other relevant international
bodies'.[4]

These mandates are carried over to the COP/MOP and Secretariat under the
Kyoto Protocol.[5]

3   Linkages with other environmental regimes

This section explores four key environmental issues that are related to
climate change, and on which concrete steps have been taken by the respective
regimes to foster greater cooperation: stratospheric ozone depletion, biodiversity
loss, desertification, and conservation of wetland ecosystems.

3.1   *Stratospheric ozone depletion*

3.1.1   Substantive linkages

Physical and chemical processes in the atmosphere mean that climate
change and stratospheric ozone depletion are closely related in many complex
ways.[6] Stratospheric ozone depletion is addressed through the 1987 Montreal Protocol on Substances That Deplete the Ozone Layer and its various amendments
and adjustments, founded on the 1985 Vienna Convention for the Protection of
the Ozone Layer.[7] The Parties to the FCCC largely coincide with the 187 Parties to
the Montreal Protocol.

In most respects, the objectives of the climate change and ozone regimes are
complementary. Ozone-depleting substances (ODS) controlled through the ozone
regime, notably CFCs and halons, are also GHGs, whose direct GWPs are typically
thousands of times greater than CO_2. Moreover, ozone layer depletion increases the
amount of ultraviolet (UV) radiation reaching the earth's surface, which damages
certain plants and marine phytoplankton, reducing their capacity to act as carbon
'sinks'.[8] Cutting the use of ODS and combating ozone depletion thus contributes,

---

[3] FCCC Article 9.2. See chapter 15.   [4] FCCC Article 8.2 (e).   [5] See chapter 13.

[6] See, in general, Ozone Secretariat, 2000; IPCC, 2001c, chapter 3, Appendix; Ozone Secretariat,
1999a; Scientific Assessment Panel, 2002; Environmental Effects Assessment Panel, 2002.

[7] See www.unep.org/ozone. For a summary of the ozone regime, see Depledge, 2001a.

[8] See Oberthür, 2001.

in turn, to climate change mitigation. Climate change also has repercussions for ozone depletion. The Montreal Protocol's Scientific and Environmental Effects Assessment Panels have warned that climate change could delay the expected recovery of the ozone layer, and therefore amplify the negative effects of ozone depletion on the incidence of skin cancer and cataracts, as well as growth of flora and fauna.[9] Once again, therefore, tackling the two problems is a complementary exercise.

Not all the interactions between the climate change and ozone regimes, however, are mutually reinforcing. Ironically, stratospheric ozone is itself a GHG, so that ozone layer depletion over the past three decades, and its consequent cooling effect, may have masked the true warming impact of climate change, which will make itself felt as the ozone layer recovers. The Scientific Assessment Panel estimates that the decrease in stratospheric ozone since 1980 has offset about 20 per cent of warming due to GHGs over the same period.[10] Moreover, the additional UV radiation entering the atmosphere as a result of ozone depletion has the effect of shortening the lifetimes of methane, HFCs and other GHGs that contain hydrogen, thus reducing their overall impact on the climate.[11] Both these interactions, however, are not so great as to counteract the benefits for climate change mitigation of phasing out ODS.

In terms of response measures, a central element to the relationship between climate change and ozone layer depletion concerns the group of chemicals known as HFCs and PFCs. These substances do not deplete the ozone layer, and have properties that allow them to perform similar functions to some ODS. Because of this, HFCs in particular have been introduced as substitutes in some applications (especially refrigeration and air conditioning) as countries seek to comply with their ODS phase-out schedules under the Montreal Protocol. PFCs are much less widely used, but have been marketed as ODS substitutes in refrigerants, solvents and fire extinguishers.[12] However, HFCs and, especially, PFCs, have high GWPs,[13] and are now covered by the Kyoto Protocol's emission targets for Annex I Parties.[14]

---

[9] Scientific Assessment Panel, 2002, and Environmental Effects Assessment Panel, 2002. Also Ozone MOP-14 report, paragraph 224.

[10] Scientific Assessment Panel, 2002, Executive Summary, pp. 6 and 20.

[11] See Oberthür, 2001.   [12] Ozone Secretariat, 1999b: p. 40.

[13] HFCs used as substitutes for ODS have GWPs ranging from 140 to (rarely) 11,700. The GWPs of PFCs range from 7,000 to 9,200. The GWPs of HFCs are typically lower than those of the ODS that they replace, although the GWPs of PFCs are typically higher. See IPCC, 2001c, chapter 3, Appendix, Section A3.1.

[14] Some analysts question the overall impact of HFCs on climate change, noting that use of HFCs can increase the efficiency of appliances, thus cutting GHG emissions. A technique known as lifecycle climate performance (LCCP) analysis can be used to analyse the total impact on the climate, including use of chemical and energy efficiency concerns (see Ozone

This issue has gained added salience by the fact that the Multilateral Fund of the Montreal Protocol, which supplies financial assistance to developing countries to facilitate their ODS phase-out, along with the GEF, which performs a similar function for EITs, grants funding for projects that introduce HFCs as substitutes for ODS.[15] As of 1999, some 7 per cent of ODS replaced by Multilateral Fund projects had used HFCs as alternatives, as these typically offer the cheapest alternative to CFCs, primarily due to safety factors.[16] In 1995, the Executive Committee of the Multilateral Fund introduced a 35 per cent discount on the cost-effectiveness threshold of hydrocarbon technology (which does not contribute to climate change) in the funding approval process to reduce its economic disadvantage relative to HFCs.[17] The 1995 Operational Strategy of the GEF similarly stated that funding should be given to 'the technology with the least impact on global warming that is technically feasible, environmentally sound and economically acceptable', bearing in mind both GWP and energy efficiency concerns.[18] However, despite these measures, HFCs remain a significant substitute for CFCs in projects funded by both bodies. A review of GEF funding, for example, found that 'all refrigeration projects foresaw use of HFC refrigerants as substitutes (irrespective of whether they were planned before or after adoption of the GEF Operational Strategy)'.[19]

3.1.2   Treaty provisions on linkages

The FCCC recognises the interconnections between climate change and ozone depletion. In its Preamble, it recalls the Vienna Convention, the Montreal Protocol and the London Amendment,[20] the ozone treaties that were in place at the time of its adoption.

Of particular importance, the FCCC establishes a clear division of labour between the climate change and ozone regimes, determining that the scope of the Convention, subsequently carried over to the Kyoto Protocol, shall be limited to 'greenhouse gases not controlled by the Montreal Protocol'.[21] The Kyoto Protocol

---

Secretariat, 1999b, and IPCC, 2001c, chapter 3, Appendix). Overall, however, these substances are considered part of the problem for climate change, yet part of the solution to ozone depletion.

[15] No PFC project, however, has ever been approved by the Multilateral Fund. Ozone Secretariat, 1999b: p. 40.

[16] Ozone Secretariat, 1999b: pp. 22–3.

[17] See Oberthür, 2001, also Ozone ExCom-17 report, 1995.

[18] Operational Strategy of the Global Environment Facility, approved by the GEF council in 1995. Available from www.gefweb.org.

[19] Oberthür et al., 2000: pp. 16–17.   [20] FCCC Preamble, paragraph 13.

[21] The reference to 'greenhouse gases not controlled by the Montreal Protocol' appears throughout the Convention.

also includes a definition of 'Montreal Protocol'[22] (there is no such definition in the FCCC), specifying that references to the Montreal Protocol also cover subsequent adjustments and amendments. This is important as additional ODS, including some with GWP, have been added to the Montreal Protocol through amendments adopted subsequent to the FCCC and the Kyoto Protocol. For more on this division of labour, see chapter 5.

The Montreal Protocol itself expresses consciousness of 'the potential climatic effects' of ODS in its Preamble,[23] but does not go further, reflecting its early adoption when the impacts of ODS and their replacements on the global climate were not well understood.

The climate change and ozone regimes are also institutionally linked by their use of the GEF to provide financial assistance to Parties, although in the case of the ozone regime, the GEF only assists those Parties – mostly EITs – not eligible under the regime's own Multilateral Fund.

3.1.3   Institutional cooperation

The adoption of the Kyoto Protocol, and the inclusion of HFCs and PFCs in Annex I Parties' quantified commitments, prompted both the climate change and ozone Parties to launch discussions on the coherence of rules and their implementation in the two regimes.

In response to an initial Sri Lankan initiative in the ozone regime, [24] the Montreal Protocol's Technology and Economic Assessment Panel (TEAP) and the IPCC proposed to hold a joint scientific workshop on the limitation of HFCs/PFCs. These developments prompted Switzerland to call for a discussion in the climate change regime on linkages with the Montreal Protocol. This led to the adoption, at FCCC COP-4 in 1998, of a decision whose thrust was to endorse the proposed workshop, and to request Parties, the TEAP, IGOs and NGOs to submit information on 'available and potential ways and means of limiting emissions of HFCs and PFCs, including their use as replacements for ozone-depleting substances'.[25] The Parties to the Montreal Protocol, meeting immediately after FCCC COP-4, adopted a 'mirror' decision, endorsing the workshop.[26]

These parallel decisions prompted a flurry of activity in the area of research and assessment. The joint IPCC/TEAP workshop produced a joint report that was

---

[22] KP Article 1.4.   [23] Montreal Protocol Preamble, paragraph 3.

[24] See Ozone OEWG-17 report, paragraphs 131–4.

[25] Decision 13/CP.4, Relationship between efforts to protect the stratospheric ozone layer and efforts to safeguard the global climate system: issues related to hydrofluorocarbons and perfluorocarbons, paragraph 1.

[26] MP Decision X/16, Implementation of the Montreal Protocol in the light of the Kyoto Protocol.

presented to both the ozone and climate change regimes.[27] In addition, the TEAP established a Task Force[28] to advance its work on analysing alternatives to HFCs/PFCs, producing a further report that was circulated to both the climate change and ozone regimes.[29] TEAP members were also invited to serve as lead authors for a section of the IPCC TAR examining 'options to reduce global warming contributions from substitutes for ozone-depleting substances'.[30] The general conclusion of these various scientific assessment exercises was that the implementation of the two Protocols need not necessarily conflict, as alternatives to HFCs already exist or are under development for most applications, and that financial assistance could help developing countries and EITs 'leapfrog' HFC technology in those applications.

Consideration of this issue in the climate change regime has continued to focus on research and assessment, and the exchange of information. Indeed, a follow-up decision taken at COP-5 mandated the SBSTA to consider only the 'information aspects'[31] of the climate change/ozone interface. The climate change Secretariat has received numerous submissions on technological and policy options for limiting HFC/PFC use following the request issued at COP-4 (and a subsequent request for updates by the SBSTA[32]), and has placed these submissions on its website,[33] as well as compiling and synthesising them in a single summary document.[34]

Moving forwards in the gathering and assessment of information, COP-8 in 2002 requested the IPCC and the TEAP jointly to produce 'a balanced, scientific, technical and policy-relevant' special report that would help Parties and stakeholders evaluate ODS alternatives in light of their implications for both the ozone layer and climate change.[35] This special report, to be prepared according to IPCC procedures,[36] is due to be published in 2005.

Consistent with its focus on research and assessment, the climate change regime has placed the onus firmly on Parties themselves to make informed choices on their ozone and climate change policies, rather than taking measures to ensure policy coherence at the intergovernmental level. In the decision adopted at COP-5, for example, the COP invited '*each Party* to give consideration' (emphasis added) to

---

[27] See Ozone Secretariat, 1999c.

[28] The TEAP has numerous task forces, which are formed and disbanded as needed.

[29] Ozone Secretariat, 1999b.   [30] IPCC, 2001c, chapter 3, appendix.

[31] Decision 17/CP.5, Relationship between efforts to protect the stratospheric ozone layer and efforts to safeguard the global atmosphere, paragraph 3.

[32] See SBSTA-15 report, paragraph 56 (b).

[33] See www.unfccc.int/program/mis/wam/index.html.   [34] See FCCC/SBSTA/2002/INF.1.

[35] Decision 12/CP.8, Relationship between efforts to protect the stratospheric ozone layer and efforts to safeguard the global climate system: issues relating to hydrofluorocarbons and perfluorocarbons.

[36] See chapter 15.

the information received by the Secretariat on options for limiting HFC/PFC use, taking account of a range of considerations, including those related to health, safety and energy efficiency.[37] Several Annex I Parties – particularly the US, given its withdrawal from the Kyoto Protocol[38] and its early, widespread conversion from CFCs to HFCs – are reluctant to constrain their use of HFCs as ODS alternatives. For their part, developing countries that already use HFCs fear that the HFC imports on which they depend may be cut off if any such constraints are imposed. The above-mentioned COP-8 decision thus simply encourages Parties to ensure that their actions to tackle ozone depletion 'are undertaken in a manner that also contributes to the objective of the Convention', while also encouraging further research and development on ODS alternatives, including through partnerships between government and industries.

In a similar vein, while the COP-8 decision recognises, in its preamble, that the Montreal Protocol's Multilateral Fund is, in some cases, funding the replacement of ODS by alternatives with GWPs, it stops short of advocating, in even the weakest terms, a switch in funding to other options. Instead, it invites the climate change Parties to consider additional project funding, in particular through the GEF and the CDM. Such funding would presumably be aimed at covering the incremental costs of a more expensive switch from ODS to technologies that avoid HFCs, or the costs of a second switch for those countries that have already converted to this technology. The Multilateral Fund and GEF only supply funding for a single conversion from ODS to an alternative substance, and not for a second conversion to another alternative.

Consideration of the issue of HFCs/PFCs has now been suspended in the climate change regime until receipt of the IPCC/TEAP special report. In a move apparently aimed at lowering the issue's profile, discussion in the SBSTA on receipt of the special report will continue under the general agenda item 'Cooperation with relevant international organizations', rather than a dedicated agenda item, as had been the case.[39]

For their part, the Parties to the ozone regime, meeting after FCCC COP-8, adopted a decision requesting the TEAP to work with the IPCC in preparing the special report.[40] The decision specifies, however, that the special report will then

---

[37] Decision 17/CP.5, paragraph 1.

[38] Since the announcement by the US of its intention not to ratify the Kyoto Protocol, SBSTA conclusions and the COP-8 decision relating to HFCs and PFCs have avoided making reference to the Kyoto Protocol.

[39] Decision 12/CP.8, paragraph 9.

[40] MP Decision XIV/10, Relationship between efforts to protect the stratospheric ozone layer and efforts to safeguard the global atmosphere: issues relating to hydrofluorocarbons and perfluorocarbons.

be considered by the ozone regime only 'in so far as it relates to actions to address ozone depletion'. This reflects the position of the US, which could not agree to language that might encourage discussion in the ozone regime of policy interconnections with climate change.[41]

The ozone regime, however, continues to be actively engaged in scientific assessment in this area. The environmental linkages between climate change and ozone depletion were discussed in some detail in the 2002 reports of the Scientific and Environmental Effects Assessment Panels.[42] Given the new findings it uncovered, the Environmental Effects Assessment Panel gave special emphasis to climate change in this latest report, entitling it 'Environmental Effects of Ozone Depletion *and its Interactions with Climate Change*' (emphasis added). Analysis of interactions with climate change also features strongly in the agreed terms of reference for the next reports of the three Assessment Panels.[43]

3.2   *Biodiversity loss and desertification*

3.2.1   Substantive linkages

Climate change will affect biodiversity by disrupting ecosystems that cannot adapt or migrate rapidly enough as weather patterns change, climatic zones shift and sea levels rise.[44] The impact will be particularly severe for species that are already vulnerable or under stress from human activities. Although climate change may bring benefits for some species, such as warm-water fish, these will be outweighed by negative impacts and will, in turn, affect the balance of ecosystems and food chains. Examples of particularly vulnerable systems include coral reefs and mangrove swamps, as well as others with restricted habitats or low population numbers, such as high-mountain, island and polar ecosystems. According to the IPCC, climate change has already begun to affect biodiversity, with changes observed, for example, in the breeding, flowering, distribution and migration of some species. Impacts on biodiversity will, in turn, feed back into further repercussions on the climate, by affecting the ability of ecosystems to absorb CO_2 and other GHGs, and modifying rates of evapotranspiration. The goals of combating climate change and biodiversity loss are therefore overwhelmingly mutually supportive.

Climate change and desertification are similarly closely linked through feedbacks between land degradation and climatic conditions, which again render

---

[41] See debate recorded in the Ozone MOP-14 report, paragraphs 122–7.

[42] These are available from www.unep.org.

[43] See MP Decision XV/53, Terms of reference for the Scientific Assessment Panel, the Environmental Effects Assessment Panel and the Technology and Economic Assessment Panel.

[44] This discussion is taken from IPCC, 2002, and IPCC, 2001b.

tackling the two problems a complementary exercise.[45] Changes in rainfall, temperature and wind patterns, including the greater frequency and severity of drought, threaten to aggravate other factors that contribute to desertification, such as unsustainable agricultural practices. Africa is particularly vulnerable in this regard, with 43 per cent of the continent, home to 40 per cent of its population, already classified as arid, semi-arid or dry sub-humid areas.[46] Desertification will, in turn, impact on climate change as loss of vegetation cover reduces the land's sink capacity, and CO_2 is released through cleared and dead vegetation.

Biodiversity is primarily addressed in the international arena through the CBD,[47] which was signed together with the FCCC in 1992 at the Earth Summit in Rio de Janeiro, Brazil. Desertification is covered by the UNCCD,[48] whose negotiation was launched at the Earth Summit and which was adopted in 1994. The Parties to the CBD (188) and UNCCD (191)[49] overlap closely with those of the FCCC, with the exception of the US, which has not joined the biodiversity regime.

Some of the causal factors that drive climate change, biodiversity loss and desertification are very similar. Deforestation and devegetation, for example, are important contributors to all three problems. The LULUCF sector thus serves as a critical nexus in the interactions between climate change, biodiversity loss and desertification. Policies to encourage afforestation and reforestation, or to halt deforestation, in order to tackle climate change should, in principle, also help to combat desertification and conserve or restore biodiversity. Likewise, measures to conserve biodiversity, such as designation of protected areas, can help mitigate climate change through carbon sequestration, as well as providing physical protection against sea level rise (e.g. mangrove swamps and coral reefs) and helping natural ecosystems to adapt to climate change by securing a viable habitat.

The reality, however, is more complex. For example, forest policy under the climate change regime aimed solely at maximising carbon absorption could lead to the cultivation of fast-growing single species, thus negatively affecting biodiversity. Similarly, forest projects in one area could simply shift ongoing deforestation to another, again with repercussions for biodiversity and desertification. Both the biodiversity and desertification regimes thus have a considerable stake in developments in the climate change regime.[50]

---

[45] The discussion below draws on IPCC, 2001b, especially section 10.2.6. See also ICCD/COP(3)/9.

[46] IPCC, 2001b: section 10.2.6.1.   [47] See www.biodiv.org.   [48] See www.unccd.int.

[49] For up-to-date figures on ratification, see the respective regime websites.

[50] For a more detailed discussion of the linkages between climate change and biodiversity, see IPCC, 2002. UNEP/CBD/SBSTTA/6/11; and analysis by the CBD Secretariat available at http://www.biodiv.org/programmes/cross-cutting/climate/.

3.2.2   Treaty provisions on linkages

The CBD and UNCCD are linked politically to the climate change regime by their origins in the 1992 Earth Summit process. They are often referred to collectively as the 'Rio Conventions', and viewed as sharing the common goal of sustainable development, a concept that was enshrined by the Earth Summit as a leading goal of the intergovernmental community.

In its Preamble, the FCCC makes reference to the 'pertinent provisions of General Assembly resolution 44/172 . . . on the implementation of the Plan of Action to Combat Desertification'.[51] The Convention also includes a number of provisions that take account of biodiversity and desertification issues, without explicitly referring to the CBD or UNCCD, which were adopted after it. These include the following:

- A component of the Convention's objective is 'to allow ecosystems to adapt naturally'.[52]
- Article 4.1 (d) calls on Parties to 'Promote . . . and cooperate in the conservation and enhancement . . . of . . . biomass, forests and oceans as well as other terrestrial, coastal and marine ecosystems'.
- Article 4.1 (e) requires Parties to elaborate 'appropriate and integrated plans . . . for the protection and rehabilitation of areas, particularly in Africa, affected by drought and desertification'.
- In its list of categories of developing countries particularly vulnerable to climate change, Article 4.8 includes those with areas 'liable to drought and desertification' and 'with fragile ecosystems, including mountainous ecosystems' (subparagraphs (e) and (g), respectively).

The Kyoto Protocol, as well as incorporating the preambular language of the Convention, its objective, and the categorisation under Article 4.8, includes a further provision in its article on policies and measures, which, by implication, alludes to the CBD and UNCCD. This calls on Annex I Parties to implement any policies and measures regarding the protection and enhancement of GHG sinks and reservoirs 'taking into account [their] commitments under *relevant international environmental agreements*'[53] (emphasis added). This clause thereby establishes an explicit link between the fulfilment of commitments under the Kyoto Protocol

---

[51] FCCC Preamble, paragraph 12. UNGA Resolution 44/172, adopted by the UNGA in 1989, addressed problems with the implementation of the 1977 Plan of Action to Combat Desertification, including inadequacy of financial resources, and called on the forthcoming Earth Summit to accord high priority to this issue.

[52] FCCC Article 2.   [53] KP Article 2.1 (a) (ii).

and other related regimes, albeit a soft, general one, and without naming the regimes concerned.

The CBD does not include any specific references to climate change. In terms of its institutional arrangements, however, the CBD is more explicit in referring to cooperation with other *conventions*, and not just international bodies in general. It mandates its COP to 'contact, through the Secretariat, the executive bodies of conventions dealing with matters covered by this Convention with a view to establishing appropriate forms of cooperation with them'. Like the climate change Secretariat, the CBD Secretariat is also mandated to 'coordinate with other relevant international bodies'.[54] Although not expressly called for under the Convention, the CBD's Subsidiary Body for Scientific, Technical and Technological Advice (SBSTTA) plays a key role in promoting and managing coordination with other bodies.

The UNCCD, which was negotiated after the adoption of the two other Rio Conventions, makes explicit reference to linkages with both the FCCC and the CBD, noting in its Preamble, 'the contribution that combating desertification can make to achieving the[ir] objectives'.[55] The UNCCD further calls on its Parties to 'encourage the coordination of activities' with other relevant international agreements, particularly the FCCC and the CBD, 'in order to derive maximum benefit from activities under each agreement while avoiding duplication of effort'.[56] The UNCCD uses similar language to the FCCC to mandate its COP to, 'as appropriate, seek the cooperation of, and utilize the services of and information provided by, competent bodies or agencies, whether national or international, intergovernmental or non-governmental'; its Secretariat, in turn, is mandated to 'coordinate its activities with the secretariats of other relevant international bodies *and conventions*'[57] (emphasis added). The UNCCD's Committee on Science and Technology (CST) is also involved in facilitating inter-MEA cooperation.

The FCCC, CBD and UNCCD are also institutionally linked by their use of the GEF to channel funding to their eligible Parties. The GEF serves as the operating entity of the financial mechanism of the biodiversity regime and, having recently added land degradation to the list of its focal areas, the GEF will now also provide financial assistance to UNCCD Parties.[58]

3.2.3   Institutional cooperation

Cooperation[59] between the FCCC, the CBD and the UNCCD has been pursued under the rubric of their common identity as Rio Conventions. This

---

[54] CBD Articles 23.4 (h) and 24.1 (d), respectively.   [55] UNCCD Preamble, paragraph 23.

[56] UNCCD Article 8.1.   [57] UNCCD Articles 22.2 (h) and 23.2 (d).   [58] See GEF Council, 2002.

[59] For a general discussion of the issues, see Jacquemont and Caparros, 2002.

cooperation began in earnest following the adoption of the Kyoto Protocol, whose inclusion of the LULUCF sector threw light on the environmental linkages between the three conventions and opened up new areas of potential cooperation between them.[60] The establishment of the CDM was also viewed by the other conventions as a possible means of pursuing their own environmental goals through the climate change regime, harnessing the additional resources that the mechanism would attract.

The UNCCD and, in particular, the CBD, have been active in initiating cooperation with the climate change regime. They have been similarly active in relation to other conventions, institutions and processes. The CBD, for example, has entered into formal memoranda of cooperation with such institutions as the World Bank and UNESCO, and has developed joint work programmes with, among others, the Ramsar Convention.[61] The UNCCD has taken a similar approach.[62] These vigorous efforts to promote cooperation reflect, in part, the particular mandates and structures of the CBD and UNCCD. The intention behind the CBD was precisely to coordinate related biodiversity and ecosystem treaties, while the UNCCD is structured according to regions, also implying a more proactive approach to cross-cutting issues. The climate change regime, for its part, has taken a reactive rather than proactive stance to cooperation, mostly responding to initiatives, rather than instigating them.

3.2.3.1 COP decisions   The CBD COP-4, meeting in 1998, requested its Executive Secretary to 'strengthen relationships' with the FCCC and the UNCCD, 'with a view to making implementation activities and institutional arrangements mutually supportive'.[63] In further decisions, the CBD COP also requested its Executive Secretary to 'liaise and cooperate' with the two secretariats on forest biodiversity issues, and to discuss the possibility of joint information initiatives.[64]

In response to a statement by the CBD Executive Secretary, FCCC COP-4, meeting later in 1998, agreed that matters of mutual concern to the FCCC and the CBD should be addressed through the FCCC SBs.[65] The CBD Executive Secretary subsequently presented a discussion note to FCCC COP-6 in 2000 on interactions

---

[60] See IPCC, 2002: section 7.

[61] See CBD Decision IV/15, The relationship of the Convention on Biological Diversity with the Commission on Sustainable Development and biodiversity-related conventions, other international agreements, institutions and processes of relevance.

[62] See ICCD/COP(5)/6.

[63] CBD Decision IV/15, paragraph 13. Since 'retired'. See www.biodiv.org.

[64] CBD Decision IV/2, Review of the operations of the clearing house mechanism, paragraph 10 (g) and CBD Decision IV/7, Forest biological diversity, paragraph 9. Since 'retired'.

[65] See COP-4 report, part I, paragraph 92; and part II, section III, paragraph 1.

between climate change and biological diversity.[66] This followed further decisions taken at CBD COP-5 earlier that year, summarised below:

- Decision V/3, in its text on coral bleaching, notes 'significant evidence that climate change is the primary cause of the recent and severe extensive coral bleaching, and that this evidence is sufficient to warrant remedial measures being taken in line with the precautionary approach'. It 'transmits that view' to the FCCC, urging it 'to take all possible actions to reduce the effect of climate change on water temperatures and to address the socio-economic impacts on the countries and communities most affected by coral bleaching'.[67] The decision goes on to identify, as a priority area for action, joint implementation support activities with the FCCC (and the Ramsar Convention), such as assessing the vulnerability of coral bleaching to global warming and building capacity for monitoring and predicting impacts. The decision also suggests providing guidance to financial institutions, including the GEF, to support such activities.[68]
- Decision V/4 on forest biological diversity urges the FCCC and the Kyoto Protocol to ensure that their future activities 'are consistent with, and supportive of, the conservation and sustainable use of forest biological diversity'.[69] It also makes requests to the CBD's SBSTTA relating to scientific assessment of the linkages between climate change and biodiversity, as discussed further below.
- Decision V/15 urges 'Parties and other governments to explore possible ways and means by which incentive measures promoted through the Kyoto Protocol' – an oblique reference to the CDM – can 'support the objectives of the CBD'.[70]
- Decision V/21 again calls on the Executive Secretary to 'strengthen cooperation' with the FCCC and the Kyoto Protocol, identifying dry and sub-humid lands, forest biological diversity, coral reefs and incentive measures as relevant areas for such cooperation.[71]

The CBD has continued to take decisions on cooperation with the climate change regime (as well as other regimes). At its COP-6 in 2002, it recognised a need 'to take

---

[66] UNEP/CBD/SBSTTA/6/11, Annex I.

[67] CBD Decision V/3, Progress report on the implementation of the programme of work on marine and coastal biological diversity (implementation of CBD Decision IV/5), paragraph 5.

[68] CBD Decision V/3, Annex, section C.

[69] CBD Decision V/4, Progress report on the implementation of the programme of work for forest biological diversity, paragraph 16.

[70] CBD Decision V/15, Incentive measures, paragraph 6.

[71] CBD Decision V/21, Cooperation with other bodies, paragraph 3.

immediate actions' under both conventions to 'mitigate the impacts of climate change' on the biodiversity of coral reefs and 'their associated socio-economic effects'.[72]

The UNCCD has similarly taken decisions calling for greater cooperation with the climate change regime, as well as other regimes. At its first session in 1997, the UNCCD COP called on the head of its (then) interim secretariat to 'make all efforts to strengthen further the collaboration with other relevant conventions, and in particular...the FCCC'.[73] Subsequently, at its third session in 1999, the UNCCD COP requested its Executive Secretary to give 'special attention' to the forthcoming FCCC COP-6, given the inclusion of LULUCF on its agenda. The same decision called on the Executive Secretary 'to facilitate the exchange of scientific and technical information and experience, in order to enhance the linkages among various scientific bodies and promote efficiency in the reporting requirements of Parties'.[74] The UNCCD COP followed up on these decisions at its fifth session in 2001, calling on its CST to enhance cooperation with both the FCCC SBSTA and the CBD SBSTTA.[75]

The climate change COP took longer to adopt decision text on cooperation with other MEAs. The 2001 Marrakesh Ministerial Declaration, adopted at COP-7, recognised that 'synergies' between the FCCC, the CBD and the UNCCD 'should continue to be explored through various channels, in order to achieve sustainable development'.[76] In the first decision taken by the climate change COP specifically on inter-MEA cooperation, COP-8 in 2002 subsequently affirmed the 'need for enhanced cooperation' between the three Rio Conventions.[77] It established that the aim should be to ensure the conventions' 'environmental integrity' and promote 'synergies under the common objective of sustainable development', in order to 'avoid duplication of efforts, strengthen joint efforts and use available resources more efficiently'.

Efforts to promote greater cooperation among the conventions have had concrete repercussions on the climate change regime's rules. Thanks to the highlighting of environmental linkages between climate change and biodiversity by the CBD, combined with the efforts of interested Parties, the Marrakesh Accords

---

[72] CBD Decision VI/20, Cooperation with other organisations, initiatives and conventions, paragraphs 9 and 10.

[73] UNCCD Decision 13/COP.1, Collaboration with other conventions, paragraph 2.

[74] UNCCD Decision 17/COP.3, Collaboration with other conventions and international bodies, paragraphs 8 and 9.

[75] UNCCD Decision 7/COP.5, Promotion and strengthening of relationships with other relevant conventions and relevant international organisations, institutions and agencies, paragraph 5.

[76] Decision 1/CP.7, paragraph 3.   [77] Decision 13/CP.8, Cooperation with other conventions.

elaborate on biodiversity concerns as one of the principles governing the treatment of LULUCF activities when used to help meet the emission targets of Annex I Parties.[78] The modalities and procedures for including afforestation and reforestation activities under the CDM were also developed taking account of 'impacts on biodiversity and natural ecosystems'.[79] The modalities and procedures agreed at COP-9 duly require project participants to submit documentation analysing the impacts on biodiversity and natural ecosystems of any proposed CDM project involving LULUCF activities.[80] The Preamble of the decision also expresses cognisance of 'relevant provisions of international agreements'.

3.2.3.2 *Least developed countries*   The special situation of LDCs is emerging as another concrete nexus between the concerns of the FCCC and the UNCCD, providing opportunities for the two regimes to engage in common implementation support activities. Given that LDCs are particularly affected by desertification, the UNCCD is closely involved with this group of Parties, while the FCCC is paying increasing attention to, and has taken several decisions on, the particular needs of LDCs (see chapter 8). The UNCCD Secretariat has participated in meetings to develop guidelines for National Adaptation Programmes of Action (NAPAs) under the climate change regime, enabling the climate change Secretariat and Parties to benefit from its experience with related National Action Programmes, and encouraging cooperation between officials working on climate change and desertification at the local level.[81]

3.2.3.3 *Scientific assessment*   Concrete steps have also been taken in the area of scientific assessment. In 2001, the CBD's SBSTTA launched a pilot assessment of the interlinkages between biodiversity and climate change. This was in response to a request by CBD COP-5 for the SBSTTA to consider the impact of climate change on forest biodiversity, in collaboration with the FCCC SBSTA and the IPCC.[82] The CBD SBSTTA established an ad hoc technical expert group (AHTEG)[83] to conduct

---

[78] See Decision 11/CP.7, Land use, land-use change and forestry, and Draft Decision -/CMP.1 of the same title, paragraph 1 (e). See also chapter 5, section 6.4.3.

[79] See Decision 11/CP.7, paragraph 2 (e).

[80] See Decision 19/CP.9, Modalities and procedures for afforestation and reforestation project activities under the clean development mechanism in the first commitment period of the Kyoto Protocol, and Draft Decision -/CMP.1 of the same title, paragraph 12 (c) and Appendix B. See also chapter 6.

[81] See ICCD/COP(5)/6, section B.   [82] CBD Decision V/4, paragraphs 11 and 18.

[83] The CBD SBSTTA regularly establishes Ad Hoc Technical Expert Groups on various topics.

that assessment, inviting the FCCC and other regimes to participate in the work.[84] The pilot assessment was finalised in 2003.[85]

The SBSTTA invited the IPCC to contribute to the assessment by preparing a technical paper on the topic.[86] This request to the IPCC reflects the fact that the CBD does not have an equivalent body to prepare up-to-date reviews and assessments of the latest literature on biodiversity. The request was subsequently endorsed by the FCCC SBSTA, which invited the IPCC to cover also linkages with desertification.[87] The technical paper was released in April 2002.[88]

A related global scientific assessment exercise is the Millennium Ecosystem Assessment. This was launched following concerns by those involved in the CBD, UNCCD and Ramsar Convention at the absence of an effective scientific assessment process for those MEAs. The initial proposal for the Millennium Assessment was devised by the World Resources Institute (WRI), the World Bank, UNDP and UNEP, and subsequently endorsed by the CBD, UNCCD and Ramsar Convention COPs.[89] While the Millennium Assessment is specifically aimed at these conventions, it is also highly relevant to the climate change regime.[90] Although neither the FCCC COP nor the SBSTA have formally endorsed the Millennium Assessment, the climate change Secretariat is represented on its Board at a high level. The Assessment is due to be finalised by 2005, and has received funding from various organisations roughly equivalent to that spent on an IPCC Assessment.[91]

3.2.3.4 Joint liaison group   A key institutional development in promoting greater cooperation between the three Rio Conventions has been the formation of a *joint liaison group* (JLG) between their three Secretariats. This move was initially proposed by the CBD SBSTTA[92] and endorsed by the FCCC SBSTA, which requested that the UNCCD Secretariat also be invited to join. In endorsing the JLG, the FCCC

---

[84] SBSTTA recommendation VI/7, paragraphs 5 and 8.

[85] See the report on the pilot assessment in UNEP/CBD/SBSTTA/9/INF/12; and the review based thereon in UNEP/CBD/SBSTTA/9/11. See also CBD SBSTTA-9 report, section on 'Biodiversity and climate change', and SBSTA-19 report.

[86] SBSTTA recommendation VI/7, paragraph 6.   [87] SBSTA-14 report, paragraph 42 (g).

[88] IPCC, 2002.

[89] See, for example, CBD Decision VI/7, Scientific assessments: Identification, monitoring, indicators and assessments; UNCCD Decision 19/COP.5, Dryland Degradation Assessment and the Millennium Ecosystem Assessment; and Ramsar resolution VIII/7, Gaps in, and harmonisation of, Ramsar guidance on wetland ecological character, inventory, assessment and monitoring.

[90] See SBSTTA, recommendations VI/5, Scientific assessment: development of methods and identification of pilot studies; and VI/7, Biodiversity and climate change, including cooperation with the United Nations Framework Convention on Climate Change. CBD SBSTTA-6 report.

[91] See chapter 15.   [92] SBSTTA recommendation VI/7, paragraph 9.

SBSTA gave it the mandate to 'enhance coordination between the three conventions, including the exchange of relevant information' and to 'explore options for further cooperation . . . including the possibility of a joint work plan and/or a workshop'.[93] The JLG is composed of the Executive Secretaries of the three conventions, along with the officers of their subsidiary bodies and key secretariat staff members. Officers of the IPCC are also sometimes invited to participate. The first meeting of the JLG took place in December 2001. It has since met on a regular basis, on the margins of meetings of the three regimes.

The JLG has received recognition by the UN General Assembly, which, in 2002 and 2003, noted the group's ongoing work, and encouraged cooperation 'to promote complementarities among the three Secretariats respecting their independent legal status'.[94] The WSSD Plan of Implementation (see below) also made an implicit reference to the JLG by encouraging the FCCC, the CBD and the UNCCD 'to continue exploring and enhancing synergies'.[95]

Initially, the JLG's activities[96] focused on the exchange of information between the three Secretariats, who developed a joint calendar of events[97] and exchanged their respective lists of experts.[98] Cooperation has now also begun in the area of implementation support. At the request of the SBSTA, the JLG worked with the climate change Secretariat to identify cross-cutting areas between the three conventions such as technology transfer, education and public awareness, reporting, research and adaptation.[99] A workshop[100] was held in 2003 to identify options for capturing synergies in these cross-cutting areas, and prepare guidance to enhance cooperation between the national focal points of the three conventions.[101] Encouraging greater interaction between the national focal points of the various conventions, many of which have little knowledge of each other, is indeed a relatively simple way of achieving greater coherence in the implementation of the regimes. The importance of cooperation among national focal points has been highlighted by the SBSTA.[102]

In addition to the specific areas of cooperation discussed above, the Secretariats of the FCCC, UNCCD and CBD maintain good contacts with each other. They regularly attend each other's meetings, often making statements to the respective

---

[93] SBSTA-14 report, paragraph 42 (d).
[94] UNGA Resolution 57/257, Protection of global climate for present and future generations of mankind, paragraph 4.
[95] See WSSD Plan of Implementation in WSSD, 2002: paragraph 41 (c). This encouragement was proffered as part of the text on the UNCCD.
[96] See FCCC/SBSTA/2002/3.   [97] See http://unfccc.int/calendar/rioconv/index.html.
[98] In the case of the climate change regime, this is the roster of experts (see chapter 15, p. 483).
[99] See FCCC/SBSTA/2002/INF.16.   [100] See FCCC/SB/2003/1.
[101] On national focal points, see chapter 3, p. 31.   [102] See SBSTA-19 report, paragraph 44 (d).

bodies on their activities,[103] and pooled their resources to run a joint stand at the 2002 WSSD. As a further means of sharing experiences and information, a staff member is sometimes seconded from one Secretariat to another for a negotiating session. This opens up opportunities for learning between the Secretariats, especially as regards different procedures and practices employed in the various regimes.

While welcoming the activities of the JLG, conclusions adopted by the FCCC SBSTA have stressed the importance of action by Parties at the *national* level to ensure coherent implementation of the three regimes.[104] The SBSTA has also been at pains to underscore the advisory nature of the JLG, safeguarding the authority of Parties – not the JLG – to take decisions on inter-convention cooperation. It has noted, for example, that it is the 'role of the Convention Parties to take decisions on matters relating to collaboration with other conventions', and that the process of enhancing cooperation between the three conventions should 'preserve the rights of the Parties to the respective conventions'.[105]

3.3   *Wetland ecosystems*

3.3.1   Substantive linkages

The 1971 Ramsar Convention on Wetlands[106], which has 140 Parties, is another biodiversity-related MEA that has a keen interest in the work of the climate change regime. Wetlands, already under stress in many areas from human activities, are among the most fragile ecosystems threatened by a changing climate, including by drought, heavy rainfall events, and saltwater intrusion in coastal habitats. Damage to wetland ecosystems can in turn exacerbate climate change and its impacts, with wetlands serving as a carbon sink and, in coastal areas, as a defence against sea level rise. Once again, therefore, wetlands conservation and climate change mitigation are mutually supportive goals.[107]

3.3.2   Treaty provisions on linkages

While neither the FCCC nor the Kyoto Protocol make explicit reference to wetlands, their provisions relating to ecosystems cited above in the context of

---

[103] See, for example, SBSTA-17 report, paragraph 49 (a).

[104] SBSTA-14 report, paragraph 42 (a); SBSTA-15 report, paragraph 41 (k) and (l); SBSTA-16 report, paragraph 50 (f); SBSTA-17 report, paragraph 49 (f); and SBSTA-19 report, paragraph 44 (d).

[105] SBSTA-16 report, paragraph 50 (d) and SBSTA-17 report, paragraph 49 (f).

[106] The formal title of the Ramsar Convention is the Convention on Wetlands of International Importance especially as Waterfowl Habitat. See www.ramsar.org.

[107] For more on the linkages between climate change and wetlands, see Ramsar COP 8-Doc.11 and Bergkamp and Orlando, 1999.

biodiversity and desertification are also relevant. Given its early date of adoption, it is not surprising that the Ramsar Convention does not contain any reference to climate change. However, the Ramsar COP is mandated to 'request relevant international bodies to prepare reports and statistics on matters which are essentially international in character affecting wetlands'.[108] The Ramsar Convention's Scientific and Technical Review Panel (STRP) which, unlike the subsidiary bodies of the FCCC, CBD and UNCCD, is a limited membership body, is actively involved in supplying advice to the Ramsar COP, including on issues of interlinkages. The GEF provides funding for wetlands projects through the biodiversity focal area,[109] although it is not formally linked to the Ramsar Convention.

3.3.3   Institutional cooperation

The Ramsar Convention has actively sought to cooperate more closely with the climate change regime, as it has done with other regimes. One of the operational objectives of its 1997–2002 strategic plan, reconfirmed in its 2003–2008 strategic plan, was to strengthen and formalise linkages with other environment conventions.[110] To meet this objective, the strategic plan called for 'consultations with related conventions to foster information exchange and cooperation, and develop an agenda for potential joint actions'.[111]

The Global Biodiversity Forum (GBF),[112] meeting immediately before Ramsar COP-7 in 1999, concluded that 'the goals of wetland conservation and river basin management can no longer be achieved without taking climate change into account' and recommended the establishment of a memorandum of cooperation between the Ramsar Convention and the FCCC.[113] This was endorsed by Ramsar COP-7.[114] While no memorandum has been agreed, the Ramsar Convention has initiated contacts with the climate change regime, including through regular statements to the SBSTA aimed at exchanging information on the interconnections between wetland ecosystems and climate change.[115] In response to these

---

[108] Ramsar Convention, Article 6.2 (e).   [109] See GEF operational strategy, 1995.

[110] See Ramsar, 1996, Operational Objective 7.2, and Ramsar, 2002, Action 13.1.1.

[111] Ramsar, 1996, Action 7.2.1.

[112] The GBF is a multi-stakeholder forum aimed at fostering 'analysis and critical dialogue . . . on key ecological, economic, social and institutional issues related to biodiversity' in support of the CBD. Through global and regional meetings held since 1992, the GBF brings together governments, NGOs, researchers, indigenous peoples, local communities and others. See www.gbf.ch.

[113] See Global Biodiversity Forum, 1999.

[114] See Ramsar Resolution VII.4, Partnerships and cooperation with other Conventions, including harmonised information management infrastructures.

[115] Ramsar Resolution VII.4.

initiatives, the Ramsar Convention Secretariat has started to participate in the JLG, at the SBSTA's request.[116] As noted above, the Ramsar Convention is also involved in the Millennium Ecosystem Assessment.

The Ramsar COP has sought to promote coherent implementation of the climate change and wetlands regimes at the national level. In a decision on climate change adopted at its 2002 eighth session, the Ramsar COP urged its Parties to 'make every effort' to ensure that their implementation of the FCCC and the Kyoto Protocol, including through revegetation, forest management, afforestation and reforestation, 'does not lead to serious damage to the ecological character of their wetlands', using environmental impact assessment and risk assessment for this purpose.[117] It further invited its Parties to 'pay special attention to the need for building and strengthening institutional capacity and synergies between related instruments *at the national level* in order to address the linkages between climate change and wetlands' (emphasis added).[118]

The Ramsar Convention has been particularly active in the field of scientific assessment. In 1999, the Ramsar Bureau commissioned IUCN, the World Conservation Union, to prepare a document on linkages between wetlands and climate change. The resulting report[119] was presented to FCCC COP-5 and SBSTA-11 in 1999, prompting the SBSTA to call on the climate change Secretariat to liaise with the Ramsar Secretariat 'in order to determine how cooperation between the conventions could be strengthened'.[120]

Furthermore, in accordance with the Ramsar Convention Work Plan for 2000–2002 adopted at Ramsar COP-7 in 1999,[121] the Ramsar STRP prepared a report reviewing the impacts of climate change on wetland ecosystems, and the contribution that wetlands can potentially play in mitigating climate change and sea level rise. This report was presented to FCCC SBSTA-17, as well as Ramsar COP-8, in 2002.[122] Ramsar COP-8 subsequently invited the IPCC and the FCCC, with the participation of the Ramsar STRP, to 'focus some of their future work' on wetlands-related data, and improve knowledge on the vulnerability of wetlands to climate change.[123] The Ramsar COP further encouraged Parties and other organisations to undertake studies of 'the role of wetlands in carbon storage and sequestration, and in mitigating the impacts of sea-level rise'.[124] Scientific assessment of linkages

---

[116] SBSTA-16 report, paragraph 50 (e), and SBSTA-17 report, paragraph 49 (b).

[117] Ramsar Resolution VIII.3, Climate change and wetlands: impacts, adaptation, and mitigation, paragraph 17.

[118] Ramsar Resolution VIII.3, paragraph 19.   [119] See Bergkamp and Orlando, 1999.

[120] See SBSTA-11 report, paragraph 99 (c).

[121] Ramsar, 1999, and Resolution VII.27, The Convention Work Plan 2000–2002.

[122] See Ramsar COP 8-Doc.11. Also SBSTA-17 report, paragraph 49 (b).

[123] Ramsar Resolution VIII.3, paragraph 20.   [124] Ramsar Resolution VIII.3, paragraph 18.

between climate change and wetlands issues is also incorporated in the Ramsar 2003–2008 strategic plan.[125]

4   Linkages with the international trading regime

4.1   *Substantive linkages*

The interface between the climate change and international trading regimes is attracting growing attention, triggered by concern over possible policy conflicts that may arise as Annex I Parties enact measures to implement their Kyoto Protocol emission targets. Neither the FCCC nor the Kyoto Protocol include any *direct* trade-related environmental measures, that is, treaty provisions imposing restrictions on international trade to achieve climate mitigation goals.[126] However, the policies put in place by Parties in order to meet their commitments under the climate change regime could include trade measures, and could therefore have implications for the international trading regime, especially with respect to trade with non-Parties or Parties without emission targets. The potential for conflict is of course magnified in a context where Annex I Parties to the Kyoto Protocol seek to maintain their international competitiveness relative to non-Annex I Parties without targets, and where the world's largest national economy, the US, is not part of the Kyoto Protocol system.[127]

The international trading regime centres on the 1947 General Agreement on Tariffs and Trade (GATT) and subsequent agreements on specific areas of trade (e.g. intellectual property rights). Since 1995, these have been administered by the WTO.[128] The fundamental aim of the WTO is to pursue the liberalisation of international trade. To this end, it operates according to a set of principles, established in the GATT, that seek to reduce trade barriers and prohibit discrimination between 'like products' traded by different WTO members, or between domestically and internationally produced goods.[129] The WTO counts 147 countries among its members, with most major players in the climate change regime either members or candidates to join (e.g. the Russian Federation and Saudi Arabia).

---

[125] See Actions 1.2.4 and 1.2.5.

[126] Unlike, for example, the Montreal Protocol which restricts trade in ODS with non-Parties, or the 1989 Basel Convention on Transboundary Movements of Hazardous Wastes and the 1973 Convention on International Trade in Endangered Species (CITES), which explicitly regulate certain types of trade.

[127] For a more in-depth discussion of the issues, see Sampson, 1999; Chambers, 1999; Brack, 2000; Charnovitz, 2003; Brewer, 2003.

[128] See 1994 Marrakesh Agreement establishing the WTO. The GATT was originally supposed to have been administered by an International Trade Organisation (a third Bretton Woods institution together with the World Bank and the International Monetary Fund), but this never came into being.

[129] See GATT Articles I (most favoured nation) and III (national treatment).

Overall, the WTO views the relationship between trade liberalisation and environmental protection in positive terms, considering these goals to be compatible and indeed potentially mutually reinforcing. This positive perspective is also apparent in the broader UN system. The WSSD Plan of Implementation (see below), for example, calls on WTO members to '*continue to enhance* the mutual supportiveness of trade, environment and development with a view to achieving sustainable development'[130] (emphasis added). The relationship between trade and environmental protection, however, remains a complex one, and continues to be the subject of heated debate and analysis.

4.2   *Treaty provisions*

Article 3.5 of the Convention, discussed in chapter 4, concerns one aspect of the relationship between the international trading and climate change regimes. The Kyoto Protocol incorporates this principle, with Article 2.3 requiring Annex I Parties 'to strive to implement policies and measures . . . in such a way as to minimize adverse effects, including . . . on international trade'. This issue is discussed in detail in chapter 9.

None of the trading agreements under the WTO directly address environmental issues. However, GATT Article XX (general exceptions) does include provisions that have been interpreted as covering the environment. Article XX(b) provides for exceptions to the GATT's non-discrimination rules for measures that may be 'necessary to protect human, animal or plant life or health'. Similarly, Article XX(g) would permit the adoption and enforcement of measures 'relating to the conservation of exhaustible natural resources if such measures are made effective in conjunction with restrictions on domestic production or consumption'. According to the chapeau of Article XX, however, measures may only be applied if they would not 'constitute a means of arbitrary or unjustifiable discrimination between countries were the same conditions to prevail, or a disguised restriction on international trade'. In addition, in its Preamble, the 1994 Marrakesh Agreement Establishing the WTO recognises that trade goals should allow 'for the optimal use of the world's resources in accordance with the objective of sustainable development'.[131]

4.3   *Institutional arrangements*

Concurrent with the establishment of the WTO, a Committee on Trade and Environment (CTE)[132] was set up, with the mandate to 'identify the relationship between trade measures and environmental measures, in order to promote sustainable development' and make recommendations on changes that might be

---

[130] WSSD Plan of Implementation, paragraph 91.
[131] Agreement establishing the WTO, Preamble, paragraph 1.
[132] The WTO has several committees and councils on various issues.

necessary to the multilateral trading system both 'to enhance positive interaction between trade and environmental measures' and avoid protectionist trade measures.[133] Within this mandate, the CTE was given the specific task, among others, of addressing 'the relationship between the provisions of the multilateral trading system and trade measures for environmental purposes, *including those pursuant to MEAs*' (emphasis added). The CTE thus serves as the main forum for discussion within the WTO on the relationship between MEAs and the international trading regime. It does not, however, take decisions, simply making recommendations to the WTO's General Council and biannual Ministerial Conference. Although its establishment was viewed as an important step in promoting environmental concerns within the WTO, the CTE's record in reaching meaningful conclusions and actually influencing the WTO's policy-making work has been weak.

Because adversarial dispute settlement procedures are inappropriate for most global environmental problems, and because most MEAs have therefore concentrated on developing specialised non-compliance procedures (see chapter 12), the WTO's *dispute settlement procedures* have, in practice, become an important channel for WTO members to hammer out trade-related aspects of the relationship between trade and environment in the international policy-making arena.[134] Any WTO member may invoke the dispute settlement procedure if it feels another member has discriminated against it in violation of the WTO/GATT.[135] Interestingly, the most high-profile disputes to date have mostly involved environmental issues.[136] These have tested the interpretation of the GATT's provisions, such as Article XX and the definition of 'like product'. No conflict involving an MEA, or a matter directly related to climate change, has ever been brought to a dispute settlement panel, while other MEAs incorporating much more direct trade-related environmental measures (see examples above) are being implemented without challenge in the WTO. This situation, however, cannot be taken for granted.

4.4   *Institutional cooperation*

The CTE has focused its discussions on trade-related measures and dispute settlement procedures included in MEAs. It has held informal information sessions, where MEA Secretariats have been invited to make presentations to the

---

[133] Decision on Trade and Environment, 14 April 1994.

[134] See Understanding on Rules and Procedures Governing the Settlement of Disputes, Annex 2 to the Agreement establishing the WTO. A dispute settlement procedure was in place prior to the establishment of the WTO, but it was less structured, did not incorporate set timelines for steps in the process, and could be blocked by the 'losing' party.

[135] The dispute settlement procedure is succinctly explained at www.wto.org.

[136] For example, the Tuna–Dolphin cases of 1991 and 1994, and the Shrimp–Turtle cases of 1998 and 2001. These are discussed in Charnovitz, 2002.

CTE on their activities. The FCCC Secretariat has observer status with the CTE, and has made presentations at most of the CTE's information sessions, submitting written information on recent developments in the climate change regime.[137] UNEP also played an important catalytic role in bringing the WTO and MEA Secretariats together, convening a series of informal meetings between the Secretariats, NGOs and governments from 1999 to 2001 focused on identifying and enhancing synergies between the trading and environmental regimes.[138] The climate change Secretariat participated in this initiative, which initially focused on UNEP-sponsored MEAs, but expanded to others.

The WTO's fourth Ministerial Conference in Doha in November 2001 launched a new round of trade negotiations dubbed the 'Doha Development Agenda'.[139] In launching the round, the Doha Ministerial Declaration 'strongly reaffirm[ed]' WTO members' 'commitment to sustainable development' and encouraged 'efforts to promote cooperation between the WTO and related environmental organizations'. Moreover, it built on language in GATT Article XX to include an explicit reference to the environment, stating that 'no country should be prevented from taking measures for the protection of human, animal or plant life or health, *or of the environment*, at the level it considers appropriate' (emphasis added). The new round, which covers a range of trade-related topics, also includes a mandate for negotiations of particular relevance to the climate change regime on:

- The relationship between the WTO and specific trade-related obligations (STOs) in MEAs; and
- A process for regular information exchange between MEA Secretariats and relevant WTO committees, and on criteria for granting observer status to MEA Secretariats.

These mandates were agreed only after protracted negotiations, with the reluctance of many countries to link the environmental and trade agendas reflected in the proviso that the negotiations 'shall not add to, or diminish' the existing rights and obligations of WTO members. The environmental aspects of the Doha round are being conducted in special sessions of the CTE.[140] Related to the negotiations, the Doha Ministerial Declaration calls on the CTE and the WTO's Committee on

---

[137] See, for example, WT/CTE/W/174 (2002).

[138] See UNEP/DTIE, 2002. These meetings were held pursuant to mandates from the UNEP Governing Council (see Decisions 20/29, Policy and advisory services of the United Nations Environment Programme in the key area of economics, trade and financial services, and 21/14, Trade and environment).

[139] Doha Ministerial Declaration, adopted 14 November 2001. Document WT/MIN(01)/Dec/1. Unless otherwise stated, subsequent citations in this section refer to the Declaration.

[140] See, for example, TN/TE/3 (2000) and TN/TE/8 (2004).

Trade and Development to serve as forums to 'identify and debate developmental and environmental aspects of the [Doha] negotiations' with the aim of appropriately reflecting sustainable development in those negotiations. The Doha negotiating round was due to conclude by 1 January 2005, but this deadline has now been extended, following the setback in negotiations at the 2003 Cancún Ministerial Conference.

Concerning STOs in MEAs, discussions to date have revealed divergent views on the scope of this mandate, that is, over what constitutes a 'specific trade-related obligation' and therefore which MEAs should be considered. A WTO Secretariat paper included the Convention and Kyoto Protocol among fourteen treaties containing 'potential trade measures', but opinions differ among WTO members as to whether the climate change treaties should indeed be covered by the negotiations.[141] Regarding regular information exchange, the CTE has already agreed that representatives of certain MEA Secretariats, including the climate change Secretariat, may attend special negotiating sessions of the CTE as ad hoc *observers*, albeit on a provisional basis subject to review.[142]

The interface between the WTO and the FCCC has only very recently been discussed in the climate change regime.[143] For the first time, at SBSTA-18 in 2003, the FCCC Secretariat presented an information paper,[144] under the SBSTA's item on 'Cooperation with relevant international organizations', providing an overview of discussions in the CTE of relevance to the climate change regime. Consistent with its emphasis on national action in other linkage areas, the SBSTA responded by encouraging Parties to 'coordinate issues relevant to the Convention and the WTO at the *national* level'[145] (emphasis added).

5   Linkages with other intergovernmental processes

Steps taken by individual regimes to improve cooperation between themselves must be understood in the context of wider intergovernmental processes

---

[141] See WT/CTE/W/160/Rev.1; ICTSD, 2003; and TN/TE/9.

[142] TN/TE/5 (2000), paragraphs 14–16, also ICTSD, 2003. The larger question of observer participation in the Trade Negotiations Committee and the WTO General Council, however, remains unresolved. See ICTSD/IISD, 2003.

[143] Other regimes have been more active in this regard. The CBD COP has taken Decisions on cooperation with the WTO (e.g. see Decision VI/20, Cooperation with other organisations, initiatives and conventions), while Ozone MOP-14 requested the Secretariat to report to the Parties on its attendance at WTO meetings and to monitor developments in the CTE (see Decision XIV/11, The relationship between the Montreal Protocol and the World Trade Organization).

[144] See FCCC/SBSTA/2003/INF.7.   [145] See SBSTA-18 report, paragraph 42 (f).

launched within the UN system to enhance policy coherence and coordination in the environment, development and sustainable development fields.

The first such process, focused on the pursuit of 'sustainable development', was launched by the 1992 UNCED (the 'Earth Summit'). It has since been advanced through the institutions, principally the Commission on Sustainable Development (CSD), set up in the Earth Summit's wake, along with the implementation reviews of the Earth Summit that culminated in the 2002 WSSD. Linked to this process, UNEP has led renewed efforts to strengthen international environmental governance, triggered both by moves towards institutional reform in the UN and by the run up to the WSSD. Both these processes are, in turn, closely entwined with steps taken in the UN system to promote a more integrated approach to tackling global issues. These include forging agreement on comprehensive global strategies – notably the Millennium Declaration and its Development Goals – along with the strengthening of system-wide institutional coordinating mechanisms. This section explores these wider UN initiatives, and their relevance to the climate change regime.

5.1   *The 'sustainable development' agenda*

While the concept of 'sustainable development' has earlier antecedents,[146] it was launched onto the international political agenda by the 1992 Earth Summit, held in Rio de Janeiro, Brazil, which itself was convened as follow-up to the UN Conference on the Human Environment held twenty years before in Stockholm.[147] The main products of the Earth Summit were the Rio Declaration and Agenda 21, whose forty chapters – including chapter 9 on the protection of the atmosphere – were intended to set out a detailed action plan for the achievement of sustainable development.[148] The FCCC was negotiated in parallel with the Earth Summit's preparatory process, and is therefore also viewed as one of its key achievements, incorporating the pursuit of sustainable development as one of its principles.[149]

5.1.1   The Commission on Sustainable Development

The central institutional outcome of the Earth Summit was the CSD. Formally established by the UN General Assembly,[150] the CSD was charged with reviewing the implementation of the Earth Summit's outcomes, notably Agenda 21. It was also mandated to enhance international cooperation and rationalise

---

[146] See World Commission on Environment and Development, 1987.   [147] See UNCHE, 1972.
[148] See UNCED, 1992.   [149] FCCC Article 3.4.
[150] See Resolution 47/191, Institutional arrangements to follow up the United Nations Conference on Environment and Development, 22 December 1992

intergovernmental decision-making, develop options for future sustainable development activities, and forge partnerships between different actors, including civil society. The CSD is thus responsible for the pursuit of the overall sustainable development agenda within the UN, a mandate that was renewed by the WSSD.[151] It is composed of fifty-three members divided between the five UN regional groups and meets annually for two or three weeks. The CSD's legal authority is very weak in terms of mandatory reporting or regulation, thus it is largely aimed at playing a facilitative role.

The CSD has considered 'Protection of the atmosphere' as part of its review of Agenda 21, most recently in 2001, when it encouraged 'further cooperation . . . and the promotion of synergies' between the Montreal Protocol, the FCCC, the CBD and the UNCCD.[152] The CSD functions mostly as a discussion forum and its decisions and reports are not intended to affect any specific MEA directly. Rather, the CSD has helped to set in motion new institutions and treaty negotiations where gaps exist and, as the preparatory mechanism for the comprehensive reviews of Agenda 21 in 1997 and 2002, has produced negotiated text on the need to advance coordination among intergovernmental bodies and MEAs specifically. High-level CSD sessions have also facilitated ministerial consultations. The extent to which the CSD has been effective in going beyond a talk shop function to exert real influence on international and national policy-making is, however, debatable.

At its eleventh meeting in 2003, following the WSSD, the CSD agreed a new multi-year programme of work, based on seven two-year cycles structured around thematic clusters. Climate change, to be considered along with air pollution, industrial development and energy for sustainable development, will be taken up in 2006–2007.[153]

5.1.2   The 2002 World Summit on Sustainable Development

The Earth Summit review process culminated in the 2002 WSSD, held in Johannesburg.[154] While the WSSD was neither seriously expected, nor indeed mandated, to take decisions directly pertaining to the climate change process, its high profile and timing a few months after finalisation of the Marrakesh Accords exerted useful pressure on Parties to declare their intentions regarding ratification of the Kyoto Protocol. The climate change regime itself provided input to the WSSD process, notably through the Marrakesh Ministerial Declaration adopted at COP-7

---

[151] See WSSD Plan of Implementation, paragraphs 145–50.
[152] CSD Decision 9/2, Protection of the atmosphere, Ninth session of the CSD, 2001.
[153] See http://www.un.org/esa/sustdev/index.html.
[154] For an overall evaluation of the WSSD, see Pallemaerts, 2003.

(see p. 523 above). [155] The FCCC Executive Secretary also addressed the WSSD, focusing on the need to enhance synergies between the three Rio Conventions.

The main outcomes of the WSSD were the *Johannesburg Declaration on Sustainable Development* and the *Plan of Implementation of the World Summit on Sustainable Development*.[156] In its discussion of the challenges faced by the international community, the Johannesburg Declaration states that 'the adverse effects of climate change are already evident'.

5.1.2.1 The WSSD Plan of Implementation   The 65-page Plan of Implementation includes several references to climate change and the climate change regime. The Plan acknowledges that the Convention is the 'key' instrument for addressing climate change and reaffirms its objective. Reflecting difficulties in agreeing to language on ratification of the Kyoto Protocol in the context of its repudiation by the US, the Plan notes that 'States that have ratified the Kyoto Protocol strongly urge States that have not already done so to ratify the Kyoto Protocol in a timely manner.' The Plan then uncontroversially calls for action on such areas as financial assistance, technology development and scientific research and monitoring.[157] Furthermore, as noted above, the Plan of Implementation makes implicit reference to the JLG,[158] while recognising the 'scientific and technical' interconnections between climate change and ozone depletion.[159]

In addition to these specific references, climate change is implicated in other parts of the Plan of Implementation, notably its provisions on energy. Energy was one of the five areas – along with water and sanitation, health, agriculture and biodiversity, forming the so-called 'WEHAB' initiative – proposed by UN Secretary-General Kofi Annan as priority themes for the WSSD.[160] The WSSD was unable to agree concrete targets for increasing renewable energy use or for phasing out energy subsidies.[161] Instead, the Plan of Implementation calls on governments to, 'with a sense of urgency, substantially increase the global share of renewable energy sources with the objective of increasing its contribution to total energy supply', and notes that 'policies to reduce market distortions would promote energy systems compatible with sustainable development . . . including restructuring taxation and phasing out harmful subsidies, where they exist'.[162] Many other sections

---

[155] Decision 1/CP.7.   [156] See WSSD, 2002.

[157] WSSD Plan of Implementation, paragraph 38.

[158] WSSD Plan of Implementation, paragraph 41 (c).

[159] WSSD Plan of Implementation, paragraph 39 (d).   [160] See Annan, 2002.

[161] See Earth Negotiations Bulletin, 2002.

[162] WSSD Plan of Implementation, paragraph 20 (e) and (p).

of the Plan of Implementation are also relevant to climate change, including those on production and consumption patterns, transport, forests, waste and agriculture.[163]

Another significant development in the run-up to and at WSSD was growing interest in private sector involvement in tackling sustainable development issues. An important outcome in this regard was the 'partnership initiative for sustainable development'.[164] This initiative aims to engage businesses, as well as other NGOs, IGOs and government agencies, in putting the Plan of Implementation into effect by voluntarily developing projects and programmes, and registering these with the CSD Secretariat.[165] At the time of writing, over 250 such partnerships had been posted on the WSSD website, including several specifically targeting climate change concerns.[166] Given that business and industry are key actors in cutting GHG emissions, the partnerships initiative is of particular potential significance to the climate change regime.

The WSSD does not mark the end of the sustainable development process in the UN, but rather a further milestone in its evolution. Indeed, the UNGA decided, at its session following the WSSD, to 'adopt sustainable development as a key element of the overarching framework for UN activities, in particular for achieving the internationally agreed development goals, including those contained in the United Nations Millennium Declaration'[167] (see below). The implementation of the WSSD will continue to be reviewed through the CSD and other UN-wide coordinating mechanisms (see also below).

5.2   *UNEP and international environmental governance*

Responsibility for promoting coordination among MEAs and the coherence of the UN's environmental policies and programmes lies primarily with UNEP, which was established following the 1972 Stockholm UNCHE.[168] Throughout its

---

[163] See, in particular, WSSD Plan of Implementation, section III (consumption/production patterns), paragraphs 21 (transport), 22 (waste), 40 (agriculture) and 45 (forests).

[164] The partnership initiative makes up the so-called 'type 2' outcome of the WSSD, with 'type 1' referring to governmental commitments, such as the Plan of Implementation.

[165] See Guiding Principles for Partnerships for Sustainable Development ('type 2 outcomes') to be elaborated by Interested Parties in the Context of the World Summit on Sustainable Development, 7 June 2002, available at http://www.johannesburgsummit.org/html/documents/ prepcom4.html.

[166] See http://www.johannesburgsummit.org/html/sustainable_dev/ type2_part.html.

[167] Resolution 57/253, World Summit on Sustainable Development, paragraph 3.

[168] Resolution 2997 (XXVII) of 15 December 1972. On the development of UNEP's mandate, see Agenda 21, chapter 38 (h) (1); also UNEP GC Decision 19/1, Nairobi Declaration on the Role and Mandate of the United Nations Environment Programme, endorsed by the 1997 UNGA Special Session, S-19-2, paragraph 123.

lifetime, UNEP has suffered from shortage of funds, institutional weakness, and lack of will on the part of many governments to grant it political clout, while struggling to find its niche within the multitude of environmental instruments now in place in the UN system. Despite these difficulties, it has played an important role as an advocate for environmental issues on the international plane, including in the development of international environmental law, the collection and dissemination of environmental data and information, and public awareness-raising.[169]

The climate change and UNEP Secretariats work relatively closely together. The climate change Secretariat attends meetings of MEA Secretariats organised by UNEP, while its Executive Secretary addresses sessions of the UNEP Governing Council. In turn, UNEP's Executive Director, or Deputy, often speaks at key COP sessions. Unlike the ozone treaties, the CBD and other MEAs, however, the climate change regime is not administered by UNEP. Although UNEP provides services to the regime in such areas as education and public awareness, in addition to its role as an implementing agency of the GEF and one of the parent institutions of the IPCC, Parties have generally been wary of its efforts to advance coordination between the climate change regime and others. In 1998, for example, UNEP proposed to assume a role in policy coordination on HFCs and LULUCF, but its offer was rebuffed by the climate change Parties.[170]

In his 1997 report 'Renewing the United Nations: a programme for reform',[171] the UN Secretary-General undertook a review of UN activities, including in the area of the 'Environment, habitat and sustainable development'. As follow-up, a *Task Force on Environment and Human Settlements*, chaired by the UNEP Executive Director, was charged with reviewing institutional arrangements in the environmental area, and suggesting future options. The climate change Secretariat was closely involved in the Task Force, with the Executive Secretary serving as one of its twenty-one 'eminent persons'. The Task Force's 1998 report[172] led to the creation, under UNEP, of a *Global Ministerial Environment Forum* (GMEF) and an *Environmental Management Group* (EMG) to continue work on environmental governance.[173] The GMEF meets on an annual basis, while the EMG,[174] a coordinating mechanism whose members include UN bodies involved in environmental work and MEA Secretariats, meets two or three times a year, establishing 'issue-management groups' to address specific issues.

[169] For a discussion of UNEP's role and achievements, see Von Moltke, 1996; Esty and Ivanova, 2002b; Najam, 2002.
[170] See SBSTA-8 report, paragraph 27 (f).   [171] A/51/950.   [172] A/53/463.
[173] UNGA Resolution 53/242, Report of the Secretary-General on environment and human settlements, 10 August 1999.
[174] See UNEP/GC.22/4.

In the run-up to the WSSD, the GMEF launched a ministerial process on International Environmental Governance (IEG) to 'undertake a comprehensive policy-oriented assessment of existing institutional weaknesses as well as future needs and options for strengthened international environmental governance'.[175] The IEG process decided early on to adopt 'a prudent approach to institutional change . . . with preference given to making better use of existing structures'.[176] This reflects widespread hesitancy in the international community over new environmental governance structures, despite longstanding proposals to establish a 'global environment organisation' or other overarching structure to bring together the separate MEAs.[177] Donor countries bemoan the expense of doing so, developing countries fear they will lack the capacity to participate fully, many countries prefer to keep authority within the MEA COPs, and others do not wish to cede more power to their environmental ministries and argue that the real problem is lack of resources and political will rather than organisational structures.

In line with the general preference for institutional economy, the WSSD did not launch any new initiatives relating to IEG. It did, however, call for greater coherence and coordination on environmental matters within the UN system, including with bodies such as the WTO, as well as for full implementation of the outcomes of the IEG process.[178] Some of these outcomes[179] pursued by UNEP include the launch of an 'intergovernmental strategic plan for technology support and capacity-building',[180] along with the possible establishment of an 'intergovernmental panel on global environmental change' to improve scientific assessment.[181] UNEP is also developing a 'strategic framework' to encourage 'joint programming' between MEA Secretariats in areas of common interest.

While relevant to the climate change regime, the extent to which it will be implicated in such initiatives is, at present, uncertain. UNEP's achievements in coordination to date, and its aspirations for the future, mostly involve the MEAs operating under its aegis. The EMG, for example, is leading efforts to harmonise

---

[175] UNEP GC Decision 21/21, International environmental governance.

[176] A/57/25, UNEP Report of the Governing Council, Seventh Special Session (13–15 February 2002), UNGA Official Records, Fifty-seventh Session, Supplement No. 25.

[177] For a sample of such proposals, see Palmer, 1992; Esty, 1994; Biermann, 2000. For discussion and analysis of the various proposals, see chapters in Brack and Hyvarinen, 2002; also Ulfstein, 1999.

[178] WSSD Plan of Implementation, paragraphs 140 (d) and 151.

[179] See UNEP/GC.22/4.   [180] See also chapter 7.

[181] UNEP GC Decision 22/17, I, Follow-up to General Assembly Resolution 57/251 on the report of the seventh special session of the United Nations Environment Programme Governing Council/Global Ministerial Environmental Forum, paragraph 6; and UNEP GC Decision 22/1, A, Strengthening the scientific base of the United Nations Environment Programme, paragraph 3; also UNEP/GC.22/4, section II.

reporting among biodiversity-related conventions. Attempts to promote more fundamental policy-level coordination in terms of coherence of rules and implementation, along with process-coordination such as streamlining of meetings and co-location of Secretariats, have now taken a backseat on UNEP's agenda, reflecting the rather lukewarm support that such proposals garnered during the IEG process.

5.3   *The wider UN system*

The climate change regime was launched by the UNGA and remains firmly anchored within the UN system. Every year, the UNGA reviews the issue of climate change, adopting a resolution entitled 'Protection of global climate for present and future generations of mankind'.[182] This resolution, however, is typically general in nature and does not attempt to impact politically on the climate change negotiations.[183]

5.3.1   The Millennium Summit

The 'dawn of a new millennium' provided an important symbolic opportunity for the UN to take stock of pressing issues on the international agenda and how to move forward on these.[184] The UN seized this opportunity by convening a Millennium Summit in September 2000, attended by heads of state. The Summit took an integrated approach to global problems, stating that the 'central challenge' faced by the international community is ensuring 'that globalization becomes a positive force for all the world's peoples'.[185] The Millennium Declaration that emerged from the Summit addressed the whole spectrum of global issues, from peace and poverty eradication, to protecting the common environment. Of specific relevance to climate change, heads of state resolved, as one of six 'first steps', 'to make every effort to ensure the entry into force of the Kyoto Protocol, preferably by the tenth anniversary of [the Earth Summit] in 2002, and to embark on the required reduction in emissions of greenhouse gases'.[186] This language was subsequently recalled in the WSSD Plan of Implementation. Eight Millennium Development Goals, including time-bound and measurable targets, were distilled from the Millennium Declaration, with a commitment to achieve

---

[182] See resolutions on the UN's website, www.un.org.

[183] The exception being the annual decision on whether to continue to fund conference-servicing costs for the climate change regime from the UN budget. See chapter 16.

[184] UNGA Resolution 55/2, United Nations Millennium Declaration, 18 September 2000, paragraph 1.

[185] UNGA Resolution 55/2, paragraph 5.

[186] UNGA Resolution 55/2, paragraph 23, first bullet.

these by 2015. These include the Goal to 'ensure environmental sustainability' and, under that heading, the target to 'integrate the principles of sustainable development into country policies and programmes and reverse the loss of environmental resources'.[187]

The UN, through consultations among its various agencies, including the FCCC Secretariat, subsequently identified a series of indicators for measuring progress towards the Millennium Development Goals.[188] Indicators of relevance to climate change include:

- Energy use, measured in terms of global average kilograms of oil equivalent used per $1,000 of GDP (ppp); and
- CO_2 emissions, measured in terms of global average tons per capita.

The inclusion of the latter indicator is particularly noteworthy, given that discussing emissions in both *global* terms on the one hand, and *per capita* terms on the other, is contentious in the climate change regime in light of political sensitivities over the future evolution of commitments.[189]

Progress in implementing the UN Millennium Declaration will be reviewed annually by the UNGA, based on a report by the UN Secretary-General, and subject to a comprehensive review after five years.[190] Climate change featured strongly in the Secretary-General's first such report.[191] He characterised the Kyoto Protocol as 'the major tool' of the international community 'to combat further climate change', highlighting failure to bring it into force by the WSSD and the fact that 'many countries that contributed significantly to past pollution levels' had not yet ratified. He also noted that 'both industrialized countries and developing countries can cooperate to reduce emissions globally', identifying, among others, emissions trading and ending subsidies for fossil fuels as means of doing this. Trends in the indicators, which were presented in this first report, will also be reviewed on a yearly basis, thus providing an additional platform for discussion of climate change on the international stage.

5.3.2   UN-wide coordination mechanisms

The UN's highest-level forum for coordinating the work of its various agencies is the United Nations System Chief Executives Board for Coordination (CEB).[192] Chaired by the UN Secretary-General, the CEB meets twice a year, and is composed

---

[187] The other quantified targets under this Goal focus on local environmental problems, namely, improving access to drinking water and the lives of slum dwellers.

[188] See A/57/270.   [189] See chapter 18.

[190] See UNGA Resolution 57/144, Follow-up to the outcome of the Millennium Summit.

[191] A/57/270, paragraphs 76, 78 and 79.

[192] Formally the Administrative Committee on Coordination.

of the heads of the main UN agencies, including UNEP and WMO, but not MEA Secretariats. Following up on the global framework identified above, the CEB's work for 2003 was structured around the themes of 'financing for development' and 'strategies for sustainable development', including UN-wide collaboration on energy issues and preparations for the 2005 comprehensive review of the Millennium Development Goals.[193]

In a related move, the UNGA, at its fifty-seventh session, established an open-ended ad hoc Working Group of the General Assembly (WGGA) to develop concrete recommendations on how best to ensure 'an integrated and coordinated follow-up' to recent UN conferences and summits, including the Millennium Summit, the WTO Doha Ministerial Conference and the WSSD.[194] The follow-up to these conferences will continue to be discussed by the UNGA at future sessions.

While the climate change regime is not directly involved in these UN-wide coordinating mechanisms, their attempts at developing a more integrated approach to addressing global issues provide the intellectual and political context in which the regime, as part of the international system, operates. Moreover, the fact that climate change itself implicates both environment and development concerns, and thus lies at the heart of the pursuit of sustainable development, means that such attempts are undoubtedly relevant to it.

[193] See http://ceb.unsystem.org.

[194] UNGA Resolution 57/270, Integrated and coordinated implementation of and follow-up to the outcomes of the major United Nations conferences and summits in the economic and social fields.

18

Evolution of the regime

1   Introduction

Like most modern MEAs, the Convention and the Protocol are framework agreements that allow the regime's institutions to review and assess commitments in response to changing scientific, technical and legal information and experience with implementation.[1] The main mechanism to foster evolution of the regime is the establishment of a COP and COP/MOP with built-in powers to review and adopt instruments containing new commitments, including legally binding instruments in the form of amendments, annexes and protocols, as well as rules and procedures that define how, and in some cases when, negotiations about commitments may proceed. This chapter explains the review provisions contained in the FCCC and the Kyoto Protocol and the various kinds of legal instruments relevant to the evolution of commitments under the climate regime. The institutional mandate of the COP and structures and techniques deployed in negotiating processes are critical components in understanding how the climate regime will address evolution of commitments and are explained in depth in chapters 13 and 14. Section 2 explains what is meant by commitments, different types of commitments, how they are created under the climate change regime and their resulting legal effect. The review procedures of the Convention and the Protocol are explained in section 3.

The final section explains briefly how developments taking place outside the international negotiations on climate change can have an important impact in framing the discussions on future commitments.

---

[1] See chapter 15.

544

2   Meaning, type and form of commitments

2.1   *Meaning*

International commitments are simply promises made by one state to other states to limit its future freedom by behaving in a certain way or achieving a specific result. Commitments are created through negotiation and subsequent ratification and entry into force of treaties.[2] Legally binding obligations relevant to protecting the environment as a whole can also arise on the basis of general principles, customary international law and through decisions of international courts, although these are not termed 'commitments'. The reciprocal exchange of promises or commitments creates certainty, ensuring that states act where costs are significant but benefits widely dispersed, as is the case in climate change. The quality of the promise or commitment made by a state has an important bearing on the legal consequences that flow. Some promises are political. Although failure to achieve such commitments may attract disapproval, it does not result in legal responsibility and there is no duty to deliver upon the promise or make good consequences flowing from its breach.[3] Legally binding commitments entail such responsibility. For this reason legally binding commitments generate a higher level of certainty and trust because states are legally bound to implement them through enactment of national laws, regulations and administrative structures. Actors whose behaviour is affected by the subject matter of the commitment therefore take binding commitments more seriously. It should also be noted that where effective means of checking compliance and/or enforcement mechanisms are lacking, a legally binding commitment may not have much more 'bite' than a political one. In the climate regime, international commitments – some binding, others not and some a mixture of the two – serve as 'the glue' that helps hold the regime together.[4] The Convention and the Protocol, and ironically its rejection by the US, confirm that Parties regard the reciprocal exchange of commitments, binding or otherwise, as the evolutionary engine of the climate regime.

2.2   *Types*

In much climate policy literature on regime evolution, the term 'commitments' is often used synonymously with 'mitigation commitments'. Other kinds of commitments, however, are relevant to the evolution of the climate change regime. The type of commitments currently contained in the Convention and the

---

[2] See chapter 1, p. 12 on treaties and custom.   [3] See chapter 1, p. 7, on state responsibility.
[4] Bodansky, 2003: p. 2.

Protocol can be divided up roughly into five broad issue areas:

- Mitigation
- Adaptation
- Consideration of special needs and circumstances
- Resource flows (financial, technological and human and institutional)
- Institutional and procedural (reporting, review, compliance and enforcement)

Because the Convention mandated a review of the mitigation commitments of Annex I Parties by COP-1, the focus of attention has been on mitigation commitments, including after the adoption of the Kyoto Protocol, on how to extend quantitative mitigation commitments to developing countries. The Marrakesh Accords negotiations brought strengthening of other types of commitments more fully into focus, signalling that the regime's evolution will need to take into account several different types of commitments, rather than addressing mitigation issues in a piecemeal and isolated fashion. Since the US announced its position on the Kyoto Protocol, the need for commitments that create incentives for countries to remain within the regime as well as appropriate, and perhaps punitive, consequences and options for countries that choose not to do so has become more pertinent and will require further consideration in the evolution of the climate regime.

2.3   *Form*

The form in which a commitment is expressed creates strong, but not determinative, presumptions about its legal status. The COP's deliberations result in a range of outputs with different legal status, including decisions, resolutions, declarations, amendments, annexes and protocols, which can be used individually and in combination to develop commitments beyond the current framework.

2.3.1   Decisions

Because COP decisions are non-legally binding they are generally considered inappropriate for altering existing commitments or establishing new ones.[5] Provided they generate legal certainty that they will be abided by and only altered in accordance with agreed criteria, COP decisions can, however, be used to great effect in elaborating existing commitments or providing long-term, detailed guidance on implementation. This is well demonstrated by the Marrakesh Accords, aspects of which elaborate issues of a fundamental legal character, such as

---

[5] Chapter 13, box 13.2, describes the general role and use of COP decisions, resolutions and declarations.

establishment of the Protocol's compliance procedures and modalities for including additional sinks, and eligibility and use of the Kyoto mechanisms.

In the immediate future, however, COP decisions will play an important procedural role in defining how and when the evolution of the climate regime will be considered. Although proposals for a COP decision setting out a procedural 'evolution mandate' were put forward at COP-3 and again at COP-4, Parties have yet to agree on the nature, scope, timing and inputs relevant to defining the process for considering future commitments.[6] Whilst there has been much discussion 'behind the scenes' on the content of such a mandate – conducted by COP Presidents, bilateral negotiations and various independent think tanks – the COP has been unable to agree a process to formally solicit Parties' views on the nature, scope, timing, inputs and other considerations that might help inform the design of new commitments. This is due, in part, to developing country Parties' refusal since COP-3 to allow issues that might involve discussion of additional commitments for them to be placed on the COP agenda.[7]

2.4   Amendments

FCCC: Article 15 of the Convention sets forth procedures for the adoption and entry into force of amendments. Only Parties may propose amendments. Proposals must be adopted at an ordinary (not an extraordinary) 'session' of the COP, provided the text of the proposal is circulated to Parties via the Secretariat at least six months before the 'meeting' at which it is proposed for amendment.[8]

If all efforts to reach consensus on the adoption of a proposed amendment have failed, Article 15.3 allows amendments to be adopted by a three-fourths majority vote of Parties present and voting at the meeting (which Article 15.4 clarifies means Parties present and casting an affirmative or negative vote). Although voting rarely takes place in MEAs, the *possibility* of voting ensures that no Party, or small group of Parties, can veto evolution of the regime in the face of widespread agreement. Because the content of any protocol can to all extents and purposes be converted in the form of an amendment, Article 15.3 has implications for the adoption of protocols notwithstanding the fact that the Convention is silent about whether protocols should be adopted by consensus or by majority voting. Thus, in the run-up to COP-3, the text of the Protocol also existed in the form of an amendment

---

[6] COP-3 report, on JUSSCANZ proposal for post-Kyoto regime. COP-4 report, proposal by President of COP-4.

[7] See chapter 14, p. 436 on the COP agenda.

[8] See chapter 13, p. 407. A 'session' of the COP comprises a series of COP 'meetings'. The ruling given by UNOLA on the amendment proposed by Kuwait in the run-up to Kyoto confirmed that if a COP session commenced on 1 December, then an amendment proposal submitted on 2 June could only validly be considered after 2 December and not on 1 December.

to the Convention to counter threats made by some OPEC members to veto its adoption.[9]

Upon adoption, the amendments must be communicated by the Secretariat to the Depository, the UN Secretary-General, and to Parties for their acceptance. Instruments of acceptance by Parties that wish to be bound by the amendment must be deposited with the Depositary. The amendment enters into force ninety days after at least three-fourths of the Parties to the Convention have accepted the amendment. This ensures a broad measure of support for the amendment but preserves the sovereign right of each Party not to accept new commitments. Amendments thus allow Parties choice about whether to accept/reject commitments whilst still participating fully in the policy-making processes of the regime. The difficulty and slowness in obtaining instruments of ratifications from such a large number of FCCC Parties speaks against amendments, and this was the reason why in 1997 Parties chose to adopt the Kyoto Protocol with its own tailor-made entry-into-force requirements. Unfortunately, for reasons discussed below, the Protocol's entry-into-force requirements have not proved successful in avoiding the lengthy hold-out by Russia.

Amendments are still an extremely useful evolutionary tool where the subject matter lends itself to limited substantive or structural changes to the original regime, where these would not require Parties to enter into protracted ratification procedures at a domestic level and/or where it does not matter too much whether some Parties accept the amendment as legally binding and others do not. These considerations did not hold true at Kyoto and it remains to be seen whether they will in the period beyond Kyoto. Certainly, assessment and revision of future commitments will encompass a greater diversity of country needs and circumstances and, given the economic, political and social realities of globalisation, an even greater need for reciprocity in the exchange of commitments – symmetrical or otherwise.

Kyoto: Procedures for proposing amendments to the Protocol and entry-into-force requirements are set out in Article 20. These are exactly the same as for the Convention.

Rule development: The AGBM negotiations elicited a number of proposals, some in the form of amendments and others as protocol, all of which formed the input for the Kyoto Protocol.[10] Apart from these, only two amendments to the Convention have been proposed and neither of these were adopted. The proposal by the EU prior to COP-3 would have allowed protocols to be adopted by majority voting and for this amendment to be applied provisionally pending its formal entry

---

[9] FCCC/TP/2000/2.

[10] FCCC/TP//2000/2 contains references to all proposals submitted during the AGBM.

into force.[11] The other proposal, submitted by Kuwait largely in response to the EU, sought to rewrite the financial provisions set out in Article 4.3 of the Convention to make Annex II Parties liable for the full costs of implementing measures under Article 4.1 as well as measures taken by developing countries to implement any future protocol to the Convention.[12] Both proposals were designed essentially to give leverage to these Parties over COP-3 proceedings. Both were withdrawn by mutual consent upon agreement that the adoption of the Protocol would not be vetoed and that OPEC concerns would be taken into account.[13]

2.5   *Annexes*

        FCCC: Like other MEAs, the Convention's annexes provide a more expedient way of incorporating material of an essentially factual nature into the regime than is possible through the use of amendments. Article 16 sets out the procedure for adoption of new annexes and amendments for new ones. Article 16.1 specifies that annexes to the Convention shall be restricted to 'lists, forms and any other material of a descriptive nature that is of a scientific, technical, procedural or administrative character'. The proposal and adoption of such annexes is subject to the same procedures as amendments set forth in paragraphs 2–4 of Article 15.

The essential difference between amendments and annexes relates to entry into force. Because material in annexes is not intended to create commitments for Parties, the entry-into-force requirements for annexes are simplified. These procedures, set out in Article 16.3, mean that, once adopted, annexes enter into force and bind *all* Parties except those that have submitted notices of 'non-acceptance' to the Depository within six months of the adoption of the annex. Obviously, if the adoption of an annex or an amendment to an annex involves an amendment to the Convention (i.e. affects substantive commitments), it would be imprudent to allow the annex to enter into force before the substantive amendment enters into force. Article 16.5 clarifies that in such a case the annex will only enter into force when the substantive amendment enters into force.

Kyoto: Annexes A and B of the Protocol are fundamental to defining the scope and quantity of each Annex I Party's quantified commitments. The procedures for adoption and entry into force of annexes set out in Article 21 therefore distinguish between amendments to Annexes A and B and other kinds of annexes that might in future be proposed for the Protocol (and amendments to these). Procedures for 'new' annexes, and amendments to these, set out in Article 21, are exactly the same as for the Convention.

---

[11] FCCC/SBI/1997/15; Yamin and Clarke, 1997.
[12] FCCC/SBI/1997/15 contains the text of the Kuwait proposal.
[13] Chapter 9 discusses OPEC concerns about the impact of response measures.

So far as amendments to Annexes A and B are concerned, they have to follow the adoption and entry into force procedures for amendments as set out in Article 20 of the Protocol. Additionally, in view of the gravity of binding commitments these annexes create, Article 21.7 stipulates that 'any amendment to Annex B shall be adopted only with the written consent of the Party concerned'. These provisions provide important sovereignty safeguards against the imposition of commitments on individual Parties by the majority.

Rule development: A number of changes to the Convention's annexes have been proposed. These relate to the listing of countries to be included in Annex I, discussed in chapter 5, and deletion of the name of Turkey from the list in Annex II of the Convention, discussed in chapter 10, box 10.2.[14]

2.6   *Protocols*

Article 17 of the Convention states the COP may adopt protocols at its ordinary sessions. The text of any proposed protocol must be communicated to Parties via the Secretariat at least six months before such a session. Although Article 17 does not say it, it is assumed that only Parties may propose protocols. Because substantive negotiations continued late into the night at COP-3, during the AGBM the requirement to submit 'the text' six months ahead was interpreted to mean that the substance of proposals should be communicated six months ahead.

Article 17 specifies that the entry-into-force requirements of a protocol must be established by that instrument. It also states that only Parties to the Convention may be Parties to the protocol and decisions under the protocol shall only be taken by the Parties to the protocol concerned. Apart from these provisions, and Article 7 of the Convention, which allows the COP to keep under review the implementation of any protocols, the Convention does not address institutional modalities determining how the COP and the decision-making structures established by any future protocol should work. The relationship between the COP and the COP/MOP is thus clarified in greater detail in the text of the Protocol. The relationship between the COP and the COP/MOP will have a key bearing on the evolution of the regime and is discussed in chapter 13.

Article 17 is silent on the adoption procedure for protocols. Combined with the impasse on the Convention's rules of procedure on the issue of majority voting, this silence tends to strengthen the hand of Parties that want to limit evolution of the regime not only for themselves but less legitimately also for Parties that are willing to move ahead. Although the Kyoto Protocol was in the end adopted unanimously, much political capital, backed by resort to use of legal and procedural

---

[14] FCCC/SBI/1997/15 contains the text of proposals submitted by Pakistan and Azerbaijan concerning Turkey.

techniques (ranging from reliance on converting proposals into Article 15 amendments, provisional application of majority voting as well as voting on the basis of the Chairman's ruling), had to be expended to achieve this result. Thus, although the lack of agreed voting rules for adoption of subsequent protocols creates a procedural hurdle, rather than a bar, to the evolution of the climate regime, this has to be factored into the dynamics of regime development.

2.7   *Entry into force, reservations and withdrawals*

Conditions setting the terms upon which a country can become a Party, triggers defining when international legal obligations commence and in what circumstances a Party ceases to be bound by them are three important parameters affecting the evolution of any regime. These matters are dealt with in provisions dealing with reservations, entry into force and withdrawal respectively.

Article 24 of the Convention and Article 26 of the Protocol state that no reservations can be made by a country that wants to become a Party to these instruments. Allowing reservations gives individual countries an opportunity to unpick multilaterally agreed rules in a manner that could undermine the reciprocal exchange of commitments which are often based on a fine balance of considerations and trade-offs. The prohibition on reservations – the 'take it or leave it' approach – creates incentives for countries to negotiate multilaterally agreed rules to cater for their specific circumstances in advance of their adoption, as well as ensuring a coherent and uniform legal regime for those who subsequently join.

The entry into force triggers are quite different for the Convention and the Protocol because they serve very different policy needs. Article 23 of the Convention provided for entry into force ninety days after fifty countries had deposited instruments of ratification, approval or accession. This inclusive approach, with each country's instrument counting equally, helped ensure the rapid entry into force of the Convention.

Article 25 of the Protocol, on the other hand, creates a double trigger, similar to the one included in the Montreal Protocol, to ensure there is a critical mass of Annex I Parties on board before the commitments in the Protocol become binding for any one of them. Article 25 provides that the Protocol will only enter into force on the ninetieth day after fifty-five countries have deposited their instruments of ratification, acceptance or approval, 'incorporating Parties included in Annex I which accounted in total for at least 55 per cent of the total carbon dioxide emissions for 1990'. To ensure legal certainty, Article 25.2 defines the total carbon dioxide emissions for 1990 to mean the amount communicated on or before the date of adoption of the Protocol by Annex I Parties in their first national communications with the Report of COP-3 setting out the amount contributed by each

Annex I Party in 1990.[15] The calibration of the trigger at 55 per cent was intended to avoid giving the US a veto over the entry into force of the Protocol. Nevertheless, given the decision by the US not to ratify the Protocol, the Russian Federation now has veto power and can prevent the entry into force of the Protocol notwithstanding its ratification by nearly 120 countries.

Climate change is a long-term problem and the Convention and Protocol envisage ongoing commitment to the regime by Parties. Somewhat surprisingly therefore, both instruments allow Parties to withdraw any time after three years from the date on which the instrument in question entered into force for them. Article 25 of the Convention and Article 27 of the Protocol contain virtually identical provisions in this regard. These specify that notice of withdrawal must be given to the Depository and takes effect upon expiry of one year from the date of receipt of the notification or at any later date if specified. A withdrawal from the Convention is deemed to be a withdrawal from the Protocol.

Although such withdrawal provisions are fairly standard in international treaties, the withdrawal of Parties from the Kyoto Protocol may be problematic because it is not clear, for example, what would happen to a Party's assigned amount and their transactions under the Kyoto mechanisms. Although highlighted in policy discussions, these concerns remain to be addressed but obviously have implications for the manner in which a Party chooses to exit from the regime pursuant to its rights under Article 27.[16]

3   Review procedures

FCCC: The COP is empowered to review the implementation of the Convention and the Protocol pursuant to the provisions of Article 7. These provisions allow the COP to make, within its mandate, appropriate decisions to promote the effective implementation of the Convention, including adoption of amendments, protocols and annexes. Article 7.2 (a) mandates the COP periodically to examine Parties' obligations, as well as the institutional arrangements under the Convention, in the light of Article 2 and 'experience gained in its implementation and the evolution of scientific and technical knowledge'. It is important to note that the COP's mandate does not explicitly authorise it to examine the obligations of individual Parties.

In addition to the general mandate set out in Article 7.2 (a), the Convention contains built-in review provisions that prompt certain reviews at particular times,

---

[15] Emissions of some Annex I Parties, such as Ukraine, that had not submitted their first national communication by this date are not included in the trigger.

[16] Yamin, 1999.

specifying what kinds of informational inputs should be considered in the reviews. So far as mitigation commitments are concerned, the Convention contains three such reviews. Article 4.2 (d) mandated COP-1 to review of the adequacy of Article 4.2 (a) and (b), which led to the adoption of the Berlin Mandate and the Kyoto Protocol, with a second review of the adequacy of these subparagraphs mandated to take place no later than 31 December 1998 and 'thereafter at regular intervals determined by the COP until the objective of the Convention is met'. Reviews are to be based on the 'best available scientific information and assessment of climate change and its impacts, as well as relevant technical, social and economic information' is to be considered. This is generally taken to mean information provided by the IPCC although increasingly, as the regime matures, information from Parties' national communications is likely to be an important additional source of information.

A third review provision is set out in Article 4.2 (f) which requires the COP to review, not later than 31 December 1998, the lists in Annex I and Annex II with the approval of the Party concerned. Rule development related to these provisions is discussed in box 5.4, chapter 5 on mitigation and in box 10.2, chapter 10.

In addition to the review of countries included in Annex II under Article 4.2 (f), Article 11.4 of the Convention mandates the COP to review the financial mechanism four years after making arrangements to implement the interim financial arrangements set out in Article 21. Rule development related to these provisions is set out in chapter 10.

Finally, Article 7.2 (a) requires the COP periodically to examine the institutional arrangements under the Convention. Although the interim institutional arrangements specified in Article 21 have long since been resolved, more recent developments in the Convention's institutional machinery, including the establishment of a number of specialised bodies, have given rise to the need to examine an interrelated set of institutional concerns that could best be examined under the broader mandate set out in Article 7.2 (a).[17] Unfortunately there is no time-bound review for examining the COP's institutional machinery and the resulting concerns are addressed in a piecemeal fashion.

Kyoto: The general review provisions are set out in Articles 9 and 13 of the Protocol. The reviews are general in the sense that they encompass the review of the commitments of all Parties – developing and developing – as well as mitigation and non-mitigation related commitments. These review provisions of the Protocol are similar in approach to those of the Convention but aim to coordinate any review of commitments under the Convention with reviews under the Protocol.

---

[17] See chapter 19.

Article 13.4 (b) requires the COP/MOP periodically to examine Parties' obligations, 'giving due recognition' to any reviews under Articles 4.2 (d) and 7.2 (b) of the Convention. Such reviews are to be conducted in the light of the Convention's objective, experience gained in its implementation and evolution of scientific and technological knowledge, and consideration of regular reports on the implementation of the Protocol mentioned in Article 13.4 (b). Like the COP, the COP/MOP can then take 'appropriate action' which would include adoption of amendments and annexes.

Article 9.1 contains a very similar, although slightly more detailed general review provision. Article 9.1 mandates the COP/MOP periodically to review the Protocol as a whole, stating the review is to be in the light of the 'best available scientific information and assessments on climate change and its impacts, as well as relevant technical, social and economic information'. Again, the need to take into account reviews undertaken by the COP is explicitly highlighted. The only significant detail added by Article 9 is the timing of the first review which Article 9.2 states must take place at the second session of the COP/MOP. The timing of subsequent reviews has been left for the COP/MOP to determine, although there is a requirement that these should take place 'at regular intervals and in a timely manner'.

In addition to these review provisions, and because the Kyoto architecture is based on the concept of sequential commitment periods, the Protocol contains built-in review provisions related to these. Article 3.9 states that commitments for subsequent periods for Annex I Parties shall be established in the form of amendments to Annex B of the Protocol which shall be adopted in accordance with Article 21.7. This means that future commitments of Annex I Parties are envisioned to be in a legally binding form. Importantly, such amendments are not subject to a double trigger to enter into force but 'simply' require three-fourths of the Parties to the Protocol to deposit instruments of ratification (provided, of course, that each Annex I Party has given its written consent to the amendment). The COP/MOP is mandated to initiate the consideration of such commitments at least seven years before the end of the first commitment period, i.e. by 31 December 2005.

Finally, Article 3.2 of the Protocol deserves mention here because it requires each Annex I Party to have made demonstrable progress by 2005 towards achieving its commitments under this Protocol. The submission of reports to enable a review of such progress to take place was mandated by COP-7 and COP-8, and is discussed in more detail in chapter 11.

4   Other evolutionary mechanisms

Multilateral negotiations under the auspices of the COP and the COP/MOP are only one procedural means to address the evolution of the regime. Other mechanisms and forums can also supplement and support the regulatory efforts made by the Convention and Protocol bodies. These are important because much social science research confirms that 'the real business of responding to climate change may well be through smaller, often less formal, agreements among states; states and firms; and firms, non-governmental organizations, and communities'.[18] The first half of this section sets out mechanisms of a formal legal character that can contribute to the evolution of commitments. The second half describes other kinds of informal, non-regulatory mechanisms, typically initiated by non-governmental actors, including multi-stakeholder initiatives, which advance the evolution of the regime.

4.1   *Formal governmental initiatives*

Many other international and regional organisations have competence over activities and sources that generate GHG emissions or affect sequestration by carbon sinks. For example, the role of the ICAO and the IMO in regulating activities that produce bunker fuels is formally recognised by the Protocol.[19] Developments in other MEAs such as the CBD, Ramsar and the UNCCD will also influence the evolution of the climate regime.[20] And because oil is the most valuable globally traded commodity in the world, linkages with economic and trade bodies, including the WTO, will remain significant.[21]

Vulnerable countries and communities may begin to make use of national and international dispute settlement procedures and these cases could affect the future direction and substantive content of regime commitments. Other judicial courts and tribunals not directly established or referenced in the climate regime, but which have competence over aspects related to climate change, such as dispute settlement procedures of the WTO and UNCLOS, could also shape the legal landscape in which existing commitments are implemented or future climate commitments are made.[22]

Regulation by city, state and provincial governments cannot create international commitments but can advance evolution of the climate regime by creating sub-national or sector-specific legal frameworks that drive behaviour towards achievement of the Convention's ultimate objective. Many such initiatives are now underway in the US and Australia and are being crafted to be Kyoto-consistent.[23] Standard-setting by supranational organisations such as the EU can also create binding rules for members of such organisations. Such standards create assured

---

[18] Rayner and Malone, 1998b: p. 14.   [19] See chapter 5, pp. 83–7.   [20] See chapter 17.

[21] See chapters 9 and 17.

[22] For a description of international courts, tribunals and their respective competencies see Sands et al., 1999. See also Sands, 1998.

[23] Rabe, 2002. For a summary of US initiatives see Cogan, 2003.

markets in climate-friendly products and services and exert a 'ratcheting' effect on trading partners and neighbouring countries.

Another supplement to international regulation in this regard is mutual recognition of permits and licences issued by national bodies, as provided for by many MEAs and non-environmental agreements, which may be particularly relevant for the global evolution of the Kyoto mechanisms and Kyoto-consistent trading concepts.[24]

Finally, because leadership demonstrates the moral, political and economic case for combating climate change, countries that want to advance evolution of the regime can adopt unilateral national targets to supplement or exceed those contained in the Convention and the Protocol – as happened in the early phases of the negotiations of both instruments. Such targets do not create international commitments but they create a backbone of expectations to guide future negotiations on commitments. The importance of national initiatives has recently been emphasised by the UK Prime Minister, Tony Blair, who warned that the consequences of environmental degradation and climate change are 'just as devastating in their potential impact' as weapons of mass destruction and went on to announce a new policy to cut the UK's carbon dioxide emissions by 60 per cent over the next half century.[25] Ambitious, long-term national targets such as these provide additional certainty for all actors that the future is carbon constrained. These statements are important because competitiveness concerns often make states reluctant to pledge too much unilaterally.

4.2   Other initiatives

Leadership from various organs of government is important, but desirable changes often occur without governmental invention, or indeed, in spite of it.

Voluntary actions by businesses, municipalities, research bodies and epistemic networks, religious groups and consumer and civil society organisations are arguably as significant as international policy-making in instigating behavioural changes necessary to move towards low- or-zero carbon-emitting economies.[26] Thus again, whilst such actions do not generate commitments, they provide the know-how, technical capacity, stakeholder involvement and political pressures upon which legitimate and effective forms of commitments can be successfully built.

Many of the multi-stakeholder initiatives recently taken outside the international regulatory sphere exemplify this contribution, and a small selection of these is set out in box 18.1. Here it is important to note that, although some of these

---

[24] Sands, 1992: p. 22.   [25] Prime Minister Tony Blair, 2003.
[26] Rayner and Malone, 1998b.

activities are showcased at side-events at COP and SB meetings, the frequency, timing and content of such events is dictated largely by the needs of the formal negotiating process rather than the learning needs of climate policy-makers and the contribution such activities make to the evolution of the regime. A more systematic approach to accessing and evaluating this body of initiatives could play an important role in regime evolution. An information network facilitating access to such activities that is linked to, or part of, the information network clearing house for Article 6 activities concerning education, training and public awareness activities, could provide a starting point.[27]

Box 18.1   Recent multi-stakeholder initiatives advancing evolution

It is impossible to summarise here all the evolution-related initiatives being undertaken by non-state agents. This small selection is thus illustrative only and focuses on initiatives to facilitate voluntary actions to reduce GHGs over and above those mandated by existing commitments. The Greenhouse Gas Protocol developed by WRI and WBCSD 'road tests' GHG reporting and tracking on a company level, as this kind of reporting is currently not mandatory for the vast majority of corporate actors. Corporate partnerships with environmental groups such as the WRI's Climate Protection Initiative, EDF's Partnership for Climate Actions and WWF's Climate Savers Programme, engage progressive companies in going beyond legalities to identify strategic opportunities that will boost their profits and productivity in a carbon-constrained world. Shareholder activism combined with existing legal security exchange requirements to disclose 'material risks' such as climate change – which constitutes a significant potential 'off-balance-sheet' risk for many major companies – is also driving companies to examine their carbon liabilities, assets and future opportunities more closely.[28] These issues have been highlighted through recent initiatives such as the Carbon Disclosure Project and by CERES (now comprising a coalition of investors and environmental groups), working on corporate environmental responsibility representing more than $300 billion in assets – 300 times more than the current GEF replenishment.[29] The 'market creation' functions of initiatives such as the World Bank Prototype Carbon Fund (PCF) and efforts to create a 'gold standard' for CMD projects by broad coalitions of

---

[27] See chapter 7 and FCCC/SBI/2003/4.   [28] Cogan, 2003.
[29] Carbon Disclosure Project, 2003. For details about CERES see Cogan, 2003.

NGOs also deserve mention.[30] On the adaptation side, businesses and international and non-governmental organisations have come together under the UNEP Finance Initiative which is highlighting the role of the financial services industry in preventing and adapting to climate change.[31]

Understanding the role and substantive contribution of such initiatives to the design and future direction of the climate regime begs a broader question about the role of institutional learning in the climate change regime itself.[32] Because institutions tend to stabilise around a common procedural culture that governs learning, role playing, sharing, competing and justifying, there is a tendency for all institutions to build up coherent worldviews or mindsets resulting in 'core' ideas and norms which are very hard to change.[33] Institutional learning refers to the process whereby individuals engaged in a regime, and the collective entities that constitute it (such as the COP, IPCC and the GEF), amass new knowledge and incorporate it into their pre-existing framework and set of working assumptions.[34]

Institutional learning provides important insights ranging from who needs to learn what, to how and why some good policy ideas might be more difficult than others to incorporate into a regime. These considerations are important because devising new climate policies that are responsive to economic, social and technological changes, emergence of new problems, 'shocks' such as the US announcement on Kyoto, and internal divisions, such as those created by the Russian Federation's hold-out over Kyoto and developing country intransigence over commitment evolution, may well require more than incremental changes to the 'core' framework. The kind of knowledge relevant to advancing consideration of these matters is likely to be complex, i.e. where the boundaries between the technical and normative elements are intertwined, and to be harshly contested amongst participants.[35]

Thus, devising institutional processes and 'spaces' – virtual or physical – where such knowledge can be articulated, shared, critiqued and justified among existing and new entrants has become the central and prior task in regime design rather than funding the production of knowledge dressed up as final policy solutions. The climate regime will be better served by policy processes that emphasise incentives, innovation and learning between actors because 'uncertainty, variety,

[30] Details of the PCF can be found at http://prototypecarbonfund.org/splash.html. Details of the 'gold standard' can be found at www.panda.org/about_wwf/what_we_do/climate_change/ what_we_do/ business_industry/gold_standard.cfm#necessary.

[31] UNEP, 2002.   [32] Rayner and Malone, 1998a: chapter 5.   [33] Rayner and Malone, 1998a.

[34] Laird, 1999.   [35] Jasanoff, 1990.

surprise and sometimes chaos characterize the evolution of complex natural and social systems more often than equilibrium and stability'.[36] The creation of policy processes emphasising learning and adaptability, and involving a much broader range of actors than currently involved in international negotiations, is vital if the evolution of an effective, inclusive and equitable climate regime is to be achieved.

[36] Berkhout et al., 2003: chapter 1, p. 25.

19

Conclusion: taking stock and moving forward

1   Introduction

The previous chapters of this book presented a comprehensive and objective guide to the rules, institutions and procedures of the climate regime. Our main aim in doing so was to make the regime more accessible. An additional hope was to encourage an informed assessment of the merits of what has been achieved, as well of the limitations that remain. We realise that few policy-makers have the time to reflect deeply on the overall direction of climate rules and the 'health' of climate institutions to see if these are performing at their best. Increased specialisation, policy linkages and travel commitments, on top of the demands of deepening domestic implementation processes, all take a toll. And, of course, climate change is not the only global challenge. Eradicating poverty, funding AIDS research, creating financial stability, progressing gender equality, financing biodiversity conservation, and securing peace and security, to name a few, compete for resources and time, notwithstanding the vital contribution each makes to achieving sustainable development and the Millennium Development Goals which climate change itself now potentially threatens.

Writing this book gave us the opportunity to think beyond the immediate demands of COP meetings. Although the achievements of the climate regime are impressive, it is also true to say that nearly all Parties are struggling to implement their commitments, and new challenges seem to emerge faster than older ones can be solved. In this concluding chapter we look to the future and provide comments and suggestions that policy-makers could consider as they address three key challenges that now face the regime: challenges relating to implementation of the Convention and the Protocol, challenges relating to strengthening commitments beyond the current framework, and finally challenges relating to the institutional health of the regime itself.

2   Implementation challenges

The FCCC entered into force in 1994. What progress has the climate change regime made since then in achieving the objective of the Convention – to prevent dangerous anthropogenic interference with the climate system? How should we judge the regime's effectiveness? One focus could be on its ability to produce outputs in the form of COP decisions or the number of countries that have ratified the Kyoto Protocol. Another could be on implementation by key actors and the resulting impact on GHG emission trends. Is the regime making full use of the information generated by the climate regime itself (e.g. national communications)? What indicators and metrics has the regime utilised to check if the behaviour of key actors is changing? These questions underlie many of the policy debates in climate negotiations but are rarely addressed in a coherent and consistent manner across the many relevant COP agenda items.

The climate regime's system of national communications, their in-depth reviews, and the compilation and synthesis documents are an impressive achievement, and huge amounts of effort and time are expended nationally and by the Secretariat to ensure their timely delivery, which, compared to other regimes, is generally very good. But this 'backbone' of the climate regime is at present a vastly underutilised resource. Collectively, the documents generated by the national communications process provide extensive in-depth information on the climate policies of Parties, and factors influencing their successes, failures, challenges and constraints. Yet these documents are subject to only brief and general debate by the SBI in an open plenary faced with a heavy agenda. There are at least two good reasons to engage in a more thorough analysis of national communications and their accompanying documents: first, to find out more about national experiences with tackling climate change around the world in order to learn more about what works, what does not and why; and second, to undertake a review of the overall implementation of the Convention, as indeed the COP is specifically mandated to do. Options to promote a more thorough discussion could include the convening of a series of workshops on specific elements in the national communications, or the establishment of a group of experts who could give detailed consideration to the communications. Both these options, and others, are currently under consideration in the regime.[1]

---

[1] See FCCC/SBI/2002/INF.6, Consideration of the review of national communications from Annex I Parties, paragraph 17.

Recent discussion of methodological work under the Convention and the Proto-col has drawn attention to the fact that much of the information that is generated by the regime is difficult for the regime participants to access for their own analyt-ical and planning purposes. Addressing the information needs of Parties, but also of key economic institutions and the development community, will enhance their capacity to mainstream climate mitigation and adaptation over the coming years. Because mainstreaming climate considerations is a key implementation challenge for the regime, the scope, structure and resources required to provide informa-tion should be accorded higher priority by the COP, particularly if the regime is to encourage those unfamiliar with climate change to become more engaged in climate processes. There are encouraging signs post COP-9 that this is beginning to happen, but making information more accessible costs money. And there are many calls on the regime's budget, particularly due to the current US stance not to fund activities that are in any way related to the Kyoto Protocol, even if these also contribute to efforts to achieve the Convention's objective. Clear ways of monitor-ing whether, and how, the information generated by the regime is being used, and to what effect, would ensure that money is well spent and that such information remains responsive to the needs of all those that need to be involved.

In the final analysis, the regime's success will be judged by whether or not rising GHG emission trends are curbed. But climate policy takes a long time to impact on GHG emissions, so that charting the progress various actors are actually making in switching to less GHG intensive pathways remains an important dimension. A series of tools, or metrics, against which to measure the progress the regime as a whole is making on various key agenda items could assist the COP to understand better how key actors are responding to international climate policy. These tools would not be used to assess the progress made by individual Parties, but rather to track progress made by the collective efforts of all those engaged in the climate regime towards agreed ends. Creating such tools would give the COP a better han-dle on how to assess the strides *the regime has made as a whole* in moving forward in achieving the objective of the Convention. Additionally, these tools and metrics would provide an overarching vision and purpose to the consideration of infor-mation across the regime, generate greater 'buy in' and support implementation of the Convention and the Protocol among a wider range of institutions, espe-cially those supporting carbon-intensive business-as-usual practices which need urgently to move towards low-carbon-emission pathways. Policy-makers could dis-cuss if R & D expenditure in particular technologies, such as renewables, is rising and whether the penetration of existing low-carbon technologies is increasing, where and why. Institutional metrics might include tracking how many coun-tries have been able to establish national climate change offices with a certain percentage of full-time staff; or how many articles about climate change have been published in non-English language natural and social science journals, as this is one way of gauging current and future research and training priorities in developing countries.

The climate regime has been successful in making the business sector and others aware that the future is carbon-constrained by including long-term targets, such as in Article 2 of the Convention, and, in the shorter term, the quantified targets in Article 3 of the Protocol. But the COP now needs a better understanding of why climate policies in various countries are moving at their current speed and what could be done to increase the pace and depth of implementation. Adopting a more actor-orientated perspective, whereby the policy-making community looks at the policy needs and institutional problems actually facing business, might help climate policy-makers understand better, for example, what impact the climate regime is having on project pipelines in the various multilateral institutions. Are they 'greener' than they used to be? Does the climate regime have tools to anticipate and monitor investment trends in GHG emitting sectors or is another UN body doing this already? Is greater use of the analysis undertaken by the OECD Development Assistance Committee on tracking Rio Convention finances possible? And how could this better feed into the regime's financial mechanism, which continues to be under-resourced in relation to the many demands for deepening implementation processes, both from the climate change regime and other international conventions?

These questions are important for understanding, from an institutional perspective, whose behaviour the regime has affected (or failed to), why and by how much. Focusing on the policy needs of various actors is important because it is becoming clear that the legal and policy uncertainties surrounding the climate regime itself – Will the Protocol enter into force? When will the US re-engage in climate abatement? – could be having a more significant effect on business than the scientific uncertainties surrounding climate change. Strategic questions about the progress the regime is making towards the Convention's objectives need to be posed and answered with some regularity to ensure that climate rule-making remains responsive to realities. These types of questions, and devising tools and metrics to assist policy-makers to understand better the impact the regime is having, could form part of the 'standing agenda' for the COP. They could be examined, in particular, by ministers to enable them to chart progress on a regular basis so they are better able to provide strategic guidance to the regime. This would be a good way to ensure that the input of ministers leaves a more indelible imprint on the rules, institutions and procedures of the regime than just a formal summary of their discussions at roundtable forums.

The examination by COP-9 of the synthesis of third national communications and the GHG inventory data from Annex I Parties for 1990–2001 provides a positive example in this regard as, at least to some extent, it successfully achieved a review of implementation of existing commitments by Annex I Parties by delinking this issue from the consideration of future commitments. The COP needs to approach other implementation-related issues, such as policies and measures, in this constructive, non-adversarial fashion. Creating institutional spaces to allow Parties to learn lessons from each other's implementation, to celebrate achievements and also to admit to some failures forms a logical next step, as does the long overdue consideration of the information generated by the IPCC TAR, which COP-9 agreed will form the basis of two new agenda items concerning mitigation and adaptation.

Given the complexity and relative youth of the climate regime, policy-makers have increasingly given greater emphasis to awareness issues and particularly to training future climate personnel, as reflected in the COP-8 Delhi programme of work on Article 6 of the Convention concerning education, training and public awareness. One reason for increased emphasis on training is that the climate change regime has been remarkably successful in spawning a set of sophisticated, generally well-functioning institutions, including a number of specialised bodies, where members must possess high levels of technical knowledge, such as the Executive Board of the CDM, the Article 6 Supervisory Committee and the Compliance Committee, as well as the Expert Group on Technology Transfer and the LDC Expert Group. Training future potential members of all these bodies, including how they might discharge responsibilities to communicate aspects of their work to the constituencies that elected them, is important for enhancing their long-term effectiveness and legitimacy. What kind of training is needed and who should provide it should be considered as part of implementation and under future steps. Because Parties remain sensitive about encroachment on their choice of members, ministers may need to give leadership to insist that training is a criteria for membership and to ensure this is provided by the regime (as will be the case for expert review team members) so that these bodies discharge their functions to the highest standards possible.

The regime's experimentation with allowing limited membership bodies to support and/or oversee implementation also has broader policy implications. The different negotiating histories and mandates of the bodies means that their procedures and practices differ in many ways – this is not necessarily a problem in itself, but it does create confusion as delegates are unsure of how the various bodies operate, or should operate. The debate over the participation of observers and NGOs in these bodies pays testimony to this issue. More thought needs to be given as to whether the procedures of these bodies – where they are not already set out in COP decisions – should be standardised, or whether they should explicitly be permitted to 'go their own way'.

The increasing specialisation of the climate regime, as evidenced by these limited membership bodies, comes at a time when implementation by Parties requires an ever greater understanding of how climate issues impact upon, and in turn can be integrated into, other policy areas. Cooperation with other international organisations and the exploration of synergies and potential conflicts between climate and other policy areas, such as trade, has justifiably risen up the COP policy agenda. Increased knowledge of, and cooperation with, other regimes is obviously a good thing, and something the climate regime needs to invest in after years of conversing and negotiating largely with itself. But after an initial learning phase, agreed objectives and deliverables must emerge from the exploration of synergies. A better understanding of the impacts of prospective conflicts too, such as that between climate change and trade, would be desirable and could initially be promoted through informal discussions on the margins of SB meetings. Increased use of domestic and international legal processes is burgeoning and, where it appears advantageous, it is only a matter of time before countries, companies and individuals sue, or get sued, on climate-related matters. Thus, an understanding of the motivations, possibilities and implications of such actions is of deep interest to all countries, and requires a wide variety of regulatory and judicial bodies to come together. Again, defining the right institutional space for climate policy-makers to reflect upon how broader trends such as this might impact on the COP agenda is part of the institutional challenges facing the regime, as discussed further below.

Finally, another dimension of sharing experiences relevant to implementation is learning by doing. The CDM was intended to be a major channel for learning by doing on the transfer of technology that would help green investment. It was also a market-based mechanism that developing countries themselves devised collectively, with support from the US and other interested delegations, as one concrete way for developing countries to learn how they could contribute to mitigation reductions in a quantified manner while pursuing sustainable development. Emission reductions from CDM projects, coupled with the learning and experimentation generated by the CDM across a wide range of key stakeholders, serves the objective of the Convention as much as it serves the Protocol which, of course, shares that objective. For these reasons, the prompt start of the CDM clearly deserves the full administrative and financial support of all Parties to the Convention.

3   Strengthening commitments

All Parties have agreed that the current commitments of Annex I Parties under the Convention are inadequate. The Kyoto Protocol was the regime's answer to strengthening these commitments. As evidenced by its ratification by more than 120 Parties, and expressions of support from large sections of the business community and civil society, the Protocol remains 'the only show in town'. No country has come forward with an alternative that would command greater international support. Ratification of the Kyoto Protocol by all remaining Annex I Parties would ensure that future multilateral efforts to strengthen commitments beyond those contained in the Convention and the Protocol can commence as swiftly as possible – as they need to if the Convention's objective is to be achieved. But what kind of additional commitments are needed? Whose commitments should be strengthened and over what time-frame? Do we need more targets, flexibility mechanisms and stricter compliance procedures? Does agreement on these issues need to be universal? Should the regime begin to address ways in which it can deal with free-riders? These questions are important, and a large number of side events at COP-9 reported on various initiatives underway to address them, notwithstanding the fact that such issues remain politically too controversial to be accepted onto the formal COP agenda. We do not wish to use this concluding chapter to examine the various suggestions for designing the future architecture of the climate regime, but aim more modestly to highlight concerns that might feed into discussions about next steps.

First, the trend of rising GHG emissions evident from a close examination of national communications indicates that the first priority of Annex I Parties at this juncture is to continue to implement mitigation commitments to modify long-term emissions trends, through domestic action and through the CDM, without waiting for the Protocol to enter into force. A clear commitment to this effect is needed by all Parties – including the ones that are not ratifying the Protocol – because the mitigation commitments of the Convention do not countenance business-as-usual emission trends.

Secondly, the Convention and the Protocol are finely balanced instruments addressing both mitigation and adaptation, with a scientifically justifiable lean towards mitigation that enjoys broad political support. Scientifically, cutting emissions at source is a clear and quantifiable way to tackle climate change in a way that broader goals such as achieving sustainable development or enhancing 'adaptive capacity' are *currently* not. This is not to say that the regime should not be investing in adaptation or trying to achieve sustainable development: it is indeed a fundamental legal tenet that Parties should do both. It is merely to point out that we know what contribution a tonne of carbon *not emitted* makes to tackling climate change better than we know what an additional dollar or euro does to improving the adaptive capacity of the Earth and its people to cope with climate impacts. Research to quantify and measure whether our actions will enhance adaptive capacity, and whether these efforts will be sufficient to cope with climate impacts, including large-scale disruptions, shocks and surprises, is much needed, but current science, backed by the precautionary principle, another foundational regime tenet, requires anticipatory and preventative steps. The recent emphasis on adaptation issues by developing countries does not seek to displace, but simply to reinforce, their historic demand for Annex I Parties to cut domestic emissions to reflect the principle of 'main responsibility' which stresses preventative action by polluters. Understanding the adaptive capacity of ecosystems, and of human societies to cope with climate impacts, will require much greater attention in international climate policy. It is true that some of the implications of Article 2 of the Convention are poorly understood, but many adaptation implications are well understood and have been deliberately misconstrued to justify inaction, particularly in relation to financing of adaptation measures.

Thirdly, one striking feature of the climate regime is the external presentation of the regime by its participants as one based on global cooperation driven by science, as compared with the fractious politics experienced by those within, whereby science routinely plays second fiddle to economic or political considerations. One reason for lack of engagement by some stakeholders is that what is agreed scientifically continues to be misconstrued by private interests – including through the regime's procedures concerning scientific and technical advice as well as media channels. Greater effort is needed to help alert the global, increasingly interconnected, media to the skewed use made of climate science by some regime participants to obfuscate the scientific basis for strengthening commitments. Action by the COP and other stakeholders to get greater, fairer and more ongoing coverage for climate change so that the short-term economic activities of a few US fossil fuel companies and oil-producing countries do not dominate, is vital for supporting activities on education, training and public awareness. This would help create momentum and synergies among a broad spectrum of social actors across and among Parties. Increased public awareness would also support the negotiation and implementation of strengthened commitments in years to come.

A fourth consideration is that, given the fragmented nature of global environmental governance, some of the most important next steps for the climate regime may need to be taken by bodies that are not formally constituted by that regime. Since the 1992 Earth Summit, sustainable development has become a powerful emerging legal concept increasingly accepted as the overarching framework for the aspirations of the international community. Its precise implementation is subject to evolving state practice and will always be context-specific, but at its core sustainable development requires integration of environmental protection in economic and social policy. However, too many international institutions, and national ones, still treat the environment and development separately. Certainly, searching questions have to be asked by the governing bodies of key economic institutions as to why their contribution to addressing climate change remains so modest. For integration to take place, it is these institutions, and those who work within them, that have to be more engaged in the climate regime, and this includes having a say in its future design. Part of the explanation for the modest level of interest may lie in the fact that the climate change regime has been engaged in an intensive cycle of rule development, leaving little time to connect to non-climate change epistemic and policy-making communities. Because strengthening commitments will require climate change to be mainstreamed to a much larger extent, tools and methodologies are urgently needed to engage the development community in climate issues and actively seek their assistance in the design of the future climate regime.

A final consideration that is foundational to possible next steps is how the climate regime measures and assesses the contribution each country and various sectors and stakeholders make, or ought to make, to the global effort. The US is currently focusing much of its effort on long-term R & D. This is a critical component for developing carbon-free pathways but, unless accompanied by actual mitigation actions, US climate policy will shift the risks of coping with climate impacts for others to face. Could we live in a world where some Parties choose to direct their resources into risky, long-term R & D investments, developing, for example, sequestration technologies, whilst others focus on more immediate reductions as a sort of international division of labour or burden-sharing? The question is political, but again finding the institutional space in which it can be examined on its merits in a transparent and legitimate manner requires further thought.

The institutional and procedural experience of the negotiations leading to the Kyoto Protocol might be useful here, as defining the nature and commensurability of Annex I mitigation commitments was a central task. Annex I countries form a cohesive group with strong economies, robust political and administrative institutions and increasingly interconnected and shared cultures. These big picture factors explain why, notwithstanding the diversity of their individual circumstances, each country eventually accepted legally binding *quantitative* targets, voluntarily assumed, as a sensible approach to creating a stable and transparent international architecture for global cooperation. The imminent implementation of an emissions trading scheme across most of Europe, of a kind first proposed by the US, is also evidence that policy differences (emissions trading versus taxes/policies and measures) that seemed insuperable can, with the benefit of mutual learning and reflection, dissipate – and to good effect.

Substantive progress will be more likely if countries first understand the underlying reasons behind the existing stalemate on future next steps. Additionally, seeing fellow negotiators as regulatory *counterparts* – rather than as political adversaries – would enable countries to formulate new, constructive questions, rather than articulate demands that favour entrenched negativities.

Seeing things through the lens of existing political formations is problematic in climate change because these groupings poorly match the functional and policy cleavages that actually exist. On flexibility mechanisms, sinks, targets, compliance and pretty much every other major policy choice facing the regime, interests and alliances cut across the North/South and Annex I/non-Annex I divide, with enthusiasts and laggards in every bloc, and many cases where countries feel they do not quite fit into any bloc. A training-based initiative focused on building the capacity of regulatory counterparts could be a means of enhancing mutual understanding of national circumstances and building functional relationships that allow participants to speak to each other as colleagues engaged in a joint venture, instead of opponents from different camps. Such an initiative might help with future work on a key issue: what metric(s) capture the efforts made by countries with divergent capabilities and responsibilities? Answering this is critical, because, unlike the relatively cohesive Annex I group, non-Annex I Parties have very diverse social, economic and political circumstances and cultures, calling for bespoke solutions rather than 'off the peg' solutions. Although there is some analytical work on what kind of additional steps might be undertaken by developing countries, a great deal of this (though by no means all) has been conceptualised in the North, largely in response to political problems facing Annex I policy-makers. There is an urgent need for broader groupings of researchers, particularly from the South, to take the lead in conceptualising future next steps, and to scrutinise and challenge methodological, technological and political assumptions in response to realities on the ground.

Finally, a full analysis of the institutional and procedural 'lessons learnt' from the negotiation of the Kyoto Protocol, its subsequent rejection by the US and tardy ratification by the Russian Federation, would also help. There is no reason to suppose that the top-down approach to setting international commitments that failed to engage stakeholders and the public in the US on the key issue of what it was actually willing to deliver, will be any more successful if applied to other countries where the current level of public and political engagement with climate change is still low. Substantively, the wealth of proposals submitted as possible future next steps during the negotiations on the Kyoto Protocol should be revisited to assess what insight the adoption of some, and rejection of others, might generate for the future steps the regime is now beginning to consider. Because efforts to prepare for the review of Annex I Parties' mitigation commitments commenced almost as soon as the Convention was adopted in 1992, it is more accurate to say that the process that culminated in the Kyoto Protocol actually took five years. Add the six years we have spent since completing its unfinished business, only for its entry into force now to hang in the balance in the hands of the two largest emitters in Annex I, and you have some compelling reasons to ask whether launching something similar to the Berlin Mandate is seriously the best institutional and procedural form we can now imagine for discussing future next steps. Instead of focusing efforts on launching a poorly institutionalised 'next round' in the interest of speed, we suggest ministers and policy-makers make use of this relative 'pause' in climate negotiations to think through more deeply the institutional, procedural and substantive aspects of future negotiations on new commitments. We present some thoughts about how this might be achieved, and the kinds of issues that might be discussed, below.

4   Institutional challenges and beyond

Some may be puzzled that in addressing the future we have given the last word to institutional issues. This is simply because we believe the ultimate direction in which we are heading is important, but so too is the institutional framework needed to get us there. The two are related, and neglecting one to the exclusion of the other would be imprudent. Yet, in our view, institutional issues tend to receive much less attention from policy-makers, who are often too preoccupied with finding the right solution to think much about the process of generating agreements. For this reason, we have emphasised here that this current phase of the climate change process might be used to good effect to conduct a wide-ranging review of the institutional machinery of the regime. Such a review might include some of the suggestions outlined above, including, for example, dealing with national communications in a different way and utilising the presence of ministers to provide the climate regime with more strategic and proactive guidance.

The potential for adverse climate impacts means a more profound review of the financial, institutional and technical infrastructure of the regime than the current structure of the COP agenda may allow. Enhancing adaptive capacity may, for example, require a radical rethink of present modalities for delivering climate adaptation finance within the context of broader changes to the international financial architecture. Creating appropriate institutional policy spaces to discuss strategic choices about how international resources can best be channelled to support adaptation – the bulk of which will be small-scale and inherently unreplicable – will be critical, particularly against the backdrop of diversion of aid to reconstruct other parts of the world. The articulation of developing country needs and service delivery by the Convention's financial machinery have improved, but existing channels of communication, formalised by COP guidance to the GEF, may need strengthening to ensure that new channels, such as the Marrakesh Funds, enhance support for adaptation without imposing additional transactions costs and procedural complexity. Additionally, ideas such as upstream coordination of donors may help reduce transaction costs associated with the increased proliferation of donors/funds in the climate regime without a consequent increase in the total amount of resources available.

How to meet the constantly evolving scientific information needs of the regime is another area where serious institutional reconsideration is needed. While the IPCC has done an admirable job of supplying analysis on climate change issues to the regime, it operates within the confines of its mandate and procedures, which makes it difficult for it to respond quickly (e.g. within one or two SB sessions) to requests for information, to proactively identify knowledge gaps and emerging issues, or to present accessible and relevant policy-related analysis on socio-economic issues. Of course, the IPCC's mandate and mode of operation could be adjusted for it to meet these challenges better, while the FCCC roster of experts could also be used more fully as a means of providing rapid expertise to the climate change regime. Other options include requesting and relying more on Secretariat input, which would require an acceptance of less guarded and rigidly non-committal analysis from this source. The financial implications of the 'arm's length' relationship between the climate regime and components of the scientific infrastructure that supports it, such as GCOS, are part of this challenge. These issues require a thorough institutional examination of the 'mediation' by SBSTA of the scientific information generated by the IPCC and other bodies to make this more effective, particularly as COP-9 has now sanctioned discussions of the implications of the TAR for mitigation and adaptation.

Another important concern is for the 'health' of the Trust Fund for Participation, which finances attendance by one or two delegates from eligible countries to sessions of the COP, SBs and some other meetings. At a time when developing countries are being asked to consider further steps and deeper engagement, the Fund looks increasingly low. The current system, whereby (mostly Annex II) countries pledge money on an ad hoc basis, is unpredictable, so that neither the Secretariat nor developing country/EIT Parties themselves can be sure that funding will be available to finance the participation of their delegates. The fact that money received by the Trust Fund has been declining over the years, and that, for the first time in many years, insufficient funds were available to fund eligible participants at SB-18, is a deeply troubling cross-cutting issue that the COP needs urgently to fix. We recommend an urgent review of the modalities for replenishment of the Trust Fund, with Parties being invited to submit views on how funding could be better arranged to provide the continuity that is often absent from many developing country delegations. Participation funds could become part of the core budget, or another option might be for each developing country to be made a 'budget holder' of a certain amount of funds that would cover a three-to-five-year cycle of meetings, to ensure continuity, enhance advance planning and reduce donor transaction costs.

Further initial questions that could be addressed as part of a review of the institutional machinery of the regime include:

- Does an annual COP, or an annual high-level segment, best serve the needs of the regime? And how can ministers make a more effective contribution?
- Does the proliferation of workshops really help to advance the work of the regime? If so, could the procedures for holding workshops (including funding for eligible participants) be usefully standardised, so that, whenever a workshop is convened, the general arrangements are understood by all?
- Could the Bureau be given a greater mandate to take procedural decisions, and should its work be made more transparent (e.g. through publication of minutes of its meetings/decisions)?
- Do *all* issues on the agenda really need to be addressed at each COP? Where the pace of developments is less than one year, an alternative might be to develop a three (or more) year plan, identifying 'themes' and issues to be covered for each COP session over that period. This would enable issues to be addressed in more depth, and might also help with establishing linkages for cross-cutting matters, such as finance.

Some regimes, notably the CBD, have reviewed their institutional arrangements with a view to improving their efficacy. And it may well turn out that there is no need for major changes to the climate change regime's machinery for now. After all, the survival of the climate regime in the face of its predicted demise bears witness to its underlying resilience and dynamism which is rooted in shared values, a commitment to multilateral solutions to solve global challenges and a problem-solving ethos, qualities which bode well for the turbulent future that lies ahead. But at least such a review would provide an opportunity for all involved in the regime to reassure themselves that the current institutional structures and procedures are the ones that best suit their needs. The formal discussions and side events at COP-9 indicated different political views about the short- to medium-term role of the Convention, ranging from those who see its role at this juncture as facilitating information-sharing and bottom-up exchanges of practical experiences, to those who see it as a top-down forum for designing mitigation and other commitments. Thus the expectations and approaches negotiators bring to the table affect how questions relating to the effectiveness of climate institutions will be addressed. The debates over what to include and exclude on the COP agenda demonstrate that procedural and institutional issues are also laced with values and political choices. The politicisation of certain items on the COP agenda, decried by some, is simply evidence that political differences exist and these must be resolved if more substantive results are to be achieved. Creating institutional processes which help policy-makers understand the reasons for these political differences will help foster compromises based on workable solutions. The increased reliance placed on informal meetings and side events, as witnessed at COP-8 and COP-9, suggests the regime is following parallel tracks – an official process and an unofficial process, with the latter picking up on issues that are too controversial for the official agenda. In the long term, however, new types of meetings with broader representation can also be imagined to ensure a large input into this agenda-setting stage of negotiations which often sets the expectations and framework for what is to come.

We believe there is certainly scope for 'fine tuning' the institutional machinery of the climate regime. To this end, we have emphasised a number of areas where new thinking is required and for which it may be wise to construct new policy spaces where those interested in the climate change regime can meet and talk honestly about what the world might look like if we venture beyond the current framework. At the very least, such institutional learning could yield observations, insights and anecdotes to enrich, guide and amuse the next generation of climate negotiators who will, of course, write the next chapter of the climate story.

Appendix I
List of Parties, their groups and key statistics

Party	GDP per capita 2000 (US$)[1]	Total CO$_2$ emissions 2000[2]	CO$_2$ emissions per capita 2000[2]	CO$_2$ emissions per unit of GDP[3] (kg CO$_2$/ 1995 US$) 2000	FCCC Annex	UN regional group for purposes of climate change regime[4]	UN list[5]	Other main international group[6]	Other climate change group
Afghanistan	100	247	0.01	–[7]	NAI	Asia	LDC	G-77	
Albania	1,197	780	0.25	0.99	NAI	CEE			CACAM
Algeria	1,663	24,404	0.80	1.36	NAI	Africa		G-77 – OPEC	
Angola	590	1,747	0.13	0.68	NAI	Africa	LDC	G-77	
Antigua & Barbuda	10,204	96	1.48	–	NAI	GRULAC	SIDS	G-77 – AOSIS	
Argentina	7,678	37,715	1.02	0.44	NAI	GRULAC		G-77	
Armenia	506	958	0.25	0.96	NAI	CEE			CACAM
Australia	20,298	94,094	4.91	0.73	AI/AII	WEOG		OECD	Umbrella
Austria	23,357	16,607	2.05	0.24	AI/AII	WEOG		OECD – EU	
Azerbaijan	655	7,926	0.99	6.94	NAI	CEE			
Bahamas	14,147	490	1.62	–	NAI	GRULAC	SIDS	G-77 – AOSIS	
Bahrain	9,929	5,322	7.70	1.96	NAI	Asia		G-77	
Bangladesh	362	7,984	0.06	0.55	NAI	Asia	LDC	G-77	
Barbados	9,721	321	1.20	–	NAI	GRULAC	SIDS	G-77 – AOSIS	
Belarus	1,022	16,144	1.61	2.01	AI/EIT[8]	CEE			
Belgium	22,323	27,905	2.72	0.38	AI/AII	WEOG		OECD – EU	
Belize	3,345	213	0.85	–	NAI	GRULAC		G-77 – AOSIS	
Benin	349	442	0.07	0.55	NAI	Africa	LDC	G-77	

Bhutan	232	108	–	NAI	Asia	LDC	G-77	
Bolivia	995	3,020	0.96	NAI	GRULAC		G-77	
Bosnia & Herzegovina	1,074	5,254	2.53	NAI	CEE		G-77	OBG
Botswana	3,225	1,051	–	NAI	Africa		G-77	
Brazil	3,484	83,930	0.38	NAI	GRULAC		G-77	
Bulgaria	1,508	11,556	3.48	AI/EIT	CEE			CG
Burkina Faso	204	281	–	NAI	Africa	LDC	G-77	
Burundi	124	66	–	NAI	Africa	LDC	G-77	
Cambodia	237	145	–	NAI	Asia	LDC	G-77	
Cameroon	626	1,785	0.28	NAI	Africa		G-77	
Canada	22,778	118,957	3.87	AI/AII	WEOG	OECD	OECD	Umbrella
Cape Verde	1,299	38	0.75	NAI	Africa	LDC, SIDS	G-77 – AOSIS	
Central African Rep.	241	74	0.02	NAI	Africa	LDC	G-77	

[1] Source: Statistics Division of the UN Secretariat and International Labour Office. Updated data available at http://unstats.org.

[2] CO_2 emissions from fossil-fuel burning, cement production and gas flaring. Total CO_2 emissions are expressed in thousand metric tons of carbon (not CO_2). National per capita estimates are expressed in metric tons of carbon. From the Carbon Dioxide Information Analysis Centre (CDIAC), Source: G. Marland, T. Boden and B. Andres (2002), Global, Regional and National Fossil Fuel CO_2 emissions. Updated data available at http://cdiac.esd.ornl.gov/.

[3] Source: International Energy Agency (IEA), Key World Energy Statistics, 2002 edition. Updated data available at www.iea.org. CO_2 emissions from fossil fuel consumption, calculated using IEA's energy balances and the Revised IPCC 1996 guidelines (see chapter 11).

[4] Source: www.staff.city.ac.uk/p.willetts/UN/UN-GRPS/doc; and FCCC Secretariat.

[5] Source: www.unctad.org; www.sidsnet.org/sids_list.html.

[6] Source: www.g 77.org; www.sidsnet.org/aosis; FCCC Secretariat.

[7] '–' indicates data unavailable from this source.

[8] Belarus is not listed in Annex B to the Kyoto Protocol as it was not a Party to the Convention when the Kyoto Protocol was adopted.

Appendix I (cont.)

Party	GDP per capita 2000 (US$)	Total CO₂ emissions 2000	CO₂ emissions per capita 2000	CO₂ emissions per unit of GDP (kg CO₂/ 1995 US$) 2000	FCCC Annex	UN regional group for purposes of climate change regime	UN list	Other main international group	Other climate change group
Chad	112	34	0	–	NAI	Africa	LDC	G-77	
Chile	4,669	16,239	1.07	0.59	NAI	GRULAC		G-77	
China[9]	866	761,586	0.60	2.88	NAI	Asia		Associate G-77	
Colombia	1,930	15,955	0.38	0.59	NAI	GRULAC		G-77	
Comoros	248	22	0.03	–	NAI	Africa	LDC, SIDS	G-77 – AOSIS	
Congo	1,005	494	0.16	0.23	NAI	Africa		G-77	
Cook Islands	3,975	8	0.42	–	NAI	Asia	SIDS	AOSIS	
Costa Rica	3,964	1,480	0.39	0.31	NAI	GRULAC		G-77	
Cote d'Ivoire	668	2,859	0.17	0.53	NAI	Africa		G-77	
Croatia	4,089	5,344	1.22	0.79	AI/EIT	CEE			CG
Cuba	2,384	8,437	0.75	1.15	NAI	GRULAC		G-77 – AOSIS	
Cyprus	11,231	1,753	2.32	0.59	NAI	Asia		G-77 – AOSIS – EU	
Czech Republic	4,942	32,416	3.16	2.18	AI/EIT	CEE		OECD – EU	
DPR Korea	540	51,544	2.31	20.14	NAI	Asia		G-77	
DR of the Congo	129	745	0.01	0.44	NAI	Africa	LDC	G-77	
Denmark	30,141	12,174	2.28	0.24	AI/AII	WEOG		OECD – EU	
Djibouti	847	105	0.17	–	NAI	Africa	LDC	G-77	
Dominica	3,803	28	0.38	–	NAI	GRULAC	SIDS	G-77 – AOSIS	

Country									
Dominican Republic	2,982	6,859	0.81	1.03	NAI	GRULAC	SIDS	G-77	
Ecuador	1,088	6,946	0.55	0.95	NAI	GRULAC		G-77	
Egypt	1,355	38,817	0.61	1.38	NAI	Africa		G-77	
El Salvador	2,103	1,819	0.29	0.48	NAI	GRULAC		G-77	
Equatorial Guinea	2,628	56	0.12	–	NAI	Africa	LDC	G-77	
Eritrea	202	166	0.05	0.93	NAI	Africa	LDC	G-77	
Estonia	3,569	4,367	3.19	2.31	AI/EIT	CEE		EU	
Ethiopia	102	1,522	0.03	0.43	NAI	Africa	LDC	G-77	
EC	n/a	n/a	n/a	–	AI/AII	n/a[10]		OECD – EU	
Fiji	2,031	198	0.24	–	NAI	Asia	SIDS	G-77 – AOSIS	
Finland	23,377	14,582	2.82	0.33	AI/AII	WEOG		OECD – EU	
FYR Macedonia	1,641	3,053	1.50	1.64	NAI	CEE			OBG
France	21,848	98,917	1.68	0.21	AI/AII	WEOG		OECD – EU	
Gabon	3,988	955	0.79	0.25	NAI	Africa		G-77	
Gambia	311	74	0.05	–	NAI	Africa	LDC	G-77	
Georgia	573	1,684	0.32	2.41	NAI	CEE			CACAM
Germany	22,753	214,386	2.61	0.31	AI/AII	WEOG		OECD – EU	
Ghana	251	1,609	0.09	0.59	NAI	Africa		G-77	
Greece	10,680	24,455	2.44	0.63	AI/AII	WEOG		OECD – EU	
Grenada	4,391	58	0.57	–	NAI	GRULAC	SIDS	G-77 – AOSIS	
Guatemala	1,659	2,698	0.24	0.50	NAI	GRULAC		G-77	

[9] Entries refer to mainland China only.

[10] The EC is not a UN member but, along with several other intergovernmental entities, has a standing invitation to participate as an observer in the General Assembly and maintains a permanent office at Headquarters.

Appendix I (cont.)

Party	GDP per capita 2000 (US$)	Total CO$_2$ emissions 2000	CO$_2$ emissions per capita 2000	CO$_2$ emissions per unit of GDP (kg CO$_2$/1995 US$) 2000	FCCC Annex	UN regional group for purposes of climate change regime	UN list	Other main international group	Other climate change group
Guinea	397	353	0.04	–	NAI	Africa	LDC	G-77	
Guinea-Bissau	279	72	0.06	–	NAI	Africa	LDC	G-77 – AOSIS	
Guyana	846	436	0.57	–	NAI	GRULAC		G-77 – AOSIS	
Haiti	432	388	0.05	0.48	NAI	GRULAC	LDC, SIDS	G-77 – AOSIS	
Honduras	919	1,307	0.20	0.97	NAI	GRULAC		G-77	
Hungary	4,649	14,782	1.47	1.01	AI/EIT	CEE		OECD – EU	
Iceland	30,681	589	2.10	0.25	AI/AII	WEOG		OECD	Umbrella
India	476	292,265	0.29	2.01	NAI	Asia		G-77	
Indonesia	723	73,572	0.35	1.29	NAI	Asia		G-77 – OPEC	
Iran	4,690	84,689	1.33	2.78	NAI	Asia		G-77 – OPEC	
Ireland	25,066	11,527	3.04	0.39	AI/AII	WEOG		OECD – EU	
Israel	19,521	17,221	2.85	0.59	NAI	WEOG			
Italy	18,653	116,859	2.02	0.35	AI/AII	WEOG		OECD – EU	
Jamaica	2,801	2,942	1.12	2.08	NAI	GRULAC	SIDS	G-77 – AOSIS	
Japan	37,494	323,281	2.55	0.20	AI/AII	Asia		OECD	Umbrella
Jordan	1,556	4,244	0.86	1.81	NAI	Asia		G-77	
Kazakhstan	1,129	33,099	2.22	5.46	NAI[11]	Asia			CACAM
Kenya	342	2,553	0.08	0.94	NAI	Africa		G-77	
Kiribati	531	7	0.08	–	NAI	Asia	LDC, SIDS	G-77	AOSIS

Party								
Kuwait	19,871	13,070	5.97	2.33	NAI	Asia		G-77 – OPEC
Kyrgyzstan	265	1,266	0.26	1.05	NAI	Asia		G-77
Lao PDR	324	113	0.02	–	NAI	Asia	LDC	G-77
Latvia	2,952	1,635	0.67	1.06	AI/EIT	CEE		EU
Lebanon	4,788	4,138	1.18	1.13	NAI	Asia		G-77
Lesotho	448	–	–	–	NAI	Africa	LDC	G-77
Liberia	247	109	0.04	–	NAI	Africa	LDC	G-77
Libya	5,667	15,591	2.95	1.14	NAI	Africa		G-77 – OPEC
Liechtenstein	33,394	–	–	–	AI	WEOG		
Lithuania	3,039	3,239	0.88	1.48	AI/EIT	CEE		EU
Luxembourg	43,372	2,315	5.31	0.33	AI/AII	WEOG		OECD – EU
Madagascar	249	619	0.04	–	NAI	Africa	LDC	G-77
Malawi	141	209	0.02	–	NAI	Africa	LDC	G-77
Malaysia	4,035	39,414	1.69	0.95	NAI	Asia		G-77
Maldives	1,985	136	0.50	–	NAI	Asia	LDC, SIDS	G-77 – AOSIS
Mali	230	152	0.01	–	NAI	Africa	LDC	G-77
Malta	9,069	768	1.96	0.57	NAI	WEOG		G-77 – AOSIS – EU
Marshall Islands	1,925	–	–	–	NAI	Asia	SIDS	G-77 – AOSIS
Mauritania	296	838	0.31	–	NAI	Africa	LDC	G-77
Mauritius	3,886	790	0.67	–	NAI	Africa	SIDS	G-77 – AOSIS
Mexico	5,805	115,713	1.19	0.96	NAI	GRULAC		OECD
Micronesia	1,934	–	–	–	NAI	Asia	SIDS	G-77 – AOSIS
Monaco[12]	21,848	–	–	–	AI	WEOG		EIG

[11] Kazakhstan will be an Annex I Party for the purposes of the Kyoto Protocol, but not for the Convention.

[12] Included in figures for France for total emissions and emissions per capita.

Appendix I (cont.)

Party	GDP per capita 2000 (US$)	Total CO_2 emissions 2000	CO_2 emissions per capita 2000	CO_2 emissions per unit of GDP (kg CO_2/ 1995 US$) 2000	FCCC Annex	UN regional group for purposes of climate change regime	UN list	Other main international group	Other climate change group
Mongolia	391	2,046	0.86	–	NAI	Asia		G-77	
Morocco	1,101	9,975	0.35	0.74	NAI	Africa		G-77	
Mozambique	195	322	0.02	0.35	NAI	Africa	LDC	G-77	
Myanmar	726	2,497	0.05	0.60	NAI	Asia	LDC	G-77	
Namibia	1,981	497	0.27	0.44	NAI	Africa		G-77	
Nauru	2,533	37	3.07	–	NAI	Asia	SIDS	AOSIS	
Nepal	230	928	0.04	0.54	NAI	Asia	LDC	G-77	
Netherlands	23,294	37,900	2.39	0.36	AI/AII	WEOG		OECD – EU	
New Zealand	13,441	8,752	2.28	0.46	AI/AII	WEOG		OECD	Umbrella
Nicaragua	478	1,020	0.20	1.49	NAI	GRULAC		G-77	
Niger	170	323	0.03	–	NAI	Africa	LDC	G-77	
Nigeria	244	9,866	0.09	1.35	NAI	Africa		G-77 – OPEC	
Niue	–	1	0.42	–	NAI	Asia	SIDS	AOSIS	
Norway	36,198	13,623	3.03	0.20	AI/AII	WEOG		OECD	Umbrella
Oman	7,811	5,397	2.25	1.65	NAI	Asia		G-77	
Pakistan	458	28,604	0.21	1.38	NAI	Asia		G-77	
Palau	6,163	66	3.48	–	NAI	Asia	SIDS	G-77 – AOSIS	
Panama	3,508	1,729	0.61	0.52	NAI	GRULAC		G-77	
Papua New Guinea	710	662	0.14	–	NAI	Asia	SIDS	G-77 – AOSIS	
Paraguay	1,405	999	0.18	0.35	NAI	GRULAC		G-77	

Peru	2,085	8,063	0.31	0.43	NAI	GRULAC		G-77	
Philippines	988	21,160	0.28	0.78	NAI	Asia		G-77	
Poland	4,082	82,245	2.13	1.79	AI/EIT	CEE		OECD – EU	
Portugal	10,603	16,330	1.63	0.46	AI/AII	WEOG		OECD – EU	
Qatar	29,100	11,104	19.65	3.04	NAI	Asia		G-77 – OPEC	
Republic of Korea	9,782	116,543	2.47	0.70	NAI	Asia		OECD	EIG
Republic of Moldova	299	1,793	0.49	2.35	NAI	CEE			CACAM
Romania	1,635	23,548	1.05	2.64	AI/EIT	CEE		G-77	CG
Russian Federation	1,726	391,664	2.69	4.21	AI/EIT	CEE			Umbrella
Rwanda	187	156	0.02	–	NAI	Africa	LDC	G-77	
St Kitts & Nevis	8,539	28	0.69	–	NAI	GRULAC	SIDS	G-77 – AOSIS	
St Lucia	4,735	92	0.62	–	NAI	GRULAC	SIDS	G-77 – AOSIS	
St Vincent & Grenadines	3,021	46	0.41	–	NAI	GRULAC	SIDS	G-77 – AOSIS	
Samoa	1,419	38	0.22	–	NAI	Asia	LDC, SIDS	G-77 – AOSIS	
San Marino[13]	18,653	–	–	–	NAI	WEOG			
Sao Tome & Principe	336	24	0.18	–	NAI	Africa	LDC, SIDS	G-77 – AOSIS	
Saudi Arabia	8,309	102,168	4.77	1.87	NAI	Asia		G-77 – OPEC	
Senegal	468	1,140	0.12	0.62	NAI	Africa	LDC	G-77	

[13] Included in figures for Italy for total emissions and emissions per capita.

Appendix I (*cont.*)

Party	GDP per capita 2000 (US$)	Total CO$_2$ emissions 2000	CO$_2$ emissions per capita 2000	CO$_2$ emissions per unit of GDP (kg CO$_2$/ 1995 US$) 2000	FCCC Annex	UN regional group for purposes of climate change regime	UN list	Other main international group	Other climate change group
Serbia & Montenegro[14]	1,094	11,399	1.07	3.27	NAI	CEE			OBG
Seychelles	7,272	62	0.76	–	NAI	Africa	SIDS	G-77 – AOSIS	
Sierra Leone	142	154	0.04	–	NAI	Africa	LDC	G-77	
Singapore	22,959	16,115	3.90	0.37	NAI	Asia		G-77 – AOSIS	
Slovakia	3,570	9,663	1.79	1.68	AI/EIT	CEE		OECD – EU	
Slovenia	9,118	3,986	2.01	0.62	AI/EIT	CEE		EU	
Solomon Islands	598	45	0.10	–	NAI	Asia	LDC, SIDS	G-77 – AOSIS	
South Africa	2,954	89,323	2.04	1.73	NAI	Africa		G-77	
Spain	14,054	77,220	1.95	0.40	AI/AII	WEOG		OECD – EU	
Sri Lanka	854	2,779	0.14	0.65	NAI	Asia		G-77	
Sudan	353	1425	0.05	0.58	NAI	Africa	LDC	G-77	
Suriname	1,584	578	1.33	–	NAI	GRULAC		G-77 – AOSIS	
Swaziland	1,507	104	0.11	–	NAI	Africa		G-77	
Sweden	25,903	12,812	1.44	0.19	AI/AII	WEOG		OECD – EU	
Switzerland	33,394	10,660	1.46	0.12	AI/AII	WEOG		OECD	EIG
Syria	2,702	14,789	0.91	3.85	NAI	Asia		G-77	
Tajikistan	143	1,084	0.18	1.86	NAI	Asia			
Tanzania	210	1175	0.03	0.24	NAI	Africa	LDC	G-77	
Thailand	1,945	54,216	0.87	0.86	NAI	Asia		G-77	
Togo	306	490	0.11	0.85	NAI	Africa	LDC	G-77	

Tonga	1,460	33	0.33	–	NAI	Asia	SIDS	G-77 – AOSIS	
Trinidad & Tobago	6,239	7,195	5.58	2.27	NAI	GRULAC	SIDS	G-77 – AOSIS	
Tunisia	2,058	5,020	0.53	0.75	NAI	Africa		G-77	
Turkey	2,998	60,468	0.93	1.00	AI	Asia		OECD	
Turkmenistan	934	9,441	1.99	4.78	NAI	Asia		G-77	CACAM
Tuvalu	1,491	–	–	–	NAI	Asia	LDC, SIDS	AOSIS	
Uganda	257	416	0.02	–	NAI	Africa	LDC	G-77	
Ukraine	639	93,551	1.89	6.79	AI/EIT	CEE		G-77	Umbrella
United Arab Emirates	20,457	16,079	6.17	1.39	NAI	Asia		G-77 – OPEC	
UK	24,058	154,979	2.59	0.41	AI/AII	WEOG		OECD – EU	
US	34,637	1,528,796	5.40	0.63	AI/AII	WEOG		OECD	Umbrella
Uruguay	6,009	1,476	0.44	0.26	NAI	GRULAC		G-77	
Uzbekistan	543	32,376	1.31	9.57	NAI	Asia		G-77	CACAM
Vanuatu	1,140	22	0.11	–	NAI	Asia	LDC, SIDS	G-77 – AOSIS	
Venezuela	5,017	43,054	1.78	1.61	NAI	GRULAC		G-77 – OPEC	
Vietnam	401	15,683	0.20	1.46	NAI	Asia		G-77	
Yemen	465	2,303	0.13	1.67	NAI	Asia	LDC	G-77	
Zambia	336	498	0.05	0.43	NAI	Africa	LDC	G-77	
Zimbabwe	572	4,040	0.32	1.71	NAI	Africa		G-77	

[14] Known as the Federal Republic of Yugoslavia until February 2003.

Appendix II
Annex I Party fact sheets: emissions, targets and projections for Annex I Parties and groupings

MALTE MEINSHAUSEN, ETH ZURICH

This appendix sets out information about Annex I Parties' GHG emissions, including whether each Party has achieved the 'stabilisation aim' under the FCCC and is likely to achieve its quantified commitments under the Kyoto Protocol. It also sets out such information for a number of Annex I Party groupings such as Annex I, Annex II, the EU-15/25, EITs and JUSSCANNZ. Further information about these fact sheets, including periodic updates, can be obtained from the Institute of Development Studies website: www.ids.ac.uk/ids/env/climatechange.html.

Prepared by Malte Meinshausen, Swiss Federal Institute of Technology, ETH Zurich, 8092 Zurich, Switzerland. The author is particularly thankful to Bill Hare for joint work on an earlier database, Jeroen Peters and Jos Olivier for providing the EDGAR data, James Grabert for his help with the FCCC data and Fiona Koza for editing support. Any remaining errors remain, of course, with the author. This data compendium can be referenced as M. Meinshausen, "Emissions, Targets and Projections for Annex I Parties", in F. Yamin and J. Depledge, *The International Climate Change Regime: A Guide to Rules, Institutions and Procedures* (Cambridge, Cambridge University Press, 2004).

Explanatory notes for the fact sheets

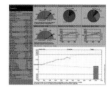

Past emissions, projections and targets

Key data in relation to the Kyoto Protocol targets is compiled in this graph. Available inventory data for Annex A emissions is given from 1990 until the latest inventory year as a percentage of base year emissions. Projections, if available, are displayed from 2000 to 2010 ('with measures' (orange dotted line); 'with additional measures' (orange dashed line)). Note that the projection base in the year 2000 might be inconsistent with year 2000 inventory data. Furthermore, the 'allowed emissions' are displayed for the period 2008–2012 as well as any categories of 'Sink Allowances' and the 'Single Project Exemption', if applicable. A linear interpolation between base year emissions (assumed in 1990) and 'Kyoto targets' (thin blue dotted line) puts the current emission trends into perspective and indicates whether countries' emissions are 'on track' to meet the Kyoto Protocol commitments. The colour code of the bar chart is given in the table on the left. Since any net emissions from afforestation and deforestation activities (denoted by '-' in the table on the left) can be fully compensated by removals related to forest management (see 'For.Mng.II'), both sink categories are consequently not displayed in the case of net emissions under Art. 3.3.

Base year

Base years for emissions under the Kyoto Protocol for carbon dioxide (CO_2), methane (CH_4), nitrous oxide (N_2O) and fluorinated gases (HFCs, PFCs and SF_6).

- CO_2, CH_4, N_2O: The base year is 1990 with the following exceptions: Bulgaria (1988), Hungary (1985–1987), Poland (1988), Romania (1989) and Slovenia (1986).
- *HFCs, PFCs, SF_6*: The base year is 1990 (with the same exceptions as for CO_2, CH_4, N_2O), or 1995 if a Party prefers (KP Article 3.8). In these fact sheets, it is assumed that 1995 is chosen, if (a) the GWP-weighted sum of fluorinated gas emissions was higher in 1995, or (b) no fluorinated gas emissions were reported for 1990. Parties must make their choice by 1 January 2007. See chapter 11.

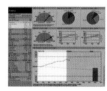

Emissions

Greenhouse gas emissions from gases and sources as in Annex A of the Kyoto Protocol. Not included in Annex A are emissions or removals from LULUCF activities (except some agricultural sources) and emissions from international marine transport and aviation (bunker fuels). *Units*: Million tonnes of carbon dioxide equivalent per year ($MtCO_2e/yr$), using GWPs in accordance with Decision 2/CP.3 ("1995 IPCC GWP values"). Emissions are also given as a percentage of base year (B.Yr.) emissions.

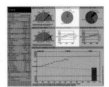

Emissions by gas

The pie charts display the relative share of CO_2, CH_4, N_2O and fluorinated gases (sum of HFCs, PFCs, and SF_6 weighted by GWPs) of Annex A emissions in the year 2000. In the trend chart, emissions of Annex A gases from 1990 until the latest inventory year are displayed as a percentage of their respective base year emissions.

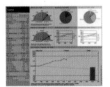

Emissions by sector

The pie charts display the relative share of total Annex A emissions in the year 2000, broken down by sector. The sectors are energy (without transport) (ENE), transport (TRA), industrial processes (IND), solvents and other product use (SOL), agriculture (AGR) and waste (WAS), according to the Revised 1996 IPCC Reporting Guidelines. In the trend chart, emissions by Annex A sectors from 1990 until the latest inventory year are displayed as a percentage of their respective base year emissions.

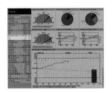

LULUCF

Net removals by LULUCF for years 1990 and 2000. LULUCF emissions comprise the following emission categories: 'Changes in Forest and Other Woody Biomass Stocks', 'Forest and Grassland Conversion', 'Abandonment of Managed Lands' and 'CO_2 Emissions and Removals from Soil', as defined in the Revised 1996 IPCC Guidelines. Note that these LULUCF categories overlap, but are not congruent with the categories that can or must be accounted for compliance purposes under the Kyoto Protocol (cp. 'Sink Allowances' below). *Units*: The net LULUCF emissions (+) or removals (−) for the years 1990 and 2000 are given in $MtCO_2e$/yr and as a percentage of the respective years' Annex A emissions (% Yr.).

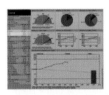

Int. bunker fuels

Emissions by international transport (aviation and marine) for years 1990 and 2000. Units: $MtCO_2e$/yr and as percentage of 1990 or 2000 Annex A emissions (% Yr.).

Projections

Projections of Annex A emissions until 2010 under the assumptions 'with measures' and 'with additional measures'.

- *2000 (projection base)*: Emissions for 2000 in the projections section of the third National Communications are sometimes not fully consistent with the reported emissions for 2000 in the inventory submissions. This is generally due to different underlying assumptions (e.g. projections relying on older inventory data), or different coverage of sectors and gases.

- *2010 'with measures'*: Projections that are classified 'with measures (WM)' incorporate the effects of policies and measures that are implemented or committed to in the national communication. Thirty of the thirty-two third National Communications analysed in FCCC/SBI/2003/7/Add.3 provided 'with measures' scenarios (orange dotted line).
- *2010 'with additional measures'*: Projections 'with additional measures (WAM)' include the effects of additional measures under consideration and as specified by the Party. Twenty-one of the thirty-two third National Communications analysed in FCCC/SBI/2003/7/Add.3 provided 'with additional measures' scenarios (orange dashed line).

For detailed notes on the projection data, consult the document FCCC/SBI/2003/7/Add.3 or the Parties' third National Communications, available at http://unfccc.int/.

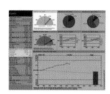

FCCC aim

Progress towards the FCCC objective to return to 1990 emission levels by 2000. Each individual country's performance under the FCCC objective (FCCC Art. 4.2 (a) and (b)) is indicated by the difference between its actual emissions in year 2000 ('Actual') and its 1990 emissions ('Allowed'). The emissions counted are those indicated under the section 'Emissions' (see above) plus bunker fuel emissions, if available. In cases where a country's emissions in 2000 were below 1990 levels, the indicator arrow points to the left (lower emissions; '-'). *Units*: $MtCO_2e/yr$ and percentage of 1990 emissions (% 1990).

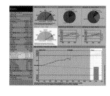

Kyoto target

Emission targets under the Kyoto Protocol for 2008–2012.

- *Allowed 2008–2012 (An.B)/(EU)*: The 'Allowed Emissions' are defined here as a country's base year emissions times the percentage listed in Annex B of the Kyoto Protocol (with the exception of the EU15 member countries, where the EU Burden Sharing Agreement serves as the basis for calculating the targets). Thus, the 'Allowed Emissions' as defined here are identical to the 'assigned amounts' as defined in the Marrakesh Accords (paragraph 5 of Annex to -/CMP.1, Decision 19/CP.7, with the exception of those countries that account for deforestation in their baseline pursuant to KP Article 3.7 (see 'Sink allowances' below).

- *Distance from year X*: Necessary emission reductions below latest inventory data (e.g. 2001) in order to reach the 'Allowed Emissions' level. A positive (negative) value means that further emission reductions are (not) necessary in order to reach the target.
- *Distance from WM*: Necessary emission reductions below projected levels under the 'with measures' scenario for 2010 (where WM projections are available).
- *Distance from WAM*: Necessary emission reductions below projected levels under the 'with additional measures' scenario for 2010 (where WAM projections are available).

Units: $MtCO_2e/yr$ and percentage of base year Annex A emissions (% B.Yr.). *Sources*: Annex B of the Kyoto Protocol; for the EU Burden Sharing Agreement, see conclusions of 2106th Council meeting ENVIRONMENT Luxembourg, 16–17 June 1998, available online at http://www.eel.nl/council/2106.htm.

Sink allowances

Potential credits and debits for the first commitment period related to the accounting of LULUCF activities. This section attempts to quantify the magnitude of LULUCF-related credits that each Party could potentially claim. These LULUCF categories comprise those in the Kyoto Protocol (Art. 3.3) and additional categories or caps provided for in the Marrakesh Accords (Art. 3.4). *Units*: $MtCO_2e/yr$ and percentage of base year emissions.

- *CDM sinks*: Eligible LULUCF activities under the CDM are afforestation and reforestation activities. The acquisition (addition to assigned amount) of these CDM sink credits is limited to 1 per cent of a country's base year emissions (see paragraph 14, in Decision 11/CP.7). For countries for which KP Art. 3.7 applies (deforestation in the base year – see above), the calculation of allowed CDM sink credits takes into account this change in the base year emissions.
- *For. Mng. I (AppZ)*: A country is allowed to account for forest management up to the country-specific limit given here (Appendix to Decision 11/CP.7 and Decision 12/CP.7).
- *Agr. Mng.*: This category comprises credits due to cropland management, grazing land management and revegetation. No caps apply to this category of credits, and estimates are uncertain due to incomplete and uncertain removal projections up to 2010.

- *Cropland management*: In order to derive a rough estimate of cropland management credits, the following assumptions have been made. A country's cropland area has been assumed to be equal to the 'arable land and permanent cropland' area as estimated by the FAO for the year 2001. The carbon uptake factor for cropland management activities was chosen to be 0.32 tC/ha/yr in accordance with an average estimate for Annex I countries (IPCC, 2000a). Furthermore, it has been assumed that 20 per cent of the total cropland area might be carbon-managed in addition to 1990 management practices ('implementation factor'). Multiplication of the area, the implementation factor and the carbon uptake factor lead to the rough estimates presented here. Note that no emissions or removals from non-CO_2 gases have been taken into account in this estimate, although N_2O emissions can be assumed to increase and partially offset CO_2 sequestration (see Table 4-4, IPCC, 2000a:199). *Sources*: FAO database available at http://apps.fao.org/page/collections; Carbon uptake factors taken from Table 4.1, IPCC, 2000a:184.
- *Grazing land management*: For cropland management, grazing land area has been assumed equal to the 'permanent pasture' area based on FAO estimates for 2001. The carbon uptake factor for grazing land management activities was chosen to be 0.53 tC/ha/yr in accordance with an average estimate for Annex I countries (see Table 4.1, IPCC, 2000a:184). Furthermore, it has been assumed that 10 percent of the total cropland area might be carbon-managed ('implementation factor'). The implementation factor is assumed to be lower than for cropland management due to the less beneficial side effects of carbon management on grazing lands, such as acidification, erosion, increased energy use and reduced biodiversity (see Table 4.4, IPCC, 2000a:199). Note that, as for cropland management, no emissions from non-CO_2 gases have been taken into account.
- *Revegetation*: Credits for 'revegetation' were only assumed for Australia (+0.59 MtCO_2e/yr) and Iceland

($+0.014$ MtCO$_2$e/yr), the only two countries that presented estimates in their August 2000 submissions (see FCCC/SBSTA/2000/9/Add.1 and FCCC/SBSTA/2000/MISC.6/Add.1). For other countries, there are no official estimates for the 'revegetation' potential, partially due to a vague definition of 'revegetation' (see definition in Decision 11/CP.7).

- *Aff & Def (est.)*: The estimates for afforestation and deforestation-related emissions (KP Art. 3.3) are from countries' own projections as provided in their submissions in August 2000 under IPCC definitions (FCCC/SBSTA/2000/9/Add.1). Updated estimates that were subsequently provided by some countries (Austria, Netherlands, Portugal, Spain and United Kingdom) have been taken into account (European Environmental Agency, 2003 *Greenhouse Gas Emission Trends and Projections in Europe 2003*, Environmental Issue Report No. 36).

- *For.Mng. II*: Beyond the credits under 'For.Mng I (AppZ)', a country is allowed to account for forest management in order to offset any potential debits under Art. 3.3. A country's forest management potential is assumed to be sufficiently high to compensate any Art. 3.3. 'debits' beyond the allowances under 'For.Mng. I (AppZ)'.

- *Defo in B.Yr.*: The second part of Art. 3.7 requests Parties to include emissions and removals from deforestation activities in their base year emissions if all LULUCF activities (according to the Revised 1996 IPCC Guidelines) were a net source in the base year. This provision is only applicable to a limited number of countries – with Australia's base year emissions likely to be the most affected (see country specific notes).

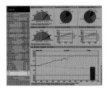

Single projects

The possible exemption of certain single project emissions is presented for Iceland and Monaco, which are the only two countries eligible to exclude up to 1.6 MtCO$_2$e/yr. Units: MtCO$_2$e/yr and percentage of base year emissions. Sources: third National Communication of Iceland, pp. 20–2, and Decision 14/CP.7

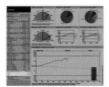

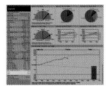

Per capita

As one simple indicator to compare emissions across countries, the per capita emissions are given for 1990 and 2000 (or the latest available year). Per capita emissions are given in tCO_2e per capita per year (tCO_2e/per/yr) comprising 'Annex A' and bunker fuel emissions. *Source*: Population data from FAO, available at: http://apps.fao.org/page/collections.

Main data sources

If not stated otherwise, the data is drawn from the country's official inventory submissions to the FCCC.

- 'CRF 2003': The country's 2003 submission in the Common Reporting Format (CRF) was used, as available at http://unfccc.int/program/mis/ghg/submis2003.html.
- 'ghg.unfccc.int': Since no 'CRF 2003' submission was available, data was drawn from the GHG online database as of 2002, available at ghg.unfccc.int.
- EDGAR: Where no FCCC data was available, the EDGAR database has been used (see http://arch.rivm.nl/env/int/coredata/edgar/). Where indicated by an asterisk in the table, remaining data gaps for international bunker fuels were filled by using the nearest datapoints in the EDGAR database from 1985 to 1995. (J. G. J. Olivier and J. J. M. Berdowski, 'Global Emissions Sources and Sinks', in: J. Berdowski, R. Guicherit and B. J. Heij (eds.), *The Climate System* (2001), pp. 33–78 (A. A. Balkema Publishers/Swets & Zeitlinger Publishers, Lisse, The Netherlands) and J. G. J. Olivier, 'Part III: Greenhouse Gas Emissions: 1. Shares and trends in greenhouse gas emissions; 2. Sources and, methods; Greenhouse gas emissions for 1990 and 1995', in: CO_2 *Emissions from Fuel Combustion 1971–2000*, 2002 edn, pp. III.1–III.31 (International Energy Agency (IEA), Paris).

Country specific notes

- Australia: There is some uncertainty as to whether Australia qualifies for an inclusion of its deforestation emissions in the base year ('Defo in B.Yr.'). The 1990 net emissions due to LULUCF are uncertain, especially the contribution from 'vegetation thickening', and could be negative. In this case, Australia's effective commitments would be about 30 per cent lower.

- Iceland: Note that special projections for Iceland 'with add. measures I' (WAM I) and 'with add. measures II' (WAM II) are displayed instead of WM and WAM. The scenarios are taken from Iceland's third National Communication (pp. 20–2) including emissions fulfilling 14/CP.7 (single projects).
- Turkey: Due to a lack of FCCC data, Turkey's fact sheet is solely based on the EDGAR database.
- Slovakia: Int. bunker fuel data for 2000 has been assumed equal to the latest available estimate in the EDGAR database (1995).
- Netherlands: Int. bunker fuel data includes CO_2 emissions only.
- Ukraine, Russian Federation and Belarus: Transport-related emissions were not reported separately and are therefore presented as part of the energy-related emissions. This affects as well the relevant aggregated fact sheets.
- Russian Federation: Russian inventory data has been updated by the information provided in its third National Communication up to 1999. Projections SCEN II and SCEN III are based on Russia's own CO_2 projections '2' and '3', as reported in Table V.4 of the third National Communication, and the assumption that an equal growth rate applies for the non-CO_2 gases.

Aggregated fact sheets

Individual country data has been aggregated for different groupings, namely Annex I, Annex II, EIT, EU-15, EU-25 and JUSSCANNZ. Some assumptions had to be made in order to aggregate the official FCCC data. For those countries, categories and years where FCCC data was missing, linear interpolation between the reported data points has been performed in order to fill data gaps. For the countries which did not report up until 2001, constant emissions have been assumed from the latest available data point onwards, except for the Russian Federation, where the CO_2 energy growth rate according to the IEA statistics (IEA, 2003) has been assumed for all gases and sources after the most recent reported data, 1996.

- Annex I: Aggregated data for all Annex I countries except Turkey, Belarus and Kazakhstan.
- Annex II: Aggregated data for all countries inscribed in Annex II of the FCCC. Turkey is excluded.

- EIT: Aggregated data for EITs, namely the Russian Federation, other Annex I states of the former Soviet Union and Eastern Europe. Belarus and Kazakhstan are not included. Note that the Russian Federation and Ukraine did not separately report transport-related emissions. Thus, the presented transport emissions are only a subset of the overall transport emission in EIT countries.
- EU-15: Aggregated data for the European Union's fifteen member states as given in the EU's CRF submission 2003. Sink allowances represent net aggregates over all member country estimates which lead to net positive emission for the 'Defo in B.Yr.', 'Aff&Def' as well as the 'For.Mng. II' category.
- EU-25: Aggregated data for the European Union's twenty-five member states as of 2004.
- JUSSCANNZ: Aggregated data for non-EU developed countries, namely Japan, US, Switzerland, Canada, Australia, Norway and New Zealand.

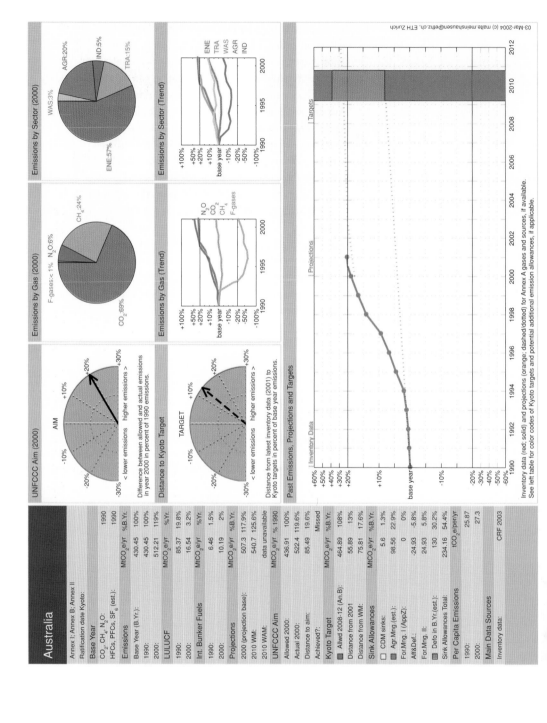

Australia

Annex I; Annex B; Annex II		
Ratification date Kyoto:		
Base Year		
CO_2, CH_4, N_2O:		1990
HFCs, PFCs, SF_6 (est.):		1990
Emissions	$MtCO_2e/Yr$	%B.Yr.
Base Year (B.Yr.):	430.45	100%
1990:	430.45	100%
2000:	512.21	119%
LULUCF	$MtCO_2e/Yr$	%Yr.
1990:	85.37	19.8%
2000:	16.54	3.2%
Int. Bunker Fuels	$MtCO_2e/Yr$	%Yr.
1990:	6.46	1.5%
2000:	10.19	2%
Projections	$MtCO_2e/Yr$	%B.Yr.
2000 (projection base):	507.3	117.9%
2010 WM:	540.7	125.6%
2010 WAM:	data unavailable	
UNFCCC Aim	$MtCO_2e/Yr$	% 1990
Allowed 2000:	436.91	100%
Actual 2000:	522.4	119.6%
Distance to aim:	85.49	19.6%
Achieved?:		Missed
Kyoto Target	$MtCO_2e/Yr$	%B.Yr.
▣ Allwd 2008-12 (An.B):	464.89	108%
Distance from 2001	55.89	13%
Distance from WM:	75.81	17.6%
Sink Allowances	$MtCO_2e/Yr$	%B.Yr.
☐ CDM sinks:	5.6	1.3%
▣ Agr.Mng.(est.):	98.56	22.9%
For.Mng. I (AppZ):	0	0%
Aff&Def.:	-24.93	-5.8%
For.Mng. II:	24.93	5.8%
▣ Defo in B.Yr.(est.):	130	30.2%
Sink Allowances Total:	234.16	54.4%
Per Capita Emissions		$tCO_2e/per/yr$
1990:		25.87
2000:		27.3
Main Data Sources		
Inventory data:		CRF 2003

UNFCCC Aim (2000)

AIM

+10% +20% +30%

-10%

-20%

-30%

< lower emissions   higher emissions >

Difference between allowed and actual emissions in year 2000 in percent of 1990 emissions.

Distance to Kyoto Target

TARGET

+10% +20%

-10%

-20%

-30%

< lower emissions   higher emissions >

Distance from latest inventory data (2001) to Kyoto targets in percent of base year emissions.

Emissions by Gas (2000)

F-gases:< 1% N_2O:6%

CH_4:24%

CO_2:69%

Emissions by Gas (Trend)

+100%
+50%
+20%
+10%
base year
-10%
-20%
-50%
-100%

1990   1995   2000

N_2O
CO_2
CH_4
F-gases

Emissions by Sector (2000)

WAS:3%
AGR:20%
IND:5%
TRA:15%
ENE:57%

Emissions by Sector (Trend)

+100%
+50%
+20%
+10%
base year
-10%
-20%
-50%
-100%

1990   1995   2000

ENE
TRA
WAS
AGR
IND

Past Emissions, Projections and Targets

| Inventory Data | Projections | Targets

+60%
+50%
+40%
+30%
+20%
+10%
base year
-10%
-20%
-30%
-40%
-50%
-60%

1990 1992 1994 1996 1998 2000 2002 2004 2006 2008 2010 2012

Inventory data (red; solid) and projections (orange; dashed/dotted) for Annex A gases and sources, if available. See left table for color codes of Kyoto targets and potential additional emission allowances, if applicable.

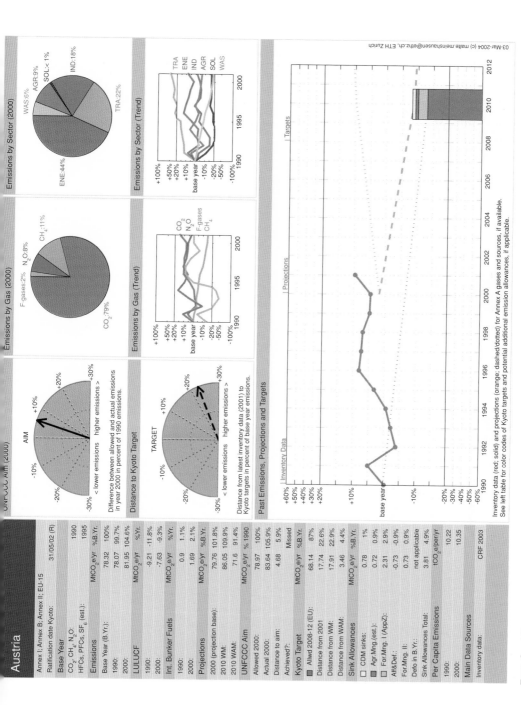

Austria

Fact sheet 2

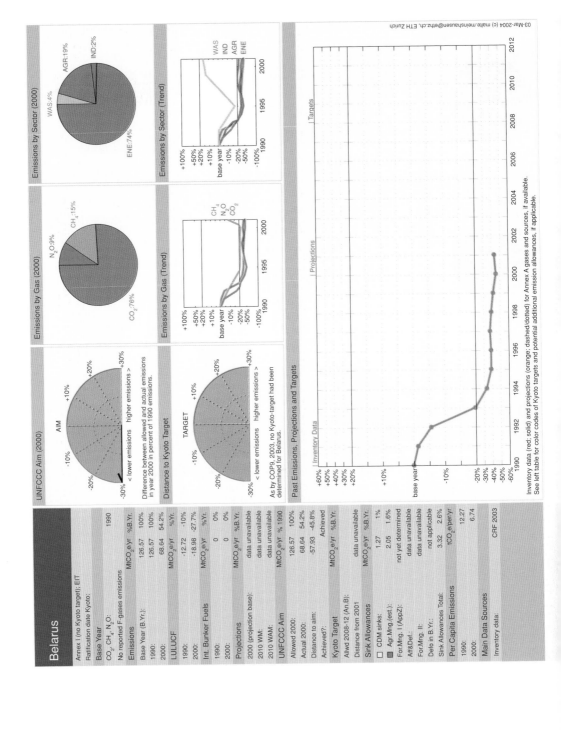

Belarus

Annex I (no Kyoto target); EIT

Ratification date Kyoto:

Base Year	1990

CO_2, CH_4, N_2O:
No reported F-gases emissions

Emissions	MtCO₂e/yr	%B.Yr.
Base Year (B.Yr.):	126.57	100%
1990:	126.57	100%
2000:	68.64	54.2%

LULUCF	MtCO₂e/yr	%Yr.
1990:	-12.72	-10%
2000:	-18.98	-27.7%

Int. Bunker Fuels	MtCO₂e/yr	%Yr.
1990:	0	0%
2000:	0	0%

Projections	MtCO₂e/yr	%B.Yr.
2000 (projection base):	data unavailable	
2010 WM:	data unavailable	
2010 WAM:	data unavailable	

UNFCCC Aim	MtCO₂e/yr	% 1990
Allowed 2000:	126.57	100%
Actual 2000:	68.64	54.2%
Distance to aim:	-57.93	-45.8%
Achieved?:	Achieved	

Kyoto Target	MtCO₂e/yr	%B.Yr.
Allwd 2008-12 (An.B):	data unavailable	
Distance from 2001	MtCO₂e/yr	%B.Yr.

Sink Allowances

☐ CDM sinks:	1.27	1%
■ Agr.Mng.(est.):	2.05	1.6%
For.Mng. I (App2):	not yet determined	
Aff&Def.:	data unavailable	
For.Mng. II:	data unavailable	
Defo in B.Yr.:	not applicable	
Sink Allowances Total:	3.32	2.6%

Per Capita Emissions	tCO₂e/per/yr
1990:	12.27
2000:	6.74

Main Data Sources	
Inventory data:	CRF 2003

UNFCCC Aim (2000)

AIM

Difference between allowed and actual emissions in year 2000 in percent of 1990 emissions.

Distance to Kyoto Target

TARGET

As by COP9, 2003, no Kyoto-target had been determined for Belarus.

Emissions by Gas (2000)

N_2O:9%

CH_4:15%

CO_2:76%

Emissions by Sector (2000)

WAS:4%

AGR:19%

IND:2%

ENE:74%

Emissions by Gas (Trend)

Emissions by Sector (Trend)

Past Emissions, Projections and Targets

Inventory data (red; solid) and projections (orange; dashed/dotted) for Annex A gases and sources, if available.
See left table for color codes of Kyoto targets and potential additional emission allowances, if applicable.

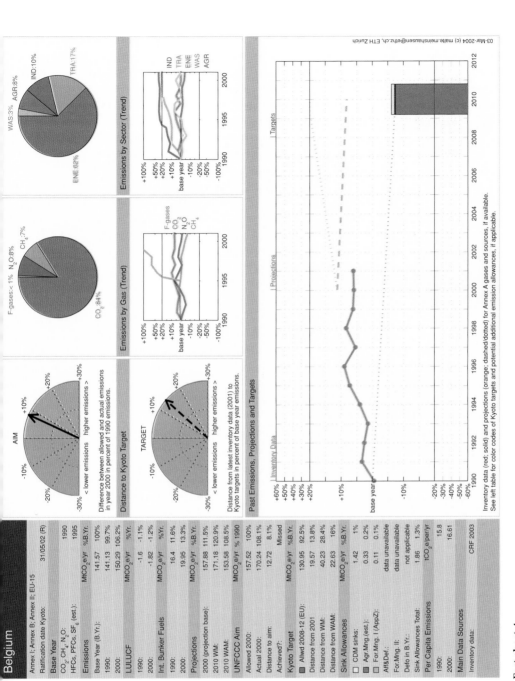

Belgium

Annex I; Annex B; Annex II; EU-15	
Ratification date Kyoto:	31/05/02 (R)

Base Year

CO_2, CH_4, N_2O:	1990
HFCs, PFCs, SF_6 (est.):	1995

Emissions

	MtCO$_2$e/yr	%B.Yr.
Base Year (B.Yr.):	141.57	100%
1990:	141.13	99.7%
2000:	150.29	106.2%

LULUCF

	MtCO$_2$e/yr	%Yr.
1990:	-1.6	-1.1%
2000:	-1.82	-1.2%

Int. Bunker Fuels

	MtCO$_2$e/yr	%Yr.
1990:	16.4	11.6%
2000:	19.95	13.3%

Projections

	MtCO$_2$e/yr	%B.Yr.
2000 (projection base):	157.88	111.5%
2010 WM:	171.18	120.9%
2010 WAM:	153.58	108.5%

UNFCCC Aim

	MtCO$_2$e	% 1990
Allowed 2000:	157.52	100%
Actual 2000:	170.24	108.1%
Distance to aim:	12.72	8.1%
Achieved?:		Missed

Kyoto Target

	MtCO$_2$e/yr	%B.Yr.
■ Allwd 2008-12 (EU):	130.95	92.5%
Distance from 2001	19.57	13.8%
Distance from WM:	40.23	28.4%
Distance from WAM:	22.63	16%

Sink Allowances

	MtCO$_2$e/yr	%B.Yr.
☐ CDM sinks:	1.42	1%
■ Agr.Mng.(est.):	0.33	0.2%
■ For.Mng. I (App2):	0.11	0.1%
Aff&Def.:	data unavailable	
For.Mng. II:	data unavailable	
Defo in B.Yr.:	not applicable	
Sink Allowances Total:	1.86	1.3%

Per Capita Emissions

	1CO$_2$e/per/yr
1990:	15.8
2000:	16.61

Main Data Sources

Inventory data:	CRF 2003

AIM

Difference between allowed and actual emissions in year 2000 in percent of 1990 emissions.

Distance to Kyoto Target

TARGET

Distance from latest inventory data (2001) to Kyoto targets in percent of base year emissions.

Emissions by Gas (Trend)

F-gases
CO_2
N_2O
CH_4

Emissions by Sector (Trend)

IND
TRA
ENE
WAS
AGR

F-gases:< 1% N_2O:8%
CH_4:7%
CO_2:84%

WAS:3%   AGR:8%
IND:10%
TRA:17%
ENE:62%

Past Emissions, Projections and Targets

| Inventory Data | | Projections | | Targets |

Inventory data (red: solid) and projections (orange: dashed/dotted) for Annex A gases and sources, if available.
See left table for color codes of Kyoto targets and potential additional emission allowances, if applicable.

03-Mar-2004 (c) malte.meinshausen@eth z.ch, ETH Zurich

Fact sheet 4

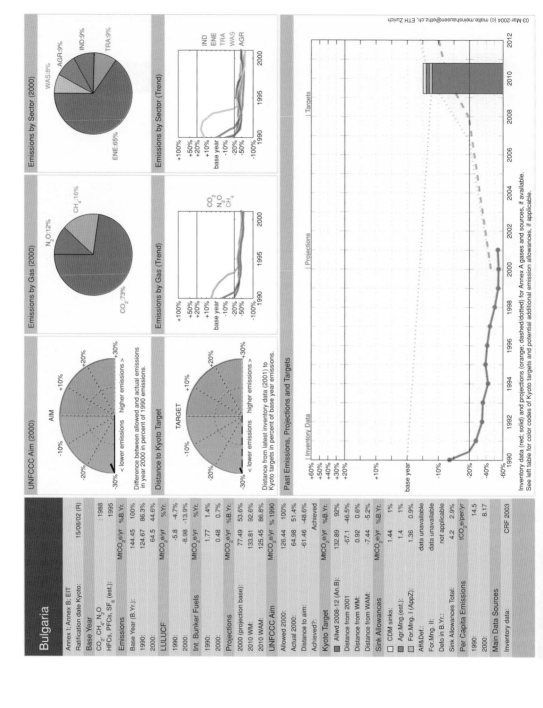

Bulgaria

Annex I: Annex B: EIT	
Ratification date Kyoto:	15/08/02 (R)

Base Year	
CO_2, CH_4, N_2O	:1988
HFCs, PFCs, SF_6 (est.):	1995

Emissions	$MtCO_2e/yr$	%B.Yr.
Base Year (B.Yr.):	144.45	100%
1990:	124.67	86.3%
2000:	64.5	44.6%

LULUCF	$MtCO_2e/yr$	%Yr.
1990:	-5.8	-4.7%
2000:	-8.98	-13.9%

Int. Bunker Fuels	$MtCO_2e/yr$	%Yr.
1990:	1.77	1.4%
2000:	0.48	0.7%

Projections	$MtCO_2e/yr$	%B.Yr.
2000 (projection base):	77.49	53.6%
2010 WM:	133.81	92.6%
2010 WAM:	125.45	86.8%

UNFCCC Aim	$MtCO_2e/yr$	% 1990
Allowed 2000:	126.44	100%
Actual 2000:	64.98	51.4%
Distance to aim:	-61.46	-48.6%
Achieved?:		Achieved

Kyoto Target	$MtCO_2e/yr$	%B.Yr.
Allwd 2008-12 (An.B):	132.89	92%
Distance from 2001	-67.1	-46.5%
Distance from WM:	0.92	0.6%
Distance from WAM:	-7.44	-5.2%

Sink Allowances	$MtCO_2e/yr$	%B.Yr.
CDM sinks:	1.44	1%
Agr.Mng.(est.):	1.4	1%
For.Mng. I (App2):	1.36	0.9%
Afft&Def.:	data unavailable	
For.Mng. II:	data unavailable	
Defo in B.Yr.:	not applicable	
Sink Allowances Total:	4.2	2.9%

Per Capita Emissions	$tCO_2e/per/yr$
1990:	14.5
2000:	8.17

Main Data Sources	
Inventory data:	CRF 2003

UNFCCC Aim (2000)

AIM

+20%
+10%
-10%
-20%
-30%
+30%

< lower emissions   higher emissions >

Difference between allowed and actual emissions in year 2000 in percent of 1990 emissions.

Distance to Kyoto Target

TARGET

+20%
+10%
-10%
-20%
-30%
+30%

< lower emissions   higher emissions >

Distance from latest inventory data (2001) to Kyoto targets in percent of base year emissions.

Emissions by Gas (2000)

N_2O:12%
CH_4:16%
CO_2:73%

Emissions by Gas (Trend)

+100%
+50%
+20%
+10%
base year
-10%
-20%
-50%
-100%

1990   1995   2000

CO_2
N_2O
CH_4

Emissions by Sector (2000)

WAS:8%
AGR:9%
IND:9%
TRA:9%
ENE:65%

Emissions by Sector (Trend)

+100%
+50%
+20%
+10%
base year
-10%
-20%
-50%
-100%

1990   1995   2000

IND
ENE
TRA
WAS
AGR

Past Emissions, Projections and Targets

| Inventory Data | Projections | Targets |

+60%
+50%
+40%
+30%
+20%
+10%
base year
-10%
-20%
-40%
-60%

1990 1992 1994 1996 1998 2000 2002 2004 2006 2008 2010 2012

Inventory data (red: solid) and projections (orange: dashed/dotted) for Annex A gases and sources, if available.
See left table for color codes of Kyoto targets and potential additional emission allowances, if applicable.

03-Mar-2004 (c) malte.meinshausen@eth z.ch, ETH Zurich

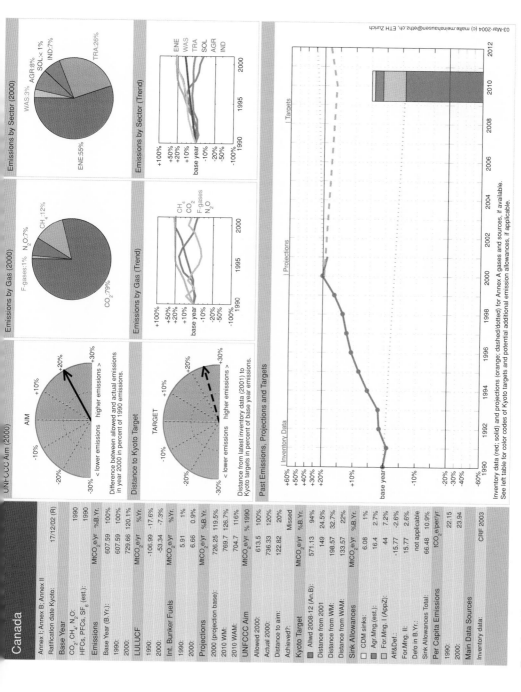

Canada

Annex I: Annex B: Annex II	
Ratification date Kyoto:	17/12/02 (R)

Base Year

CO_2, CH_4, N_2O:	1990
HFCs, PFCs, SF_6 (est.):	1990

Emissions · MtCO₂e/yr · %B.Yr.

	MtCO$_2$e/yr	%B.Yr.
Base Year (B.Yr.):	607.59	100%
1990:	607.59	100%
2000:	729.66	120.1%

LULUCF · MtCO₂e/yr · %Yr.

	MtCO$_2$e/yr	%Yr.
1990:	-106.99	-17.6%
2000:	-53.34	-7.3%

Int. Bunker Fuels · MtCO₂e/yr · %Yr.

	MtCO$_2$e/yr	%Yr.
1990:	5.91	1%
2000:	6.66	0.9%

Projections · MtCO₂e/yr · %B.Yr.

	MtCO$_2$e/yr	%B.Yr.
2000 (projection base):	726.25	119.5%
2010 WM:	769.7	126.7%
2010 WAM:	704.7	116%

UNFCCC Aim · MtCO₂e/yr · % 1990

	MtCO$_2$e/yr	% 1990
Allowed 2000:	613.5	100%
Actual 2000:	736.33	120%
Distance to aim:	122.82	20%
Achieved?:	Missed	

Kyoto Target · MtCO₂e/yr · %B.Yr.

	MtCO$_2$e/yr	%B.Yr.
■ Allwd 2008-12 (An.B):	571.13	94%
Distance from 2001	149	24.5%
Distance from WM:	198.57	32.7%
Distance from WAM:	133.57	22%

Sink Allowances · MtCO₂e/yr · %B.Yr.

	MtCO$_2$e/yr	%B.Yr.
☐ CDM sinks:	6.08	1%
■ Agr.Mng.(est.):	16.4	2.7%
■ For.Mng. I (AppZ):	44	7.2%
Afl&Def.:	-15.77	-2.6%
For.Mng. II:	15.77	2.6%
Defo in B.Yr.:	not applicable	
Sink Allowances Total:	66.48	10.9%

Per Capita Emissions · tCO₂e/per/yr

	tCO$_2$e/per/yr
1990:	22.15
2000:	23.94

Main Data Sources	
Inventory data:	CRF 2003

UNFCCC Aim (2000)

AIM

+30% / +20% / +10% / -10% / -20% / -30%

< lower emissions   higher emissions >

Difference between allowed and actual emissions in year 2000 in percent of 1990 emissions.

Distance to Kyoto Target

TARGET

+30% / +20% / +10% / -10% / -20% / -30%

< lower emissions   higher emissions >

Distance from latest inventory data (2001) to Kyoto targets in percent of base year emissions.

Past Emissions, Projections and Targets

Emissions by Gas (2000)

F-gases:1% N_2O:7%
CH_4:12%
CO_2:79%

Emissions by Gas (Trend)

CH_4 / CO_2 / F-gases / N_2O

+100% / +50% / +20% / +10% / base year / -10% / -20% / -50% / -100%

1990   1995   2000

Emissions by Sector (2000)

WAS:3% AGR:8% SOL:< 1% IND:7%
TRA:26%
ENE:55%

Emissions by Sector (Trend)

ENE / WAS / TRA / SOL / AGR / IND

+100% / +50% / +20% / +10% / base year / -10% / -20% / -50% / -100%

1990   1995   2000

Inventory data (red; solid) and projections (orange: dashed/dotted) for Annex A gases and sources, if available.
See left table for color codes of Kyoto targets and potential additional emission allowances, if applicable.

03-Mar-2004 (c) malte.meinshausen@ethz.ch, ETH Zurich

Fact sheet 6

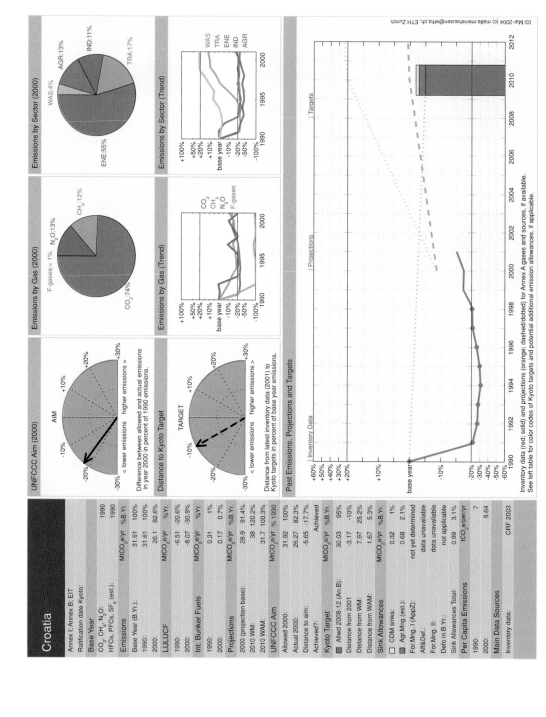

Croatia

Annex I: Annex B: EIT		
Ratification date Kyoto:		
Base Year		
CO_2, CH_4, N_2O:		1990
HFCs, PFCs, SF_6 (est.):		1990
Emissions	MtCO$_2$e/yr	%/B.Yr.
Base Year (B.Yr.):	31.61	100%
1990:	31.61	100%
2000:	26.1	82.6%
LULUCF	MtCO$_2$e/yr	%/Yr.
1990:	-6.51	-20.6%
2000:	-8.07	-30.9%
Int. Bunker Fuels	MtCO$_2$e/yr	%/Yr.
1990:	0.31	1%
2000:	0.17	0.7%
Projections	MtCO$_2$e/yr	%/B.Yr.
2000 (projection base):	28.9	91.4%
2010 WM:	38	120.2%
2010 WAM:	31.7	100.3%
UNFCCC Aim	MtCO$_2$e/yr	% 1990
Allowed 2000:	31.92	100%
Actual 2000:	26.27	82.3%
Distance to aim:	-5.65	-17.7%
Achieved?:		Achieved
Kyoto Target	MtCO$_2$e/yr	%/B.Yr.
Allwd 2008-12 (An.B):	30.03	95%
Distance from 2001	-3.17	-10%
Distance from WM:	7.97	25.2%
Distance from WAM:	1.67	5.3%
Sink Allowances	MtCO$_2$e/yr	%/B.Yr.
☐ CDM sinks:	0.32	1%
☐ Agr.Mng.(est.):	0.68	2.1%
For.Mng. I (AppZ):	not yet determined	
Aff&Def.:	data unavailable	
For.Mng. II:	data unavailable	
Defo in B.Yr.:	not applicable	
Sink Allowances Total:	0.99	3.1%
Per Capita Emissions	tCO$_2$e/per/yr	
1990:	7	
2000:	5.64	
Main Data Sources		
Inventory data:	CRF 2003	

UNFCCC Aim (2000)

Difference between allowed and actual emissions in year 2000 in percent of 1990 emissions.

Distance to Kyoto Target

Distance from latest inventory data (2001) to Kyoto targets in percent of base year emissions.

Emissions by Gas (2000)

F-gases: < 1%   N$_2$O: 13%
CH$_4$: 12%
CO$_2$: 74%

Emissions by Sector (2000)

WAS: 4%   AGR: 13%   IND: 11%
TRA: 17%
ENE: 55%

Emissions by Gas (Trend)

CO$_2$
CH$_4$
N$_2$O
F-gases

Emissions by Sector (Trend)

WAS
TRA
ENE
IND
AGR

Past Emissions, Projections and Targets

Inventory data (red; solid) and projections (orange; dashed/dotted) for Annex A gases and sources, if available. See left table for color codes of Kyoto targets and potential additional emission allowances, if applicable.

03-Mar-2004 (c) malte.meinshausen@env.ethz.ch, ETH Zurich

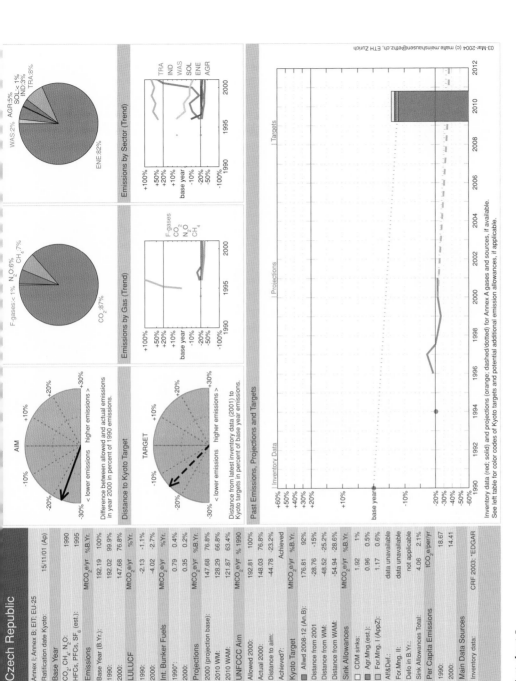

Czech Republic

Annex I; Annex B; EIT; EU-25	
Ratification date Kyoto:	15/11/01 (Ap)

Base Year	
CO₂, CH₄, N₂O:	1990
HFCs, PFCs, SF₆ (est.):	1995

Emissions	MtCO₂e/yr	%B.Yr.
Base Year (B.Yr.):	192.19	100%
1990:	192.02	99.9%
2000:	147.68	76.8%

LULUCF	MtCO₂e/yr	%Yr.
1990:	-2.13	-1.1%
2000:	-4.02	-2.7%

Int. Bunker Fuels	MtCO₂e/yr	%Yr.
1990*:	0.79	0.4%
2000:	0.35	0.2%

Projections	MtCO₂e/yr	%B.Yr.
2000 (projection base):	147.68	76.8%
2010 WM:	128.29	66.8%
2010 WAM:	121.87	63.4%

UNFCCC Aim	MtCO₂e/yr	% 1990
Allowed 2000:	192.81	100%
Actual 2000:	148.03	76.8%
Distance to aim:	-44.78	-23.2%
Achieved?:		Achieved

Kyoto Target	MtCO₂e/yr	%B.Yr.
☐ Allwd 2008-12 (An.B):	176.81	92%
Distance from 2001:	-28.76	-15%
Distance from WM:	-48.52	-25.2%
Distance from WAM:	-54.94	-28.6%

Sink Allowances	MtCO₂e/yr	%B.Yr.
☐ CDM sinks:	1.92	1%
☐ Agr.Mng.(est.):	0.96	0.5%
☐ For.Mng. I (AppZ):	1.17	0.6%
Aff&Def.:		data unavailable
For.Mng. II:		data unavailable
Defo in B.Yr.:		not applicable
Sink Allowances Total:	4.06	2.1%

Per Capita Emissions	tCO₂e/per/yr
1990:	18.67
2000:	14.41

Main Data Sources	
Inventory data:	CRF 2003; EDGAR

Fact sheet 8

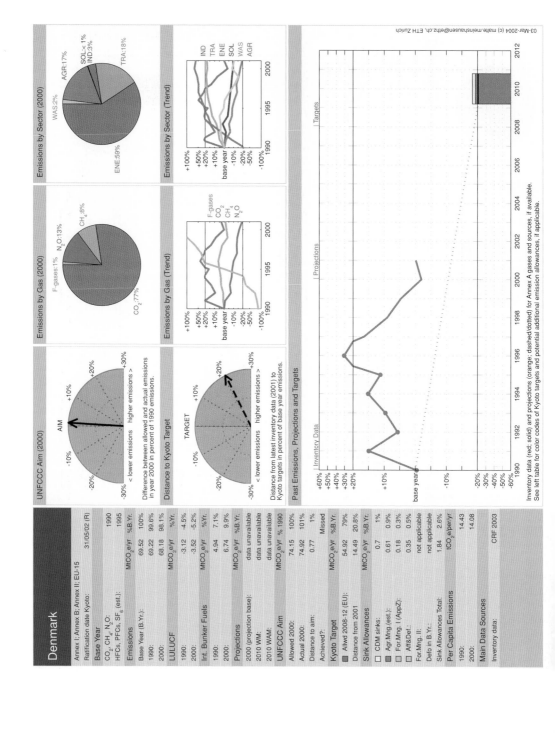

Denmark

Annex I; Annex B; Annex II; EU-15

Ratification date Kyoto: 31/05/02 (R)

Base Year
CO2, CH4, N2O: 1990
HFCs, PFCs, SF6 (est.): 1995

Emissions | MtCO2e/yr | %B.Yr.
Base Year (B.Yr.): | 69.52 | 100%
1990: | 69.22 | 99.6%
2000: | 68.18 | 98.1%

LULUCF | MtCO2e/yr | %Yr.
1990: | -3.12 | -4.5%
2000: | -3.52 | -5.2%

Int. Bunker Fuels | MtCO2e/yr | %Yr.
1990: | 4.94 | 7.1%
2000: | 6.74 | 9.9%

Projections | MtCO2e/yr | %B.Yr.
2000 (projection base): | data unavailable
2010 WM: | data unavailable
2010 WAM: | data unavailable

UNFCCC Aim | MtCO2e/yr | % 1990
Allowed 2000: | 74.15 | 100%
Actual 2000: | 74.92 | 101%
Distance to aim: | 0.77 | 1%
Achieved?: | Missed

Kyoto Target | MtCO2e/yr | %B.Yr.
■ Allwd 2008-12 (EU): | 54.92 | 79%
Distance from 2001 | 14.49 | 20.8%

Sink Allowances | MtCO2e/yr | %B.Yr.
☐ CDM sinks: | 0.7 | 1%
■ Agr.Mng.(est.): | 0.61 | 0.9%
☐ For.Mng. I (App2): | 0.18 | 0.3%
☐ Aff&Def.: | 0.35 | 0.5%
For.Mng. II: | not applicable
Defo in B.Yr.: | not applicable

Per Capita Emissions | tCO2e/per/yr
1990: | 1.84 | 2.6%
2000: | 14.43
| 14.08

Main Data Sources

Inventory data: | CRF 2003

UNFCCC Aim (2000)

Difference between allowed and actual emissions in year 2000 in percent of 1990 emissions.

Distance to Kyoto Target

Distance from latest inventory data (2001) to Kyoto targets in percent of base year emissions.

Past Emissions, Projections and Targets

Inventory data (red; solid) and projections (orange; dashed/dotted) for Annex A gases and sources, if available. See left table for color codes of Kyoto targets and potential additional emission allowances, if applicable.

Emissions by Sector (2000)

Emissions by Gas (2000)

Emissions by Sector (Trend)

Emissions by Gas (Trend)

03-Mar-2004 (c) malte.meinshausen@env.ch, ETH Zürich

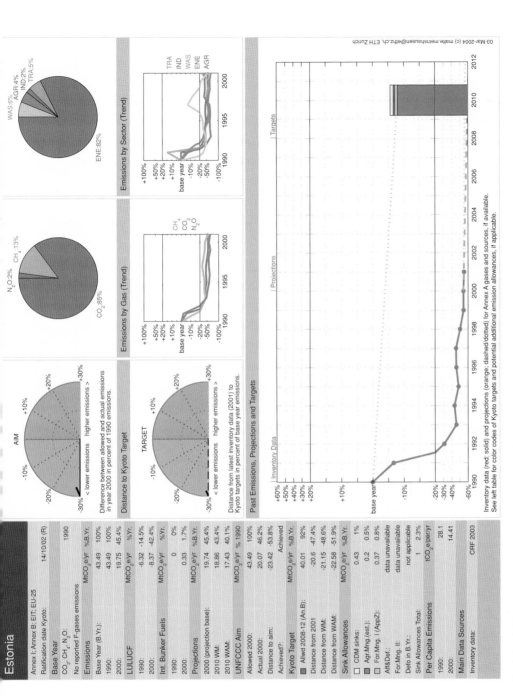

Estonia

Annex I; Annex B; EIT; EU-25	
Ratification date Kyoto:	14/10/02 (R)

Base Year

Base Year	1990
CO$_2$, CH$_4$, N$_2$O:	
No reported F-gases emissions	

Emissions

	MtCO$_2$e/yr	%B.Yr.
Base Year (B.Yr.):	43.49	100%
1990:	43.49	100%
2000:	19.75	45.4%

LULUCF

	MtCO$_2$e/yr	%Yr.
1990:	-6.32	-14.5%
2000:	-8.37	-42.4%

Int. Bunker Fuels

	MtCO$_2$e/yr	%Yr.
1990:	0	0%
2000:	0.33	1.7%

Projections

	MtCO$_2$e/yr	%B.Yr.
2000 (projection base):	19.74	45.4%
2010 WM:	18.86	43.4%
2010 WAM:	17.43	40.1%

UNFCCC Aim

	MtCO$_2$e/yr	% 1990
Allowed 2000:	43.49	100%
Actual 2000:	20.07	46.2%
Distance to aim:	-23.42	-53.8%
Achieved?:		Achieved

Kyoto Target

	MtCO$_2$e/yr	%B.Yr.
Allwd 2008-12 (An.B):	40.01	92%
Distance from 2001	-20.6	-47.4%
Distance from WM:	-21.15	-48.6%
Distance from WAM:	-22.58	-51.9%

Sink Allowances

	MtCO$_2$e/yr	%B.Yr.
☐ CDM sinks:	0.43	1%
☐ Agr.Mng.(est.):	0.2	0.5%
☐ For.Mng. I (App2):	0.37	0.8%
Aff&Def.:		data unavailable
For.Mng. II:		data unavailable
Defo in B.Yr.:		not applicable
Sink Allowances Total:	1	2.3%

Per Capita Emissions

	tCO$_2$e/per/yr
1990:	28.1
2000:	14.41

Main Data Sources

Inventory data:	CRF 2003

AIM

Difference between allowed and actual emissions in year 2000 in percent of 1990 emissions.

Distance to Kyoto Target

TARGET

Distance from latest inventory data (2001) to Kyoto targets in percent of base year emissions.

Emissions by Gas (Trend)

CH$_4$
CO$_2$
N$_2$O

Emissions by Sector (Trend)

TRA
IND
WAS
ENE
AGR

N$_2$O:2% CH$_4$:13%

CO$_2$:85%

WAS:6%
AGR:4%
IND:2%
TRA:5%

ENE:82%

Past Emissions, Projections and Targets

| Inventory Data | | Projections | | Targets |

Inventory data (red: solid) and projections (orange: dashed/dotted) for Annex A gases and sources, if available. See left table for color codes of Kyoto targets and potential additional emission allowances, if applicable.

03-Mar-2004 (c) malte.meinshausen@ethz.ch, ETH Zurich

Fact sheet 10

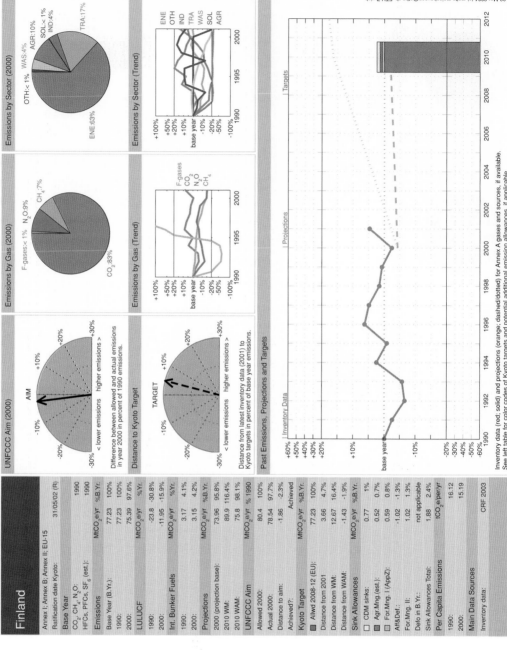

Finland

Annex I: Annex B: Annex II: EU-15		
Ratification date Kyoto:	31/05/02 (R)	

Base Year

CO_2, CH_4, N_2O:		1990
HFCs, PFCs, SF_6 (est.):		1990

Emissions

	$MtCO_2e/yr$	%B.Yr.
Base Year (B.Yr.):	77.23	100%
1990:	77.23	100%
2000:	75.39	97.6%

LULUCF

	$MtCO_2e/yr$	%Yr.
1990:	-23.8	-30.8%
2000:	-11.95	-15.9%

Int. Bunker Fuels

	$MtCO_2e/yr$	%Yr.
1990:	3.17	4.1%
2000:	3.15	4.2%

Projections

	$MtCO_2e/yr$	%B.Yr.
2000 (projection base):	73.96	95.8%
2010 WM:	89.9	116.4%
2010 WAM:	75.8	98.1%

UNFCCC Aim

	$MtCO_2e/yr$	% 1990
Allwed 2000:	80.4	100%
Actual 2000:	78.54	97.7%
Distance to aim:	-1.86	-2.3%
Achieved?:		Achieved

Kyoto Target

	$MtCO_2e/yr$	%B.Yr.
Allwd 2008-12 (EU):	77.23	100%
Distance from 2001:	3.66	4.7%
Distance from WM:	12.67	16.4%
Distance from WAM:	-1.43	-1.9%

Sink Allowances

	$MtCO_2e/yr$	%B.Yr.
☐ CDM sinks:	0.77	1%
☐ Agr.Mng.(est.):	0.52	0.7%
☐ For.Mng. I (App2):	0.59	0.8%
Aff&Def.:	-1.02	-1.3%
For.Mng. II:	1.02	1.3%
Defo in B.Yr.:	not applicable	
Sink Allowances Total:	1.88	2.4%

Per Capita Emissions

	$tCO_2e/per/yr$	
1990:	16.12	
2000:	15.19	

Main Data Sources

Inventory data:	CRF 2003

UNFCCC Aim (2000)

AIM

-30% < lower emissions   higher emissions > +30%

Difference between allowed and actual emissions in year 2000 in percent of 1990 emissions.

Distance to Kyoto Target

TARGET

-30% < lower emissions   higher emissions > +30%

Distance from latest inventory data (2001) to Kyoto targets in percent of base year emissions.

Emissions by Gas (2000)

F-gases:< 1% N_2O:9% CH_4:7%

CO_2:83%

Emissions by Gas (Trend)

F-gases
CO_2
N_2O
CH_4

Emissions by Sector (2000)

OTH:< 1%   WAS:4%
AGR:10%
SOL:< 1%
IND:4%
TRA:17%

ENE:63%

Emissions by Sector (Trend)

ENE
OTH
IND
TRA
WAS
SOL
AGR

Past Emissions, Projections and Targets

| Inventory Data | Projections | Targets

Inventory data (red; solid) and projections (orange; dashed/dotted) for Annex A gases and sources, if available.
See left table for color codes of Kyoto targets and potential additional emission allowances, if applicable.

03-Mar-2004 (c) malte.meinshausen@ethz.ch, ETH Zürich

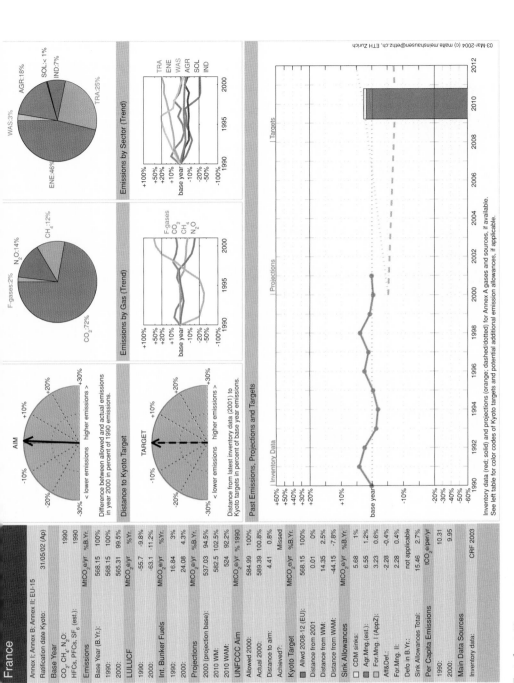

France

Annex I: Annex B: Annex II: EU-15		
Ratification date Kyoto:	31/05/02 (Ap)	

Base Year

CO_2, CH_4, N_2O:		1990
HFCs, PFCs, SF_6 (est.):		1990

Emissions	$MtCO_2e/yr$	%B.Yr.
Base Year (B.Yr.):	568.15	100%
1990:	568.15	100%
2000:	565.31	99.5%

LULUCF	$MtCO_2e/yr$	%Yr.
1990:	-55.7	-9.8%
2000:	-63.1	-11.2%

Int. Bunker Fuels	$MtCO_2e/yr$	%Yr.
1990:	16.84	3%
2000:	24.08	4.3%

Projections	$MtCO_2e/yr$	%B.Yr.
2000 (projection base):	537.03	94.5%
2010 WM:	582.5	102.5%
2010 WAM:	524	92.2%

UNFCCC Aim	$MtCO_2e/yr$	% 1990
Allowed 2000:	584.99	100%
Actual 2000:	589.39	100.8%
Distance to aim:	4.41	0.8%
Achieved?:	Missed	

Kyoto Target	$MtCO_2e/yr$	%B.Yr.
▇ Allwd 2008-12 (EU):	568.15	100%
Distance from 2001:	0.01	0%
Distance from WM:	14.35	2.5%
Distance from WAM:	-44.15	-7.8%

Sink Allowances	$MtCO_2e/yr$	%B.Yr.
☐ CDM sinks:	5.68	1%
☐ Agr.Mng.(est.):	6.55	1.2%
☐ For.Mng. I (AppZ):	3.23	0.6%
Aff&Def.:	-2.28	-0.4%
For.Mng. II:	2.28	0.4%
Defo in B.Yr.:	not applicable	
Sink Allowances Total:	15.46	2.7%

Per Capita Emissions	$tCO_2e/per/yr$	
1990:	10.31	
2000:	9.95	

Main Data Sources

Inventory data:	CRF 2003

AIM

-10% / +10% / -20% / +20% / -30% / +30%

< lower emissions   higher emissions >

Difference between allowed and actual emissions in year 2000 in percent of 1990 emissions.

Distance to Kyoto Target

TARGET

-10% / +10% / -20% / +20% / -30% / +30%

< lower emissions   higher emissions >

Distance from latest inventory data (2001) to Kyoto targets in percent of base year emissions.

Past Emissions, Projections and Targets

WAS:3% / AGR:18% / SOL:< 1% / IND:7% / TRA:25% / ENE:46%

F-gases:2% / N_2O:14% / CH_4:12% / CO_2:72%

Emissions by Gas (Trend)

F-gases / CO_2 / CH_4 / N_2O

+100% / +50% / +20% / +10% / base year / -10% / -20% / -50% / -100%

1990 / 1995 / 2000

Emissions by Sector (Trend)

TRA / ENE / WAS / AGR / SOL / IND

+100% / +50% / +20% / +10% / base year / -10% / -20% / -50% / -100%

1990 / 1995 / 2000

| Inventory Data | Projections | Targets |

+60% / +50% / +40% / +30% / +20% / +10% / base year / -10% / -20% / -30% / -40% / -50% / -60%

1990 / 1992 / 1994 / 1996 / 1998 / 2000 / 2002 / 2004 / 2006 / 2008 / 2010 / 2012

Inventory data (red; solid) and projections (orange; dashed/dotted) for Annex A gases and sources, if available.
See left table for color codes of Kyoto targets and potential additional emission allowances, if applicable.

Fact sheet 12

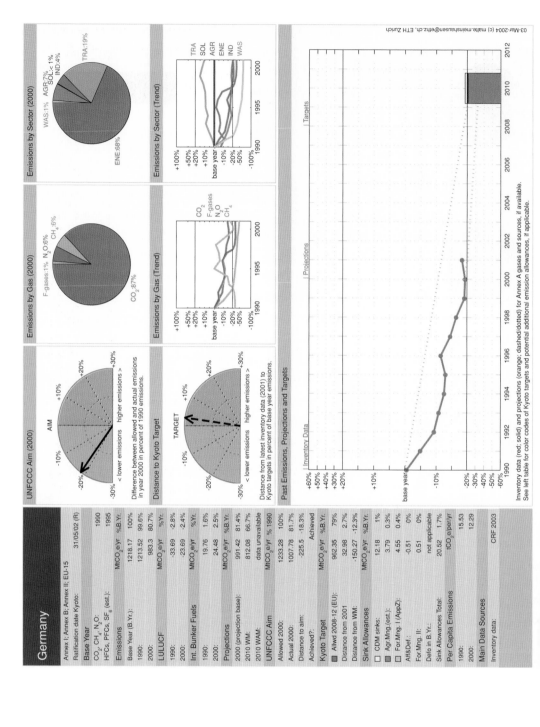

Germany

Annex I; Annex B; Annex II; EU-15	
Ratification date Kyoto:	31/05/02 (R)

Base Year
CO₂, CH₄, N₂O:	1990
HFCs, PFCs, SF₆ (est.):	1995

Emissions
	MtCO₂e/yr	%B.Yr.
Base Year (B.Yr.):	1218.17	100%
1990:	1213.52	99.6%
2000:	983.3	80.7%

LULUCF
	MtCO₂e/yr	%Yr.
1990:	-33.69	-2.8%
2000:	-23.69	-2.4%

Int. Bunker Fuels
	MtCO₂e/yr	%Yr.
1990:	19.76	1.6%
2000:	24.48	2.5%

Projections
	MtCO₂e/yr	%B.Yr.
2000 (projection base):	991.42	81.4%
2010 WM:	812.08	66.7%
2010 WAM:	data unavailable	

UNFCCC Aim
	MtCO₂e/yr	% 1990
Allowed 2000:	1233.28	100%
Actual 2000:	1007.78	81.7%
Distance to aim:	-225.5	-18.3%
Achieved?:	Achieved	

Kyoto Target
	MtCO₂e/yr	%B.Yr.
Allwd 2008-12 (EU):	962.35	79%
Distance from 2001	32.98	2.7%
Distance from WM:	-150.27	-12.3%

Sink Allowances
	MtCO₂e/yr	%B.Yr.
CDM sinks:	12.18	1%
Agr.Mng.(est.):	3.79	0.3%
For.Mng. I (AppZ):	4.55	0.4%
Aff&Def.:	-0.51	0%
For.Mng. II:	0.51	0%
Defo in B.Yr.:	not applicable	
Sink Allowances Total:	20.52	1.7%

Per Capita Emissions
	tCO₂e/per/yr
1990:	15.53
2000:	12.29

Main Data Sources
Inventory data:	CRF 2003

UNFCCC Aim (2000)

AIM

-30% -20% -10% +10% +20% +30%

< lower emissions   higher emissions >

Difference between allowed and actual emissions in year 2000 in percent of 1990 emissions.

Distance to Kyoto Target

TARGET

-30% -20% -10% +10% +20% +30%

< lower emissions   higher emissions >

Distance from latest inventory data (2001) to Kyoto targets in percent of base year emissions.

Emissions by Gas (2000)

F-gases:1% N₂O:6% CH₄:6%

CO₂:87%

Emissions by Gas (Trend)

+100%
+50%
+20%
+10%
base year
-10%
-20%
-50%
-100%

1990   1995   2000

CO₂
F-gases
N₂O
CH₄

Emissions by Sector (2000)

WAS:1% AGR:7% SOL:< 1%
IND:4%
TRA:19%

ENE:68%

Emissions by Sector (Trend)

+100%
+50%
+20%
+10%
base year
-10%
-20%
-50%
-100%

1990   1995   2000

TRA
SOL
AGR
ENE
IND
WAS

Past Emissions, Projections and Targets

| Inventory Data | Projections | Targets |

+60%
+50%
+40%
+30%
+20%
+10%
base year
-10%
-20%
-30%
-40%
-50%
-60%

1990 1992 1994 1996 1998 2000 2002 2004 2006 2008 2010 2012

Inventory data (red; solid) and projections (orange; dashed/dotted) for Annex A gases and sources, if available.
See left table for color codes of Kyoto targets and potential additional emission allowances, if applicable.

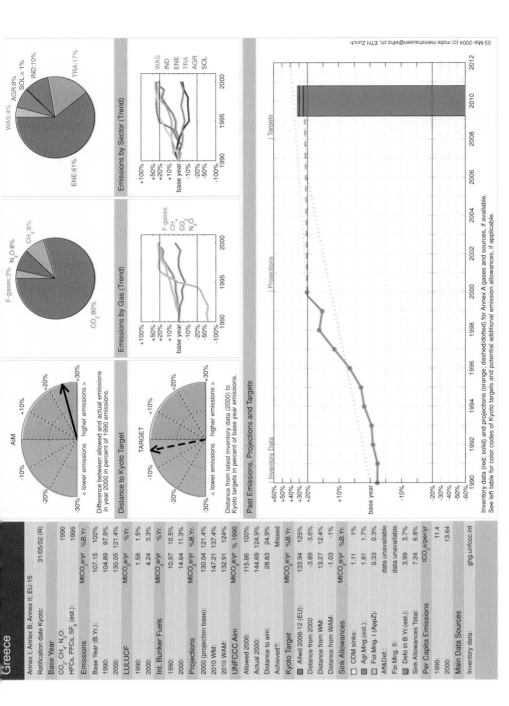

Greece

Annex I; Annex B; Annex II; EU-15	
Ratification date Kyoto:	31/05/02 (R)

Base Year

CO_2, CH_4, N_2O:	1990
HFCs, PFCs, SF_6 (est.):	1995

Emissions

	$MtCO_2e/yr$	%B.Yr.
Base Year (B.Yr.):	107.15	100%
1990:	104.89	97.9%
2000:	130.05	121.4%

LULUCF

	$MtCO_2e/yr$	%Yr.
1990:	1.58	1.5%
2000:	4.24	3.3%

Int. Bunker Fuels

	$MtCO_2e/yr$	%Yr.
1990:	10.97	10.5%
2000:	14.64	11.3%

Projections

	$MtCO_2e/yr$	%B.Yr.
2000 (projection base):	130.04	121.4%
2010 WM:	147.21	137.4%
2010 WAM:	132.91	124%

UNFCCC Aim $MtCO_2e/yr$ % 1990

Allowed 2000:	115.86	100%
Actual 2000:	144.69	124.9%
Distance to aim:	28.83	24.9%
Achieved?:		Missed

Kyoto Target

	$MtCO_2e/yr$	%B.Yr.
Allwd 2008-12 (EU):	133.94	125%
Distance from 2000	-3.89	-3.6%
Distance from WM:	13.27	12.4%
Distance from WAM:	-1.03	-1%

Sink Allowances $MtCO_2e/yr$ %B.Yr.

CDM sinks:	1.11	1%
Agr.Mng.(est.):	1.81	1.7%
For.Mng. I (AppZ):	0.33	0.3%
Aff&Def.:	data unavailable	
For.Mng. II:	data unavailable	
Defo in B.Yr.(est.):	3.99	3.7%
Sink Allowances Total:	7.24	6.8%

Per Capita Emissions $tCO_2e/per/yr$

1990:	11.4
2000:	13.64

Main Data Sources

Inventory data:	ghg.unfccc.int

AIM

< lower emissions   higher emissions >

Difference between allowed and actual emissions in year 2000 in percent of 1990 emissions.

Distance to Kyoto Target

TARGET

< lower emissions   higher emissions >

Distance from latest inventory data (2000) to Kyoto targets in percent of base year emissions.

Past Emissions, Projections and Targets

F-gases:3% N_2O:8%

CH_4:8%

CO_2:80%

WAS:4% AGR:8%

SOL:< 1%

IND:10%

TRA:17%

ENE:61%

Emissions by Gas (Trend)

F-gases
CH_4
CO_2
N_2O

Emissions by Sector (Trend)

WAS
IND
ENE
TRA
AGR
SOL

Inventory data (red; solid) and projections (orange; dashed/dotted) for Annex A gases and sources, if available.
See left table for color codes of Kyoto targets and potential additional emission allowances, if applicable.

03-Mar-2004 (c) malte.meinshausen@ethz.ch, ETH Zurich

Fact sheet 14

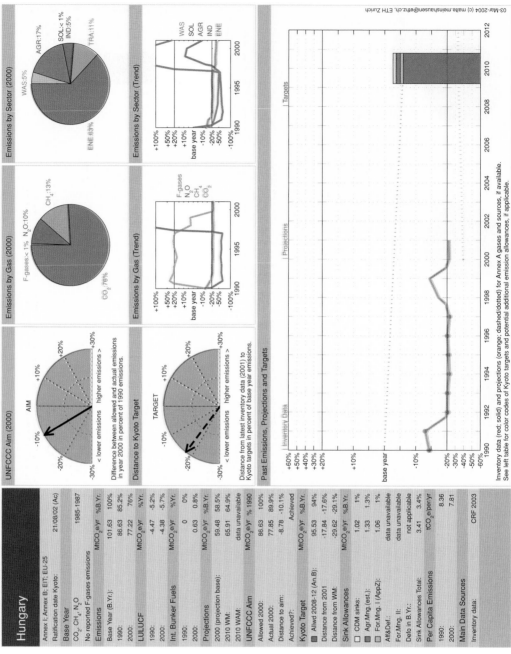

Hungary

Annex I; Annex B; EIT; EU-25		
Ratification date Kyoto:	21/08/02 (Ac)	

Base Year	1985-1987	
CO_2, CH_4, N_2O		
No reported F-gases emissions		

Emissions	$MtCO_2e/yr$	%B.Yr.
Base Year (B.Yr.):	101.63	100%
1990:	86.63	85.2%
2000:	77.22	76%

LULUCF	$MtCO_2e/yr$	%Yr.
1990:	-4.47	-5.2%
2000:	-4.38	-5.7%

Int. Bunker Fuels	$MtCO_2e/yr$	%Yr.
1990:	0	0%
2000:	0.63	0.8%

Projections	$MtCO_2e/yr$	%B.Yr.
2000 (projection base):	59.48	58.5%
2010 WM:	65.91	64.9%
2010 WAM:	data unavailable	

UNFCCC Aim	$MtCO_2e/yr$	% 1990
Allowed 2000:	86.63	100%
Actual 2000:	77.85	89.9%
Distance to aim:	-8.78	-10.1%
Achieved?:	Achieved	

Kyoto Target	$MtCO_2e/yr$	%B.Yr.
■ Allwd 2008-12 (An.B):	95.53	94%
Distance from 2001	-17.84	-17.6%
Distance from WM:	-29.62	-29.1%

Sink Allowances	$MtCO_2e/yr$	%B.Yr.
☐ CDM sinks:	1.02	1%
■ Agr.Mng (est.):	1.33	1.3%
☐ For.Mng. I (AppZ):	1.06	1%
Aff&Def.:	data unavailable	
For.Mng. II:	data unavailable	
Defo in B.Yr.:	not applicable	
Sink Allowances Total:	3.41	3.4%

Per Capita Emissions	$tCO_2e/per/yr$	
1990:	8.36	
2000:	7.81	

Main Data Sources		
Inventory data:	CRF 2003	

Emissions by Sector (2000)

ENE:63%
WAS:5%
AGR:17%
SOL:< 1%
IND:5%
TRA:11%

Emissions by Gas (2000)

CO_2:76%
F-gases:< 1%
N_2O:10%
CH_4:13%

UNFCCC Aim (2000)

AIM

+10% +20% +30%
-10% -20% -30%

< lower emissions   higher emissions >

Difference between allowed and actual emissions in year 2000 in percent of 1990 emissions.

Distance to Kyoto Target

TARGET

+10% +20% +30%
-10% -20% -30%

< lower emissions   higher emissions >

Distance from latest inventory data (2001) to Kyoto targets in percent of base year emissions.

Emissions by Sector (Trend)

+100% +50% +20% +10%
base year
-10% -20% -50% -100%

1990   1995   2000

WAS SOL AGR IND ENE

Emissions by Gas (Trend)

+100% +50% +20% +10%
base year
-10% -20% -50% -100%

1990   1995   2000

F-gases N_2O CH_4 CO_2

Past Emissions, Projections and Targets

Inventory Data | Projections | Targets

+60% +50% +40% +30% +20% +10%
base year
-10% -20% -30% -40% -50% -60%

1990 1992 1994 1996 1998 2000 2002 2004 2006 2008 2010 2012

Inventory data (red; solid) and projections (orange; dashed/dotted) for Annex A gases and sources, if available.
See left table for color codes of Kyoto targets and potential additional emission allowances, if applicable.

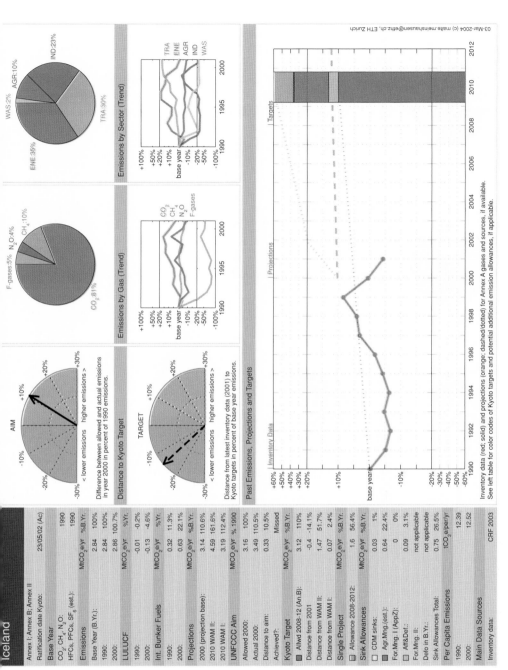

Fact sheet 16

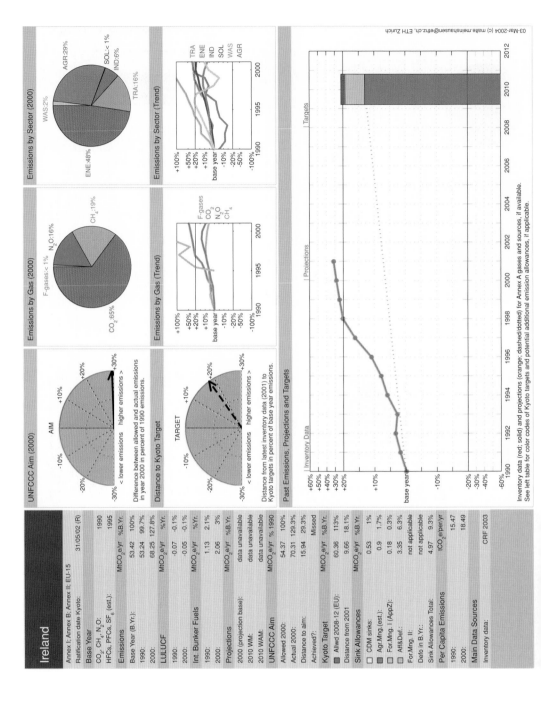

Ireland

Annex I: Annex B: Annex II; EU-15	
Ratification date Kyoto:	31/05/02 (R)

Base Year	
CO_2, CH_4, N_2O:	1990
HFCs, PFCs, SF_6 (est.):	1995

Emissions	$MtCO_2e/yr$	%B.Yr.
Base Year (B.Yr.):	53.42	100%
1990:	53.24	99.7%
2000:	68.25	127.8%

LULUCF	$MtCO_2e/yr$	%Yr.
1990:	-0.07	-0.1%
2000:	-0.05	-0.1%

Int. Bunker Fuels	$MtCO_2e/yr$	%Yr.
1990:	1.13	2.1%
2000:	2.06	3%

Projections	$MtCO_2e/yr$	%B.Yr.
2000 (projection base):	data unavailable	
2010 WM:	data unavailable	
2010 WAM:	data unavailable	

UNFCCC Aim	$MtCO_2e/yr$	% 1990
Allowed 2000:	54.37	100%
Actual 2000:	70.31	129.3%
Distance to aim:	15.94	29.3%
Achieved?:	Missed	

Kyoto Target	$MtCO_2e/yr$	%B.Yr.
Allwd 2008-12 (EU):	60.36	113%
Distance from 2001	9.66	18.1%

Sink Allowances	$MtCO_2e/yr$	%B.Yr.
☐ CDM sinks:	0.53	1%
☐ Agr.Mng.(est.):	0.9	1.7%
☐ For.Mng. I (AppZ):	0.18	0.3%
☐ Aff&Def.:	3.35	6.3%
For.Mng. II:	not applicable	
Defo in B.Yr.:	not applicable	
Sink Allowances Total:	4.97	9.3%

Per Capita Emissions	tCO_2e/yr
1990:	15.47
2000:	18.49

Main Data Sources	
Inventory data:	CRF 2003

UNFCCC Aim (2000)

AIM

-20% -10% +10% +20% +30%

< lower emissions   higher emissions >

Difference between allowed and actual emissions in year 2000 in percent of 1990 emissions.

Distance to Kyoto Target

TARGET

-20% -10% +10% +20% +30%

< lower emissions   higher emissions >

Distance from latest inventory data (2001) to Kyoto targets in percent of base year emissions.

Emissions by Gas (2000)

F-gases:< 1% N_2O:16%

CH_4:19%

CO_2:65%

Emissions by Gas (Trend)

+100% +50% +20% +10% base year -10% -20% -50% -100%

1990   1995   2000

F-gases
CO_2
N_2O
CH_4

Emissions by Sector (2000)

AGR:29%   SOL:< 1%   IND:6%

WAS:2%

TRA:16%

ENE:48%

Emissions by Sector (Trend)

+100% +50% +20% +10% base year -10% -20% -50% -100%

1990   1995   2000

TRA
ENE
IND
SOL
WAS
AGR

Past Emissions, Projections and Targets

| Inventory Data | Projections | Targets |

+60% +50% +40% +30% +20% +10% base year -10% -20% -30% -40% -60%

1990 1992 1994 1996 1998 2000 2002 2004 2006 2008 2010 2012

Inventory data (red: solid) and projections (orange: dashed/dotted) for Annex A gases and sources, if available.
See left table for color codes of Kyoto targets and potential additional emission allowances, if applicable.

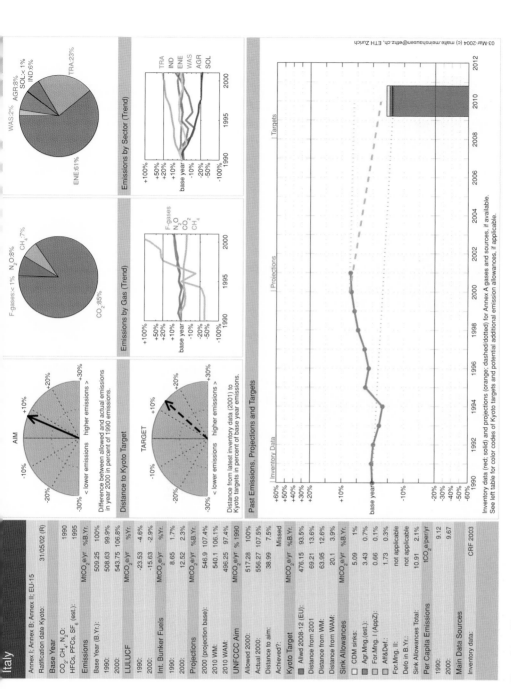

Italy

Annex I; Annex B; Annex II; EU-15	
Ratification date Kyoto:	31/05/02 (R)

Base Year

CO₂, CH₄, N₂O:	1990
HFCs, PFCs, SF₆ (est.):	1995

Emissions

	MtCO₂e/yr	%B.Yr.
Base Year (B.Yr.):	509.25	100%
1990:	508.63	99.9%
2000:	543.75	106.8%

LULUCF

	MtCO₂e/yr	%Yr.
1990:	-23.53	-4.6%
2000:	-15.63	-2.9%

Int. Bunker Fuels

	MtCO₂e/yr	%Yr.
1990:	8.65	1.7%
2000:	12.52	2.3%

Projections

	MtCO₂e/yr	%B.Yr.
2000 (projection base):	546.9	107.4%
2010 WM:	540.1	106.1%
2010 WAM:	496.25	97.4%

UNFCCC Aim

	MtCO₂e/yr	% 1990
Allowed 2000:	517.28	100%
Actual 2000:	556.27	107.5%
Distance to aim:	38.99	7.5%
Achieved?:		Missed

Kyoto Target

	MtCO₂e/yr	%B.Yr.
▨ Allwd 2008-12 (EU):	476.15	93.5%
Distance from 2001	69.21	13.6%
Distance from WM:	63.95	12.6%
Distance from WAM:	20.1	3.9%

Sink Allowances

	MtCO₂e/yr	%B.Yr.
☐ CDM sinks:	5.09	1%
▨ Agr.Mng.(est.):	3.43	0.7%
☐ For.Mng. I (AppZ):	0.66	0.1%
☐ Alf&Def.:	1.73	0.3%
For.Mng. II:	not applicable	
Defo in B.Yr.:	not applicable	
Sink Allowances Total:	10.91	2.1%

Per Capita Emissions

	tCO₂e/per/yr
1990:	9.12
2000:	9.67

Main Data Sources

Inventory data:	CRF 2003

Emissions

F-gases:< 1% N₂O:8% CH₄:7%

CO₂:85%

WAS:2% AGR:8% SOL:< 1% IND:6%
TRA:23%

ENE:61%

Emissions by Gas (Trend)

F-gases
N₂O
CO₂
CH₄

+100%
+50%
+20%
+10%
base year
-10%
-20%
-50%
-100%

1990   1995   2000

Emissions by Sector (Trend)

TRA
IND
ENE
WAS
AGR
SOL

+100%
+50%
+20%
+10%
base year
-10%
-20%
-50%
-100%

1990   1995   2000

AIM

+10%   +20%   +30%

-10%

-20%

-30%

< lower emissions   higher emissions >

Difference between allowed and actual emissions in year 2000 in percent of 1990 emissions.

Distance to Kyoto Target

TARGET

+10%   +20%   +30%

-10%

-20%

-30%

< lower emissions   higher emissions >

Distance from latest inventory data (2001) to Kyoto targets in percent of base year emissions.

Past Emissions, Projections and Targets

| Inventory Data | | Projections | | Targets |

+60%
+50%
+40%
+30%
+20%
+10%
base year
-10%
-20%
-30%
-40%
-50%
-60%

1990 1992 1994 1996 1998 2000 2002 2004 2006 2008 2010 2012

Inventory data (red; solid) and projections (orange; dashed/dotted) for Annex A gases and sources, if available.
See left table for color codes of Kyoto targets and potential additional emission allowances, if applicable.

Fact sheet 18

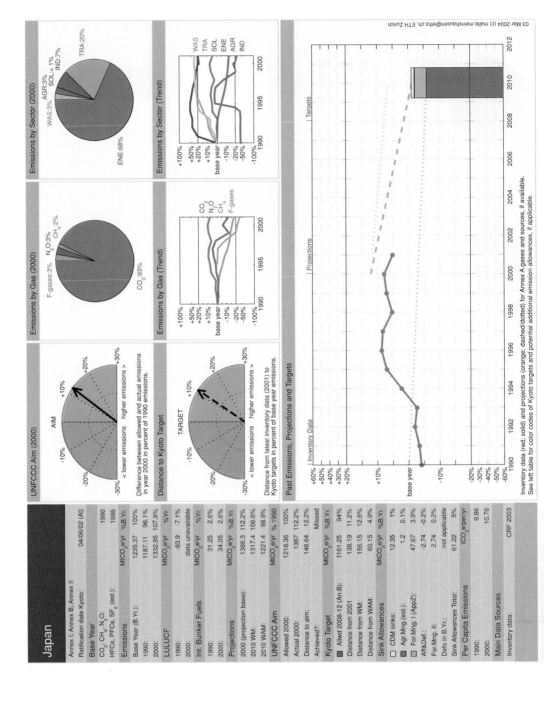

Japan

Annex I; Annex B; Annex II	
Ratification date Kyoto:	04/06/02 (At)

Base Year

CO_2, CH_4, N_2O:	1990
HFCs, PFCs, SF_6 (est.):	1995

Emissions

	$MtCO_2e$/yr	%B.Yr.
Base Year (B.Yr.):	1235.37	100%
1990:	1187.11	96.1%
2000:	1332.95	107.9%

LULUCF

	$MtCO_2e$/yr	%Yr.
1990:	-83.9	-7.1%
2000:	data unavailable	

Int. Bunker Fuels

	$MtCO_2e$/yr	%Yr.
1990:	31.25	2.6%
2000:	34.05	2.6%

Projections

	$MtCO_2e$/yr	%B.Yr.
2000 (projection base):	1386.3	112.2%
2010 WM:	1317.4	106.6%
2010 WAM:	1221.4	98.9%

UNFCCC Aim

	$MtCO_2e$	% 1990
Allowed 2000:	1218.36	100%
Actual 2000:	1367	112.2%
Distance to aim:	148.64	12.2%
Achieved?:	Missed	

Kyoto Target

	$MtCO_2e$/yr	%B.Yr.
Allwd 2008-12 (An.B):	1161.25	94%
Distance from 2001	138.19	11.2%
Distance from WM:	156.15	12.6%
Distance from WAM:	60.15	4.9%

Sink Allowances

	$MtCO_2e$/yr	%B.Yr.
☐ CDM sinks:	12.35	1%
☐ Agr.Mng.(est.):	1.2	0.1%
☐ For.Mng. I (AppZ):	47.67	3.9%
Aff&Def.:	-2.74	-0.2%
For.Mng. II:	2.74	0.2%
Defo in B.Yr.:	not applicable	
Sink Allowances Total:	61.22	5%

Per Capita Emissions tCO_2e/per/yr

1990:	9.86
2000:	10.76

Main Data Sources

Inventory data:	CRF 2003

UNFCCC Aim (2000)

Emissions by Gas (2000)

Emissions by Sector (2000)

AIM

Difference between allowed and actual emissions in year 2000 in percent of 1990 emissions.

Distance to Kyoto Target

TARGET

Distance from latest inventory data (2001) to Kyoto targets in percent of base year emissions.

Emissions by Gas (Trend)

Emissions by Sector (Trend)

Past Emissions, Projections and Targets

Inventory data (red; solid) and projections (orange; dashed/dotted) for Annex A gases and sources, if available.
See left table for color codes of Kyoto targets and potential additional emission allowances, if applicable.

03-Mar-2004 (c) malte.meinshausen@env.ethz.ch, ETH Zürich

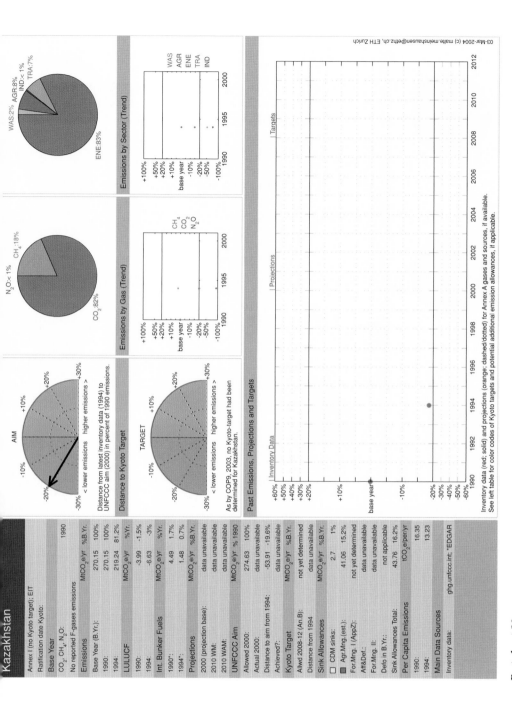

Kazakhstan

Annex I (no Kyoto target): EIT

Ratification date Kyoto:

Base Year

CO_2, CH_4, N_2O: 1990

No reported F-gases emissions

Emissions	MtCO₂e/yr	%B.Yr.
Base Year (B.Yr.):	270.15	100%
1990:	270.15	100%
1994*:	219.24	81.2%

LULUCF	MtCO₂e/yr	%Yr.
1990:	-3.99	-1.5%
1994:	-6.63	-3%

Int. Bunker Fuels	MtCO₂e/yr	%Yr.
1990*:	4.49	1.7%
1994*:	1.48	0.7%

Projections	MtCO₂e/yr	%B.Yr.
2000 (projection base):	data unavailable	
2010 WM:	data unavailable	
2010 WAM:	data unavailable	

UNFCCC Aim	MtCO₂e/yr	% 1990
Allowed 2000:	274.63	100%
Actual 2000:	data unavailable	
Distance to aim from 1994:	-53.91	-19.6%
Achieved?:	data unavailable	

Kyoto Target	MtCO₂e/yr	%B.Yr.
Allwd 2008-12 (An.B):	not yet determined	
Distance from 1994	data unavailable	

Sink Allowances	MtCO₂e/yr	%B.Yr.
☐ CDM sinks:	2.7	1%
■ Agr.Mng.(est.):	41.06	15.2%
For.Mng. I (App2):	not yet determined	
Afl&Def.:	data unavailable	
For.Mng. II:	data unavailable	
Defo in B.Yr.:	not applicable	
Sink Allowances Total:	43.76	16.2%

Per Capita Emissions	tCO₂e/per/yr
1990:	16.35
1994:	13.23

Main Data Sources

Inventory data: ghg.unfccc.int; *EDGAR

AIM

< lower emissions   higher emissions >

Distance from latest inventory data (1994) to UNFCCC aim (2000) in percent of 1990 emissions.

Distance to Kyoto Target

TARGET

< lower emissions   higher emissions >

As by COP9, 2003, no Kyoto-target had been determined for Kazakhstan.

Past Emissions, Projections and Targets

Emissions by Gas (Trend)

CH_4
CO_2
N_2O

Emissions by Sector (Trend)

WAS
AGR
ENE
TRA
IND

N_2O:<1% CH_4:18%

CO_2:82%

WAS:2%   AGR:8%
IND:<1%   TRA:7%

ENE:83%

Inventory data (red; solid) and projections (orange; dashed/dotted) for Annex A gases and sources, if available.
See left table for color codes of Kyoto targets and potential additional emission allowances, if applicable.

03-Mar-2004 (c) malte.meinshausen@ethz.ch, ETH Zurich

Fact sheet 20

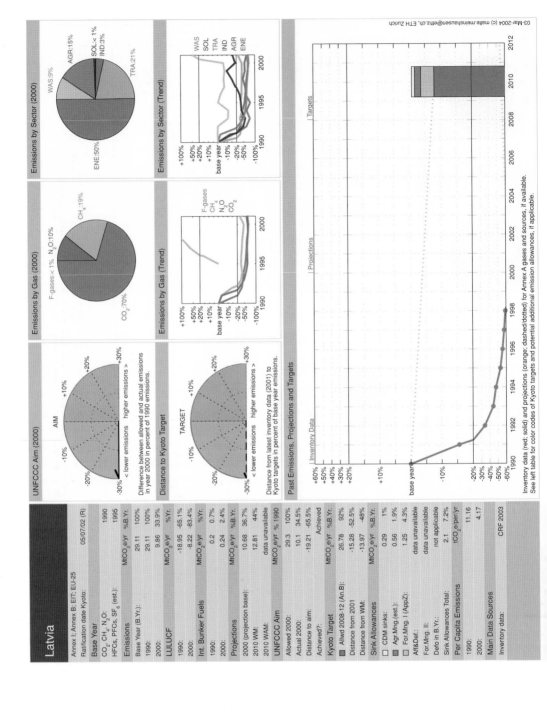

Latvia

Annex I; Annex B: EIT; EU-25	
Ratification date Kyoto:	05/07/02 (R)

Base Year

CO_2, CH_4, N_2O:	1990
HFCs, PFCs, SF_6 (est.):	1995

Emissions

	$MtCO_2e/yr$	%B.Yr.
Base Year (B.Yr.):	29.11	100%
1990:	29.11	100%
2000:	9.86	33.9%

LULUCF

	$MtCO_2e/yr$	%Yr.
1990:	-18.95	-65.1%
2000:	-8.22	-83.4%

Int. Bunker Fuels

	$MtCO_2e/yr$	%Yr.
1990:	0.2	0.7%
2000:	0.24	2.4%

Projections

	$MtCO_2e/yr$	%B.Yr.
2000 (projection base):	10.68	36.7%
2010 WM:	12.81	44%
2010 WAM:	data unavailable	

UNFCCC Aim

	$MtCO_2e/yr$	% 1990
Allowed 2000:	29.3	100%
Actual 2000:	10.1	34.5%
Distance to aim:	-19.21	-65.5%
Achieved?:	Achieved	

Kyoto Target

	$MtCO_2e/yr$	%B.Yr.
Allwd 2008-12 (An.B):	26.78	92%
Distance from 2001:	-15.28	-52.5%
Distance from WM:	-13.97	-48%

Sink Allowances

	$MtCO_2e/yr$	%B.Yr.
CDM sinks:	0.29	1%
Agr.Mng.(est.):	0.56	1.9%
For.Mng. I (App.Z):	1.25	4.3%
Aff&Def.:	data unavailable	
For.Mng. II:	data unavailable	
Defo in B.Yr.:	not applicable	
Sink Allowances Total:	2.1	7.2%

Per Capita Emissions $tCO_2e/per/yr$

1990:	11.16
2000:	4.17

Main Data Sources

Inventory data:	CRF 2003

Emissions by Gas (2000)

F-gases:< 1% N_2O:10% CH_4:19%
CO_2:70%

Emissions by Sector (2000)

AGR:15%   SOL:< 1%   IND:3%
WAS:9%   TRA:21%   ENE:50%

UNFCCC Aim (2000)

AIM

-30% -20% -10% +10% +20% +30%

< lower emissions   higher emissions >

Difference between allowed and actual emissions
in year 2000 in percent of 1990 emissions.

Distance to Kyoto Target

TARGET

-30% -20% -10% +10% +20% +30%

< lower emissions   higher emissions >

Distance from latest inventory data (2001) to
Kyoto targets in percent of base year emissions.

Emissions by Gas (Trend)

+100% +50% +20% +10% base year -10% -20% -50% -100%
1990   1995   2000
F-gases CH_4 N_2O CO_2

Emissions by Sector (Trend)

+100% +50% +20% +10% base year -10% -20% -50% -100%
1990   1995   2000
WAS SOL TRA IND AGR ENE

Past Emissions, Projections and Targets

Inventory Data	Projections	Targets

+60% +50% +40% +30% +20% +10% base year -10% -20% -30% -40% -50% -60%

1990 1992 1994 1996 1998 2000 2002 2004 2006 2008 2010 2012

Inventory data (red; solid) and projections (orange; dashed/dotted) for Annex A gases and sources, if available.
See left table for color codes of Kyoto targets and potential additional emission allowances, if applicable.

03-Mar-2004 (c) malte.meinshausen@etx.ch, ETH Zurich

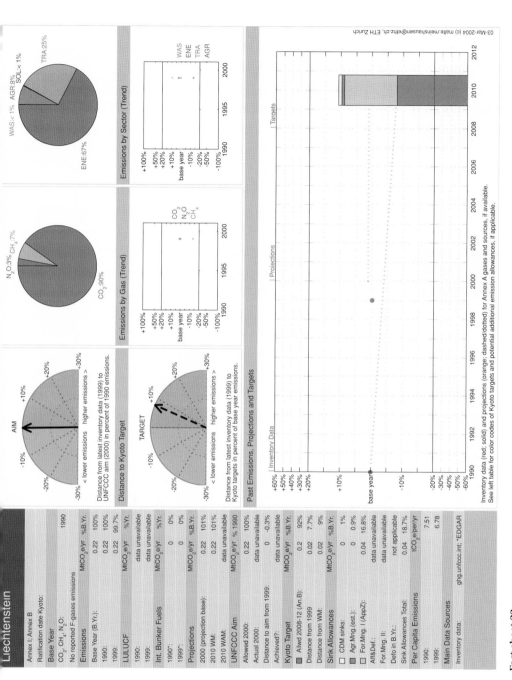

Liechtenstein

03-Mar-2004 (c) malte.meinshausen@ethz.ch, ETH Zurich

Annex I: Annex B		
Ratification date Kyoto:		
Base Year		1990
CO_2, CH_4, N_2O:		
No reported F-gases emissions		
Emissions	MtCO$_2$e/yr	%B.Yr.
Base Year (B.Yr.):	0.22	100%
1990:	0.22	100%
1999:	0.22	99.7%
LULUCF	MtCO$_2$e/yr	%Yr.
1990:	data unavailable	
1999:	data unavailable	
Int. Bunker Fuels	MtCO$_2$e/yr	%Yr.
1990*:	0	0%
1999*:	0	0%
Projections	MtCO$_2$e/yr	%B.Yr.
2000 (projection base):	0.22	101%
2010 WM:	0.22	101%
2010 WAM:	data unavailable	
UNFCCC Aim	MtCO$_2$e/yr	% 1990
Allowed 2000:	0.22	100%
Actual 2000:	data unavailable	
Distance to aim from 1999:	0	-0.3%
Achieved?:	data unavailable	
Kyoto Target	MtCO$_2$e/yr	%B.Yr.
▨ Allwd 2008-12 (An.B):	0.2	92%
Distance from 1999:	0.02	7.7%
Distance from WM:	0.02	9%
Sink Allowances	MtCO$_2$e/yr	%B.Yr.
☐ CDM sinks:	0	1%
☐ Agr.Mng. (est.):	0	0.9%
▨ For.Mng. I (AppZ):	0.04	16.8%
Alf&Def.:	data unavailable	
For.Mng. II:	data unavailable	
Defo in B.Yr.:	not applicable	
Sink Allowances Total:	0.04	18.7%
Per Capita Emissions	tCO$_2$e/per/yr	
1990:	7.51	
1999:	6.78	
Main Data Sources		
Inventory data:	ghg.unfccc.int; *EDGAR	

Distance from latest inventory data (1999) to
UNFCCC aim (2000) in percent of 1990 emissions.

Distance to Kyoto Target

Distance from latest inventory data (1999) to
Kyoto targets in percent of base year emissions.

Emissions by Gas (Trend)

CO_2
N_2O
CH_4

Emissions by Sector (Trend)

WAS
ENE
TRA
AGR

WAS:< 1% AGR:8%
SOL:< 1%
TRA:25%

ENE:67%

N_2O:3% CH_4:7%

CO_2:90%

Past Emissions, Projections and Targets

Inventory Data | Projections | Targets

Inventory data (red; solid) and projections (orange; dashed/dotted) for Annex A gases and sources, if available.
See left table for color codes of Kyoto targets and potential additional emission allowances, if applicable.

Fact sheet 22

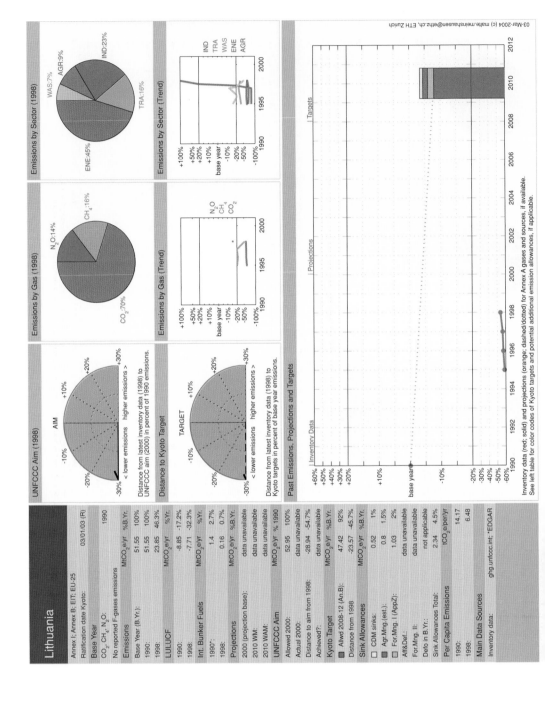

Lithuania

Annex I; Annex B; EIT; EU-25		
Ratification date Kyoto:	03/01/03 (R)	
Base Year		
CO_2, CH_4, N_2O:	1990	
No reported F-gases emissions		
Emissions	MtCO₂e/yr	%B.Yr.
Base Year (B.Yr.):	51.55	100%
1990:	51.55	100%
1998:	23.85	46.3%
LULUCF	MtCO₂e/yr	%Yr.
1990:	-8.85	-17.2%
1998:	-7.71	-32.3%
Int. Bunker Fuels	MtCO₂e/yr	%Yr.
1990*:	1.4	2.7%
1998:	0.16	0.7%
Projections	MtCO₂e/yr	%B.Yr.
2000 (projection base):	data unavailable	
2010 WM:	data unavailable	
2010 WAM:	data unavailable	
UNFCCC Aim	MtCO₂e/yr	% 1990
Allowed 2000:	52.95	100%
Actual 2000:	data unavailable	
Distance to aim from 1998:	-28.94	-54.7%
Achieved?:	data unavailable	
Kyoto Target	MtCO₂e/yr	%B.Yr.
Allwd 2008-12 (An.B):	47.42	92%
Distance from 1998:	-23.57	-45.7%
Sink Allowances	MtCO₂e/yr	%B.Yr.
☐ CDM sinks:	0.52	1%
☐ Agr.Mng.(est.):	0.8	1.5%
☐ For.Mng. I (AppZ):	1.03	2%
Aff&Def.:	data unavailable	
For.Mng. II:	not applicable	
Defo in B.Yr.:	data unavailable	
Sink Allowances Total:	2.34	4.5%
Per Capita Emissions	tCO₂e/per/yr	
1990:	14.17	
1998:	6.48	
Main Data Sources		
Inventory data:	ghg.unfccc.int; *EDGAR	

UNFCCC Aim (1998)

AIM

Distance from latest inventory data (1998) to
UNFCCC aim (2000) in percent of 1990 emissions.

Distance to Kyoto Target

TARGET

Distance from latest inventory data (1998) to
Kyoto targets in percent of base year emissions.

Emissions by Gas (1998)

N_2O:14%
CH_4:16%
CO_2:70%

Emissions by Gas (Trend)

N_2O
CH_4
CO_2

Emissions by Sector (1998)

WAS:7%
AGR:9%
IND:23%
TRA:16%
ENE:45%

Emissions by Sector (Trend)

IND
TRA
WAS
ENE
AGR

Past Emissions, Projections and Targets

Inventory Data | Projections | Targets

Inventory data (red; solid) and projections (orange; dashed/dotted) for Annex A gases and sources, if available.
See left table for color codes of Kyoto targets and potential additional emission allowances, if applicable.

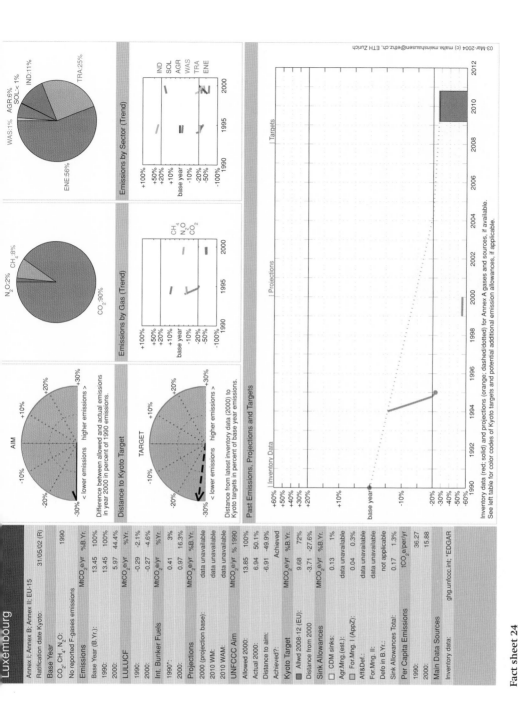

Luxembourg

Annex I; Annex B; Annex II: EU-15		
Ratification date Kyoto:	31/05/02 (R)	

Base Year		
CO_2, CH_4, N_2O:	1990	
No reported F-gases emissions		

Emissions	MtCO$_2$e/yr	%B.Yr.
Base Year (B.Yr.):	13.45	100%
1990:	13.45	100%
2000:	5.97	44.4%

LULUCF	MtCO$_2$e/yr	%Yr.
1990:	-0.29	-2.1%
2000:	-0.27	-4.6%

Int. Bunker Fuels	MtCO$_2$e/yr	%Yr.
1990*:	0.41	3%
2000*:	0.97	16.3%

Projections	MtCO$_2$e/yr	%B.Yr.
2000 (projection base):	data unavailable	
2010 WM:	data unavailable	
2010 WAM:	data unavailable	

UNFCCC Aim	MtCO$_2$e/yr	% 1990
Allowed 2000:	13.85	100%
Actual 2000:	6.94	50.1%
Distance to aim:	-6.91	-49.9%
Achieved?:	Achieved	

Kyoto Target	MtCO$_2$e/yr	%B.Yr.
▇ Allwd 2008-12 (EU):	9.68	72%
Distance from 2000	-3.71	-27.6%

Sink Allowances	MtCO$_2$e/yr	%B.Yr.
☐ CDM sinks:	0.13	1%
Agr.Mng.(est.):	data unavailable	
☐ For.Mng. I (AppZ):	0.04	0.3%
Aff&Def.:	data unavailable	
For.Mng. II:	data unavailable	
Defo in B.Yr.:	not applicable	
Sink Allowances Total:	0.17	1.3%

Per Capita Emissions	tCO$_2$e/per/yr
1990:	36.27
2000:	15.88

Main Data Sources	
Inventory data:	ghg.unfccc.int; *EDGAR

AIM

+10%
+20%
-10%
-20%
-30%   +30%

< lower emissions   higher emissions >

Difference between allowed and actual emissions in year 2000 in percent of 1990 emissions.

Distance to Kyoto Target

TARGET

+10%
+20%
-10%
-20%
-30%   +30%

< lower emissions   higher emissions >

Distance from latest inventory data (2000) to Kyoto targets in percent of base year emissions.

Past Emissions, Projections and Targets

| Inventory Data | Projections | Targets |

+60%
+50%
+40%
+30%
+20%
+10%
base year
-10%
-20%
-30%
-40%
-50%
-60%

1990 1992 1994 1996 1998 2000 2002 2004 2006 2008 2010 2012

N$_2$O:2% CH$_4$:8%

ENE:56%

WAS:1% AGR:6% SOL:< 1% IND:11%

TRA:25%

CO$_2$:90%

Emissions by Gas (Trend)

+100%
+50%
+20%
+10%
base year
-10%
-20%
-50%
-100%

1990 1995 2000

CH$_4$
N$_2$O
CO$_2$

Emissions by Sector (Trend)

+100%
+50%
+20%
+10%
base year
-10%
-20%
-50%
-100%

1990 1995 2000

IND
SOL
AGR
WAS
TRA
ENE

Inventory data (red: solid) and projections (orange: dashed/dotted) for Annex A gases and sources, if available.
See left table for color codes of Kyoto targets and potential additional emission allowances, if applicable.

03-Mar-2004 (c) malte.meinshausen@ethz.ch, ETH Zurich

Fact sheet 24

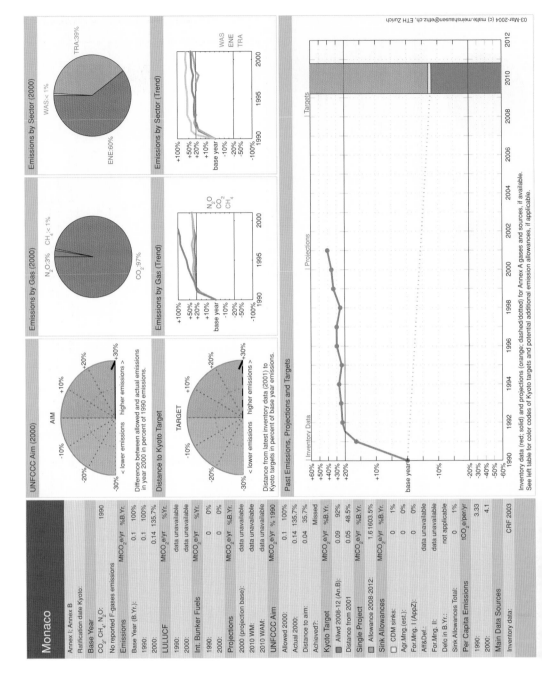

Monaco

Annex I: Annex B	
Ratification date Kyoto:	
Base Year	
CO_2, CH_4, N_2O:	1990
No reported F-gases emissions	

Emissions	MtCO$_2$e/yr	%B.Yr.
Base Year (B.Yr.):	0.1	100%
1990:	0.1	100%
2000:	0.14	135.7%

LULUCF	MtCO$_2$e/yr	%Yr.
1990:	data unavailable	
2000:	data unavailable	

Int. Bunker Fuels	MtCO$_2$e/yr	%Yr.
1990:	0	0%
2000:	0	0%

Projections	MtCO$_2$e/yr	%B.Yr.
2000 (projection base):	data unavailable	
2010 WM:	data unavailable	
2010 WAM:	data unavailable	

UNFCCC Aim	MtCO$_2$e/yr	% 1990
Allowed 2000:	0.1	100%
Actual 2000:	0.14	135.7%
Distance to aim:	0.04	35.7%
Achieved?:	Missed	

Kyoto Target	MtCO$_2$e/yr	%B.Yr.
▨ Allwd 2008-12 (An.B):	0.09	92%
Distance from 2001	0.05	48.5%

Single Project	MtCO$_2$e/yr	%B.Yr.
▨ Allowance 2008-2012:	1.6	1603.5%

Sink Allowances	MtCO$_2$e/yr	%B.Yr.
☐ CDM sinks:	0	1%
Agr.Mng.(est.):	0	0%
For.Mng. I (AppZ):	0	0%
Afk&Def.:	data unavailable	
For.Mng. II:	not applicable	
Defo in B.Yr.:	0	1%
Sink Allowances Total:		

Per Capita Emissions	tCO$_2$e/per/yr
1990:	3.33
2000:	4.1

Main Data Sources	
Inventory data:	CRF 2003

UNFCCC Aim (2000)

AIM

Difference between allowed and actual emissions in year 2000 in percent of 1990 emissions.

Distance to Kyoto Target

TARGET

Distance from latest inventory data (2001) to Kyoto targets in percent of base year emissions.

Past Emissions, Projections and Targets

Emissions by Gas (2000)

N_2O:3% CH_4:< 1%

CO_2:97%

Emissions by Gas (Trend)

N_2O
CO_2
CH_4

Emissions by Sector (2000)

WAS:< 1%   TRA:39%

ENE:60%

Emissions by Sector (Trend)

WAS
ENE
TRA

Inventory data (red; solid) and projections (orange; dashed/dotted) for Annex A gases and sources, if available.
See left table for color codes of Kyoto targets and potential additional emission allowances, if applicable.

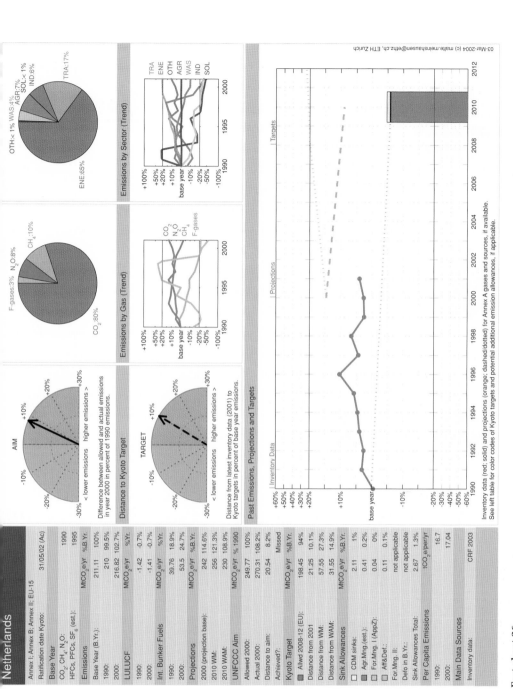

Netherlands

Annex I: Annex B: Annex II:	EU-15	
Ratification date Kyoto:	31/05/02 (Ac)	

Base Year

| CO_2, CH_4, N_2O: | 1990 |
| HFCs, PFCs, SF_6 (est.): | 1995 |

Emissions	MtCO$_2$e/yr	%B.Yr.
Base Year (B.Yr.):	211.11	100%
1990:	210	99.5%
2000:	216.82	102.7%

LULUCF	MtCO$_2$e/yr	%Yr.
1990:	-1.42	-0.7%
2000:	-1.41	-0.7%

Int. Bunker Fuels	MtCO$_2$e/yr	%Yr.
1990:	39.76	18.9%
2000:	53.5	24.7%

Projections	MtCO$_2$e/yr	%B.Yr.
2000 (projection base):	242	114.6%
2010 WM:	256	121.3%
2010 WAM:	230	108.9%

UNFCCC Aim	MtCO$_2$e/yr	% 1990
Allowed 2000:	249.77	100%
Actual 2000:	270.31	108.2%
Distance to aim:	20.54	8.2%
Achieved?:	Missed	

Kyoto Target	MtCO$_2$e/yr	%B.Yr.
Allwd 2008-12 (EU):	198.45	94%
Distance from 2001	21.25	10.1%
Distance from WM:	57.55	27.3%
Distance from WAM:	31.55	14.9%

Sink Allowances	MtCO$_2$e/yr	%B.Yr.
CDM sinks:	2.11	1%
Agr.Mng.(est.):	0.41	0.2%
For.Mng. I (App2):	0.04	0%
Aff&Def.:	0.11	0.1%
For.Mng. II:	not applicable	
Defo in B.Yr.:	not applicable	
Sink Allowances Total:	2.67	1.3%

Per Capita Emissions	tCO$_2$e/per/yr
1990:	16.7
2000:	17.04

Main Data Sources	
Inventory data:	CRF 2003

AIM

-10% | +10% | +20%
-20%
-30% | +30%

< lower emissions   higher emissions >

Difference between allowed and actual emissions in year 2000 in percent of 1990 emissions.

Distance to Kyoto Target

TARGET

-10% | +10% | +20%
-20%
-30% | +30%

< lower emissions   higher emissions >

Distance from latest inventory data (2001) to Kyoto targets in percent of base year emissions.

Past Emissions, Projections and Targets

OTH:< 1% WAS:4%
AGR:7%   SOL:< 1%
IND:6%
TRA:17%
ENE:65%

Emissions by Sector (Trend)

TRA ENE OTH AGR WAS IND SOL

+100%
+50%
+20%
+10%
base year
-10%
-20%
-50%
-100%
1990   1995   2000

F-gases:3% N_2O:8%
CH_4:10%
CO_2:80%

Emissions by Gas (Trend)

CO_2
N_2O
CH_4
F-gases

+100%
+50%
+20%
+10%
base year
-10%
-20%
-50%
-100%
1990   1995   2000

Inventory Data   Projections   Targets

Inventory data (red; solid) and projections (orange; dashed/dotted) for Annex A gases and sources, if available. See left table for color codes of Kyoto targets and potential additional emission allowances, if applicable.

03-Mar-2004 (c) malte.meinshausen@ethz.ch, ETH Zurich

Fact sheet 26

New Zealand

Annex I: Annex B: Annex II		
Ratification date Kyoto:	19/12/02 (R)	

Base Year

CO_2, CH_4, N_2O:		1990
HFCs, PFCs, SF_6 (est.):		1990

Emissions	MtCO2e/yr	%B.Yr.
Base Year (B.Yr.):	61.75	100%
1990:	61.75	100%
2000:	70.35	113.9%

LULUCF	MtCO2e/yr	%Yr.
1990:	-21.77	-35.3%
2000:	-23.71	-33.7%

Int. Bunker Fuels	MtCO2e/yr	%Yr.
1990:	2.41	3.9%
2000:	2.55	3.6%

Projections	MtCO2e/yr	%B.Yr.
2000 (projection base):	76.95	124.6%
2010 WM:	88.09	142.6%
2010 WAM:	84.14	136.3%

UNFCCC Aim	MtCO2e/yr	% 1990
Allowed 2000:	64.16	100%
Actual 2000:	72.9	113.6%
Distance to aim:	8.73	13.6%
Achieved?:	Missed	

Kyoto Target	MtCO2e/yr	%B.Yr.
Allwd 2008-12 (An.B):	61.75	100%
Distance from 2001:	10.63	17.2%
Distance from WM:	26.34	42.6%
Distance from WAM:	22.39	36.3%

Sink Allowances	MtCO2e/yr	%B.Yr.
☐ CDM sinks:	0.62	1%
■ Agr.Mng.(est.):	3.49	5.6%
■ For.Mng. I (AppZ):	0.73	1.2%
☐ Aff&Def.:	28.29	45.8%
For.Mng. II:	not applicable	
Defo in B.Yr.:	not applicable	
Sink Allowances Total:	33.13	53.6%

Per Capita Emissions	tCO2e/per/yr
1990:	19.1
2000:	19.29

Main Data Sources

Inventory data:	CRF 2003

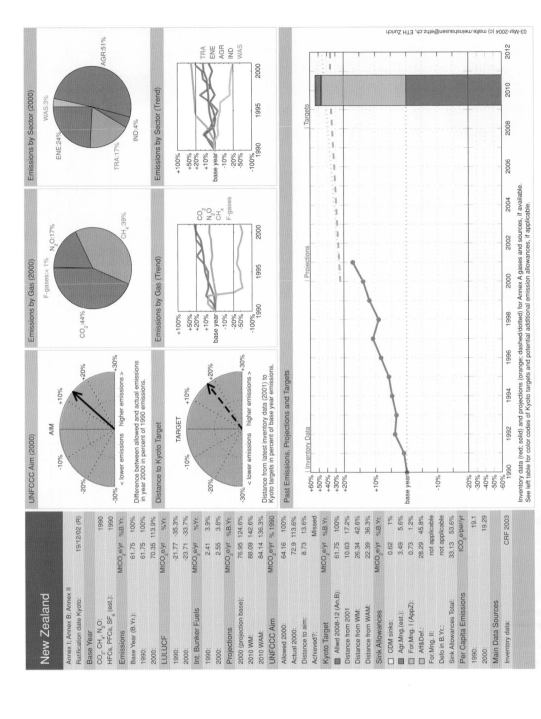

UNFCCC Aim (2000)

AIM
−30% < lower emissions · higher emissions > +30%

Difference between allowed and actual emissions in year 2000 in percent of 1990 emissions.

Distance to Kyoto Target

TARGET
−30% < lower emissions · higher emissions > +30%

Distance from latest inventory data (2001) to Kyoto targets in percent of base year emissions.

Emissions by Gas (2000)

CO_2:44% · N_2O:17% · F-gases:< 1% · CH_4:39%

Emissions by Gas (Trend)

CO_2 · N_2O · CH_4 · F-gases

Emissions by Sector (2000)

WAS:3% · ENE:24% · AGR:51% · IND:4% · TRA:17%

Emissions by Sector (Trend)

TRA · ENE · AGR · IND · WAS

Past Emissions, Projections and Targets

Inventory Data | Projections | Targets

Inventory data (red; solid) and projections (orange; dashed/dotted) for Annex A gases and sources, if available. See left table for color codes of Kyoto targets and potential additional emission allowances, if applicable.

03-Mar-2004 (c) malte.meinshausen@env.ethz.ch, ETH Zurich

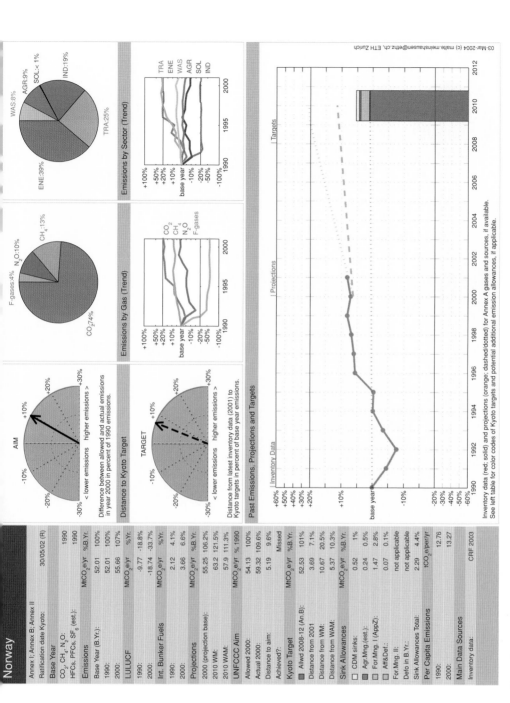

Norway

Annex I: Annex B: Annex II		
Ratification date Kyoto:	30/05/02 (R)	
Base Year		
CO₂, CH₄, N₂O:	1990	
HFCs, PFCs, SF₆ (est.):	1990	
Emissions	MtCO₂e/yr	%B.Yr.
Base Year (B.Yr.):	52.01	100%
1990:	52.01	100%
2000:	55.66	107%
LULUCF	MtCO₂e/yr	%Yr.
1990:	-9.77	-18.8%
2000:	-18.74	-33.7%
Int. Bunker Fuels	MtCO₂e/yr	%Yr.
1990:	2.12	4.1%
2000:	3.66	6.6%
Projections	MtCO₂e/yr	%B.Yr.
2000 (projection base):	55.25	106.2%
2010 WM:	63.2	121.5%
2010 WAM:	57.9	111.3%
UNFCCC Aim	MtCO₂e/yr	%1990
Allowed 2000:	54.13	100%
Actual 2000:	59.32	109.6%
Distance to aim:	5.19	9.6%
Achieved?:		Missed
Kyoto Target	MtCO₂e/yr	%B.Yr.
■ Allwd 2008-12 (An.B):	52.53	101%
Distance from 2001	3.69	7.1%
Distance from WM:	10.67	20.5%
Distance from WAM:	5.37	10.3%
Sink Allowances	MtCO₂e/yr	%B.Yr.
☐ CDM sinks:	0.52	1%
■ Agr.Mng.(est.):	0.24	0.5%
☐ For.Mng. I (AppZ):	1.47	2.8%
☐ Alf&Def.:	0.07	0.1%
For.Mng. II:	not applicable	
Defo in B.Yr.:	not applicable	
Sink Allowances Total:	2.29	4.4%
Per Capita Emissions	tCO₂e/per/yr	
1990:	12.76	
2000:	13.27	
Main Data Sources		
Inventory data:	CRF 2003	

Emissions by Gas (Trend)

CO₂:74%
CH₄:13%
N₂O:10%
F-gases:4%

Emissions by Sector (Trend)

ENE:39%
TRA:25%
IND:19%
WAS:8%
AGR:9%
SOL:< 1%

AIM

< lower emissions   higher emissions >

Difference between allowed and actual emissions in year 2000 in percent of 1990 emissions.

Distance to Kyoto Target

TARGET

< lower emissions   higher emissions >

Distance from latest inventory data (2001) to Kyoto targets in percent of base year emissions.

Past Emissions, Projections and Targets

| Inventory Data | Projections | Targets |

Inventory data (red; solid) and projections (orange; dashed/dotted) for Annex A gases and sources, if available.
See left table for color codes of Kyoto targets and potential additional emission allowances, if applicable.

03-Mar-2004 (c) malte.meinshausen@ethz.ch, ETH Zurich

Fact sheet 28

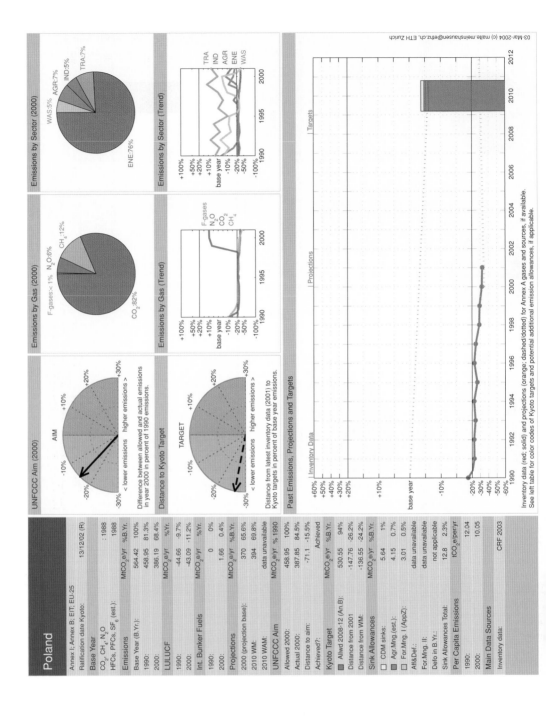

Poland

Annex I; Annex B; EIT; EU-25	
Ratification date Kyoto:	13/12/02 (R)

Base Year

CO_2, CH_4, N_2O	:1988
HFCs, PFCs, SF_6 (est.):	1988

Emissions

	$MtCO_2e/yr$	%B.Yr.
Base Year (B.Yr.):	564.42	100%
1990:	458.95	81.3%
2000:	386.19	68.4%

LULUCF

	$MtCO_2e/yr$	%Yr.
1990:	-44.66	-9.7%
2000:	-43.09	-11.2%

Int. Bunker Fuels

	$MtCO_2e/yr$	%Yr.
1990:	0	0%
2000:	1.66	0.4%

Projections

	$MtCO_2e/yr$	%B.Yr.
2000 (projection base):	370	65.6%
2010 WM:	394	69.8%
2010 WAM:	data unavailable	

UNFCCC Aim

	$MtCO_2e/yr$	% 1990
Allowed 2000:	458.95	100%
Actual 2000:	387.85	84.5%
Distance to aim:	-71.1	-15.5%
Achieved?:		Achieved

Kyoto Target

	$MtCO_2e/yr$	%B.Yr.
Allwd 2008-12 (An.B):	530.55	94%
Distance from 2001	-147.76	-26.2%
Distance from WM:	-136.55	-24.2%

Sink Allowances

	$MtCO_2e/yr$	%B.Yr.
CDM sinks:	5.64	1%
Agr.Mng.(est.):	4.15	0.7%
For.Mng. I (AppZ):	3.01	0.5%
Aff&Def.:	data unavailable	
For.Mng. II:	not applicable	
Defo in B.Yr.:	12.8	2.3%
Sink Allowances Total:		

Per Capita Emissions

	$tCO_2e/per/yr$
1990:	12.04
2000:	10.05

Main Data Sources

Inventory data:	CRF 2003

UNFCCC Aim (2000)

AIM

< lower emissions   higher emissions >

Difference between allowed and actual emissions in year 2000 in percent of 1990 emissions.

Distance to Kyoto Target

TARGET

< lower emissions   higher emissions >

Distance from latest inventory data (2001) to Kyoto targets in percent of base year emissions.

Past Emissions, Projections and Targets

Inventory Data   Projections   Targets

Emissions by Gas (2000)

F-gases:< 1% N_2O:6%

CH_4:12%

CO_2:82%

Emissions by Gas (Trend)

F-gases
N_2O
CO_2
CH_4

Emissions by Sector (2000)

WAS:5%   AGR:7%

IND:5%

TRA:7%

ENE:76%

Emissions by Sector (Trend)

TRA
IND
AGR
ENE
WAS

Inventory data (red; solid) and projections (orange; dashed/dotted) for Annex A gases and sources, if available.
See left table for color codes of Kyoto targets and potential additional emission allowances, if applicable.

03-Mar-2004 (c) malte.meinshausen@ethz.ch, ETH Zurich

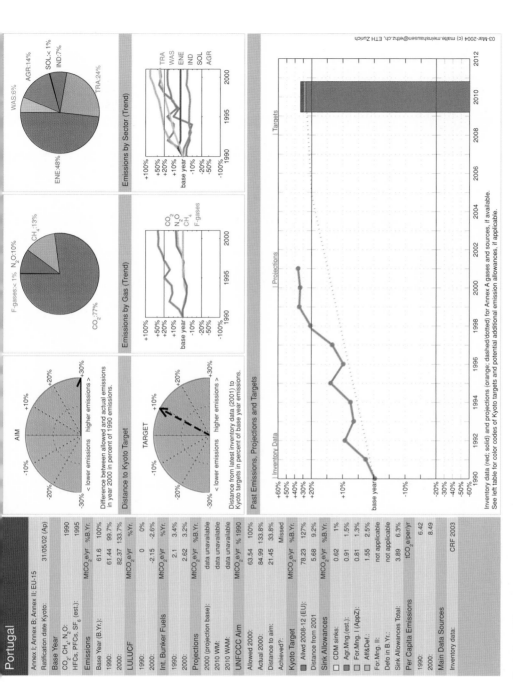

Portugal

Annex I; Annex B; Annex II; EU-15		
Ratification date Kyoto:	31/05/02 (Ap)	

Base Year		
CO_2, CH_4, N_2O:		1990
HFCs, PFCs, SF_6 (est.):		1995

Emissions	MtCO$_2$e/yr	%B.Yr.
Base Year (B.Yr.):	61.6	100%
1990:	61.44	99.7%
2000:	82.37	133.7%

LULUCF	MtCO$_2$e/yr	%Yr.
1990:	0	0%
2000:	-2.15	-2.6%

Int. Bunker Fuels	MtCO$_2$e/yr	%Yr.
1990:	2.1	3.4%
2000:	2.62	3.2%

Projections	MtCO$_2$e/yr	%B.Yr.
2000 (projection base):	data unavailable	
2010 WM:	data unavailable	
2010 WAM:	data unavailable	

UNFCCC Aim	MtCO$_2$e/yr	% 1990
Allowed 2000:	63.54	100%
Actual 2000:	84.99	133.8%
Distance to aim:	21.45	33.8%
Achieved?:		Missed

Kyoto Target	MtCO$_2$e/yr	%B.Yr.
■ Allwd 2008-12 (EU):	78.23	127%
Distance from 2001	5.68	9.2%

Sink Allowances	MtCO$_2$e/yr	%B.Yr.
☐ CDM sinks:	0.62	1%
■ Agr.Mng.(est.):	0.91	1.5%
■ For.Mng. I (AppZ):	0.81	1.3%
☐ Aff&Def.:	1.55	2.5%
For.Mng. II:	not applicable	
Defo in B.Yr.:	not applicable	
Sink Allowances Total:	3.89	6.3%

Per Capita Emissions	tCO$_2$e/per/yr	
1990:	6.42	
2000:	8.49	

Main Data Sources		
Inventory data:		CRF 2003

AIM

Difference between allowed and actual emissions in year 2000 in percent of 1990 emissions.

Distance to Kyoto Target

TARGET

Distance from latest inventory data (2001) to Kyoto targets in percent of base year emissions.

F-gases:< 1% N_2O:10%

CH_4:13%

CO_2:77%

Emissions by Gas (Trend)

WAS:6%   AGR:14%

SOL:< 1%   IND:7%

TRA:24%

ENE:48%

Emissions by Sector (Trend)

Past Emissions, Projections and Targets

| Inventory Data | Projections | Targets |

Inventory data (red; solid) and projections (orange; dashed/dotted) for Annex A gases and sources, if available.
See left table for color codes of Kyoto targets and potential additional emission allowances, if applicable.

03-Mar-2004 (c) malte.meinshausen@ethz.ch, ETH Zurich

Fact sheet 30

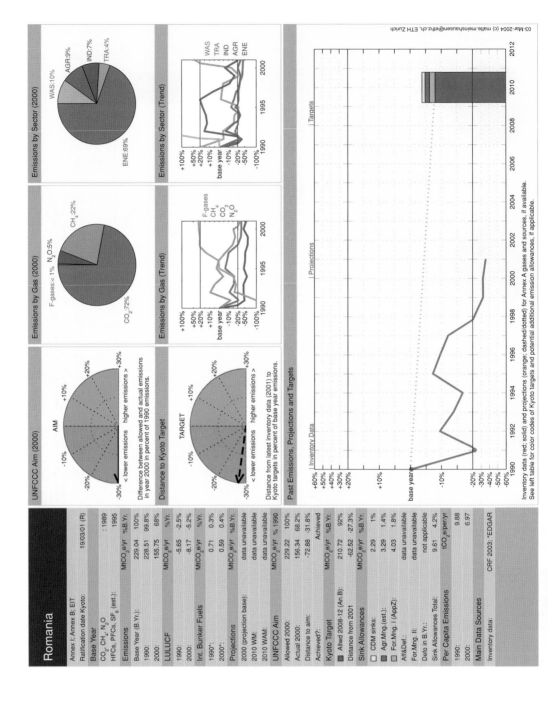

Romania

Annex I: Annex B; EIT	
Ratification date Kyoto:	19/03/01 (R)

Base Year
CO_2, CH_4, N_2O	: 1989
HFCs, PFCs, SF_6 (est.):	1995

Emissions
	$MtCO_2e/yr$	%B.Yr.
Base Year (B.Yr.):	229.04	100%
1990:	228.51	99.8%
2000:	155.75	68%

LULUCF
	$MtCO_2e/yr$	%Yr.
1990:	-5.65	-2.5%
2000:	-8.17	-5.2%

Int. Bunker Fuels
	$MtCO_2e/yr$	%Yr.
1990*:	0.71	0.3%
2000*:	0.59	0.4%

Projections
	$MtCO_2e/yr$	%B.Yr.
2000 (projection base):	data unavailable	
2010 WM:	data unavailable	
2010 WAM:	data unavailable	

UNFCCC Aim
	$MtCO_2e/yr$	% 1990
Allowed 2000:	229.22	100%
Actual 2000:	156.34	68.2%
Distance to aim:	-72.88	-31.8%
Achieved?:		Achieved

Kyoto Target
	$MtCO_2e/yr$	%B.Yr.
Allwd 2008-12 (An.B):	210.72	92%
Distance from 2001	-62.52	-27.3%

Sink Allowances
	$MtCO_2e/yr$	%B.Yr.
☐ CDM sinks:	2.29	1%
■ Agr.Mng.(est.):	3.29	1.4%
■ For.Mng. I (AppZ):	4.03	1.8%
Aff&Def.:	data unavailable	
For.Mng. II:	not applicable	
Defo in B.Yr.:		
Sink Allowances Total:	9.61	4.2%

Per Capita Emissions
	tCO_2e/per/yr
1990:	9.88
2000:	6.97

Main Data Sources
Inventory data:	CRF 2003; *EDGAR

UNFCCC Aim (2000)

AIM

< lower emissions   higher emissions >

Difference between allowed and actual emissions in year 2000 in percent of 1990 emissions.

Distance to Kyoto Target

TARGET

< lower emissions   higher emissions >

Distance from latest inventory data (2001) to Kyoto targets in percent of base year emissions.

Emissions by Gas (2000)

F-gases:< 1% N_2O:5%

CH_4:22%

CO_2:72%

Emissions by Gas (Trend)

F-gases
CH_4
CO_2
N_2O

Emissions by Sector (2000)

WAS:10%
AGR:9%
IND:7%
TRA:4%

ENE:69%

Emissions by Sector (Trend)

WAS
TRA
IND
AGR
ENE

Past Emissions, Projections and Targets

| Inventory Data | Projections | Targets |

Inventory data (red: solid) and projections (orange: dashed/dotted) for Annex A gases and sources, if available. See left table for color codes of Kyoto targets and potential additional emission allowances, if applicable.

03-Mar-2004 (c) malte.meinshausen@ethz.ch, ETH Zurich

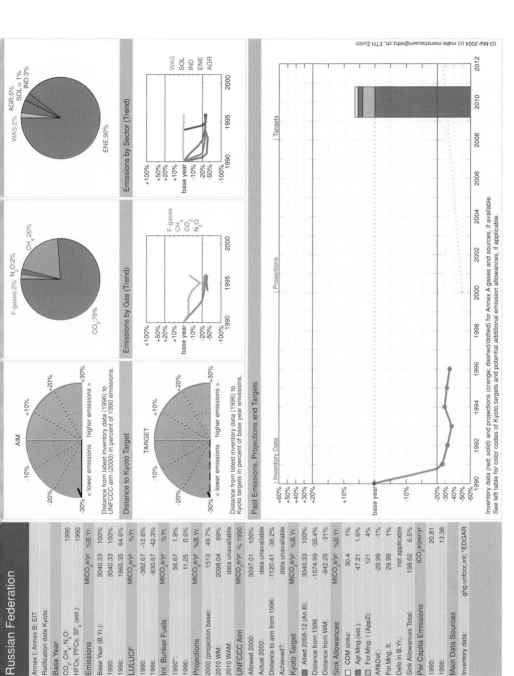

Russian Federation

Annex I: Annex B; EIT		
Ratification date Kyoto:		
Base Year		
CO_2, CH_4, N_2O:		1990
HFCs, PFCs, SF_6 (est.):		1990
Emissions	MtCO₂e/yr	%B.Yr.
Base Year (B.Yr.):	3040.33	100%
1990:	3040.33	100%
1996:	1965.35	64.6%
LULUCF	MtCO₂e/yr	%Yr.
1990:	-382.67	-12.6%
1996:	-830.67	-42.3%
Int. Bunker Fuels	MtCO₂e/yr	%Yr.
1990*:	56.67	1.9%
1996:	11.25	0.6%
Projections	MtCO₂e/yr	%B.Yr.
2000 (projection base):	1510	49.7%
2010 WM:	2098.04	69%
2010 WAM:	data unavailable	
UNFCCC Aim	MtCO₂e/yr	% 1990
Allowed 2000:	3097.01	100%
Actual 2000:	data unavailable	
Distance to aim from 1996:	-1120.41	-36.2%
Achieved?:	data unavailable	
Kyoto Target	MtCO₂e/yr	%B.Yr.
▓ Allwd 2008-12 (An.B):	3040.33	100%
Distance from 1996	-1074.99	-35.4%
Distance from WM:	-942.29	-31%
Sink Allowances	MtCO₂e/yr	%B.Yr.
☐ CDM sinks:	30.4	1%
▓ Agr.Mng.(est.):	47.21	1.6%
▓ For.Mng. I (AppZ):	121	4%
Aff&Def.:	-29.99	-1%
For.Mng. II:	29.99	1%
Defo in B.Yr.:	not applicable	
Sink Allowances Total:	198.62	6.5%
Per Capita Emissions	tCO₂e/per/yr	
1990:	20.81	
1996:	13.38	
Main Data Sources		
Inventory data:	ghg.unfccc.int; *EDGAR	

Fact sheet 32

03-Mar-2004 (c) malte.meinshausen@ethz.ch, ETH Zurich

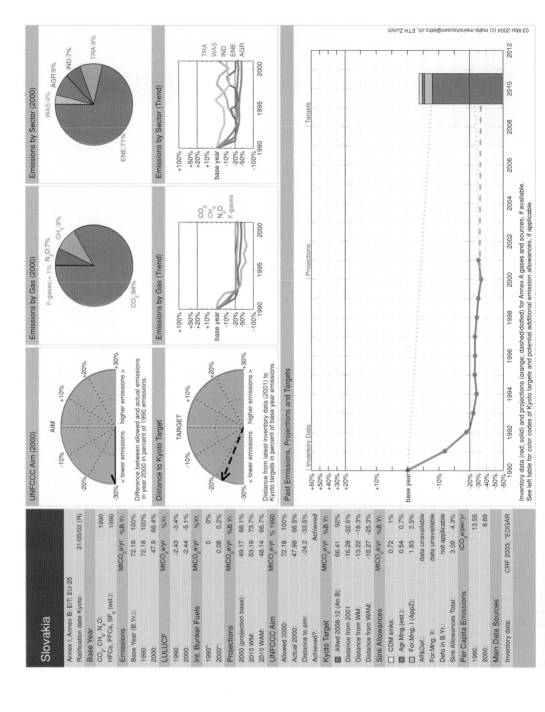

Slovakia

Annex I: Annex B; EIT; EU-25		
Ratification date Kyoto:	31/05/02 (R)	

Base Year
CO_2, CH_4, N_2O:		1990
HFCs, PFCs, SF_6 (est.):		1990

Emissions
	MtCO₂e/yr	%B.Yr.
Base Year (B.Yr.):	72.18	100%
1990:	72.18	100%
2000:	47.9	66.4%

LULUCF
	MtCO₂e/yr	%Yr.
1990:	-2.43	-3.4%
2000:	-2.44	-5.1%

Int. Bunker Fuels
	MtCO₂e/yr	%Yr.
1990*:	0	0%
2000*:	0.08	0.2%

Projections
	MtCO₂e/yr	%B.Yr.
2000 (projection base):	49.17	68.1%
2010 WM:	53.19	73.7%
2010 WAM:	48.14	66.7%

UNFCCC Aim
	MtCO₂e/yr	% 1990
Allowed 2000:	72.18	100%
Actual 2000:	47.98	66.5%
Distance to aim:	-24.2	-33.5%
Achieved?:		Achieved

Kyoto Target
	MtCO₂e/yr	%B.Yr.
Allwd 2008-12 (An.B):	66.41	92%
Distance from 2001	-16.28	-22.6%
Distance from WM:	-13.22	-18.3%
Distance from WAM:	-18.27	-25.3%

Sink Allowances
	MtCO₂e/yr	%B.Yr.
☐ CDM sinks:	0.72	1%
☐ Agr.Mng.(est.):	0.54	0.7%
☐ For.Mng. I (AppZ):	1.83	2.5%
Aff&Def.:	data unavailable	
For.Mng. II:	data unavailable	
Defo in B.Yr.:	not applicable	
Sink Allowances Total:	3.09	4.3%

Per Capita Emissions
	tCO₂e/per/yr	
1990:	13.55	
2000:	8.89	

Main Data Sources
Inventory data:	CRF 2003; *EDGAR	

UNFCCC Aim (2000)

AIM

+20%
+10%
-10%
-20%
-30%   +30%

< lower emissions   higher emissions >

Difference between allowed and actual emissions in year 2000 in percent of 1990 emissions.

Distance to Kyoto Target

TARGET

+20%
+10%
-10%
-20%
-30%   +30%

< lower emissions   higher emissions >

Distance from latest inventory data (2001) to Kyoto targets in percent of base year emissions.

Past Emissions, Projections and Targets

| Inventory Data | Projections | Targets |

+60%
+50%
+40%
+30%
+20%
+10%
base year
-10%
-20%
-30%
-40%
-50%
-60%

1990 1992 1994 1996 1998 2000 2002 2004 2006 2008 2010 2012

Inventory data (red; solid) and projections (orange; dashed/dotted) for Annex A gases and sources, if available.
See left table for color codes of Kyoto targets and potential additional emission allowances, if applicable.

Emissions by Sector (2000)

WAS:4%
AGR:9%
IND:7%
TRA:9%
ENE:71%

Emissions by Sector (Trend)

+100%
+50%
+20%
+10%
base year
-10%
-20%
-50%
-100%

1990 1995 2000

TRA
WAS
IND
ENE
AGR

Emissions by Gas (2000)

F-gases:< 1% N_2O:7%
CH_4:9%
CO_2:84%

Emissions by Gas (Trend)

+100%
+50%
+20%
+10%
base year
-10%
-20%
-50%
-100%

1990 1995 2000

CO_2
CH_4
N_2O
F-gases

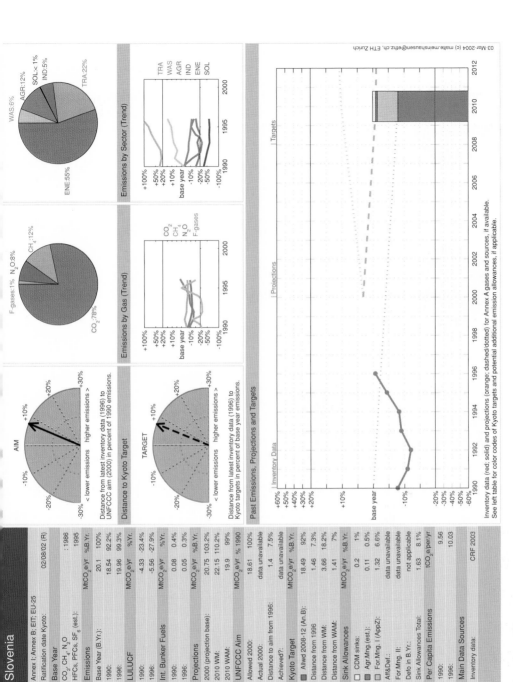

Slovenia

Annex I: Annex B; EIT; EU-25		
Ratification date Kyoto:	02/08/02 (R)	

Base Year

CO_2, CH_4, N_2O	:1986	
HFCs, PFCs, SF_6 (est.):	1995	

Emissions	$MtCO_2e$/yr	%B.Yr.
Base Year (B.Yr.):	20.1	100%
1990:	18.54	92.2%
1996:	19.96	99.3%

LULUCF	$MtCO_2e$/yr	%Yr.
1990:	-4.33	-23.4%
1996:	-5.56	-27.9%

Int. Bunker Fuels	$MtCO_2e$/yr	%Yr.
1990:	0.08	0.4%
1996:	0.05	0.3%

Projections	$MtCO_2e$/yr	%B.Yr.
2000 (projection base):	20.75	103.2%
2010 WM:	22.15	110.2%
2010 WAM:	19.9	99%

UNFCCC Aim	$MtCO_2e$/yr	% 1990
Allwed 2000:	18.61	100%
Actual 2000:	data unavailable	
Distance to aim from 1996:	1.4	7.5%
Achieved?:	data unavailable	

Kyoto Target	$MtCO_2e$/yr	%B.Yr.
■ Allwd 2008-12 (An.B):	18.49	92%
Distance from 1996:	1.46	7.3%
Distance from WM:	3.66	18.2%
Distance from WAM:	1.41	7%

Sink Allowances	$MtCO_2e$/yr	%B.Yr.
☐ CDM sinks:	0.2	1%
☐ Agr.Mng.(est.):	0.11	0.5%
☐ For.Mng. I (AppZ):	1.32	6.6%
Aff&Def.:	data unavailable	
For.Mng. II:	data unavailable	
Defo in B.Yr.:	1.63	8.1%
Sink Allowances Total:		not applicable

Per Capita Emissions	tCO_2e/per/yr	
1990:	9.56	
1996:	10.03	

Main Data Sources		
Inventory data:	CRF 2003	

AIM

< lower emissions   higher emissions >

Distance from latest inventory data (1996) to UNFCCC aim (2000) in percent of 1990 emissions.

Distance to Kyoto Target

TARGET

< lower emissions   higher emissions >

Distance from latest inventory data (1996) to Kyoto targets in percent of base year emissions.

Emissions by Gas (Trend)

CO₂
CH₄
N₂O
F-gases

Emissions by Sector (Trend)

TRA
WAS
AGR
IND
ENE
SOL

Past Emissions, Projections and Targets

| Inventory Data | | Projections | | Targets |

Inventory data (red: solid) and projections (orange: dashed/dotted) for Annex A gases and sources, if available. See left table for color codes of Kyoto targets and potential additional emission allowances, if applicable.

F-gases:1%   N₂O:8%
CH₄:12%
CO₂:78%

WAS:6%
AGR:12%   SOL:< 1%
IND:5%
ENE:55%
TRA:22%

03-Mar-2004 (c) malte.meinshausen@ethz.ch, ETH Zurich

Fact sheet 34

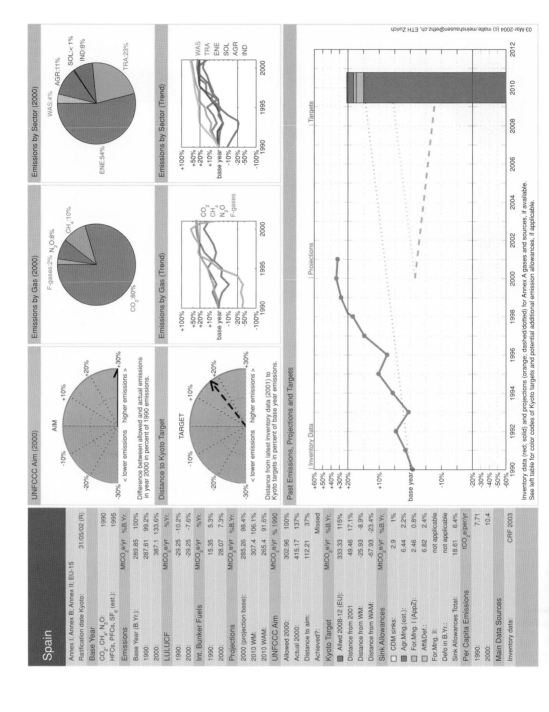

Spain

Annex I; Annex B; Annex II; EU-15		
Ratification date Kyoto:	31/05/02 (R)	

Base Year
CO₂, CH₄, N₂O:		1990
HFCs, PFCs, SF₆ (est.):		1995

Emissions
	MtCO₂e/yr	%B.Yr.
Base Year (B.Yr.):	289.85	100%
1990:	287.61	99.2%
2000:	387.1	133.6%

LULUCF
	MtCO₂e/yr	%Yr.
1990:	-29.25	-10.2%
2000:	-29.25	-7.6%

Int. Bunker Fuels
	MtCO₂e/yr	%Yr.
1990:	15.35	5.3%
2000:	28.07	7.3%

Projections
	MtCO₂e/yr	%B.Yr.
2000 (projection base):	285.26	98.4%
2010 WM:	307.4	106.1%
2010 WAM:	265.4	91.6%

UNFCCC Aim
	MtCO₂e/yr	% 1990
Allowed 2000:	302.96	100%
Actual 2000:	415.17	137%
Distance to aim:	112.21	37%
Achieved?:		Missed

Kyoto Target
	MtCO₂e/yr	%B.Yr.
Allwd 2008-12 (EU):	333.33	115%
Distance from 2001	49.46	17.1%
Distance from WM:	-25.93	-8.9%
Distance from WAM:	-67.93	-23.4%

Sink Allowances
	MtCO₂e/yr	%B.Yr.
CDM sinks:	2.9	1%
Agr.Mng.(est.):	6.44	2.2%
For.Mng. I (AppZ):	2.46	0.8%
Aff&Def.:	6.82	2.4%
For.Mng. II:	not applicable	
Defo in B.Yr.:	not applicable	
Sink Allowances Total:	18.61	6.4%

Per Capita Emissions
	tCO₂e/per/yr
1990:	7.71
2000:	10.4

Main Data Sources
Inventory data:	CRF 2003

UNFCCC Aim (2000)

AIM

Difference between allowed and actual emissions in year 2000 in percent of 1990 emissions.

Distance to Kyoto Target

TARGET

Distance from latest inventory data (2001) to Kyoto targets in percent of base year emissions.

Past Emissions, Projections and Targets

| Inventory Data | Projections | Targets |

Emissions by Gas (2000)

F-gases:2% N₂O:8% CH₄:10%

CO₂:80%

Emissions by Gas (Trend)

CO₂
CH₄
N₂O
F-gases

Emissions by Sector (2000)

WAS:4% AGR:11% SOL:< 1% IND:8%

TRA:23%

ENE:54%

Emissions by Sector (Trend)

WAS
TRA
ENE
SOL
AGR
IND

Inventory data (red; solid) and projections (orange; dashed/dotted) for Annex A gases and sources, if available. See left table for color codes of Kyoto targets and potential additional emission allowances, if applicable.

03-Mar-2004 (c) malte.meinshausen@ethz.ch, ETH Zurich

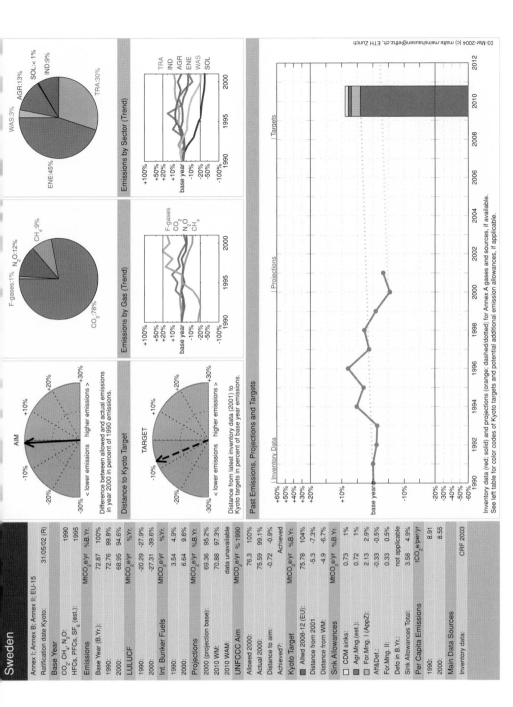

Sweden

Annex I; Annex B; Annex II; EU-15	
Ratification date Kyoto:	31/05/02 (R)

Base Year

CO_2, CH_4, N_2O:	1990
HFCs, PFCs, SF_6 (est.):	1995

Emissions	$MtCO_2e/yr$	%B.Yr.
Base Year (B.Yr.):	72.87	100%
1990:	72.76	99.8%
2000:	68.95	94.6%

LULUCF	$MtCO_2e/yr$	%Yr.
1990:	-20.29	-27.9%
2000:	-27.31	-39.6%

Int. Bunker Fuels	$MtCO_2e/yr$	%Yr.
1990:	3.54	4.9%
2000:	6.64	9.6%

Projections	$MtCO_2e/yr$	%B.Yr.
2000 (projection base):	69.36	95.2%
2010 WM:	70.88	97.3%
2010 WAM:	data unavailable	

UNFCCC Aim		$MtCO_2e/yr$ % 1990
Allowed 2000:	76.3	100%
Actual 2000:	75.59	99.1%
Distance to aim:	-0.72	-0.9%
Achieved?:		Achieved

Kyoto Target	$MtCO_2e/yr$	%B.Yr.
Allwd 2008-12 (EU):	75.78	104%
Distance from 2001	-5.3	-7.3%
Distance from WM:	-4.9	-6.7%

Sink Allowances	$MtCO_2e/yr$	%B.Yr.
☐ CDM sinks:	0.73	1%
☐ Agr.Mng.(est.):	0.72	1%
☐ For.Mng. I (AppZ):	2.13	2.9%
Aff&Def.:	-0.33	-0.5%
For.Mng. II:	0.33	0.5%
Defo in B.Yr.:		not applicable
Sink Allowances Total:	3.58	4.9%

Per Capita Emissions	$tCO_2e/per/yr$
1990:	8.91
2000:	8.55

Main Data Sources	
Inventory data:	CRF 2003

AIM

Difference between allowed and actual emissions in year 2000 in percent of 1990 emissions.

Distance to Kyoto Target

TARGET

Distance from latest inventory data (2001) to Kyoto targets in percent of base year emissions.

Past Emissions, Projections and Targets

Inventory data (red: solid) and projections (orange: dashed/dotted) for Annex A gases and sources, if available. See left table for color codes of Kyoto targets and potential additional emission allowances, if applicable.

Emissions by Gas (Trend)

Emissions by Sector (Trend)

03-Mar-2004 (c) malte.meinshausen@ethz.ch, ETH Zurich

Fact sheet 36

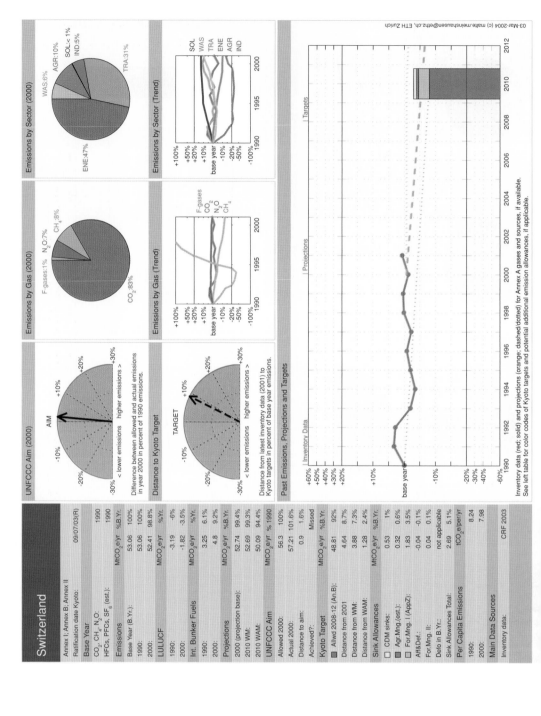

Inventory data (red; solid) and projections (orange; dashed/dotted) for Annex A gases and sources, if available.
See left table for color codes of Kyoto targets and potential additional emission allowances, if applicable.

03-Mar-2004 (c) malte.meinshausen@ethz.ch, ETH Zürich

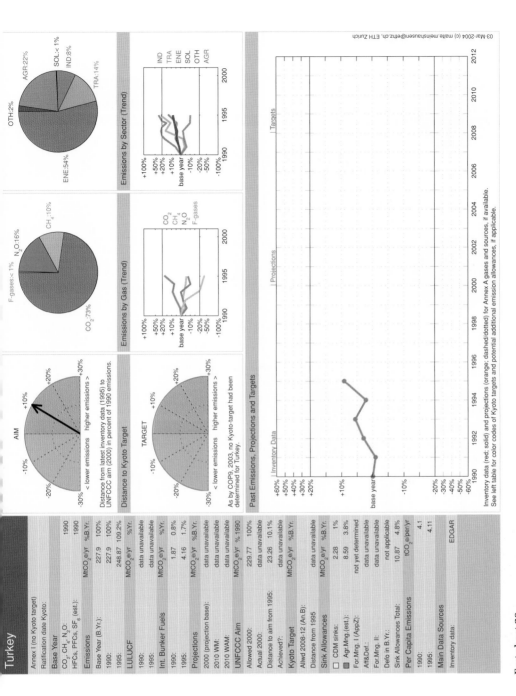

Turkey

Annex I (no Kyoto target)		
Ratification date Kyoto:		
Base Year		
CO₂, CH₄, N₂O:		1990
HFCs, PFCs, SF₆ (est.):		1990
Emissions	MtCO₂e/yr	%B.Yr.
Base Year (B.Yr.):	227.9	100%
1990:	227.9	100%
1995:	248.87	109.2%
LULUCF	MtCO₂e/yr	%Yr.
1990:	data unavailable	
1995:	data unavailable	
Int. Bunker Fuels	MtCO₂e/yr	%Yr.
1990:	1.87	0.8%
1995:	4.16	1.7%
Projections	MtCO₂e/yr	%B.Yr.
2000 (projection base):	data unavailable	
2010 WM:	data unavailable	
2010 WAM:	data unavailable	
UNFCCC Aim	MtCO₂e/yr	% 1990
Allowed 2000:	229.77	100%
Actual 2000:	data unavailable	
Distance to aim from 1995:	23.26	10.1%
Achieved?:	data unavailable	
Kyoto Target	MtCO₂e/yr	%B.Yr.
Allwd 2008-12 (An.B):	data unavailable	
Distance from 1995	data unavailable	
Sink Allowances	MtCO₂e/yr	%B.Yr.
☐ CDM sinks:	2.28	1%
■ Agr.Mng.(est.):	8.59	3.8%
For.Mng. I (AppZ):	not yet determined	
Aff&Def.:	data unavailable	
For.Mng. II:	not applicable	
Defo in B.Yr.:	data unavailable	
Sink Allowances Total:	10.87	4.8%
Per Capita Emissions		tCO₂e/per/yr
1990:		4.1
1995:		4.11
Main Data Sources		
Inventory data:		EDGAR

Pie chart labels: OTH:2%, AGR:22%, SOL:< 1%, IND:8%, TRA:14%, ENE:54%

Pie chart labels: F-gases:< 1%, N₂O:16%, CH₄:10%, CO₂:73%

AIM
−20%, −10%, +10%, +20%, +30%
< lower emissions   higher emissions >

Distance from latest inventory data (1995) to UNFCCC aim (2000) in percent of 1990 emissions.

Distance to Kyoto Target

TARGET
−20%, −10%, +10%, +20%, +30%
< lower emissions   higher emissions >

As by COP9, 2003, no Kyoto-target had been determined for Turkey.

Emissions by Gas (Trend)
+100%, +50%, +20%, +10%, base year, −10%, −20%, −50%, −100%
1990, 1995, 2000
CO₂, CH₄, N₂O, F-gases

Emissions by Sector (Trend)
+100%, +50%, +20%, +10%, base year, −10%, −20%, −50%, −100%
1990, 1995, 2000
IND, TRA, ENE, SOL, OTH, AGR

Past Emissions, Projections and Targets
| Inventory Data | Projections | Targets |

+60%, +50%, +40%, +30%, +20%, +10%, base year, −10%, −20%, −30%, −40%, −50%, −60%
1990, 1992, 1994, 1996, 1998, 2000, 2002, 2004, 2006, 2008, 2010, 2012

Inventory data (red: solid) and projections (orange: dashed/dotted) for Annex A gases and sources, if available.
See left table for color codes of Kyoto targets and potential additional emission allowances, if applicable.

03-Mar-2004 (c) malte.meinshausen@ethz.ch, ETH Zürich

Fact sheet 38

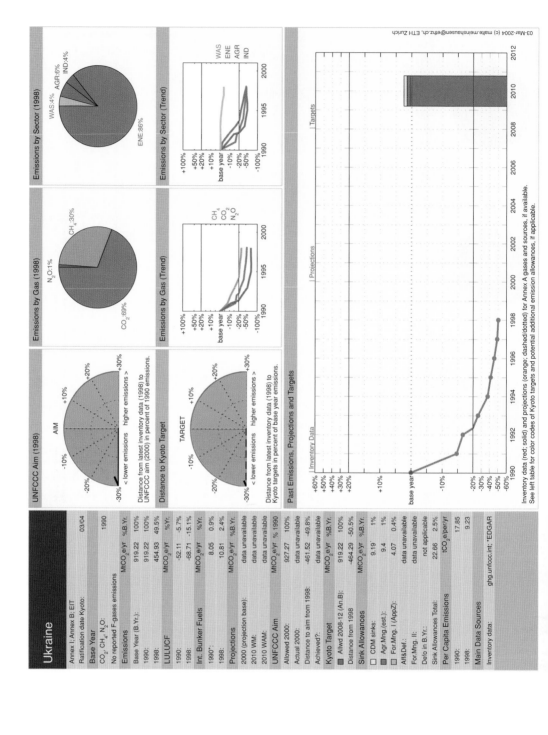

Ukraine

Emissions by Sector (1998)

WAS:4%   AGR:6%   IND:4%

ENE:86%

Emissions by Gas (1998)

N_2O:1% CH_4:30%

CO_2:69%

UNFCCC Aim (1998)

AIM

-10%   +10%
-20%   +20%
-30%   +30%

< lower emissions   higher emissions >

Distance from latest inventory data (1998) to
UNFCCC aim (2000) in percent of 1990 emissions.

Distance to Kyoto Target

TARGET

-10%   +10%
-20%   +20%
-30%   +30%

< lower emissions   higher emissions >

Distance from latest inventory data (1998) to
Kyoto targets in percent of base year emissions.

Emissions by Sector (Trend)

+100%
+50%
+20%
+10%
base year
-10%
-20%
-50%
-100%

1990   1995   2000

WAS
ENE
AGR
IND

Emissions by Gas (Trend)

+100%
+50%
+20%
+10%
base year
-10%
-20%
-50%
-100%

1990   1995   2000

CH_4
CO_2
N_2O

Past Emissions, Projections and Targets

Inventory Data   Projections   Targets

+60%
+50%
+40%
+30%
+20%

+10%

base year

-10%

-20%
-30%
-40%
-50%
-60%

1990 1992 1994 1996 1998 2000 2002 2004 2006 2008 2010 2012

Inventory data (red: solid) and projections (orange: dashed/dotted) for Annex A gases and sources, if available.
See left table for color codes of Kyoto targets and potential additional emission allowances, if applicable.

Annex I: Annex B: EIT		03/04
Ratification date Kyoto:		
Base Year		1990
CO_2, CH_4, N_2O:		
No reported F-gases emissions		
Emissions	MtCO₂e/yr	%B.Yr.
Base Year (B.Yr.):	919.22	100%
1990:	919.22	100%
1998:	454.93	49.5%
LULUCF	MtCO₂e/yr	%Yr.
1990:	-52.11	-5.7%
1998:	-68.71	-15.1%
Int. Bunker Fuels	MtCO₂e/yr	%Yr.
1990*:	8.05	0.9%
1998:	10.81	2.4%
Projections	MtCO₂e/yr	%B.Yr.
2000 (projection base):	data unavailable	
2010 WM:	data unavailable	
2010 WAM:	data unavailable	
UNFCCC Aim	MtCO₂e/yr	% 1990
Allowed 2000:	927.27	100%
Actual 2000:	data unavailable	
Distance to aim from 1998:	-461.52	-49.8%
Achieved?:	data unavailable	
Kyoto Target	MtCO₂e/yr	%B.Yr.
Allwd 2008-12 (An.B):	919.22	100%
Distance from 1998	-464.29	-50.5%
Sink Allowances	MtCO₂e/yr	%B.Yr.
☐ CDM sinks:	9.19	1%
☐ Agr.Mng (est.):	9.4	1%
☐ For.Mng. I (AppZ):	4.07	0.4%
Aff&Def.:	data unavailable	
For.Mng. II:	data unavailable	
Defo in B.Yr.:	not applicable	
Sink Allowances Total:	22.66	2.5%
Per Capita Emissions	tCO₂e/per/yr	
1990:	17.85	
1998:	9.23	
Main Data Sources		
Inventory data:	ghg.unfccc.int; *EDGAR	

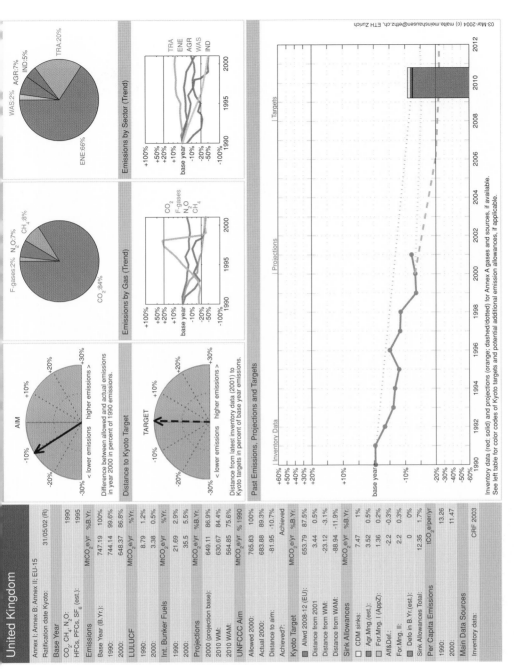

United Kingdom

Annex I: Annex B: Annex II:	EU-15	
Ratification date Kyoto:	31/05/02 (R)	

Base Year		
CO_2, CH_4, N_2O:	1990	
HFCs, PFCs, SF_6 (est.):	1995	

Emissions	$MtCO_2e/yr$	%B.Yr.
Base Year (B.Yr.):	747.19	100%
1990:	744.14	99.6%
2000:	648.37	86.8%

LULUCF	$MtCO_2e/yr$	%Yr.
1990:	8.79	1.2%
2000:	3.38	0.5%

Int. Bunker Fuels	$MtCO_2e/yr$	%Yr.
1990:	21.69	2.9%
2000:	35.5	5.5%

Projections	$MtCO_2e/yr$	%B.Yr.
2000 (projection base):	649.11	86.9%
2010 WM:	630.67	84.4%
2010 WAM:	564.85	75.6%

UNFCCC Aim	$MtCO_2e/yr$	% 1990
Allowed 2000:	765.83	100%
Actual 2000:	683.88	89.3%
Distance to aim:	-81.95	-10.7%
Achieved?:		Achieved

Kyoto Target	$MtCO_2e/yr$	%B.Yr.
Allwd 2008-12 (EU):	653.79	87.5%
Distance from 2001	3.44	0.5%
Distance from WM:	-23.12	-3.1%
Distance from WAM:	-88.94	-11.9%

Sink Allowances	$MtCO_2e/yr$	%B.Yr.
☐ CDM sinks:	7.47	1%
☐ Agr.Mng.(est.):	3.52	0.5%
☐ For.Mng. I (AppZ):	1.36	0.2%
Aff&Def.:	-2.2	-0.3%
For.Mng. II:	2.2	0.3%
☐ Defo in B.Yr.(est.):	0	0%
Sink Allowances Total:	12.35	1.7%

Per Capita Emissions		$tCO_2e/per/yr$
1990:		13.26
2000:		11.47

Main Data Sources		
Inventory data:		CRF 2003

03-Mar-2004 (c) malte.meinshausen@ethz.ch, ETH Zurich

Inventory data (red: solid) and projections (orange: dashed/dotted) for Annex A gases and sources, if available.
See left table for color codes of Kyoto targets and potential additional emission allowances, if applicable.

Fact sheet 40

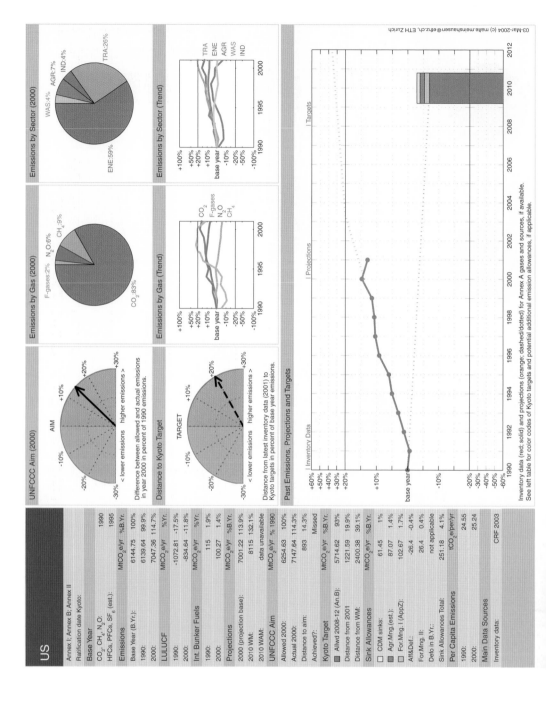

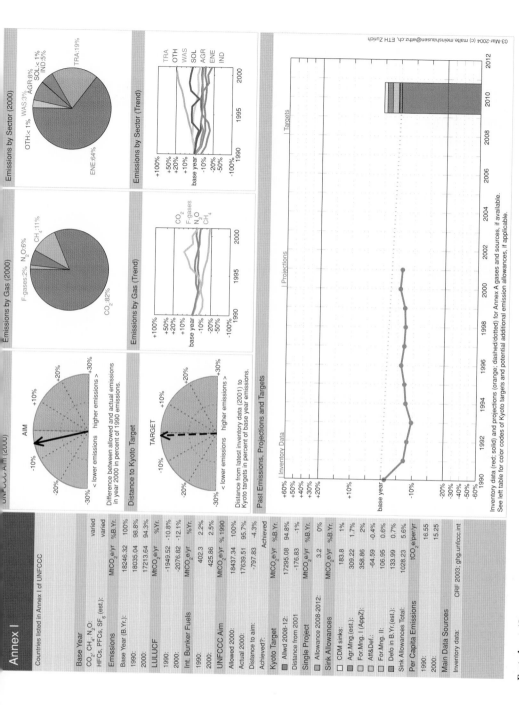

Annex I

Countries listed in Annex I of UNFCCC

Base Year

CO_2, CH_4, N_2O:		varied
HFCs, PFCs, SF_6 (est.):		varied

Emissions | | MtCO₂e/yr | %B.Yr.
Base Year (B.Yr.):	18246.32	100%
1990:	18035.04	98.8%
2000:	17213.64	94.3%

LULUCF | | MtCO₂e/yr | %Yr.
| 1990: | -1949.52 | -10.8% |
| 2000: | -2076.82 | -12.1% |

Int. Bunker Fuels | | MtCO₂e/yr | %Yr.
| 1990: | 402.3 | 2.2% |
| 2000: | 425.86 | 2.5% |

UNFCCC Aim | | MtCO₂e/yr | % 1990
Allowed 2000:	18437.34	100%
Actual 2000:	17639.51	95.7%
Distance to aim:	-797.83	-4.3%
Achieved?:		Achieved

Kyoto Target | | MtCO₂e/yr | %B.Yr.
| ▣ Allwd 2008-12: | 17295.08 | 94.8% |
| Distance from 2001 | -176.83 | -1% |

Single Project | | MtCO₂e/yr | %B.Yr.
| ▣ Allowance 2008-2012: | 3.2 | 0% |

Sink Allowances | | MtCO₂e/yr | %B.Yr.
☐ CDM sinks:	183.8	1%
▣ Agr.Mng. (est.):	309.22	1.7%
▣ For.Mng. I (AppZ):	358.86	2%
☐ Aff&Def.:	-64.59	-0.4%
☐ For.Mng. II:	106.95	0.6%
☐ Defo in B.Yr.(est.):	133.99	0.7%
Sink Allowances Total:	1028.32	5.6%

Per Capita Emissions | | | tCO₂e/per/yr
| 1990: | | 16.55 |
| 2000: | | 15.25 |

Main Data Sources

Inventory data:	CRF 2003; ghg.unfccc.int

UNFCCC Aim (2000)

AIM

+10% +20% +30%

-10%

-20%

-30%   < lower emissions   higher emissions >

Difference between allowed and actual emissions in year 2000 in percent of 1990 emissions.

Distance to Kyoto Target

TARGET

+10% +20% +30%

-10%

-20%

-30%   < lower emissions   higher emissions >

Distance from latest inventory data (2001) to Kyoto targets in percent of base year emissions.

Past Emissions, Projections and Targets

Emissions by Gas (2000)

F-gases 2% N₂O 6%
CH₄ 11%

CO₂ 82%

Emissions by Gas (Trend)

+100%
+50%
+20%
+10%
base year
-10%
-20%
-50%
-100%

1990   1995   2000

CO₂
F-gases
N₂O
CH₄

Emissions by Sector (2000)

OTH:< 1% WAS 3%
AGR 8% SOL:< 1%
IND 5%
TRA:19%

ENE 64%

Emissions by Sector (Trend)

+100%
+50%
+20%
+10%
base year
-10%
-20%
-50%
-100%

1990   1995   2000

TRA
OTH
WAS
SOL
AGR
ENE
IND

+60%
+50%
+40%
+30%
+20%

+10%

base year

-10%

-20%
-30%
-40%
-50%
-60%

1990 1992 1994 1996 1998 2000 2002 2004 2006 2008 2010 2012

| Inventory Data | Projections | Targets

Inventory data (red; solid) and projections (orange; dashed/dotted) for Annex A gases and sources, if available. See left table for color codes of Kyoto targets and potential additional emission allowances, if applicable.

Fact sheet 42

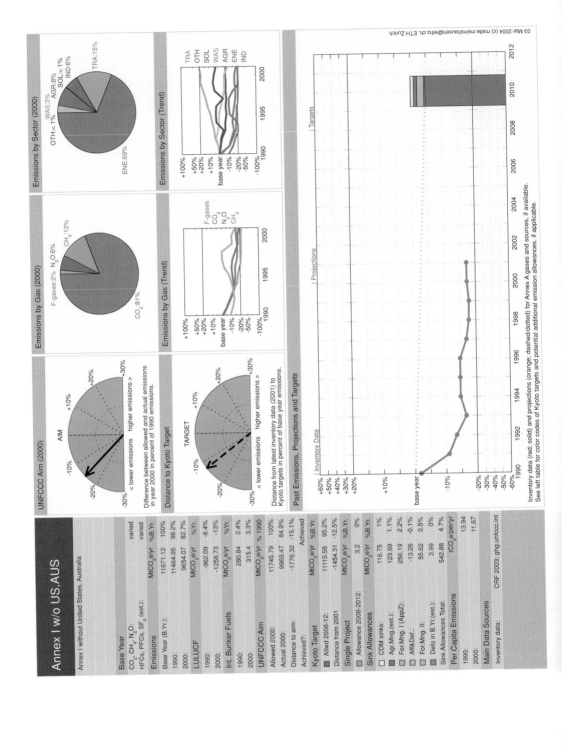

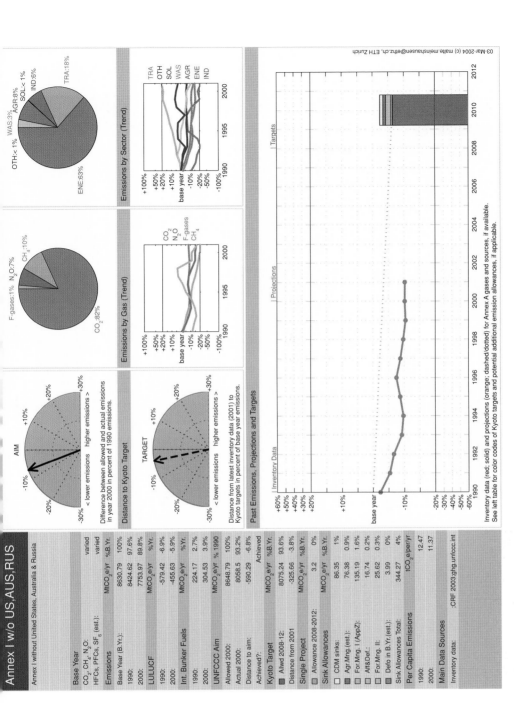

Annex I w/o US,AUS,RUS

Annex I without United States, Australia & Russia

Base Year

CO₂, CH₄, N₂O:	varied
HFCs, PFCs, SF₆ (est.):	varied

Emissions

	MtCO₂e/yr	%B.Yr.
Base Year (B.Yr.):	8630.79	100%
1990:	8424.62	97.6%
2000:	7753.97	89.8%

LULUCF

	MtCO₂e/yr	%Yr.
1990:	-579.42	-6.9%
2000:	-455.63	-5.9%

Int. Bunker Fuels

	MtCO₂e/yr	%Yr.
1990:	224.17	2.7%
2000:	304.53	3.9%

UNFCCC Aim

	MtCO₂e/yr	% 1990
Allowed 2000:	8648.79	100%
Actual 2000:	8058.5	93.2%
Distance to aim:	-590.29	-6.8%
Achieved?:		Achieved

Kyoto Target

	MtCO₂e/yr	%B.Yr.
■ Alwd 2008-12:	8075.24	93.6%
Distance from 2001	-325.66	-3.8%

Single Project

	MtCO₂e/yr	%B.Yr.
□ Allowance 2008-2012:	0	0%

Sink Allowances

	MtCO₂e/yr	%B.Yr.
□ CDM sinks:	3.2	0%
■ Agr.Mng.(est.):	86.35	1%
□ For.Mng. I (AppZ):	76.38	0.9%
□ Aff&Def.:	135.19	1.6%
□ For.Mng. II:	16.74	0.2%
■ Defo in B.Yr.(est.):	25.62	0.3%
	3.99	0%
Sink Allowances Total:	344.27	4%

Per Capita Emissions

	tCO₂e/per/yr
1990:	12.47
2000:	11.37

Main Data Sources

Inventory data: :CRF 2003;ghg.unfccc.int

AIM

Difference between allowed and actual emissions in year 2000 in percent of 1990 emissions.

Distance to Kyoto Target

TARGET

Distance from latest inventory data (2001) to Kyoto targets in percent of base year emissions.

Emissions by Gas (Trend)

CO₂
N₂O
F-gases
CH₄

Emissions by Sector (Trend)

TRA
OTH
SOL
WAS
AGR
ENE
IND

F-gases:1% N₂O:7%
CH₄:10%
CO₂:82%

OTH:< 1% WAS:3%
AGR:8%
SOL:< 1%
IND:6%
TRA:18%
ENE:63%

Past Emissions, Projections and Targets

Inventory data (red; solid) and projections (orange; dashed/dotted) for Annex A gases and sources, if available. See left table for color codes of Kyoto targets and potential additional emission allowances, if applicable.

03-Mar-2004 (c) malte.meinshausen@ethz.ch, ETH Zurich

Fact sheet 44

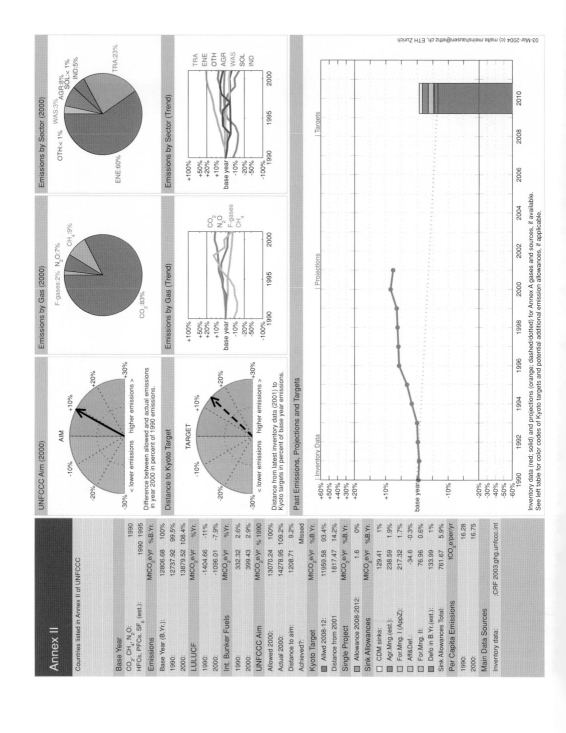

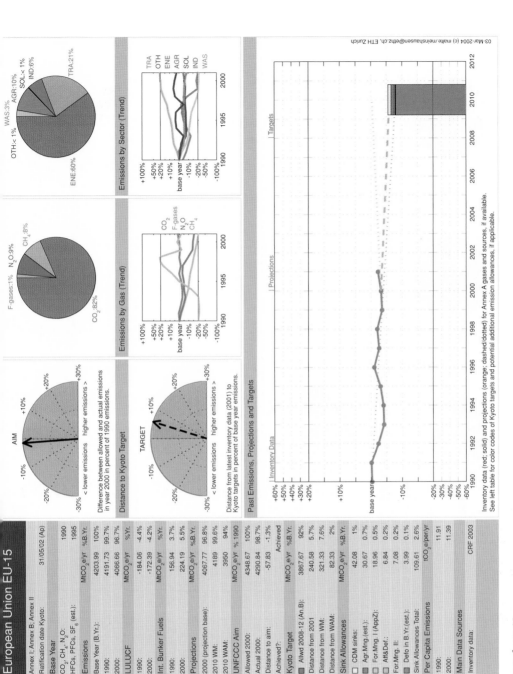

European Union EU-15

Annex I: Annex B: Annex II		
Ratification date Kyoto:	31/05/02 (Ap)	

Base Year

Base Year		1990
CO₂, CH₄, N₂O:		1995
HFCs, PFCs, SF₆ (est.):		

Emissions

Emissions	MtCO₂e/yr	%B.Yr.
Base Year (B.Yr.):	4203.99	100%
1990:	4191.73	99.7%
2000:	4066.66	96.7%

LULUCF

LULUCF	MtCO₂e/yr	%Yr.
1990:	-184.06	-4.4%
2000:	-172.39	-4.2%

Int. Bunker Fuels

Int. Bunker Fuels	MtCO₂e/yr	%Yr.
1990:	156.94	3.7%
2000:	224.19	5.5%

Projections

Projections	MtCO₂e/yr	%B.Yr.
2000 (projection base):	4067.77	96.8%
2010 WM:	4189	99.6%
2010 WAM:	3950	94%

UNFCCC Aim

UNFCCC Aim	MtCO₂e/yr	%1990
Allowed 2000:	4348.67	100%
Actual 2000:	4290.84	98.7%
Distance to aim:	-57.83	-1.3%
Achieved?:		Achieved

Kyoto Target

Kyoto Target	MtCO₂e/yr	%B.Yr.
▮ Allwd 2008-12 (An.B):	3867.67	92%
Distance from 2001	240.58	5.7%
Distance from WM:	321.33	7.6%
Distance from WAM:	82.33	2%

Sink Allowances

Sink Allowances	MtCO₂e/yr	%B.Yr.
☐ CDM sinks:	42.08	1%
▨ Agr.Mng.(est.):	30.67	0.7%
▮ For.Mng. I (AppZ):	18.96	0.5%
☐ Aff&Def.:	6.84	0.2%
For.Mng. II:	7.08	0.2%
☐ Defo in B.Yr.(est.):	3.99	0.1%
Sink Allowances Total:	109.61	2.6%

Per Capita Emissions

Per Capita Emissions	tCO₂e/per/yr	
1990:	11.91	
2000:	11.39	

Main Data Sources

Main Data Sources		
Inventory data:		CRF 2003

AIM

Difference between allowed and actual emissions in year 2000 in percent of 1990 emissions.

Distance to Kyoto Target

Distance from latest inventory data (2001) to Kyoto targets in percent of base year emissions.

Emissions by Gas (Trend)

Emissions by Sector (Trend)

Past Emissions, Projections and Targets

Inventory data (red; solid) and projections (orange; dashed/dotted) for Annex A gases and sources, if available.
See left table for color codes of Kyoto targets and potential additional emission allowances, if applicable.

03-Mar-2004 (c) malte.meinshausen@eth z.ch, ETH Zürich

Fact sheet 46

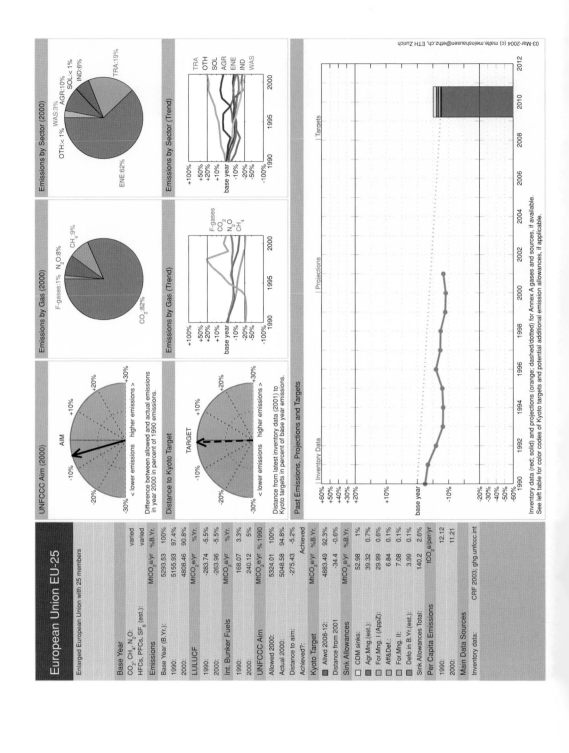

Emissions by Sector (2000)

OTH:<1%   WAS:3%   SOL:<1%
AGR:10%
IND:6%
TRA:19%
ENE:62%

Emissions by Gas (2000)

F-gases:1% N₂O:8%
CH₄:9%
CO₂:82%

UNFCCC Aim (2000)

AIM
-30% < lower emissions   higher emissions > +30%

Difference between allowed and actual emissions in year 2000 in percent of 1990 emissions.

Distance to Kyoto Target

TARGET
-30% < lower emissions   higher emissions > +30%

Distance from latest inventory data (2001) to Kyoto targets in percent of base year emissions.

Emissions by Sector (Trend)

TRA
OTH
SOL
AGR
ENE
IND
WAS

Emissions by Gas (Trend)

F-gases
CO₂
N₂O
CH₄

Past Emissions, Projections and Targets

Inventory Data | Projections | Targets

Inventory data (red; solid) and projections (orange; dashed/dotted) for Annex A gases and sources, if available.
See left table for color codes of Kyoto targets and potential additional emission allowances, if applicable.

03-Mar-2004 (c) malte.meinshausen@env.ethz.ch, ETH Zurich

European Union EU-25

Enlarged European Union with 25 members

Base Year		
CO₂, CH₄, N₂O:	varied	
HFCs, PFCs, SF₆ (est.):	varied	
Emissions	MtCO₂e/yr	%B.Yr.
Base Year (B.Yr.):	5293.53	100%
1990:	5155.93	97.4%
2000:	4808.46	90.8%
LULUCF	MtCO₂e/yr	%Yr.
1990:	-283.74	-5.5%
2000:	-263.96	-5.5%
Int. Bunker Fuels	MtCO₂e/yr	%Yr.
1990:	168.07	3.3%
2000:	240.12	5%
UNFCCC Aim	MtCO₂e/yr	% 1990
Allowed 2000:	5324.01	100%
Actual 2000:	5048.58	94.8%
Distance to aim:	-275.43	-5.2%
Achieved?:		Achieved
Kyoto Target	MtCO₂e/yr	%B.Yr.
■ Allwd 2008-12:	4883.49	92.3%
Distance from 2001:	-34.4	-0.6%
Sink Allowances	MtCO₂e/yr	%B.Yr.
☐ CDM sinks:	52.98	1%
☐ Agr.Mng.(est.):	39.32	0.7%
☐ For.Mng.-I (AppZ):	29.99	0.6%
☐ Aff&Def.:	6.84	0.1%
☐ For.Mng. II:	7.08	0.1%
☐ Defo in B.Yr.(est.):	3.99	0.1%
Sink Allowances Total:	140.2	2.6%
Per Capita Emissions	tCO₂e/per/yr	
1990:	12.12	
2000:	11.21	
Main Data Sources		
Inventory data:	CRF 2003; ghg.unfccc.int	

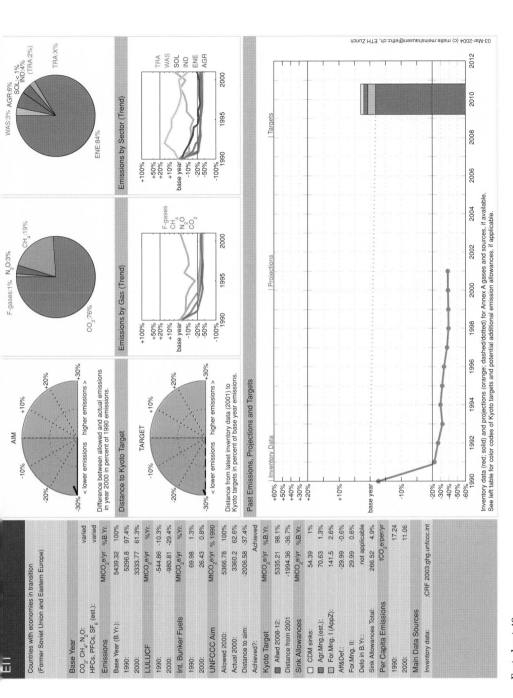

EIT

Countries with economies in transition
(Former Soviet Union and Eastern Europe)

Base Year		
CO₂, CH₄, N₂O:	varied	
HFCs, PFCs, SF₆ (est.):	varied	

Emissions	MtCO₂e/yr	%B.Yr.
Base Year (B.Yr.):	5439.32	100%
1990:	5296.8	97.4%
2000:	3333.77	61.3%

LULUCF	MtCO₂e/yr	%Yr.
1990:	-544.86	-10.3%
2000:	-980.81	-29.4%

Int. Bunker Fuels	MtCO₂e/yr	%Yr.
1990:	69.98	1.3%
2000:	26.43	0.8%

UNFCCC Aim	MtCO₂e/yr	% 1990
Allowed 2000:	5366.78	100%
Actual 2000:	3360.2	62.6%
Distance to aim:	-2006.58	-37.4%
Achieved?:	Achieved	

Kyoto Target	MtCO₂e/yr	%B.Yr.
▨ Allwd 2008-12:	5335.21	98.1%
Distance from 2001	-1994.36	-36.7%

Sink Allowances	MtCO₂e/Yr	%B.Yr.
☐ CDM sinks:	54.39	1%
▨ Agr.Mng.(est.):	70.63	1.3%
▨ For.Mng. I (AppZ):	141.5	2.6%
Afk&Def.:	-29.99	-0.6%
For.Mng. II:	29.99	0.6%
Defo in B.Yr.:	not applicable	
Sink Allowances Total:	266.52	4.9%

Per Capita Emissions	tCO₂e/per/yr
1990:	17.24
2000:	11.06

Main Data Sources
Inventory data: :CRF 2003:ghg.unfccc.int

AIM

Difference between allowed and actual emissions in year 2000 in percent of 1990 emissions.

Distance to Kyoto Target

TARGET

< lower emissions   higher emissions >

Distance from latest inventory data (2001) to Kyoto targets in percent of base year emissions.

Past Emissions, Projections and Targets

| Inventory Data | Projections | Targets |

Emissions by Gas (Trend)

F-gases:1% N₂O:3%

CH₄:19%

CO₂:76%

Emissions by Sector (Trend)

WAS:3% AGR:6%
SOL:<1%
IND:4%
(TRA:2%)

TRA:X%

ENE:84%

Inventory data (red: solid) and projections (orange: dashed/dotted) for Annex A gases and sources, if available.
See left table for color codes of Kyoto targets and potential additional emission allowances, if applicable.

Fact sheet 48

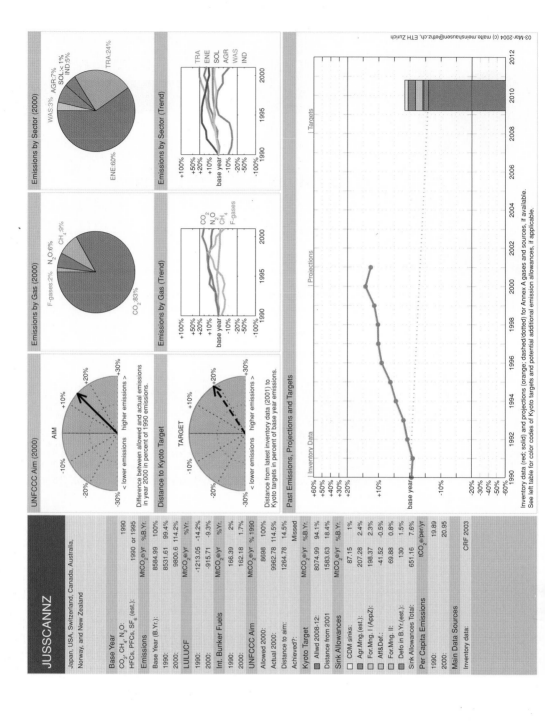

JUSSCANNZ

Japan, USA, Switzerland, Canada, Australia, Norway, and New Zealand

Base Year		
CO₂, CH₄, N₂O:		1990
HFCs, PFCs, SF₆ (est.):		1990 or 1995

Emissions	MtCO₂e/yr	%B.Yr.
Base Year (B.Yr.):	8584.99	100%
1990:	8531.61	99.4%
2000:	9800.6	114.2%

LULUCF	MtCO₂e/yr	%Yr.
1990:	-1213.05	-14.2%
2000:	-915.71	-9.3%

Int. Bunker Fuels	MtCO₂e/yr	%Yr.
1990:	166.39	2%
2000:	162.18	1.7%

UNFCCC Aim	MtCO₂e/yr	% 1990
Allowed 2000:	8698	100%
Actual 2000:	9962.78	114.5%
Distance to aim:	1264.78	14.5%
Achieved?:		Missed

Kyoto Target	MtCO₂e/yr	%B.Yr.
■ Allwd 2008-12:	8074.99	94.1%
Distance from 2001	1583.63	18.4%

Sink Allowances	MtCO₂e/yr	%B.Yr.
☐ CDM sinks:	87.15	1%
■ Agr.Mng. (est.):	207.28	2.4%
■ For.Mng. I (AppZ):	198.37	2.3%
☐ Aff&Def.:	-41.52	-0.5%
☐ For.Mng. II:	69.88	0.8%
■ Defo in B.Yr.(est.):	130	1.5%
Sink Allowances Total:	651.16	7.6%

Per Capita Emissions	tCO₂e/per/yr
1990:	19.89
2000:	20.95

Main Data Sources	
Inventory data:	CRF 2003

Emissions by Sector (2000)

WAS:3% AGR:7% SOL:< 1% IND:5% TRA:24% ENE:60%

Emissions by Sector (Trend)

TRA ENE SOL AGR WAS IND

Emissions by Gas (2000)

F-gases:2% N₂O:6% CH₄:9% CO₂:83%

Emissions by Gas (Trend)

CO₂ N₂O CH₄ F-gases

UNFCCC Aim (2000)

AIM

< lower emissions   higher emissions >

Difference between allowed and actual emissions in year 2000 in percent of 1990 emissions.

Distance to Kyoto Target

TARGET

< lower emissions   higher emissions >

Distance from latest inventory data (2001) to Kyoto targets in percent of base year emissions.

Past Emissions, Projections and Targets

Inventory Data   Projections   Targets

Inventory data (red; solid) and projections (orange; dashed/dotted) for Annex A gases and sources, if available. See left table for color codes of Kyoto targets and potential additional emission allowances, if applicable.

03-Mar-2004 (c) malte.meinshausen@eflz.ch, ETH Zurich

Appendix III
Table of Articles, issues and COP Decisions

For each Article of the Convention and Kyoto Protocol, the table below indicates:

- the issue that it covers;
- the COP Decisions elaborating on the Article; and
- the chapter of this book in which the Article and Decisions are discussed.

This table, which is intended to assist the reader in quickly locating information on a particular topic, is complemented by the standard index at the end of this book. Decisions in **bold** are part of the Marrakesh Accords.

Article	Issue[1]	Decisions[2]	Chapter
		Convention	
Preamble	Preambular paragraphs	–	4, 5, 8
Article 1	Definitions	–	5, 8
Article 2	Objective	–	4
Article 3	Principles	–	4
Article 4	Commitments	(see specific paragraphs)	5
Article 4.1	General commitments for all Parties	(see specific paragraphs)	5
Article 4.1 (a)	Prepare/publish emission inventories	See FCCC Articles 12, 4.2(c)	5, 11
Article 4.1 (b)	Prepare/publish programmes to mitigate/adapt to climate change	(integral to implementation of FCCC)	5, 8
Article 4.1 (c)	Technology transfer	See FCCC Article 4.5	5, 10
Article 4.1 (d)	Conservation/enhancement of sinks and reservoirs	No decision specifically on this subparagraph, but see KP Article 3.3/3.4	5
Article 4.1 (e)	Adaptation	No decision specifically on this subparagraph, but see FCCC Article 4.8 and 4.9. See also 10/CP.9 on sci/tech/socio-ec aspects	8, 10
Article 4.1 (f)	Take climate considerations into account	–	5, 8
Article 4.1 (g)	Research and systematic observation	See FCCC Article 5	5, 7
Article 4.1 (h)	Information exchange	See FCCC Article 5	5, 7
Article 4.1 (i)	Education, training, public awareness	See FCCC Article 6	5, 7
Article 4.1 (j)	Reporting	See FCCC Article 12	5, 11
Article 4.2	Specific commitments for Annex I Parties	(see specific subparagraphs)	
Article 4.2 (a) and (b)	'aim' to return GHG emissions to 1990 levels by 2000; report policies and measures to this effect	1/CP.1, 1/CP.9	5, 11

Article	Title	Key Decisions	
Article 4.2 (c)	Methodologies	4/CP.1; 2/CP.3 See also FCCC Article 12	11
Article 4.2 (d)	Review of adequacy	1/CP.1	18
	Joint implementation	AIJ: 5/CP.1; 8/CP.2; 10/CP.3; 6/CP.4; 13/CP.5; **8/CP.7**; 14/CP.8; 20/CP.8	6
Article 4.2 (e) (i)	Coordination of economic/administrative instruments	(cited in KP Article 2.1 (b))	5, 9
Article 4.2 (e) (ii)	Review of policies leading to higher emissions	Included in Annex I reporting guidelines – see FCCC Article 12	
Article 4.2 (f)	Review of Annexes I and II	4/CP.3; 15/CP.4; 26/CP.7	18, 5
Article 4.2 (g)	Notification of intent to be bound by Article 4.2 (a) and (b)	–	5
Article 4.3	Financial assistance	See FCCC Article 11	10
	Technology transfer	See FCCC Article 4.5	
Article 4.4	Assistance for Parties particularly vulnerable to climate change	See FCCC Articles 4.3 and 11	8, 10
Article 4.5	Technology transfer	13/CP.1; 7/CP.2; 9/CP.3; 4/CP.4; 9/CP.5 **4/CP.7**; 10/CP.8	10, 8
Article 4.6	Flexibility for EITs	Reporting guidelines – 9/CP.2; 3/CP.5	5, 11
Article 4.7	Implementation by DCs dependent on financial assistance and technology transfer; priority to development/poverty eradication	See FCCC Articles 4.3, 4.4, 4.5, 11	5, 10

[1] This column does not always use the formal title of Articles as included in the Convention.

[2] This column does not exhaustively reference all Decisions that mention a particular Article, but rather includes the key Decisions that develop the Article in question.

Article	Issue	Decisions	Chapter
Article 4.8 (a)–(h)	Specific needs of DCs from adverse effects of climate change or implementation of response measures	3/CP.3; 5/CP.4; 12/CP.5; 5/CP.7	8, 9
Article 4.9	Specific needs of LDCs	3/CP.3; 5/CP.4; 12/CP.5; 5/CP.7; Resolution 2/CP.6	8, 10, 11
		NAPAs: 28/CP.7; 9/CP.8; 8/CP.9	
		LEG: 29/CP.7; 7/CP.9	
		LDC fund: 7/CP.7; 27/CP.7; 8/CP.8; 6/CP.9	
Article 4.10	Parties with economies vulnerable to implementation of response measures	–	9
Article 5	Research and systematic observation	8/CP.3; 14/CP.4; 5/CP.5; 11/CP.9	7
Article 6	Education, training and public awareness	11/CP.8	7
Article 7	COP		13, 14
Article 7.2	Functions of COP	Integral to all the COP decisions cited in this table. Specific functions not covered elsewhere:	13
Article 7.2 (f)	Adopt/publish regular reports on implementation	7/CP.1	13
Article 7.2 (k)	Adopt rules of procedure	–	14
Article 7.2 (l)	Adopt financial rules	15/CP.1	16
Article 7.2 (l)	Cooperation with IGOs/NGOs	IGO/NGOs: see FCCC Article 7.6	3, 14, 15
		Other conventions: 13/CP.8	17
Article 7.3	Adopt rules of procedure, incl. decision-making majorities	–	14
Article 7.4 and 7.5	Convening of sessions	Dates/venues: 21/CP.1; 1/CP.2; 5/CP.3; 2/CP.5; 2/CP.6; 37/CP.7; 15/CP.8; 14/CP.9	13, 14
		Calendar: 19/CP.4	
Article 7.6	Observers	18/CP.4	3, 14, 15

Article	Topic	Decisions	
Article 8	Secretariat	Arrangements for Secretariat support: 16/CP.1; 3/CP.2; 14/CP.2; 15/CP.2; 17/CP.3; 39/CP.7; Institutional linkage: 14CP.1; 22/CP.5; 6/CP.6; Admin/financial matters: 17/CP.4; 4/CP.6; 16/CP.8; 15/CP.9	16
Article 8.2	Secretariat functions	Support of Secretariat integral to all COP decisions covered by this table. Functions leading to specific decisions include:	
Article 8.2 (c)	Facilitate assistance to developing countries	3/CP.2	10, 11
Article 8.2 (e)	Coordinate with other Secretariats	13/CP.8	17
Article 9	SBSTA	Functions, division of labour: 6/CP.1; 13/CP.3	13, 14, 15
Article 10	SBI	Functions, division of labour: 6/CP.1; 2/CP.2; 13/CP.3	13, 14
Article 11	Financial mechanism	Guidance: 11/CP.1; 11/CP.2; 2/CP.4; **6/CP.7**; 27/CP.7; 6/CP.8; 7/CP.8; 4/CP.9 Arrangements/MOU: 9/CP.1; 10/CP.1; 12/CP.2; 13/CP.2; 12/CP.3 Review: 11/CP.3; 3/CP.4; 5/CP.8 GEF report: 12/CP.1; 3/CP.9 Special climate change fund: **7/CP.7**; 7/CP.8; 5/CP.9 LDC fund: See Article 4.9	10

Article	Issue	Decisions	Chapter
Article 12	Reporting	*Annex I reporting*	11
		NC guidelines: 9/CP.2; 4/CP.5; 34/CP.7;	
		Inventory guidelines: 3/CP.5; 34/CP.7; 18/CP.8; 13/CP.9	
		Review process: 2/CP.1; 6/CP.3; 34/CP.7; 6/CP.5; 19/CP.8; 12/CP.9	
		General: 3/CP.1; 6/CP.3; 11/CP.4; 33/CP.7; 4/CP.8; 1/CP.9	
		Non-Annex I reporting	
		Guidelines: 10/CP.2; 17/CP.8	
		CGE: 8/CP.5; 31/CP.7; 3/CP.8	
		Comp&Synthesis: 7/CP.5; 3/CP.6; 30/CP.7; 2/CP.8; 2/CP.9	
		Other: 8/CP.1; 3/CP.2; 12/CP.4; 32/CP.7	
Article 13	Multilateral consultative process (AG13)	20/CP.1; 4/CP.2; 5/CP.2; 14/CP.3; 10/CP.4	12
Article 14	Settlement of disputes	–	12
Article 15	Amendments	–	18
Article 16	Adoption and amendment of annexes	4/CP.3; 26/CP.7	18
Article 17	Protocols	1/CP.3	18
Article 18	Right to vote	–	1, 14
Article 19	Depositary	–	1, 18
Article 20	Signature	–	1
Article 21	Interim arrangements:		
	GEF	9/CP.1 – see also FCCC Article 11	10
	IPCC	6/CP.2; 7/CP.3; 19/CP.5; 25/CP.7; 10/CP.9	15, 11

Article	Issue	Decisions	Chapter
Article 3.10–3.12	Acquisition/transfer of units pursuant to JI, ET and the CDM	7/CP.4; **15/CP.7; 19/CP.7**	6
Article 3.13	'Carry over' of excess units	**19/CP.7**	5
Article 3.14	Minimisation of impacts on DCs	5/CP.4; 12/CP.5; 5/CP.7; 9/CP.7	8, 9
Article 4	Joint fulfilment ('bubble')	19/CP.7	5
Article 5	Methodologies	2/CP.3; 8/CP.4; **20/CP.7; 21/CP.7; 20/CP.9**	11
Article 6	Joint implementation	1/CP.3; 7/CP.4; 14/CP.5; **15/CP.7; 16/CP.7**	6
Article 7	Reporting	8/CP.4; **22/CP.7; 22/CP.8**	11
Article 7.4	Accounting of assigned amounts	8/CP.4; **15/CP.7; 19/CP.7; 24/CP.8**	5, 6, 11
Article 8	Review of reporting	8/CP.4; **23/CP.7; 22/CP.8; 23/CP.8; 21/CP.9**	11
Article 9	Review of the Protocol	–	18
Article 10	General commitments	–	5
Article 11	Financial mechanism	Adaptation fund: see KP Article 12	10
Article 12	CDM	1/CP.3; 7/CP.4; 14/CP.5; **15/CP.7; 17/CP.7**	6
		Guidance to EB: 21/CP.8, 18/CP.9	
		Adaptation fund: **10/CP.7**	8, 10
		LULUCF projects: 19/CP.9	6
Article 13	COP/MOP	17/CP.9	13
Article 14	Secretariat	–	13
Article 15	SBSTA and SBI	–	13,
			15 (SBSTA)
Article 16	Multilateral consultative process	8/CP.4	12
Article 17	Emissions trading	1/CP.3; 7/CP.4; 14/CP.5; **15/CP.7; 18/CP.7**	6
Article 18	Compliance system	8/CP.4; 15/CP.5; **24/CP.7**	12
Article 19	Dispute settlement	–	12

Article 20	Amendments	–	18
Article 21	Adoption/amendment of annexes	–	18
Article 22	Right to vote	–	14
Article 23	Depositary	–	1
Article 24	Signature and ratification	–	1
Article 25	Entry into force	–	18
Article 26	Reservations	–	18
Article 27	Withdrawal	–	18
Article 28	Authentic texts	–	1

Cross-cutting issues or issues not covered by any particular article

'Umbrella' decisions	1/CP.4 (Buenos Aires Plan of Action)	2 and throughout book
	1/CP.5 (Implementation of BAPA)	
	1/CP.6 (Implementation of BAPA)	
	5/CP.6 (Bonn Agreements)	
Declarations	Geneva Ministerial Declaration (not adopted)	13 and throughout book
	1/CP.7 Marrakesh Ministerial Declaration	
	1/CP.8 Delhi Ministerial Declaration	
Capacity-building	10/CP.5; 11/CP.5; 2/CP.7; 3/CP.7; 9/CP.9	10
Bunker fuels under FCCC	4/CP.1; 18/CP.5	5, 11
	Reporting guidelines – see FCCC Article 12	
	Bunker fuels under KP – see KP Article 2.2	
Linked to lists in FCCC Annexes I and II	Clarification of status of non-Annex I EITs	35/CP.7	3, 5, 10
	Participation of women	36/CP.7	13
	Impact of single projects (under KP)	1/CP.3; 16/CP.4; 14/CP.7	5

Article	Issue	Decisions	Chapter
Linked to inclusion of HFCs/PFCs/SF$_6$ in KP; exclusion of GHGs controlled by Montreal Protocol in scope FCCC and KP	Linkages with the Montreal Protocol	13/CP.4; 17/CP.5; 12/CP.8	5, 17
	Volume of documentation	17/CP.2; 18/CP.3	14
	Programme budgets	17/CP.1; 18/CP.1; 19/CP.1; 15/CP.3; 20/CP.5; 38/CP.7; 16/CP.9	16
	Financial performance	16/CP.2; 16/CP.3; 21/CP.5; 39/CP.7; 15/CP.9	16
	Thanks to host governments	Resolutions 1/CP.1; 1/CP.2; 1/CP.3; 2/CP.4; 3/CP.6; 1/CP.7; 1/CP.8; 1/CP.9	13
	Expressions of solidarity	Resolutions 1/CP.4; 1/CP.6	13
	Tribute (to Executive Secretary)	Resolution 2/CP.7	16

Bibliography

UNFCCC and other UN documentation

All CBD documents (UNEP/CBD/...) are available at www.biodiv.org

All GEF documents are available at www.gefweb.org

All IPCC documents are available at www.ipcc.ch

All Montreal Protocol documents (UNEP/OzL.Pro./...) are available at
www.unep.ch/ozone

All Ramsar documents are available at www.ramsar.org

All UN documents (A/[no.]..., A/CONF..., or ST/...) are available at www.un.org

All UNCCD documents (ICCD/...) are available www.unccd.org

All UNFCCC documents (FCCC/... or A/AC/...) are available at www.unfccc.int

All WTO documents (WT/... or TN/...) are available at www.wto.org

UNFCCC documentation

A/AC.237/74, 1994, Modalities for the functioning of operational linkages between the
Conference of the Parties and the operating entity or entities of the financial
mechanism: legal opinion of the United Nations Office of Legal Affairs

A/AC.237/81 and Corr.1, 1994, First review of information communicated by each
Party included in Annex I to the Convention. Compilation and synthesis of
national communications from Annex I parties

A/AC.237/Misc.1/Add.3, 1991, Proposal for an Insurance Mechanism submitted by
Vanuatu on behalf of AOSIS

COP-1 report, part I, Proceedings, FCCC/CP/1995/7, Berlin

COP-1 report, part II, Action taken, FCCC/CP/1995/7/Add.1, Berlin

COP-2 report, part I, Proceedings, FCCC/CP/1996/15, Geneva

COP-2 report, part II, Action taken, FCCC/CP/1996/15/Add.1, Geneva

COP-3 report, part I, Proceedings, FCCC/CP/1997/7, Kyoto

COP-3 report, part I, Action taken, FCCC/CP/1997/7/Add.1, Kyoto

COP-4 report, part I, Proceedings, FCCC/CP/1998/16, Buenos Aires

COP-4 report, part II, Action taken, FCCC/CP/1998/16/Add.1, Buenos Aires

COP-5 report, part I, Proceedings, FCCC/CP/1999/6, Bonn

COP-5 report, part II, Action taken, FCCC/CP/1999/6/Add.1, Bonn

COP-6 part I report, part I, Proceedings, FCCC/CP/2000/5/Add.1, The Hague

COP-6 part I report, part II, Action taken, FCCC/CP/2000/5/Add.2, The Hague

COP-6 part II report, parts I and II, FCCC/CP/2001/5, Bonn

COP-7 report, part I, Proceedings, FCCC/CP/2001/13, Marrakesh

COP-7 report, part II, Action taken, FCCC/CP/2001/13/Adds.2–4, Marrakesh

COP-8 report, part I, Proceedings, FCCC/CP/2002/7, New Delhi

COP-8 report, part II, Action taken, FCCC/CP/2002/7/Adds.1–3, New Delhi

COP-9 report, part I, Proceedings, FCCC/CP/2003/6, Milan

COP-9 report, part II, Action taken, FCCC/CP/2003/6/Adds.1–3, Milan

FCCC/AG13/1998/2, Report of AG13 on its sixth session

FCCC/AGBM/1996/MISC.2, Implementation of the Berlin Mandate: Proposals from
    Parties

FCCC/CP/1995/4, GEF Report to COP-1

FCCC/CP/1996/2, Draft rules of procedure of the Conference of the Parties and its
    subsidiary bodies

FCCC/CP/1996/6/Add.2, Administrative and financial matters

FCCC/CP/1996/12 and Adds.1–2, Second compilation and synthesis of first national
    communications from Annex I Parties

FCCC/CP/1996/MISC.1, Legal arrangements for the effective discharge of the functions
    of the Convention secretariat in the Federal Republic of Germany

FCCC/CP/1997/3, GEF Report to COP-3

FCCC/CP/1997/5, Adoption of the rules of procedure. Report by the President of COP 2

FCCC/CP/1997/INF.1, Programme Budget for 1998–9

FCCC/CP/1998/8/Add.1, Administrative and financial matters

FCCC/CP/1998/9, Audited financial statements for the biennium 1996–7: Report of the
    United Nations Board of Auditors

FCCC/CP/1998/11 and Adds.1–2, Second compilation and synthesis of second national
    communications from Annex I Parties

FCCC/CP/1999/7, UNFCCC guidelines on reporting and review

FCCC/CP/2000/3/Add.1, Review of the GEF of its climate change enabling activities

FCCC/CP/2001/12, Letter from CACAM on their status under the convention

FCCC/CP/2001/MISC.4, Statements Made in connection with the approval of the Bonn
    Agreements on the implementation of the Buenos Aires Plan of Action

FCCC/CP/2002/1, Provisional agenda (COP-8)

FCCC/CP/2002/2, Agreement between the European Community and its Member States
    under Article 4 of the Kyoto Protocol

FCCC/CP/2002/3, First Report of the CDM Executive Board to the COP

FCCC/CP/2002/4, GEF Report to COP-8

FCCC/CP/2002/8, National Communications: GHG Guidelines: UNFCCC Guidelines for
    reporting and review

FCCC/CP/2002/INF.2, List of participants (COP-8)

FCCC/CP/2003/2 and Add.1, Annual Report of the EB to the COP

FCCC/CP/2003/3, GEF Report to COP-9

FCCC/SB/1997/3, Secretariat Note: progress note on development and transfer of technology

FCCC/SB/1999/9, Note by SBSTA Chairman on workshop on Article 4.8 and 4.9

FCCC/SB/2000/2, Note by the Chairmen of the SBs on implementation of Article 4.8 and 4.9 of the Convention and Article 2.3 of the Protocol

FCCC/SB/2000/INF.1, Secretariat Note on capacity-building needs in developing countries

FCCC/SB/2000/INF.5, List of participants SB-12

FCCC/SB/2002/INF.2, Report on national greenhouse gas inventory data for Annex I Parties from 1990 to 2000

FCCC/SB/2003/1, Report of the workshops on possible synergy and joint action with the other multilateral environmental conventions and agreements, and on enhancing cooperation with other conventions

FCCC/SBI/1996/7, Advice of the Office of Legal Affairs to the Executive Secretary of the Climate Change Convention, 18 December 1995

FCCC/SBI/1996/10, Secretariat activities relating to technical and financial support to Parties: progress report

FCCC/SBI/1997/12, Volume of documentation

FCCC/SBI/1997/14, Mechanisms for consultations with NGOs

FCCC/SBI/1997/19 and Add.1, First compilation and synthesis of second national communications from Annex I Parties

FCCC/SBI/1997/MISC.6, Mechanisms for consultations with non-governmental organizations

FCCC/SBI/1998/4, Administrative and financial matters

FCCC/SBI/1999/INF.11, Report on activities to facilitate the provision of financial and technical support and information on communications from Parties not included in Annex I to the Convention

FCCC/SBI/2000/2, Late payment of contributions: response options

FCCC/SBI/2000/9, Audited financial statements for the biennium 1998–9: Report of the United Nations Board of Auditors

FCCC/SBI/2000/16, Report of the first meeting of the Consultative Group of Experts on national communications from Parties not included in Annex I to the Convention

FCCC/SBI/2001/2, Report of the second meeting of the Consultative Group of Experts on national communications from Parties not included in Annex I to the Convention

FCCC/SBI/2001/3, Report of the third meeting of the Consultative Group of Experts on national communications from Parties not included in Annex I to the Convention

FCCC/SBI/2001/15, Report of the CGE on national communications from Parties not included in Annex I

FCCC/SBI/2001/17/Add.1, Proposed programme budget for the Convention

FCCC/SBI/2002/2, Report of the fourth meeting of the Consultative Group of Experts on national communications from Parties not included in Annex I to the Convention

FCCC/SBI/2002/5, Matters relating to the LDCs: Secretariat Note

FCCC/SBI/2002/8, Fourth compilation and synthesis of initial national communications from Parties not included in Annex I to the Convention: Summary

FCCC/SBI/2002/10, Audited financial statements for the biennium 2000–1: Report of the United Nations Board of Auditors

FCCC/SBI/2002/11, Interim financial performance for the biennium 2002–3

FCCC/SBI/2002/12, Arrangements for the first session of the Conference of the Parties serving as the meeting of the Parties to the Kyoto Protocol

FCCC/SBI/2002/13, Effective participation in the Convention process

FCCC/SBI/2002/15, Report of the fifth meeting of the CGE on national communications from Parties not included in Annex I

FCCC/SBI/2002/16, Fourth compilation and synthesis of initial national communications from Parties not included in Annex I to the Convention

FCCC/SBI/2002/INF.6, Consideration of the review of national communications from Annex I Parties

FCCC/SBI/2002/INF.12, Information on activities by the Global Environment Facility

FCCC/SBI/2002/INF.13, Status of contributions as at 15 October 2002

FCCC/SBI/2002/INF.14, LEG input on development of NAPAs

FCCC/SBI/2002/INF.15, Secretariat Note: Progress on implementing capacity-building frameworks

FCCC/SBI/2002/MISC.8, Parties' Submissions: Effective participation

FCCC/SBI/2003/3, Arrangements for the first session of the Conference of the Parties serving as the meeting of the Parties to the Kyoto Protocol

FCCC/SBI/2003/4, FCCC Article 6, Proposal for an information clearing house

FCCC/SBI/2003/6, Secretariat Note: Implementation of Article 4.8/4.9

FCCC/SBI/2003/7 and Adds.1–4, Compilation and synthesis of third national communications from Annex I Parties

FCCC/SBI/2003/11, Report on Insurance Workshops

FCCC/SBI/2003/12, Income and budget performance as at 30 June 2003

FCCC/SBI/2003/13, Fifth compilation and synthesis of initial national communications from Parties not included in Annex I to the Convention

FCCC/SBI/2003/14, Secretariat Note: Capacity-building framework

FCCC/SBI/2003/15, Revised programme budget for the biennium 2004–2005

FCCC/SBI/2003/17, Secretariat Note: Synthesis of views on Article 6

FCCC/SBI/2003/INF.3, Parties' views on SCCF

FCCC/SBI/2003/INF.12 and Add.1, Views from LEG and EGTT on SCCF

FCCC/SBI/2003/INF.14, An initial assessment of steps taken by non-Annex I Parties to reduce emissions and enhance removals of greenhouse gases

FCCC/SBI/2003/INF.15, Information on activities by the Global Environment Facility

FCCC/SBI/2003/INF.18, Status of contributions as at 31 October 200

FCCC/SBI/2003/MISC.1, Parties' views on SCCF

FCCC/SBI/2003/MISC.2, GEF Submission: Capacity-building

FCCC/SBI/2003/MISC.8, Parties' submissions on experiences with GEF

FCCC/SBSTA/1996/6, Scientific assessments: Cooperation with the Intergovernmental Panel on Climate Change

FCCC/SBSTA/1997/MISC.4, Structure and contents of the Third Assessment Report by the IPCC. Comments by Parties

FCCC/SBSTA/1998/MISC.1, Structure and contents of the Third Assessment Report by the IPCC. Additional comments by Parties

FCCC/SBSTA/1999/11, Secretariat Note: Status of consultative process on technology transfer

FCCC/SBSTA/1999/MISC.11, Secretariat Note: Options to accelerate coastal adaptation technologies

FCCC/SBSTA/2000/2, Note by SBSTA Chairman on workshop on good practices in policies and measures

FCCC/SBSTA/2001/6, Sectetariat Note: Integration of Article 6 activities

FCCC/SBSTA/2001/INF.1, Intersessional Report: Emissions from international transportation

FCCC/SBSTA/2001/INF.5, Note by SBSTA Chairman on workshop on good practices in policies and measures

FCCC/SBSTA/2002/2, Secretariat Note: Workshop on GHG Reporting Guidelines

FCCC/SBSTA/2002/3 Cooperation with other conventions: progress report on the work of the joint liaison group between the secretariats of the UNFCCC, the CBD and the UNCCD

FCCC/SBSTA/2002/8, Secretariat Note: Synthesis Report on AIJ

FCCC/SBSTA/2002/9, EGTT Annual Report

FCCC/SBSTA/2002/10, Secretariat Note: Progress Report on implementation of technology transfer

FCCC/SBSTA/2002/CRP.7, EGTT Second Meeting Report

FCCC/SBSTA/2002/INF.1, Synthesis of information submitted by Parties and organizations

FCCC/SBSTA/2002/INF.6, Secretariat Note: Beijing Workshop on Technology Transfer

FCCC/SBSTA/2002/INF.13, Secretariat Report: Good practices in policies and measures

FCCC/SBSTA/2002/INF.15, First compilation and synthesis of national reports on GCOS

FCCC/SBSTA/2002/INF.16, Cross-cutting thematic areas and activities under the United Nations Convention to Combat Desertification, Convention on Biological Diversity and United Nations Framework Convention on Climate Change

FCCC/SBSTA/2002/MISC.10, GCOS Report to SBSTA 16

FCCC/SBSTA/2003/9, Secretariat Note: Issues relating to GCOS

FCCC/SBSTA/2003/INF.3, Secretariat Note: Emissions from international aviation and maritime transportation

FCCC/SBSTA/2003/INF.4, Secretariat Note: Ghent workshop on enabling environments

FCCC/SBSTA/2003/INF.7, Cooperation with International Organisations: World Trade Organization

FCCC/TP/1997/3, Technical Paper: Adaptation Technologies

FCCC/TP/1999/1, Technical Paper: Coastal Zone Technologies

FCCC/TP/2000/2, Technical Paper: Tracing the origins of the Kyoto Protocol: an article-by-article textual history

FCCC/TP/2002/2, Technical Paper: Treatment of confidential information by international treaty bodies and organisations

FCCC/TP/2002/3, Technical Paper: Registries under the Kyoto Protocol

FCCC/TP/2003/2, Technical Paper: Enabling environments for technology transfer

FCCC/WEB/2002/3, Activities of IGOs and NGOs on Article 6 activities

FCCC/WEB/2002/7, Technical Paper: Policies and measures reported by Annex I Parties in their third national communications: Database information

FCCC/WEB/2002/8, List of projects submitted by Parties not included in Annex I to the Convention in accordance with Article 12, paragraph 4 of the Convention

FCCC/WEB/2002/9, Status of preparation of national communications from non-Annex I Parties

FCCC/WEB/2002/10, Report on national greenhouse gas inventory data from Annex I Parties for 1990–2000

FCCC/WEB/2002/11, 'Good practices' in policies and measures among Annex I Parties Submissions from international and intergovernmental organisations

FCCC/WEB/2002/13, Effective participation in the Convention process: Submission by a non-governmental organisation

FCCC/WEB/2002/14, Effective participation in the Convention process

FCCC/WEB/2003/4, Status of the preparation of national communications from Parties not included in Annex I to the convention

INC-5 report, part II, A/AC.237/18 (part II) and Add.1

INC-9 report, part II, A/AC.237/55

INC-11 report, part II, A/AC/237/91/Add.1

SBI-1 report, FCCC/SBI/1995/5, Report of the Subsidiary Body for Implementation on the work of its first session, Geneva, 31 August 1995

SBI-4 report, FCCC/SBI/1996/14, Report of the Subsidiary Body for Implementation on the work of its fourth session, Geneva, 10–11 December 1996

SBI-5 report, FCCC/SBI/1997/6, Report of the Subsidiary Body for Implementation on the work of its fifth session, Bonn, 25 February–7 March 1997

SBI-14 report, FCCC/SBI/2001/9, Report of the Subsidiary Body for Implementation on the work of its fourteenth session, Bonn, 24–27 July 2001

SBI-16 report, FCCC/SBI/2002/6, Report of the Subsidiary Body for Implementation on the work of its sixteenth session, Bonn, 10–14 June 2002

SBI-17 report, FCCC/SBI/2002/17, Report of the Subsidiary Body for Implementation on the work of its seventeenth session, New Delhi, 23 October–1 November 2002

SBI-18 report, FCCC/SBI/2003/8, Report of the Subsidiary Body for Implementation on the work of its eighteenth session, Bonn, 4–13 June 2003

SBSTA-1 report, FCCC/SBSTA/1995/3, Report of the Subsidiary Body for Scientific and Technological Advice on the work of its first session, Geneva, 28 August–1 September 1995

SBSTA-3 report, FCCC/SBSTA/1996/13, Report of the Subsidiary Body for Scientific and Technological Advice on the work of its third session, Geneva, 9–16 July 1996

SBSTA-4 report, FCCC/SBSTA/1996/20, Report of the Subsidiary Body for Scientific and Technological Advice on the work of its fourth session, Geneva, 16–18 December 1996

SBSTA-6 report, FCCC/SBSTA/1998/6, Report of the Subsidiary Body for Scientific and Technological Advice on the work of its sixth session, Bonn, 28 July–5 August 1997

SBSTA-7 report, FCCC/SBSTA/1997/14, Report of the Subsidiary Body for Scientific and Technological Advice on the work of its seventh session, Bonn, 20–28 October 1997

SBSTA-8 report, FCCC/SBSTA/1998/6, Report of the Subsidiary Body for Scientific and Technological Advice on the work of its eighth session, Bonn, 2–12 June 1998

SBSTA-10 report, FCCC/SBSTA/1999/6, Report of the Subsidiary Body for Scientific and Technological Advice on the work of its tenth session, Bonn, 31 May–11 June 1999

SBSTA-11 report, FCCC/SBSTA/1999/14, Report of the Subsidiary Body for Scientific and Technological Advice on the work of its eleventh session, Bonn, 25 October– 5 November 1999

SBSTA-12 report, FCCC/SBSTA/2000/5, Report of the Subsidiary Body for Scientific and Technological Advice on the work of its twelfth session, Bonn, 12–16 June 2000

SBSTA-14 report, FCCC/SBSTA/2001/2, Report of the Subsidiary Body for Scientific and Technological Advice on the work of its fourteenth session, Bonn, 24–27 July 2001

SBSTA-15 report, FCCC/SBSTA/2001/8, Report of the Subsidiary Body for Scientific and Technological Advice on the work of its fifteenth session, Marrakesh, 29 October–6 November 2001

SBSTA-16 report, FCCC/SBSTA/2002/6, Report of the Subsidiary Body for Scientific and Technological Advice on the work of its sixteenth session, Bonn, 5–14 June 2002

SBSTA-17 report, FCCC/SBSTA/2002/13, Report of the Subsidiary Body for Scientific and Technological Advice on the work of its seventeenth session, New Delhi, 23– 29 October 2002

SBSTA-18 report, FCCC/SBSTA/2003/10, Report of the Subsidiary Body for Scientific and Technological Advice on the work of its eighteenth session, Bonn, 4–13 June 2003

SBSTA-19 report, FCCC/SBSTA/2003/15, Report of the Subsidiary Body for Scientific and Technological Advice on the work of its nineteenth session, Milan, 1–9 December 2003

UNFCCC Secretariat, 2002, *A Guide to the Climate Change Process*, Bonn: Climate Change Secretariat

UNFCCC Workshop for the Development of a Work Programme on Article 6 of the Convention background paper: 'Education, Training and Public Awareness', Bonn, 2–3 June 2002, available in UNFCCC website

Other UN documentation

A/45/696/Add.1, Annex III, 1990, Progress achieved in the implementation of resolution 44/207 on protection of global climate for present and future generations of mankind, Ministerial Declaration

A/50/7/Add.15, 1996, ACABQ Report on conference servicing of the Conference of the Parties and its subsidiary bodies

A/51/950, 1997, Renewing the United Nations: a programme for reform

A/53/463, 1998, Environment and human settlements: Report by the Secretary-General

A/57/25, 2002, UNEP Report of the Governing Council, Seventh Special Session (13–15 February 2002), UNGA Official Records, Fifty-seventh Session, Supplement No. 25

A/57/270, 2002, Implementation of the United Nations Millennium Declaration: Report of the Secretary-General, Annex

A/520/Rev.15, 1984, Rules of procedure of the General Assembly

A/CONF.198/11, 2002, Report of the International Conference on Financing for Development, Monterrey, Mexico, 18–22 March 2002

A/RES/55/2, United Nations Millennium Declaration

CBD COP-1 report, 1994, Report of the First Meeting of the Conference of the Parties to the Convention on Biological Diversity, UNEP/CBD/COP/1/17

CBD SBSTTA-6 report, 2001, Report of the Sixth Session of the Subsidiary Body on Scientific, Technical and Technological Advice, UNEP/CBD/COP/6/3

CBD SBSTTA-9 report, 2003, Report of the Subsidiary Body on Scientific, Technical and Technological Advice on its Ninth Session, UNEP/CBD/COP/7/4

Environmental Effects Assessment Panel, 2002, 'Environmental Effects of Ozone Depletion and its Interactions with Climate Change', UNEP report

GEF, 1997, Operational Guidelines for Expedited Financing of Initial Communications from non-Annex I Parties, Annex F: Enabling Activities and Related Measures – A Glossary of Terms

GEF, 1999, Operational Guidelines for Expedited Financing of Climate Change Enabling Activities, Part II, Expedited Financing for (interim) Measures for Capacity-building in Priority Areas.

GEF, 2001a, A Guide for Self-Assessment of Country Capacity Needs for Global Environmental Management, September

GEF, 2001b, Operational Guidelines for Expedited Funding of National Self Assessments of Capacity-Building Needs

GEF, 2001c, Operational Program Number 11, Promoting Environmentally Sustainable Transport

GEF, 2002, Operational Guidelines for Expedited Funding for Preparation of NAPAs by LDCs

GEF Council, 2002, Joint summary of the Chairs, GEF Council Meeting 14–15 October 2002

GEF/C.7/Inf.5, Incremental costs, February 1996

GEF/C.7/Inf.10, Operational criteria for enabling activities: Climate change, February 1996

GEF/C.13/Inf.7, Pipelines of the Implementing Agencies, April 1999

GEF/C.14/5, Report on incremental costs, November 1999

GEF/C.19/Inf.7, Note on GEF support for National Adaptation Plans of Action, May 2002

GEF/C.19/6, Arrangements for the establishment of the new climate change funds, April 2002

GEF/C.19/Inf.12, GEF Support to National Focal Points and Council members
representing Constituencies, 7 May 2002

GEF/C.20/6, Co-financing, September 2002

GEF/C.21/5/Rev.1, Operation of the LDC Trust Funds, 21 April 2003

GEF/C.21/Inf.4, Action Plan to respond to the Recommendations of the Second GEF
Assembly, the Policy Recommendations of the Third Replenishment, the Second
Overall Performance Study of the GEF and the WSSD, April 2003

GEF/C.21/Inf.10, A proposed GEF approach to Adaptation to Climate Change, April 2003

ICCD/COP(3)/9, Collaboration and synergies among Rio Conventions for the
implementation of the UNCCD

ICCD/COP(5)/6, Review of activities for the promotion and strengthening of
relationships with other relevant conventions and relevant international
organisations, institutions and agencies

IPCC, 1993, Procedures for preparation, review, acceptance, approval and publication
of its reports. Approved at the ninth session, Geneva, June 1993

   1994, *IPCC Technical Guidelines for Assessing Climate Change Impacts and Adaptations*
   (T. Carter et al.)

   1995a, *Climate Change 1995: The Science of Climate Change. Contribution of Working
   Group I to the Second Assessment of the Intergovernmental Panel on Climate Change*
   (J. T. Houghton et al., eds.), Cambridge University Press

   1995b, *Climate Change 1995: Impacts, Adaptations and Mitigation of Climate Change:
   Scientific–Technical Analyses. Contribution of Working Group II to the Second Assessment
   of the Intergovernmental Panel on Climate Change* (R. T. Watson et al., eds.), Cambridge
   University Press

   1995c, *Climate Change 1995: Economic and Social Dimensions of Climate Change.
   Contribution of Working Group III to the Second Assessment of the Intergovernmental Panel
   on Climate Change* (J. P. Bruce et al., eds.), Cambridge University Press

   1996a, Financial procedures for the IPCC, adopted at the twelfth session, Mexico
   City, 11–13 September 1996

   1996b, *Revised 1996 IPCC Guidelines for National Greenhouse Gas Inventories*
   (J. T. Houghton et al., eds.)

   1997, The IPCC Third Assessment Report, Decision Paper, adopted at the thirteenth
   session, Maldives, 22 and 25–28 September 1997

   1998, Principles governing IPCC work, approved at the fourteenth session, Vienna,
   1–3 October 1998

   1999, Procedures for the preparation, review, acceptance, adoption, approval and
   publication of IPCC reports, approved at the fifteenth session, San José, 15–18
   April 1999

   2000a, *Land use, Land-use Change and Forestry*. Special Report of the Intergovernmental
   Panel on Climate Change (R. T. Watson et al., eds.), Cambridge University Press

   2000b, *Good Practice Guidance and Uncertainty Management in National Greenhouse Gas
   Inventories* (J. Penman et al., eds.)

   2000c, *Methodological and Technological Issues in Technology Transfer* (B. Metz et al., eds.),
   Cambridge University Press

2001a, *Climate Change 2001: The Scientific Basis. Contribution of Working Group I to the Third Assessment Report of the Intergovernmental Panel on Climate Change* (J. T. Houghton et al., eds.), Cambridge University Press

2001b, *Climate Change 2001: Impacts, Adaptation and Vulnerability. Contribution of Working Group II to the Third Assessment Report of the Intergovernmental Panel on Climate Change* (J. McCarthy et al., eds.), Cambridge University Press

2001c, *Climate Change 2001: Mitigation. Contribution of Working Group III to the Third Assessment Report of the Intergovernmental Panel on Climate Change* (B. Metz et al., eds.), Cambridge University Press

2001d, *Climate Change 2001: Synthesis Report* (R. Watson et al., eds.), Cambridge University Press

2002, *Climate Change and Biodiversity*, IPCC Technical Paper V (H. Gitay et al., eds.)

2004, *Good Practice Guidance for Land Use, Land-Use Change and Forestry* (J. Penman et al., eds.)

IPCC-8 report, 1992, Applicable excerpts from the Report of the eighth session, Harare, 11–13 November 1992

IPCC-18 report, 2001, IPCC-XIX/Doc.2, Report of the eighteenth session, Wembley, UK, 23–29 September

IPCC-19 report, 2002, Report of the nineteenth session, Geneva, 17–20 (a.m. only) April

IPCC-20 report, 2003, Report of the twentieth session, Paris, 19–21 February

IPCC-21 report, 2003, Draft report of the twenty-first session, Vienna, 3 and 6–7 November

IPCC-XX/Doc.19, 2003, Proposal for a Special Report on Carbon Storage and Capture

IPCC-XXI/Doc.4, 2003, IPCC programme and budget for 2004 to 2007

Ozone ExCom-17 report, 1995, Report of the seventeenth meeting of the Executive Committee of the Multilateral Fund for the Implementation of the Montreal Protocol, UNEP/OzL.Pro/ExCom/17/60, decision 17/14, available at www.unmfs.org

Ozone MOP-14 report, 2003, Report of the fourteenth meeting of the Parties to the Montreal Protocol on Substances That Deplete the Ozone Layer, UNEP/OzL.Pro.14/9

Ozone OEWG-17 report, 1998, Report of the seventeenth meeting of the Open-Ended Working Group of the Parties to the Montreal Protocol, UNEP/OzL.Pro.WG1/17/3

Ozone Secretariat, 1999a, Synthesis of the Reports of the Scientific, Environmental Effects and Technology and Economic Assessment Panels of the Montreal Protocol: A Decade of Assessments for Decision-makers regarding the Protection of the Ozone Layer 1988–1999, available at www.unep.org/ozone

1999b, The Implications to the Montreal Protocol of the Inclusion of HFCs and PFCs in the Kyoto Protocol. Report of the HFC and PFC Task Force of the Technical and Economic Assessment Panel, available at www.unep.org/ozone

1999c, Options for the Limitation of Emissions of HFCs and PFCs. Proceedings of Joint IPCC/TEAP Expert Meeting, Petten, The Netherlands, 26–28 May 1999, available at www.ipcc.ch

2000, Action on Ozone, available at www.unep.org/ozone

2003, Handbook for the International Treaties for the Protection of the Ozone Layer, available at www.unep.org/ozone

Ramsar, 1996, Strategic Plan 1997–2002

1999, Convention Work Plan 2000–2002

2002a, Strategic Plan 2003–2008

2002b, COP 8-Doc.11, Climate Change and Wetlands: Impacts, Adaptations and Mitigation

Scientific Assessment Panel, 2002, Scientific Assessment of Ozone Depletion, WMO Global Ozone Research and Monitoring Project, report no. 47

ST/SGB/2002/1, Staff rules: Staff regulations of the United Nations and Staff rules 100.1 to 112.8 1 January 2002

TN/TE/3, 2002, Report by the Chairperson of the Special Session of the Committee on Trade and Environment to the Trade Negotiations Committee, December

TN/TE/W/9, 2002, Energy Taxation, Subsidies and Incentives in OECD Countries and their Economic and Trade Implications: Submission by Saudi Arabia

TN/TE/5, 2003, Report by the Chairperson on the Special Session of the Committee on Trade and Environment to the Trade Negotiations Committee, February

TN/TE/8, 2004, Report by the Chairperson of the special session of the Committee on Trade and Environment to the Trade Negotiations Committee

TN/TE/9, 2004, Trade and Environment negotiations: State of Play

UNCED, 1992, Report of the United Nations Conference on Environment and Development, Rio de Janeiro, 3–14 June 1992, UN Publication, Sales no. E.93.I.8, available at www.un.org/esa/sustdev/agenda21text.htm

UNCHE, 1972, Report of the United Nations Conference on the Human Environment, Stockholm, 5–16 June 1972, UN Publication, Sales no. E.73.II.A.14

UNCTAD, 2001, 'Greenhouse Gas Market Perspectives: Trade and Investment Implications of the Climate Change Regime: Recent Research on Institutional and Economic Aspects of Carbon Trading', UNCTAD/DITC/TED/MISC.9, available at www.ictsd.org

2002, 'The Least Developed Countries, 2002 Report: Escaping the Poverty Trap'

UNDP, 1994, Document DP/1994/9, Report on the Second Regular Session

UNEP, 1994, Governing Council, Resolution ss.iv.1, Adoption of the Instrument for the Establishment of the Restructured Global Environment Facility

1998, *Handbook on Methods for Climate Change Impact Assessment and Adaptation Strategies* (J. Feenstra, I. Burtan, J. Smith and R. Tol, eds.)

2001, *Managing Technological Change, An Explanatory Summary of the IPCC Special Report, Methodological and Technological Issues in Technology Transfer*, Nairobi: UNEP

2002, *Climate Change and the Financial Services Industry*, Nairobi: UNEP

UNEP/CBD/SBSTTA/6/11, 2001, Note by the Executive Secretary: Biological diversity and climate change, including cooperation with the United Nations Framework Convention on Climate Change

UNEP/CBD/SBSTTA/9/11, 2003, Climate change: Review of interlinkages between biological diversity and climate change: Advice on the integration of biodiversity into the implementation of the UNFCCC and Kyoto Protocol

UNEP/CBD/SBSTTA/9/INF/12, 2003, Report of the Ad Hoc Technical Expert Group on Biodiversity and Climate Change

UNEP/DTIE, 2002, Enhancing synergies and mutual supportiveness of MEAs and the WTO: A synthesis, available at www.unep.org

UNEP/GC.22/4, 2002, Implementing the outcomes of the World Summit on Sustainable Development: international environmental governance. Report of the Executive Director, available at www.unep.org

UNGA Press release, 2000, GA/9850, 'Assembly approves new scale of assessments, as it concludes main part of its millennium session', 23 December, available at www.un.org

UNITAR report with the Consortium for North–South Dialogue on Climate Change, 2001, 'Who Needs What to Implement the Kyoto Protocol? An Assessment of Capacity Building Needs in 33 Developing Countries', Geneva

UNOLA, 1993, Unpublished memorandum dated 4 November 1993 from Carl Fleischhauer, Under-Secretary-General for Legal Affairs, United Nations Office of Legal Affairs, to Michael Zammit Cutajar, Executive Secretary, Intergovernmental Negotiating Committee for a Framework Convention on Climate Change, on Arrangements for the implementation of the provisions of Article 11 of the UN Framework Convention on Climate Change concerning the financial mechanism

WSSD, 2002, Report of the World Summit on Sustainable Development, Johannnesburg, 26 August–4 September 2002, A/Conf.199/20

WT/CTE/W/160/Rev.1, 2001, Committee on Trade and Enviroment, Matrix on trade measures pursuant to selected MEAs. Note by the Secretariat

WT/CTE/W/174, 2002, Committee on Trade and Environment, Communication from the United Nations Framework Convention on Climate Change

WT/MIN(01)/DEC/1, Doha Declaration, World Trade Organisation, adopted 14 November 2001

Secondary Material

Ackerman, D., 2001, *Congressional Research Service Report*, 'Global Climate Change: Selected Legal Questions about the Kyoto Protocol'

Agrawala, S., 1998, 'Context and Early Origins of the Intergovernmental Panel on Climate Change', *Climatic Change*, vol. 39, no. 4, pp. 605–20

Aldy, J., Baron R. and Tubiana, L., 2003, 'Addressing Cost: The Political Economy of Climate Change', Pew Center Paper

American Law Institute, 1987, *Restatement (Third) of the Foreign Relations Law of the United States*, vol. 1

Anderson, M., 2002a, 'Verification under the Kyoto Protocol', in T. Findlay and O. Meier (eds.), *Verification Yearbook*, London: Vertic, p. 156

2002b, Vertic Briefing Paper 02/02, 'Verification of the Kyoto Protocol: filling in the detail', available at www.vertic.org

Anderson, D., Grubb, M. and Depledge, J., 1997, *Climate Change and the Energy Sector: A Country-by-Country Analysis of National Programmes*, vol. I: *The European Union*, FT Management Report, London: FT Energy

Andresen, S. and Skjaerseth, J. B., 1999, 'Can International Environmental Secretariats Promote Effective Co-operation?', paper presented at the International Conference on Synergies and Co-ordination between Multilateral Environmental Agreements, United Nations University, Tokyo, 14–16 July 1999

Annan, K., 2002, 'Towards a Sustainable Future', American Museum of Natural History's Annual Environmental Lecture, 14 May 2002, available at http://www.johannesburgsummit.org/html/media_info/ speeches/sg_speech_amnh.pdf

Arnell, N. W., Cannell, M. G. R., Hulme, M., Kovats, R. S., Mitchell, J., Nicholls, R. J., Parry, M. L., Livermore, M. T. J. and White, A., 2002, 'The Consequences of CO_2 Stabilisation for the Impacts of Climate Change', *Climatic Change*, vol. 53, no. 4, pp. 413–46

Asian–African Legal Consultative Committee, 1992, 'UNFCCC: A Preliminary Study', on file with author

Australian Department of Foreign Affairs and Trade Discussion Paper, 2000, 'Climate Change: Options for the Kyoto Protocol Compliance System'

Bailey, S., 1984, *The General Assembly of the United Nations: A Study of Procedure and Practice*, rev. edn

Barnett, J., and Dessai, S., 2002, 'Articles 4.8/4.9 of the UNFCCC: The Adverse Effects and the Impacts of Response Measures', *Climate Policy*, vol. 2, issue 3, pp. 231–9

Barnett, J., Dessai, S. and Webber, M., 2004, 'Will OPEC Lose from the Kyoto Protocol?' *Energy Policy*, vol. 32, issue 18, pp. 2077–88

Bartsch, O. and Müller, B., 2000, *Fossil Fuels in a Changing Climate*, Oxford University Press

Benioff, R., Guill, S. and Lee, J. (eds.), 1996, *Vulnerability and Adaptation Assessments: An International Handbook*, Dordrecht: Kluwer

Bergkamp, G. and Orlando, B., 1999, 'Wetlands and Climate Change: Exploring Collaboration between the Convention on Wetlands (Ramsar, Iran, 1971) and the UN Framework Convention on Climate Change', IUCN October 1999, available at http://www.ramsar.org/key_unfccc_bkgd.htm

Berk, M. M., van Minnen, J. G., Metz, B., Moomaw, W., den Elzen, M. G. J., van Vuuren, D. P. and Gupta, J., 2002, 'Climate Options for the Long Term (COOL) Global Dialogue – Synthesis Report', Report 410 200 118, Bilthoven: RIVM

Berkhout, F. et al., 2003, 'Shifting Perspectives in Environmental Social Sciences', in F. Berkhout, M. Leach and I. Scoones (eds.), *Negotiating Environmental Change, New Perspectives from Social Sciences*, Edward Elgar, pp. 1–32

Biermann, F., 2000, 'The Case for a World Environment Organisation', *Environment*, vol. 42, no. 9, pp. 22–31

Birnie, P. and Boyle, A., 2002, *International Law and the Environment*, 2nd edn, Oxford

Blair, Prime Minister Tony, 2003, 'Concerted International Effort Necessary to Fight Climate Change', speech delivered in London, 24 February, available at http://www.number-10.gov.uk/output/page5.asp

Bodansky, D., 1993, 'The United Nations Framework Convention on Climate Change: A Commentary', *Yale Journal of International Law*, vol. 18, no. 2, pp. 451–558

2001, 'Bonn Voyage, Kyoto's Uncertain Revival', *The National Interest* (Fall)

2003, 'Climate Commitments: Assessing the Options', Pew Center Paper

Bodansky, D. and Brunnee, J., 1998, 'The Role of National Courts in the Field of International Environmental Law', RECIEL, Special Issue, *Judicial Application of International Environmental Law*, vol. 7, no. 1, pp. 11–20

Boehmer Christiansen, S., 1994a and b 'Global Climate Policy: The Limits of Scientific Advice': Parts 1 and 2, *Global Environmental Change*, vol. 4, no. 2, pp. 140–59; and vol. 4, no. 3, pp. 185–200

Brack, D., and Gray, K., 2003, 'Multilateral Environmental Agreements and the WTO', RIIA/IISD Report

Brack, D. and Grubb, M., 1996, 'Climate Change: A Summary of the Second Assessment Report of the IPCC', Briefing Paper 32, London: Royal Institute of International Affairs

Brack, D., with Grubb, M. and Windram, C., 2000, *International Trade and Climate Change Policies*, London: RIIA/Earthscan

Brack, D. and Hyvarinen, J., 2002, 'Global Environmental Institutions: Perspectives on Reform', Royal Institute of International Affairs, Sustainable Development Programme, available at www.riia.org

Brewer, T., 2003, 'The Trade Regime and the Climate Regime: Institutional Evolution and Adaptation', *Climate Policy*, vol. 3, issue 4, pp. 329–41

Brown, P., 1996, *Global Warming: Can Civilization Survive?* London: Blandford

Brown Weiss, E. and Jacobson, H. K., 1998, *Engaging Countries: Strengthening Compliance with International Environmental Accords*, MIT Press

Burgiel, S.W. and Cohen, S, 1997, *The GEF: From Rio to New Dehli, A Guide for NGOs*, IUCN

Cameron, J. and Zealke, D., 1990, 'Global Warming and Climate Change – An Overview of International Legal Process', *American Journal of International Law*, vol. 5, no. 2, p. 248

Carbon Disclosure Project, 2003, 'Carbon Finance and Global Equity Markets', available at http://www.cdproject.net

Carpenter, C., 2001, 'Businesses, Green Groups and the Media: The Role of Non-Governmental Organizations in the Climate Change Debate', *International Affairs*, vol. 77, no. 2, pp. 313–28

Cassese, A., 2001, *International Law*, Oxford

Chambers, W. B., 1999, 'International Trade Law and the Kyoto Protocol', in W. B. Chambers (ed.), *Global Climate Governance: Inter-linkages between the Kyoto Protocol and Other Multilateral Regimes*, United Nations University, Tokyo, pp. 39–58

Charnovitz, S., 2002, 'The Law of Environmental "PPMs" in the WTO: Debunking the Myth of Illegality', *Yale Journal of International Law*, vol. 27, no. 11, pp. 59–110

2003, 'Trade and Climate: Potential Conflicts and Synergies', in *Beyond Kyoto: Advancing the International Effort against Climate Change*, Pew Center

Chayes, A. and Chayes, A. H., 1995, *The New Sovereignty. Compliance with International Regulatory Agreements*, Cambridge, MA: Harvard University Press

Cheng, B., 1965, 'United Nations Resolutions on Outer Space: "Instant" International Customary Law?' *Indian Journal of International Law*, vol. 5, pp. 23–43

Chinkin, C., 2000, 'Normative Developments in the International Legal System', in D. Shelton (ed.), *Commitment and Compliance, The Role of Non-Binding Norms in the International Legal System*, Oxford University Press, p. 27

Chossudovsky, M., 1998, 'The G7 "Solution" to the Global Financial Crisis – A Marshall Plan for Creditors and Speculators', available at http://www.transnational.org/features/g7solution.html

Christoffersen, L., et al., 2002, 'Overall Performance Study of GEF' (OPS-2), GEF/A.2/4

Churchill, R. and Ulfstein, G., 2000, 'Autonomous Institutional Arrangements in Multilateral Environmental Agreements: A Little-noticed Phenomenon in International Law', *American Journal of International Law*, vol. 94, no. 4, pp. 623–59

Cibils, A. et al., 2002, 'Argentina Since Default: The IMF and the Depression', Centre for Economic and Policy Research Paper, September

Claussen, E. and McNeilly, L., 1998, 'Equity and Global Climate Change: The Complex Elements of Fairness', Pew Center Paper

Climate Change Information Kit, 'Biodiversity and Ecosystems', Sheet 12, available at http://unfccc.int/resource/iuckit/

Climate Change Information Kit, 'How Human Activities Produce Greenhouse Gases', Sheet 22, available at http://unfccc.int/resource/iuckit/

'Climate Change Mitigation in Developing Countries, Brazil, China, India, Mexico, South Africa and Turkey', 2002, Pew Center Paper

Climate Policy, 2003, Special Issue: *EU – Implementation Challenges*, vol. 3, issue 1

Cogan, D., 2003, 'Corporate Governance and Climate Change: Making the Connection', a CERES Sustainable Governance Project Report, prepared by the Investor Responsibility Research Centre

Dahl, A., 2000, 'Competence and Subsidiarity', in J. Gupta, and M. Grubb (eds.), *Climate Change and European Leadership: A Sustainable Role for Europe?* Dordrecht: Kluwer, pp. 203–20

Depledge, J., 2001a, 'New Challenges for the Ozone Regime', *Global Environmental Change*, vol. 11, no. 4, pp. 343–7

2001b, 'The Organization of the Kyoto Protocol Negotiations: Lessons for Global Environmental Decision-making', PhD thesis, University of London

2002, 'Climate Change in Focus: The IPCC Third Assessment Report', Briefing Paper 29, London: Royal Institute of International Affairs

DFID, 2003, *Poverty and Climate Change: Reducing the Vulnerability of the Poor through Adaptation*, prepared by DFID, World Bank, ADB, African Development Bank, UNDP, OECD, UNEP, European Commission, Dutch Ministry for Development Cooperation and German Ministry for Economic Cooperation and Development

Earth Negotiations Bulletin, 2002, 'Summary of the World Summit on Sustainable Development: 26 August–4 September 2002', vol. 22, no. 51

Ecologic, 2002, 'Participation of Non-Governmental Organizations in International Environmental Governance: Legal Basis and Practical Experience', on behalf of the Umweltbundesamt, final report, June 2002, available at www.ecologic.de

Elias, T. O., 1974, *The Modern Law of Treaties*

Estrada, R., 1999, 'What Policy-makers Need', paper prepared for the IPCC Experts Meeting on Costing Issues for Mitigation and Adaptation to Climate Change, Tokyo, 29 June–1 July 1999, on file with author

Esty, D., 1994, *Greening the GATT: Trade, Environment and the Future*, Washington DC: Institute for International Economics

Esty, D. C. and Ivanova, M. H. (eds.), 2002a, *Global Environmental Governance: Options and Opportunities*, Yale School of Forestry and Environmental Studies

2002b, 'Revitalizing Global Environmental Governance: A New Function-driven Approach', in Brack and Hyvarinen, pp. 5–18

European Commission, 1997, *The Law of Sustainable Development: General Principles*

1998, 'An Analysis of the Kyoto Protocol', Commission Staff Working Paper, prepared at the request of the Environment Council, Brussels, 13 March 1998

2001, Third Communication from the European Community under the UN Framework Convention on Climate Change. Commission Staff Working Paper SEC(2001)2053, 30 November 2001, available at www.unfccc.int

Fisher, J. and Grubb, M., 1997, 'The Use of Economic Models in Climate Change Policy Analysis', Energy and Environmental Programme Climate Change Briefing Paper 5, London: Royal Institute of International Affairs.

Flavin, C., 1998, 'Last Tango in Buenos Aires', *WorldWatch* (Nov./Dec.), 11–18

Freestone, D., 1999, 'Caution or Precaution: A Rose by Any Other Name', *Yearbook of International Environmental Law*, vol. 10, p. 25

Freestone, D. and Hey, E., 1995, *The Precautionary Principle and International Law*, Kluwer Law International

Fry, I., 2002, 'Twists and Turns in the Jungle: Exploring the Evolution of Land Use, Land-Use Change and Forestry Decisions within the Kyoto Protocol', RECIEL, vol. 11, issue 2, pp. 159–69

Gelbspan, R., 1997, *The Heat Is On: The High Stakes Battle Over Earth's Threatened Climate*, Reading, MA: Addison-Wesley Publishing

Global Biodiversity Forum, 1999, Statement of the 13th Global Biodiversity Forum: Supporting the Ramsar/CBD work programme, 7–9 May 1999, San José, Costa Rica, available at www.gbf.ch/

Grossman, D. A., 2003, 'Warming Up to a Not-so-radical Idea: Tort-based Climate Change Litigation', *Columbia Journal of Environmental Law*, vol. 28, pp. 1–61

Grubb, M., Vrolijk, C. and Brack, D., 1999, *The Kyoto Protocol, A Guide and Assessment*, Earthscan/RIIA

Grubb, M. and Yamin, F., 2001, 'Climate Collapse at The Hague: What Happened, Why, and Where Do We Go from Here?' *International Affairs*, vol. 77, no. 2, pp. 261–76

Gupta, J., 1997, *The Climate Change Convention and Developing Countries: From Conflict to Consensus?* Dordrecht: Kluwer

Gupta, J. and Grubb, M. (eds.), 2000, *Climate Change and European Leadership: A Sustainable Role for Europe?* Dordrecht: Kluwer

Haites, E., 2000, 'Article 4 and the Kyoto Mechanisms', paper on file with author

Haites, E. and Aslam, M. A., 2000, 'The Kyoto Mechanisms and Global Climate Change: Coordination Issues and Domestic Policies', Pew Center Paper

Haites, E. and Mullins, F., 2003, 'Linking National Emissions Trading Schemes', CATEP Paper, OECD Workshop, on file with authors

Haites, E. and Yamin, F., 2000, 'The Clean Development Mechanism: Proposals for its Operation and Governance', *Global Environmental Change*, vol. 10, issue 1, pp. 27–45

Hare, B., 2001, 'Dangerous Interference with the Climate System: Implications of the IPCC TAR for Article 2 of the Convention', *Greenpeace Briefing Paper*

Harremoes, P., Gee, D., MacGarvin, M., Stirling, A., Keys, J., Wynne, B. and Guedes Vaz, S., 2002, *The Precautionary Principle in the 20th Century, Late Lessons from Early Warnings*, Earthscan

Harsch, E., 1998, 'Africa Tenses for Asian Aftershocks: Global Financial Crisis Hitting African Growth, Exports and Investment Flows', *Africa Recovery*, vol. 12, no. 2

Holtwisch, C., 2003, 'Study on Compliance Concerning the Kyoto Protocol', unpublished manuscript on file with author

Honkanen, M. L., Von Moltke, K., Hisschemoller, M. et al., 1999, Report of the Concerted Action on the Effectiveness of International Environmental Agreements, Noordwijk Workshop, 15–18 October 1998, Report no. R-99/05, Amsterdam: IVM

Househam, I., Hauff, J., Missfeldt, F. and Grubb, M., 1998, *Climate Change and the Energy Sector: A Country-by-Country Analysis of National Programmes*, vol. III: *The Economies in Transition*, FT Management Report, London: FT Energy

Huq, S., Rahman, A., Konate, M., Sokona Y. and Reid, H., 2003, 'Mainstreaming Adaptation to Climate Change in Least Developed Countries', London: IIED

ICTSD, 2003, 'WTO Environment Committee Allows Ad Hoc Attendance to MEA Secretariats', *Bridges*, vol. 7, no. 6, available at www.ictsd.org

ICTSD/IISD, 2003, Doha Round Briefing Series: Developments since the Fourth WTO Ministerial Conference, vol. 1 no. 9, available at www.ictsd.org

IMO, 2000, Study of GHG Emissions from Ships, Final Report to the IMO, Issue no. 2, 31 March 2000

International Affairs, 2001, 'The Climate Change Debate', vol. 77, no. 2

Jacob, T. R., 2003, 'Report on UNFCCC Subsidiary Body Meetings, Bonn, June 2003', *Climate Policy*, vol. 3, issue 3, pp. 309–14

Jacquemont, F. and Caparros, A., 2002, 'The Convention on Biological Diversity and the Climate Change Convention 10 Years after Rio: Towards a Synergy of the Two Regimes?' RECIEL, vol. 11, issue 2, p. 169

Jasanoff, S., 1990, *The Fifth Branch: Science Advisers as Policymakers*, Cambridge, MA: Harvard University Press

Kashyap, A. K., 2002, 'Sorting out Japan's Financial Crisis', NBER Working Paper

Kimball, L. and Boyd, W., 1992, 'International Institutional Arrangements for Environment and Development: A Post-Rio Assessment', RECIEL, vol. 1, issue 3, pp. 295–306

Krasner, S. D., 1982, 'Structural Causes and Regime Consequences: Regimes as Intervening Variables', *International Organizations*, vol. 36, no. 21, p. 186

Laird, F., 1999, 'Institutional Learning and Development: The Case of Renewable Energy', paper delivered at the 1999 Annual Meeting of the American Political Sciences Association, Atlanta, USA

Lang, W., 1989, 'The Role of Presiding Officers in Multilateral Negotiations', in F. Mautner-Markhof (ed.), *Processes of International Negotiations*, Boulder, CO: Westview Press, pp. 23–42

Lang, W. (ed.), 1995, *Sustainable Development and International Law*, Kluwer Law International

Lannon, A., 1999, 'The World Financial Crisis: Made in the USA, February', Institute for Global Communication

Lefeber, R., 2001, 'From The Hague to Bonn to Marrakesh and Beyond: A Negotiating History of the Compliance Regime under the Kyoto Protocol', *Hague Yearbook of International Law*, vol. 17, pp. 25–54

Leggett, J., 1999, *The Carbon War, Global Warming and the End of the Oil Era*, Penguin

Linnerooth-Bayer, J., Mace, M. J. and Verheyen, R., 2003, 'Insurance-Related Actions and Risk Assessment in the Context of the UNFCCC', Background Paper for May 2003 UNFCCC Workshop on Insurance

Lusthaus, C., Adrien, M. and Morgan, P., 2000, 'Integrating Capacity Development into Project Design and Evaluation', GEF Monitoring and Evaluation Working Paper 5

McCaughey, J., 1996, 'Pearlman before Swine etc.', *Energy Economist*, vol. 179, pp. 8–11

Meinshausen, M. and Hare, 2003, *An Analysis of the CDM Sinks Agreement at COP-9*, Greenpeace International, December

Mertens, S., 1996, *An NGO Guide to the GEF, Climate Network Europe*, Brussels: CAN

Metz, B., Berk, M., den Elzen, M., de Vries, B. and van Vuuren, D., 2002, 'Towards an Equitable Global Climate Change Regime: Compatibility with Article 2 of the Climate Change Convention and the Link with Sustainable Development', *Climate Policy*, vol. 2, issue 2–3, pp. 211–30

Michaelowa, A., 2003, Background Paper prepared for UNFCCC Secretariat workshop on insurance-related actions related to adverse impacts and impacts of response measures, available from UNFCCC website

Miles, E., Uderdal, A., Andresen, S., Wettestad, J., Birger Skjaerseth, J., Skodvin, T. and Carlin, E., 2002, *Environmental Regime Effectiveness: Confronting Theory with Evidence*, Cambridge, MA: MIT

Mitchell, R., 1996, 'Compliance Theory: An Overview', in J. Cameron, J. Werksman and P. Roderick (eds.), *Improving Compliance with International Environmental Law*, Earthscan

Mott, R. N., 1991, *Looking Through America's Climate Change Strategy*, ECO

Mwandosya, M., 2000, *Survival Emissions: A Perspective from the South on Global Climate Change Negotiations*, Dar es Salaam: Dar es Salaam University Press and Centre for Energy, Environment, Science and Technology

Najam, A., 2002, 'The Case against GEO, WEO, or Whatever-else-EO', in Brack and Hyvarinen, pp. 32–43

Newell, P., 2000, *Climate for Change: Non-State Actors and the Global Politics of the Greenhouse*, Cambridge University Press

Nobs, B., 2002, 'Compromise Group – Switzerland', in C. Bail, R. Falkner and H. Marquard, *The Cartagena Protocol on Biosafety: Reconciling Trade in Biotechnology with Environment and Development?* London: Earthscan/RIIA, pp. 186–92

Nollkaemper, A., 2002, *Year Look of International Environmental Law*, vol. 13, pp. 165–99

O'Riordan, T. and Cameron, J. (eds.), 1994, *Interpreting the Precautionary Principle*, Earthscan

Oberthür, S., 2000, 'The EU in International Environmental Regimes and the Energy Charter Treaty', in J. Gupta and M. Grubb (eds.), *Climate Change and European Leadership*, Dordrecht: Kluwer

    2001, 'Linkages between the Montreal and Kyoto Protocols: Enhancing Synergies between Protecting the Ozone Layer and the Global Climate', *International Environmental Agreements: Politics, Law and Economics*, vol. 1, no. 3, pp. 357–77

    2003, Institutional Interaction to Address GHG Emissions from International Transportation: ICAO, IMO and the Kyoto Protocol, *Climate Policy*, vol. 3, pp. 191–205

Oberthür, S. et al., 2000, Study of Impacts of GEF Activities on Phase-out of Ozone Depleting Substances, *GEF Evaluation Report*, available at www.gefweb.org

Oberthür, S. and Ott, H., 1999, *The Kyoto Protocol: International Climate Policy for the 21st Century*, Berlin: Springer Verlag

OECD, 2002a, Report, 'Integrating Rio Conventions into Development Cooperation'
    2002b, Report, 'Aid Targeting the Objectives of the Rio Conventions, 1998–2000'
    2003, Summary Report, OECD Workshop, Benefits of Climate Policy: Improving Information for Policy Makers CD Forum, December 2002, OECD, ENV/EPOC/GSP (2003)3/REV 1

OECD and IEA, 2003, Information Paper, 'Technology Innovation, Development and Diffusion', COM/ENV/EPOC/IEA/SLT (2003) 4, 3 June

Oppenheim's *International Law*, ed. Sir Robert Jennings and Sir Arthur Watts, 9th edition, 1992, Longman

Pallemaerts, M., 2003, 'Is Multilateralism the Future? Sustainable Development or Globalisation as "a Comprehensive Vision of the Future of Humanity"', *Environment, Development and Sustainability*, vol. 5, pp. 275–95

Palmer, G., 1992, 'New Ways to Make International Environmental Law', *American Journal of International Law*, vol. 86, no. 2, pp. 259–83

Pershing, J., 2002, *Fossil Fuel Implications of Climate Change Mitigation Responses*, IEA

Pershing, J. and Tudela, F., 2003, 'A Long-term Target: Framing the Climate Effort', Pew Center Paper

Porter, G., Clemencon, R., Ofosu-Amaah, W. and Phillips, M., 1997, 'Study of the GEF's Overall Performance' (OPS-1), available at http://www.gefweb.org/MaE/ops.pdf

Purdy, R. and MacRory, R., 2004, 'Geological Carbon Sequestration: Critical Legal Issues', Tyndall Centre for Climate Change Research, Working Paper no. 45

Rabe, B. G., 2002, 'Greenhouse and Statehouse: The Evolving State Government Role in Climate Change', Pew Centre Paper

Ragazzi, M., 1997, *The Concept of International Obligations Erga Omnes*, Oxford University Press

Rajamani, L., 2000, 'The Principle of Common but Differentiated Responsibility and the Balance of Commitments Under the Climate Regime', RECIEL, vol. 9, issue 2, pp. 120–31

Rayner, S. and Malone, E., 1998a, *Human Choice and Climate Change*, vol. I, *The Societal Framework*, Battelle Press, chapter 5

1998b, *Human Choice and Climate Change*. vol. IV, *What Have We Learned*? Battelle Press

Reinstein, R. A., 1994, 'The FCCC: Developed Country Commitments on Greenhouse Emissions', paper on file with authors

Ringius, L., 1999, 'Differentiation, Leaders and Fairness: Negotiating Climate Commitments in the European Union', *International Negotiation*, vol. 4, no. 2, pp. 133–66

Sabel, R., 1997, *Procedure at International Conferences: A Study of the Rules of Procedure of International Inter-governmental Conferences*, Cambridge University Press

Sampson, G., 1999, 'WTO Rules and Climate Change: The Need for Policy Coherence', in Chambers, *Global Climate Governance*, pp. 29–38

Sand, P. H., 1990, *Lessons Learned in Global Environmental Governance*, World Resources Institute

1994, *Trusts for the Earth: New Financial Mechanisms for International Environmental Protections*, Hull University Press

Sandford, R., 1994, 'International Environmental Treaty Secretariats: Stage-hands or Actors?' in Fridtjof Nansen Institute, *Green Globe Yearbook of International Cooperation on Environment and Development*, Oxford University Press, pp. 17–30

Sands, P., 1992, 'UN Framework Convention on Climate Change', RECIEL, vol. 1, issue 41, p. 272

1995a, 'International Law in the Field of Sustainable Development', *British Yearbook of International Law* vol. 65, p. 303

1995b, *Principles of International Environmental Law, Frameworks, Standards and Implementation,* Manchester University Press

1998, 'International Environmental Litigation: What Future?' RECIEL, vol. 7, issue 1, pp. 1–3

2003, *Principles of International Environmental Law*, 2nd edn, Cambridge University Press

Sands, P., Mackenzie, R. and Shany, Y., 1999, *Manual on International Courts and Tribunals*, Butterworths

Schermers, H. G. and Blokker, N. M., 1995, *International Institutional Law: Unity with Diversity*, 3rd edn, The Hague: Martinius Nijhoff Publishers

Schlamadinger, B. and Marland, G., 2000, 'Land-use and Global Climate Change: Forests, Land Management, and the Kyoto Protocol', Pew Center Paper

Schoeters, K., 2003, 'CAN International Opts to Toughen Structure', *Hotspot*, issue 26, CAN-Europe

Shackley, S., 1997, 'Consensual Knowledge and Global Politics', *Global Environmental Change*, vol. 7, no. 1, pp. 77–80

Shelton, D. (ed.), 2000, *Commitment and Compliance, The Role of Non-Binding Norms in the International Legal System*, Oxford University Press

Sjoberg, H. 1996, 'The Global Environment Facility', in J. Werksman (ed.), *Greening International Institutions*, Earthscan

Skodvin, T., 1999a, 'Making Climate Change Negotiable: The Development of the Global Warming Potential Index', CICERO Working Paper 1999:9, available at www.cicero.uio.no

1999b, 'Science-policy Interaction in the Global Greenhouse: Institutional Design and Institutional Performance in the Intergovernmental Panel on Climate Change', CICERO Working Paper 1999:3, available at www.cicero.uio.no

Smit, B., Burton, I., Klein, R. and Wandel, J., 2000, 'An Anatomy of Adaptation to Climate Change and Variability', *Climatic Change*, vol. 45, no. 1, pp. 233–51

Smith, J. and Hitz, S., 2003, Background Paper, 'Estimating Global Impacts from Climate Change', Stratus Consulting Inc., Colorado, United States, OECD, Paris, ENV/EPOC/GSP (2002) 12/FINAL

Soroos, M. S., 1997, *The Endangered Atmosphere*, Columbia: University of South Carolina Press

Spalding-Fecher, R. (ed.), 2002, *The CDM Guidebook: A Resource for Clean Development Mechanism Project Developers in Southern Africa*, Energy and Development Research Centre, University of Cape Town

Sperling, F. (ed.), Multi-Agency Report, 2003, *Poverty and Climate Change: Reducing the Vulnerability of the Poor through Adaptation*, World Bank, Washington DC

Stone, C., 1990, 'Afterword: The Global Warming Crisis, If There is One, and the Law', *American Journal of International Law*, vol. 5, no. 2, p. 497

2004, 'Common But Differentiated Responsibilities: A Legal, Economic and Ethical Critique', *American Journal of International Law*, vol 98, no. 2, pp. 270–302

Széll, P., 1993, 'Negotiations on the Ozone Layer', in G. Sjöstedt (ed.), *International Environmental Negotiation*, London: Sage, pp. 31–47

1996, 'Decision-making under Multilateral Environmental Agreements', *Environmental Policy and Law*, vol. 26, no. 5, pp. 210–14

Taalab, A., 1998, *Rising Voices against Global Warming*, Frankfurt: IZE

UK Department of the Environment, 1992, Analysis of the UNFCCC, on file with author

UK Royal Commission on Environmental Pollution, 2000, 'Energy, The Changing Climate', RCEP's 22nd Report

Ulfstein, G., 1999, 'The Proposed GEO and its Relationship to Existing MEAs', paper presented at the International Conference on Synergies and Coordination between Multilateral Environmental Agreements, United Nations University, Tokyo, 14–16 July 1999

United States, Department of State, 1994, Transmittal documents sent to the President, Article-by-Article Analysis of the UNFCCC, annexed to the Ratification Decision by George Bush, 13 October, on file with author

Van Beers, C. and de Moors, A., 2001, *Public Subsidies and Policy Failures, How Subsidies Distort the Natural Environment, Equity and Trade and How to Reform them*, Cheltenham: Edward Elgar Publishers

Verheyen, R., 2002, 'Adaptation to the Impacts of Anthropogenic Climate Change: The International Legal Framework, RECIEL, vol. 11, issue 2, pp. 129–43

Von Moltke, K., 1996, 'Why UNEP Matters', in Fridtjof Nansen Institute, *Green Globe Yearbook of International Cooperation on Environment and Development*, Oxford University Press

Vrolijk, C., 2002, 'A New Interpretation on the Kyoto Protocol, Outcomes from The Hague, Bonn and Marrakesh', available at www.riia.org

Wang, X. and Wiser, G., 2002, 'The Implementation and Compliance Regimes under the Climate Change Convention and its Kyoto Protocol', RECIEL, vol. 11, no. 2, pp. 181–99

Werksman, J., 1995, 'Consolidating Governance of the Global Commons: Insights from the Global Environment Facility', *Yearbook of International Environmental Law*, vol. 6, pp. 27–65

　　1996, 'The Conference of the Parties to Environmental Treaties', in J. Werksman (ed.), *Greening International Institutions*, London: Earthscan

　　1998, 'Compliance and the Kyoto Protocol: Building a Backbone into a "Flexible" Regime', *Yearbook of International Environmental Law*, vol. 9, pp. 48–104

　　1999a, 'Procedural and Institutional Aspects of the Emerging Climate Change Regime: Do Improvised Procedures lead to Impoverished Rules?' paper presented at the concluding workshop for the project to enhance policy-making capacity under the Framework Convention on Climate Change and the Kyoto Protocol, London, 17–18 March 1999

　　1999b, 'Greenhouse Gas Emissions Trading and the WTO', RECIEL, vol. 8, no. 3, pp. 251–64

　　1999c, 'WTO Issues Raised by the Design of an EC Emissions Trading System', paper prepared for the European Commission

　　Forthcoming, 'The Negotiation of a Kyoto Compliance System', in J. Hovi, O.S. Stokke and G. Ulfstein (eds.), *International Compliance: Implementing the Climate Regime*

Wettestad, J., 2000, 'The Complicated Development of EU Climate Policy', in Gupta and Grubb, *Climate Change and European Leadership*, pp. 25–45

Wilkins, H., 2002, 'What's New in the CDM?' RECIEL, vol. 11, no. 2, pp. 144–59

Williams, M., 1997, 'The Group of 77 and Global Environmental Politics', *Global Environmental Change*, vol. 7, no. 3, pp. 295–8

Wiser, G., 1999a, 'The Clean Development Mechanism versus the World Trade Organization: Can Free-market Greenhouse Gas Emissions Abatement Survive Free Trade?' *Georgetown International Environmental Law Review*, vol. 11, no. 3, pp. 531–98

　　1999b, 'Compliance Systems Under Multilateral Agreements / A Survey for the Benefit of Kyoto Protocol Policy Makers', CIEL, available at www.ciel.org

WMO, 1991, Basic Documents No. 1, 1991 edn, WMO-No. 15

Wollansky, G. and Freidrich, A., 2003, 'A Guide to Carrying out Joint Implementation and Clean Development Mechanism Projects', version 1.1, produced for and published by Austrian Federal Ministry of Agriculture, Forestry, Environment and Water Management, Vienna

World Bank, Board of Governors, 1994, Resolution No. 487, Protection of the Global Environment 7 July

World Bank, Executive Directors, 1994, Resolution No. 94–2, Global Environment Facility Trust Fund: Restructuring and First Replenishment of the Global Environment Facility

World Commission on Environment and Development, 1987, *Our Common Future*, Oxford University Press

Yamin, F., 1998a, 'The Kyoto Protocol: Origins, Assessment and Future Challenges', RECIEL, vol. 7, issue 2, pp. 113–27

    1998b, 'The Clean Development Mechanism and Adaptation', background paper for the FCCC Secretariat Workshop, Capacity Building for Project Based Mechanisms, Abidjan, 17–18 September

    1999, 'Equity, Entitlements and Property Rights under the Kyoto Protocol: The Shape of Things to Come', RECIEL, vol. 8, issue 3, pp. 265–75

    2000, 'Joint Implementation', *Global Environmental Change*, vol. 10, issue 1

    2001, 'NGOs and International Environmental Law: A Critical Evaluation of their Roles and Responsibilities', RECIEL, vol. 10, issue 2, pp. 149–62

Yamin, F., Burniaux, J-M. and Nentjes, A., 2001, 'Kyoto Mechanisms: Key Issues for Policy-Makers', *International Environmental Agreements: Politics, Law and Economics* vol. 1, pp. 187–218

Yamin, F. and Clarke, F., 1997, 'Provisional Application: Precedents and Use in the United Nations Framework Convention on Climate Change', FIELD Working Paper

Yefimov, G. K., 1989, 'Developing a Global Negotiating Machinery', in F. Mautner-Markhof (ed.), *Processes of International Negotiations*, Boulder, CO: Westview Press, pp. 55–64

Index